CAMBRIDGE LIBRARY COLLECTION

Books of enduring scholarly value

The Nav

The *Naval Chronicle*, published in 4
key source for British maritime and
by those researching family historie
(and often reprinted with correction
in London, and bound up into two v ... economically,
on paper of varying weights and often with very small type, the extant copies have been heavily used over the course of two centuries, present significant conservation challenges, and are difficult to find outside major libraries. This reissue is the first complete printed reproduction of what was the most influential maritime publication of its day. The subjects covered range widely, including accounts of battles, notices of promotions, marriages and deaths, lists of ships and their tonnages, reports of courts martial, shipwrecks, privateers and prizes, biographies and poetry, notes on the latest technology, and letters. Each volume also contains engravings and charts relating to naval engagements and important harbours from Jamaica to Timor, Newfoundland to Canton, and Penzance to Port Jackson.

Volume 15

Volume 15 (1806) contains addenda to the biography of Lord Nelson published in Volume 14, including an account of his last months and details of his funeral. Biographies of William Dannett and Cuthbert, Lord Collingwood are included, together with the sixth Report of the Commissioners of Naval Inquiry and maps and descriptions of the Caribbean islands of Guadeloupe and St Lucia.

Cambridge University Press has long been a pioneer in the reissuing of out-of-print titles from its own backlist, producing digital reprints of books that are still sought after by scholars and students but could not be reprinted economically using traditional technology. The Cambridge Library Collection extends this activity to a wider range of books which are still of importance to researchers and professionals, either for the source material they contain, or as landmarks in the history of their academic discipline.

Drawing from the world-renowned collections in the Cambridge University Library, and guided by the advice of experts in each subject area, Cambridge University Press is using state-of-the-art scanning machines in its own Printing House to capture the content of each book selected for inclusion. The files are processed to give a consistently clear, crisp image, and the books finished to the high quality standard for which the Press is recognised around the world. The latest print-on-demand technology ensures that the books will remain available indefinitely, and that orders for single or multiple copies can quickly be supplied.

The Cambridge Library Collection will bring back to life books of enduring scholarly value (including out-of-copyright works originally issued by other publishers) across a wide range of disciplines in the humanities and social sciences and in science and technology.

The Naval Chronicle

Containing a General and Biographical History of the Royal Navy of the United Kingdom with a Variety of Original Papers on Nautical Subjects

Volume 15: January-June 1806

Edited by James Stanier Clarke and John McArthur

Cambridge University Press

CAMBRIDGE UNIVERSITY PRESS

Cambridge, New York, Melbourne, Madrid, Cape Town, Singapore,
São Paolo, Delhi, Dubai, Tokyo

Published in the United States of America by Cambridge University Press, New York

www.cambridge.org
Information on this title: www.cambridge.org/9781108018548

This edition first published 1806
This digitally printed version 2010

ISBN 978-1-108-01854-8 Paperback

NAVAL CHRONICLE.

VOL. XV.

J. T. Lee Esq. del. H. R. Cook Sc.

Funeral Carr

Published 30th June 1806, by J. Gold, No. 103, Shoe Lane.

THE

Naval Chronicle,

FOR 1806:

CONTAINING A

GENERAL AND BIOGRAPHICAL HISTORY

OF

THE ROYAL NAVY

OF THE

UNITED KINGDOM;

WITH A

VARIETY OF ORIGINAL PAPERS

ON

NAUTICAL SUBJECTS:

UNDER THE GUIDANCE OF SEVERAL

LITERARY AND PROFESSIONAL MEN.

VOLUME THE FIFTEENTH.

(*FROM JANUARY TO JUNE.*)

"ENGLAND EXPECTS EVERY MAN WILL DO HIS DUTY."

NELSON AND BRONTE.

London:

PRINTED AND PUBLISHED BY JOYCE GOLD, SHOE-LANE.

And sold by Messrs. LONGMAN, HURST, REES, and ORME, Mr. SYMONDS, and Mr. WALKER, Paternoster Row; Mr. WHITE, Fleet-street; Messrs. VERNOR, HOOD, and SHARPE, Poultry; Mr. ASPERNE, and Messrs. RICHARDSON, Cornhill; Messrs. A. & J. BLACKS and H. PARRY, Leadenhall-street; Messrs. CROSBY and Co., Stationers' Hall Court; Mr. OSTELL, and Mr. LAW, Avemaria-lane; Mr. MOTTLEY, Portsmouth; Mr. HAYDON, Plymouth; Messrs. NORTON and SON, Bristol; Mr. ROBINSON, and Mr. JONES, Liverpool; Messrs. MANNERS and MILLER, Mr. CREECH, and Mr. CONSTABLE, Edinburgh; Mr. ARCHER, Dublin; and the principal Booksellers in the different Seaport Towns throughout the United Kingdom.

MDCCCVI.

TO

THE RIGHT HONOURABLE

CUTHBERT LORD COLLINGWOOD,

VICE-ADMIRAL OF THE RED,

THIS FIFTEENTH VOLUME OF THE

Naval Chronicle

IS RESPECTFULLY DEDICATED

BY THE EDITORS.

PLATES IN VOLUME XV.

From Original Designs.

PREFACE

TO THE FIFTEENTH VOLUME.

DURING the progress of the present Volume a new Ministry has been established, and a new Board of Admiralty appointed by His Majesty. The veteran Lord Barham, and the veteran Cornwallis, and the veteran Sir A. S. Hammond, have retired. Whilst the Minister, who so long guided the destinies of this country, and weathered some of the most violent storms that ever agitated the political hemisphere, has followed his favourite Hero, our lamented Nelson, to the tomb.

Attached to no party, and wedded to no system; we yet, in common with the rest of our independent countrymen, dread those sudden and continual changes, which, like the uncertain temperature of our climate, render the minds of men feverish and irritable: they are always followed by storms of thunder, and of lightning. The angry spirit of party that had subsided, or been repressed, blazes forth anew; and the modest unassuming exertions of some of the ablest servants of the public, are sunk in an ungrateful oblivion.

The present Government, and the present Board of Admiralty, present an assemblage of talent, and of integrity, from which every thing may be expected: and we sincerely trust, that the impetuosity, and too decided character of a few individuals, will be chastened and overcome, by the candour and mild deportment of some of the leading members in the present administration.

In detailing the services, and describing the character and opinions of such members of this administration, as are connected with the great object which this CHRONICLE has in view, our readers will sometimes find, that we insert the sentiments both of friends and of enemies:

Fas est, et ab Hoste doceri!

Yet even this, we trust, will be done in a manner that is consistent with candour and impartiality; and will never deviate from our earliest profession, "That the leading objects in this publication, are to do good, and to give pain to no one*."

To some persons our pages have on the contrary given offence, for what they term an uniform sacrifice of praise, and of undue commendation, to officers who did not merit it. To this we must reply: that every man has two characters; and surely his biographer may be allowed to select the most favourable: besides, our great object has been, and ever will be, to collect facts, and authentic dates, to supply the hitherto meagre and incorrect page of our naval history. Some of our memoirs, and perhaps the most valuable, are obtained from the relations of the officers concerned; when partiality, and a laudable affection, will have a natural effect on the writer. Yet at the same time that we acknowledge this, we trust we do not deserve to be classed with the herd of flatterers; or to be suspected of any intention to palliate imperfections. Like the portrait painter, if we sometimes

* See Preface to our first Volume.

heighten the expression, and soften the lineaments, we trust the outline is always, or at least in general, correct.

The present Volume, among other biographical memoirs, has given the lives of the late gallant Captain George Duff; of Admiral Lord Collingwood; and of Rear-Admiral the Earl of Northesk, from the first and most undoubted sources of information: yet even these, perhaps, will after all vary in point of merit; and the fastidious critic will discover, that the introduction to Lord Collingwood's is too long; the extracts from poor Duff's letters too minute; and that many things might have been added, that would impart additional interest to our account of the services of the Earl of Northesk. Remember, gentle Reader, the fable of the Man and his Ass. Like all other periodical works, the NAVAL CHRONICLE is not without its faults. But as long as we are open to conviction, and give that information to the British Navy, and the public at large, which they could not otherwise obtain; we trust we merit our meed of praise, and that the labourer is worthy of his hire.

Amongst the various nautical papers which are inserted in this Volume, the following will be found particularly worthy of attention:—

"Letter from a Poor Post Captain," (page 195.)—On the "Printing of Scientific Tracts relative to Navigation," (page 196.)—"Remarks on some of the recent proceedings of the American Senate, relative to the impressing of seamen, and the non-importation of British commodities," (page 307.)—"Narrative of the proceedings on board the armed lugger Aristocrat, commanded by Captain Wilkins, July 15, 1795," (page 310.) Surely what has been so confidently asserted, respecting the fate of Captain Wright, (page 190,) demands more consideration and notice than it has hitherto received.—Our Addenda to the first, and previous memoir of the lamented Nelson, which closed, (pages 222—235,) has, we trust, comprehended every circumstance that could at the time be collected respecting that extraordinary man; and to complete the whole, we have subjoined, as a frontispiece, a faithful representation of the Car which conveyed his remains to St. Paul's.—Our account of the Rules and Orders observed at the Royal Academy at Portsmouth, (page 401,) may perhaps render that noble Institution more generally known.—The various private letters we have inserted, will throw additional light and interest on the different actions that have reflected so much honour on our Navy: particularly these at page 118, from Mr. Aikenhead; from Captain Lee, relative to the attack on the Rattlesnake in 1799, (page 119.)—Defence of the Diamond Rock, (page 123.)—Letter written by an officer of the Bellerophon, December 2, 1805, (page 203.)—From the Ramillies, one of Sir J. B. Warren's squadron, (page 407.)—From a Midshipman on board the Marengo, (page 413.)—And from Mr. Horseburgh, of Walworth, for his communication relating to the loss we have sustained in the China Sea, owing to shipwrecks, and the treachery of the Malays.—We have also given at considerable length (page 477) an account of Lord Melville's Trial, which we thought it our duty to lay before our readers, and have no doubt it will prove interesting, particularly to such as reside abroad.

The arrival of Earl St. Vincent in London will probably make a change in the present administration, particularly if Lord Howick is already tired of his situation. Report says, that the Admiral has purposely been sent for. Rumours of an approaching peace are daily gaining ground: perhaps Buonaparté is mindful of part of the advice which Louis XIV gave, when dying, to his successor:—

"You are soon going to be King over a great Kingdom: what I most earnestly recommend to you is, never to forget the obligations you have to God; remember, that it is to him you owe every thing. *Endeavour to preserve peace with your neighbours: I have been too fond of war:* imitate me not in that, no more than in my too great expenses. Take advice in all things; and endeavour to distinguish the best, that you may always follow it. Relieve your people as much as you can, and do what I have had the misfortune not to be able to do myself."

We cannot conclude our Preface without returning our best thanks to the various Correspondents that have favoured us with their communications; as also to our friends Mr. John Theophilus Lee, and Amor, for the Drawings which they forwarded to us.

All communications intended for insertion in the NAVAL CHRONICLE are requested to be sent to Mr. GOLD, 103, Shoe Lane, London.

WILLIAM DOMETT ESQ.R

Rear Admiral of the White Squadron

Pub.d by J Gold 103 Shoe Lane Jan.y 31st 1806

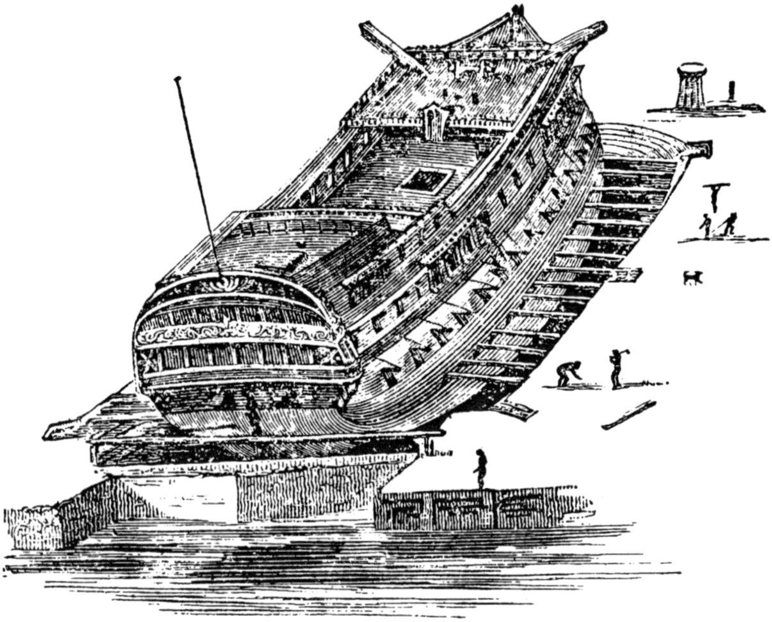

Portrait of His Majesty's ship Impetueux, by Mr. Pocock, taken by Lord Hugh Seymour on the first of June, 1794, and then called l'Amerique. She was afterwards named Impetueux, from the ship of that name which was burnt in Portsmouth harbour. She was fitted out expressly under the late Admiral J. W. Payne's directions, who placed the Crest of The Prince in the centre of her beautiful stern. For further particulars, see our first and third Volumes.

BIOGRAPHICAL MEMOIR OF

WILLIAM DOMETT, Esq.

REAR-ADMIRAL OF THE WHITE SQUADRON.

" Hope, rising, bids us mourn, but not despair.
Trust, Britain, to thy naval sons! for there
See, from his Phœnix ashes future Nelsons spring!"
Anon.

THOUGH we cannot but lament, with deep sorrow, and heart-felt anguish, the loss of the departed Nelson; despair, while we have so many " heroes of the dark rolling sea," is a sentiment that can never enter the British bosom. We feel a cheering consciousness of superiority; satisfied that, from the acknowledged excellence of our naval tactics, and the proved valour of our seamen, we must ever retain that superiority; unless, indeed, for some wise purpose, a higher power than that of man should inflict the stroke of defeat.

The first name which we shall inscribe on our FIFTEENTH COLUMN, is that of Rear-Admiral Domett, *another* friend of the illustrious Nelson! He is, we doubt not, impressed with a due sense of the honour, as it proves him to be deserving of his country's esteem.

This gentleman, who was born in the year 1754, is descended from a respectable family in Devonshire. In 1769, he embarked, as a Midshipman, under the patronage of Captain Hood (now Lord Bridport), on board His Majesty's ship Quebec, commanded by the present Lord Ducie *, and served in that ship upwards of three years in the West Indies. On the return of the Quebec to England, in 1773, when she was paid off, Mr. Domett went on board His Majesty's ship Scorpion, under the command of Lord Keith, in the Mediterranean. He remained in this ship until her return to England, in the spring of the year 1775, when he was removed into the Marlborough, commanded by the present Lord Hood. He served only a few weeks in the Marlborough, and then embarked as Master's Mate of His Majesty's ship Surprise, commanded by the late Admiral Robert Linzee, and employed on the Newfoundland station.

In the month of March, 1777, the Surprise sailed from Plymouth for Quebec, which was then besieged by an American army; and, after a very boisterous passage, and lying in the Gulf of St. Lawrence, entirely surrounded with ice, for more than three weeks, she was the first ship that arrived at Quebec. She immediately proceeded up the river, above that town, to annoy as much as possible the American army in its retreat; the siege having been raised on its being known that reinforcements had arrived in the river.

The Surprise was soon afterwards sent to Newfoundland; and, on her arrival in St. John's harbour, Mr. Domett was, by

---

* This nobleman, then Captain Francis Reynolds Morton, succeeded to the title of Lord Ducie, on his brother's death in 1785; in consequence of which he resigned his rank in the navy, and his country lost the future services of a good, gallant, and most able officer. His Lordship is Provost Marshal of the island of Barbadoes, a *sinecure* office, which has been held in his family many years.

the recommendation of Captain Linzee, taken into the Romney, the flag-ship of the late Admiral John Montagu, then Governor and Commander in Chief on that station. He served as acting Lieutenant of that ship, until her return to England in the fall of the year 1777; when, by the desire of his first patron, Lord Bridport, he was made a Lieutenant, and appointed to the Robust, then under his Lordship's command*. Mr. Domett was second Lieutenant of the Robust, in the battle between the fleet commanded by Admiral Keppel, and that of the French, under the command of Admiral the Count d'Orvilliers, on the 27th of July 1778†.

In the beginning of the following year, Lord Bridport quitting the command of the Robust, Captain (now Admiral) Cosby was appointed to that ship‡; and Lieutenant Domett had the honour of serving under him till the summer of 1781. He was his first Lieutenant in the battle which took place off the Chesapeak§, in North America, between a squadron of His Majesty's ships commanded by Admiral Arbuthnot, and a French squadron that had been for some time in that country, under the Chevalier de Ternay; in which action the Robust, as we have fully stated in our memoir of Admiral Cosby, bore an important part, being very much disabled, and suffering more in killed and wounded than any other ship in the squadron. The complimentary letter, addressed by Admiral Arbuthnot to Captain Cosby ||, is a sufficient proof of the high estimation in which the conduct of the officers and crew of the Robust was held by the Commander in Chief on that occasion.

In the autumn of 1781, Lieutenant Domett was removed to His Majesty's ship Invincible, commanded by the present Sir Charles Saxton, and was on board that ship in Admiral Graves's action with the French fleet off the Chesapeak, in the month of September¶. Soon after this he was taken into the Barfleur,

---

* *Vide* NAVAL CHRONICLE, Vol. I, page 273.

† *Ibid.*; and Vol. VII, page 296, *et seq.*

‡ *Vide* NAVAL CHRONICLE, Vol. XIV, page 357.

§ *Ibid.*, page 358, *et seq.* || *Ibid.*, page 360.

¶ *Vide* NAVAL CHRONICLE, Vol. V, page 391.

by his friend Lord Hood, and had the honour of serving under him as signal officer, during the memorable and masterly manœuvres of his Lordship at St. Kitt's, and the several actions which took place on that occasion *. He was also in the glorious battle of the 12th of April, 1782 †; when, on the Count de Grasse, in the Ville de Paris, striking to the Barfleur, and the first Lieutenant being sent to take possession of that ship, Mr. Domett was appointed to succeed him in that situation.

Some days after the battle, Lord Hood was allowed to pursue the flying enemy with such ships of his division as had been the least disabled; and, on the morning of the 19th of April, he got sight of five sail of the fugitives. On perceiving the British squadron, they pushed for the Mona Passage, in hopes, from the shallowness of the water, that they would not be pursued. Determined, however, if possibility would admit, to effect his object, Lord Hood threw out the signal for a general chase. As the enemy approached the Passage, the wind died away, and they lay some time becalmed, which gave our ships greatly the advantage, and enabled Captain Goodall, in the Valiant, at three P.M. to get alongside of the Caton, of 64 guns, which struck at the first broadside. This brave officer, leaving her to be picked up by the ships astern, proceeded on and attacked the Jason, of the same force, with so much impetuosity, that, after a stout resistance for twenty minutes, she also hauled down her colours. Captain Robert Linzee, in the Magnificent, took l'Aimable, of 32 guns; and Captain Alexander Hood, in the Champion, the Ceres, of 16 guns. The only remaining ship of the enemy, l'Astrée, of 32 guns, although closely pursued, effected her escape. Mr. Domett, who had very actively exerted himself on this occasion, was appointed to the command of the Ceres, which proved to be an English sloop, formerly taken from us by a French frigate.—Subsequently to this, our officer remained some time cruising with Lord Hood off St. Domingo, and was then sent home by Lord Rodney, with the account of the capture of the before-mentioned ships in the Mona Passage.

* *Vide* NAVAL CHRONICLE, Vol. II, page 14, *et seq.* † *Ibid.*, page 21.

On the 9th of September, in the same year, 1782, Captain Domett was made Post; and, by the particular desire of his steady friend, Lord Bridport, who hoisted his flag, as Rear-Admiral of the White, on board His Majesty's ship Queen, of 90 guns, he was appointed to that ship. Lord Bridport assumed the command of the second, or larboard division, in the fleet sent under the command of Lord Howe to relieve Gibraltar. Captain Domett consequently proceeded with the expedition to that port, and was in the battle which took place on the 19th of October *.

On the restoration of peace, in 1783, the Queen was paid off; and this was the first time that Captain Domett had been out of actual service, since his first embarking, in 1769, in the Quebec frigate. His period of relaxation, however, was not of a protracted nature; for, in the beginning of the year 1785, he was again called into service, by being appointed to the Champion frigate, of 24 guns, and employed as the senior officer on the Leith station, where he remained until the Dutch armament in October 1787. He was then superseded, in order to be appointed to the London, intended to bear the flag of Lord Bridport; but, an accommodation immediately taking place with Holland, Captain Domett did not take the command of the London, but was, in the spring of the following year, appointed to the Pomona, in which he went to the coast of Africa, and proceeded thence to the West Indies.

On his return to England, in the beginning of the year 1789, he was removed from the Pomona to the Salisbury, at the request of the late Admiral Milbanke, who hoisted his flag in that ship, having been appointed Governor and Commander in Chief at Newfoundland. Captain Domett continued in the Salisbury till the month of June 1790, when, in consequence of an armament that took place on account of the dispute with Spain respecting Nootka Sound, he was appointed to the command of the London, to which he had once before been nominated. This appointment, as well as the former, pro-

* *Vide* NAVAL CHRONICLE, Vol. I, pages 17 and 275.

ceeded from the influence, and was made at the express desire of Lord Bridport, who had chosen that ship for the reception of his flag. The London proceeded to Torbay, where a fleet was assembled under the command of Lord Howe; but, the misunderstanding with Spain having been accommodated, the fleet was paid off in the month of December, in the same year; and Captain Domett was immediately appointed to the command of the Pegasus frigate, and again employed on the Newfoundland station. In the fall of the year 1791, he proceeded from Newfoundland to Cadiz and Lisbon; and, on his arrival in England, about the latter end of December, in the same year, the Pegasus was paid off.

The services of Captain Domett were in such estimation, that he did not remain long inactive. In the spring of 1792, he was appointed to the Romney, at the request of Admiral Goodall*, who hoisted his flag in that ship, and proceeded to the Mediterranean, as Commander in Chief on that station. Captain Domett continued to serve in the Romney, with his friend Admiral Goodall, till the commencement of the late war in 1793, when he was again applied for by his steady friend and patron Lord Bridport, to be his Captain in the Royal George. To this ship he was appointed in the month of May, and was employed, in the western squadron, under Earl Howe, during the remainder of the year 1793. Captain Domett continued to command the Royal George; and, on the glorious 1st of June, 1794†, he distinguished himself in a very gallant manner. The Royal George, as we have stated in our memoir of Lord Bridport, commenced the action on the 29th of May, and, during that and the 1st of June, she was exposed to an incessant and fierce cannonade; by which the foremast, with the fore and main-top-mast, were shot away; and twenty men were killed and seventy-two wounded.

Captain Domett, on this occasion, was honoured with a gold chain and medal from His Majesty.

* Captain of the Valiant, at the capture of the French ships in the Mona Passage, on the 19th of April, 1782. *Vide* page 4, preceding.

† *Vide* NAVAL CHRONICLE, Vol. I, pages 20 and 277.

Colossus, Captain J. Monckton—4 seamen and 1 soldier killed; 26 seamen and two soldiers wounded.—Lieut. Mends, and Mr. John Whyley, Midshipman, wounded.

Sans Pareil, Right Hon. Lord Hugh Seymour, Captain Browell—7 seamen and 1 soldier killed.—Lieut. C. M. Stocker, 2d Lieutenant; Lieut. W. Jephcott, 2d Lieutenant of marines, killed; Lieut. F. J. Nott, and Mr. Richard Spencer, Midshipman, wounded.

London, Captain E. Griffith—2 seamen wounded.—Mr. J. E. Baker, Midshipman, wounded.

Queen, Vice-Admiral Sir A. Gardner, Captain Bedford—None killed or wounded.

Prince George, Captain Edge—None killed or wounded.

Royal George, Admiral Lord Bridport, Captain Domett—5 seamen and 1 soldier wounded.

Royal George, at Sea, June 24. BRIDPORT.

Captain Domett continued in the command of the Royal George for a considerable time after Lord Bridport struck his flag; amounting, in the whole, to a period of about seven years and a half; a greater length of time, perhaps, than ever fell to the lot of an individual successively to command a first rate. During this period, too, the Royal George was considered as one of the best disciplined and most expert ships, in all her manœuvres, in His Majesty's Navy.

For a short time, while he commanded her, Lord St. Vincent hoisted his flag on board, and appointed our officer to act as Captain of the fleet.

In the month of November, 1800, in consequence of the Royal George being wanted to bear the flag of Sir Hyde Parker, Captain Domett was removed from that ship, and appointed to the command of the Belleisle, one of the French prizes taken by Lord Bridport off l'Orient.

On a promotion of flag officers taking place, on the 1st of January 1801, by which the Colonelcies of Marines became vacant, Captain Domett had the honour of receiving His Majesty's appointment to be Colonel of the Portsmouth division of that distinguished *corps*.

In the succeeding month, Captain Domett was removed from the Belleisle, and appointed Captain of the fleet, in the London, of 98 guns, under the command of Sir Hyde Parker, to be employed in the Baltic. He accordingly proceeded with him in that capacity to Copenhagen; and, after the battle which took place off that city*, and Sir Hyde Parker had left the fleet to return to England, Captain Domett, at the solicitation of Lord Nelson, on whom the command devolved, remained with his Lordship, as Captain of the fleet, until Admiral Sir C. M. Pole arrived, and took the command thereof.

In June 1801, Captain Domett returned to England with his friend Lord Nelson, and immediately resumed the command of his old ship the Belleisle, then with the Channel fleet off Ushant. In a short time afterwards, Admiral Cornwallis applied for him to be appointed Captain of the Channel fleet, in which situation he continued to serve until the peace of Amiens, when the Admiral struck his flag, and the fleet was paid off.

The cessation of hostilities afforded but a short relief to Captain Domett; for, not many months after, he was appointed senior officer, with a broad pendant, on the Coast of Ireland, where, we believe, he continued to be employed until the commencement of the present war. At that period he was again requested by Admiral Cornwallis, then appointed to command the Channel fleet, to resume his old station of Captain thereof. In this capacity he continued to share with the gallant and persevering Commander in Chief, the duties and fatigues of service, in an unusually long protracted blockade, during the severest season of the year, and until the month of April, 1804, when he was promoted to the rank of Rear-Admiral of the Blue Squadron.

Soon after this promotion, he was ordered to hoist his flag in the North Sea; but, in consequence of ill health, he was under the necessity of declining the proffered command.

* We have had such repeated occasion to enter at large into the merits of the glorious battle off Copenhagen, in which Captain Domett had the honour of sustaining a part, that, in the present instance, repetition would be superfluous. The reader is therefore referred, for particulars, to our Biographical Memoir of Sir Hyde Parker, Vol. V, page 281, *et seq.*; to several other parts of the same Volume; to our Addenda to the Life of Lord Nelson, Vol. XIV, page 391, *et seq.*; to our Memoir of Captain Sir F. Thesiger, Vol. XIV, page 441, &c.

bluntly said, "*I thank you, stay where you are; you will do more good there:*" he then went down by himself to the cockpit. The Surgeon (who respected him) would willingly have attended him, in preference to others, whose wounds were less alarming; but Main would not admit of it, saying, "*Avast, not until it comes to my turn, if you please.*" The Surgeon soon after amputated the shattered part of the arm, near the shoulder; during which, with great composure, smiling, and with a steady clear voice, he sang the whole of "*Rule Britannia.*" The cheerfulness of this rough son of Neptune has been of infinite use in keeping up the spirits of his wounded shipmates, and I hope this recital may be of service to him.

Plymouth, December 1.

I am sorry to inform you, that the above-mentioned fine fellow died since writing the above, at Gibraltar Hospital, of a fever he caught, when the stump of his arm was nearly well.

H. B.

SHERIDAN'S LINES, ON THE DEATH OF COLONEL BULLER, APPLIED TO THE DEATH OF LORD NELSON.

AMONG the multitude of verses produced on the lamented death of Lord Nelson, we regret to observe that scarcely any thing has appeared worthy the occasion, or the illustrious subject. The following Lines, concluding a little Poem which found its way into print at the time, written by R. B. Sheridan, Esq., and addressed to his present Lady, on the death of her near relation, Colonel Buller, who was killed in Flanders in the last war, we cannot but think singularly applicable to the last moments of our departed Hero. We wish the acknowledged patriotism of the Author would induce the same pen to an exertion upon an occasion which calls upon every talent the country possesses, to assist the national gratitude in the expression of its feelings:—

"Fall'n with the brave, e'er number'd with the slain,
His mind, unwounded, sooths his body's pain—
Half rais'd he leans—see Friendship bending o'er,
But ah! with looks that promise life no more!

Hopeless—but not dismay'd—with fearless eye
He reads the doom that tells him he must die;
Lays his brave hand upon his bleeding breast,
And feels his glory while he finds his rest—

Then yields the transient breath which Nature gave,
And sure of prouder life, o'erlooks the grave:
Sweet is the meed that waits his laurell'd bier,
'Tis Valour's hope—'tis Honour's praise sincere—
'Tis Friendship's manly sigh, and gentle Beauty's tear."

BOULTON'S TRAFALGAR MEDAL.

MR. BOULTON, the scientific and venerable proprietor of Soho, whose public exertions have so uniformly been distinguished by a patriotism the best directed, has solicited the permission of Government, that he might be allowed to strike a Medal, at his own expense, in commemoration of the brilliant victory off Cape Trafalgar, and to present one to every seaman who served that day on board the British Fleet. The permission was immediately granted, with the warmest approbation of so laudable a design. In a short time the Medals will be sent down to the several ports, to be distributed among the valorous tars by His Majesty's Commissioners, thus enabling the heroic defenders of their country, to carry to their wives, and sweethearts, the most honourable testimony—

"That their own true Sailor he was one!"

JACK TAR IN THE PLAYHOUSE.

AT Covent Garden Theatre, shortly after the news of Lord Nelson's death had arrived, the following interesting incident occurred:—

In the pit, at an early part of the evening, a sailor, apparently about thirty years of age, and of very healthy appearance, with the blunt and honest manner of a real tar, bawled loudly for those aloft (meaning the galleries) *to stow their jabber*, (or cease their noise); increasing thereby the confusion which prevailed. Jack, at length, raising himself on one of the seats, exclaimed—"*Messmates aloft—three hearty cheers for* Nelson *and the* Nile!—Jack was obeyed; nor were the shouts confined to the galleries only.

Jack, from the attention paid to him, was now inclined to indulge himself further, and producing a medal, to which he fastened a black riband, he gave the audience to understand that "it was a medal which had been struck to commemorate the Battle of the Nile; and which, as the brave Nelson was no more, and it bore his head, he offered it to their notice, (pointing to the black riband) in mourning!—Much applause followed; and the medal in mourning was conspicuously waved by the sailor many times during the remainder of the night.

Jack having repeatedly called to the musicians between the acts of the tragedy, for "*Rule Britannia*," without being attended to, at the conclusion of the play forced his way, through all impediments in the pit, to the orchestra, when he again waved his black riband with the medal affixed to it, and insisted upon his favourite tune, and with which he was at this time indulged.

Much applause followed; and Jack, as he twirled round his black riband, lost the medal, which found its way to the stage. A gentleman in one of the boxes beckoned to a performer whom he observed standing against one of the wings at the side of the stage, to take up and bring to him the medal which the sailor had lost, which was accordingly done, and Jack soon after was again in possession of his prize.

The honest sailor then, until the close of the entertainment, continued tranquil; when he suddenly clambered over the orchestra; and succeeded in taking possession of the stage! Shouts, accompanied with much laughter, now predominated in the house, and Jack made several ineffectual attempts to *speechify*. The audience, however, at length became silent, to listen to what he had to say, when he addressed them in the following words:—

"*Ladies and Gentlemen*,

"Shall I give you a *handspike* (meaning a hornpipe) or a song?"

A song! a song! was exclaimed by many at the same time in the gallery; but Jack being beckoned to by a performer from the right hand stage-door, he retired before he had performed the vocal part of the task he had voluntarily undertaken to attempt.

Nothing more was heard of the sailor until the final piece, "*Nelson's Glory*," was nearly concluded; when Mr. Incledon stepped forward to the front of the stage, and spoke the following words:—

"*Ladies and Gentlemen*,

"One of the brave crew of the Victory begs your permission to appear before you on this occasion, that he may join in the chorus of "*Rule Britannia*."

This extraordinary request was instantly granted, with very loud reiterated applause; when the honest sailor, of whom we have been speaking, again appeared, and, *sans ceremonie*, seized the British flag, which one of the performers supported, and exultingly continued to wave it above the head of Incledon, till the song of "*Rule Britannia*" was concluded.

This made a wonderful impression on the minds of the spectators; and the final curtain at length dropped amidst the loudest plaudits, in which the ladies in the boxes, and, in fact, every individual present most heartily joined.

When the honest tar indicated a resolution not to part with the flag, although importuned by the performer whose office it was to bear it, the theatre resounded with the highest acclamations of spontaneous approbation.

HORRIBLE INSTANCE OF FRENCH CRUELTY.

THE following statement, relative to the capture of the Esther, Captain Irving, is copied from a late American paper.

Charlestown, November 5.

WE mentioned yesterday the critical situation in which the British ships Esther and Minorca were left on Sunday evening, with the French privateer in company, and the probability that one or both of the ships would be taken. We regret that our fears have been realized, by the capture of the Esther, accompanied with such a bloody massacre, that our feelings revolt at the bare recital of the dreadful tale. The circumstances, as far as we have been able to collect, are these:—

On Monday morning, about seven o'clock, the privateer bore down on the Esther, but was kept off by the gallant and well-directed fire of the brave Captain Irving and his crew. for nearly an hour; the wind, however, becoming so light, that the ship could not answer her helm, the privateer, taking the advantage with her sweeps, got alongside, and grappled. In this situation the contest was continued for three quarters of an hour, when the Frenchmen succeeded in getting on board the ship: here they were kept at bay, for nearly twenty minutes, by the ship's crew; but Captain Irving being severely wounded in the thigh, and having five of his men killed, ordered the colours to be struck, and retired to his cabin. Mr. Lowdon, the third Mate, after having hauled down the colours, was coming forward, when he was shot, and thrown overboard. Four of the privateer's men then followed Captain Irving into the cabin, where he was shot, and most cruelly mangled, and his body was thrown over the side before life was extinct. Mr. Edwards, the second Mate, a fine young man, while in the act of supporting his dying Captain in his arms, was stabbed in several places with a small sword, and otherwise so severely cut in his head, that no hopes are entertained of his recovery. By this time the residue of the crew were driven below, when the Frenchmen, having complete possession of the ship, the inhuman monster, Ross, ordered the prisoners to be brought on deck, and put to death. This being remonstrated against, by some of the privateer's men, he ordered them to fire upon them, when several muskets were discharged into the hatchway, which killed the Carpenter, and mortally wounded two seamen, who have since died.

The privateer is called the Creole, mounts six guns, of different calibre; is commanded by one Pierre Burgman; and had on board, at the commencement of the action, 111 men. They state their loss to be six killed, seven severely wounded, and a number missing, supposed to have been knocked overboard and drowned.

The wounded Englishmen were yesterday put on board one of our pilot boats. Two of the seamen died before she reached town. Mr. Ashton, the first Mate, died on board, at the wharf; one poor fellow died while they were conveying him to the hospital. Two seamen at the hospital, and thirteen others, are so dreadfully cut up, that it is supposed only two of the number can possibly recover.

The Captain of the privateer was wounded in the fleshy part of the arm by a musket ball, and Ross slightly in the wrist—they were both knocked overboard, but succeeded in regaining the privateer. We are sorry to state, that three of the seamen (a Venetian and two Portuguese) belonging to the Esther, have entered on board the privateer, notwithstanding they had stood to their quarters and behaved well during the action. The privateer has gone off with the Esther. She was a fine ship, and had on board a valuable cargo of sugars, &c.; but being in a leaky condition, doubts are entertained of her reaching port. She made 16 inches of water per hour.

ADMIRAL RAINIER.

Madras Gazette, 2d March, 1805.

ON Tuesday evening, the Civil Servants of the Honourable Company gave an elegant entertainment at the Pantheon, to his Excellency Vice-Admiral Rainier, on the occasion of his departure for Europe.

The Admiral was received by the Stewards, who were appointed for the occasion, in the front room of the Pantheon; and the Right Honourable the Governor, accompanied by his Excellency

Sir John Craddock, and the Honourable Sir Arthur Wellesley, arrived shortly after.

A trumpet announced dinner being on the table, and was followed by the band striking up the popular tune of "God save the King!"—the company now passed through the theatre, and descended to a building which had been erected for the purpose.

On entering the pavilion, the eye was immediately attracted by the elegance and splendour with which it was fitted up; the whole was covered with fine white linen, richly embossed with stars of gold, and fringed with variegated colours, to which were attached small reflecting globes, which presented the most grand *coup d'œil* the imagination can conceive—the superb pillars, by which the whole was supported, were alternately gold, and blue and white—the whole evidently displaying the taste of the gentleman who had the management of this part of the entertainment.

The chandeliers and lamps which illuminated this spacious and grand building were distributed with an equal degree of simplicity and elegance.

THE DINNER.—The Admiral was conducted to the centre of the table, on the right hand of the senior Civil Servant, the Governor and Sir Arthur Wellesley to the left, and the Commander in Chief and Mr. Petrie to the opposite side—At regulated spaces two Stewards were placed throughout the whole length, by which means the utmost regularity prevailed; and notwithstanding the number of visitors that were present, a private entertainment could not have been conducted with more order and regularity.

The tables were covered with every luxury that munificence could produce; every thing was of its best kind, and what is scarcely to be paralleled, was quite hot. The wines were cool, excellent, and in great abundance. The claret had been selected with the greatest attention, and the other wines were of the best importations.

After dinner the following toasts, among others, were drunk:—

THE KING—Tune, *God save the King!*

THE NAVY.—*Rule Britannia.*

THE ARMY—*Britons strike home!*

ADMIRAL RAINIER, and a pleasant passage to him. This toast was received with the greatest applause, and drank with three times three, the band playing *Hearts of Oak.*

THE HONOURABLE COMPANY—*Money in both Pockets.*

MARQUIS WELLESLEY AND THE GOVERNMENT IN INDIA—*St. Patrick's Day in the Morning.*

The company were obligingly entertained, by several gentlemen of the Presidency, with many select and choice songs, and the gallant Admiral sang three or four during the evening.

The following complimentary song, written in haste for the occasion, was introduced by a gentleman present, in the most happy manner :—

I.

'Twas on a day, when Albion's foes
Had bled beneath her conquering arm,
And shatter'd by a thousand blows,
Shrunk trembling from her stern alarm ;
That rising from the troubled wave,
Britannia thus her orders gave :—
" Victory, go forth, and to my longing sight
Place those my favourite Chiefs, the bulwarks of the fight."

II.

Victory the mandate, pleas'd, obeys,
And, fix'd in her triumphal car,
The semblance, first, of *Howe* displays,
The *Father* of the thundering war!
On his right hand, with threatening mien,
And fearless, was *St. Vincent* seen ;
The Spanish flag, no more the prop of pride,
Bath'd in its Country's blood, hung drooping by his side.

III.

Scotland's fam'd Hero next appears :
Duncan, of great and just renown ;
Fair Victory high her banner rears
To hail the *Chief of Camperdown!*
While *Nelson*, rushing from the Main,
Egypt's dread Warriors in his train,
Tells how the Battle of the Nile was won,
And proud Britannia springs to greet her darling son !—

IV.

" Yet not enough"—the Goddess cried—
" One *Veteran*, still, I pant to see,
Alike his grateful Country's pride,
Alike thy *boast*, O Victory!
And tho' relentless Time hath spread
His silver honours o'er his head,
While *Commerce* triumphs in her India's fame,
Rainier! her happy sons shall venerate thy name."

The Right Honourable the Governor did not rise from the table until past twelve, and it was near three o'clock before the Admiral departed from this well supplied and hospitable board.

A more splendid and well conducted entertainment has never been given at this Presidency; and if we may judge from the hilarity and pleasantry of the company, which may be deemed a just criterion in these cases, few have been partaken of, productive of more pleasure and satisfaction.

The Committee who had the management were,

Messrs. Oakes,	Buchan,
Dick,	Hodgson,
Roebuck,	Hurdis,
Balfour,	Garrow,
Smith,	Greenway, and
Ogilvie,	Higginson.

CAPTURE OF THE SHANNON AND TRIMMER.

Bombay Courier, Feb. 16, 1805.

THE following particulars regarding the unfortunate capture of the Shannon and Trimmer, by the pirates infesting the Gulf of Persia, are communicated by a letter received from Captain Babcock, of the former vessel, dated Bussora, January 6, 1805:—

It is with much regret I have to inform you of the melancholy and unfortunate circumstance that happened to me on board the Shannon, on the 1st day of December last, in my passage up the Gulf, near the island of Polior, after a short but pretty smart engagement with fifteen pirate dows and botillas. At three in the afternoon they boarded the Shannon with swords and spears in hand, and I am sorry to acquaint you that I had one man killed outright, and four more severely wounded, besides myself. You will be sorry to learn that I have had my left hand taken off at the wrist, my left shoulder dislocated, and eight wounds in my body. In this deplorable state, being stript quite naked, I lay eight days weltering in my gore, exposed to the weather, not being permitted to go below. I was fortunate in getting some biscuit and a few bottles of wine the next day, but the crew were not allowed any fire or food for three days.

I am sorry to add that the Trimmer was taken on the same day, at about half past ten in the forenoon. The only person wounded was the officer, who will, I believe, lose the use of his right hand. On the 11th they put me again in possession of the Shannon, with only two cables and anchors, a compass, two guns, a part of an old English ensign, and a frail of dates, bidding me go where I pleased; first having put on board the Shannon, Captain Cumming, and all the christians belonging to the Trimmer. On the 29th of December we arrived safe at Bussora, where we were kindly received by Mr. Manesty, whose attentions not a little contributed to the relief of our distresses.

I expect to sail for Bombay in about a month, and am happy to inform you that it is likely I may recover in a short time from the severity of my wounds. The loss of my hand however is irretrievable, and being plundered of all my clothes, &c. I am now ready for the *newest fashion.*

THE LATE CAPTAIN DUFF.

THE following account of the late gallant Captain Duff, of the Mars, has appeared in the Scotch papers:—

Upon the general promotion in the navy, which took place in April 1804, Captain Duff was appointed to the command of the Mars, of 74 guns, and immediately proceeded to join her off Ferrol. He cruised off that port, and successively off Rochefort and Brest, as one of the Channel fleet, till, in May last, he was detached to Cadiz, under Vice-Admiral Collingwood, whose small squadron of four ships of the line, afterwards increased to eight, continued to keep their station off that port, unawed by the arrival of the combined fleet.

Vice-Admiral Lord Nelson having, in the end of September, returned from England, to resume the command upon that most important station, made a disposition of his increased force into two divisions, one of which was to be led by himself, and the other by Vice-Admiral Collingwood. Rear-Admiral Louis having been detached to the Mediterranean with seven sail of the line, Captain Duff had the honour, upon his departure, though there were senior Captains in the fleet, to be appointed Commodore of the advanced squadron of four sail of the line, by the recommendation, no doubt, of Vice-Admiral Collingwood, who selected the Mars to be second to himself in his division of the fleet.—On the 21st of October, in the ever-memorable battle off Trafalgar, Captain Duff acted with such judgment and intrepidity, that, though his ship sailed ill, and there was little wind, he was the third in action; and was one of four ships which, owing to an unfortunate calm, had to maintain the conflict for a considerable time with the leeward division of the enemy's fleet. He continued to exert himself with the most undaunted heroism, having at one time to contend with no less than four of the enemy's ships, till he was struck dead by a cannon shot, one hour and five minutes after the commencement of the battle; about the same time that the companion of his youth, Captain Cooke, was killed in the Bellerophon, and that their Commander in Chief, the great Lord Nelson, was mortally wounded on board the Victory!

Captain Duff was a man of fine stature, strong and well made, above six feet in height, and had a manly, open, benevolent countenance. During thirty years' service, he had not been four years unemployed; about twenty months after his return from the West Indies in 1787, and not quite two years after the last war. Although he went early to sea, he lost no opportunity of improving himself in the theory, as well as in the practice of his profession, and acted the part of an instructor and father to the numerous young men who were under his command. By his beloved wife he had five children, of whom a boy and two girls remain, together with their disconsolate mother, to mourn their father's death. His son, thirteen years of age, had joined him as a Midshipman on the 19th of September last; and soon after his arrival on board the Mars, wrote exultingly to his mother, that his father's ship had been put in the post of honour, next to Vice-Admiral Collingwood, in his division of the fleet. This spirited youth, who has commenced his career in so interesting a manner, was, after the transcendant victory off Trafalgar, removed by Admiral, now Lord Collingwood, with the kindest attention, from on board the Mars to the Euryalus frigate, which was soon after sent with dispatches to England. The Hon. Captain Blackwood, the distinguished officer who commands that ship, has undertaken, in the handsomest manner, to continue to take charge of the son of his respected friend, the late Captain Duff, than whom, he has been pleased to say, "His Majesty's service could not boast of a better or more gallant officer." We can add, with the greatest truth, that he was also a tender husband, an affectionate parent, a dutiful son, and a sincere friend. In the navy he was called Worthy Duff.

CAPTURES FROM THE FRENCH.

SPANISH and French men of war taken, destroyed, or blown up, with the amount of guns and seamen captured from these powers, by the wonderful exertions of our gallant tars and royal marines, from July 23 to Nov. 5, 1805, on the European seas, or western station:—

By Rear-Admiral Calder, July 23, 1805.

Names.	Guns.	Men.
La Firme, S.	74	850
San Raphael, S.	84	1000
By the Phœnix, 44, Captain Baker.		
La Didon, F.	48	370
By l'Egyptienne, 40, Hon. Captain Fleming.		
L'Acteon, F.	22	150
By Goliath, 74, and our cruisers.		
La Torche, F.	20	180
La Faune, F.	18	160
By the late Vice-Admiral Lord Nelson, Lord Collingwood, and the Earl of Northesk, off Trafalgar, Oct. 21, 22, 28.		
Twenty sail of the line; viz.		
14 French / 6 Spanish / From 110 guns to 74 guns.	1648	21,210
By Rear-Admiral Strachan, Nov. 4, off Cape Ortegal.		
Le Formidable, F. Admiral Dumanoir	84	990
Mont Blanc, F.	74	750
Du Guay Trouin, F.	74	750
Scipion, F.	74	750
Total,	2220	27,120

Privateers omitted in the above list.

Recapitulation.

Loss of the enemy, 26 ships of the line, from 110 to 74 guns, 1 frigate of 48 guns, and 3 corvettes.

Men of war, 30.

Guns, 2220. Calibre, 42-pounders to 12 pounders.

Seamen and soldiers, amongst which are all the prime seamen of France and Spain, 27,120.

LORD NELSON.

THE exact circumstances under which our lamented Hero fell, have not yet been stated. Captain Hardy and himself had walked the quarter-deck for some minutes, conversing upon the business of the pending contest. They had been silent about a minute, and Captain Hardy had continued his walk to the end of the quarter-deck, before he perceived that Lord Nelson had turned, three or four paces short of him, and had fallen. Two sailors were then in the act of raising him. Captain Hardy took his hand and said, "I hope, my Lord, you are not badly wounded?" Lord Nelson said, "Yes—my back is broke, Hardy, they have caught me at last." (Those were the exact words.) As the seamen were carrying his Lordship down, he said, "Put something over my face; don't say a word about *me*." Thus careful was he to prevent any check from being given to the ardent spirit he had previously excited among the crew.

Of all the merits, by which this wonderful man was distinguished, perhaps the most remarkable was the union of so great a degree of coolness and deliberation in forming his plans, with such astonishing heroism and ardour in executing them. It is not much known, but is true, that during his pursuit of the combined fleets from the West Indies, he had formed *seven* distinct plans for attacking them, each calculated to suit some difference in the positions of his fleet and theirs, or in the direction of the wind, or in the degree of nearness to a port. Of each of those plans a sufficient number of copies was written out for the Captains, so that if the enemy had been seen under circumstances corresponding with any one of them, not a moment would have been lost in preparing suitable orders for circulation through the fleet.

CORRESPONDENCE.

MR. EDITOR,

HAVING read in the fourteenth Volume of your NAVAL CHRONICLE*, some extracts from a very excellent and appropriate sermon preached by the Rev. Mr. Clarke, on the Thanksgiving day, and received great pleasure from his sketch of the piety of a seaman's feelings, I think an extract from one preached by the Rev. J. Symons, Rector of Whitburn, to the soldiers at his church on the 17th of November, upon the news of Lord Nelson's victory and lamented death, may not be unacceptable to your readers. I wish that the same means to form the soldiers' mind to a like pious confidence in Providence, were still in use in that branch of the service, and that every regiment, as every ship of war, had its Chaplain to perform

* Page 487.

"the holy service of the established church" with the same solemnity and devotion that Mr. Clarke describes on board our squadrons. Yours, &c.

PHILO NAUT.

After pointing out the influence of christianity in forming the military and moral character of a soldier, and considering this as the genuine source of the truest courage, he thus proceeds to illustrate his doctrine by the apposite example which had been so recently afforded in our late great naval victory.

Did there need a proof of this, we have an example at hand most convincing and satisfactory: and, though that example is taken from another service, it is equally applicable to your own. The recent and splendid victory which has been achieved by one branch of our national force over an enemy so superior in numbers, shows what discipline and courage directed and inspired by principle can do.

It presents the gratifying picture of a christian hero in the hour of battle. Skilful, experienced, intrepid, fortunate above all other men, yet not, like the idol of our enemies, intoxicated with his successes, and boasting of the command of fortune, but humbly relying for future, as in his past successes, upon God.—Prepared for victory if it should please the Lord of all power and might to crown his well concerted plans with success—prepared to receive it with humble praise if he should live to witness the glorious triumph—prepared to resign himself into the hands of God, if he should not be permitted to share in the joy which his country would feel upon the occasion.

It presents a christian warrior about to enter into an arduous conflict, on which depended not merely the safety or existence of his own country, but of the whole civilized world. Cool, collected, and undismayed by superiority of numbers or advantage of position, he advances to the battle with that dignified superiority and confidence which nothing but duty and a full trust in God could inspire.

Mark the last orders that he gave as he entered into the tremendous contest—words that should be engraved on every helmet and inscribed on every soldier's breast—"ENGLAND EXPECTS EVERY MAN TO DO HIS DUTY."—And what but duty—what but a strong sense of duty, and a confidence in that Almighty Power who ruleth the events of war could have inspired the whole band of patriots, as well as their brave leaders, to achieve the wonders that they did?

Well they knew the character of their nations and their accustomed triumphs over the enemy they had to encounter. Well they knew their country is not ungrateful. Well might they anticipate the joy with which that country would receive the news of this addition to the glories which it had so often received at the hands of its brave defenders: but something more is wanting, at such a time, to animate men to deeds like theirs. The honours would be confined to few. The rewards with which their country is never backward to distinguish meritorious services are small compared with the perils of the contest: and though in the character of their nation, and the benefits to be derived to their country, every man would share in the glory and advantage to be obtained, this was no more than the enemy might feel in common with themselves.

No. It was this that must inspire them with courage and confidence to brave and surmount the arduous and perilous contest, that every man was *doing his duty*—discharging his duty to his King and Country—acting under the dictates of a conscientious principle, that would not suffer any man to fall short of any other man in fulfilling the duties of his profession.

The previous discipline which prepared them for the contest was founded on the principle of conscientious obedience that I have been describing. It was this principle that paved the way for that good order and discipline which are so necessary to the success of every enterprize. It was this principle which inspired them with that courage which their Commander describes to have been *irresistible*. It was the principle of religion that prepared them to look death in the face with that coolness which we see to have been the case with our departed Hero, and which, if their individual feelings could have been collected, no doubt each individually felt. It was a confidence in God, in that Providence which had so often and so signally displayed his power in the protection and defence of their country against all its enemies. It was this strong assurance, that though without their own accustomed bravery the battle could not be theirs, yet after every man in his respective station had done all that men could do, it was God that must give them success. For we not only see in the event the beneficial effects of that discipline founded upon duty which the subject has led me to speak of, but strong and unequivocal proofs of their confidence in the power and goodness of an overruling Providence.

The great event which I allude to presents (would it had been otherwise ordained in the counsels of the Most High!) a sight afflicting indeed to his country, but honourable to himself—a Christian Hero in the hour of death, expiring in the moment of a victory rising above all the rest, as all his former ones had risen one above another, and appearing as the very summit to which human skill and prowess could aspire.

As in the conflict we see in this great warrior an example of the highest fortitude, under the guidance of consummate skill—that fortitude which religion inspires, and which did for his country all that his country could hope in her unbounded confidence in this her darling son, so in the hour of death did he display like fortitude in braving that king of terrors which his duty led him to meet so much sooner than in the common course of nature he might have done. But he counts not his life dear unto himself so that he may finish his course with joy. With the feelings which are common to our nature he would have wished to share in the joy of his countrymen—to die in his own land, "to breathe his last upon British ground," but he resigns himself to the divine Disposer of events. He feels that the hour is at hand in which he must close his career of earthly glory; but with an interest still alive to the event of this important day, and that love of his country which ever ruled in his heart, he wishes, ere his soul depart to its everlasting home, to know the state of the battle; and when he finds it to be so near to the consummation of his wishes, he breathes out his soul in thanks to the Almighty for the victory which his country had obtained; and for himself in pious resignation yields to his decree, saying, "*THE WILL OF GOD BE DONE.*"

And in the survivor of his glory, and the sharer of his honours, we see alike a pattern of humble praise in the hour of victory, as in himself of christian resignation in the hour of death: not in the fervour of triumphant joy elated with proud glory and exultation, and ascribing his successes to the arm of flesh, but to the living God: not flying from the scene of carnage which he had witnessed to scenes of riot and excess, to drown the remembrance of the lost companions of his danger, and express an unbefitting and tumultuous joy; but calmly and serenely reviewing the path of glory with the feelings of religious praise; and calling upon the companions of his victory to join in the humblest acknowledgment and devoutest expression of their grateful feelings "to Him whose arm is strength," and who had given them victory in the day of battle.

From these expressions of their pious sentiments in the two great leaders of this signal victory, and the immediate appointment of a solemn day of humiliation and thanksgiving among all who had shared in the dangers and glories of it, it is fair to conclude that the same principle animated the whole mass, and to ascribe their heroic deeds to their pious trust and confidence in the Being to whom they so justly attribute their success. It however furnishes an example both to commanders and men of every rank and description, whether naval or military, to look unto God for strength, and to ascribe their successes to Him who ruleth alike the ragings of the sea and the events of war: and great as the benefits of this unexampled victory will be to our own country, and in our own day, the benefit of that example of devout and religious praise which the relation of this event both in the language and spirit which it breathes, will extend to other countries and future times, may be greater in a moral point of view than it is even in a political. It is by the extension and prevalence of such principles that an end shall be put to the necessity of war. Then when the same spirit which breathes in the language of this victory, and the same just conceptions of Providence shall animate the kings of the earth and the rulers of the people (and the example will not be without its effect), then may "our swords be turned into ploughshares;" then, and not before, will they cease to furnish the occasion; and with the cause of provocation the effect will cease, "neither shall they learn war any more."

After such patterns, however, none need hereafter fear to unite the character of the christian with the soldier. That to which they did not think beneath such great conquerors to ascribe their success, humbler ranks of the profession need not shrink to avow All may safely rank under the banners of such pious chieftains; and while they bear the character of warriors, glory in the name of christians. And this I will venture to assure them, that in proportion as they adopt this principle and copy the example in a moral respect, they will find the advantage in the military. They will find their duty easier, their men more orderly, more easily and better disciplined, more intrepid in danger, and more useful to their country in the line of their profession. They will also be better prepared, both themselves and men, for that event which it may bo their lot to experience in the day of battle.

Death, you see, spares not the choicest of our heroes. In this great and glorious action, which we contemplate with alternate feelings of joy and grief, the soldier sees, what every other action will confirm, that no rank, or skill, or bravery, can escape the shafts of death—that the commander is no more secure from the fate of war than the common man; nay often exposed to greater danger, as in the present case, where the envied and the dreaded name of him who had so often triumphed over the enemy in battle, and chased them from sea to sea to add this fresh laurel to his country's brow, became the marked object of their revenge; as if the death of him were victory to themselves, or the fate of the action depended upon the life of him whose unrivalled intrepidity and powers they so well knew and feared.

His great and dreaded powers hastened perhaps the hour of his fall; but every man of whatever rank should be prepared for this: and there is no other preparation than the faith and fear of God; to live such lives that they may be always in a state to meet it; always ready to be called out whenever the Captain of their salvation may require them.

No man is safe who is not always "ready to depart and be with Christ;" but the soldier above all other men should be always in readiness for an event which none can escape; but which he, from the nature of his profession, should consider to be ever near at hand. Called as he may be in a few hours into the field of battle, how shall he face the enemy with that undaunted courage which he ought if he be not prepared to die?

MR. EDITOR,

THE following account of the exploits and public funeral of Admiral the Earl of Sandwich, about a century and a half ago, bears so curious an accordance and coincidence with that of our ever-to-be-lamented Nelson, that I conceive it may be thought worthy of notice in your Chronicle: it is extracted from "Allusive Arms of Families in Great Britain, collected by an Antiquary:"—

Admiral Edward Montague was very instrumental in the restoration of King Charles II, by gaining the fleet to his interest. He commanded the fleet that brought over the exiled Monarch, on his return to his dominions. The King had so just a sense of his services, that, two days after his landing at Dover, he sent the Admiral the Ensigns of the Most Noble Order of the Garter, which were presented to him on board his ship, riding in the Downs, and shortly after he created him Earl of Sandwich, in Kent, &c. and constituted him Lieutenant-Admiral to His Royal Highness James Duke of York, then Lord High Admiral of England. On the 3d of June, 1665, he bore a distinguished part in the action with the Dutch fleet, under Admiral Opdam, leading his squadron into the centre of the enemy, by which he put them into such confusion, as to end in their defeat, with the loss of *nineteen* of their ships! In September following, he took eight sail of Dutch men of war, with twenty sail of merchantmen, and, on his coming to Court, was received by the King with distinguished marks of favour.

On the 28th of May 1672, he was again in the great sea fight with the Dutch, in Southwold Bay, on the coast of Suffolk. He on that day commanded the Royal James, of 1000 men, and was finally blown up in her. Thus perished this gallant Earl, who was the idol of the seamen.—On the 10th of June, his body was perceived floating on the ocean, being known by the star on his coat. It was brought in a yacht to Deptford, and from thence was conveyed in a sumptuous barge, to Westminster, attended by the barges of the King, Duke of York, several of the Nobility, the Lord Mayor, and the different Companies of the City of London, equipped suitably to the melancholy occasion, with trumpets, and other music adapted to the solemnity: the Tower guns, and those at Whitehall, being discharged as the procession passed, and all the bells tolling. Eight Earls attended his son, the chief mourner; no circumstance of magnificence being spared, that could testify the universal and unaffected sorrow that prevailed for the loss of this heroic Admiral.

B. B.

MR. EDITOR, *Dover, December 16, 1805.*

I AM just come from on board the Victory: she is very much mauled, both in her hull and rigging; has upwards of 80 shot between wind and water: the foremast is very badly wounded indeed, and though strongly fished, has sunk about six inches: the mainmast also is badly wounded, and very full of musket shots; she has a jury mizen-mast, and fore and main-top-masts, and has a great many shot in her bowsprit and bows; one of the figures which support the arms has both the legs shot off. I clearly ascertained that Lord Nelson was killed by a shot from the maintop of the Redoubtable: he was standing on the starboard side of the quarter-deck, with his face to the stern, when the shot struck him, and was carried down into one of the wings: he lived about one hour, and was perfectly sensible until within five minutes of his death. When carrying down below, although in great pain, he observed the tiller ropes were not sufficiently tight, and ordered tackles to be got on them, which now remain; the ship he engaged was so close, that they did not fire their great guns on board the enemy, but only musketry, and manned the rigging to board, but nearly the whole that left the deck were killed; the ship had 25 guns dismounted with the Victory's fire; a shot carried away four spokes from the wheel of the Victory, and never killed or wounded any of the men steering; temporary places have been fitted up between decks for the wounded men, which are warmed by stoves.

R. J.

MR. EDITOR,

IN return for the pleasure, which a letter from a young seaman, gave me, at page 491, Vol. XIV, I have sent you another, describing the feelings of a young mind on first encountering the perils of the ocean. It was addressed to his father.

BLUE PETER.

DEAR FATHER, *Falmouth, Dec.* 18, 1805.

Here I am alive, and pretty well. We set sail from Dartmouth, Friday the thirteenth, and arrived here on Monday the sixteenth; after being tossed about three nights, going a voyage of ten hours. An hour after we sailed, which was about five in the evening, I began to be worked; and after I had cascaded two or three times, I laid me down on the hen coops, where I slept about two hours, although it was blowing a gale of wind. I then crawled up, and got down into one of the cabins, where I remained shivering a good three hours. I then got some clothes on, and swallowed quantities of tea, and bread and butter; and turning into my cot, remained asleep until Monday morning. Whilst I remained in an oyster state, between asleep and awake, I heard the Master sing out—All ready!

When I arrived on deck, I saw the land to my surprise, for nobody had called out. Whilst I continued in a sort of oyster state, between asleep and awake, I heard the Master—All ready! Then let go! and about half a minute afterwards, I was tumbled over to the other side, and cracked my crown. We could not haul the sails, owing to bad blocks: we ran foul of one ship's cable, and then letting it out,—Let go!—so they lost their anchor. Our bowsprit was by this time within two yards of a ship. —O Father! now there was bustle!—Let go the anchor!—No! hold on!—No! no! let go!

All on board join in chorus, that our ship is the best in the service, and a great beauty. Be that as it may, she is a pure bold one. We have no fire; and ever since Monday morning to Tuesday night, I was so bitter cold, that I could feel nothing—and my hands are now only half thawed. I thought I should like the service, but I hate it confoundedly: and if we go to America, as is expected, I shall never come back. I suppose I have wished myself at home twice as many times as I wished myself at sea before. However, I am yet only half pickled; perhaps when I have taken in more brine, I shall be as tough as a bit of old junk. This hoping, I remain, dear father,

Your dutiful and affectionate son,

—— P——.

MR. EDITOR,

THE following is much at your service.

W. T..

RECEIPT TO RESTORE THE COLOUR IN SCARLET CLOTH.

Four ounces of aqua fortis.—A quarter part of two ounces and a half of block tin.

Melt the tin, and drop it as gently as possible into a bason of water.—Put the particles of tin into the aqua fortis, and stir them with the stem of a pipe till dissolved.

If they should not dissolve quickly, take a tea spoonful of fine salt (dried) and put a little in from time to time, till the whole heat and dissolve.—Add to this three half pints of good water, poured on the mixture gradually.

Of this mixture take three ounces, and add about a quart of water. Spunge the cloth over entirely, and let it remain an hour: then spunge it again with clean water, and hang it to dry without wringing. It is advisable to make an experiment with a piece of spotted cloth at first, and by tasting the diluted liquor it will be easily perceived whether it requires more mixture or water, as it must not be acrid to the tongue.

N.B. Tried repeatedly on board the Sans Pareil last war with complete success.

PLATE CXCVI.

THE Drawing from which the accompanying Plate is engraved, was made and presented to us by Mr. JOHN THEOPHILUS LEE, a son of the late Captain Lee, of the Royal Navy.

The Plate represents the situation of His Majesty's ship Defence, and her prize, the St. Ildefonso, on the morning following the battle of Trafalgar.

Cadiz and Rota are in the distance, and several of the captured ships ashore on the coast.

Mr. John Theophilus Lee del.
Hall sculp.
Published 31st Jan. 1808, by J. Gold, 103, Shoe Lane, Fleet Street

ADDENDA

TO

THE BIOGRAPHICAL MEMOIR

OF THE LATE RIGHT HONOURABLE

HORATIO LORD VISCOUNT NELSON, K.B.

AND DUKE OF BRONTE;

VICE-ADMIRAL OF THE WHITE SQUADRON.

(Continued from Vol. XIV, page 504.)

" THE TEAR IS ON THE CHEEK OF THE KING,
FOR TERRIBLE WAS HIS SON IN WAR."

OSSIAN.

THE following has been handed about as an extract of the last private letter which Lord Nelson ever wrote. It is dated *off Cadiz, Victory, October* 3:—

The reception I met with on joining the fleet caused the sweetest sensation of my life. The officers who came on board to welcome my return forgot my rank as Commander in Chief in the enthusiasm with which they greeted me. As soon as these emotions were past, I laid before them the plan I had previously arranged for attacking the enemy, and it was not only my pleasure to find it generally approved, but clearly perceived and understood. The enemy are still in port, but something must be immediately done to provoke or lure them to a battle. My duty to my country demands it, and the hopes centered in me, I hope in God, will be realized. In less than a fortnight expect to hear from me, or of me, for who can foresee the fate of battle? Put up your prayers for my success, and may God protect all my friends!

The LAST *official** communication from Lord Nelson, appeared in the Gazette of Saturday, November the 9th. It is an acknowledgment of the services of some of the ships under his command, and is dated eight days previously to the battle which terminated his invaluable life.

In our preceding Volume †, we gave, from the best information which could be obtained, at the period when that portion of these *Addenda* was written, a sketch of the manner of his Lordship's death. His fall was then understood to have been

* Vol. XIV, page 425. † *Vide* page 413, *et seq.*

occasioned by a shot from the main-round-top of the Santissima Trinidada. The ball is now supposed to have been fired from the mizen-top of the French ship Redoubtable. For this, and for some other slight corrections, we are indebted to the following interesting statement, which has been authenticated by Mr. Beatty and Mr. Bourke, the Surgeon and Purser of the Victory.—

A few minutes before Lord Nelson was wounded, Mr. Bourke was near him. He looked stedfastly at him, and said, "Bourke, I expect every man to be upon his station!" Mr. Bourke took the hint, and went to his proper situation in the cockpit.

At this time his Lordship's Secretary, Mr. Scott, who was not, as has been represented, either receiving directions from him, or standing by him, but was communicating some orders to an officer at a distant part of the quarter-deck, was cut almost in two by a cannon-shot. He expired on the instant, and was thrown overboard. Lord Nelson observed the act of throwing his Secretary overboard, and said, as if doubtful, to a Midshipman who was near him, "Was that Scott?" The Midshipman replied, he believed it was. He exclaimed, "Poor fellow!"

He was now walking the quarter-deck, and about three yards from the stern, the space he generally walked before he turned back. His Lordship was in the *act of turning* on the quarter-deck, with his face towards the enemy, when he was mortally wounded in the left breast by a musket-ball, supposed to have been fired from the mizen top of the Redoubtable, French ship of the line, which the Victory had attacked early in the battle.

He instantly fell. He was not, as has been related, picked up by Captain Hardy. In the hurry of the battle, which was then raging in its greatest violence, even the fall of their beloved Commander did not interrupt the business of the quarter-deck. Two sailors, however, who were near his Lordship, raised him in their arms, and carried him to the cockpit. He was immediately laid upon a bed, and the following is the substance of the conversation which *really* took place in the cockpit, between his Lordship, Captain Hardy, Mr. Bourke, and Mr. Beatty :—

Upon seeing him brought down, Mr. Bourke immediately ran to him. "I fear," he said, "your Lordship is wounded!"—"Mortally! mortally!"—"I hope not, my dear Lord; let Mr. Beatty examine your wounds."—"It is of no use," exclaimed the dying Nelson; "he had better attend to others."

Mr. Beatty now approached to examine the wound. His Lordship was raised up; and Beatty, whose attention was anxiously fixed upon the eyes of his patient, as an indication the most certain when a wound is mortal, after a few moments glanced his eye on Bourke, and expressed his opinion in his countenance. Lord Nelson now turned to Bourke, and said, "Tell Hardy to come to me." Bourke left the cockpit. Beatty now said, "Suffer me, my Lord, to probe the wound with my finger; I will give you no pain." Lord Nelson permitted him, and, passing his left hand round his waist, he probed it with the fore-finger of his right.

When Bourke returned into the cockpit with Captain Hardy, Lord Nelson told the latter to come near him. "Kiss me, Hardy!" he exclaimed.—Captain Hardy kissed his cheek.—"I hope your Lordship," he said, "will still live to enjoy your triumph."—"Never, Hardy!" he exclaimed; "I am dying—I am a dead man all over—Beatty will tell you so—bring the fleet to an anchor—you have all done your duty—God bless you!" Captain Hardy now said, "I suppose Collingwood, my dear Lord, is to command the fleet?"—"Never," exclaimed he, "whilst I live;"—meaning, doubtless, that, so long as his gallant spirit survived, he would never desert his duty.

What passed after this was merely casual: his Lordship's last words were to Mr. Beatty, whilst he was expiring in his arms, "I could have wished to have lived to enjoy this; but God's will be done!"—"My Lord," exclaimed Hardy, "you die in the midst of triumph!"—"Do I, Hardy?"—He smiled faintly—"God be praised!" These were his last words before he expired.

The above account is fully confirmed by the following official statement, with which we have been favoured by Mr. Beatty himself:—

His Majesty's Ship Victory, 15th Dec. 1805.

About the middle of the action with the combined fleets, on the 21st of October last, the late illustrious Commander in Chief, Lord Nelson, was mortally wounded in the left breast by a musket ball, supposed to be fired from the mizen-top of the Redoubtable, French ship of the line, which the Victory fell on board of early in the battle. His Lordship was in the act of turning on the quarter-deck, with his face towards the enemy, when he received his wound; he instantly fell, and was carried to the cockpit, where he lay about two hours. On his being brought below, he complained of acute pain about the sixth or seventh dorsal vertebra; of privation of sense, and motion of the body, and inferior extremities; his respiration short and difficult; pulse weak, small, and irregular. He frequently declared his back was shot through; that he felt every instant a gush of blood within his breast; and that he had sensations which indicated to him the approach of death. In the course of an hour, his pulse became indistinct, and was gradually lost in the arm; his extremities and forehead became soon afterwards cold: he retained his wonted energy of mind, and exercise of his faculties, until the latest moment of his existence; and when victory, as signal as decisive, was announced to him, he expressed his pious acknowledgments thereof, and heartfelt satisfaction at the glorious event, in the most emphatic language. He then delivered his last orders with his usual precision; and in a few minutes afterwards expired without a struggle.

COURSE AND SITE OF THE BALL, ASCERTAINED SINCE DEATH.

The ball struck the fore part of his Lordship's epaulette, and entered the left shoulder immediately before the processus acromium scapulæ, which it slightly fractured; it then descended obliquely into the thorax, fracturing the second and third ribs; and after penetrating the left lobe of the lungs, and dividing in its passage a large branch of the pulmonary artery, it entered the left side of the spine, between the sixth and seventh dorsal vertebra; fractured the left tranverse process of the sixth vertebra, wounded the medula spinalis, and fracturing the right transverse process of the seventh vertebra, it made its way from the right side of the spine, directing its course through the muscles of the back, and lodged therein about two inches below the inferior angle of the eighth scapula.

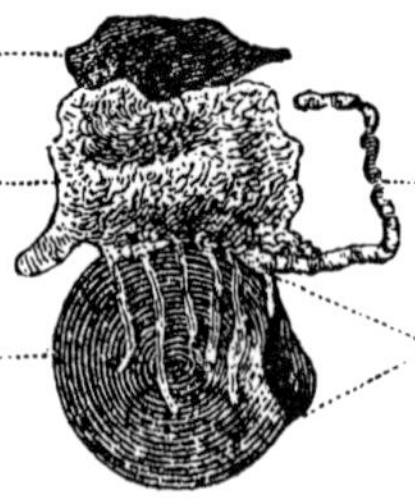

On removing the ball *, a portion of the gold lace, and pad of the epaulette, with a small piece of his Lordship's coat, was found firmly attached to it.

W. BEATTY,
Surgeon of His Majesty's Ship Victory.

* The accompanying engraving is copied from the original drawing, in possession of Sir Isaac Heard.

We here subjoin the following

Abstract of the last Will and Testament, and Codicils thereto annexed, of Lord Viscount NELSON, *as proved in the Commons by his Executors, Earl* NELSON *and* WILLIAM HAZLEWOOD, *Esq. on Monday, December the* 23*d*, 1805.

"Horatio Viscount Nelson, of the Nile, and of Burnham Thorpe, in the county of Norfolk, and Duke of Bronté, in the kingdom of Farther Sicily.

"First,—In the event that he shall die in England, he desires to be buried in the Parish Church of Burnham Thorpe, unless His Majesty shall signify it to be his pleasure that he shall be buried elsewhere.

"Gives the sum of 100*l.* to the poor of the several parishes of Burnham Thorpe, Sutton, and Merton, in the county of Norfolk; viz. one-third part to each parish: the same to be divided at the discretion of the Curates or Ministers.

"Gives to Emma Lady Hamilton, Widow of the Right Hon. Sir William Hamilton, K.B., his diamond star, as a token of his friendship; also the silver cup which she presented to him.

"Gives to his Brother, the Rev. Wm. Nelson, D.D. (Earl Nelson), the gold box presented to him by the City of London; also his gold sword, presented to him by the Captains who fought with him at the Nile.

"Gives to his Sister Catherine Matcham, the sword presented to him by the City of London.

"Gives to his Sister Susannah Bolton, the silver cup presented to him by the Turkey Company.

"Gives to A. Davison, of St. James's-square, Esq. his Turkish gun and canteen.

"Gives to his worthy friend Captain Hardy, all his telescopes and sea-glasses, and 100*l.*

"Gives to each of his Executors 100*l.*

"Gives to his Brother, and William Haslewood, Esq. of Craven-street, Strand, all the residue of his goods, chattels, and personal estate, (except the household goods, &c. which shall be in his house at Merton, at his decease, and also except his diamond sword and jewels, and any other articles which he should, by any codicil to his will, otherwise dispose of), to hold to them and their executors and administrators, upon the trusts following; namely:— Upon trust, that his said trustees and executors shall, as soon as may be, after his death, convert into money such personal estate as does not consist of money, and lay out and invest the same in the purchase of 3 per cent. consols; and also the money which shall belong to him at his death, so that the dividends and interest may produce the clear yearly sum of 1000*l.*, of which they shall stand possessed, upon trust, that, during the life of Frances Herbert, Viscountess Nelson, his Wife, his said trustees do, and shall, fully authorize and empower the said Viscountess Nelson, his Wife, and her assigns, to receive the dividends, when the same shall become due, in addition to all other provisions made by him at any time heretofore for her, and in addition to the sum of 4000*l.* lately given her, which sums to be taken in lieu and satisfaction of all dower, and right and title of dower, of her the said Viscountess Nelson. And in case the annual income to be produced from the Bank Annuities, to be purchased with the residue of his personal estate, shall be insufficient to answer and pay the sum of 1000*l.* a year, then the deficiency to be made up to his Wife, out of his barony, town, and lands, in Farther Sicily; so that his said Wife may be entitled to receive a clear income of 1000*l.*; and, after the decease of his said Wife, to divide the said 1000*l.* between the said William Nelson, Susannah Bolton, and Catherine Matcham."

CODICIL

"I, Horatio, Viscount Nelson of the Nile, of Burnham Thorpe, in the County of Norfolk, and of the United Kingdom of Great Britain and Ireland, and Duke of Bronté, in the Kingdom of Farther Sicily, having, to my last Will and Testament, which bears date on or about the 10th day of May, in the year of our Lord, 1803, made and published a Codicil, bearing date the 13th day of the same month, do make and publish a farther Codicil to the same last Will and Testament in manner following:—That is to say, I give and bequeath to Miss Horatia Nelson Thompson, who was baptized on the 13th day of May last, in the parish of St. Mary la bonne, in the county of Middlesex, by Benjamin Laurence, Curate, and John Willock, Assistant Clerk, (and who I acknowledge as my adopted daughter,) the sum of 4,000*l.* sterling money of Great Britain, to be paid at the expiration of six months after my decease, or sooner if possible; and I leave my dearest friend Emma, Lady Hamilton, sole guardian of the said Horatia Nelson Thompson, until she shall have arrived at the age of eighteen years; and the interest of the said 4,000*l.* to be paid to Lady Hamilton, for her education and maintenance. This request of guardianship I earnestly make of Lady Hamilton, knowing that she will educate my adopted child in the paths of religion and virtue, and give her those accomplishments which so much adorn herself; and I hope make her a fit wife for my dear nephew, Horatio Nelson, whom I wish to marry her, if he prove worthy, in Lady Hamilton's estimation, of such a treasure, as I am sure she will be. Farther, I direct that the legacies by this my Codicil, as well as those by my last Will and Testament, given and bequeathed, shall be paid and discharged from and out of my personal estate only, and shall not be charged, or chargeable, upon my real estates in the United Kingdom of Great Britain and Ireland, and in the Kingdom of Farther Sicily, or any or either of them, or any part thereof. In all other respects, I ratify and confirm my said last Will and Testament and former Codicil. In witness whereof, I, the said Horatio Viscount Nelson and Duke of Bronte, have to this Codicil, all in my own hand-writing, and contained in one sheet of paper, set my hand and seal this sixth day of September, in the year of Our Lord One Thousand Eight Hundred and Three.

(Signed) " NELSON AND BRONTE."

Signed, sealed, and published by the Right Hon. Horatio Viscount Nelson, Duke of Bronte, as and for a Codicil to his last Will and Testament, in the presence of

" GEORGE MURRAY, First Captain of the Victory.
" JOHN SCOTT, Secretary."

" Lord Nelson, in his Will, has directed. that if it shall please his Sovereign to grant a continuance of his pension of one thousand pounds per annum to Lady Nelson, that the direction in his Will to raise a sum of money to be vested in the Funds, to pay her Ladyship an annuity of one thousand pounds per annum shall be void.

" A Codicil, in his own hand-writing, directs, that one hundred pounds per annum be paid to the Widow of his brother Maurice.

" The last Codicil annexed to his Lordship's Will, is dated in September last, and gives to Lady Hamilton all the hay on his estate at Merton.

" His Lordship has given full power to his Trustees, to dispose or exchange the whole of his Italian estates."

We must not close these *Addenda* without taking some notice of Lord Nelson's senatorial character. His professional services did not allow him many opportunities of attending to parliamentary duty; and, from a certain portion of natural modesty which he possessed, he seldom, if ever, delivered his sentiments in the House, unless on questions immediately relating to naval affairs. He was no professed orator; yet, when he spoke, he expressed himself with such energy and ability, that he commanded the attention and respect of all who heard him.—On the 30th of October, 1801, when Earl St. Vincent moved for the thanks of the House of Lords to Admiral Sir James Saumarez, for his conduct in the action off Algesiras, Lord Nelson recounted the memorable services of Sir James, and, in the handsomest manner, seconded the motion* In the succeeding month, when the preliminaries of peace with France were taken into consideration, and Ministers were censured for consenting to give up Malta, his Lordship offered some remarks on the importance of that island. He observed that, "when he was sent down the Mediterranean, Malta was in the hands of the French, and on his return from Aboukir it was his first object to blockade the island, because he deemed it an invaluable service to rescue it from their possession. In any other view it was not of much consequence, being at too great a distance from Toulon to watch the enemy's fleet from that port in time of war. In peace it would require a garrison of 7000 men, in war of twice that number, without being of any real utility. The Cape of Good Hope would be equally detrimental if retained by Great Britain: and though it certainly ought not to be given up to the French, this cession would be preferable to keeping it. Though the war had been long, he believed His Majesty had seized the first opportunity of making peace, and he was satisfied it was the best that existing circumstances admitted."

In December 1802, on the second reading of the Bill for the correction of abuses committed by certain boards employed in

* *Vide* NAVAL CHRONICLE, Vol. VI, page 418.

the naval department of the public service, and by prize agents, Lord Nelson stood forward as a zealous supporter of the measure *. He conceived it to be for the interest and honour of the country, that the neglect and frauds, which had so long prevailed in the payment of prize-money should be removed; and that, in future, no difficulty should be thrown in the way of our brave tars in obtaining the hard-earned remuneration of their gallant services.

Thus, in whatever point of view we contemplate the character of our departed Hero, we behold him, with the most amiable and philanthropic intentions, exerting himself for the good of his country. In the words of our immortal bard, " he was a man, take him for all in all, we shall not look upon his like again!"

We now pass onward to the last solemn scene, which closed for ever from our eyes the remains of the first of heroes.

On the 4th of December, about noon, the Victory hove in sight at Portsmouth; and, at two o'clock, she came to anchor at St. Helen's, the tide not answering for her to proceed to Spithead. His Lordship's flag was flying at half-mast; and, soon after the Victory's arrival, the Port Admiral made the signal for the ships at Spithead and in the harbour to lower their flags and pendants to half-mast. It had been arranged, that the Victory should immediately proceed round to Woolwich with the body; but, in consequence of her shattered state, it was afterwards expected that she would be under the necessity of landing his Lordship's remains at Portsmouth, and that they would be conveyed thence to London by land. This, however, was otherwise ordered; and, having received the necessary repairs, with the body still on board, the Victory got under weigh for the Nore on the 10th of the month. On the evening of the 12th, she came to an anchor, a little to the westward of Dover, where she remained till the morning of the 16th, when she weighed anchor, and endeavoured to proceed; but, owing to the wind coming short, she was compelled to bring up on the

---

* *Vide* NAVAL CHRONICLE, Vol. IX, page 60.

South Foreland. She was not able to reach the Downs before the 17th. On the 19th she sailed direct for the Nore.

On the preceding Sunday, (the 15th), the remains of Lord Nelson were taken from the vessel of spirits in which they had been immersed for preservation, and deposited in a plain elm coffin, which was placed in the after cabin of the main deck, under a canopy of colours. With the exception of a little discolourment on the left ancle, neither the features nor body had undergone any change of appearance. In this state, the last tribute of respect was paid to his memory, by a number of visitors, who daily went off for that purpose, during the stay of the Victory in the Downs.

On the morning of the 21st, Mr. Whitby, the Master Attendant at Woolwich, with Mr. Tyson, who, for several years, had been Secretary to Lord Nelson, arrived at Sheerness with the exterior coffin (of which the subjoined description will convey some idea to the reader) for the reception of his Lordship's corpse.

This coffin, which is considered as the most elegant and superb ever seen in Europe, is the production of Mr. France, undertaker, of Pall Mall. The emblematical devices with which it is ornamented, were executed from designs, by Ackerman, of the Strand. The covering is of fine black velvet, with treble rows of double gilt nails, the whole finely enriched with gold matt, enclosed, and chased.

The Head-piece represents a monument supported by eagles, the emblem of victory, with the portrait of the deceased Hero, in bass relief, surmounted by an urn, containing his ashes, over which reclines the figure of Grief. At the base are seen the British Lion, with one of his paws laid on the Gallic Cock, Sphinxes, and other trophies, intended to commemorate the brilliant Victory which the gallant Admiral obtained on the shores of Egypt, and to indicate that he might fairly claim the Sovereignty of the Ocean.

Next is a Viscount's coronet, the reward of his Lordship's services to his King and Country.

The breast-plate, of gold, thirteen inches by nine, the same size as that of the late Duke of Gloucester, prepared by His Majesty's goldsmith, with the following inscription:—

DEPOSITUM.
The Most Noble Lord HORATIO NELSON,
Viscount and Baron NELSON of the NILE,
and of
Burnham Thorpe, in the County of Norfolk.
Baron NELSON of the Nile, and of Hilborough, in the said County.
Knight of the Most Honourable Order of the Bath;
Vice-Admiral of the White Squadron of the Fleet;
and
Commander in Chief of His Majesty's Ships and Vessels in the Mediterranean.
Also,
Duke of BRONTE, in Sicily;
Knight Grand Cross of the Sicilian Order of St. Ferdinand,
and of Merit.
Member of the Ottoman Order of the Crescent;
and
Knight Grand Commander of the Order of St. Joachim.
Born September 29, 1758.
After a series of transcendant and heroic Services, this Gallant Admiral fell gloriously, in the moment of a brilliant and decisive Victory over the Combined Fleets of France and Spain, off Cape Trafalgar, on the 21st of October, 1805.

Lower down is the first Crest which His Majesty granted him after the battle of Cape St. Vincent, where Lord Nelson boarded and took the San Josef, the motto "*Faith and Works.*"

The last ornament on the lid, is an Egyptian weeping figure (a cast from the antique) wrapped up in drapery, with the face hidden, emblematical of grief.

On the left hand side of the Coffin, next to the head, is the British Lion, with the Union Flag, the Supporter of England, as also that of Lord Nelson's Arms.

Lower down, about the shoulder, on the same side, is a display of the *insignia* of the Most Honourable Military Order of the Bath, with the motto, *Tria juncta in Uno.*

Directly in the centre, on the same side, is a beautiful composition of Britannia and Neptune riding triumphant on the Ocean, drawn by Sea-horses, and led by Fame; while Neptune is pointing to a shield, which bears this motto "*Viro immortali.*"

Next is the Order of St. Ferdinand, which Lord Nelson received of the King of Naples, with the motto, "*Fide a merito.*"

The last ornament, towards the feet, on this side, is a crocodile, allusive to the Battle of the Nile.

The first device, on the right hand side of the coffin, at the head, is the Sphynx, the emblem of Egypt.

Corresponding with the Order of the Bath, on the opposite side, is the Order of the Great Crescent, which was transmitted to the

Noble Admiral by the Grand Seignior after the glorious Battle of the Nile.

In the centre, on the right hand, are again Britannia and Neptune riding triumphant on the Ocean, drawn by Sea horses, &c. as on the opposite side.

Lower down, corresponding with the Order of St. Ferdinand, on the opposite side, is the Order of St. Joachim, transmitted to Lord Nelson by the Emperor Paul, as Grand Master of the Knights of Malta, with the motto, "*Junxit Amicos Amor.*"

The last ornament on the right hand side, towards the foot, is a Dolphin, the noblest fish of the sea, and formerly claimed by the Heir of France.

The device, at the head end of the coffin, is composed of naval and military trophies, with Lord Nelson's arms on a shield.

That at the foot end, is also a composition of naval and military trophies.

Commissioner Grey's yacht, the Chatham, went from Sheerness to the Nore, on the morning of the 22d, for the purpose of meeting the Victory and receiving the body. The Victory hove in sight about twelve o'clock, but the wind blowing strong at S.W. prevented her coming nearer to the Nore than five or six miles. As soon as it was known that she had arrived, the ships at the Nore, and in the harbour, lowered their colours half-mast high.

On the morning of the 23d, the body was received on board the Chatham, which immediately proceeded for Greenwich. The coffin, covered with an ensign, was placed on the deck. All the vessels, while the yacht was passing, hoisted colours half mast high; and, at Tilbury and Gravesend, the forts fired minute guns. The bells were tolled, and afterwards rung a muffled peal.—In the evening, the body was received by Lord Hood, with the greatest privacy, at Greenwich, and deposited in a private apartment, where it remained until the requisite arrangements were made for its lying in state in the Painted Chamber.

It was not until the 27th of December that it was finally settled for the funeral to take place on Thursday the 9th of January following. The determination was then communicated by Lord

Hawkesbury to the Board of Works, and orders were immediately sent from that department to St. Paul's Cathedral, addressed to all the principal artificers there employed, desiring them to expedite the finishing of their different orders on or before the 7th of January.

On Saturday, the 4th of January, the preparations for the public to pay their last tribute to the remains of the immortal Nelson were completely finished; and, about one o'clock, the Princess of Wales, attended by her retinue, entered the saloon, where she remained for a considerable time, contemplating with silent sorrow the last solemn obsequies paid to the remains of the gallant Hero. After her departure a few persons of respectability were also admitted by the Governors, to see the body lie in state.

The Rev. Mr. Scott, Lord Nelson's favourite Chaplain, whom in his last moments he earnestly requested to pay particular attention to his remains till they were interred, accompanied by Mr. France's partner, of Pall Mall, the undertaker, remained with the body the whole of the night; and on Sunday, at eleven o'clock, the hall and gate were opened for the admission of strangers.

The painted chamber had been fitted up for this melancholy spectacle with peculiar taste and elegance.

A platform was erected along the chamber, with two divisions, one for the ingress and the other for the egress of the spectators; at the farther end of which, elevated six feet, a portion was railed off, in the form of a crescent, within which a canopy was erected of black cloth, festooned with gold; the festoons ornamented with the plume of triumph; the coronet and the stem of the San Josef, a Spanish Admiral's ship, already quartered in his Lordship's arms, and the back field with an escutcheon of his Lordship's arms. Motto, "*Palmam qui meruit ferat,*" surmounted by a laurel wreath, encircling Neptune's trident, and a palm branch in *sattier;* and above the whole, a golden wreath, with the word TRAFALGAR inscribed within it. Solar rays surrounded his Lordship's shield, bearing the motto, "*Tria juncta in uno,*" were appropriately interspersed in the back ground. The coffin, richly ornamented, as already described, containing the body, lying beneath it, covered with a black velvet pall, lined with white satin, turned up at the foot, so as to expose the lower part of the coffin (which was turned towards the entrance) to the spectators. On the top was Lord Nelson's coronet supported on a black velvet cushion richly fringed; at the head of which sat the Rev. Mr.

Scott, Chaplain of the Victory, as Chief Mourner, seated in an elbow chair, dressed in his cassock, and without powder; and at the foot was a pedestal covered with black velvet, trimmed with rich fringe, black and yellow alternately, and supporting models, richly gilt, of his Lordship's shields, gauntlets, sword and helmet, surmounted by a naval crown and chelengk, or triumphal plume, presented to his Lordship by the Grand Seignior, in approbation of his glorious victory at the Nile. Ten mourners, appointed from the Lord Chamberlain's office, also attended, two on each side the coffin, and three on each side the canopy; the former standing, the latter sitting: they were dressed in deep mourning, with black scarfs, full powdered, and wearing bag wigs. Ten banners, exhibiting various quarterings of his Lordship's arms, belonging to the several orders, and each bearing the motto inscribed on the escutcheon, elevated on staves, were pendant towards the coffin. Four high benches, covered with black cloth, were placed two on each side the coffin, supporting twelve elegant silver *trestles*, with two wax candles in each. The railing was in the form of a crescent, about three feet in height, outside of which the spectators viewed the funeral saloon, and on the inside were stationed several persons from the Lord Chamberlain's office, appropriately dressed. Volunteers belonging to the Greenwich and Deptford Association, remained at the head of each avenue, and round the railing, to prevent riot, and to keep the throng in continual motion onward. The steps leading to, and coming from the saloon, were covered with matting and black cloth, as was the whole of the chamber floor.—Double rows of sconces, highly plated, each with two branches, and containing wax lights, were suspended around the saloon, with escutcheons bearing two shields, and a coronet between each pair; above them a white satin belt was brought all round as a relief from the dead black; single rows of sconces and escutcheons were fixed in a similar manner to the other parts of the chamber. A large black curtain, festooned, was suspended at the entrance to the saloon. At the end of the avenue for egress a guard was placed, who directed the spectators as they came out of the hall, to pass on to the back gate of the hospital, and depart, to prevent confusion.

This solemn exhibition continued for three days—Sunday, Monday, and Tuesday. On the last day, some slight alterations were made in the arrangements in the saloon. The sable pall was cast from the coffin, which was fully exposed to view, and upon it was placed the cushion supporting the coronet, with two armorial shields, appropriately emblazoned. The ten mourners, who before were seated at the head of the coffin, to the right and left of the canopy, now took their places, five on each side, outside of the benches on which the tressels stood, and facing inwards. The effect was thus rendered much more solemn and impressive.

On the afternoon of Tuesday, a little before four o'clock, the brig Elizabeth and Mary, from off Chatham, hove in sight at Greenwich, having on board a chosen band of seamen and marines, belonging to the brave crew of the Victory, who were intended to fall into the funeral procession of their deceased Commander.—The St. George's jack, at the mast-head of the brig, was lowered half-mast high, as a funeral salute, which was immediately returned by the colours of all the ships in sight from the terrace.

Lieutenant Brown, the commanding officer of the seamen and marines, came on shore to take orders for their proceeding. The Lieutenant-Governor of Greenwich then proceeded to inform Lord Hood of their arrival; when that gallant Admiral, accompanied by a party of the river fencibles, armed with their pikes, proceeded to the north gate, next the river, and ordered the HEROES OF TRAFALGAR to be brought on shore. The brig then hauled up alongside the quay, and the brave tars landed, amidst the warm greetings and grateful acclamations of the surrounding throng.

At this interesting moment, what must have been the sensations of these gallant fellows! What must have been the sensations of British spectators, witnessing the arrival of their noble protectors, to heighten the funeral solemnities of their beloved Nelson! It was a mingled feeling, of rapture and of agony, that could find no utterance by words, but which burst forth with irresistible eloquence in every eye.

Brave seamen! how different would *your* feelings have been, had you arrived, to swell, with songs of joy, and banners of conquest, the triumphal entry of Trafalgar's immortal Hero!

It was remarked by a person present, that, if this little band, consisting of forty-six seamen and fourteen marines, each bearing his hammock, exhibited a fair specimen of their messmates in the Victory, their triumph was the less wonderful; for each appeared a true-bred cub of the British Lion, and most of them bore the honourable scars which they had received on the day that their lamented leader fell.

On their passing within the gates, they were ordered by Lord Hood, who approached them, to stow their baggage in the Royal Charlotte ward of the hospital; after which, his Lordship informed them, they should be gratified with a view of their heroic leader's body lying in state, though he was sure that it would be to them no pleasant sight. To this remark his gallant auditors bowed an expressive assent.

They then proceeded to stow their hammocks in the ward appointed, and were afterwards escorted, by a part of the military, to the great hall, whence they were conducted to the saloon, where the remains of their beloved Commander lay. Silently they eyed the coffin, with melancholy respect and admiration, while the manly tears glistened in their eyes, and stole reluctant down their weather-beaten cheeks. Strangers were excluded during this affecting scene.

On the return of the seamen and marines to the parade in front, they were again warmly greeted by the multitude, who seemed deeply to participate in their feelings.

After this part of the ceremony, the doors and gates were closed, and an immense concourse of people, extending almost from Greenwich to London, were under the necessity of returning, ungratified with the sight for which they had so anxiously pressed forward.

It was calculated, that, notwithstanding the extreme avidity of the populace, and the ceremony of lying in state lasting for three days, not more than 15,000 persons obtained admission.

(To be continued.)

Naval Reform.

THE SIXTH REPORT OF THE COMMISSIONERS

Appointed by an Act of the Forty-third Year of the Reign of his present Majesty, entitled, "An Act for appointing Commissioners to inquire and examine into any Irregularities, Frauds, or Abuses, which are or have been practised by Persons employed in the several Naval Departments therein mentioned, and in the Business of Prize Agency, and to report such Observations as shall occur to them for preventing such Irregularities, Frauds, and Abuses, and for the better conducting and managing the Business of the said Departments, and of Prize Agency, in future."

[Continued from Vol. XIV, page 320.]

PLYMOUTH YARD.

THE Naval Arsenal at Plymouth Dock was first established in the year 1691; and it appears by the Records, that, previous to that time, the Master Shipwright and the artificers were borne on board one of His Majesty's ships fitted for their accommodation.

The affairs of the dock-yard are conducted under the general superintendance of a Commissioner, chosen from the Captains in His Majesty's Navy: he has authority over all persons employed in the yard, but he has no power to reward, promote, or even to cause a man to be entered into the service; and from this circumstance, the Commissioner, although the principal, appears to have less influence over the workmen than any other officer. This seems to be a defect in the system, as we conceive all principals should have it more or less in their power to distinguish and reward the ability, zeal, and industry of those employed under them; and without such power, we apprehend authority will seldom be respected. The principal duty of the Commissioner is to enforce obedience to the orders and regulations of the Navy Board, which are sent to him to be delivered to the respective officers: no orders originate with him, except in cases of emergency, such as the issuing stores to, or repairing any ships which the Commander in Chief of the port may represent as wanted for immediate and special service: and as all the returns and accounts are sent by the respective officers to the Navy Board, the duty of the Commissioner, which is not well defined, appears to relate more particularly to the executive business of the yard.

Over each department an officer presides, who is individually responsible for the due execution of the business entrusted to his management.—In His Majesty's yard at Plymouth, the principal officers consist of—

A Master Shipwright,	A Storekeeper,
Two Masters Attendant,	A Clerk of the Survey,
A Clerk of the Check,	A Clerk of the Rope Yard.

The duties of the Master Shipwright are multifarious and important: he has the direction and superintendance of nearly the whole operative business of the dock-yard; in the execution of which he is assisted by four subordinate professional officers, termed "Assistants to the Master Shipwright;" one of whom is particularly entrusted with the management and conversion of timber, and is stiled "Timber Master;" of which office we shall have occasion to speak more at large in a subsequent Report.

It is likewise the peculiar duty of the Master Shipwright to inspect the quality of all stores received from contractors, which are used in his department, and to attest their fitness for the Service; to survey and value all vessels hired or purchased into His Majesty's Navy; to keep an account, and certify to the Navy Board, the quantity of all works performed by contract in the dock-yard; and to keep an account of the earnings of the respective artificers under his superintendance, and to certify the amount from time to time to the Clerk of the Check.

The duty of the Master's Attendant is to superintend the works carrying on in the sail-loft and rigging-house; to muster and direct the employment of the persons borne in the ordinary; to attend the launching, docking, masting, and ballasting His Majesty's ships; to attend to the ships coming into and going out of port, and their removal from one part of the Harbour to another, and to take care that proper moorings be provided for them; to see to the timely provision of the rigging and sails of the ships preparing for sea; to inspect the quality of all stores used in their department, either purchased or served in upon contract, and to certify to the Navy Board their fitness for the Service.

The duty of the Clerk of the Check is to muster the several persons belonging to the yard, upon their coming to or quitting work; to keep an account of their wages; to make out, quarterly, the pay books of the yard and ordinary; to muster the companies of His Majesty's ships in commission, and the persons employed on board the ships in ordinary, and to check the absentees of their provisions; to muster at certain periods the marines at head quarters; to view, in conjunction with the other officers, the quality of all stores received, and to make out certificates of the quantities, when required by the contractors, in order to their obtaining payment of the Navy Board; to attend in turn with the Storekeeper and Clerk of the Survey, the receipt of all stores, and the delivery of lots of old stores to the purchasers: he likewise pays bounty to volunteer seamen, and the contingencies of the yard.—Several other payments have been imposed on this officer, by recent acts of parliament, relating to seamen's wages, which are totally unconnected with his situation in the dock-yard, and will become the subject of our future observation.

The Storekeeper has charge of, and is accountable for all stores received into the dock-yard; it is likewise his duty, in rotation with the Clerk of the Check and Clerk of the Survey, to attend the survey and receipt of all stores from contractors, and the delivery of lots of old stores to the purchasers; and to check the certificates made out by the Clerk of the Check, for stores received upon contract.

The duty of the Clerk of the Survey is, in conjunction with the Master

Shipwright and Master Attendant, to direct the issues of all stores to the warrant officers of ships, and for the use of the yard, and to keep a charge against the persons to whom they are issued; to survey all articles returned into store, and with the Clerk of the Check and Storekeeper, to attend the survey and receipt of all stores from contractors, and the delivery of lots of old stores to the purchasers; and to examine the certificates made out by the Clerk of the Check of the stores received, by which the contractors obtain payment.

The duty of the Clerk of the Rope Yard combines the offices of the Clerk of the Check and Storekeeper: he musters the people in that department, upon their coming to and quitting work; and is charged with the hemp, tar, and other articles, used in rope-making, of the expenditure of which he keeps an account.

From a consideration of the various and important duties entrusted to the officers in His Majesty's yards, it would be expected that upon their appointment they should be furnished with full and sufficient instructions for the regulation of their conduct; but upon inquiry of the officers of His Majesty's yard at Plymouth, we find that the instructions under which they act are of very ancient date (prior to the year 1700); that they have not been revived since their establishment, and have in great part been abrogated by orders issued by the Navy Board from time to time, adapted to the various circumstances of the service as they have arisen. These occasional orders or instructions have accumulated to a great extent, superseding each other as the opinions of those entrusted with the direction of the civil department of the Navy have varied; and as no abstract of them, under the particular heads of service to which they relate, has been kept at Plymouth yard, it is only by a reference to the documents themselves, voluminous and often contradictory, that an officer upon his appointment can (and that with much industry and application) gain a knowledge of the duties of his station.

It will appear by the evidence of the * Clerk of the Check, that the

---

* *The Examination of Richard Pering, Esq., Clerk of the Check of Plymouth Yard; taken upon Oath the 23d day of August,* 1803.

How long have you been in your present situation?—I was appointed, I think, in December 1801.

How long have you been employed in His Majesty's yards, and in what line?—I believe about twenty-one years. I was first brought up in the shipwright line under Sir John Henslow, to whom I served my apprenticeship; from thence I went into the Navy Office as a Clerk in the Surveyor's Office, and in about a year and a half afterwards was appointed Clerk of the Survey at Sheerness: I was afterwards Storekeeper at Sheerness, removed to the same situation at Woolwich, and from thence I came to this yard.

Are the instructions now shown you a copy of those given to you for the regulation of your conduct, at the time of your appointment as Clerk of the Check?—I do not recollect ever to have received any instructions as Clerk of the Check.

instructions, however insufficient for the regulation of his conduct, have not even been given to him, either at the time of, or subsequent to his appoint-

---

Did you receive a copy of such instructions from your predecessor in office? —I did not.

Is there any general printed or written code of instructions in your office, under which you now act?—There is not; I am obliged to have reference to the different orders in the Office.

Do you consider the general printed instructions now shown you to be obsolete?—In many instances.

At what time were they first issued, and when were they last revised?—I do not know.

Is there any general abstract in your office of the several warrants and letters of the Navy Board, which contain instructions for your guidance?—A collection has been made of certain warrants of the Navy Board, which contain standing orders from the year 1729 to 1791. They are directed to be read quarterly in the presence of the Commissioner and the officers; but they have only been read once since I have been here, owing, I conceive, to a great part of them being obsolete.

Can you collect, readily and distinctly, by reference to the books and papers in your office, the instructions and intentions of the Navy Board on every particular branch of your duty?—It is very difficult to be done, owing to the multiplicity of orders, and the succeeding warrants contradicting the former ones sometimes in part, sometimes in whole.

By what authority, by whose nomination, and after what examination or approbation, are the clerks, artificers, labourers, and others, entered on the books of the yard?—The clerks are nominated by the officers, and approved by the Commissioner and the Navy Board. The Master Shipwright nominates all the workmen, except the sailmakers, riggers, and riggers' labourers, and they are named by the Masters Attendant; but none are entered without the approbation of the Commissioner. On their coming to my office, I take the descriptions of their persons, and see that they come within the standing rules of the yard with respect to their age, as none are to be entered over the age of thirty-five; and, upon the production of a certificate from the Surgeon, of their having no bodily infirmity, they are entered. The ropemakers are a distinct branch, under the superintendance of the Clerk of the Rope Yard.

Is there any actual or implied contract entered into by the artificers and labourers at the time of their admission, with respect to forfeitures for non-attendance, or any other circumstance?—None, that ever I heard of.

Is there any fee paid by the artificers and labourers on their entry?—There were fees paid to the clerks before the abolition of fees, but there are none at present.

How often are the artificers and labourers mustered, or called, and by whom? —They are mustered in the morning on coming into the yard, and when they go out of the yard to dinner, they are mustered on their return, and again on their leaving work in the evening. The first clerk musters the shipwrights, caulkers, cabin keepers, oakum boys, and pitch heaters; the rest of the artificers and labourers are mustered by the third clerk.

Do you ever superintend the muster or calls; how often, and when?—Frequently, both in the morning and evening. I think, upon an average, I attend the musters three or four times a week.

ment; nor were they delivered to him with the other official documents by his predecessor, on his entering upon office.

Is there a daily report made, and to whom, of the persons who may absent themselves from their duty?—None daily; but a return is made once a week to the Commissioner, of the men who absent themselves three successive days within the week.

After what period are men discharged who absent themselves without leave?—It depends, at present, entirely on the discretion of the Commissioner. But the standing orders direct men to be discharged who absent themselves, without leave, for six successive days.

Is there any penalty or forfeiture attached to persons absenting themselves without leave?—No penalty; but he has no pay while absent; and if he absents himself frequently, it is a bar to his promotion.

Does the Surgeon of the yard furnish you, or any other officer, with a list of the persons that may be sick, and incapable of performing their duty?—He furnishes me with a list of those that are hurt in the yard, but not with those who are sick.

How do you distinguish those who are sick from those who absent themselves from other causes, and without leave?—There is no knowing but from the people answering for them at the Call Office; and if they are said to be sick, they are so set off in the muster book.

When the men are answered for as being sick, does the Surgeon visit them to see that they are so?—No, he does not.

What officers grant leave of absence to the artificers and labourers of the yard?—The officers in the several departments grant leave, with the approbation of the Commissioner, which is signified to me by a note, to which the Commissioner subscribes his approval.

Is their pay continued to them during their absence?—No.

Are copies of the muster or call book sent to the Navy Board, and at what periods?—They are never sent.

Is there any return of the musters of the yard made to the Navy Board?—There is no return of the musters made to the Navy Board; but the time they work is set off in the pay book.

When artificers are employed on board ships in the Sound or Cawsand Bay, does your clerk muster them when he musters the company of the ship?—They used not to be mustered; but they have been within these twelve months.

How have the different classes of artificers and labourers been paid?—The artificers working by task and job were paid till the 8th of March last, at the rate of double days in the single day hours, and for the extra time they have wrought they have been paid in addition; since that time they have been and are to be paid for the work performed, according to the prices allowed by the Navy Board in the schemes of job and task work, which schemes being incomplete, the works for which prices are not therein fixed, are transmitted to the Navy Board. with prices proposed, for their approval.—The labourers have been paid at the rate of two for one by job in the single day hours, and for the extra time by note, according to the hours they remained in the yard; but at present, a certificate is given by the Master Shipwright to the Clerk of the Check, certifying, that they have performed a sufficient quantity of work to entitle them to two days' pay for one in the single day hours; and at present about one half of the labourers are

We understand that the Navy Board, in the year 1785, had it in contemplation to make a general collection and digest of their standing orders

---

employed one hour extra in the morning, two hours extra at dinner time, and two hours extra in the evening, making five hours extra, which, by the Navy Board's order, is considered equal to a single day's work; but the Master Shipwright has granted a certificate for two tides only, conceiving such extra (making their wages three shillings a day, exclusive of an allowance of threepence a day in lieu of chips) adequate to the labour performed. The remainder of the labourers, with two exceptions, (an infirm man, and the Clerk of the Chapel,) are allowed, by a certificate from the Master Shipwright, two days' pay for one for working the common hours of the yard, making their pay two shillings and fourpence a day, exclusive of the threepence a day in lieu of chips.

Are there any descriptions of labourers employed by contractors in the yard, and how are they paid?—The men employed by the contractor for horses to drive the teams, who stay in the yard all the working hours, are allowed, I believe, eleven shillings a week by the contractor, and threepence a day from Government, for driving the dogs or hooks into the timber to be removed.

What is the price of common labour in this neighbourhood, from six o'clock in the morning to six o'clock in the evening?—I cannot speak positively; but, I believe, from half a guinea to twelve shillings a week.

What is the employment of scavelmen in the yard?—The scavelmen are a description of labourers, selected from the labourers of the yard, who attend to clean and pump the docks, and in general assist the shipwrights.

How are they now paid?—They have been employed by job the general extra of the yard, but they are now employed two for one in the single day hours, upon a certificate from the Master Shipwright, the same as the labourers, making their pay three shillings a day, exclusive of threepence a day in lieu of chips.

If the artificers and labourers of the yard are not employed upon job or task, and do not work extra, do they receive more than a common day's pay?—There are no men in the yard who do not receive more than a single day's pay, although not employed in the common day hours, except the two instances I have before stated: the additional wages are paid to them by task or job note, or certificate from the Master Shipwright, Master Attendants, or Storekeeper, for the men in their different departments.

What is the distinction between job and task work?—I conceive task work to be men working on new ships, and job work to consist in pulling to pieces and repairing.

Have there been no instances in this yard of artificers being paid according to the scheme of job on new work?—Not that I recollect.

When was the present rate of pay to artificers and labourers established?—I believe in the reign of Queen Anne.

Is the scheme of prices for job and task work now shown you, a copy of that by which the earnings of the artificers are now set off on the pay books?—I believe it is.

What is the nature of a job note?—It is now an actual statement of the work performed by job and task, with the prices of the labour set against each article; but, when I came to the yard, the men were set off by a general note given by the then Master, under the authority of the Navy Board, without any accoun or regulations; and that an abstract of the dates of them up to the 31st of December, 1784, arranged under different heads, was actually formed and

of the work performed being sent to the Check Office.—The following is a copy of the note:—

"MR. LLOYD,

"All the artificers, &c., now employed at the rate of two for one by job in the single day hours, and two tides extra after bell-ringing, are to continue working by job, also to work one night extra after bell-ringing in the evening, to expedite the works in hand, till further notice, agreeably to the Honourable Navy Board's warrant of the 28th instant.

"JOHN MARSHALL,
"Master Shipwright."

"*January* 30, 1801."

Is there any particular form of job or task note?—Yes; the following is a copy of the form which has been introduced by the present Master Shipwright:—

"CANOPUS.

"MR. PERING,

"John Pratlent, William Provo, Francis Langdon, quartermen of the shipwrights and their gangs, have performed the following works by job on the Canopus, between the 28th and 31st March 1803 (except George Bone), including William Brenton and his gang, between the 29th and 31st, (except Spencer Dominey), agreeable to the schedule per Honourable Navy Board's warrant, 2d January, 1802:

		No. Thick.	Quantity.	Rate.			Value.		
		Inches.	Feet.	£.	s.	d.	£.	s.	d.
Hold	Trimmed and fastened bulkheads	5	28	0	0	7½	0	17	6
		3	390	0	0	4½	7	6	3
		2	381	0	0	3½	5	11	1½
	Coppered the light room, &c.—Sheets	No. 79	each.	0	0	9	2	19	3
Orlop trimmed and fastened, the flat		Inches. 3	182	0	0	3	2	5	6
Quarter deck taken up, deck flat		3	122	0	0	1½	0	15	3
TOTAL ......£.							19	14	10½
Value of works to complete the above, sent for the Hon. Navy Board's approbation, and approved of by their warrant, 21st June, 1803...							59	5	11½
TOTAL, ...£.							79	0	10

"J. TUCKER, Master Shipwright,
"R. PERING, Clerk of the Check."

"These are to certify, that the whole of the above works have been performed, and the prices charged for the same are either in conformity to the schedule of rates, or by subsequent orders from the Hon. Navy Board.

"J. ANCELL, Assistant to the Master Shipwright,
"J. ATKINS, Foreman of the New Work."

forwarded to the officers of Plymouth yard, who were acquainted that a general collection was preparing; that it should be sent to them when completed; and that in future they should be furnished with the substance and dates of all standing regulations, in order to their being added to such

---

How much have the artificers and labourers been, and are now, allowed to earn?—Formerly their earnings were restricted to two days for one, and two tides or three for one, as the Navy Board thought proper; but now the artificers are permitted to earn as much as they can by the schedule of prices for job and task work—I should think the present average earnings of the shipwrights to be about seven shillings and sixpence per day.

Do you know what shipwrights are paid by the day in this neighbourhood?—I do not.

How are the earnings by job or task set off on the pay books?—The money earned by job or task is divided amongst the artificers employed, agreeably to the time they worked.

RICHARD PERING.

Chs. M. Pole.
John Ford.
Henry Nicholls.

The Examination of Richard Pering, Esq.; continued on the 24th of August, 1803.

Do you consider yourself authorized in setting off to the men all the earnings for which job notes may be made out?—Yes.

Are the job notes examined by the call book, previous to their being set off?—Always.

Is such an examination an effectual check upon any improper allowance of wages? –It is no check as to the amount of the wages, as the examination only goes to the proper division of the money among the men.

Has it ever been a practice in the Clerk of the Check's office at this port, to make application to the executive officers for job notes, in order to give the men more pay?—Prior to my appointment to this yard, I understand that no job notes for the shipwrights at all were sent to the check office. But, on the first job notes coming to my office, I think in (a) Christmas quarter last, the earnings by them were on calculation found to fall short of two days' pay for one, and were so set off on the pay books; on which the men petitioned the Navy Board, who gave directions by warrant on the 7th of April, 1803, that the whole of the men employed at the dock side should have two for one for the months of September, October, November, and December, 1802, in consequence of their having been employed in working up old materials, and on iron-fastened ships.

Did the artificers and labourers receive considerably more pay in consequence of such order, than they would have done if paid only for the work they actually performed?—Yes, they did; but I have my doubts whether the quartermen delivered a proper statement of the works performed.

Would it be difficult to ascertain the account of the increase of wages granted by the Navy Board's order?—No; it would not.

What was the amount of the increase of wages so granted?—It amounted in Christmas quarter 1802, to three hundred and sixty-one pounds one shilling and eleven pence.

collection. It is much to be regretted that this very useful work was not accomplished, as it would have greatly facilitated the business of the dock-yard, and afforded to the Navy Board a comprehensive view of their standing regulations, whereby they would have been enabled to have kept a better check upon the due observance of them, than in the course of this Report will appear to have existed.

Do such men as may be absent by sickness continue to receive their pay, and how long?—No men absent by sickness ought to receive any pay, except such as are hurt when on duty, and their pay is continued to them at the rate of single day for six weeks, by a note from the Surgeon; but I have reason to believe that men formerly received pay upon a Doctor's note without having been hurt in the service.

Has the pay of such men who have not answered their calls or musters, been always stopped?—Since I have been here, I believe it has; except the men who may have been hurt, and certified by the Surgeon to be incapable of attending their muster.

Who makes out the pay books of the yard?—There are two sets of pay books, ordinary, and extraordinary; the ordinary, for the pay of the officers' clerks, and such other persons as are paid by annual salaries, and the men borne in the ordinary; and the extraordinary, for the different classes of artificers and labourers in the dock-yard: they are made out by the clerks in my office.

By whom are they examined, and by whom are they signed?—They are examined by the clerks in my office, and signed by myself.

How often is the yard paid, and for what periods?—The yard is paid quarterly, one quarter being always kept in arrears.

Are the pay books, and the several vouchers from which they are made out, sent to the Navy Board for examination previous to their being paid upon?—Never.

Are the vouchers from which the earnings of the men are set off on the pay books, regularly preserved?—They have been regularly preserved since I came here; but not before that time.

How often are the men, put on the list for superannuation, mustered; what work do they perform, and what pay do they receive?—They are mustered every day. In some instances they have performed no work; and in others they have been employed, and are paid the single day's pay of the class to which they belong. If they do not attend their musters, they are checked of their pay.

How long have you known a person continued on the superannuation list, before he has been actually superannuated?—In the instance of Thomas Davis, joiner, as appears by the books of this yard, he was put on the list for superannuation in July 1797, and was superannuated in June 1800; several men placed on the superannuation list in October 1798, were superannuated in June 1800, and there are many instances of a similar nature.

Do you know why they were kept on the superannuation list so long, without being superannuated?—I do not know.

Have you reason to believe, that men who have been recommended for superannuation, or who ought to have been recommended, have received more than a single day's pay?—Yes, I think in several instances they have received agreeably to the general extra of the yard.

[To be continued.]

BASS'S STRAIT.

SINCE the discovery of Bass's Strait, which divides Vandieman's Land from the south coast of New Holland, some pains appear to have been taken to conceal from public knowledge the name of him to whom we are obliged for this discovery, and, if possible, to allow to those, who had no more to do with it than the Emperor of China, the credit of the discovery. In order to do common justice to a man, too modest to assert his own claim in a public newspaper, and with whose character, judgment, and ability as a seaman, navigator, and naval officer, we profess ourselves to be perfectly acquainted, we cannot, therefore, resist the desire we feel to represent the manner in which the discovery of this strait has been made.

About the 20th of January, 1788, Governor Phillips, with his little convoy of convicts intended for the establishment of a settlement in New South Wales, arrived there; and, having fixed upon Port Jackson in preference to Botany Bay, for the seat of government, they established themselves at Sydney Cove, in that harbour. Whilst the Governor was fully employed in forming regulations for carrying on the various works he had to accomplish, Captain John Hunter *, second Captain of His Majesty's ship Sirius, was engaged in making a maritime survey of that extensive harbour, for the direction of such ships as might be sent out after their arrival was known.

In the end of 1788, and beginning of 1789, Captain Hunter had occasion to sail a second and third time along the south part of that coast. When between the latitudes of 39° and 42°, he had before made observation, that the ship was always set off to the eastward. After seriously and maturely considering what could have occasioned this effect, he remembered that Captain Cook, on his first coming upon this coast from that of New Zealand, had fallen in with the land at Point Hicks, and had seen very little to the southward of that point; and that Captain Furneaux, after his discovery of Furneaux's Islands, had not sailed to the northward of them; that there remained between those two discoveries a certain space in which no land had been seen. Captain Hunter, therefore, from these considerations, and his own observations of this part of the coast, ventured, in 1789, to suggest the existence

* For the Biographical Memoir of Governor Hunter, see NAVAL CHRONICLE, Vol. VI, page 349.

of either a very large or deep gulf, or a strait, which would probably be found to separate Vandieman's land (which he considered a group of islands) from the south coast of New Holland, or New South Wales; and that suggestion may be seen in his Journal, published by Stockdale in 1792 or 1793, and, as near as we can recollect, at page 124 or 125.

This suggestion was never taken any notice of, nor any attempts made to discover whether or not it was well founded, until, upon the resignation of Governor Phillips, on account of his ill health, Captain Hunter was appointed to succeed to the government of the colony. His instructions were such, relative to the employment of the two ships which he took out with him, that it was not in his power, consistent with those instructions, to employ them on discoveries, otherwise to realize his former conjecture would have been one of his first attempts. Those ships, after each having performed a voyage from the colony to the Cape of Good Hope, were found so very bad as to require considerable repairs. During the time the Reliance was under that repair which her weak condition required, Mr. George Bass, her Surgeon, a man of considerable enterprise and ingenuity, a strong and comprehensive mind, with the advantage of a vigorous body and healthy constitution, requested Governor Hunter would employ him in some way in which he could render himself useful, for an idle life he could not endure. The Governor inquired in what way he could employ him that might meet his own wishes? he replied, by giving him the use of a boat, and allow him to sail along and examine the coast. The Governor expressed his wishes to get all the information he could obtain on the neighbouring coast, and said he would prepare for him his own whale-boat, the best vessel of that kind in the colony, with which Mr. Bass was quite delighted. He sailed from Port Jackson manned with volunteers from the Reliance, and victualled for twelve weeks, the time to which the Governor had limited his absence. The history of his voyage may be seen in Colonel Collins's second volume of the History of the English Settlement in New South Wales, and with which Governor Hunter had supplied him. This journal of Mr. Bass's voyage in the whale-boat served strongly to strengthen Captain Hunter's conjectures respecting the existence of a strait.

The Governor about this time having occasion to send a small colonial schooner to Furneaux's Islands, sent Lieutenant Flinders, of the Reliance (a young man clever and expert in maritime surveying), to make what observations he could relative to anchorage amongst those islands. His observations there, with the strength and direction of the tides, &c. were another argument in favour of Captain Hunter's original conjecture that a strait existed thereabout.

After Mr. Flinders and Bass's return, the Governor ordered a small decked boat, sloop rigged, of about sixteen tons burthen, which had been built at Norfolk Island, to be fitted in the most secure manner. In this vessel Lieutenant Flinders was directed to embark, with particular instructions how he was to proceed in the examination of this part of the coast, and that if a passage through to the westward was found, he was to go through, and to circumnavigate Vandieman's Land. Mr. Bass, who had recovered the fatigues of his last trip, requested he might be allowed to accompany Mr. Flinders, and in this little vessel they proved the existence of a strait. The journals of those different attempts to examine this part of the coast of New South Wales, were supplied by Governor Hunter to Colonel Collins, and they appear in his second volume of his history of that country. During this last trip of Lieutenant Flinders, he connected into one chart his own observations amongst the islands on the south side the strait, and those made by Mr. Bass on the north side, or coast of the main land, which he passed along in his whale-boat, together with such islands as they had an opportunity of seeing to lie scattered between. When Mr. Flinders laid his chart before Governor Hunter, he considered it only a tribute of justice due to the bold exertions and perseverance of that able and excellent young man, Mr. George Bass, to give the strait his name. This is a plain and correct statement of the manner in which the discovery of this strait has been made, and it will appear that Captain Hunter's conjecture of its situation had not been much mistaken, for he says he conceives, if it does exist, it lies between the latitudes of 39° and 42° south; it is now known to be between the parallels of 39° and 41° south.

Having thought it our duty to put the public in possession of these facts, we have only further to add, that whatever merit may arise from the discovery of Bass's Strait, no person surely has a greater right to claim it than Governor Hunter, who first suggested the probability of, and afterwards realized, under his own immediate authority, the existence of this passage, together with those gentlemen whom he selected, and who so ably executed his orders in ascertaining its correct situation.

Naval Poetry.

The Heart's remote recesses to explore,
And touch it's Springs, when Prose avail'd no more.

FALCONER.

Epicedium upon the Death of Vice-Admiral Lord Viscount NELSON, *who, after a series of heroic and transcendant Services, fell gloriously in the Battle of Trafalgar, Oct.* 21, 1805, "*In the hour of Victory.*"—By the Rev. SAMUEL BULLER, Master of the Free School, Shrewsbury.

WHILE notes of triumph swell the gale,
Why sits Britannia sad and pale
In the hour of Victory?

She mourns her gallant Hero dead,
She weeps that matchless Nelson bled,
And pensive bows her laurel'd head
In the hour of Victory!

O Chief! she cries, to Britons dear,
For thee we shed Britannia's tear,
In the hour of Victory!

Chief of the Lions, dauntless soul,
From Egypt's shore to Norway's pole,
'Twas thine to bid my thunders roll
In the hour of Victory!

For thee shall spotless Honour grieve,
And cypress 'midst his laurels weave
In the hour of Victory!

On thee shall grateful memory dwell,
And ages yet unborn shall tell,
How NELSON fought, how NELSON fell
In the hour of Victory!

Heir of Immortal Glory now,
Example of the brave be thou
In the hour of Victory!

Teach thou the valiant, good, and great,
Thy high exploits to emulate
And fearless smile, like thee, on fate
In the hour of Victory!

LINES
ON THE
DEATH OF LORD VISCOUNT NELSON.

(From the Morning Chronicle.)

WHILE Britain's ensigns, on the subject main,
Wave o'er the humbled pride of France and Spain;
While Britain's triumphs every muse employ,
Whence flows the tear that mingles with our joy?
Too dearly bought, our trophies we deplore—
The hand that rais'd those trophies is no more.
Oh! ever mournful, ever glorious day,
That snatch'd our pride, our brightest hope away!
Oh! fatal moment, when his parting breath
Hail'd the fresh laurels purchas'd with his death!
Yet had his bliss surpass'd the bounds of fate,
Had Heaven prolong'd it to a later date.

Lo! where the Corsican Usurper reigns
O'er servile hordes and subjugated plains,
With talents eminent, though misapplied,
Through wild ambition and despotic pride;
While Peace and Virtue curse the fatal hour
When civil triumphs led to regal power.
But patriotic valour scorns to know
Repose or pleasure in the public wo,
And feels that glory rightly understood
Guides but to one great end—its Country's good.
By worth like this, in Freedom's earlier days,
Victorious Greece and Rome aspir'd to praise;
By worth like this immortal NELSON shone,
And on BRITANNIA's glories rais'd his own.
Lamented shade! to thee the veteran tar,
Thy try'd companion 'mid the storms of war,
Who brav'd each form of death without a fear,
Pays the pure tribute of an honest tear.
The steady patriot unus'd to feel
A private sorrow in the public weal,
The hind, rough tenant of the peaceful vale,
Oft as he lingers on the mournful tale,
With manly pride restrains the rising sigh,
Till grief as manly glistens in his eye.

Such is the general grief—and long shall flow
The generous tide of unaffected wo;
Long shall each parent to his lisping son
Recount the palms thy matchless valour won,
Dwell with fond rapture on thy honour'd name,
And proudly aid him t'emulate thy fame.

How at that name the youthful soul aspires!
How glows the generous breast with patriot fires!
What heroes, form'd by thy example, rise,
Proud to exalt our glories to the skies,
While grateful millions shall exult to tell
How NELSON conquer'd, and how NELSON fell.

THE VICTORY OF TRAFALGAR.

THOUGH half round the globe, in pursuit of the foe,
Undaunted, unwearied, brave Nelson had sail'd;
While fate, for a season, suspended the blow,
Yet at length was the Hero with Victory hail'd:
Trafalgar's wide shore
Saw the flag which he bore,
And Cadiz far off heard his cannons' loud roar;
The heart of the foe was soon sunk in despair,
No hope could he cherish, for Nelson was there.

With tactic unusual Villeneuve form'd his line,
The Crescent's nice curve was his order of battle;
But fruitless his courage, and vain his design,
When in peals British thunder began its dread rattle.
Then close alongside,
Each ship fiercely tried
For the laurel of glory, in blood deeply dyed;
But nothing from Britain that laurel could tear,
While her favourite, her Hero, her Nelson was there.

The shock was resistless, the foe was o'erthrown;
What annals can boast of a Victory so great?
Their Chief, and just twenty proud flags were pulled down,
All from ships of the line, and from two of first rate.
Trafalgar's wide shore
Heard the last awful roar,
But the Hero of Britain, alas! was no more!
Death had clos'd his bright course of achievements so rare,
Though his Spirit rejoicing, still, still, linger'd there.

And blest be that Spirit wherever it goes,
Through ether's pure regions, to realms of delight!
Eternal his bliss, undisturb'd his repose,
As his fame througn this life was unsullied and bright,
And while o'er his grave
Bend the gallant and brave,
May we cherish the brilliant example he gave!
And the foes of our country behold in despair,
Wherever our flag flies his spirit's still there. G. C.

ON THE DEATH OF LORD NELSON, AND THE BATTLE OFF TRAFALGAR, ON THE 21ST OF OCT. 1805.

AND art thou gone, great Hero of the Nile,
Protector of this favour'd Isle!
How is the voice of rapture fled,
Since thou art number'd with the dead!
Perhaps thy blessed Spirit hovers o'er,
To guard with watchful care thy native shore.
Fain wou'd I spare,
Ah! fain forbear,
T' express the tide of wo,
That will in torrents flow,
At recollection of domestic love:
Who will assuage the Widow's grief,
Who to her sorrow give relief;
And who a kinsman to thy kindred prove?
The Nation, fam'd for liberal deeds,
Provides for his, who for his country bleeds.
Nelson, thy loss will every Briton mourn,
Full many are the laurels thou hast worn;
Immortal fame
Adorns thy name.
Thy soul hath mounted to the blest abode,
Where reigns the Giver of all Victory—GOD,
But 'midst our grief for thee
Forget we not the Heroes *yet our own*:
Let us prepare to give the merit due,
To every valiant Leader and his crew,
With gratitude, and high reward, *their labours crown.*

C.

MR. EDITOR,

DURING the blockade of Cadiz, which preceded the late glorious victory of Trafalgar, the officers on board His Majesty's ship Britannia, the flag-ship of Lord Northesk, sometimes amused themselves by the performance of theatrical entertainments. On one of these occasions, the following very neatly pointed Occasional Address was spoken by Lieutenant L. B. Halloram, of the royal marines. The prediction towards the conclusion has been happily fulfilled by the triumph of the British Arms, but unfortunately with the loss of the first of British Heroes.

Your insertion of it will, I doubt not, afford considerable gratification to many of your readers. Yours, &c.

H.

ADDRESS

SPOKEN ON BOARD HIS MAJESTY'S SHIP BRITANNIA, OFF CADIZ.

MY *Lord** and *Gentlemen*—alas! off Cadiz,
How hard it is we can't address the *Ladies!*
For "if the *brave* alone deserve the *fair*,"
BRITANNIA's Sons should surely have *their* share!
But, since their valour, tho' upon record,
Like other merits, is its own reward;
Tho' *female* charms inspire us not—again
We welcome *you*—my *Lord* and *Gentlemen!*
You, too, brave fellows! who the *back ground* tread,
Alike we welcome—jackets *blue* or *red!*
And humbly hope, "That while we give our aid,
To cheer the tedium of a dull blockade;
To banish *ennui* for a few short hours,
However feeble our theatric powers,
Our well-meant efforts—to amuse awhile—
Will meet the wish'd reward—*your fav'ring smile.*"

For tho', while thro' our parts we swell and pant,
We stun your *ears* with *mock-heroic rant*,
We trust "to pay *their* suff'rings through your *eyes*,"
By the bright splendors of the gay disguise;
In which our heroes (nor let Critics grin)
Bedight in robes of "*bunting* laced with *tin*,"
As Kings or Emperors, with mimic rage,
Strut their short hour upon this "*floating stage*."
In times of Yore, as grave old Authors write,

---

* Rear-Admiral the Earl of Northesk, who, with his usual condescension and good nature, honoured these performances with his presence.

Poets possess'd a kind of "*second sight*;"
And could (tho' *entre nous*, 'twas all a *hum*,)
Inform you clearly of "*events to come!*"
Oh! could the Bard, who to amuse your time,
Has manufactur'd all this "doggrel rhyme;"
From mortal mists clear his desiring eyes,
And pry into *your* future destinies:
He would foretell—(nor ask you, as a charm,
Like other Soothsayers—"*to cross his palm*);"
What—yes! he sees—*must* on your courage wait,
"An happy fortune, and a glorious fate!"
Yes!—he foresees—(confirm his prospects, Heav'n!)
* "*Yon coop'd up boasters*" to your wishes giv'n!
Sees their proud Ensigns from their Standards torn,
Their vanquish'd Navies in glad triumph borne;
Sees added laurels grace our Nelson's brow,
And VICTORY hov'ring o'er his glowing prow;
His conqu'ring banners o'er the waves unfurl'd,
And BRITAIN's thunder rule the wat'ry world!
If aught of pre-science to the muse belong,
Soon, soon the scenes that animate her song,
In glowing colours shall salute your eyes,
And Heav'n shall bid th' auspicious morn arise,
When France and Spain shall be again subdued,
And your "*brave Leader's*" Victories renew'd!

Then, to reward your persevering toils,
With honours crown'd—enrich'd with hostile spoils—
(Her bravest Sons—her guardian Sailor's Friend),
"*Your grateful Country*" shall her arms extend,
To greet your glad return with conscious pride,
And in her bosom bid your cares subside!

And, while our fam'd BRITANNIA shall resort,
In awful grandeur to her wish'd-for Port,
Her loveliest Daughters shall with pleasure meet,
And bless "the Heroes of the *British Fleet!*"
Your Wives, your Children, and your Friends shall come,
With tears of joy to bid you "*welcome home!*"
Nor storms nor battle more your bliss shall mar,
"But, *Peace and Plenty crown the toils* of War!"

* The combined fleets, who, though superior to the British blockading fleet by eight sail of the line, remained under the protection of their batteries in disgraceful security.

AN ADDRESS TO ENGLAND
UPON
HER NELSON'S DEATH.

WRITTEN BY WM. THOS. FITZGERALD, ESQ.

——— *breve et irreparabile Tempus*
Omnibus est VITÆ; *sed* FAMAM *extendere* FACTIS,
HOC VIRTUTIS OPUS!

WHILE ENGLAND beams one universal blaze,
The faithful tribute of a nation's praise!
For naval deeds achiev'd of high renown,
And honours added to the British Crown,
Is there a Briton's breast that does not beat
At NELSON's triumph, and the foe's defeat?
However poor, he shares the gen'rous flame,
And glows exulting at the Hero's name.—
Immortal NELSON!—here my throbbing heart,
Swelling with sorrow, acts no borrow'd part—
May I not say, and say it with a tear,
That with his death the Triumph's bought too dear?
But who can murmur, glorious was his doom,
THE HEART OF EVERY BRITON IS HIS TOMB!
The NATION'S FAVORITE, and His SOVEREIGN's pride,
He rul'd despotic Lord of Ocean's tide!
Each coast, remember'd for some deed of fame,
Was made illustrious by great NELSON's name;
DENMARK, IBERIA, EGYPT's trophied shore,
Heard the dread thunder of his cannons' roar!
While laurels won from ev'ry hostile fleet,
He laid, in triumph, at his Monarch's feet;
And history ever shall record the day,
Bright with his glory! in Trafalgar's Bay.
In torrid climes, where nature pants for breath,
Or tainted gales bring pestilence and death;
Where hurricanes are born, and whirlwinds sweep,
The raging billows of th' Atlantic deep,
NELSON had sought, but long had sought in vain,
The still *retreating* fleets of France and Spain:
When found at last, he crush'd them on the flood,
And seal'd the awful conquest with his blood!

Yet as he lived, so did the Hero fall—
Crouch'd at his feet, he saw the humbled Gaul;
Saw hostile navies into ruins hurl'd,
And ENGLAND'S TRIDENT RULE THE WAT'RY WORLD!
Then did he—laurel-crown'd, and rapt in fire,
Upborne on Vict'ry's out-spread wing, expire!
Suspended by the shouts that rend the skies—
ENGLAND'S TRIUMPHANT!—but her NELSON dies!
A grateful Nation mourns her Hero dead,
And dews with tears the laurels on his head—
Laurels for ever green!—for ever new!—
Bequeath'd with NELSON'S dying breath to YOU!

NAVAL HISTORY OF THE PRESENT YEAR, 1806.

(January.)

RETROSPECTIVE AND MISCELLANEOUS.

THE melancholy but splendid funeral of our Naval Rolla; the trial of Sir Robert Calder; and the death of Mr. Pitt, are events which have successively demanded the public attention during the short period of the preceding month. The proud triumphs of the wily Corsican come not within the limits of our Chronicle; and we leave to other hands the painful task of investigating the causes which have enabled a ferocious horde of *Gauls* to dictate an ignominious peace to the Emperor of Germany, in the very metropolis of his kingdom; to trample upon the honours and high military character of the house of Austria; and to project the restoration of the kingdom of Poland in the person of Kosciusko. No power, but that of England, seems able to withstand this sanguinary Usurper; with inferior force it baffled all his deceit and wary attempts on the plains of Acre, and purified the sacred land of Egypt from the overwhelming inroad of his legions. Is it then reserved by Providence for this inconsiderable island alone to check the mad ambition of this self-created Emperor? If such is the will of Heaven, the threats, and calumnies, and falsehoods of this low-born and narrow-minded soldier, will be called forth with fresh virulence against our beloved country. But there is a sacred Bulletin on record, which will reflect light upon the cause of Liberty and of Religion, and may one day dazzle the hitherto blinded eyes of this modern *Rab-shakeh*. "BE NOT AFRAID OF THE WORDS WHICH THOU HAST HEARD! BEHOLD! I WILL SEND A BLAST UPON HIM, AND HE SHALL HEAR A RUMOUR, AND SHALL RETURN TO HIS OWN LAND; AND I WILL CAUSE HIM TO FALL BY THE SWORD IN HIS OWN LAND!"

On Monday, December 9, was opened, in the north transept of St. Paul's Cathedral, a monument to the memory of Captain G. BLAGDON WESTCOTT, of the Majestic, who fell in the Battle of the Nile, 1798. The Captain is represented expiring in the arms of Victory, who holds a crown of laurel over his head: this groupe is placed on a pedestal, in the form of a sarcophagus. In front is a figure in a recumbent posture, representing the Nile—the sphynx, and palm trees, farther indicate the Egyptian shore. Ships, in action, are introduced on each side of the sarcophagus, one of which is l'Orient, blowing up. This monument, which is a companion to the one voted to Captain BURGES, was, with that, the last production of our late eminent soulptor, Thomas Banks, Esq. R. A.

Letters on Service,

Copied verbatim from the LONDON GAZETTE.

[Continued from Vol. XIV, page 510.]

ADMIRALTY-OFFICE, DEC. 31, 1805.

Copy of a Letter from Lieutenant Phillips Cosby Handfield, of the Egyptienne, to Wm. Marsden, Esq., dated in Cawsand Bay, the 29th Instant.

SIR,

I HAVE the honour to enclose, for the information of the Lords Commissioners of the Admiralty, a copy of my letter to Admiral Cornwallis, respecting the capture of the French frigate la Libre by His Majesty's ships Loire, Captain F. L. Maitland, and Egyptienne, at present under my command, on the 24th instant, off Rochefort. I have the honour to be, &c.

P. C. HANDFIELD, Lieut.

SIR, *His Majesty's ship Egyptienne, off Ushant, Dec. 28, 1805.*

I have the honour to acquaint you with the capture of the French frigate la Libre, on the afternoon of the 24th instant, off Rochefort, by His Majesty's ships la Loire, Captain F. L. Maitland, and Egyptienne, at present under my command, both coming up at the same time, and joining in the attack.

La Libre, commanded by Monsieur Descorches, Capitaine de Fregate, mounts twenty-four eighteen-pounder guns on the main deck, six thirty-six-pounder carronades, and ten nine-pounder guns on the quarter deck and forecastle, with a complement of 280 men. She submitted after an obstinate defence of half an hour, having twenty men killed and wounded, and received so much damage, that all her masts went overboard soon after we took possession. She sailed from Flushing on the 14th November, in company with a French frigate of 48 guns, from whom she parted in a gale of wind on the 9th instant, on the coast of Scotland.

I have much pleasure in communicating to you the good conduct of the officers and men of the Egyptienne in this affair, and have only to regret that the inferior force of the enemy did not give room for the full extent of their services. Enclosed is a list of the wounded, and I am sorry to add that one is since dead.

Captain Maitland, of la Loire, has taken charge of the prize, from whom I parted on the 25th, when he had her in tow.

I have the honour to be, &c.

The Hon. W. Cornwallis, P. C. HANDFIELD, Lieut.
Commander in Chief, &c.

A List of the Wounded on board His Majesty's ship the Egyptienne, in the action with la Libre French frigate, the 24th of December, 1805.

None killed.

Wounded.

Mr. Thomas Robinson, Boatswain, slightly; William Thinn, Seaman, dangerously (since dead); John Williams, seaman, badly; John Davis, seaman, slightly; Thomas Lucas, seaman, slightly; John Strutton, Quarter-master, slightly; James M'Guire, royal marine, badly; James Evans, royal marine, slightly.

P. C. HANDFIELD, Lieut.

JANUARY 11, 1806.

Copy of a Letter from Sir Edward Pellew, Bart. Rear-admiral of the Red, &c. to Wm. Marsden, Esq., dated on board the Culloden, in Madras Roads, the 27th June, 1805.

SIR,

I forward, for the satisfaction of the Lords Commissioners of the Admiralty, a letter from Lieutenant Bell, Acting Commander of His Majesty's sloop Victor, dated Busheer, 23d May, announcing his having captured, and subsequently destroyed, a small French privateer named les Amis Reunis (alias le Vingt Cinq), on the 7th ultimo, at the entrance of the Persian Gulf.

I have the honour to be, &c.

E. PELLEW.

His Majesty's sloop Victor, Busheer Road,
May 23, 1805,

SIR,

With pleasure I inform your Excellency, that His Majesty's ship Victor, under my command, on the 7th of this month captured les Amis Reunis, a French privateer of fifty tons, two long four-pounders, and manned with thirty-eight men, just within the entrance of the Persian Gulf, the Coins bearing E. N. E. five or six leagues; out eighty days from the Isle of France; had not taken any thing. I was prompted to destroy her by having the convoy in company, which arrived hither safe three days since. I have the honour to be, &c.

GEORGE BELL.

To Sir Edward Pellew, Bart. Commander in Chief, &c.

JANUARY 14.

Copies of four Letters (with Enclosures) from Vice-Admiral Dacres, Commander in Chief of His Majesty's ships and vessels at Jamaica, to Wm. Marsden, Esq.

SIR, *Shark, Port Royal, October 23, 1805.*

You will receive herewith, for the information of the Lords Commissioners of the Admiralty, the copy of a letter I have received from Captain Chambers, of the Port Mahon, acquainting me of his having captured his Catholic Majesty's packet el Galgo. I am, &c.

J. R. DACRES.

His Majesty's sloop Port Mahon, Sept. 30, 1805,
Trinidad de Cuba, N. E. by N. distant twenty-six leagues.

SIR,

His Majesty's sloop Port Mahon, under my command, this morning crossed upon a schooner, lying to; but, on our near approach, made sail from us. I have the honour of informing you, she was captured after a chase of two hours, and proves His Catholic Majesty's packet el Galgo, commanded by Lieutenant Ignacio Guosquez, with thirty men; pierced for fourteen guns, but only four brass swivels mounted. She is a very fine vessel, coppered and copper-fastened, well found, and sails fast; left Cadiz on the 9th of August, had delivered dispatches at Camana, and was bound, with others, to Trinidad de Cuba and Vera Cruz, which were thrown overboard. I have, &c.

James Richard Dacres, Esq. SAM. CHAMBERS.
Commander in Chief, &c.

SIR, *Port Royal, Oct. 31, 1805.*

I am to request you to acquaint the Lords Commissioners of the Admiralty, that I have received a letter from Captain Macdonnell, of the Franchise, informing me of the boats of that ship having captured the General Ferrand felucca privateer, of one six-pounder, two four-pounder swivels, musketry, &c belonging to Santo Domingo. She had sailed from Saint Jago four days, and had taken nothing. I am, &c.

J. R. DACRES.

SIR, *Shark, Port Royal, Oct. 31, 1805.*

Herewith you will receive, for the information of the Lords Commissioners of the Admiralty, the copy of a letter I have received from Captain Wright, of the Swift, enclosing a letter from Lieutenant Smith, of that sloop, acquainting him with the success of an enterprise conducted with great bravery, which reflects great credit to the party engaged in it, particularly to Mr. Bowler, who has not been two years at sea. I am, &c.

J. R. DACRES.

His Majesty's sloop Swift, Port Royal,
October 27, 1805.

SIR,

In consequence of information I received while on my station at Honduras, that a schooner guarda costa had taken several vessels trading to that settlement, and if not captured, was likely to do much more mischief, I was determined to detach Mr. James Smith, Second Lieutenant of the ship I command, with a party of men, to see what could be effected; and I take the honour to refer you to a perusal of his letter to me for an account of his success, which, for execution and bravery, has been acknowledged to bid fair for protection and countenance.

La Caridad Perfecta is a very fine new vessel, and, in my opinion, every way fit for His Majesty's service. I remain, Sir, &c.

To Rear-Admiral Dacres, &c., Port Royal. J. WRIGHT.

SIR, *Mariamne schooner, Balize, Sept. 4, 1805.*

I beg leave to acquaint you, that, in pursuance of your orders, I proceeded with the schooner you placed under my command to the southward; and, while cruising on that station, and off the island of Bonacca, received information from the Caribbean fishermen, that a guarda costa was at anchor under the batteries of Truxillo, and that she had lately captured and carried into that port the schooner Admiral Duckworth, of Jamaica, with another vessel, name unknown, from Honduras; I therefore maturely considered the incalculable injury such a vessel might cause to the settlement, and conceiving it a duty incumbent on myself to prevent, if possible, further depredations, summoned the people aft, and, on my stating the case to them, they very readily volunteered to make an attempt to cut her out. Accordingly, on the evening of the 13th ultimo, I stood over, under cover of the night, for the harbour of Truxillo, and got well into the bay without being discovered, when I manned two small boats, with six men in each, under charge of Mr. Walker, Boatswain, in the one, and Mr. Bowler, Midshipman, in the other, with directions to pull in close along shore, and examine if our information was correct, standing in, at the same time, with the schooner to cover the boats, if occasion required. Shortly after we got in sight of the vessel we were in pursuit of, which was immediately boarded with great bravery by the boat's crew under charge of Mr. Bowler (the other, from pulling heavy, not being able to get up), and, after some resistance from the people on deck, they very gallantly got possession of her, the Captain and others jumping overboard: the noise this contest occasioned alarmed the forts, which opened on us a very heavy fire. The cables were then cut, and sail made, the forts keeping a continual fire on us till out of gun-shot, which was returned from both vessels. She proves to be la Caridad Perfecta, schooner rigged, copper bottomed, and pierced for sixteen guns, but mounted only with twelve, and had on board but fifteen men, the remainder of her complement being on shore at the time.

I am happy to add, that in performing this service no person has been hurt.

I have the honour to be, &c.

To John Wright, Esq., commanding His Majesty's ship Swift, Honduras. JAMES SMITH.

SIR, *Hercule, November 2, 1805.*

I enclose you, for the information of the Lords Commissioners of the Admiralty, the copy of a letter I have received from Captain M'Kenzie, of the Wolf, acquainting me of his having recaptured an American ship, and run on shore the privateer that captured her. I am, &c.

J. R. DACRES.

His Majesty's sloop Wolf, at Sea,
SIR, *October 20, 1805.*

I have to acquaint you, that yesterday evening, in consequence of information I received from the shore, I gave chase to two sail in the offing, and soon came up with a ship, which proved to be an American, captured a few minutes before by a Spanish privateer then standing in shore. I dropped a boat to take possession of her, and stood after the privateer; but it falling calm shortly after, I dispatched two boats in chase; they came up with, and boarded her at the very moment she struck on a reef near the shore, and about ten miles to leeward of Falmouth: every effort proved ineffectual to get her off, and she went to pieces soon after. She proved to be la Precieusa, a new cutter, out six days from St. Jago Cuba, commanded by Galana Garsa, carrying three small guns and twenty-three men, five of whom made their escape in a canoe previous to her being boarded; had made no other captures. I have the honour to be, &c.

To James Richard Dacres, Esq., Rear-Admiral of the Red, &c., Jamaica. G. C. M'KENZIE.

Imperial Parliament.

HOUSE OF LORDS, TUESDAY, JAN. 21.

THE Session of Parliament was opened by Commissioners appointed by His Majesty, to whom it was not convenient to attend in person. Lord Ellenborough, one of the Commissioners, read the following Speech :—

" *My Lords and Gentlemen,*

" In pursuance of the authority given to us by His Majesty's commission, under the great seal, amongst other things, to declare the cause of his holding this parliament, His Majesty has directed us particularly to call your attention to the most decisive success with which Providence has vouchsafed to bless His Majesty's arms at sea, since you were last assembled in parliament.

" The activity and perseverance of His Majesty's fleets have been conspicuously displayed in the pursuit and attack of the different squadrons of the enemy, and every encounter has terminated to the honour of the British flag, and the diminution of the naval force of the powers with whom His Majesty is at war; but the victory obtained over the combined fleet of France and Spain off Cape Trafalgar has manifested, beyond any exploit recorded even in the annals of the British Navy, the skill and enterprise of His Majesty's officers and seamen; and the destruction of so large a proportion of the naval strength of the enemy has not only confirmed, in the most signal manner, the maritime superiority of this country, but has essentially contributed to the security of His Majesty's dominions.

" His Majesty most deeply regrets that the day of that memorable triumph should have been unhappily clouded by the fall of the heroic Commander under whom it was achieved : and he is persuaded that you will feel that this lamented but glorious termination of a series of transcendant exploits claims a distinguished expression of the lasting gratitude of the country; and that you will therefore cheerfully concur in enabling His Majesty to annex to those honours which he has conferred on the family of the late Lord Viscount Nelson, such a mark of national munificence, as may preserve to the latest posterity the memory of his name and services, and the benefit of his great example.

" His Majesty has commanded us further to inform you, that, whilst the superiority of his arms at sea has been thus uniformly asserted and maintained, he has not been wanting in his endeavours to apply the means, which were so liberally placed at his disposal, in aid of such of the powers of the continent as evinced a determination to resist the formidable and growing encroachments of France. He has directed the several treaties entered into for this purpose to be laid before you; and, though he can not but deeply lament that the events of the war in Germany have disappointed his hopes, and led to an unfavourable issue, yet His Majesty feels confident, that, upon a review of the steps which he has taken, you will be of opinion, that he has left nothing undone on his part to sustain the efforts of his allies, and that he has acted in strict conformity to the principles declared by him, and recognized by parliament as essential to the interest and security of his own dominions, as well as to the general safety of the continent.

" It is a great consolation to His Majesty, and one in which he is persuaded you will participate, that although the Emperor of Germany has felt himself compelled to withdraw from the contest, His Majesty continues to receive from his august ally the Emperor of Russia, the strongest assurances of unshaken adherence to that generous and enlightened policy by which he has hitherto been actuated; and His Majesty has no doubt that you will be fully sensible of the important advantages to be derived from preserving at all times the closest and most intimate connexion with that Sovereign.

" *Gentlemen of the House of Commons,*

" His Majesty has directed the estimates for the year to be laid before you, and he has commanded us to inform you that they are framed upon that scale of exertion which the present situation of the country renders indispensable. His Majesty fully relies upon your granting him such supplies as, upon due deliberation, the public exigencies may appear to require. It is his earnest wish to contribute, by every means in his power, to alleviate the additional burthens which must necessarily be imposed upon his people, and with this view he has directed the sum of one million sterling, part of the proceeds arising from the sale of such prizes made on the powers with which he is at war, as are by law vested in the crown, to be applied to the public service of the year.

" *My Lords and Gentlemen,*

" His Majesty is fully persuaded, that whatever pride and confidence you may feel in common with him, in the success which has distinguished the British arms, in the course of the present contest, you will be sensible how much the events of the war on the continent, by which the predominant power and influence of France have been so unhappily extended, require the continuance of all possible vigilance and exertion. Under this impression, His Majesty trusts that your attention will be invariably directed to the improvement of those means which are to be found in the bravery and discipline of his forces, in the zeal and loyalty of every class of his subjects, and in the unexhausted resources of his dominions, for rendering the British empire invincible at home, as well as formidable abroad; satisfied that, by such efforts alone, the contest can be brought to a conclusion consistent with the safety and independence of the country, and with its rank amongst the nations of the world."

Earl *Nelson* was introduced by the Earls of Macclesfield and Bristol, attended by the Earl Marshal, and Garter King at Arms: and after the usual oaths took his seat.

The Earl of *Essex*, in moving the Address on the Speech, said, Every one of your Lordships must feel much more forcibly than any words of mine can express, the highest sentiments of satisfaction at that most brilliant and decisive victory which was lately gained over the combined fleets of France and Spain—a victory which has crowned our country with new glory, and tended most effectually to establish its permanent security against all the hostile attempts which the enemy may meditate against us. I am confident that all your Lordships participate in the generous and tender feelings expressed in His Majesty's Speech, for the loss of that heroic Commander, to whose great talents, to whose consummate valour and skill, the whole kingdom is indebted for the victory in question. Such services as these are entitled to the highest honours and the highest rewards which it is in the power of the nation to confer; and I trust your Lordships will cheerfully concur in the magnanimous recommendation of His Majesty to make a suitable provision for the family of the late illustrious Lord Nelson.

Lord Viscount *Carleton*, in seconding the Address, spoke nearly as follows:—My Lords, most of the topics alluded to in His Majesty's Speech are such as must meet your concurrençe. The glorious victory of Trafalgar is an event of such magnitude and importance, that it is hardly possible for the imagination to conceive any other more transcendant: it is superior to almost every other naval action for which our history is so famous. The unparalleled valour displayed by all the individuals engaged in that action, and the unexampled ability and skill with which it was conducted, has been a subject of admiration to this country and the whole world. Never was so great an enemy so completely destroyed. The naval skill and the valour displayed on that glorious occasion was never equalled, and will never be surpassed. Every man who recollects the signal given by the Hero who achieved the successes—"*England expects that every man will do his duty*"—must be struck with a still higher degree of admiration of his character. We never can speak or think with sufficient admiration of this great victory, nor sufficiently lament the fate of him whose great mind planned the attack that was crowned with such brilliant success. I have thus far expressed my feelings on this subject, because I wish to direct your attention to the importance of that part of His Majesty's Speech, which recommends a munificent recompense to the representatives of the deceased Hero, to whom every individual in the country, from the highest to the lowest, is so greatly indebted for his security.

In the course of the debate, Lord *Grenville* took an opportunity of saying:—My Lords, I most heartily concur in that part of the Address which relates to the brilliant and important victory gained over the combined fleets of the enemy. Every man possessed of an English heart and an English head must concur in all the praises that have so justly been bestowed on the persons who achieved that most glorious victory; and all must cheerfully concur in pledging the national gratitude towards the family of the illustrious Hero who fell on that memorable occasion; and in acknowledging their claim to every remuneration a generous and grateful country can bestow. The part of the Address, therefore, which alludes to that event, has my full and heartfelt approbation.

Lord *Hawkesbury* was happy to find that there existed but one opinion on the subject of the great and brilliant services which the late naval victory produced; and that there was only one opinion also on the manner in which it was proposed those services should be rewarded. His Lordship also gave notice, that on Friday he would move the Thanks of the House to Admiral Lord Collingwood, and the other Officers, together with the Seamen and Marines, who were engaged in the late action off Cape Trafalgar.

WEDNESDAY, JAN. 22.

Lord *Melville* delivered in at the table a plea of NOT GUILTY to the charges exhibited against him by the Commons. In consequence of which,

On the motion of Lord *Walsingham*, Mr. Adam, Mr. Plumer, and another Gentleman, were appointed to assist his Lordship in the necessary arrangements relative to his defence.

HOUSE OF COMMONS, TUESDAY, JAN. 21.

The speech on commencing the session having been read by the Speaker,

Lord *F. Spencer* rose for the purpose of moving an address thereto. In the course of which, he observed, that nothing could be more consolatory than a review of our naval glory. The activity and perseverance of His Majesty's fleets had never been more displayed than in the present war, and had rendered His Majesty's arms every where victorious by sea. The late victory obtained over the combined fleets of France and Spain, was an unquestionable proof of the skill and enterprise of our Navy, and had given a death blow to the remaining force of the enemy. This victory, though dearly purchased by the death of the gallant Hero who contributed so much to achieve it, while the death of that Hero was matter of condolence, must give the greatest satisfaction to every lover of his country, and place us in a commanding situation amid the nations of Europe; and the House he thought could have no hesitation in seconding the munificent intentions of His Majesty respecting the family of that noble Lord, who had fallen so gloriously in the defence of the naval glory of the country.

Lord *Henry Petty* declared, that no member in the House could feel more sensibly than he did the loss that accompanied the late Naval Victory; and none could be more forward than he felt himself disposed to be in seconding any measures to acquit ourselves of the debt of gratitude due by the country to the gallant Officer whose loss they lamented. As when alive he united all around him in the admiration of his character, so also would his memory ever unite all hearts. With respect to the munificent intentions, therefore, of His Majesty towards the family of the late noble Lord, there could be but one opinion, and to that part of the Address he could have no objection.

Lord *Castlereagh* gave notice of his intention to move, on Friday next, a Vote of Thanks to the Officers, Seamen, and Marines, who had so eminently distinguished themselves at the memorable Battle of Trafalgar.

WEDNESDAY, JAN. 22.

The papers respecting the repairs of ships, which were ordered last Session, were presented by Mr. W. Dickinson, from the Admiralty. On the motion of Admiral Markham, they were ordered to be printed.

A person from the Commissioners of Naval Inquiry, brought up the 12th Report of those Commissioners, together with observations by way of supplement, which were read, and, on the motion of Sir C. Pole, ordered to be printed.

Mr. *Whitbread* moved that the resolutions of the 26th of June, for appointing a Committee to conduct the Impeachment against Lord Viscount Melville be now read. The resolutions being read, he moved that the said Committee sit and proceed on the matters referred to them to-morrow morning.—Ordered.

TRIAL

OF

VICE-ADMIRAL SIR ROBERT CALDER, BART.

FIRST DAY, PORTSMOUTH, DECEMBER 23, 1805.

THIS morning the signal for a Court Martial was hoisted on board the Prince of Wales, to inquire into the conduct and proceedings of Vice-Admiral Sir Robert Calder, with His Majesty's squadron under his command, on the 23d day of July last, and the two following days. The Court was composed of the following Officers :—

GEORGE MONTAGU, Esq., Admiral of the White, and Commander in Chief of His Majesty's ships and vessels of war at Portsmouth and Spithead, President.

Vice-Admiral HOLLOWAY	Vice-Admiral ROWLEY
Vice-Admiral THORNBOROUGH	Rear-Admiral Sir I. COFFIN, Bart.
Rear-Admiral SUTTON	Captain IRWIN
Captain OLIVER	——— SEATER
——— WOOD	——— LARMOUR
——— CAPEL	——— BISSET.

The prosecution was conducted by Moses Greetham, Esq., Judge Advocate, assisted by C. Bicknell, Esq., Solicitor to the Admiralty. The Court opened at half past ten o'clock, and Vice-Admiral Sir R. Calder being called in, entered with the usual formalities.

The terms of the inquiry and of the charges were as follow :—

" Which Court is hereby required and directed to inquire into the conduct and proceedings of the said Vice-Admiral Sir R. Calder, with His Majesty's squadron under his command, on the said 23d day of July last, and also into his subsequent conduct and proceedings, until he finally lost sight of the enemy's ships, and to try him for not having done his utmost to renew the said engagement, and to take or destroy every ship of the enemy, which it was his duty to engage accordingly."

The President then said, Sir Robert Calder, one of your witnesses, Captain Prouse, is unavoidably absent; we do not wish you to proceed without him, if you feel his evidence to be necessary to your defence.—Sir R. Calder. I am perfectly willing to proceed without him.—Sir R. Calder's letter of the 30th of September to the Admiralty, demanding a Court Martial, was then read.

Mr. Josiah Hope, the Master of the Prince of Wales, produced the log-book of the Prince of Wales.

Q. Is that the log-book of the Prince of Wales? A. It is.

Q. Are the contents of it, to the best of your knowledge, true? Yes.

Mr. Gorthine Parker produced the Triumph's log-book, and deposed that the contents, to the best of his knowledge, were true.

Mr. Henry Craddock, Master of the Glory, produced the log-book of that ship, and swore to the truth of the contents.

Mr. William Glen, Master of the Warrior, produced her log-book, and pointed out two places where the entry had been erroneous.

Mr. Edward Shode, the Master of the Hero, produced her log-book, and verified the contents,

Extracts from the log of Sir Robert Calder were then produced. They were the same he transmitted to Admiral Cornwallis, by order of the Lords Commissioners of the Admiralty.

Admiral Charles Stirling sworn.—Examined by Mr. Bicknell.

Q. Be so good as to state to the Court, on board what ship your flag was flying on the 23d of July last, and the subsequent day, and until you lost sight of the enemy.—A. The Glory.

Q. What was the force and disposition of the British fleet under the command of Vice-Admiral Calder on those days?—A. It consisted of fifteen sail of the line, two frigates, a lugger, and a cutter. At day-light part of the van was far advanced to the enemy, the body of the fleet lying to; the Malta, the Thunderer, the two frigates, the Egyptienne and Sirius, and the two prizes captured the day before, were not in sight.

Q. What was the force of the enemy's fleet on the morning of the 23d of July, at day-break?—A. The enemy was so distant at day-light, and the weather so hazy, that we could not see them all; but as they approached us nearer when the weather cleared, I considered that their force was eighteen sail of the line, and seven or eight others.

Q. Will you have the goodness to state to the Court all the circumstances that came within your knowledge and observation, respecting the British fleet and the combined fleet, from the time you came in sight of the enemy, on the 23d of July, till you lost sight of them on the following day?—A. When the day advanced, the British van bore up to join the Admiral, and soon after the fleet wore, and ran to the leeward, till we joined the Malta and Thunderer with the prizes, when we hauled our wind with the main-top-sail to the mast; the enemy had come down towards us, and the British fleet had hauled their colours, but about the time of our showing our wind, they hauled theirs. We were not in any order of sailing or of battle, and therefore we sometimes had our main-top-sail full, or kept it aback, to keep such distance from the Admiral as I thought he would approve. A look-out frigate from the enemy having come down to reconnoitre in the course of the forenoon, the Triumph was sent to chase her, and afterwards lay to between the two fleets. The Dragon was sent to take the Windsor Castle in tow. About noon, the enemy, I think, bore for the North-west by North to West, and by North; the wind was North-west and by North, according to my idea; the logs will better state it with accuracy. The crippled ships stood on the lar board tack, and it appeared to me that the Admiral's object was to keep company with them.——The enemy sometimes during the day, besides the time I before mentioned, bore up in line of battle, and then hauled their wind, not approaching us, I believe, nearer than four leagues, or being further than six from us, keeping near in the same line of bearing. About midnight firing was heard in the direction where the enemy was, when the wind shifted to the Northward, or rather came to the Eastward of North, and, at daylight in the morning they were seen steering away about South-east. I do not remember seeing them from the deck any part of the day, therefore can only speak of their bearings from the report of such officers as I sent up to look after them, who told me they kept receding from us, till about six o'clock, when I understood they could be no longer seen from the Glory. About eight, the British fleet were with their head to the north-west. The wind, as the day advanced, had come round to the eastward.

Q. Was a signal made from the Vice-Admiral's ship on Tuesday morning, the 23d of July, and at what hour, to ask what ships had occasion to lie by to refit?—A. A signal was made to that effect, about the time of our wearing; I do not recollect the exact time.

Q. What was the answer from your ship?—A. We answered in the negative, not having occasion to lie by.

Q. Did the British fleet, by going to leeward, increase their distance from the enemy?—A. They would have increased their distance, if the enemy had lain to; but as they bore up in the manner I have before stated, they came nearer to us than they were at day-light in the morning.

Q. If the British fleet had gone on in the same course, instead of steering a more easterly course, would not the captured ships have been equally protected?—A. If the British fleet had kept their wind, they would not have afforded any protection to the captured ships, as they would have drifted out of sight; we did not steer precisely in the same course throughout the day, sometimes we sprung our luff; the Admiral sometimes bore down towards them, from their not being able to keep their wind; but when the enemy vauntingly bore up, he occasionally hauled his wind, and then edged down to near the prizes. I say vauntingly, because the enemy might have brought us to action when they chose, during the 23d. By the crippled ships I mean the prizes, and the Windsor Castle, which were in tow. The Dragon had the Windsor Castle, and the frigates the prizes.

Q. Could the two frigates have secured the captured ships, and thereby left the Thunderer and Malta at liberty to join the fleet?—A. The Thunderer and Malta did join the fleet when we formed a junction with the prizes.

Q. Considering the wind, and the relative situation of the two fleets, during the day of the 23d, could the British fleet have neared the enemy, and renewed the action?—A. That is a mere matter of opinion. It is impossible for me to say whether we could have neared the enemy's fleet or not; we did not lay our heads towards them. I have before mentioned my belief, that the wind was N. W. and by N. on the 23d, and that the enemy bore from N. W. to W. and by N., consequently we could not have fetched them any part of the 23d, if they had chosen to avoid us, I mean by going a contrary tack.

Q. Did the Vice-Admiral make any signal, or show any disposition to endeavour to renew the action on that day?—A. I have before stated, that it appeared to me that the Admiral's object was to keep company with the crippled ships on that day, and I saw no other signal indicative of a disposition to renew the combat, after he asked if any ships wanted to lie to.

Q. Did the Vice Admiral take any step to direct the British fleet to bear up after the enemy on the 24th?—A. The British fleet continued standing from the enemy till the time I have before mentioned that we wore.

Q. Could the British fleet have pursued the enemy with advantage on the 24th, they bearing southward and eastward, and the wind north and by east?—A. I do not know any objection to the British fleet following the enemy, if the Admiral thought proper to do so.

Q. Did the Vice-Admiral at any time, on the 24th, show any disposition to renew the action?—A. I think that question answered by the preceding; we continued steering from the enemy.

Q. Did the Vice-Admiral, from your remarks and observations, do all he might have done between the 23d of July at day-light, and the time you lost sight of the enemy, to renew the engagement, and to take or destroy every ship which it was his duty to engage?—A. We never attempted to renew the action, or to lay our heads towards the enemy: and I have said before, it appeared to me that the Admiral's object was to cover the crippled ships.

Cross-examined by the Court.

Q. At the time the British fleet bore down to the crippled ships, in what state was the Windsor Castle?—A. She appeared to have lost her foretop-mast, and not able to make sail.

Q. What other ships of the British fleet were unable to keep company with the Vice-Admiral, had he endeavoured to bring the enemy to action?—I do not know that any other ship was disabled.

Q. From the 23d to the 25th, what other ships were not able to give him succour?—I do not know of any other ship being disabled.

Cross-examined by Admiral Calder.

Q. Under what sail, and at what rate did we edge down to the crippled ships on the morning of the 23d?—A. I believe the body of the fleet under their three top-sails.

Q. What rate of sailing?—A. I do not know; the log will tell.

Q. Was there not a heavy swell, and so little wind in the morning of the 24th, so much so that I made the signal for sailing in open order?—A. There was a considerable swell, but I do not recollect the signal. I think there was little wind in the early part of the day.

Q. Were you acquainted with the returns which had been made of the damages the squadron had received at sea?—A. No.

Q. Were you acquainted with the orders under which I acted?—A. No.

Q. What force had the enemy at Rochefort when you left it to put yourself under my command?—A. From report, one 3-decker, two 80 guns ships, three 74's, and some smaller vessels.

Q. Do you mean to say no frigates; whether two or three frigates?—A. I do not know; there were several smaller vessels.

Q. On what day was that?—A. I believe my order to put myself under Sir Robert's command was on the 16th July.

Q. Recollect yourself; I believe you came under my command on the 15th?—A. It was so: it was three days before I joined you that I received the order: it must have been the 12th.

Q. In what state did you leave the Rochefort squadron?—A. I understand they were ready for sea, and meant to take the first opportunity of pushing out, and the signal had been made to me on that morning, the morning I left them, that the enemy was moving.

Q. Had those ships been frequently under sail during the time you was off Rochefort?—A. I know no other time but that day.

Q Were they under sail?—A. Some of them were: I did not see them: it was mere report. Captain Fleming's signal that they were moving was by telegraph. I ran down nearer with the squadron, and found them at anchor again.

Q. Could they have put to sea with the wind with which you came to me?—A. Certainly.

Q. Have you since learnt they did put to sea on or about the 18th of July; or at what other time?—A. Yes, I understood they put to sea about that time; but I know not the precise date.

Q. Did you receive a letter from me on service after the action?—A. Yes: I had two letters from Sir Robert Calder after the action, of different dates.

Q. Did the first give you any reasons for standing to the northward with the Windsor Castle and Precious?—A. I can produce the letter (the letter was produced and read, it was dated Prince of Wales, 24th July); the Admiral begged he might be permitted to return thanks to Admiral Stirling for his unremitted attention to the service, and the gallant support he had given him during the whole action. Had the weather been favourable, and they could have seen the signal, so as to have availed themselves of the mistakes of the enemy, they should have captured more of their ships. He added, that he was going to Cape Finisterre to meet Lord Nelson, and concert measures with him for attacking the combined fleet.

Q. Is this the answer to that letter?—A. It is not an answer to that letter, but was written in reply. I sent by the same conveyance a letter to the Vice-Admiral, on public service. I should not have written such a letter to my Commander if it had been on public service; it was a private letter. The cutter brought me that letter.

It was produced and read. It began by thanking Admiral Calder for his letter; and stated that he meant to give him all the support in his power. It stated Admiral Stirling's hope that Admiral Calder had got a good tale for John Bull, who could not but be pleased that he had taken two ships from a superior force.

I believe that letter was sent to the Admiral on the 25th, and I had the honour to wait upon him in the afternoon, by his permission; and, to the best of my recollection, that was my reason for not returning an official answer. I do not remember any other communication with the Admiral from about midnight of the 22d.

After some conversation, another letter from Admiral Stirling was read. It was dated 24th July, and congratulated him on the capture of two ships of the line, from a force so superior. He thought that if the three ships which showed a disposition to support them, had followed their intention, the consequences might have been decisive.

Q. Did I not always place the squadron between the squadron of the enemy and the Windsor Castle and captured ships, when in tow by our ships?—A. The British fleet was always between them.

Q. Was not the English squadron always placed by me between the enemy and the port of Ferrol as long as the enemy remained in sight?—A. The British fleet was nearer to Ferrol than the enemy, till they crossed our stern on the 24th.

Q. When they crossed our stern, could they have fetched Ferrol?—A. I don't think they could.

Q. By the Court. What distance was the British fleet from Rochefort the morning after the action?—A. I do not know, the chart will tell. I recollect by the Master's reckoning. By the Master's reckoning we were in long. 44. 13. and about 39 leagues N. W. from Cape Finisterre.

Henry Craddock, the Master of the Glory, sworn.

Q. What was the distance of the British fleet on the 23d and 24th July last from the port of Ferrol and Rochefort?—A. On the 23d July, at noon, to the best of my remembrance, Cape Finisterre bore the nearest; the difference will be very little. It bore about 39 leagues south east by east; Ferrol much the same distance; it might be about three leagues more. I cannot say the distance of Rochefort without a chart.

Q. Do you know the port of Ferrol?—A. Yes, by looking in, and having a plan of the harbour.

Q Can an enemy's ship come out of that port with a wind at north, or any wind that you had, between the time of the action and Wednesday the 24th, at 8 P. M.?—A. I hardly recollect the wind at 8 P. M. With the wind at N. N. W. they could not, in my opinion, and I hardly suppose they could with the wind at north.

Admiral Calder. I never can ask that genlteman any questions.

Admiral George Martin sworn.

Be so good as to state all the circumstances, &c. (*See the question as put to Admiral Stirling*)—A. Not having made any minutes, or expecting to be called on before a Court-Martial, I do not feel myself prepared to relate a narrative, or answer the question. I left the Barfleur on account of ill health; and am not prepared.

State as many facts as you can. Q. Was a signal made from the Vice-Admiral's ship on Tuesday morning, July 23, and what hour, to ask what ships had occasion to lie by to refit?—A. The signal was made generally.

Q. At what time?—A. I cannot say; early in the morning.

Q. What was the answer from your ship?—A. In the negative, that I did not require to lie to.

Q. What was the relative situation of the two fleets on Tuesday the 23d, at day-break?—A. At day-break, on Tuesday the 23d, the Barfleur was five miles to leeward of the enemy, and nearly five miles to windward of the fleet; the Barfleur, Hero, Triumph, and, I think, Agamemnon, were about midway between the two fleets.

Q. How was the wind at the time?—A. I think about W. N. W. from N. W. to N. N. W.

Q What course were the two fleets then steering?—A. The two fleets were standing on the larboard tack, the precise course I do not recollect. The Malta and some other ships were to leeward with the prizes, and were not seen by us till the following morning, about eight o'clock of the 23d.

Q. Did the British fleet alter their course by sailing from the wind more to the eastward, thereby increasing their distance from the enemy?—A. Upon a signal being made by one of the ships of the squadron, when I do not recollect, the Malta and prizes to leeward, the British fleet bore up to close them.

Q. Considering the wind, and the relative situation of the two fleets on the 23d of July, could the British fleet have neared the enemy, and renewed the engagement?—A. The enemy being rather abaft the beam, the British fleet naturally would have neared them had they tacked; but whether they would have renewed the engagement I cannot say: that must in a great measure have depended on the enemy.

Q. Did the Vice-Admiral make any signal ,or show any disposition to endeavour to renew the action on that day?—A. No

Q. Were the lights of the enemy's fleet seen at any time during the night of the 23d?—A. In the early part of the evening they were; just when I went to bed they were not reported to me as having been seen.

Sir Robert Calder.—I admit I did not show any disposition to do so, except by hawling the wind when I saw them bearing down, as, by doing so, I must have separated myself from the crippled ships.

Q. At day-light on the 24th what was the relative situation of the two fleets, and how was the wind?—A. Very moderate, nearly calm; at seven or eight o'clock in the morning a breeze sprung up from the N. N. E. which brought the enemy a litle on the quarter, at that time a considerable distance off, the whole of the fleet not being in sight from the deck.

Q, Did the enemy on the morning of the 24th, and at what hour, bear away to the southward and eastward?—A. I cannot say the precise hour the enemy bore away, but their heads were to the S. E. and they did not appear close to the wind.

Q. Could the British fleet have pursued the enemy the 24th with a prospect of advantage?—A. Every ship but the Windsor Castle appeared to me to be in a situation. I can only speak from appearances, not having an opportunity of knowing their internal situation.

Q. Did the Vice-Admiral, at any time on the 24th, show any disposition to renew the engagement?

Admiral Calder.—I did not; for reasons which I will hereafter state.

Q. Did the Vice-Admiral, from your remarks and observations, do all he might have done, between the 23d of July at day-light, and the time you lost sight of the enemy, to renew the engagement, and to take or destroy every ship which it was his duty to engage?—A. I consider that I have already answered, that the Vice-Admiral never did stand towards the enemy on either of those days.

Cross-examined by Sir Robert Calder.

Q. Did the enemy ever chase or make any attempt to force me to action either on the 23d or 24th of July?—A. The enemy bore up shortly after, in the afternoon, on the day of the 23d, as I then thought to renew the engagement, but by their hauling to the wind again, as soon as they closed with the leeward ship, I believe it was only intended for that purpose.

Q. Did I keep my wind when the enemy bore down?—Yes; I observed you haul to the wind when the enemy bore down.

Y. Was there not a swell, and so little wind, that I gave the signal to keep the ships in open order?—A. I have already mentioned there was little wind, and I do recollect the signal to keep open order.

Q. Could I have pursued the enemy on the 24th without separating the rest of the squadron from the Windsor Castle and prizes and frigates?—A. Certainly not, without separating them from the prizes, and not under a press of sail without separating from the Windsor Castle.

Q. Did I not always place the squadron between that of the enemy and the Windsor Castle, and the prizes in tow by our ships?—A. It appeared to me to be the intention of Sir Robert Calder, from the time of the action, to keep company with them till they separated by signal.

Q. Was not the English squadron always placed by me between that of the enemy and the port of Ferrol, as long as the enemy remained in sight?—A. We certainly were between them; it did not appear to me, that any particular situation was chosen.

Mr. Craddock, examined by the Court.

Q. You have said that an enemy could not come out of Ferrol with a N.N.W. wind. Do you know how the wind was on the 24th? The witness referred to the log. It appears it was at N. N. E.; from eight A. M. to eight P. M. it was from N. N. E. to N. E.

Q. Could an enemy's ship have come out of Ferrol with a wind from N. N. E. to N. E?—A. They could at N. E., but, to the best of my judgment, it would be attended with some difficulty at N. N. E.

Captain Philip Charles Durham.

Q. Was you ordered to reconnoitre the enemy's fleet, and to observe their motions on the 24th July?—I was.

Q. At what time?—A. Between six and seven.

Q. Did you at any time make a signal to the Vice-Admiral to ask if you should keep the enemy's fleet in sight?—A. I did.

Q. At what time?—A About six, or between five and six in the evening. It was in the afternoon, after four o'clock.

Q. Was you to windward of the enemy's fleet at that time?

By the Court.

Q. When you last saw the enemy's fleet, under what sail were they standing and what course were they steering?—A. They were under their top-sails, top-gallant sails, and fore-sails, in general steering S. E. and by S.

Q. How did the British fleet then bear from the enemy?—A. The enemy bore about S. S. W. of me, and the Admiral nearly N. or N. N. E. and by E.

Q. At the time you returned to the British fleet, under what sail were they standing, and what course were they steering?—A. They were steering by the wind on the larboard tack, I should suppose about S. E. and by E.

Q. What sail were they under when you returned?—A. I think under topsail and foresail; when I returned to the fleet we lay about S. E.

Q. What distance were you at that time from Ferrol by your reckoning?—A. When I made the signal, shall I keep sight of the enemy? we were 125 miles from Ferrol, as near as a seaman can reckon.

Q. Do you recollect the bearings of Ferrol at that time?—A. If I recollect right, about south east by compass.

Q. When you returned to the fleet, do you recollect what ships of the British fleet appeared to you to be in a disabled state?—A. The Windsor Castle had no fore-top-mast up; no other ship appeared to me to want any thing.

Q. What ships had the prizes in tow at that time?—A. I think the Egyptienne and Sirius frigates.

Admiral Calder.—I can ask Captain Durham no questions whatever; I beg leave to observe that to the Court.

Captain Henry Inman sworn.

Q. Was you at any time on the 23d or 24th July ordered by the Vice-Admiral to reconnoitre the enemy's fleet?—A. No; it was to chase a frigate.

Q. Was you ordered at any time to chase a frigate of the enemy that appeared to be reconnoitring?—A. Yes; on the morning of the 23d, between nine and ten, my signal was made to tack and chase a French frigate reconnoitring, about three or four miles to windward, abaft the beam.

Q. What motions did you observe of the enemy's fleet?—A. They were in line of battle to windward of this frigate, on our weather beam, about three or four miles, apparently repairing their damages, and hoisting up top-sails.

Q. Did you observe what damages?—A. Yes

State to the Court what damages.—A. I will, to the best of my recollection: one of the ships of the rear appeared to have the head of her bowsprit gone, and apparently in tow of another; a second with her fore yard down, and fore top-gallant-mast; another with her top-sail yard down, and three or four ships shifting top-sails during the time I lay there.

Q. Was the situation you have just described reported to the Vice-Admiral?—A. No, not till two or three days after the business was over.

Q. Was any signal made by the Vice-Admiral to know the situation of the enemy's fleet?—A. No.

By Admiral Calder.

Q. Was your ship in danger of carrying away her masts on the 23d of July, when I made you a signal to chase the French frigate, then reconnoitring the squadron?—A. Yes; and I very much wonder the main-mast did not go; the bowsprit might also be very badly wounded, and the foremast also being sprung, though fished.

Q. Did you report to me this when you came on board the Prince of Wales?—A. Yes, some few days afterwards.

Q. Was you obliged to leave the Admiral afterwards to relieve Admiral Stirling, and go into port?—A. Three carpenters declared the main-mast to be unsafe to carry a top-mast, on which Admiral Stirling ordered me into port, where the fore-mast, main-mast, and bowsprit, were shifted.

Q. Was the English squadron always kept by me between that of the enemy and the port of Ferrol, as long as the enemy were in sight?—A. Yes.

Q. (By the Court.) Did you make the signal of inability when you were ordered to chase the frigate?—A. No; I did not consider it a time to make a signal of distress or inability.

Captain Durham was called to correct some part of his evidence with respect to bearings.

Mr. Bicknell, the Solicitor to the Admiralty, said he had closed all the evidence he had to offer for the prosecution. The Court immediately adjourned till next day.

SECOND DAY, DEC. 24.

The Court assembled at ten o'clock, when Sir Robert Calder, addressing the President, said, that, not conceiving the evidence for the prosecution would have closed so early as it had done, he had not had sufficient time to prepare his defence in the way in which he wished to present it to the Court: he therefore hoped for their indulgence, and assured the Court he should be ready to-morrow.

The President observed, that the Court was disposed to grant every indulgence in their power. They would, consequently, adjourn till to-morrow at ten.

Admiral Calder asked if it was the intention of the Court to proceed on Christmas day?

Admiral Montagu.—Yes, I do certainly. I do not feel that the Service will admit of any delay. [*To be continued.*]

Promotions and Appointments.

Captain T. Bertie, to the St. George; Captain Laroche, to the Uranie; Captain Mitchell, of the Zealand, to the command of the Sea Fencibles at Brighton; Hon. Captain Paget, to the Egyptienne; Hon. Captain Capel, to the Endymion; Captain Oswald, to the Phœbe. Lieutenant Quilliam, of the Victory, to be a Post Captain; and Lieutenants Pascoe, Williams, and Youle, of the same ship, to be Commanders. Lieutenant Pillford, who was acting Commander of the Ajax; Lieutenant J. Stockham, who was acting Commander of the Thunderer; Captain Digby, of the Beagle, and the First Lieutenants of the Mars and Bellerophon, whose Captains were killed in the action off Trafalgar, are promoted to Post Captains. The first Lieutenants of the other ships engaged off Trafalgar, the second Lieutenant of the Royal Sovereign (Lord Collingwood's flag ship,) and the first Lieutenants of Sir R. Strachan's squadron, are to be Commanders.—They take rank according to the seniority as Lieutenants. Four Midshipmen, or Master's Mates of the Victory; three of the Royal Sovereign; two of the Britannia; one of each of the other line of battle ships and of the frigates, selected by their respective Captains), according to merit, are made Lieutenants, and will rank according to their seniority in passing.

Captain George Cockburn, removed from the Phaeton to the Howe; Edward Ratsey, acting Captain of the Howe, appointed Commander of the Harrier; Captain Wm. Wooldridge, promoted from the Harrier to la Psyche; Captain John Wood, removed from the Concorde to the Phaeton; Captain J. Cranmer, promoted from the Rattlesnake to the Concorde; Wm. James Lye, acting Captain of the Cornwallis, appointed Commander of the Rattlesnake; Captain Charles Johnstone, removed from the Dedaigneuse to the Cornwallis; Captain John Duer, promoted from the Albatross to the Dedaigneuse; James Murray Gordon, Lieutenant of the Dedaigneuse, promoted to be Commander of the Albatross; Captain Lord George Stuart, late of the Sheerness, to the Duncan; Charles Hawtayne, acting Captain of the Duncan, appointed Governor of the Navy Hospital, Madras; Captain Larmour, acting, to the Audacious; Captain Burlton, to the Resolution; Captain C. Richardson, to the Cæsar, *vice* Shortland; Captain Mowbray, to the Harpy; Captain J. Rose, to the Africa, *vice* Digby.

C. Matson, Esq., of Havants, is appointed Purser of His Majesty's ship Lion of 64 guns.

The Hon. Captain Blackwood, to the Ajax; Captain M. Robinson, to the Gibraltar; Captain Cuming, to the Isis; Captain Caulfield, to the Russell, *vice* Williams; Captain H. Laroche, to the Kangaroo; Lieutenant John Lucas, to the impress service at Bristol.

Captain Sir Samuel Hood is appointed to the Centaur; Captain Bedford, to the Prince of Wales; Captain Inglis, to the Hibernia; Captain J. Stewart, to the Sea Horse; Captain W. Green, to the Spitfire; Captain E. Haywood, to the Rosario; Hon. Captain Pakenham, to the Sparrow; Captain Burrowes, to the Confiance; Hon. Captain Poulet, to the Orestes; Lieutenant W. Vosper, to the signal-post at Christchurch.

Captain James Ross Farquharson, of Invercauld, second son of the late Admiral Sir John Lockhart Ross, of Balnagown, Bart., is appointed to the Gibraltar, of 80 guns.

BIRTHS.

At Edinburgh, the lady of Captain Halkett, of the Royal Navy, of a daughter.

On the 17th of December, the lady of Nathaniel Belcher, Esq., of the Royal Navy, of a daughter.

MARRIAGES.

Edward O'Reilly, Esq., a Captain in the Warwickshire Militia, to Miss Eliza Wood, youngest daughter of the late Captain Charles Wood, Royal Navy, and sister of Sir Francis Wood, Baronet.

Lieutenant Augustus Keppel Colley, Adjutant of the Chatham division of Royal Marines, to Miss Smith.

Captain Carter, of the Royal Navy, to Miss Graydon, eldest daughter of the late Robert Graydon, Esq., many years Representative in Parliament for Kildare in Ireland.

Captain Mitchell, of the Royal Artillery, to Miss Breedon, daughter of the late Captain Breedon, of the Royal Marines.

On the 16th of January, Mr. Cliverton, Purser in the Royal Navy, to Miss M. A. Rowe, daughter of Mr. G. Rowe, Surgeon, Portsea.

On the 95th of January, at Alverstoke Church, near Gosport, Captain G. P. Wingrove, of the Royal Marines, to Miss Laugherne, eldest daughter of the late Captaiu T. Laugherne, of the Royal Navy.

OBITUARY.

During the funeral procession of Lord Nelson up the river, a lady of the name of Bayne, related to the late Captain William Bayne, who lost his life in the West Indies, under Lord Rodney, was so affected at the scene, that she fell into hysterics, and died a few minutes after.

Captain T. Affleck, of the Navy.

Lieutenant Skrymsher, of the signal post at Christchurch.

A few days since, Captain Richardson, of His Majesty's ship Utile.

On Saturday the 28th of December, at Totness, Captain R. Cuthbertson, of His Majesty's Royal Marine forces.

At Lady Laforey's, Miss Laforey, second daughter of the late Admiral Sir John Laforey, Bart.

At Lisbon, where he went for the recovery of his health, Mr. Charles Hope, second son of Commissioner Hope, of Chatham Dock-yard.

We are truly sorry to state the loss of Lieutenant Smith and seven men belonging to the Namur, lying at St. Helen's:—On Thursday, 16th January, during the very dreadful gale which blew on that day, the launch of that ship broke adrift with two men in it; two cutters were manned and sent after the launch; one of them returned to the ship with the launch; but the other, with the above persons in it, was suddenly lost sight of; from which it is imagined, that she struck on the Wolleners and overset, in attempting to enter Langston Harbour, and that every person perished. A cutter, with six oars, and the body of a seaman, is drifted on shore at Hayling Island.

A most melancholy accident occurred at Plymouth, during the hurricane of the 16th and 17th January:—The launch of the Hibernia, Admiral Douglas, was sent ashore with old stores, and to receive new, manned with a Lieutenant, a Midshipman, and 43 seamen: after having loaded, the launch, they went off to join the Hibernia, in Cawsand Bay, it blowing then hard; but, before the launch could near the Indiamen in the bite of Cawsand Bay, it was found necessary to bear away, and endeavour to weather the Mew-stone, and get into Yealm River for the night, but in doing this the mast went over the side; the launch missed weathering the Mew-stone, and got, it being near the high water, between the Shag, Rock and the land. She then struck on the deceitful Rannie Rocks, between the Shag-stone and the land, and overset. The Lieutenant and eighteen men were by some providential means washed ashore, but the Midshipman and twenty-three men were unfortunately drowned. The poor young Midshipman and sixteen bodies were washed ashore, and decently buried together in Wembury churchyard. One seaman with his leg broke, and jammed to pieces, contrived to crawl up a rock, and his comrade, almost exhausted, crept to his side for warmth: in the morning, when the quarry-men came to their assistance, the wounded man was found still alive, but his companion a lifeless corpse. The wounded seaman was conveyed to the Royal Naval Hospital.

Lloyd's Marine List

OF

SHIPS LOST, DESTROYED, CAPTURED, AND RECAPTURED, &c.

FROM MAY 24 TO JUNE 18, 1805.

The Jafon, Martin, from Liverpool to Surinam, reported to be retaken, is carried into Martinique.

The Sufannah, (an American), Wigley, from Liverpool to New Orleans, has been taken, retaken, and carried into Antigua.

The Emilia, Schol, from Lubeck to Ferrol, is totally loft on the Ifland of Ameland.

The Fabius, Atkins, from Bourdeaux to America, is detained by the Ponfonby privateer of Liverpool, and arrived at that port.

The Brig Active, of Sunderland, in ballaft, Wilfon, Mafter, is totally loft on Deal Beach.

A Spanifh brig, from Cuba, with fugar and hides, is taken by the Phœnix and Brunfwick of London, bound to Jamaica, and paffed Antigua, in company, on the 26th March.

The Betfey, Carnegie, from London to Montferrat, is taken and carried into Guadaloupe.

The Heroine, Harwood, from London to St. Kitt's, arrived at Antigua 2d ult., after being taken by a French brig, run on fhore and deferted by the French.

The Liberty, Heppinftal, of London; the Hamilton, Derbyfhire; and the Sarah, Jacks, of Liverpool; were burnt at Montferrat, by the French fquadron from Rochfort, on the 9th of March.

The Odefiord, Erbe, from Saloe to Amfterdam, is detained by the Neptune Letter of Marque, of Greenock, and arrived in the Clyde.

The Betfey, ———, of Rye, from London to Dymchurch, is loft near Broadftairs.

The Induftry, M'Carthy, from Cork to Barbadoes, has been taken, retaken, and arrived at St. Vincent's.

The Sarah, Crand, from Eckwarden to Philadelphia, after being out 170 days, was fallen in with by a fchooner bound to Barbadoes, in want of every thing, having 260 people on board. The Captain of the fchooner took upwards of 200 on board his veffel, and would have brought the refidue from the Sarah, when a gale of wind prevented his proceedings, and the Ship went down with thofe that were in her. With his fchooner he bore away for Barbadoes, but before he reached that Ifland upwards of 40 of the paffengers perifhed for want.

The under-mentioned veffels; viz. Good Intent, Phelan; Friends, Kavanagh; Eliza, Lufhman; Ranger, Phelan; Endeavour, Efford; Peggy, Brennock, all from Waterford; Good Fortune, Richardfon; and Creon, Shellebear, both from Dartmouth, failed from Cork the 9th May for Newfoundland, and on the 13th, in lat. 49 deg. 49 min., long. 15 deg. 25 min., were fallen in with by the Sylph French corvette, of 18 guns, which it is fuppofed captured them all. The Friends, and the Good Intent are arrived at Waterford, after being plundered; the Topaze and Rofario have retaken two of them; the Sylph had alfo taken the Margaret, Chappell; and the Hunter, Stevens, of Arbroath; and the Bowman, Prieftman, of Workington.

The Young William, Young, from Cork to Weftport, is taken by a Spanifh corvette, of 20 guns, which is fince taken by the Topaze frigate.

The Napoleon Privateer has taken and carried into Paffage an Englifh Veffel, from 200 to 260 tons, laden with logwood and mahogany. Journal du Commerce, 20th May.

The Maria, Berry, from Malaga to Embden, was loft 1ft May near Ufhant.

The Mary, White, from Mogadore to London; the Brig James, of 180 tons, from Plymouth, were taken and carried into Calais, 11th inftant; and the Sloop Kingfton, of Woodbridge, of about 100 tons, is taken and carried into Ambleteufe.—Journal du Commerce, 16th and 18th May.

The Harmoine, Seur, from Embden to ———, is detained and fent into Yarmouth, by the Hunter Revenue cutter.

The American Ship Eliza, Evans, from Jamaica to Virginia, has been captured by a privateer, and fince run on fhore.

The Rattler, Dalmond, from Honduras to London, is totally wrecked on the Carysfort Reef in the Gulf of Florida; part of the cargo faved.

The Hope, French, from Liverpool to Berbice, was captured 3d February, near Berbice, by a Privateer from Guadaloupe; and funk after being plundered.

Ninety-feven Veffels were detained and fent into Malta by Britifh cruifers, between the 11th of October, 1804, and 18th March, 1805, viz. 38 Spanifh, 7 French, 12 Ragufan, 17 Imperial, 3 Ottoman, 4 Swedes, 6 Danes, 4 Ruffian, 1 American, 3 Genoefe, 1 Pruffian, 1 Neapolitan; among them the following; 22d Nov., Favorite, Davis, from Philadelphia; 4th Dec., Pomona, Rolender; 15th, Eleanor, Alfseir; 13th Jan., Eidenburg, Muller, all from Smyrna, bound to Amfterdam.

The Induftry, of St. Ive's, Quick, from Dublin to Galway, was loft the 10th May, off the Dorfeys; Crew faved.

The Fame, Nicholfon, from Rotterdam to St. Lucar, is loft at the entrance of St. Lucar's.

The Diana, Rowling, from Memel to Pappenberg, is detained and fent into Yarmouth by the Lynx Sloop of War.

The Creon, Shellebere, from Liverpool to Newfoundland, has been taken by a Spanifh Privateer, retaken by the Phœnix and another Privateer of Jerfey, and arrived at Penzance.

The Etruria packet from St. Sebaftian's to Vera-Cruz, was taken 14th May near Madeira, by the Eolus Privateer of Guernfey, and fent for that Ifland. The Eolus is arrived at Plymouth.

The Atalanta, Gammell, from Grenada to Halifax, was loft the 29th January at Torbay on the coaft of America. Part of the cargo faved.

The Francifco del Protigedo, from Carthagena to Ceuta, with 1200 barrels of gunpowder; and the Divina Conception, from Cadiz to Barcelona, with logwood, are captured by the Seahorfe Frigate, and fent into Gibraltar 8th May.

The Jane, Storey, from London to Quebec, was taken and funk 14th April by the Sylph French Privateer.

The Stork, Webber, from Lisbon to Newfoundland, is retaken by the Milbrook Schooner, and arrived at Oporto.

The Active, White, from Cork to Grenada, was taken, and carried into Guadaloupe on the 16th March.

The Frederica, Bakker; the Stadt, Berlin; the Jonge Conrad, Johannes; the Johan and Carl; the Maria Francifco, all from Bourdeaux, are detained, and fent into Plymouth; the former by the Naiad Frigate, the others by the Lord Nelfon Privateer.

The China, M'Pherfon, from Batavia to Philadelphia, is loft near the Delaware; part of the cargo faved.

The Edward and Mary, Gibbons, from Naples to London, is taken, and carried into Algefiras.

The Eliza, ———, from Waterford to Newfoundland, was captured by a Spanifh Privateer, off Cape Clear, fince retaken by the Weftmoreland, Goodall, and fent for Liverpool.

The Commerce, Ray, from Philadelphia to Antwerp, arrived off Falmouth the 5th; the Captain reports that the Elizabeth, of Liverpool, from New York to Liverpool, foundered off the Banks of Newfoundland, 13 of the crew faved.

The Mary, White, from Mogadore to London; and the William, of Shields, in ballaft, were captured the 10th of May by a French Privateer, and carried into Calais. Captain White was dangeroufly wounded, and died two days following.

The Gerhard, Wold, (a Dane,) from Hull to Meffina, Venice, &c., was captured the 25th April, by five Spanifh Privateers, and carried into Algeziras; it is expected the cargo will be condemned.

[To be continued.]

Ridley & Holl sc.

THE HON.BLE HENRY EDWYN STANHOPE

Vice Admiral of the Blue Squadron.

Pub. by I. Gold, 103, Shoe Lane, Feb.y 28, 1806

BIOGRAPHICAL MEMOIR OF THE

HONOURABLE HENRY EDWYN STANHOPE,

VICE-ADMIRAL OF THE BLUE SQUADRON.

" So mild, so gentle, so compos'd a mind,
To such heroic warmth, and courage join'd!
He, too, like Sydney, nurs'd in learning's arms,
For nobler war, forsook her softer charms!"

Lord Littleton.

THE union of scholastic acquisitions with personal courage, imparts an exalted interest to public character. This union, though it has never been ostentatiously displayed, is eminently conspicuous in the subject of the present memoir.

The Hon. Henry Edwyn Stanhope, at a very early age, commenced his education in a school at East Hill, Wandsworth, which was then regarded as a seminary of the first respectability. Having imbibed the rudimental branches of learning, he was thence removed to Winchester College; where, under the tuition, and indeed particular favour, of the learned and Rev. Dr. Wharton, he attained the head of that institution. He was next placed under the private superintendance of the Rev. Monsieur de Giffendier, preparatory to his being entered at the University of Oxford.

He had passed but a short time at that national seat of instruction, when, evincing an unusual activity of mind, he was, at the suggestion of the late Earl of Besborough, equipped for the sea service. He accordingly embarked at Sheerness, in May 1768, on board the Rose, of 20 guns, commanded at that time by Captain (now Admiral) Caldwell*, and sailed for the American station.

Soon after his arrival at Boston, he was removed to the Romney, then bearing the broad pendant of Commodore (now Admiral Lord) Hood, as Commander in Chief.—For the benefit, however, of his professional education, he returned to

* *Vide* Naval Chronicle, Vol. XI, page 5.

the Rose in the spring; when, cruising in the Bay of Massachussetts, to protect the regular trade, he accompanied Lieutenant Henry Penton to search a brig, called the Pitt Packet. The crew, suspecting the visit to be for the purpose of impressing some of them, pierced the Lieutenant with a harpoon; which, passing the jugular vein, occasioned his instant death.—The culprit being afterwards tried at the Court of Admiralty, at Boston, Mr. Stanhope was particularly noticed as an evidence, especially in the cross-examination by the counsel for the prisoner.

After the usual term of three years, the Rose returned to England; and, being paid off, Mr. Stanhope prepared to take his degree at Oxford. In order that he might not neglect the profession which his family intended for him, he was afterwards, for a short time at the Naval Academy of Mr. Charles Bettesworth, at Portsea. About this period, we trace him to the Lennox, under the command of the present Admiral Roddam; but cannot learn that he ever embarked in her.

In the month of June, 1771, he was Midshipman of the Chatham, commanded by Captain (afterwards Vice-Admiral) Sir Charles Thompson, then bearing the flag of Vice-Admiral Parry, Commander in Chief at the Leeward Islands. In this ship he sailed for Antigua; but, labouring under an ill state of health, from repeated bilious attacks, he was under the necessity of returning to Europe.

After his arrival he took his degree at Oxford, and did not return to the service till March 1775; when he sailed for Boston, in the Otter sloop, Captain (late Rear-Admiral) Squires, in time to bear a part in the unfortunate battle of Bunker's Hill.—Having an appointment to act as Lieutenant of the Glasgow, of 20 guns, Captain Tyringham, he commanded a division of flat boats; and imprudently marching up with the troops unarmed, under the expectation that the Americans would leave their works on the appearance of the King's troops, he furnished himself with the firelock of one of the slain on that disastrous occasion. Thus armed, he pursued the enemy, after the marines had most gallantly stormed the redoubt*.

Returning to his ship, she was ordered to Newport, Rhode Island; and, having been appointed Prize-master to an American brig, he took a large schooner, and carried them both into Boston, where he had been directed to embark, with his men, as passengers in a sloop to Rhode Island. But, on his arrival at Boston, on learning that some American privateers were cruising in the bay, he turned the master of the sloop, and the passengers, ashore; and, assuming the command of her, went upon a cruise, took two prizes, and, falling in with the Swan sloop, Captain Ayscough, sailed with her to Newport, where the vessel was returned to the owners.

On the arrival of the Rose, commanded by the late Sir James Wallace, the ship in which Mr. Stanhope had first embarked, he was removed to her; and, officiating as Lieutenant, he took a schooner out of Stonington harbour, on the Naragansett shore, in the night. Mr. Stanhope used her as a tender; and, being furnished with swivels from the Rose, he proceeded in her, with a convoy of prizes, to Boston, where he procured six three-pounders; and receiving a cargo of powder for the fleet, he sailed for Rhode Island.

On his passage, he fell in with the Hancock privateer, of 14 guns, commanded by —— Manly; and, after an action of an hour and a half, in which the tender was very much disabled, only twelve men of her crew remaining, he was necessitated to proceed on his destination. He was much mortified on his arrival, at being removed from his little command by Captain Howe; but his removal was eventually overruled by Captain Wallace.

* At the beginning of this action, the rebels had at least 5000 men: the loss which they sustained in killed and wounded was very considerable. Many of them they conveyed off in waggons, during the conflict, as only 30 of their killed were found in their works when the King's troops forced them; among which number was their Commander, Dr. Warren, a physician, who on this occasion had acted as a Major General.—The loss sustained by the British troops, considering the numbers that were engaged, was great beyond example. Eighteen officers, and upwards of 200 men, were killed upon the spot; and 68 officers, and 758 men, were wounded; many of whom died, or were completely disabled from farther service.——*Vide* BEATSON'S *Naval and Military Memoirs*, Vol. IV, p. 73.

One evening, being accidentally on board the Glasgow, with his old messmates, Captain Howe ordered him to go ashore at Newport, in search of some deserters, who had run off with the boat. It is not to be supposed that this order was very agreeable to Lieutenant Stanhope, as the town was known to be ill-affected towards the King's government. He went, however; but scarcely had he reached the head of the wharf, when he was struck down with a cutlass; and to the providential circumstance of the weapon striking against the button of a Dutch cap, worn for disguise, was he alone indebted for the preservation of his life.—Mr. Stanhope was soon marched to Providence, and committed to gaol; whence, after various occurrences of little moment, he was sent upon his parole to Northampton, in the state of Massachussetts. There now appeared to be a stop to all promotion; but, what greatly aggravated the evil, was his having been appointed Lieutenant of the Nautilus, at Boston, whither he was to have sailed on the day succeeding that of his being made prisoner.

At Northampton he found many of his brother officers, all of whom lived in the most friendly intimacy. But of this the Committee of Safety soon became so jealous, that they determined to abridge the privilege enjoyed by the tenor of their parole. This was ill-relished by Lieutenant Stanhope, who long opposed it, but at length yielded to the universal opinion of his fellow-sufferers; declaring his resolution, however, not to consent to any farther encroachment by the Committee, without the express order of General Washington; clearly foreseeing their evil intention, which soon displayed itself by an order for their being in their respective apartments by sun-set. To this Lieutenant Stanhope positively refused to accede; averring, that if it were insisted on, he should consider it as an infraction of his parole. The Committee were peremptory; and, conceiving himself no longer bound by his parole, he made his escape on horseback, in company with the present Captain George Gregory. The fugitives reached Middleton, in Connecticut; but being discovered, they were seized, conveyed back to Northampton, and committed to gaol, as close prisoners, for nine months. At length, accompanied by Mr. Arnald, Master of the Falcon sloop, (now Lieutenant, and serving under the Transport Office), he again effected his escape; and, after numerous most extraordinary adventures, during a walk of seven hundred miles, in various disguises, he reached Salem. From that place, on the receipt of particular intelligence, ventured to go to Sir Archibald Campbell, then a prisoner at Reading; and being charged by him with important papers and information for General Sir William Howe, the Commander in Chief, he rejoined his friend and fellow traveller, Arnald, at Salem. They were eventually obliged to return to Boston, whence they took a fishing vessel, in the night, and sailed for Marblehead, where the officer commanding a cartel refused to receive them. Reluctantly, and at great risk, they sailed back to Boston, quitted the vessel, and proceeded by land to Marblehead. They remained there for some time, living in disguise, and acting in various capacities, till they contrived to make their escape on board another cartel, whose commanding officer had more consideration for their fate, and at length arrived safely at Halifax, in Nova Scotia.

From Halifax, acting as Lieutenant of the Milford, under an order from Sir George Collier, Captain of the Rainbow, and senior officer, and subsequently in the Liverpool, Captain Bellew, he reached Plymouth in March 1777.

On his arrival he experienced a severe mortification. From an omission of Vice-Admiral Graves, who had commissioned him to the Nautilus, in neglecting to make a return to the Admiralty of his appointment, his name did not appear upon the list of Lieutenants. His chagrin, however, was but of short duration; for, having communicated the circumstance to his family, the return of post brought him a commission as first Lieutenant of the Nonsuch; and, on the tenth day from the Liverpool's anchoring in the Sound, he sailed for New York, under the command of the late Captain Walter Griffith.

In December, after various services in the Chesapeak and Delaware, Lieutenant Stanhope went to Newport; where, no operation of moment occurring, and the Nonsuch being stationary, he solicited and obtained the command of the Pigott galley.

In this vessel, among other services, he sailed close under an American battery, at Bristol Ferry; and, being hailed, was permitted to pass unmolested, under the character of Jemmy Pierce, who was known to be in the service of the Americans, with powder and shot for their galley, called the Spitfire, lying many miles above, in the Swansea River. Lieutenant Stanhope succeeded in capturing the Spitfire, and repassed the battery with little loss.

In a second attempt, however, he was less fortunate, as the Pigott grounded under the guns of the battery, and was nearly knocked to pieces.

In the course of a few months after, she was on the advanced post, subsequently to the arrival of the French fleet under le Comte d'Estaing; when, being threatened by a part of that force, Lieutenant Stanhope ran her ashore upon the island, and, escaping with his crew into the town of Newport, having set her on fire, she soon afterwards blew up.

The Americans having landed, in great numbers, under General Sullivan, to co-operate with the French fleet, the very small force that was intended for the protection of the island was necessarily withdrawn within the lines, to defend the town; and the American army, advancing, took post upon Honeyman's and Tomyni Hills, within point blank shot.

The naval force, under Captain Brisbane, of the Flora*, landed from the different men of war and merchant ships, which it was found expedient to destroy, as they must otherwise have become prizes to the enemy. The men were appointed to act with the troops, under General Sir Robert Pigot. Lieutenant Stanhope assisted in the command of this force, until the little army was reduced to considerable extremity; when, being pressed on every side, it became necessary to seek assistance from head quarters. The vessels and boats, that attempted to escape, being either lost or taken, Lieutenant Stanhope volunteered his

* Captain Brisbane assumed the command, as senior officer, when Captain Griffith, in the Nonsuch, sailed for New York.

services in a whale boat; which, having carried over land, and launched from Easton's beach, at some distance from the harbour's mouth, he steered for the body of the enemy's fleet, knowing that the skirts would be more narrowly guarded. Rowing under the French Admiral's stern about midnight, he was hailed; but answering in French, (a language which he speaks fluently,) that he was the guard-boat, he was permitted to pass. On the second morning he arrived at New York, having encountered a gale which dismasted two French men of war, and was very graciously received by Lord Howe, who directed him to do duty in the Monmouth, Captain (now Admiral Lord) Collingwood, who at that time had a broad pendant: the present Commissioner, Harwood, formerly of the Falcon sloop, sunk at Rhode Island, was his Captain. That gentleman having been removed, to perform a service of more importance, Lieutenant Stanhope succeeded to his situation.

After the relief of Rhode Island, and Commodore Collingwood having struck his pendant, on going to the West Indies, Lieutenant Stanhope prepared to return to England. He accordingly embarked, in October 1778, with the other officers whose ships and vessels had been sunk and destroyed at Rhode Island, on board the Leviathan, Captain (now Vice-Admiral) Brown; and arriving at Plymouth Sound in November, hastened to town.

In April, 1779, he was appointed first Lieutenant of the Portland, Captain Anthony Hunt; in which ship, under the flag of Rear-Admiral Richard Edwards, Commander in Chief, he sailed for Newfoundland. On that station he was, on the 6th of August following, promoted, by the Rear-Admiral, to the rank of Master and Commander, in the Trepassey, an American privateer. This vessel was ill adapted to the service; a circumstance which, indirectly at least, occasioned Captain Stanhope to be tried by a Court Martial, at his own solicitation, on some reflection having been cast upon him by the Admiral, who had rejected his application to succeed Captain (now Rear-Admiral) Thomas Drury, in command of the Cygnet, a fine sloop.

The result of the trial was, in every respect, highly honourable to Captain Stanhope.

Despairing of ever gaining the least reputation in a vessel altogether unfit for a man of war, as was verified by her subsequent capture, and conceiving that there did not exist the least hope of promotion, he came to England, in the Fairy sloop, in the fall of the year 1780.

From that time, we hear nothing farther of Captain Stanhope, until the April following, when he went passenger in the Ranger cutter, Lieutenant Alexander Hood, with dispatches to the West Indies. On their passage they fell in with the fleet under Sir George Rodney, whose private signals not being known, was supposed to be the enemy. Captain Stanhope, with that spirit by which his conduct has been uniformly characterised, took the cutter, manned with volunteers, at the close of day, and ran down to the fleet to reconnoitre. On discovering them to be friends, he was received on board the Pegasus, commanded by his relation, Captain J. Stanhope; and the signals previously determined on having been made, the Ranger joined the fleet.—On their arrival at Barbadoes, Sir George Rodney appointed Captain Stanhope to the Salamander fire-ship; and, on the 16th of June, promoted him to the rank of Post Captain, in the Terrible of 74 guns. He remained but a short time in that ship, being subsequently appointed to the Russell, of the same force, which he commanded in the action off St. Kitt's. After the engagement, being charged with Sir Samuel (now Admiral Viscount) Hood's dispatches, he sailed for England, in the Tisiphone, in February 1782, in such an extremely ill state of health, as to have little expectation of reaching his native country alive.

In the course of the summer, however, Captain Stanhope experienced a renovation of health; and in the month of September he was appointed to the Mercury frigate, then lying in the Downs. He sailed thence to the Orkneys, for the Hudson's Bay ships; and returning in December to Sheerness, was refitted; after which he proceeded to Spithead.

At the conclusion of the war the Mercury was paid off; but being re-commissioned, Captain Stanhope sailed, in June 1783, for New York, with the definitive treaty of peace.

Previous to the evacuation of New York, he proceeded to the coast of Nova Scotia, where the Mercury continued for the usual period of three years. In the course of that time, he was sent to Boston, by Commodore Sawyer, to convoy some small vessels, which were to take on board live stock, hay, &c. for Shelbourne, and some of the other new settlements. On Captain Stanhope's arrival, he waited on the Governor, as a matter of ceremony; but when returning to his boat, the inhabitants not approving of his errand, he was insulted by a mob, which had collected for the purpose, and himself, his officers, and people, extremely ill treated. This circumstance, with various other insults experienced by Captain Stanhope at Boston, produced a correspondence between him and Governor Bowdoin; which, on the part of the former, though indicative of the most earnest desire, that all animosity should be forgotten, breathed that proper spirit which is inherent in the guardians of the British flag. The share of Bowdoin in the correspondence, evinced, on the contrary, a high portion of that supercilious *hauteur*, so frequently the result of republican principles, when unexpectedly exalted to superior station.—The following are copies of the letters which passed on the occasion:—

SIR, *Mercury, Boston Harbour, August* 1, 1785.

I AM sorry to be obliged to represent to your Excellency the continued insults and disgraceful indignities offered by hundreds in this town to me and my officers, which hitherto we have taken no notice of, nor of the illiberal and indecent language with which the newspapers have been filled; nor should I have troubled you now, had I not been pursued, and my life, as well as that of one of my officers, been endangered by the violent rage of a mob, yesterday evening, without provocation of any sort.

I trust it is needless to recommend to your Excellency to adopt such measures as may discover the ringleaders, and bring them to public justice, as well as protect us from further insults.

I have the honour to be

Your Excellency's most obedient humble servant,

E. H. STANHOPE.

To His Excellency Governor Bowdoin.

SIR, *Commonwealth of Massachussetts. Boston, August* 1, 1785.

YOUR letter of this date is now before me.—It is a great misfortune that the subjects or citizens of different countries, which have been at enmity, cannot easily recover that degree of good humour which should induce them to treat each other with proper decorum, when the governments to which they respectively belong have entered into a treaty of amity, and sheathed the sword. But you must have observed, that disturbances arising from this source too frequently happen, especially in popular sea-port towns.

If you have been insulted, and your life has been endangered, in manner as you have represented to me, I must inform you, that our laws afford you ample satisfaction. Foreigners are entitled to the protection of the law, as well as amenable to it, equally with any citizen of the United States, while they continue within the jurisdiction of this commonwealth.

Any learned practitioner in the law, if applied to, will direct you to the mode of legal process in the obtaining a redress of injury, if you have been injured; and the judiciary court will cause due inquiry to be made, touching riotous and unlawful assemblies, and their misdemeanors, and inflict legal punishment on such as by verdict of a jury may be found guilty.

I have the honour to be, &c.

To Captain Stanhope. ——— BOWDOIN.

SIR, *Mercury, Boston Harbour, August* 1785.

WHEN I had the honour of applying to your Excellency to discountenance the disgraceful attacks made upon me and the officers of His Britannic Majesty's ship Mercury, under my command, and to afford us your protection, it was upon your positive assurance to that effect, in their presence, I rested my hopes. How much your conduct contradicts both that and my expectations is too obvious either to satisfy me or even to do credit to yourself; for your Excellency must excuse me, when I remark, that I never received a letter so insulting to my senses, as your answer to my requisition of yesterday. I am however happy in finding a much better disposition in the first class of inhabitants, whose assistance, I am glad to acknowledge, is the more acceptable after your apparent evasion from the substance of my letter; and however well informed your Excellency may believe yourself upon the laws and customs of nations in similar cases, allow me to assure you, there is not one, no not even the ally of the States, that would not most severely reprobate, either the want of energy in government, or the disinclination of the governor, to correct such notorious insults to public characters, in which light only we can desire to be received.

I have the honour to be, &c.

E. H. STANHOPE.

To His Excellency Governor Bowdoin.

CAPTAIN STANHOPE,

YOUR letter, dated the 2d instant, was delivered to me by your Lieutenant, Mr. Nash, at four o'clock this morning.

I hereby let you know, that as the letter is conceived in terms of insolence and abuse altogether unprovoked, I shall take such measures concerning it, as the dignity of my station, and a just regard to the honour of this commonwealth, connected with the honour of the United States in general, shall require.

——— BOWDOIN.

Boston, August 3, 1785, six o'clock P.M.

SIR, *Mercury, Nantasket Road, Aug. 4, 1785, half-past 12 A.M.*

I AM to acknowledge the honour of your Excellency's letter, this moment received, and have to assure you, I shall most cheerfully submit to the worst consequences that can arrive from our correspondence, which I do not conceive, on my part, to have been couched in terms of either insolence or abuse, which is more than I could venture to say of yours; and however exalted your Excellency's station is, I know not of any more respectable than that I have the honour to fill.

I have the honour to be, &c.

E. H. STANHOPE.

To His Excellency Governor Bowdoin.

In 1786, the Mercury returned to England, and was paid off. Captain Stanhope, after eighteen years of steady employment, then sought, in time of peace, some relaxation from the fatigues of service; and having a taste for the classics, endeavoured to recover what, in the course of his professional pursuits, it may be supposed he had in some measure lost.

The tranquillity of this country having been again disturbed by our ancient enemy, Captain Stanhope was called from his retirement; and in September, 1794, he was appointed to the command of the Ruby, at Spithead.

After various duties in the Channel till February 1795, he

sailed with the America, Stately, and Echo, for the Cape of Good Hope, under the orders of Captain (late Rear-Admiral) Blanket, who had a distinguishing pendant on board the America.

During the passage, Captain Stanhope had a most severe bilious attack, which nearly proved fatal; but reaching the Cape, his health was soon restored; notwithstanding the occurrence of an event extremely unfavourable to his recovery. At the instance of the junior Lieutenant, he was tried by a Court Martial, for a variety of alleged offences, contrary to the order and discipline of service; but, to the satisfaction and honour of Captain Stanhope, the charges were declared by the Court to be "frivolous, malicious, ill-grounded, not supported, tending to subvert that due subordination which is the basis of all military service." He was therefore fully acquitted.

Soon after the surrender of the Cape, being in very indifferent health, he was charged with the Commander in Chief's dispatches; and leaving the Cape in October 1795, he reached England on the 5th of February following.

Nothing can be more distressing to a feeling man, than to meet with a chilling reception where he conceives himself entitled to the welcome of cordiality. Such, however, was the case with Captain Stanhope, on his arrival at St. James's; but an explanation eventually terminated so much to his honour, that Lord Spencer, then presiding at the Admiralty, was the means of his being again restored to favour at Court, and on the 25th of March gave him the command of the Neptune, a new ship of 98 guns, then fitting at Woolwich. In this ship he was appointed to a very arduous task, as a member of the Court Martial for the trial of Richard Parker and the other mutineers at the Nore, which lasted two months. On its termination, he carried the Neptune round to the Nore, and was succeeded in the command by Captain (now Sir Erasmus) Gower.

In June 1798, Captain Stanhope took command of the Achille, a new 74, at Chatham; and, though not in very good health, he persevered until his arrival at Spithead, in January 1799; when, having suffered severely under repeated dangerous attacks of bilious colic, he obtained a month's leave of absence, and was at length reluctantly constrained to resign the command.

He was subsequently appointed to the Cornish Fencibles; but, shortly after, he experienced another most dangerous attack of his old complaint. On his recovery, he was removed to the Fencibles in Devonshire, where he remained until the promotion of flags, on the Union, in 1801, when he was advanced to the rank of Rear-Admiral of the Blue; and in April 1804, to the same rank in the Red Squadron.

The Rear-Admiral at this time having leisure to pursue his literary studies, to which he has ever been much attached, applied himself diligently to the Hebrew, being desirous to read the Old Testament in the original; and we have been informed, that he has nearly completed a Bible, with the accented pronunciation of the proper names, according to their derivations from the Hebrew and Greek.

In February 1805, he was appointed to command in the River Thames, and hoisted his flag on board the Matilda, at Woolwich.

On the recent promotion, since the victory of Trafalgar, he was advanced to the rank of Vice-Admiral of the Blue Squadron.

Vice-Admiral Stanhope's flag still continues on board the Matilda; but we look forward to a time when, should his health permit, he may be employed in the more active service of his country.

HERALDIC PARTICULARS.

Vice-Admiral the Hon. Henry Edwyn Stanhope, is the only son of the Hon. Edwyn Francis Stanhope, cousin to the Earl of Chesterfield, and the Right Hon. Lady Catherine, daughter of John Marquis of Caernarvon, eldest son of James Duke of Chandos, Baroness Chandos, by right of writ of summons in the reign of Edward the IIId, to his ancestor, Sir John Chandos, which descends to the Admiral.

NAVAL ANECDOTES, COMMERCIAL HINTS, RECOLLECTIONS, &c.

NANTES IN GURGITE VASTO.

THE FRENCH ADMIRAL MIESSESEY.

ADMIRAL MIESSESEY, who commands the Rochefort squadron now in the West Indies, was born at Toulon, where his father was director of the marine artillery. He is, at present, about 50 years old, and had the rank of Lieutenant in the navy at the commencement of the revolution. He is an enterprising and active officer, without being distinguished by any extraordinary talent. The following anecdote is not much to the credit of the clearness of his intellectual faculties. He, under the patronage of M. de Chabert, compiled a system of signals, which was printed at the royal press; but neither the patron nor the *protegé* could ever prevail on any officer to give it a trial, Among the multitude of signals which he had laid down, the following occurred: *Night signals, for discontinuing the engagement; three guns to be fired.*

HYDROSTATIC QUERY.

THE following communication on a curious fact in the science of hydrostatics, is extracted from a New York paper:—

I have heard marines assert, that if an empty glass bottle be corked tight, and sunk in the ocean by weights to a certain depth, that the bottle when drawn up would be found full of water, by means of the cork being forced in by the pressure of the sea. To those who are acquainted with the principles of hydrostatics this will not appear improbable, and I have no doubt of its being a fact. The experiment, however, has been lately made, by a person now in this city, and attended with a different and very surprising result. A bottle was corked perfectly tight, and the cork secured in such manner, by means of tarred cloth, as to prevent the forcing in of the cork. It was then sunk seventy fathoms deep, and when drawn up was found full of water without any apparent removal or disturbance of the cork. The bottle with its contents is now in the possession of a gentleman in this city, in the same state as when drawn up from the ocean. From the credibility of the person who made the experiment, I have no doubt of the truth of the above circumstances. The query is, in what manner is the water forced into the bottle? Is it through the pores of the glass, or is it through the pores of the tarred cork? Let Philosophers determine.

LIEUTENANT DOYLE.

LIEUTENANT DOYLE, of the St. Fiorenzo frigate, has been presented by the Captain of the Psyche French frigate with an elegant sword, for the humanity displayed by him after he had heroically boarded and captured that ship. Lieut. Doyle has been promoted to the rank of Commander, and until he is provided with a ship, he will hold the situation of Governor of the naval officers at Madras.

NEW INVENTION.

A PLAN, the invention of an Hon. Admiral, is about to be tried in His Majesty's dock-yard at Portsmouth, of a Port Lever, for more expeditiously opening and securing the gun ports of ships of war. It forms a new kind of hinge, which opens the port, and supports it when up, and also forms a security when down. By means of this invention one man can open the port of the largest ship, which heretofore required six.

CAPTAIN VINCENT.

CAPTAIN VINCENT, (now residing near Portsmouth), whose brave defence of a convoy from the Mediterranean, in His Majesty's ship Arrow, will ever be recollected with high satisfaction, has been presented, by the Committee of the Patriotic Fund at Lloyd's, with a sword of 100 guineas value, for his conduct on that occasion.

BOSCAWEN'S ACTION.

IT was off the opposite point of Trafalgar, viz. St. Mary's, where Admiral Boscawen obtained a complete victory over the French Admiral, Mons. de St. Clue.

LIEUTENANT RAM.

LIEUTENANT RAM, who was killed on the quarter-deck of the Victory, was the son of Colonel Ram, and was a native of Hampshire. His relatives resided near Hartford Bridge. He had been in several of Lord Nelson's actions, and always distinguished himself by his good conduct. Had he lived, there is no doubt he would have proved an ornament to his profession. His death is greatly lamented, not only by his family, but by his friends and his brother officers.

REPLY TO AN AUCTIONEER.

A TAR, half-seas over, swaggered into an auction room, and hearing the auctioneer bawling out, two or three times, "who bids more than ninepence halfpenny?" asked, "May we bid what we please?"—"O yes," replied the seller, "any thing you please, Sir."—"Why then," said Jack, "I bid you a good night and be d——d to you!"

PIRACY.

THE ship Alert, Captain Morrison, from Bengal, bound to Bombay, sailed from Calcutta some time in June, in company with eight other vessels, but from some accident or other parted company from her companions.—It appears that part of her crew, consisting of from 15 to 20 Arabs, rose and murdered the commander and officers, and some other Europeans on board, to the number of nine persons, and possessed themselves of the ship: they immediately changed their course, steered for the Arabian coast, and after much difficulty made the island of Soccatra, where they continued for three weeks or a month; during which period they disposed of as much of the ship's cargo as they were able. From Soccatra they made the best of their way for Maculla Bay, and on their arrival announced themselves to the chief of that place, as belonging to Moosa, the rich Mopola at Tellicherry. Here they endeavoured for some time to get rid of the remaining part of the piece goods, of which articles it appeared a great part of her cargo had consisted.—Purchasers, it seems, they met with in abundance; for so ignorant were these wretches of the value and current price of the various articles they exposed to sale, that they offered them frequently from 50 to 75 per cent. under the actual prime cost of these articles in the markets at Bengal. This, and various other circumstances, leading to a suspicion that they could not have come by the goods fairly and honestly, and suspicion being followed up by inquiries, the foregoing catastrophe was soon discovered; but it seems, that as soon as these inquiries were set on foot, and there appeared a probability of discovery, the villains who perpetrated this horrid deed made their escape, and fled to Sahar.

INTERESTING NARRATIVE OF EVENTS, SUBSEQUENT TO THE CAPTURE OF THE FLY CRUISER.

THE following is a more detailed and circumstantial account of the melancholy fate of Captain Youl, Mr. Flower, &c. than that which appears at page 286, Vol. XIV.

When the Fly cruiser, belonging to the East India Company, with dispatches, was captured by the French privateer la Fortune, in the Gulf of Persia, the packets were thrown overboard, to prevent their falling into the hands of the enemy.

It appears that Mr. Flower, who was a passenger on board the Fly, had taken very correct bearings of the ship's situation at the time the letters were thrown overboard. When landed soon after, at Bushire, he communicated his observations to Captain Youl and Mr. Loane; and they being all strongly impressed with the idea of the possibility of recovering the packet, purchased a vessel, and having provided creepers, and other necessary apparatus, set sail towards the spot where the packet had been dropped, near the Isle of Khen. At the end of three days, their labours were crowned with success: they instantly weighed anchor, and were proceding down the gulf, on their way to Bombay, with the recovered packet, when they were unexpectedly attacked by two pirate boats belonging to Jochassum, and full of armed Arabs, who, boarding the vessel, and cutting and stabbing all whom they met, forced the whole crew overboard. Nine, out of sixteen, were wounded; and all must have perished miserably, had not a long-boat, which they accidentally picked up at sea, been in tow at the time.—In it they took refuge, and the Arabs finally took them into one of their boats, and landed them at Ejmaum, a small town on the Arab side, about thirty miles from Noselkeim: it has a good harbour, and appears to be their place of rendezvous. There they were detained thirty-three days, subject to every hardship; and, at the end of that time, to complete their misery, were about to be sold as slaves, when a Wahabee Chief, who heard that they were English, and who had known the British Resident at Bussora, interfered, and procured them a passage to Khen. They were landed at that island, after having been stripped of every thing, except their shirts and trowsers, and the packet, the great source of their labours and sufferings. Two days were now devoted to drying the letters, which had been about five weeks in the sea; and their purpose was not yet effected, when ten Jochassum boats appeared in sight. The unhappy men, instantly carrying off the packet, sought shelter among the rocks, where they remained hid for two days and nights, exposed to every hardship, and nearly perishing with hunger and thirst. Meanwhile, the pirates burned and laid waste the villages on the island, which forced the wretched inhabitants to pass over to the main land; so that on the departure of the pirates, our sufferers were left the undisturbed and solitary possessors of the island. After waiting four days longer for an opportunity of crossing over to the Continent, they obtained a passage to the neighbourhood of Ararack; on their arrival at which place they learned, that the pirate boats had anchored there, and were committing the same havoc as at Khen. Thus pursued by misfortune, they were forced to walk to Cheroo, a distance of nearly forty miles. This town is under the government of Sheik Aga Mahomed, who, at first, received them in a friendly manner; but finding them without money, and stripped of every thing valuable, he drove them from the house which he had provided for them, and treated them with the most unfeeling cruelty and contempt. For some nights, in excessive bad weather, they had no covering but an inverted boat, under which they took refuge. Finding at length no probability of being enabled to proceed on their voyage by sea, they determined to walk on foot to Bushire. After two days march from Cheroo, they reached Nochyloo, without shoes or stockings; where, to their great surprise and joy, they found that Sheik Rama had invited them to his island of Busheab, and supplied them with every thing that his house afforded with the kindest hospitality. Nevertheless, in consequence of their past sufferings, they were all seized with fever and ague. The extreme state of debility to which, from their long hardships, they were all reduced, joined with the want of medicines and medical advice, made their illness extremely severe; and though Sheik Rama gave them a boat, in which they arrived at Bushire on the 4th of January, Captain Youl, worn out with sickness and fatigue, died on the 5th, and was followed to the grave by Mr. Flower on the 7th. Some of the seamen also died. We are happy to learn that Mr. Loane, who arrived some time ago at Bombay, is quite recovered.

We understand the Bombay government has ordered a very liberal allowance to be paid to the parties concerned, and to the families of such of them as are dead.

MR. PEARCE, MIDSHIPMAN OF THE FOUDROYANT.

THE seamen of the Foudroyant, of 84 guns, Vice-Admiral Sir Thomas Graves, now at sea, out of gratitude, and in testimony of regard to Mr. Pearce, Midshipman of that ship, when last in Plymouth, unanimously voted him an elegant naval sabre, of the value of sixty guineas, for his humanity in a late cruise, when it was blowing hard, in saving the lives of three seamen, who had accidentally fallen overboard, by jumping into the sea, and keeping them afloat, by his personal exertions, till more assistance put off.

THE LATE ADMIRAL SIR R. KINGSMILL.*

THE death of Admiral Sir Robert Kingsmill was received at Cove with demonstrations of the sincerest regret for that melancholy event. Every kind and beneficent act of his (and they were many,) towards its inhabitants, were recapitulated. The humanity with which he relieved their wants in a scarce and distressing season, and the concern with which he promoted whatever could conduce to their advantage, were subjects of their gratitude. Every shop in the town was kept shut for two days, to testify their feelings.

ADMIRAL DRURY.

A VERY flattering address, accompanied by a valuable piece of plate, has been presented to Rear-Admiral Drury by the inhabitants of Cork, in testimony of their approbation of his conduct during his late command on the Irish station.

THE IMPLACABLE ENEMY OF THE BRITISH NAVY.

THE following singular sketch of his character, is from a number of the "*Charleston Courier*," which we dare say will neither appear in the *Moniteur* nor *Journal de Paris*:—

Napoleon Buonaparte, Saint and Apostle of the Gauls, Sovereign of France, and Dictator of the Continent of Europe; originally a Lieutenant of Artillery, afterwards one of the spies of the police of Paris; but having married the cast-off mistress of his patron, in consideration of her fortune, and a promise of preferment in the army, he became a General; defeated armies always inferior to his own in number; over-ran Italy by the means of numberless successful frauds; became a Hero, revolutionized it, and then became its Legislator; committed a thousand military blunders, for which, as a General, he deserved to be shot; robbed and massacred its inhabitants, for which he deserved to be hanged; promised to revolutionize England in six months, wherein he lied; set off for Egypt at the head of 47,000 choice thieves like himself, to ransack it and butcher its inhabitants, for which he deserved to be put in the pillory; contrived to rid the public of a whole fleet of men of war, for which he deserved the guillotine; poisoned his own sick soldiers, for which he deserved to be put in a boiling cauldron, conformably to the old statute in such cases made and provided; became a Mussulman, for which he deserved to be circumcised; murdered his defenceless prisoners, for which

* For the Biographical Memoir and Portrait of Admiral Kingsmill, see Vol. V.

he deserved to be buried alive; ran away from his distressed army, for which he deserved to be put to the halberts; subverted the constitution he had sworn to observe, and made himself master of France, for which he deserves to be sent among the wild beasts; cheated all his former associates, and lashed his people with a rod of scorpions, for which he deserves much praise; made himself president of the Italian Republic, for which he deserves the gallies; disturbs the peace of Switzerland, for which he deserves to be drowned in the Lake of Geneva; the eternal enemy of the British Nation, for which he deserves their thanks; a member of the National Institute, for which he deserves to be whipped at school; the implacable enemy of God and man, for which he deserves to go to ——

CAPTAIN R. W. MILLER'S MONUMENT.

THE gallant Captain Ralph Willett Miller, after a series of splendid and essential services to his country, performed in different parts of the Globe, particularly at St. Fiorenzo, Bastia, and Calvi in Corsica, in destroying the Toulon fleet, in the blockade and bombarding Cadiz, at the expedition of Teneriffe, the battles of St. Vincent and the Nile, and the defence of Acre, where he rendered the most essential services, was unfortunately killed by the accidental bursting of a bomb-shell on board his own ship the Theseus. This brave officer's memory was honoured with an equal tribute of love and respect: Lord Nelson, Earl St. Vincent, and the other commanders and officers of the fleets in which he had served, raised a monument to him in St. Paul's Cathedral, in which Britannia and Victory are represented affixing his Medallion to a Palm Tree, with the inscription, "To Captain R. Willett Miller. this Monument is raised by his companions in Victory."

CUTHBERT COLLINGWOOD, 1575.

IN the Minstrelsy of the Scottish Border, Vol. I, page 95, is the narrative of the skirmish of the Reidshire, June 7, 1575, which terminated in a complete victory on the part of the Scots, who took prisoners, among others therein named, Cuthbert Collingwood, (the ancestor of Admiral Lord Collingwood,) and who is thus described, page 103:—

"But if ye waid a Souldier search,
Among them a' were ta'en that night,
Whas name sae wordie to put in verse,
As Collingwood, that courteous knight?"

CREW OF HIS MAJESTY'S SHIP DEFENCE.

RECENTLY, a detachment of French prisoners, consisting of about 300 soldiers, taken in the late action off Trafalgar, came into Canterbury; they proceeded immediately on board the Sandwich prison-ship, which was previously prepared for their reception. Several of the crew of the Defence being on shore at the time they came in, went up to them, in their blunt way, and, with that instinctive liberality so inseparable from the character of a British seaman, distributed money among the poor fellows, over whom they had obtained so brilliant a victory; affording them a convincing proof of the generous disposition of English sailors.

HEROISM OF TWO MARINES.

IT would be endless to recount the traits of heroism exhibited by individuals in the late action; two instances have, however, come to our knowledge, which we cannot forbear to state: both instances occurred on board the Victory, and both the persons belonged to that ever gallant and meritorious body, the royal marine corps.—A Corporal, in the middle of the action, had his arm carried off by a cannon shot; he bound the stump round with the sash of an officer, who had been killed, spirited up a party to board the enemy, and was himself at the head of that party, and the first that was on board the opposing ship.—A private marine was at the point of firing his musket, when his left arm was struck off by a ball; he afterwards fired off his piece, and went, unattended, to the cockpit, carrying his musket with him in his right hand.

THE VICTORY AND TEMERAIRE.

TWO sailors went into a church at Plymouth on the Thanksgiving Day, both of whom belonged to the Temeraire in the ever-memorable battle off Trafalgar. The Clergyman, in the course of his sermon, mentioned the words "glorious victory," on which one of the tars observed to the other, "Hear, Jack, there's the Victory!" The clergyman pronounced the word "victory" a second time, on which the tar observed, "Mind, Jack, there's the Victory again." The clergyman, not long after, mentioned the word "victory" a third time, on which the irritated tar observed to his companion, "D—n my eyes, Jack, if we stop here any longer—that fellow has mentioned the Victory three times, and never mentioned the Temeraire, that was in the hottest part of the engagement, and took two ships;" when they immediately left the church.

CAPTAIN ROTHERAM, OF THE VICTORY.

A REMARKABLE instance of cool intrepidity of Captain Rotheram, Vice-Admiral Lord Collingwood's Captain, in the Royal Sovereign, of 110 guns, off Trafalgar, Oct. 21.—During the late glorious action off Trafalgar, a heavy shower of the enemy's musketry swept the quarter-deck of the Royal Sovereign, Vice-Admiral Lord Collingwood (when she had seven ships upon her), and left Captain Rotheram standing almost alone, amongst the dead, dying, and wounded, which strewed the deck.—Captain Rotheram had on his gold laced cocked hat (rather a remarkable one) and his gold epaulettes. Being asked why he exposed himself so much to the enemy's sharp shooters in that conspicuous dress? gallantly replied, "I have always fought in a cocked hat, and I always will."

BUST OF LORD NELSON.

THE bust of the late Lord Nelson is carving at Plymouth, for the head of the Conqueror, of 74 guns: more than ordinary care is to be devoted to its execution.

INCIDENT AT THE FUNERAL OF LORD NELSON.

ONE of the undertakers at Lord Nelson's funeral being without a horse, was accommodated by one belonging to a Dragoon: the trumpet, however, was no sooner sounded, than the animal galloped off to fall into the ranks. The terrified undertaker in the mean time clung, like another Gilpin, to the horse's mane, to the great amusement of the spectators, who, however, at last relieved him from his perilous situation.

INSCRIPTION ON LORD NELSON'S COFFIN.

THE brass plate affixed on the outside of the interior coffin has the following inscription:—"I do hereby certify, that every part of this coffin is made of the wood and iron of l'Orient, most of which was picked up by His Majesty's ship under my command, in the bay of Aboukir.

(Signed) "BENJ. HOLLOWELL."

"*Swiftsure, May* 23, 1799."

It is lined with white satin.

LORD NELSON'S PILLAR AT BRISTOL.

THE corporation and inhabitants of Bristol have it in agitation to erect a pillar to the memory of Lord Nelson, in Nelson Street. The base is to be constructed of granite from St. Vincent's Rock; the column is to be ornamented with a crocodile, and Egyptian hieroglyphics, and a loosened belt encircling the middle with this inscription—

"The frozen Belt relax'd thro' fear,"

supporting a figure of a first rate man of war, the Victory. On the summit is to be placed a Bust of the ever-to-be-lamented Hero, with the motto—

"Omnibus in terris quæ sunt a Gadibus usque
"Auroram et Gangem:"

thus embracing the history of his Lordship's exploits. The magnificent arched-way, lately constructed under St. John's Gate, will be embellished with appropriate Figures, and serve as a triumphal arch leading to the pillar.

LORD NELSON'S MONUMENT, CALTON HILL, EDINBURGH.

IT is proposed to erect a monument in honour of Lord Nelson on the Calton Hill, Edinburgh; a rustic tower, of the height, at least, of 100 feet, and of a proportionable breadth, on the site of the present signal staff, having convenient stairs in the interior, to lead to the top, from whence the signals are to be repeated, as at present. The upper part of the tower to be fitted up with proper accommodations for a signal officer. The under part to be divided into five or more small cabins, for the reception of deserving seamen; and the first preference to be given to those who have been wounded in battle with Lord Nelson. In addition to this, flags to be provided and put in charge of the signal officer, with the names. in large characters, of Nelson, and all our other Naval Heroes who have gained great victories within a certain period. To assist the maintenance of the seamen, a small fee to be taken at the gate from all visitors: and from the situation, being admitted to command one of the finest views in Europe, a sufficient fund for this laudable purpo e might be depended on. It is understood that from 1500*l.* to 2000*l.* would fully answer. And we are happy to hear, that a considerable sum is already subscribed.

LIBERALITY OF LORD NELSON.

A LETTER from Boston, in America, dated December 21, 1805, furnishes us with the following anecdote of the late Lord Nelson:—

During the latter part of the American war he had the command of a ship on this station, and took a schooner belonging to Plymouth, (in America,) about forty miles from Boston, the Captain of which was put on shore, to go to his home. Some time after he observed Nelson sailing up the bay of Boston, and his prize at a short distance. The Captain of the schooner immediately fitted out a boat, put one or two sheep in, and filled it with vegetables, with which he sailed for Nelson, and, on coming alongside, threw the articles on the deck, and jumped on board, and desired Captain Nelson to accept them, which he did, but observed to Captain Carver, that he must have some motive for his kindness, and desired to know what it was? Carver, with doubt and hesitation, said he had. What is it? was replied. He answered, that he could scarcely expect it, but it was to return him his schooner again—it was his all.—Nelson immediately wrote the following certificate, and gave it him:—

"These are to certify, that I took the schooner Harmony, Nathaniel Carver, Master, belonging to Plymouth; but, on account of his good services, have given him up his vessel again.—Dated on board His Majesty's ship Albemarle, 17th of Aug. 1782.

" *Boston Bay.* "HORATIO NELSON."

The above certificate is framed and glazed, and hangs in a gentleman's parlour at Boston.

MR. SMEATON.

THIS gentleman, to whom the science of civil architecture is indebted for systematic improvements which place him upon a level with its original inventor, once in conversation stated, that when, in spite of the various difficulties he had to encounter, the Eddystone light-house * was finished, notwithstanding the fate that had attended the former building, a number of persons applied to him to be appointed residents in the new erection, where, it is to be understood, two were to be constantly on duty, immured or cased in stone, in a situation where, probably for many months in every year, it was impossible to have any communication with them from the main land. Among the rest that, upon this occasion,

* For a View of the Eddystone Light-House, see Vol. XII.

attended his levee in Arundel street, was a young man, one of the journeymen to his tailor.

As this youth had frequently brought home, and tried on, clothes for him, Mr. Smeaton knew him perfectly well; but as at this time he had given no orders respecting apparel, he was astonished at his appearance, and still more so when he understood the nature of his application.

He asked him if he was *married?*

"No," he said, "he was a single man."

"What then," said Mr. Smeaton, "can induce you to wish to become an inhabitant of the Eddystone light-house?"—"Why, to confess the truth," replied the tailor, "I have a vast inclination to *see* a little more of the world; I was always fond of *liberty*, and have for many years disliked the confinement of business and my master's shop."

Mr. Smeaton could hardly keep his countenance: he, however, with that affability which was so distinguishing a trait in his character, explained to the man the nature and the danger of his situation. But no arguments that he could use had force sufficient to dissuade him. He wished to feel the advantages of *liberty*, and to obtain that knowledge of the world which, he had an idea, the prospect from a barren rock, continually beaten by, and frequently almost covered with, the waves of a boisterous ocean, would afford.

As Mr. Smeaton knew this person to be perfectly sober, and of an unexceptionable character, he no longer pressed his objections, but accordingly sent him to reside at the light-house. As he was fond of reading, his patron directed, that whensoever an opportunity offered, files of newspapers, with magazines and other books, should be sent to him; and the tailor, by his care and diligence, repaid his attention. He continued in this perilous situation for a long period, and declared that he never was so happy in his life. Fishing, in fine weather, was one of his amusements. But what was very extraordinary, he made such good use of the abundant leisure which the winter afforded, in reading, writing, and studying, that he exceedingly improved his mind, and became so capable of business, that he was by his patron, when the term of his last engagement (I think seven years) had expired, employed more advantageously, though probably not more agreeably, to himself.

NAVAL PROCESSION AT AYLSHAM, ON THE LATE THANKSGIVING DAY.

AT Aylsham (under the patronage of the noblemen, ladies, and gentlemen of the town and its vicinity), the Thanksgiving Day was observed with peculiar demonstrations of joy, accompanied at the same time with proper marks of respect to the memory of the departed Hero, whose name will survive to the latest posterity. A procession was made to church in the following order:—

Blue flag, carried by a British Sailor.
Band of music.
Red flag, carried on horseback by a British Sailor, with a drawn sword.
State horse, covered with black cloth, and led by two British Sailors, and mounted by a Captain in the Navy, wearing a black silk scarf, and carrying a sword reversed in the left arm, covered with black crape.
Flag of an Admiral of the White, borne by a British Sailor.
A ship, carried by four Sailors, bearing the flag of an Admiral of the White.
King's Arms, carried by a Volunteer in the South Erpingham Cavalry, supported by two other Volunteers of the same troop.
A Banner, with the words, "The immortal NELSON," painted on an anchor, surrounded with cannon balls, and a piece of cannon at each corner—trimmed with black crape—borne by a Lieutenant of the Navy.
Banners, with the following inscriptions, borne by British Sailors:—
"England expects every man will do his duty."
"Show me my Country's Foes the Hero cried—
"He saw, he fought, he conquer'd, and he died."
"The Combined Fleets of France and Spain, defeated off Cape Trafalgar."
"Rule Britannia."
"The Duke of YORK and the Army."
"Success to Lord COLLINGWOOD and his valiant Crew."
"Sir RICHARD STRACHAN and the British Navy."
"Earl ST. VINCENT, Sir J. B. WARREN,
"Sir SIDNEY SMITH, Viscount DUNCAN,
"ABERCROMBIE, COOKE,
"BURGESS, DUFF."
"We rejoice for our Country, but mourn for our Friend."
"The British Volunteers."
"May every Briton prove a Norfolk Hero."
"Prosperity to the town of Aylsham."
"In thee, O Lord! we put our trust."
"Almighty God has blessed His Majesty's arms."
"God save the King!"

CAPTAIN TALBOT.

THE following Address was delivered to Captain Talbot, on his taking leave of the Leander's officers, previous to his joining the Centaur.

SIR, *His Majesty's Ship Leander, at Halifax, 5th Dec.* 1805.

THE ward-room Officers of His Majesty's ship Leander, who, while under your command, have so constantly seen the correct and steady conduct of the officer happily blended with the manners of the gentleman, anxious to testify their esteem and respect, and the unfeigned regret they feel at your departure, beg leave, as a small token of their regard, to present you with a sword, value one hundred guineas; well assured it will always be drawn in the cause of honour, defending the rights of your King and Country.

To Captain Talbot.

To which Captain Talbot returned the following reply:—

His Majesty's Ship Centaur, Halifax Harbour,
December 6, 1805.

GENTLEMEN,

YOU have presented me with such a testimony of your regard as deserves my warmest acknowledgments.

I shall wear *that* sword with pride.

It is impossible for words to express my feelings on so flattering an occasion, and I have only to request you will believe I shall ever retain a due sense of the honour you have conferred on me.

I am, Gentlemen,
With great regard,
Yours, &c. &c. &c.
JOHN TALBOT.

To the Ward-room Officers of His Majesty's Ship Leander.

A Scale of the increased Pensions granted to the Widows of Officers of the Royal Navy, by His Majesty's Order in Council; the same to take place from June last.

	per annum.
Captains' Widows, if more than three years Post	£.80
Captains, if not less than three years Post	70
Commanders	60
Lieutenants returned with the rank of Commanders	45
Lieutenants, Surgeons, and Masters	40
Pursers	30
Boatswains, Gunners, Carpenters, and Hospital Mates	25

MARINE OFFICERS' WIDOWS.

Colonels	80
Lieutenant-Colonels	50
Majors	40
Captains	30
First and Second Lieutenants	20

CORRESPONDENCE.

MR. EDITOR,

AS every thing which relates to the memory of the immortal Hero of Trafalgar must be interesting to your readers, I make no apology for transmitting to you the following faithful extract of a letter, written by an officer of rank now commanding a line of battle ship, off Cadiz:—

I have another source of sorrow, which arises from the loss of a very good friend, in our late most excellent and ever-to-be-lamented Commander in Chief. The Nation may also mourn, and consider the victory, splendid as it is, dearly purchased by the death of such a man. Our list of flag officers does not afford many who are adequate to supply his loss; for in him were united more good points than I ever thought it possible for one man to possess.—Solidity of judgment, activity, energy, promptness in decision, were his leading features; to these he added mildness of manners, and the most pleasing affability of deportment. He kept every one in good humour, and knew how to produce the most astonishing efforts of human exertion from the people around him, without making one of them think himself oppressed, or giving occasion for the slightest murmur, or expression of dissatisfaction. In a word, he was beloved, admired, and respected by officers and men, at once deserving and possessing their entire confidence.

Such, Mr. Editor, are the genuine expressions of a British Officer, who committed them to paper with no intention of their being made public. I shall not apologize for the style, which to me appears particularly ingenuous, or insult the feelings of your readers by deprecating their criticism. Suffice it to say, that they are the tribute of professional gratitude paid to the memory of a departed Hero, and that they were written on those waves where the victory was won.

I am, Sir, yours, &c.

December 4, 1805. PHILO POICTIERS.

MR. EDITOR,

IT is beyond a doubt that Columbus found the continent of America inhabited wherever he landed; how the ancestors of the natives got there, perhaps will never be known to a certainty, therefore we have no other rule to go by than that of conjecture and probability: amongst the numerous hypotheses which have been advanced on the subject, the following (which I believe is not generally known) bears the strongest marks of probability; and, I think, will satisfactorily account for what has puzzled some of the wisest and greatest men of the two last centuries.

Beyond the Obi, in the immense regions of Tartary, is a great river called Kavonia, which receives the waters of another, known by the name of Lena. At the Kavonia, where it discharges itself into the frozen sea, lies a large island, frequented by a vast number of people, who resort to it for the purpose of killing certain amphibious animals which are found there in great abundance, which the people of the country call Behemots. These creatures are frequently seen asleep on the ice in the frozen sea: the hunters or fishermen often get upon the ice for the purpose of killing their prey: great assiduity is requisite on this occasion, therefore the hunters commonly take their wives with them to assist in the chase. It but too often happens, that whilst these poor people are engaged in this business, a thaw comes suddenly on, by which the immense plain of ice is broken into many floating islands. Upon some of those the hunters are sometimes wafted to the shore from which they have originally ventured; but when the wind blows from the shore, those unfortunate creatures are never seen again by their countrymen; but whether they perish through cold at sea, or are driven to some other coast, is not known.

Now it is not at all improbable that some of these floating islands may have been driven towards the point of North America, which lies at no great distance from that part of Asia which projects to the sea of Tartary. What renders this opinion extremely probable is, that the Americans, who inhabit the parts to which I allude, have exactly the same complexion and features with the Tartars who live upon the island mentioned as situated at the mouth of the Kavonia; and precisely the same species of beasts and animals are found on the borders of the sea of Tartary, that are seen in the most northern parts of the Continent of America.

Woodstock Street, Feb. 12, 1806. THOMAS BOOLE.

MR. EDITOR,

I OBSERVE a Correspondent in a newspaper suggests the idea of giving medals to all our brave defenders concerned in the late glorious victory of Trafalgar: to this there can be no objection; but first, Mr. Editor, reward them in a more beneficial manner, and instead of the poverty they are obliged to struggle against, give them a comfortable support, and a pay adequate to the rank they so deservedly hold in that country whose honour and renown they so gallantly and zealously maintain. Splendid poverty is misery.

It is a fact, but not generally noticed, that people of ordinary occupation in this country daily earn more than the pittance of pay of many respectable classes of officers in the Navy, without the station in life to support; the consequence is, that those who have no private fortune of their own, are not enabled to live in the manner that a generous public would be happy and anxious they should do; and unless fortunate enough to make prize-money, (a circumstance that does not fall to the lot of every one,) are compelled in a short time to hide their heads either in a hovel or a jail. It cannot be the wish of the nation, Mr. Editor, that those who have invariably been their protectors in the hour of danger, should afterwards pass a miserable existence.

By inserting the above in your respectable Work, to which the Navy already owe a great deal, you will oblige

A WELL-WISHER TO THE COUNTRY.

MR. EDITOR,

IN your biographical account of Captain Rotheram, in the Chronicle for December last, mention is made of his brother, Dr. John Rotheram; and it is stated, that the Doctor "resided at Turnham Green about fifteen years ago, and *conducted The Monthly Review*, of which the late Dr. Griffiths was the ostensible Proprietor and Editor."—This representation is incorrect. Dr. Rotheram was engaged by the late Dr. Griffiths to reside in his house as tutor to his son, and never had any share in the *conduct* of *The Monthly Review*, of which Dr. Griffith was the *real* (not merely the *ostensible*) Proprietor and Editor, from its commencement to his death: when the property and management of it descended to his son, above mentioned.

Turnham Green, Jan. 20, 1805. G. E. G.

MR. EDITOR,

THE following are extracts of letters from Mr. Thomas Aikenhead, late Midshipman of His Majesty's ship Royal Sovereign, to his father and sister, who reside at Portsea.

They were written a few hours previous to the late action off Trafalgar. Your readers will not fail to admire the amiable and noble sentiments which pervade them, as well as perceive the presentiment he possessed, that he should not survive the action :—

We have just piped to breakfast; thirty-five sail, besides smaller vessels, are now on our beam, about three miles off. Should I, my dear parents, fall in defence of my King, let that thought console you. I feel not the least dread on my spirits. Oh my parents, sisters, brothers, dear grandfather, grandmother, and aunt, believe me ever yours!

Accept, perhaps for the last time, your brother's love; be assured I feel for my friends, should I die in this glorious action—glorious, no doubt, it will be. Every British heart pants for glory. Our old Admiral (Admiral Collingwood) is quite young with the thoughts of it. If I survive, nothing will give me greater pleasure than embracing my dearest relations. Do not, in case I fall, grieve—it will be to no purpose. Many brave fellows will no doubt fall with me on both sides. Oh! Betsey, with what ardour I shall, if permitted by God's providence, come to England to embrace you all!

This last is dated four hours before the action commenced, in which this brave and good youth was killed. The letter to his father contains, beside, an account of his will, which he had deposited in his desk, and a general statement of the property (including money) deposited in his chest. He had saved some money at the time of making his will, and had added 10*l.* to the saving afterwards, and he says (in the above letter)—"Do not be surprised to find 10*l.* more—it is mine." There was a coolness and presence of mind in all the youth did, in that important moment, that renders his memory deservedly esteemed.

P.

MR. EDITOR,

THE subjoined letter, from Captain Lee, addressed to Commodore Losack, contains what may be considered as an official account of the attack made by la Preneuse, French frigate, of 46 guns, on His Majesty's sloop of war Rattlesnake and the Camel store-ship, when lying at anchor in Algoa Bay, on the 20th of September, 1799*.

It has not hitherto been printed; and, should it be thought worth notice, it is much at your service. Yours, &c.

* * *

SIR, *Camel, Algoa Bay, September 23, 1799.*

I AM to acquaint you, that on Friday the 20th inst., at 4 P.M., a strange sail was discovered standing to the S.W., the wind at S.E.; at 5 she wore, and stood in for the bay with Danish colours; at 6 she brought up, when the Camel guard-boat went with an intention to board her; but on the boat's getting alongside, two men were observed getting out of the ports with cutlasses in their hands, on which the boat put off and rowed on board, finding her to be a large French frigate, and sent word to the Rattlesnake to get ready to engage her, who had been previously informed by the Surprize schooner, the Star prize which was under weigh working out to proceed to join you, when the frigate came in, passed her close, who hailed him in French, but took no further notice of him; the schooner then tacked, and stood into the bay to inform the ships of it, which was not till after the guard-boat had returned. As soon as the Rattlesnake and Camel were ready, with springs on their cables, the signal was settled that the Camel, when ready to engage, was to hoist a light at the mizen-peak. The Rattlesnake began before the signal was made, about half-past 6 P.M., by firing a shot astern of the French frigate, as did also the Camel, which was taken no notice of: in a few minutes after the Rattlesnake fired a broadside, which was soon accompanied by the Camel, when the Frenchman returned to the Camel, and continued his whole force at her for near three hours, giving the Rattlesnake a shot now and then, who kept up a very brisk fire the whole of the time. At about 12 the wind suddenly shifted from the S.E. to the N.W., when the ships all canted, which occcasioned the Camel to slip her small bower cable, and veer to two cables on the best bower, to bring her broadside to bear on the enemy; at half-past 12 the Carpenter's Mate reported that the ship was making a great deal of water, and had then six feet water in the hold, which occasioned the people to break off from the guns for some time, to man the chain pump, to free the ship, when the fire was again opened on the enemy: during the Camel's fire being slack, the

* *Vide* NAVAL CHRONICLE, Vol. III, page 411.

enemy turned on the Rattlesnake, occasionally firing a few guns at the Camel, till half-past 3 A.M., when she cut or slipt, and ran out of the bay; both our ships were lying with yard and top-mast down, and top-gallant-masts on deck, and Captain Gooch and myself on shore with General Dundas, as also the first Lieutenant of the Camel, with a working party of 30 men, which was greatly against the ship, as she was not able to man all her guns; the Rattlesnake's pinnace was also on shore with the boat's crew and second Lieutenant, and so unfortunate, that the surf was so high that no boat could be got off the beach, which was tried several times by Captain Gooch and myself; every time the boat filled and upset, and some of the people nearly drowned: the surf still continuing, which prevented any boat getting off till noon, we saw the enemy from the hills at 10 A.M. on the starboard tack, standing to the S.W.; have not seen her since. General Dundas promised he would write to you the business, and send off an express.

It is with pleasure I acquaint you, that the ships were both well defended by the spirited exertions of the officers, Lieutenant Shaw, Mr. Thomas the Master, Mr. Hayslip the Gunner of the Camel, who I understand was very active on deck the whole time. Lieutenant Fothergal, of the Rattlesnake, officers, and ship's company, deserve praise for their conduct.

I herewith return you a list of killed and wounded.

Camel,—6 wounded.
Rattlesnake,—2 killed, 1 wounded, severely.
Mr. John Drew, Carpenter, killed.
William Barter, Quarter-Master, killed.

Both ships are a good deal cut in the rigging; the Camel's fore-mast, mizen-mast, main-yard, and fore-top-sail-yard wounded, several shot in the hull, and one under the magazine, which occasioned her to make a good deal of water; we are employed in repairing our damages as fast as possible: my intention was to have sailed from this place on the 22d to join you, as Major-General Dundas told me he thought the Rattlesnake would be sufficient to remain in the bay, as the south-east monsoon was coming on, which, when set in, I do not think any ships can ride at this anchorage with safety. I shall not now proceed till I hear from you, as it will not be safe to leave one ship here alone. I have to regret that it was not in my power, from the state of the two ships, to proceed after the enemy; as I think, from the long time the action lasted, that she must have suffered much; we do not know her force; the Quarter-Master who has charge of the Surprize tells me she had 15 ports of a side on her main deck, which must be 18-pounders, from the size of some of the shot which we have on board. I have the honour to be, Sir,

Your most obedient humble servant,

George Losack, Esq., Commodore and Commander in Chief, &c. JOHN LEE.

MR. EDITOR,

I TRANSMIT you the following extract of a letter from an English Merchant, detained in France, dated at Valenciennes, November 5, 1805. A. B.

I had last the pleasure of writing to you from Verdun, where we have remained till within these few days, when an order arrived for the removal of 140 of us to this place. We were marched here in three detachments, under an escort of *gens d'armes*. We walked always between 20 and 30 miles per day; and, on entering any town where we were to pass the night, we were drawn up in rank and file, called over, and then received billets on the different public houses: the same form of calling over took place again in the morning. At a town called Mezieres, about half way between this and Verdun, we were passed in review, by order of the Captain of *gens d'armerie*, who had the meanness to tell us that we were going to Valenciennes to be exchanged; and great indeed was our disappointment to find, on our arrival here, that he had been guilty of telling us a most notorious falsehood. After eight days' march we arrived here; and, on entering the town, heard the first detachment, which had preceded ours, had the liberty to remain on parole at the different hotels. Judge then of our astonishment on being immediately conducted into the citadel; there we were given to understand that the first detachment was permitted to remain on parole, because it consisted of *real* gentlemen; but we, on the contrary, were to be confined, because we were (*negocians*) merchants. We were confined in a dungeon, I cannot call it a room, no distinction between our servants and ourselves; all shared the same fate. Our furniture consisted of one dresser, two benches, and five miserable, I cannot say straw matrasses, but sacks full of stinking straw. There we were to be called over three times a day, and locked up at half-past five. Almost immediately on my arrival I sent notice of it to my worthy friends, Messrs. ———, who with great kindness came forward and offered themselves as security for my appearance when called for, upon which the Commandant had the liberality to permit me to breathe the pure air.

OFFICIAL ACCOUNT

OF THE

LOSS OF THE DIAMOND ROCK.

FROM the very animated description of the Diamond Rock, which, through the medium of a Correspondent, we were some time since enabled to lay before the public*, the reader would naturally infer, that that astonishing production of Nature was nearly impregnable. In all probability it would have proved wholly so, had it not been for the unfortunate shortness of ammunition, and the absolute want of water, under which our brave fellows laboured, at the attack previously to the late surrender.

We have much pleasure in presenting to our readers the following official details, which have not before been printed, as they place the conduct of Captain Maurice, the senior officer commanding at the Rock, in a most interesting point of view. Indeed, the man whose proceedings were sanctioned, and applauded, by so excellent a judge of merit as the late Lord Nelson, will incur little danger of censure from his countrymen.

Very little has hitherto been known in this Country relative to the loss of the Diamond Rock; but it will be obvious, on a perusal of the following papers, that Captain Maurice, though not able to "*command* success," fully "*deserved*" it.

MY LORD, *Barbadoes, June* 6, 1805.

IT is with the greatest sorrow I have to inform you of the loss of the Diamond Rock, under my command, which was obliged to surrender on the 2d inst., after three days' attack from a squadron of two sail of the line, one frigate, one brig, a schooner, eleven gun-boats, and, from the nearest calculation, 1500 troops. The want of ammunition and water was the sole occasion of its unfortunate loss. Although I shall never cease to regret the accident, yet it is some consolation to think so many valuable lives are saved to His Majesty's service, having only two killed and one wounded. The enemy, from the nearest account I have been able to obtain, lost on shore 30 killed and 40 wounded, independent of the ships and boats: they also lost three gun-boats and two rowing-boats. Allow me to speak in the

* *Vide* NAVAL CHRONICLE, Vol. XII, page 205.

highest terms of the officers and men under my command; and I trust, when the Court Martial shall have taken place, that their hardships, fatigue, and gallantry, will merit your Lordship's approbation, having been 19 nights under arms, and some of them obliged to drink their own water. I beg leave to enclose the Articles of Capitulation.

I have the honour to remain

Your Lordship's most obedient and humble Servant,

J. W. MAURICE.

Right Hon. Lord Viscount Nelson,
Duke of Bronté, &c.

ARTICLES OF CAPITULATION.

Article 1st,—That the Garrison, with all its Works, shall be delivered up entire.

2d,—That the Garrison shall be allowed to march with their Arms to the Queen's Battery, with drums beating and colours flying, and there lay down their Arms.

3d,—That all private Property shall be secured to the Officers and Men.

4th,—That the Garrison shall be sent to Barbadoes, at the expense of the French Nation; but not to serve till regularly exchanged.

5th,—That the Garrison is capable of holding out a few days longer, and two hours given for an answer, when hostilities will be re-commenced.

J. W. MAURICE.

French Squadron that attacked the Rock.

Pluton	- - 74	Berwick	- - 74
Sirene	- - 40	Argus brig	- 16

La Fien schooner, 18 swivels; and 11 gun-boats, each mounting three pieces of cannon.

SIR, *Victory at Sea, June* 8, 1805.

I HAVE received your letter of the 6th inst., acquainting me with the surrender of the Diamond Rock under your command, on the 2d of this month, to a squadron of the enemy's ships and gun-boats, therein mentioned, together with the terms of capitulation which accompanied your said letter; in answer to which, while I regret the loss of the Diamond, I have no doubt that every exertion has been used by yourself and those under your command for its defence, and that its surrender has been occasioned from the circumstances you represent. It is particularly gratifying that so few lives were lost in the contest, and I have very fully to express my approbation of the terms of capitulation, as well as with your conduct personally, and that of the officers and men under your command, which I have to request you will be pleased to communicate to them. I am, Sir,

Your most obedient humble Servant,

NELSON & BRONTE.

To Captain J. W. Maurice,
late Commander of the Diamond Rock.

SIR, *Barbadoes, June* 19, 1805.

IN my letter of the 6th inst., to the Right Honourable Lord Viscount Nelson and Bronte, stating the unfortunate loss of the Diamond Rock under my command, and from the vessel sailing directly on my arrival here, I was unable to state to his Lordship the particulars of the action. I therefore beg leave to enclose the narrative for your information.

I have the honour to remain, Sir,

Your most humble and obedient Servant,

To Rear-Admiral Cochrane. J. W. MAURICE.

SIR, *Barbadoes, June* 19, 1805.

IN my letter of the 14th May, to Sir Francis Lafforey, I informed him of the arrival of the enemy's combined squadron off the Rock, and of our having had one hour's partial action with them as they passed it: their force consisting of sixteen sail of the line, eight frigates, three brigs, one armed en flute, and His Majesty's late sloop Cyanne.

On the 16th of May, at half-past seven in the morning, saw a large ship rounding Point Saline, and from her appearance I plainly saw she was a ship of the line, and from the cut of her sails an enemy. At eight she hoisted a Spanish ensign and pendant; I immediately directed French colours to be hoisted as a decoy, which fully answered my wishes, for at twenty minutes before nine she had got under the lee of the Rock, at the distance of three quarters of a mile, when I shifted the colours, and opened a well directed fire of round and grape from Fort Diamond; the first shot striking her under the fore channels, she directly put her helm up, and in the act of wearing returned one feeble shot. From the little winds she did not get out of the range of shot until nine, but continued running before the wind until twelve. At two an enemy's brig stood out of Port Royal, and beat to windward of the Rock, where she continued to cruise. I was now fully satisfied in my own mind of the intention of the enemy to attack the Rock. From the 16th to the 29th the Rock was completely blockaded by frigates, brigs, schooners, and small boats, sloop-rigged, which prevented any supplies being thrown in to me; for on the 25th a sloop from St. Lucia, with my second Lieutenant, who had carried dispatches to Barbadoes, and the Purser, who had gone over to complete the provisions to four months, were taken under my guns, endeavouring to throw in some barrels of powder, although we covered her with a spirited fire from Fort Diamond, Centaur's Battery, and Maurice's Battery. On the 29th, at half-past five in the evening, two ships of the line, one frigate, and a schooner, with 11 gunboats in tow, stood out from Fort Royal, under all sail. I now had not the smallest doubt that the squadron was intended for the attack of the Diamond. The Rock was put into the best state of defence it could, as far as little ammunition and water would allow; but I was determined to defend it while I had any remaining. On the 30th, at sun-rise, the enemy's squadron had fallen far to leeward; but the wind unfortunately veering very much to the southward, (indeed farther than I had known it for some months, enabled them to fetch as high as St. Ann's Bay, where they continued under easy sail for the night. On the morning of the 31st, at sun-rise, they were still under easy sail, far to windward; but from the number of their signals, and having cast off their boats, I was convinced the attack would be made soon. At seven the enemy bore up in a line for the Rock, the gun-boats, &c. keeping within them, crowded with troops. Seeing the impossibility of defending the lower works against such a force, and the certainty of our being prevented from gaining the heights without considerable loss, and which could not be defended for any time without us, with the greatest reluctance I ordered the whole above the first lodgment, having a man at each gun to give the enemy their discharge, which they did, and joined me over the North Garden Pass, excepting the cook, who was made a prisoner. What powder was left below we drowned, and cut away the launch, that she might not be serviceable to the enemy. At ten minutes before eight we had every person up, and the ladders secured, when the Berwick opened her fire within pistol shot, and at eight the whole of the enemy's squadron of ships and gun-boats were in action, which was returned by Hood's Battery and Fort Diamond; the whole of the troops in the boats keeping up a heavy fire of musketry. It was a fortunate circumstance we quitted the lower works when we did, as our own stones hove down by the enemy's shot would have killed and wounded the whole of us. I was now busily employed in placing the people on the different lodgements, with small arms, to harrass the enemy as they landed, and cover themselves. I am happy to say that the execution done was considerable; for the fire of our men was so galling, that the seamen left their boats, excepting three men in each, who were shot dead, and three of the gun-boats went adrift; two of them went on shore at Martinique, and were beat to pieces, and the other went to sea. The whole of the enemy's squadron were constantly employed during this day in bombarding the Rock, as they could fetch in to windward of it. At night the whole of the men were posted on different lodgements, to harrass the enemy as they threw in supplies and reinforcements: on the 1st the enemy's squadron employed constantly bombarding the Rock, the fire from the troops much more spirited: on the 2d the enemy's squadron bombarding as before, who had been reinforced with another brig, but the fire from the troops this day very severe, as they had during the night got under the rocks in the surf, and were covered by the overhanging rocks, and as our men appeared they fired up. At four in the afternoon, on examining into our ammunition, I found we had but little powder left, and not a sufficient quantity of ball cartridges to last until dark, and being firmly of opinion the enemy meant to endeavour to carry the heights by assault that night, I thought it a duty I owed to those brave fellows who had so gallantly supported me during three days and two nights constant battle, to offer terms of capitulation; and having consulted my first Lieutenant, who was of the same opinion, at half-past four, the unhappiest moment of my life, I threw out a flag of truce, which returned at five, with honourable terms for the garrison, and the next morning we embarked on board the Pluton and Berwick, and on the fourth we were sent to Barbadoes in a cartel, agreeable to the articles, except fourteen men, which they forcibly detained unknown to me, getting men to swear they were French. I have written to Captain Kempt, Agent for prisoners of war, stating the business, as well as their endeavouring to entice the whole of my crew to enter into their service, but, thank God! I trust no Englishman, let him be ever so bad, is base enough to do it. I beg leave to recommend in the strongest terms, the able and gallant support I received from my first Lieutenant, Mr. Robert Adams Wadham, and whose services at different times in carrying dispatches to Barbadoes, relating to the enemy, merits my warmest acknowledgments. I am also much indebted to Lieutenant Watson, of the marines, for his active and able support. Those, Sir, were the only officers I had, but I needed not more, for the conduct of the whole of my people was so active, orderly, and gallant, that I shall always reflect on it with pleasure to the latest day of my life. Indeed, when you observe that we had only two killed and one wounded, you will perceive, that had not my orders been put in execution with the greatest promptness and attention, we must have met with great loss; and had I let loose their valour, I should have lost half my men. Their fatigue and hardships are beyond description, having only a pint of water during 24 hours, under a vertical sun, and not a moment's rest day or night; and several of them fainted for want of water, and obliged to drink their own. A schooner had brought out sixty scaling ladders, to attempt us that night under cover of the ships, and four more ships of the line were to have come against us the next day. Indeed the whole of the combined squadron's launches were employed on the service, and not less than three thousand men. The Captain of the Sireine frigate was wounded through the knee. My only consolation is, that although I unfortunately lost the Rock, I trust its defence was honourable, and hope it will merit your approbation.

I have the honour to remain

Your most humble and obedient Servant,

J. W. MAURICE.

At a Court Martial assembled on board His Majesty's Ship Circe, at Carlisle Bay, Barbadoes, the 24th June, 1805, for the Trial of James Wilkes Maurice, Esq., Commander, the Officers, and Crew of His Majesty's late sloop Diamond Rock, taken by a squadron of the enemy's ships on the 2d inst.

PRESENT,

Captains,

Jonas Rose, President.

George Tobin, William Champion,

R. Henderson, Joseph Nourse.

The Court being duly sworn according to Act of Parliament, in pursuance of an order from the Hon. Rear-Admiral Cochrane, commanding His Majesty's ships and vessels at Barbadoes, the Leeward Islands, &c. &c. &c. dated the 23d June, 1805, directed to Jonas Rose, Esq., Captain of His

Majesty's ship Circe, and senior officer of His Majesty's ships and vessels at Barbadoes, which being read before the Members and Judge Advocate then in open Court, and before they proceeded to trial, the letter from James W. Maurice, Esq. was read, and after having heard what the said James Wilkes Maurice, Esq., Commander, the Officers and Company of the late sloop Diamond Rock had to offer in their defence, the Court is of opinion that Captain J. W. Maurice, the Officers and Company of His Majesty's late sloop Diamond Rock, did every thing in their power to the very last, in the defence of the Rock, and against a most superior force; and Captain James W. Maurice behaved with firm and determined resolution, and did not surrender the Diamond until he was unable to make further defence for want of water and ammunition; the Court do therefore honourably acquit Captain Maurice accordingly.

The Court cannot dismiss Captain James W. Maurice without expressing their admiration of his conduct in the whole of the occasion; and also they express the highest approbation of the support given by the officers and men under his command; a circumstance that does high honour to them; does no less credit and honour to the discipline by Captain J. W. Maurice; and therefore do unanimously and honourably acquit the said Officers and ship's Company, and they are unanimously and honourably acquitted accordingly.

(Signed,) JONAS ROSE,
WILLIAM CHAMPION,
GEORGE TOBIN,
JOSEPH NOURSE,
ROBERT HENDERSON.

THOMAS HORT,
Appointed Deputy Judge Advocate upon this occasion.

The preceding documents are fully sufficient to establish the credit of Captain Maurice, relative to the defence of the Rock; but, to gratify the curiosity of our readers, we shall subjoin the French official account of the transaction.

The *Barbadoes Mercury*, of June 29, 1805, to which we are indebted for the article, which has not yet found its way into any of the publications of this country, speaking of the florid details of the French, says :—" To their bombast we do not look for Captain Maurice's panegyric, although we trace *his* valour in *their* difficulties and distress ;—from his own countrymen and brother officers, who best know how to discriminate the real hero, he has received the most honourable approval of his conduct; and on the close of the Court Martial held on him for the surrender of the Rock, the President expressed himself happy that it fell to his lot to return him his sword, which had been so honourably drawn in the cause of his country; and made no doubt, when his services were again called on, that they would be equally conspicuous. He then addressed the ship's company, and commended their conduct in the highest terms of approbation, for gallantry and discipline; and was confident that it would be an example in His Majesty's service."

The Editor of *The Martinique Gazette,* from which *The Barbadoes Mercury* translated the article, prefaces his "*Extract from the Official Report*" with the following ludicrously-gasconading remarks :—

This Rock, which was never deemed of the least importance till it struck the fancy of Commodore Hood to sink millions of money in it;—this Rock, qualified nevertheless by the British Gazettes with the pompous appellation of "The Gibraltar of the Windward Islands," and with which the administration of that country have been pleased to amuse the public by the most exaggerated accounts and poetical descriptions, was taken possession of by the French soldiers in three days. Though this conquest will be considered but trifling to our armies, accustomed to far greater triumphs, it is not the less glorious to the handful of brave men concerned in it.—It will always be said to their honour, that 200 Frenchmen conquered in a few hours, a place that nature, art, and eighteen months' incessant labour, had conjoined to render in some degree impregnable. It is true, that it cost the English much less trouble to occupy it, for nobody before Sir Samuel Hood ventured to dispute the possession of it with the reptiles and birds of the sea, who reigned there for ages without a rival.

It was a post thus fortified that the French soldiers carried in sixty hours:—had there been a French garrison upon it of 100 men, with provisions and ammunition, it would probably have held out against 10,000 men. But such is the fortune of the two belligerent Nations, that the one has the superiority in money, as the other has it in bravery; and the result to the latter must be, that it will also have the money.

On the 7th Prairial, two days before the expedition, the Captain-General, Gen. Lauriston, Admirals Villeneuve and Gravina, with a number of General and other Officers, went to the Diamond Quarter, in order to inspect the Rock as much as its distance from the shore would permit them. The Captain-General staid there till Saturday night, when he was called to Fort Royal by dispatches he received from thence, of the arrival of the French frigate Didon. General d'Houdetot remained there till the surrender of the Rock, in order to assist the besiegers in case of need.

The Editor then subjoins his

Extract of the Official Report of Chef d'Escadron, BOYER, *(Aid-de-Camp to the Captain-General,) to* VILLARET JOYEUSE, *Captain-General of Martinique and its Dependencies.*

GENERAL,

I embarked on the evening of the 9th Prairial, with the 200 men of the 82d regiment which you put under my command, for the expedition against the Diamond. The naval forces, under the command of Captain Casmao. consisted of the following ships:—

Le Pluton, 74, Captain Casmao.
Le Berwick 74, Captain Camas.
Le Sirene (Frigate), Captain Chabert.
L'Argus (brig), Captain Taillard, and
La Fine (schooner), Captain Meynard.

The troops were embarked on board the Pluton and Berwick. The current ran so strong against us during the night, that in the morning we found ourselves under the lee of St. Lucia. The whole of the 10th was spent in beating up again, so as to commence the attack the following morning: we anchored for the night off Point Borgnesse. On the morning of the 11th, the ships being all collected again, the troops were embarked in the boats, and were directed to make fast to the Argus, in order to be towed near the Rock. I divided them in two divisions: the first, which I commanded in person, was to attempt the landing near the Little Savanna, with Captains Pinede and Balossier; the second, composed of Spanish boats, and commanded by Captain Don Rosando Porlier, with the troops under Captain Cortes, Aid-de-Camp to General Houdetot, and Lieutenants Blairon and Nocus, was to land at the Patch. On the same day, between nine and ten o'clock, we effected our landing much sooner, and with less difficulty, than we had expected, notwithstanding a most brisk and determined fire which the enemy (having abandoned the lower part of the Rock) kept upon us from the heights, and particularly from the middle battery, where they had perfect command of us, and the violent manner in which the sea is constantly agitated near the Rock. We took a man prisoner, whom we found concealing himself. The fortifications of the Rock, and the positions of the enemy, were exactly as I had conceived them to be from the opposite shore. The scaling of it appeared to me there to be perfectly easy, and I had made my dispositions accordingly; but the moment we had landed, this illusion ceased—I saw nothing but immense precipices, perpendicular rocks, a threatening enemy, whom it was impossible to reach, and insurmountable difficulties on all sides. We naturally enough concluded, that from the facility with which the enemy had suffered us to occupy the bottom of the Rock, they had reserved all their force, to destroy us more securely from the heights of their inaccessible retreat. Our troops suffered severely from a most galling volley of musketry, large fragments of the rock, cannon balls, and casks filled with stones, which they poured upon us. They were entrenched in a number of cavities, which nature had formed at different heights, and to which it was impossible to attain, but by ladders of thirty or forty feet in length. From the tremendous fire of the enemy, the boats had been obliged to retreat, without having landed any of the articles with which I had furnished myself for the attack; the ships also had drifted into the offing, and we remained without support or provisions: I saw we had no resource, but to retreat into two cavities in the Rock (in one of which the enemy had erected two large forges), where we should at least be under cover: I had all our wounded carried into them, and placed a detachment over each. I committed the whole of the east side to the charge of Captain Cortes, giving him a sufficient number of men to support him, and at the same time desired him to reconnoitre the most advantageous point to commence the escalade. Captain Pinede was placed in the situation on the right, with like orders, and the like means: Captain Balossier had charge of the western side, and of the landing place. I successively visited all our detachments, and found the same ardour for the attack amongst them all, but found also the most insurmountable obstacles and innumerable dangers. In order to prevent as much as possible the effects of the enemy's destructive fire, I made all the out-posts fall back into the two caverns, to wait for the approach of night, when we might be able to form anew. Notwithstanding this, our situation was truly dreadful; we were exhausted with fatigue, and the want of nourishment was the more severely felt by the troops, who had been prevented by the sea sickness from taking any for the two preceding days that they were on board the ships. The boats had not had time to land any provisions, nor could we expect they would run the risk of bringing us any. The enemy too had now, by the quantity of shot and stones which they continued to direct at us, cut off the communication between the two caverns, notwithstanding their vicinity to each other: in short, to add to the horrors of this calamitous scene, we had nothing to offer our wounded, of whom some were in a most deplorable state, but barren consolations.

About five in the evening, a party of the soldiers came to inform me, that Lieutenant Latour, being led away by his zeal and courage, had ascended by means of ropes to a considerable height on the Rock, when he was discovered by the enemy, and, with twenty-five men, made prisoner. A few minutes afterwards, I learnt that he had been fortunate enough to disengage himself from them, with the loss of two men killed and two wounded, one of which was M. Galiois, a meritorious young man, and a volunteer, who received a ball through the arm. We found a few casks of water that the enemy had abandoned, with which, though perfectly putrid, we were obliged to relieve our wounded, and endeavour to assuage the thirst that devoured us. A canoe reached the shore, and delivered me your letter; the fire of the enemy only allowed me time to write a few hasty lines in answer, and the canoe pushed off; but I had the mortification presently to see two of her crew killed, one of whom was the man to whom I had given my note. At night, although the enemy did not at all relax in their vigorous defence, I endeavoured to reconnoitre the Rock on all sides; I sent Captain Cortes to take possession of one of the buildings, called the Great House, and establish two intermediate posts between him and me; I then caused the guns on the lower Battery, which the enemy had evacuated, to be spiked, and passed the remainder of the night in visiting our detachments. Towards midnight, a boat approached without noise, and succeeded in landing Lieutenants Dutil and Girondon, with sixty grenadiers of the 82d, and likewise some provisions, which had been sent by Captain Meynard, of la Fine. I embraced this opportunity of sending away our wounded. A second boat also attempted to land, but was swept away by the current.

On the 12th, at day-break, I relieved all our out-posts with the grenadiers newly arrived. We discovered a magazine, containing a quantity of rum, Madeira wine, and biscuit, but we were still in great want of water; and above all, of cartridges and flints. In the evening, I determined, in concert with the other officers, to summon the Garrison to surrender the following morning. In the course of the night we received provisions, ammunition, and the rest of the grenadiers of the 82d, under the command of Captain Brunet; the Commandant Richaud also arrived, and was as much surprised as I had been, to find the Diamond so very different to what it had appeared from the main land.

On the morning of the 13th, a boat laden with provisions and ammunition was seen steering for the landing place, and though exposed to the dreadful fire of the enemy, seemed determined to reach it: it was commanded by M. Berenger, a volunteer, who having seen our distressed situation on the evening of the 11th, had vowed to brave every danger to bring us assistance. He had been ordered not to attempt the landing but at night; but the current having delayed him till day-break, he was resolved to comply with his engagement, or perish in the attempt. This brave young man, with one of his sailors, was unfortunately killed; two others were dreadfully wounded, in attempting to save themselves by swimming, and were picked up under the Rock, with six of the boat's crew. Two other supplies were also seen endeavouring to approach, but the enemy's cannon obliged them to return.

On examining the Rock immediately over our cavern, it occurred to me that it could be scaled, and being joined in this opinion by the Commandant Richaud, I with his advice sent to the General commanding the troops, for a quantity of scaling ladders, boat hooks, &c., and desired Captain Brunet and Lieutenant Dutil to prepare themselves, with sixty grenadiers, for the attempt, which I intended to make at one o'clock in the morning, by which time I expected the ladders would arrive. My intention to summon the Garrison was of course dropt. My plan being formed, I gave a *carte-blanche* to all our men, recommending them to search every where for an outlet, and to harass the enemy as much as possible, forbidding them at the same time to fire on the part of the Rock above our cavern, in order that the English might have no idea of an attack from that side; and desired them to let me know whatever new they should discover or do. About nine in the morning, a number of them returned to inform me, that by various means they had succeeded in climbing pretty high up different parts of the Rock, and would have been able to maintain their dispositions, had they had more men and ammunition. I immediately sent them back with a supply of both, and about an hour after, Captain Cortes came himself to inform me that some of his detachment had got very high up the Rock, and demanded my orders. I supplied him with men and ammunition, and desired him to hasten and direct that part of the attack. Some of his men had actually gained a height which commanded the entrance to the Great House, and had fastened to the Rock some ropes which they found; but as the Rock was upwards of forty feet high, they did not descend within reach. Captain Cortes caused part of the staircase of the Great House to be brought away, which they made fast to the Rock, and were thus enabled to reach the ropes; but no one seemed inclined to ascend, till the gallant Lieut. Girandon, who hastened there, and climbed up to the summit of the height with the rapidity of an arrow, and was immediately followed by a crowd of grenadiers, marines, and soldiers. One of the stones hurled at him by the enemy wounded him in the arm, another struck him on the head so as to knock off his hat, but nothing could stop him.

To assist this attack, I caused fifty men to conceal themselves among the rocks and buildings facing the Little Savanna, in order to cut off the communication of the enemy, and to prevent their giving any support to their right flank, which our troops had attacked. In the mean time, Captain Brunet and Lieutenant Dutil had succeeded in climbing up at the head of their grenadiers; and Captain Cortes and Lieutenant Girandon overcame every thing they found in their way. In one place they discovered a quantity of wearing apparel; in another, a month's provisions; and in a third, three large casks of water, which were constantly filled by filtration from the Rock.

It was now all over with the Diamond, and we should probably have had possession of it in a few hours, when la Fine arrived with a flag of truce. Captain Meynard informed me that the Garrison had thrown out the signal for capitulation, which our situation on the Rock prevented us from perceiving. The firing was immediately stopped, and two Englishmen came down with a white flag, and announced their intentions of capitulating. One of them delivered me a letter from the Commander, wherein he offers to surrender, to prevent any further effusion of blood. Articles of Capitulation were immediately drawn up and agreed upon, subject to your ratification. I then dispatched Captain Brunet to receive possession of all the batteries and magazines on the top of the Rock, and to hoist the French flag; and desired him to offer to Captain Maurice and his Garrison whatever refreshments we had in our power. At his request he was permitted to stay on the Rock till the following morning.

At sun-rise on the 14th, he descended with his garrison, agreeably to the Articles agreed upon, and filed off in front of our troops, which I had drawn up at the Queen's Battery, and laid down their arms and their colours, and came with the rest of his officers to deliver me their swords.

To treat a vanquished enemy with respect is, I believe, General, only following your intentions, as well as the rules of French generosity; I therefore returned Captain Maurice and his officers their swords, and renewed my offers to serve them. The number of effective men amounted to 107, one half of whom were sent on board the Pluton, and the other on board the Berwick. I inspected the whole of the Rock, and had the two 18-pounders at the top of it thrown into the sea, as well as the platform, and all the powder and shot; I also cut down one of the flag-staffs, leaving only that on which the French colours were flying.

To judge from the great quantity of powder, shot, water, and provisions of all kinds, which we found in the different cavities near the summit of the Rock, it would be supposed that the enemy could have held out much longer. The prodigious buildings which they had constructed, evidently prove that they considered themselves as well established here. I cannot even yet conceive how they should be so soon dislodged:—it required, no doubt, Frenchmen to do it, and Frenchmen as brave as those you put under my command. From a hasty calculation, I am afraid we have to regret the loss of 50 men, both killed and wounded, which is certainly great, when we reflect that it is so many brave men who have fallen; but from the difficulty of the enterprise, we might have calculated upon a much greater one.

I cannot say too much in praise of the troops employed on this expedition officers, soldiers, and sailors, manifested their usual bravery, coolness, and activity. The 82d regiment, though but just raised under your auspices, has consecrated its new number in the most brilliant manner. It does not belong to me to speak of the naval forces—the behaviour of the whole of the ships employed under Captain Casmao has been generally admired. I owe a great deal both to him and Captain Camas, of the Berwick; their co-operation with the land forces, in supplying us with provisions, was of essential service, and their guns greatly assisted in seconding our efforts. Lieutenant Dodignon, of the Bucentaure, who commanded the boats, behaved with great merit and bravery; he had the misfortune to be shot through the knee with a musket ball, but is in a fair way of recovery.

I should be happy, were it in my power, to name here all the brave men who contributed to our success:..at their head I must place Captain Cortes, who particularly distinguished himself; as did also Captains Brunet, Pinede, and Balossier; Lieutenants Dutil, Blairon, Nocus, Forstal, Loubiere, Daubersmille, and Latour; and Sub-Lieutenant Girandon, who was the first that dared to ascend the lofty Rock from whence the enemy seemed to defy us.

To do the poor "*sea-sick*" French all possible credit for their achievement, we shall not withhold the closing remarks of the Martinique Editor:—

In reading (says he) this interesting report, it will no doubt be remarked with what impartiality and candour Mons. Boyer notices the whole of his comrades; and that he, in some measure, endeavours to conceal his own judicious and intrepid conduct during the whole of the expedition: but his Commanders, his fellow-soldiers, and the public, will do him more justice than he does himself. General d'Houdetot, the Commander of the troops, writes thus to the Captain-General:—"I must here add what the modesty of the Chef d'Escadron Boyer omitted.—It was impossible to do more than he did—his coolness and activity during the disembarkation, the judiciousness of his arrangements in disposing of the troops, and the firm and courageous manner of the whole of his behaviour, amply justifies the confidence we placed in him, and proves him to be a most valuable Officer."

The Captain-General, in a letter to the Colonial Prefect, thus expresses himself:—" My attachment to the Chef d'Escadron Boyer, my Aid-de-Camp, leads me to rejoice in the honour he has obtained by this expedition, by the ze , courage, and talents which he has manifested, and by his generous conduct to a vanquished enemy."

At the end of Mons. Boyer's report is that of Captain Casmao.—After giving an account of the arrangements made for landing the troops, he adds, that he made a signal to the Berwick to pass between the Diamond and the land, and to lie off the N.E. point of the Rock, in order to cover the landing which was intended to be made on that side. The English commenced a fire upon her, which was so warmly returned by Captain Camas, that he soon silenced the lower battery. Captain Casmao himself lay off the S.E. side, in order to divert the attention of the enemy, and to bombard the Hospital. The signal for disembarkation being made, the Spaniards were the first who effected a landing, and immediately hoisted the Spanish flag upon the Queen's Battery. The current having driven the squadron to leeward, they could not re-commence the fire till four o'clock in the afternoon. On the 12th, the winds and the current were so strong, that only the frigate and two corvettes could keep up the cannonade. The 13th, as the ships were about to moor, they perceived the flag of truce. Captain Casmao speaks in the most flattering terms of Captain Meynard, commanding la Fine, and of the great assistance which he afforded to the boats employed in the disembarkation.

It will not fail to strike the *English* reader, in perusing " this *interesting* report," that it is in part composed of gross exaggeration, misrepresentation, and absolute falsehood. It is even, in parts, contradictory of itself.

It will be observed, that in the French account it is stated that 260 troops reduced the Diamond (200 embarking from Martinique, in the first instance, and a reinforcement of 60 going off afterwards); while Captain Maurice, in his letters to Lord Nelson and Admiral Cochrane, estimates the number of troops at 1500; in addition to which, the crews, from the launches of the combined squadron, formed an aggregate of not less than 3000 men. This is merely point against point, Captain Maurice's word against that of M. Boyer; but, in the minutes of the Court Martial, it appears, that the first Lieutenant and the two men who carried down the flag of truce *swore* that there were 1500 under arms, beside two seventy-fours, one frigate, a brig, and eleven gun-boats.

The French say, that they found *plenty of water* on the Rock. If this be *true,* is it not extraordinary, that, when they took possession of the top, Captain Maurice should ask the French Commander *to send to the ships of war for some water for his people?*

The French, too, had the good luck to find a *great quantity of powder, shot, and provisions of all kinds,* in the cavities of the Rock; though Captain Maurice expressly states, that the surrender of the place was *solely* occasioned by the *want of water and ammunition.*

According to Boyer, the French got up the Rock; but, from the terms of capitulation, this is evidently false. The articles, written by Captain Maurice, were agreed to in five minutes. If the French had succeeded in reaching the summit, it stands to reason, and perfectly accords with the known *generosity* of the French, that they would have granted no terms.

We shall dismiss the subject with observing, that the French, instead of 50 killed and wounded, as stated by Boyer, are known, by persons who were on the spot, to have lost nearly 600!!

PLATE CXCVIII.

THE HYDROGRAPHER, (No. 3.)

GUADALOUPE.

THIS Map of Guadaloupe is drawn by Mr. Arrowsmith with his usual accuracy, and will prove, we trust, particularly interesting to our readers.

Guadaloupe, so called by Columbus, from the resemblance which its mountains have to what the Spaniards style those of our Lady of Guadaloupe in Old Spain, is the largest of the Caribbee Islands; and lies in north lat. 16° 30, west long. 61°. Its utmost length from north to south is about 55 English miles, and its greatest breadth is much the same distance. This Island is divided into Grand Terre and Guadaloupe, by la Riviere Sal, which diminishes in breadth from fifty to fifteen fathoms. Its depth is very unequal; but, towards the middle, it can only admit of small boats or canoes going through from the Petit Cul

Published Feby. 28th. 1806, by J. Gold, 103, Shoe Lane, Fleet Street.

Drawn & Engraved by Arrowsmith.

de Sac, to the Grand Cul de Sac. No Island is so well supplied with water; not less than fifty rivers, and some of them of considerable size, empty themselves into the sea. The interior is mountainous and woody: one of the mountains, la Souffrerie, is a volcano. It throws out fire and smoke: but its eruptions are neither violent nor hurtful. The capital of the whole Island is Basse-terre, on the western side, situated on a fine open bay: this town is only called Basse-terre from the citadel to the river Herbes; thence to the westward it is named St. Francis. The chief place of strength, and to which the women and children retire in case of an attack, is the Dos d'Ane; which is no more than a pass in the mountains about four or five miles from Basse-terre, the principal town and harbour of Grand Terre, at the most northerly point of the Island. The two Bays, on the two sides of the Island, are known by distinct names, and are at each mouth of la Riviere Sal. That on the north coast is called le Grand Cul de Sac, and that on the south, Petit Cul de Sac. The former contains a Bason of five or six leagues, from the point of Grosse Morne in the Basse-terre, to the point of Antigua in the Grand Terre: it is nearly three leagues broad in the widest part, and not less than one league in the narrowest. It has safe riding for ships of all rates.

The dependencies on Guadaloupe are Petit Terre Desirade, or Desiderada Island, los Santos, or les Saintes, and Marigalante, so named by Columbus in his second voyage, 1493, from his ship Maria Galanta. This latter Island was thought, on its first discovery, to want water; but an excellent stream has since been discovered. Marigalante, seen at a distance from a ship, appears like a floating Island, because as it is for the most part flat, the trees appear to swim.

The history of Guadaloupe is briefly as follows. Five hundred and fifty Frenchmen, led on by Loline and Duplessis, arrived on the 28th of June, 1635, and, according to the confession of Raynall, having neglected to supply themselves with stores from their native country, plundered the natives. War and famine were the necessary consequences; and the Colonists were reduced to graze in the fields, and to dig up dead bodies for their support. Peace was at length concluded with the savages about 1640. Guadaloupe by degrees recovered from its miseries, but did not become a flourishing Colony until it had been conquered by England in 1759, when it was taken by Major-General Hopson and Commodore Moore*. The Island was restored to the French in 1763.

---

* *Vide* NAVAL CHRONICLE, Vol. III.

ADDENDA

TO

THE BIOGRAPHICAL MEMOIR

OF THE LATE RIGHT HONOURABLE

HORATIO LORD VISCOUNT NELSON, K.B.

AND DUKE OF BRONTE;

VICE-ADMIRAL OF THE WHITE SQUADRON.

(Continued from page 52.)

ON Wednesday morning, the 8th January, at half-past seven o'clock, the Heralds, and the Naval Officers who were to assist in the Procession by water, met at the Admiralty, and thence proceeded, about eight, to Greenwich. At ten o'clock they assembled in the Governor's House within Greenwich Hospital.

The boats and gun-boats of the River Fencibles, with the whole of the establishment of the Water Bailiffs and Harbour Master, assembled off the King's Stairs at nine o'clock, and proceeded to arrange the barges and boats in the order that they were to go in the Procession, in a single line, which reached a considerable way down the River towards Woolwich. This prevented a great deal of confusion, although it in some measure occasioned more delay than might have been expected.

A large guard, composed of the Life Guards and the Greenwich Volunteers and Pikemen, kept the respective avenues as clear as possible. The pressure, however, was great, and many people were much hurt in their attempts to obtain a view of the embarkation.

The Naval Officers, who had assembled in Lord Hood's apartments, partook of a breakfast there, and were ready some time before the Lord Mayor and the City Companies arrived in state from London.

On the alighting of the latter at the Governor's House, a signal was given, and a lane of guards, consisting of the Greenwich and Deptford Volunteers, was formed across the grass plat between the houses of the Governor and Lieutenant-

Governor, to the North Gate, opening to the River. Another lane was also formed by the River Fencibles, armed with their swords and pikes, from the Volunteer line to the entrance of the Painted Chamber, through which the corpse and its attendants moved in procession to the barges on the River appointed to receive them. The body, it should be remembered, was carried from the Saloon, through the Great Hall; out at the eastern Portal, round the Royal Charlotte Ward to the North Gate.

Precisely at half-past twelve o'clock the Procession began to move forwards, passing through the lanes of Volunteers, who received it with presented arms; the River Fencibles firing minute guns from the commencement to the close of the embarkation.

The following was the order of Procession:

Four fifes, and four drums, in the royal uniform, playing the dead-march in Saul.

Five hundred of the Greenwich Pensioners, who, as they advanced from the Hospital, filed off to the right and left, and formed in front of the Volunteers, facing inwards.

Six Mourners in scarfs and hatbands.

Eight Trumpeters, sounding the 104th Psalm.

The Standard, borne by a Naval Captain, and supported by two Lieutenants.

Two Trumpeters, sounding as the former.

Two Pursuivants at Arms, properly attired.

The Guidon, borne by Captain Durham, supported by two Lieutenants, motto reversed.

Two Trumpeters, sounding as the former.

A Pursuivant at Arms.

The Banner of the Order of the Bath, emblazoned on a sable ground, borne as the Guidon.

The great Banner, borne by Captain Moorsom, and supported as the last.

Four Pursuivants at Arms.

Two Chaplains of Greenwich Hospital.

Six Lieutenants of ditto, naval uniform coats, black waistcoats, breeches, and stockings.

Four Mourners.

A Banner of emblems and armorial bearings, borne by Captain T. M. Hardy, and supported by two Lieutenants.

The Coffin, covered with the black velvet pall, borne on a bier elegantly ornamented, and carried by twelve bearers in full mourning.

Chief Mourner, Admiral Sir Peter Parker, Bart.

His Train-bearer, the Hon. Captain Blackwood.

Supporters to the Chief Mourner, Admirals Lord Hood and Radstock.

Six Assistant Mourners.

Six Vice-Admirals:—Caldwell, Hamilton, Nugent, Bligh, Sir R. Curtis, and Sir C. M. Pole; and an emblematical Banner, borne by a Captain, and supported by two Lieutenants, exhibiting Britannia, seated beneath a cypress, weeping over the armorial shield of the Hero, with the British Lion couchant at her feet, guarding her shield. The colours of France, Spain, and Holland, lowered in the back ground.

Four Captains, and six Lieutenants of the Victory.

The whole passed onwards through the North Gate, down the steps, to the River side, along the cause-way, and to the barges, the drums and trumpets halting and continuing to play.

The Body having been placed on board the State Barge, the several members of the Procession took their places on board their appointed barges, when the Lord Mayor of London, Corporation, &c. proceeded from the Painted Chamber, uncovered, to the River side, and went on board their respective barges, appropriately decorated for the solemn occasion, the great bell over the south-east Colonade tolling a funeral knell the whole time.

The whole of the Procession, properly arranged, rowed round the stern of Sir Sidney Smith's little sloop, moored off the Hospital; and, favoured by the flood tide, though opposed by the wind, it proceeded up the River for London.

The Procession moved forward at a slow rate, the flags half-staff high, and the boats of the River Fencibles firing minute guns the whole way to Whitehall stairs. Not a ship, or boat, was suffered to disturb the order. The shores, with the decks, yards, rigging, and masts of the numerous ships on the River, were lined with thousands of spectators. Every hat was off, and every countenance expressed the deepest regret.

As the Procession passed the Tower, a quarter before three o'clock, the great guns were fired at minute intervals from the wharf, and were answered, in corresponding time, by the gun-boats.

The extreme violence of the wind, it being south-westerly, much impeded the progress of the boats in their making the point of land opposite Somerset House: however, by great labour on the part of the rowers, the line of Procession was tolerably well observed to the last.

At half past two o'clock, the 7th Royal Veteran battalion, to the amount of 800, formed a lane two deep, from the Admiralty to Whitehall stairs. At a quarter before three, a large black velvet covering was brought forth, supported by eight undertakers, with bearers, and formed into a temporary awning, at the entrance of the avenue leading to Whitehall stairs. Round the awning was a deep black velvet border and fringe, gilt and festooned in rich drapery, with Coronets and the *insignia* of different Orders, &c. painted in gold.

The Procession arrived at Whitehall stairs precisely at half past three o'clock; when the whole of the boats drew up, and lay upon their oars, forming columns, in the order of a crescent, suffering the barge with the body to shoot a-head, and pass the stairs a short distance. This done, the barge tacked and brought to, when the coffin was landed and received with military honours under the above-described awning or canopy.

The respective members of the Procession then landed in order, and formed in Whitehall yard, agreeably to the arrangement by which they had proceeded from Greenwich Hospital to the place of embarkation. They moved forward, at a slow pace, and reached the Admiralty about four o'clock, when the Body was conveyed into the apartment on the left of the Great Hall, called the Captains' Room. The coffin was placed on a square platform, ascending three steps, and covered with a canopy of black velvet. The canopy was enriched with a display of armorial bearings, &c. On the top of the coffin were placed the coronet and cushion, and on each side were six large wax lights, in silver sconces. Round the room, which was lighted with wax lights to the number of eighty, were fixed the flags of different ships.

The Rev. Mr. Scott, who had sat up with the corpse during the whole time that it lay in state at Greenwich, also remained with it at the Admiralty the night previous to its interment.

Although it had been generally understood that the public were not to view the lying in state at the Admiralty, the curiosity of the populace was so great, that every door of the office was surrounded early in the evening; and many remained till a late hour at night, without succeeding in their object.

A Captain's guard, of the Invalids from the Tower, was stationed at the Admiralty during the whole of Wednesday night.

The Lord Mayor and Corporation of London, &c. did not land at Whitehall stairs, but proceeded in their barges to Palace Yard, where they landed and returned in their carriages to the City.—The boats of the River Fencibles, and others of the Procession, excepting the city barges, returned in order with the tide down stream, firing minute guns the whole way.

The preparations in the streets through which the Procession was to pass, continued, almost unremittingly, during the whole of Wednesday night.

The following is the *official account* of the ceremony observed in conveying the Body of our deceased Hero from Greenwich, on the 8th of January, to the interment of the same at St. Paul's Cathedral on the following day, and is copied *verbatim* from the London Gazette of the 18th January.

PUBLIC FUNERAL OF LORD VISCOUNT NELSON.

ON Wednesday, the 8th instant, the remains of the late Right Honourable Horatio Viscount and Baron Nelson, K. B., Vice-Admiral of the White Squadron of His Majesty's Fleet, were conveyed from the Royal Hospital of Greenwich, where they had lain in state, in the Painted Hall, on the three preceding days, to the Admiralty.

Soon after ten o'clock in the morning, the several persons, appointed to attend the remains from Greenwich, assembled at the Governor's House within the Royal Hospital; and, at about one o'clock, proceeded in the barges according to the following order, viz.

FIRST BARGE, covered with black cloth.

Drums—two trumpets, with their banners in the steerage.

The Standard, at the head, borne by Captains Sir Francis Laforey, Bart. of the Spartiate, supported by Lieutenants William Collins Barker, and George Antram, of the Royal Navy.

The Guidon, at the door-place, borne by Captain Henry William Bayntum of the Leviathan, (in the absence, by indisposition, of Captain Durham,) supported by two Lieutenants of the Royal Navy, all in their full uniform coats, with black waistcoats, breeches, and stockings, and crape round their arms and hats.

Rouge Croix and Blue Mantle, Pursuivants of Arms, in close mourning, with their tabards over their cloaks, and hatbands and scarves.

SECOND BARGE, covered with black cloth.

Four trumpets in the steerage.

Heralds of Arms, habited as those in the first barge, bearing the Surcoat, Target, and Sword, Helm and Crest, and the Gauntlet and Spurs, of the Deceased.

The Banner of the Deceased, as a Knight of the Bath, at the head, borne by Captain Edward Rotherham, of the Royal Sovereign, supported by two Lieutenants of the Royal Navy.

The Great Banner, with the augmentations, at the door-place, borne by Captain Robert Moorsom, of the Revenge, supported by Lieutenants David Key's and Nicholas Tucker, of the Nassau, all habited as those in the first barge.

THIRD BARGE,

Covered with black velvet, the top adorned with plumes of black feathers; and in the centre, upon four shields of the arms of the Deceased joining in point, a Viscount's coronet. Three bannerolls of the family lineage of the Deceased, on each side, affixed to the external parts of the barge.

Six trumpets with the banners as before, in the steerage.

Six Officers of the Royal Navy, habited as those in the other barges; one to each banneroll, viz.

Lieutenant (now Captain) John Pasco.
Lieutenant (now Captain) John Yule.
Thomas Atkinson, Master of the Victory.
Lieutenant (now Captain) —— Williams.
Lieutenant George Browne.
Lieutenant James Uzuld Purches.

THE BODY,

Covered with a large sheet, and a pall of velvet adorned with six escutcheons.

Norroy King of Arms, (in the absence by indisposition, of Clarenceux,) habited as the other Officers of Arms, and bearing, at the head of the body, a Viscount's coronet upon a black velvet cushion.

At the head of the barge the Union Flag of the United Kingdom.

Attendants on the Body while at Greenwich, in mourning.

FOURTH BARGE, covered with black cloth.

The Chief Mourner, Sir Peter Parker, Bart., Admiral of the Fleet, with his two Supporters, Admiral Samuel Viscount Hood, and Admiral William Lord Radstock; six assistant Mourners, viz. Admirals Benjamin Caldwell, Sir Roger Curtis, Knt. and Bart., Richard Rodney Bligh, Sir Charles Morice Pole, Bart., and Vice-Admirals Charles Edmund Nugent and Charles Powell Hamilton; four Supporters of the pall, viz. Vice-Admirals James Hawkins Whitshead and Thomas Taylor, Admiral Sir John Orde, Bart. (in the absence, by indisposition, of Vice-Admiral Henry Savage, who had been nominated to this station,) and Rear-Admiral Eliab Harvy; six Supporters of the canopy, viz. Rear-Admirals Thomas Drury, Sir William Henry Douglas, Bart., Thomas Wells, Sir Isaac Coffin, Bart., John Aylmer, and William Domett; and the Train-bearer of the

Chief Mourner, the Honorable Henry Blackwood, of the Euryalus; all in mourning cloaks, over their respective full uniform coats, black waistcoats, breeches, and stockings, crape round their arms, and crape hatbands.

Windsor Herald, acting for Norroy King of Arms, habited as the other Officers of Arms.

The Banner of Emblems, at the door-place, borne by Captain Thomas Masterman Hardy, of the Victory, supported by Lieutenants Andrew King and George Miller Bligh, of the Royal Navy, habited as those in the other barges.

The Barges of His Majesty, and of the Lords Commissioners for executing the office of Lord High Admiral, followed, singly; and, immediately after, the Right Honourable the Lord Mayor in the City State Barge, followed by the barges of several of the Companies of the City of London, singly, according to their rank: their respective colours half-staff.

The Procession was attended by a considerable number of gun-boats and row-boats of the River Fencibles; and the Lord Mayor, in his character of Conservator of the river Thames, highly distinguished himself upon this occasion by his Lordship's judicious and unremitting attentions to their due arrangement and order.

As the Procession passed the Tower of London, minute guns were there fired. During the time of landing the body, and the several persons from the four mourning barges, at Whitehall stairs; the King's and Admiralty barges, and those of the Lord Mayor, and the City Companies, lay on their oars.

ORDER OF THE PROCESSION FROM WHITEHALL STAIRS TO THE ADMIRALTY, ON FOOT.

Drums and Trumpets.

Rouge Croix Pursuivant of Arms.

The Standard, borne by the Captain, and supported by the two Lieutenants before mentioned.

Trumpet.

Blue Mantle Pursuivant of Arms.

The Guidon, borne and supported as in the barge.

Two Trumpets.

Rouge Dragon Pursuivant of Arms.

The Banner of the deceased as a Knight of the Bath, borne and supported as in the Barge.

Two Trumpets.

Richmond Herald.

The Great Banner, borne and supported as in the barge.

Gauntlet and Spurs, borne by York Herald.

Helm and Crest, ——— Somerset Herald.

Sword and Target, ——— Lancaster Herald.

Surcoat, ——— Chester Herald.

Six Trumpets.

Norroy King of Arms, in the absence of Clarenceux, bearing the Coronet on a black velvet cushion.

Three Bannerolls of the Family Lineage of the Deceased, borne as before mentioned.	Two Supporters of the Pall.	THE BODY, Covered with a black velvet Pall, adorned with Escutcheons, under a Canopy supported by six Admirals.	Two Supporters of the Pall.	Three Bannerolls of the Family Lineage of the Deceased, borne as before mentioned.

Garter Principal King of Arms (absent, by indisposition).

Supporter, Adm. Lord Radstock.	THE CHIEF MOURNER, Sir Peter Parker, Bart. Admiral of the Fleet.	Supporter, Adm. Viscount Hood.

Train-Bearer,
Captain the Honourable Henry Blackwood.
The Six Admirals before named, Assistant Mourners.
Windsor Herald, acting for Norroy King of Arms.
The Banner of Emblems, borne and supported as in the barge.
Attendants on the Body while at Greenwich.

Upon arrival at the Admiralty, the Body was there deposited, privately, till the following day, and the persons who were in the Procession retired.

Early in the morning of Thursday the 9th instant, His Royal Highness the Prince of Wales, their Royal Highnesses the Dukes of the Blood Royal, with several of the great Officers, and the Nobility and Gentry, in their carriages; the relations of the Deceased, with the Officers and others of his household, the Officers of Arms, and a number of Naval Officers, in mourniag coaches, assembled in Hyde Park; having been admitted at Cumberland and Grosvenor Gates upon producing tickets issued from the College of Arms; and, having there been marshalled within the rails, proceeded, one by one, across Piccadilly, into St. James's Park, by the gate at the top of Constitution Hill, and onwards, through the Horse Guards, to the Admiralty, in the order in which they were to move in the Procession.

The Chief Mourner, with his Supporters and Train-bearer, and the several Naval Officers to whom duties were assigned in the solemnity, assembled at the Admiralty: the Seamen and Marines of the Victory, the Pensioners from Greenwich Hospital, the Watermen of the Deceased, the six Conductors, the Messenger of the College of Arms, and the Marshal's-Men, with the trumpets and drums, were stationed in the Admiralty Yard.

Those persons in the Procession, who were not to wear mourning cloaks, official gowns, or habits, appeared in mourning, without weepers, and with mourning swords; Knights of the several Orders wore their Collars; Naval and Military Officers were in their full uniforms, with crape around their arms and in their hats; the Naval Officers, to whom particular duties were assigned, had black cloth waistcoats and breeches, and black stockings; and the Clergy were in their clerical habits.

Servants not in mourning, attending the carriages, were admitted with silk or crape hatbands and gloves.

The Troops, ordered by His Majesty to attend at the Funeral, under the command of General Sir David Dundas, K. B., were assembled and formed by the several General Officers under whose command they respectively were, on the Parade in St. James's Park, before the Horse Guards, at half past eight o'clock in the morning. The whole fronted towards the Horse Guards, and were formed as follows, (the Infantry being three deep), viz. four Companies of Grenadiers, with their right near to the angle of the Treasury Building: four Companies of Light Infantry, in a line with the Grenadiers, and their right to the road leading through the Horse Guards: the second Brigade of Infantry, about 60 yards behind the Grenadiers, and their right to the Treasury Wall: the first Brigade of Infantry, about 60 yards behind the second, and parallel to it.

The Cavalry formed in one line behind the Infantry; their right to the sluice cover on the parade, and extending towards the end of the Mall, being parallel to the row of trees, which were close in their rear. The Artillery assembled, and formed fronting to the Treasury, with their right at the parade gun.

This disposition being made, the march began at twelve o'clock in the following order; the General Officers and their Staff at the head of their respective Brigades.

General Sir David Dundas, K. B. Lieutenant-General Harry Burrard

A Detachment of Light Dragoons.
Four Companies of Light Infantry.
The 92d Regiment } The 79th Regiment } Commanded by the Honourable Major-General Charles Hope.
The 31st Regiment } The 21st Regiment } Commanded by the Honourable Brigadier-General Robert Meade.
The 14th—2 Squadrons } The 10th—2 Squadrons } The 2d—2 Squadrons } Commanded by Major-General William St. Leger.
The Royal Artillery, with eleven pieces of cannon.
Four Companies of Grenadiers.

Each corps marched off, and followed in succession from its left. The Infantry marched in sections of six or seven files: the Cavalry four men in front: the Artillery and its carriages two a-breast: Officers of Infantry in front of the divisions, and not on the flanks.

As soon as the Troops had passed the Admiralty, the Procession moved in the following order:

Marshal's-Men, on foot, to clear the way.

Messenger of the College of Arms, in a mourning cloak with a Badge of the College on his shoulder, his Staff tipped with silver and furled with sarsnet.

Six Conductors, in mourning cloaks, with black staves headed with Viscounts' Coronets.

Forty-eight Pensioners from Greenwich Hospital, two and two, in mourning cloaks, with badges of the crest of the Deceased on the shoulders, and black staves in their hands.

Forty-eight Seamen and Marines of His Majesty's ship the Victory, two and two, in their ordinary dress, with black neck handkerchiefs and stockings, and crape in their hats.

Watermen of the Deceased, in black coats, with their Badges.

Drums and Fifes.

Drum-Major.

Trumpets.

Serjeant Trumpeter.

Rouge Croix, Pursuivant of Arms (alone in a mourning coach), in close mourning, with his Tabard over his cloak.

The Standard, borne in front of a mourning coach, in which were Captain Sir Francis Laforey, Bart. and his two Supporters, Lieutenants William Collins Barker and George Antram, of the Royal Navy.

Trumpets.

Blue Mantle, Pursuivant of Arms (alone in a mourning coach), habited as Rouge Croix.

The Guidon, borne in front of a mourning coach, in which were Captain Edward Rotherham, of the Royal Sovereign, supported by Lieutenants James Bradshaw and Thomas Errington, of the Royal Navy.

Servants of the Deceased, in mourning, in a mourning coach.

Officers of His Majesty's Wardrobe, in mourning coaches.

Gentlemen.

Esquires.

Deputations from the Great Commercial Companies of London.

Physicians of the Deceased, in a mourning coach.

Divines, in clerical habits.

Chaplains of the Deceased, in clerical habits, and Secretary of the Deceased, in a mourning coach.

Trumpets.

Rouge Dragon and Portcullis, Pursuivant of Arms (in a mourning coach), habited as before.

The Banner of the Deceased, as a Knight of the Bath, borne in front of a mourning coach, in which were Captain Philip Charles Durham, of the Defiance, supported by Lieutenants James Usuld Purches and James Poate, of the Royal Navy.

Attendants on the Body while it lay in State at Greenwich; viz. Reverend Alexander John Scott (Chaplain to His Royal Highness the Prince of Wales), Joseph Whidbey, Esquire, and John Tyson, Esquire, in a mourning coach.

Knights Bachelors.

Sergeants at Law.

Deputy to the Knight Marshal on horseback.

Knights of the Bath; viz.

Sir Samuel Hood and Sir Thomas Trigge.

Baronets.

A Gentleman Usher (in a mourning coach) carrying a carpet and black velvet cushion, whereon the Trophies were to be deposited in the Church.

William Haslewood, Esq.; Alexander Davison, Esq.; and William Marsh, Esq.; as Comptroller, Treasurer, and Steward of the Household of the Deceased (in a mourning coach), in mourning cloaks, bearing white Staves.

Younger Sons of Barons, viz.

Honourable Augustus Cavendish Bradshaw..

Honourable Richard Ryder, M. P. Honourable Charles James Fox, M. P.

Privy Counsellors, not Peers, viz.

Right Honourable Sir Evan Nepean, Baronet, M. P., and a Lord of the Admiralty.

Right Honourable George Tierney, M. P.

Right Honourable Sir William Scott, Knt. M. P. Judge of the Admiralty.

Right Honourable William Windham, M.P.

Younger Sons of Earls, viz.

Honourable Thomas William Fermor.

Honourable ——— Bennet. Honourable Alexander Murray.

Eldest Sons of Viscounts, viz.

Honourable Thomas Newcomen. Honourable Thomas Knox.

Honourable Henry Hood.

Barons.

Lord Hutchinson, K. B. Lord Donalley.

Lord de Blaquiere, K. B. Lord Holland.

Lord Aston.

Lord Mulgrave, one of His Majesty's Principal Secretaries of State. Lord Hawkesbury, one of His Majesty's Principal Secretaries of State.

Lord Bishop of Exeter.

Younger Sons of Marquisses; viz.

Lord Henry Moore. Lord Henry Petty.

Eldest Sons of Earls; viz.

Viscount Castlereagh, Viscount Duncannon.

One of His Majesty's Principal Secretaries of State.

Lord Delvin.

Viscount Fitzharris. Lord Hervey.

Lord Ossulston.

Viscount Kirkwall. Lord Fincastle.

Viscounts.

Viscount Sidmouth.

Viscount Hawarden. Viscount Gosford.

Viscount Chetwynd. Viscount Ranelagh.

Younger Son of a Duke.

Lord Archibald Hamilton.

Eldest Son of a Marquis.

Earl of Altamont,

Earls.

Earl of Clancarty. Earl of Moira.

Earl of Fife. Earl of Bessborough.

Earl of Darnley. Earl of Westmeath.

Earl of Leicester. Earl of Buckinghamshire.

Earl of Portsmouth, Earl Cowper.

Earl of Bristol. Earl of Scarborough.

Earl of Winchelsea, K. G. Earl of Suffolk.

Earl of Dartmouth, K. G., Lord Chamberlain of His Majesty's Household.

Eldest Sons of Dukes.

Marquis of Douglas.

Marquis of Blandford. Marquis of Hartington.

Dukes.

Duke of Montrose, K. T.

Duke of Devonshire, K. G. Duke of St. Albans.

Duke of Norfolk, Earl Marshal.

Earl Camden, K. G., Lord President of the Council.

Archbishop of Canterbury.

Dukes of the Blood Royal.

His Royal Highness the Duke of Cambridge.

His Royal Highness the Duke of Sussex,

His Royal Highness the Duke of Cumberland.

His Royal Highness the Duke of Kent.

His Royal Highness the Duke of Clarence.

His Royal Highness the Duke of York, Commander in Chief.

His Royal Highness the Prince of Wales.

Richmond Herald (alone in a mourning coach), habited as the other Officers of Arms.

The Great Banner, borne in front of a mourning coach, in which were Captain Robert Moorsom, and his Supporters, Lieutenants David Keys and Nicholas Tucker, of the Royal Navy.

Gauntlet and Spurs,
Helm and Crest,
Target and Sword,
Surcoat, } In front of four mourning coaches, in which were York, Somerset, Lancaster, and Chester Heralds, habited as before.

A mourning coach, in which the Coronet of the Deceased, on a black velvet cushion, was borne by Norroy King of Arms, in the absence of Clarenceux, habited as before, and attended by two Gentlemen Ushers.

The six Lieutenants of the Royal Navy, habited as before, who were to bear the Bannerolls, in two mourning coaches.

The six Admirals, in like habits, who were to bear the Canopy, in two mourning coaches.

The four Admirals, in like habits, who were to support the Pall in a mourning coach.

THE BODY,

Placed on a Funeral Car, or open Hearse, decorated with a carved imitation of the Head and Stern of His Majesty's Ship the Victory, surrounded with escutcheons of the Arms of the Deceased, and adorned with appropriate Mottoes and emblematical Devices; under an elevated Canopy, in the form of the upper part of an ancient Sarcophagus, with six sable Plumes, and the Coronet of a Viscount in the centre, supported by four columns, representing palm trees, with wreaths of natural laurel and cypress entwining the shafts; the whole upon a four-wheeled carriage, drawn by six led horses, the caparisons adorned with armorial escutcheons.

N. B. *The black velvet Pall, adorned with six Escutcheons of the Arms of the Deceased, and the six Bannerolls of the Family Lineage, were removed from the Hearse, in order to afford an unobstructed view of the Coffin containing the Remains of the gallant Admiral.*

Garter principal King of Arms, in his official habit, with his Sceptre, (in his carriage, his servants being in full mourning), attended by two Gentlemen Ushers.

THE CHIEF MOURNER,

In a mourning coach, with his two Supporters, and his Train-bearer, all in mourning cloaks.

Six assistant Mourners, (in two mourning coaches), in mourning cloaks as before.

Windsor Herald, acting for Norroy King of Arms, in a mourning coach, habited as the other Officers of Arms, and attended by two Gentlemen Ushers.

The Banner of Emblems in front of a mourning coach, in which were Captains Thomas Masterman Hardy and Henry William Bayntun, supported by Lieutenants Andrew King and George Miller Bligh, of the Royal Navy.

Relations of the Deceased, in mourning coaches.

Officers of the Navy and Army, according to their respective ranks, the seniors nearest the Body.

Within Temple Bar the Procession was received by the Right Honourable the Lord Mayor of London, attended by the Aldermen and Sheriffs, and the Deputation from the Common Council.

The six carriages of the Deputation from the Common Council fell into the Procession between the Deputation of the Great Commercial Companies of London and the Physicians of the Deceased, a Conductor on horseback being appointed to indicate the station.

The carriages of the Aldermen and Sheriffs fell into the Procession between the Knights Bachelors and the Sergeants at Law; a Conductor on horseback being also there stationed for the purpose, as before.

The Right Honourable the Lord Mayor, on horseback, bearing the City Sword, was marshalled and placed in the Procession between His Royal Highness the Prince of Wales and the Herald of Arms, who preceded the Great Banner, in obedience to a warrant under His Majesty's Royal Signet and Sign Manual, bearing date 6th instant, directing Garter Principal King of Arms to marshal and place the Lord Mayor of London, on the present occasion, in the same station wherein his Lordship would have been placed if His Majesty had been present.

When the head of the troops arrived at St. Paul's, the light companies entered within the railing, drew up, and remained. The rest of the column proceeded round St. Paul's, down Cheapside, along the Old Jewry and Coleman-Street, to Moorfields, round which they were formed and posted.

The Grenadiers quitted the column at St. Paul's, and entered within the railing. The Light Infantry lined each side of the space from the gate of the Church-yard to the door of the Church. The Grenadiers lined the great nave of the Church on each side, from the outer door to the place where the Body was deposited, and from thence to the door of the Choir. The two Corps (who had their arms reversed during the time of their remaining at St. Paul's,) formed two deep for that purpose; and the 2d Dragoons, in passing St. Paul's, left an Officer and twenty men, who formed up, and remained within the outer gate of the iron railing.

Upon arrival of the Procession at St. Paul's Cathedral, the six Conductors, forty-eight Pensioners from Greenwich Hospital, and forty-eight Seamen and Marines of the Victory, ascended the steps, divided and ranged on each side, without the great west door; and the rest of the Procession having alighted at the west gate of the Church-yard, entered the Church, and divided on either side, according to their ranks; those who had proceeded first remaining nearest the door. The Officers of Arms and the Bearers of the Banners, with their Supporters, entered the Choir, and stood within, near the door; and all above and including the rank of Knights Bachelors, as well as the Staff Officers, and the Naval Officers who attended the Procession, had seats assigned to them in the Choir. The Lord Mayor, with the Aldermen and Sheriffs, City Officers, and Deputation from the Common Council, occupied their seats on the north side of the Choir. Near the entrance of the Church, the Dean and Prebendaries, attended by the Choir, fell into the Procession immediately after the Great Banner, and before the Heralds who bore the Trophies; the Choir singing the Sentence in the Office for Burial, "I am the Resurrection and the Life," &c. with the two following Sentences, and continuing to sing until the Body was placed in the Choir.

The Body, having been taken from the Funeral Car, was borne into the Church and Choir according to the following order:

Richmond Herald.

Supporter,	THE GREAT BANNER,	Supporter,
Lieut. Nicholas Tucker.	borne by Capt. Robert Moorsom.	Lieut. David Keys.

The Gauntlet and Spurs, borne by York Herald.

Helm and Crest, ——— Somerset Herald.

Target and Sword, ——— Lancaster Herald.

Surcoat, ——— Chester Herald.

A Gentleman Usher. { The Coronet, on a black velvet cushion, borne by Norroy King of Arms, in the absence of Clarenceux. } A Gentleman Usher.

Three Bannerolls of the Family Lineage, borne by Lieutenant (now Captain) John Pasco.

Lieutenant (now Captain) John Yule.

Thos. Atkinson, Master.

All of the Victory.

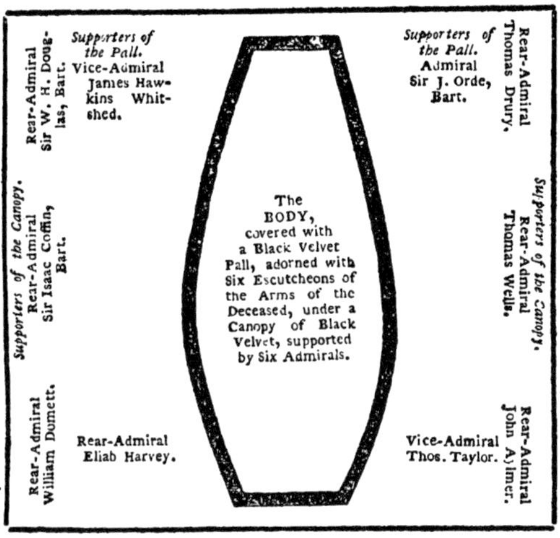

Three Bannerolls of the Family Lineage, borne by Lieutenant (now Captain) —— Williams.

Lieutenant George Browne.

Lieutenant —— Peake, (Royal Marines.)

All of the Victory.

A Gentleman Usher. Garter Principal King of Arms, (with his Sceptre.) A Gentleman Usher.

Supporter to the Chief Mourner, Admiral William Lord Radstock.	CHIEF MOURNER, Sir Peter Parker, Bart. Admiral of the Fleet.	Supporter to the Chief Mourner, Admiral Samuel Viscount Hood.

Six Assistant Mourners, viz.

Admiral Sir Roger Curtis, Knt. and Bart.	Admiral Caldwell.
Admiral Sir Charles Morice Pole, Bart.	Admiral Richard Rodney Bligh.
Vice-Admiral Charles Powell Hamilton.	Vice-Admiral Charles Edmund Nugent.

A Gentleman Usher. Windsor Herald, acting for Norroy King of Arms. A Gentleman Usher.

Supporter, Lieutenant George Miller Bligh.	The BANNER of EMBLEMS, borne by Captain Thomas Masterman Hardy, and Captain Henry William Bayntun.	Supporter, Lieutenant Andrew King.

Relations of the Deceased, viz.

Horatio Nelson, Esq. commonly called Viscount Merton, Nephew.	William Earl Nelson, sole Brother and Heir.
George Matcham, Esq. Nephew.	Thomas Bolton, Esq. Nephew.
George Matcham, Esq. Brother-in-Law.	Thomas Bolton, Esq. Brother-in-Law.

Reverend Robert Rolf,
Thomas Trench Berney, Esq.
Honorable Horatio Walpole,
Honorable George Walpole, } Cousins.

The Remainder of the Procession followed in the order as before marshalled.

The CHIEF MOURNER, his two Supporters and Train-bearer, were seated on chairs near the Body, on the side nearest the altar; and the six assistant Mourners, four Supporters of the Pall, and six Supporters of the Canopy, on stools on each side.

The Relations also near them in the Choir, and Garter was seated near the Chief Mourner.

The Body, when placed in the Choir, was not covered with the Pall, nor the Canopy borne over it; the rule in that respect being dispensed with, for the reason before mentioned. The Bannerolls were borne on each side the Body.

The Officers of the Navy, and the Staff Officers commanding the troops, were seated near the Altar.

The Carpet and Cushion (on which the Trophies were afterwards to be deposited,) were laid, by the Gentleman Usher who carried them, on a table placed near the grave, which was under the centre of the dome, and behind the place which was to be there occupied by the Chief Mourner.

The Coronet and Cushion borne by Norroy King of Arms, in the absence of Clarenceux, was laid on the Body.

During the service in the Choir, an anthem suitable to the occasion was sung; and, at the conclusion, a Procession was made from thence to the grave, with the Banners and Bannerolls as before; the Officers of Arms preceding with the Trophies; the Body borne and attended as before: the Choir singing "Man that is born of a Woman," &c. and the three following sentences. The Chief Mourner, with his Supporters, and, near them, Garter, had seats at the east end of the grave; the Train-bearer stood behind the Chief Mourner, and near him the Relations of the Deceased. At the opposite end sat the Right Reverend the Lord Bishop of Lincoln, Dean of the Cathedral, attended by three Canons Residentiaries. A Supporter of the Pall stood at each angle. The Assistant Mourners, Supporters of the Canopy, and Bearers of the Bannerolls, on either side. On the right of the Dean were the Chaplains; on the left, the Officers of the Household of the Deceased. The Great Banner was borne on the north, the Banner of the Deceased, as a Knight of the Bath, on the south of the grave; the Standard and Guidon behind the Dean; the Banner of Emblems behind the Chief Mourner; the Trophies in the angles.

Then the Dean read "Forasmuch as it hath pleased Almighty God," &c.: then the Choir sung part of an anthem "His Body is buried in peace; but his Name liveth evermore."

The service at the Interment being over, Garter proclaimed the style; and the Comptroller, Treasurer, and Steward of the Deceased, breaking their staves, delivered the pieces to Garter, who threw them into the grave.

Upon a signal given from St. Paul's that the Body was deposited, the Troops being drawn up in Moorfields, the Artillery fired their guns, and the Infantry gave vollies, by corps, three times repeated.

The interment ended, the Standard, Banners, Bannerolls, and Trophies, were deposited on the table behind the Chief Mourner; and all persons in the Procession retired.

During the whole of this solemn ceremony, the greatest order prevailed throughout the metropolis; and as the remains of the much-lamented Hero proceeded along, every possible testimony of sorrow and of respect was manifested by an immense concourse of spectators of all ranks. From the Admiralty to the Cathedral, the streets were lined with the several Volunteer Corps of London and Westminster, the Militia, and many other Military Bodies, both Cavalry and Infantry.

[To be continued.]

Naval Reform.

THE SIXTH REPORT OF THE COMMISSIONERS OF NAVAL INQUIRY.

[Continued from page 61.]

THE advantage of officers placed in situations of important public trust, being furnished with instructions for the general outline of their duty, is too obvious to need comment; and we cannot too strongly recommend a revision of the instructions to the officers of His Majesty's Yards, adapting them to the present extended scale of the naval service.

How many of the men who were superannuated by the Lords of the Admiralty, on their visitation in August 1802, were upon the list for superannuation; and how many were there on that list on the 1st of January preceding?—At the visitation there were sixty-eight; and on the 1st of January preceding there were twelve.

Was not the number placed on the list for superannuation between January and August 1802, an unusual increase in so short a period?—It was an unusual increase; but no more than ought actually to have been there: It arose from the investigation of the present Master Shipwright into the capability of the men to perform a day's work.

Whose duty is it to represent to the Navy Board the artificers and labourers who, from age and infirmities, may be incapable of performing their duty?—The Master Shipwright and Masters' Attendant, in their respective departments, give notes to the Clerk of the Check, desiring him to bear such men on the list for superannuation as they may think incapable of performing a day's work.

Has it ever been customary to muster the artificers and labourers in the presence of the officers of the yard, in order to see what men are fit for service, and who are objects for superannuation or discharge?—Never to my knowledge.

At what rate have the mastmakers of this yard been paid during the late war, and by what authority?—I cannot speak from my own knowledge; but on examining the books, I find they have been paid at the same rate of job and extra as the other shipwrights, and certified by a note from the Master Shipwright; but no particular specification, nor one article of work brought to an account that was performed by job.

What are the common working hours of this yard at different seasons of the year, which constitute a day's work?—The smiths, in the summer, from six in the morning to six in the evening; in the winter from six in the morning to bell-ringing at night: the other workmen, in summer from six in the morning to six in the evening; and in the winter from daylight in the morning till dark at night. From the 1st of November to the 1st of February, the workmen are allowed one hour for dinner; from the 2d of February to April one hour and an half; from the 23d of April to the 22d of August two hours; and from the 23d of August to the 31st of October one hour and an half.

Are they the same at all His Majesty's yards?—No, they are not; but I cannot state the different times of working in the several yards.

The inferior officers of the dock-yards have no instructions whatever for their guidance, but act immediately under the direction of their superior

---

Into what divisions of time was the extra worked by the artificers and labourers of the yard made, and what was the rate of pay for such divisions?—The extra was divided into nights and tides:—a night consisted of five hours, and a tide of an hour and an half; for the former they had a day's pay, and for the latter, rather less than the third of a day's pay; by which rule the smiths, riggers, and labourers, are still paid; but the smith's night consists only of three hours.

Is the whole of the time allowed for dinner taken into the extra?—When they work their dinner time, they are allowed the whole time; but when they stay their dinner time, and do not work, they are allowed half a tide.

When they are said to work their dinner time, are they not allowed a certain time for eating their dinners?—Yes, in general half an hour; but their dinners are brought to them in the yard.

What allowance have the artificers for sleeping on board His Majesty's ships?—One night extra, which is equal to a day's pay beyond what they work.

Do they receive lodging money when they sleep on board?—They receive their lodging money, which is twopence halfpenny a week, whether they sleep afloat or not.

Are they victualled at the King's expense during their stay on board?—Yes, they are.

Have men ever been paid the extra for sleeping on board ships when they have not done so?—Yes, it appeared it was so, upon an examination of the Navy Board in 1802, into a complaint against the foreman of the caulkers, in this yard, for including himself in the extra notes for sleeping afloat when he had not done so.

Has it been customary, when artificers have been sent on board ships in the Sound and Cawsand Bay, to send lists of them to the Captains, in order that they may be mustered, and that it may be known which of them are entitled to extra for sleeping on board, and which are not?—Since I have been here I have always done so.

What allowance have the artificers when they are working by the job on board His Majesty's ships, for the time lost in passing to and from the ships?—Lately they have had an allowance when the ships have lain in the harbour at a distance from the yard, of ninepence a day, on a certificate from the Master Shipwright; but they have had no allowance for the time lost in going into the Sound and Cawsand Bay.

Has it been customary for the artificers and labourers of this yard to receive two days' pay for one day's work, when employed only during the common working hours of the day?—Yes.

By what authority have they been so paid?—On the authority of the Navy Board's warrants of 5th June and 8th October 1802, and by notes or certificates made out by the Master Shipwright and Master Attendant.

Do you know when the order was first given by the Navy Board for allowing the artificers and labourers of the yard two days' pay for one day's work for working only in the common working hours of the day, which had previously entitled them only to one day's pay?—The Navy Board's warrant of the 7th October, 1794, authorizes the employment of the artificers and labourers of the yard two for one in the common working hours; but such as were not capable of working either by task or job, to be employed one or two tides by day work.

officers. It may be advanced, that the officer who is held generally responsible, should have the entire direction of his subordinates. In the

---

Has the work performed by job and task before the 8th of March, 1803, been a bonâ fide employment by job and task, and the men paid for the work they actually performed, or has it only been an ideal system to give the men more pay?—The work performed by task has, I believe, been a bonâ fide employment, and the men paid only for what they actually earned by the scheme for task. The work by job has in great measure been ideal, and the men so employed have been generally paid by a note from the Master Shipwright, desiring the men to be paid two for one by job in the single day hours, and one night extra after bell-ringing, instead of making out separate job notes for the works performed.

Has it been usual, when the shipwrights have been working two for one, and also two tides, and sometimes one night extra, to measure in the work performed in the whole time, as the work necessary to entitle them to two days' pay for one?—I understand, and the whole of the quartermen in the yard have certified, that all the work performed by the men from their coming into the yard to their going out, has been taken into the calculation of the work necessary to entitle them to the two for one in the common working hours; and no stint of work has been required for the extra allowed them.

When was such practice discovered?—Soon after Mr. Tucker's appointment as Master Shipwright.

Was it represented to the Navy Board, and by whom?—It was stated to the Navy Board by a general representation in March last, signed by all the officers and quartermen of the yard.

What orders were given by the Navy Board in consequence of such representation?—I think there has been no answer to the letter.

RICHARD PERING.

Charles M. Pole.
John Ford.
Henry Nicholls.

The Examination of Richard Pering, Esq.; continued on the 25th August, 1803.

Are the artificers and labourers of the yard ever mulcted of their pay, by whom, and under what circumstances?—They are mulcted of their pay for improper behaviour, neglect, or slighting their work, by the officer under whose direction they are employed, with the approbation of the Commissioner.

Have you reason to believe the schemes of prices for job and task work are fair and equitable, and that the artificers can earn, by equal exertion, as much when employed upon one article of job or task as another?—I have reason to believe the schemes of prices are very unequal, and that the men can earn considerably more upon some jobs than they can upon others.

How, and by whom, is the work performed by job or task ascertained?—The work performed by job is, in the first instance, collected by the quartermen and person superintending the work, who deliver an account of the quantity performed into the job office, where it is classed, rated, and brought under its respective heads; and such work as does not come within the schedule of prices, is valued by the Master Shipwright, and submitted to the Navy Board for their approbation.

Are the quartermen, who in the first instance give an account of the work performed to the job office, interested in the amount of the works given in as the executive branch of his business, we fully accord in this opinion; but as various accounts relating to the different classes of artificers, placed under

---

earnings of the people?—Yes, inasmuch as their own rate of pay is governed by the general earnings of their gangs.

Is there any class of persons in the yard who make out their own job notes, and value the works performed, or said to be performed, by them?—I believe there are; the leading men of the blockmakers, braziers, plumbers, and coopers, make out and sign their own notes, which are afterwards countersigned by the Master Shipwright, and sent to the Navy Board for their approbation.

Do you think a fair estimate can possibly be made of such men's work by job? —It is impossible.

Are men appointed quartermen who cannot write?—I cannot positively speak to it.

With whom does the job note originate?—It is made out in the job office, under the immediate direction of the Master Shipwright.

What is the establishment of the job office in the yard?—There is no actual establishment of a job office; but there is a place where reduced quartermen and shipwrights, who have been heretofore employed in making out job notes, are employed for that purpose.

Are the men employed in making out the job notes interested in the amount of the work therein stated to be performed?—Yes, inasmuch as they are paid in proportion to the general earnings of the companies in which they are borne.

Do you not conceive, from the quartermen who first deliver in an account of the work said to be performed by their gangs, and from the people employed in the job office, being all interested in the amount of the earnings of the shipwrights, that the working by job is thereby rendered very liable to abuse? —Yes.

By whom are the job notes directed to be signed?—By the Master Shipwright, and the Assistant and Foreman, who superintend the work, and the Master Workmen in their respective departments; but the Master Shipwright at present signs only to the value of the work, and the Assistant and Foreman sign the certificate of the work having been actually performed.

Do you apprehend that all the persons who certify the works stated in job notes to have been performed, actually measure and inspect such work?—They do not, I believe.

Are not the artificers so frequently broken off, by docking of ships, and other circumstances, as to render it very difficult, if not impossible, to pay them for their labour by job?—Yes.

Is not the present system of employing all the artificers in this yard by job or task so complicated, and the schemes of prices for the different works so incomplete, as to be likely to produce much inconvenience and expense to the public service?

Very considerable expense and inconvenience is likely to result from the mode of employing artificers by job; the difficulty of ascertaining the exact amount of wages, from the numerous jobs they are liable to be put on in the course of a quarter, and the various rates of wages of persons working in each gang, and the deduction of lost time of the different individuals, make it so extremely complicated, that it is almost impossible to cast the wages correctly.

RICHARD PERING.

Charles M. Pole.
John Ford.
Henry Nicholls.

the superintendence of these inferior officers or master workmen, are kept and rendered by them, for which they alone can in fact be held responsible, we are of opinion, that they also should have instructions for their guidance, as their present means of gaining information of the regulations of the Board on these subjects are very precarious and imperfect.

The Examination of Richard Pering, Esq.; continued upon Oath the 26th August, 1803.

What allowance have the artificers and labourers of the yard for working on Sundays?—They are allowed an extra day's pay, for which no work is required from them.

What classes of persons in the yard are now allowed apprentices?—Quartermen of shipwrights and caulkers, and the foremen of the different branches who have not fixed annual salaries, have apprentices by virtue of their offices: they were formerly allowed one servant each, and received for him the general extra pay of the gang in which he was borne, but they are now allowed two servants, who are borne at single day's pay only. Apprentices have likewise been granted by the Navy Board, as an indulgence to the most deserving of the artificers; but by a late regulation, they are not to be bound to the individuals, but to the Master Shipwright, by whom they are to be allotted to the most deserving of the artificers, to be instructed in their professions.

Who receives the pay of the apprentices?—Two-thirds of it are paid to the Master or person to whom they may be allotted by the Master Shipwright, and the other third to the parents or guardians of the boy, to maintain him, and find him tools.

Have you all the documents now in your possession, to enable you to make out the pay books of the yard for the quarter ending 30th June last?—No, I have not. The job notes for that quarter, for work for which no prices are set in the general scheme of job, not having been as yet completed and sent to the Navy Board for their approval.

Has the payment of the yard ever been, or is it likely to be, deferred beyond the usual time of payment, in consequence of the alteration in ascertaining the earnings of the men by job?—It was deferred in the last quarter about three weeks; on the day the payment became due, the whole of the job notes were not returned from the Navy Board. It is likely to be deferred longer in the ensuing quarter, although additional assistance has been granted to me by the Navy Board, to assist in casting the earnings of the men by the job notes.

RICHARD PERING.

Charles M. Pole.
John Ford.
Henry Nicholls.

Alterations made by desire of this Examinant, the 15th day of February, 1804, in his Evidence of the 24th of August, 1803.

(a) Job notes for the shipwrights were first sent to my office in Lady Quarter, 1802, and not in Christmas Quarter; and it was in the months of September, October, November, and December, 1802, that the earnings of the men fell short of two for one, and that they were so set off on the books; but afterwards paid at the rate of two for one by the Navy Board's warrant of the 7th April, 1803.

RICHARD PERING.

NAVAL HISTORY OF THE PRESENT YEAR, 1806.

(January—February.)

RETROSPECTIVE AND MISCELLANEOUS.

RESPECTING the death of our illustrious Statesman, Mr. Pitt, we never had but one opinion; and this the events, which have succeeded, have fully justified. We considered that his death, at this momentous crisis, might tend to produce an union between the opposite and leading Characters of both Houses of Parliament, and might form a Ministry that should be highly respectable both for talent, and for high political connections. Such a Ministry has been at length formed; and what renders it doubly acceptable to the country, is the knowledge, that the whole arrangement has been made to the satisfaction of our aged and beloved Monarch.

We are credibly informed, that on the day previous to his lamented death, Mr. Pitt wrote a letter to the King, in which he recommended Lord Grenville to His Majesty, as a fit and proper person to form and be placed at the head of a new Administration.

Mr. Grey, the eldest son of Lord Grey, as First Lord of the Admiralty, displays a character of undoubted integrity, without prejudice, and without ostentation. During the period of his education at Eton, his abilities were universally acknowledged: and the Profession at large has every thing to hope from the independence of his mind, and the sincerity of his character. His brother, Captain George Grey, who long served under Earl St. Vincent, is at present Commissioner at Sheerness. The following observations on Mr. Grey's appointment appeared in the Courier:—

"The appointment of Mr. Grey as First Lord of the Admiralty, is one at which we look with very considerable apprehension. Mr. Grey is a man of as high honour, of integrity as spotless, as any man in the kingdom. He is the last man in the world to do a mean thing, or to take a step which his conscience does not commend. But he is a man of a petulant, capricious temper; easily led, harsh, precipitate, and imperious: he trusts too much to his conscious rectitude, acting hastily, and with a high hand, because he feels himself strong in the honesty of his intentions. We must admire the feelings of such a man, but we cannot trust much to his prudence. Believing himself right, he regards other men as in the wrong, and he proceeds as if his own judgment were infallible. Of all men in the world this is the last for a reformer, especially a reformer of our Naval System, which should be touched with great delicacy. We would rather have seen Lord St. Vincent again First Lord of the Admiralty, than Mr. Grey. This Gentleman is avowedly placed at the head of that great Department, to carry Lord St. Vincent's plans into effect; and the strong, the old family friendship and connexion that has existed between them, leaves no doubt that Mr. Grey will be completely in his Lordship's hands. Admiral Markham, Lord St. Vincent's particular partizan, is to be one of the Lords of the Admiralty, and Mr. Grey's chief adviser. Lord St. Vincent had rendered himself very unpopular by his conduct when in office; and had he again been appointed, he would have been compelled to proceed with great caution; but Mr. Grey, unknown to the Navy, is known only to the public as a Gentleman of very high character and pure intentions. Such a man will be able to urge bad measures, should Lord St. Vincent prevail on him to adopt such, with more authority than Lord St. Vincent himself could. The St. Vincent system will be stronger in Mr. Grey's hands than in those of Lord St. Vincent. That this system should be revived is surprising, when we recollect how much it was execrated by what was called the new Opposition, by Lords Grenville and Spencer, and particularly by Mr. Windham, in whose Weekly Journal, the most gross and incessant abuse of Lord St. Vincent and his conduct, as First Lord of the Admiralty, appeared. We believe indeed that the design of the new Opposition at that time was merely to shake the Addington Ministry, of which Lord St. Vincent was a main prop; but this they cannot avow, though by reviving the system now they do in fact avow it. There is another point on which Mr. Grey has shown himself well qualified for the St. Vincent system, and that is the prosecution of the press. At the time Lord St. Vincent was at the head of the Admiralty, the lawyers' desks groaned under the load of briefs in prosecution for libels on his Lordship; and we all know how rashly Mr. Grey took up the prosecution against the Oracle last spring. He has heard from his own friends so much on that subject, that it is unnecessary we should say more, than just remind the public, that Mr. Grey will be quite as likely as Lord St. Vincent to put down with a strong hand any thing that may be published against his measures. We are extremely sorry that Lord Spencer was not appointed First Lord of the Admiralty, and we know so are the Navy and the public. His Lordship gave the highest satisfaction both to our Navy and the commercial world. From a coalition Ministry the country reckoned on the benefit of his services at least at the head of the Admiralty; but cruel must be the disappointment when they find, that instead of the Spencer they are to have the St. Vincent system. Lord Spencer, it is well known, disapproved highly of Lord St. Vincent's conduct, and we supposed he declined accepting the Admiralty, when he found that the St. Vincent system was to be revived by order of Mr. Fox. " Why is the command to be taken from Admiral Cornwallis, who has proved himself so worthy of it? Do the new ministers mean to begin by dismissing officers of great and experienced talents?—The services of Admiral Cornwallis will, we trust, be remunerated by a Peerage.

The *Tom Thumb* egotism, and impudent Bulletins of the Corsican Usurper, continues. almost without a parallel in history. He however informs his Soldiers, that they shall have a Dance, or rather Grand Festival, together, on their return; when *they shall see him surrounded with all that grandeur and splendour, which becomes the Sovereign of the first Nation in the World.* He takes no notice of the glorious victory of Trafalgar, but tells his soldiers, that *the English are skulking behind their dirty Channel:* and in a note, which has been circulated from some of his travelling printing presses, he informs his slaves—Frenchmen! your Emperor has conquered Austria, humbled Russia, silenced Prussia....England still dares to resist, but her resistance is the struggle of death, she is breathing her last....Without the permission of the Emperor of the French, a vessel shall no more dare to sail, than a fort to be built, or a cannon fired.

The noble minded Spaniards, who behaved with such true Castilian liberality after the action off Trafalgar, and were so much struck with the heroism of our countrymen, are made, by *the Prince of the Peace*, and the French emissaries, to hold the following language, in the Supplement to the Madrid Gazette, of November 29, 1805; which is entitled, *An Exhortation in behalf of the poor Widows and Orphans of the Defenders of their Country, who fell in the Bay of Cadiz on the 21st of October*......" O beloved countrymen! who have survived the glorious catastrophe of the 21st of October! to you the nation commits the task of redressing its wrongs, and avenging the victims sacrificed in that dreadful combat. It has been handed down from age to age, and the most remote posterity will look back, with pleasing admiration, on that patriotism and celerity wherewith, a few years after the destruction of the grand Armada fitted out by our King D. Philip II, all good Spaniards contributed to that formidable fleet, which covered the Spanish marine with glory, at the battle of Lepanto....Gifts of the greatest and of the smallest denomination facilitated the exertions of the Government; and even the poorest day labourers presented, with pleasure, some of them hemp and timber, some of them tar, and other productions of the sweat of their brow. The artisans deposited in their arsenals, nails, cordage, sails, and all the other articles requisite for the equipment of the new fleet. Every heart concurred in a happy patriotic co-operation, and even the poorest was able to make some small offering in order to invigorate the springs of the common weal.

" Never did SPAIN glow with more ardent transports of patriotism than at this moment. All! All to a man, are anxious to contribute to the common welfare, the national glory, and to frustrate the unjust aggressions of our enemies. Let there revive in one and all of us our immemorial and never failing constancy in bearing up against unavoidable reverses; and speedily we shall see our efforts crowned with glory and success, against *a people who are the destroyers of our happiness.* Every class of the nation feels an interest in it, and in co-operating in every thing which can add to the vigour of our royal marine. This constitutes the support of our mercantile marine........

" Our government in its wisdom is alive to all these considerations. Penetrated with the conviction, that Spain ought to be a power essentially maritime, it has issued fresh orders, and made the most effectual dispositions for equipping, with all possible expedition, a *respectable naval force;* which will continue to show itself more and more terrible to our enemies, until we have obtained the most glorious and decided triumphs by means of that valour, which is characteristic of such heroic defenders as have recently asserted the national honour, with the loss, it is true, of many lives, but with a much more copious effusion of the blood of our enemies, and in a battle much more glorious to the Spaniards than the English; who will have many occasions of learning to their cost, what our nation is capable of achieving, and that every Spaniard is an undaunted lion, who will brave every danger in gratifying the noble impulses of a just patriotic revenge......

A letter from a fore-mast-man, named James West, on board the Britannia, of a late date, gives a very good account, in a humble stile, of the memorable battle of Trafalgar. The following short extract from West's letter, is a proof of the warm work that took place on board the Britannia:—" I am sorry to inform you I am wounded in the left shoulder, and that William Hillman was killed at the same time. The shot that killed him and three others, wounded me and five more!—Another of my messmates, Thomas Crosby, was also killed; they both went to their guns like men, and died close to me. Crosby was shot in three places. Pray inform their poor friends of their death, and remind them that they died at the same time as Nelson, and in the moment of glorious victory!—Remember me to all my relations and friends, tell them I am wounded at last, but that I do not much mind it, for I had my satisfaction of my enemies, as I never fired my gun in pain; I was sure to hit them; I killed and wounded them in plenty. Should have written you sooner, but the pain in my shoulder would not let me."

Letters on Service,

Copied verbatim from the LONDON GAZETTE.

[Continued from page 75.]

ADMIRALTY-OFFICE, FEB. 1, 1806.

Copy of a Letter from the Rt. Hon. Lord Keith, K. B., Admiral of the White, &c., to Wm. Marsden, Esq.; dated on board the Edgar, off Ramsgate, the 30th January, 1806.

SIR,

I TRANSMIT, for their lordships' information, a copy of a letter from Lieutenant Smithies, commanding the Bruizer gun-vessel, to Vice-Admiral Holloway, reporting the capture of the French lugger privateer l'Impromptu, one of the enemy's cruisers, by which the trade in the narrow part of the Channel has of late been much annoyed. I have the honour to be, &c.

KEITH.

His Majesty's Brig, Bruizer,
Downs, Jan. 30, 1806.

SIR,

I have the honour to acquaint you, for the information of the Commander-in-Chief, that outstanding close in with the high land, near Folkstone, yesterday morning about two o'clock (being hazy), a lugger was observed hovering about with an intent (as I have been since informed) to board, but on finding her mistake, and His Majesty's brig bearing up, made all sail; she was captured after a chase of seven hours, during which they hove most of their gun-carriages, stores, and provisions overboard. She proves to be l'Impromptu French privateer, of Boulogne (last from Calais), commanded by Jacques Sauvage, with a complement of fifty men, fifteen guns, two only of which were mounted when captured; and she is a remarkable fine vessel; and, I am informed, the best sailer from that port; might have been a great annoyance to the trade. Last week she captured two brigs, the Mary of Pool, laden with coals; and the Caroline of Yarmouth, lade with barley. I am, &c.

T. SMITHIES, Lieut.

P. S. On coming up with the chase, the Combatant, Captain Kerr, joined company, and took out part of the prisoners.

John Holloway, Esq., Vice-Admiral
of the Red, &c.

Copy of a Letter from Vice-Admiral Lord Collingwood, Commander-in-Chief of His Majesty's Ships and Vessels in the Mediterranean, to Wm. Marsden, Esq.; dated on board His Majesty's Ship Queen, off Cadiz, the 8th January, 1806.

SIR,

I enclose, for the information of the Lords Commissioners of the Admiralty, a return of vessels captured and detained by His Majesty's ships and vessels under my command, to the 31st ultimo. I am, &c.

COLLINGWOOD.

A Report of Vessels captured and detained by the Ships and Vessels on the Mediterranean Station, under the Command of the Rt. Hon. Cuthbert Lord Collingwood, Vice-Admiral of the Blue, and Commander-in-Chief, between the 19th day of November, 1805, and the 31st day of December following.

Spanish settee St. Christo del Troa, of 14 men, and 40 tons, from la Guyra bound to Cadiz, laden with indigo, cocoa, &c.; captured by the Donnegal, &c. Nov. 19, 1805,

Ragusan ship Nemesis, of 4 guns, 18 men, and 350 tons, from the Isle of France bound to Leghorn, laden with spice, indigo, &c.; detained by the Thunderer, &c. November 25, 1805.

Spanish settee l'Avion, of 1 gun, 18 men, and 54 tons, from Cadiz bound to la Guyra, laden with Spanish wine, &c.; captured by the Martin and Bittern, Dec. 4, 1805.

Spanish brig el Baptista, 2 guns and 19 men, from Cadiz bound to la Guyra, laden with Spanish wine, &c.; captured by the Neptune, &c. December 5, 1805.

American ship Wells, of 11 men and 205 tons, from Salem bound to Marseilles, laden with sugar and coffee; detained by the Naiad, September 10, 1805.

COLLINGWOOD.

N. B. The Naiad's report of vessels detained was not received until this day.

TRIAL

OF

VICE-ADMIRAL SIR ROBERT CALDER, Bart.

[Continued from page 86.]

THIRD DAY, DEC. 25.

THE Court met this day at ten o'clock, and Sir Robert Calder having been called in, addressed the Court, and presenting a scroll, said, "Mr. President, and Gentlemen of the Court, I beg leave to deliver this as my defence, and to request your permission that a friend of mine may read it."

The President replied, "Most assuredly."

Mr. Gazelee, Sir Robert's official adviser, then read nearly as follows:— Mr. President, and Gentlemen of this Honourable Court, I appear before you in a singular, and, I may say, in almost an unprecedented situation, having served my King and Country, not only without reproach, but with honour and reputation, for a period of upwards of 46 years, (47 years! exclaimed Sir Robert Calder), during which I have been more than once honoured with distinguished marks of approbation; and, within the last six months, have, with an inferior fleet, forced into action the combined fleets of the enemy, and captured two of their line-of-battle ships. Notwithstanding these circumstances, I have found myself under the painful necessity of demanding a Naval Court of Inquiry upon my conduct, in order that I might defend my character from the aspersions which have been cast upon it, in consequence of my not renewing the action with the combined squadrons of France and Spain, after the second day from the action. The consciousness of having done my duty to my country would have been alone sufficient to have induced me to treat those aspersions with contempt, if their circulation had not been so general, that my silence must have been construed into an admission of their truth. It was therefore that I found myself under the indispensable necessity of applying to the Lords of the Admiralty, in order that I might be enabled to refute the aspersions against my character and fame. To this their Lordships assented, and, although in a subsequent letter I requested that the Court should be invested with the power of inquiring into the whole of my conduct, they have thought it right to confine the Inquiry entirely to the proceedings of the 23d July, and to my not taking and destroying every ship of the enemy, which the charge asserts it was my duty to do. I consider this, therefore, as a declaration on the part of their Lordships, that my not renewing the engagement with the enemy on the 23d, is the only part of my conduct to which any doubt attaches. At the same time, I cannot but lament that the inquiry should have been so limited as it is, for it prevents me from giving evidence of the action of the 22d; an action which, I am proud to say, added to the glory of the British Navy. I trust I shall satisfy the Court that my not renewing the engagement was, under all the circumstances, the most proper course to be adopted, and that the attempting to renew the action might have endangered my own fleet, and with it the safety of the country. I shall lay before the Court the situation in which I was placed, the orders I had received, and the reasons by which I was actuated, confident that the aspersions, of which I have been so long the object, will be dissipated, and I shall be restored with unsullied honour to that country for which I have bled and conquered. Permit me, Mr. President and Gentlemen, to make a few observations on the specific charge. It does not, strictly speaking, range itself within any of the articles of war. It assumes, that it was my duty to take and destroy every ship of the enemy. I admit that it is so much the duty of every officer, that it is incumbent on him to exert himself to his utmost means to destroy every ship of the enemy; but it is not necessary for me to prove the physical possibility of destroying them. There may be many reasons which would render the attempt rash and imprudent: those reasons must be so obvious to the Court, that it would be unnecessary to state them. Permit me, however, to observe, that mine is not the only instance where a British fleet has been lying in sight of the enemy without renewing the fight. I may name two gallant officers, who, after brilliant victories, did not think themselves justified in bringing the enemy to battle again—I mean Earl Howe in 1794, and Earl St. Vincent in 1797. Of the latter I can speak from my own personal knowledge, having served under him in that engagement. Of the propriety of the conduct of those brave officers upon each occasion, no doubt has ever been entertained. They exercised a sound discretion, acting to the best of their judgment for the advantage of the country. But it may not be improper to remark, that mine was a situation in which it was more peculiarly necessary to exercise that discretion which an officer is supposed to possess, and by which he is to determine the propriety of offering battle to a superior fleet. Upon the two memorable occasions to which I have referred, there was no apprehension of attack from any other quarter. I, on the contrary, found myself under the necessity of being on my guard against the Ferrol and Rochefort squadrons, consisting of not less than twenty-one sail of the line, one of which was at sea, and the other on the point of sailing. I will trouble the Court with a short statement of the facts. In February last I was dispatched by Lord Cornwallis to blockade the roads of Ferrol and Corunna. Besides a French squadron of five sail of the line, afterwards increased to nine sail of the line, there were several frigates then at sea. I applied to the Admiralty for two frigates and some small ships to place at the mouth of the harbour, but I was only able to obtain one frigate. I do not impute any blame to the Admiralty on this account; I well know that at that time they had abundant means of applying all the force they could collect. I am not accusing the Admiralty, I am defending myself, and the sole object is, that the Court may be aware of the situation in which I was placed. With my small force I kept my station, and forwarded the information I received to the Commander in Chief, Lord Cornwallis. The Toulon and Cadiz fleet joined. My situation now became so dangerous, that Lord Gardner desired me to join him. At this time the combined squadrons, which had gone to the West Indies, were on their return, and I was directed to be upon my guard against them. The preparations at Ferrol continued. I received information that a French Admiral at Paris was ordered to proceed to Ferrol, to relieve the Admiral, and to push to sea; and the report made to me by Captain Prouse agreed with this, so far as respected the intention of the squadron to sail. I also received information that the ships had actually began to move. In addition to this, I learnt that the enemy had erected signal posts along the coast, in order that the combined squadron, on its return, might, by sending in a small frigate, communicate their arrival to the ships at Ferrol, and direct them to push out.

Admiral Cornwallis, who had joined me, directed me to proceed 40 leagues to the N.W. of Cape Finisterre, and cruise six or eight days, in order to intercept the French and Spanish squadron, which he never supposed amounted to more than 16 sail of the line; after which I was to return to my post off Ferrol. This order was brought me on the 15th of July, on which day Admiral Stirling joined me, and we proceeded to cruise as the order directed. At that time there were nine sail of the line in Rochefort ready; and the evidence of Admiral Stirling has proved that they had sailed on the 18th. The wind was quite fair for the enemy to get out of Ferrol; the wind continued fair two or three days for that purpose, and if they took the advantage of it, they might have got from thence.—They might have sailed from Ferrol on the 24th; for though the wind was N.W. on the 23d, it was N.N.E. on the 24th. But I shall place this out of all doubt, by putting in the charts, by which it will be seen what winds would bring the squadron out of Ferrol; besides, the Court will not fail to recollect that there are frequent land winds on that part of the coast, by which they might have pushed out. These observations are only material, as they enable the Court to judge of my apprehensions that the Ferrol squadron might actually be at sea. I received an order from Lord Nelson, directed to the commanding officers in the Tagus, acquainting them, that the combined squadron had passed Antigua on their way to Europe. On the 22d of July they came in sight, twenty sail of the line, seven frigates, and two armed brigs; a much greater force than I expected them to consist of. It appears, that when they were seen off the Diamond Rock, they were only 16 sail. The force under my command amounted only to 15 sail of the line, two frigates, and two cutters. Notwithstanding this great difference in point of strength, I forced them to action:—the general result you are acquainted with. As it is not the object of inquiry, it is not necessary to take up your time by entering into it. I have never heard of any disapprobation expressed by any one as to the mode of carrying the fleet into action. The victory was decidedly ours. I have only to lament that the state of the weather prevented its being more complete. As it was, there are but few instances in which an equal number of British ships, against a superior force, have been so successful. The firing did not cease till nine o'clock; and though it has been said, by those who are unacquainted with the subject, that it might have been longer continued yet you well know, that in the latitude in which the action was fought, it is completely dark at that hour. At the time the firing ceased, the enemy were at long cannon shot. I had hailed the Windsor Castle, and desired Captain Boyle to get a mast up. He said he was afraid he could not. I said I should keep on the same tack all night, which I did, keeping the squadron between the Windsor Castle and the prizes. During the night my ship was employed in repairing the damages, the other ships were similarly employed; and being unacquainted with the state of the damages, I did flatter myself that I should be able next morning to renew the action, and I did endeavour to keep as near the enemy as I could, the captured ships not being able to keep up with the squadron, and I sent the Frisk and the Nile to take the accounts of the damages. At day-break the accounts were laid before me, and I found the damages much more considerable than I expected. I was eight or nine miles to leeward, with the Malta and Thunderer out of sight. At eight o'clock we saw the Malta, frigates, and prizes to leeward, and the Windsor Castle in tow of the Dragon. Observing that the Malta appeared to have one of the prizes in tow, I ordered her to quit her, and join me. The enemy at this time were in a body, and apparently had not materially suffered in their masts; on the contrary, on examining the accounts of the damages, I found, that of my fifteen ships, although the Windsor Castle was the only one that answered my signal in the affirmative, when I asked who wanted to lie by to refit, yet that there was not one of them in a state to carry sufficient sail to take them to windward, particularly as there was a heavy swell. That my judgment was correct requires no other proof than that early in the morning the Barfleur sprung her yard; that a few hours only after, the Repulse sprung her bowsprit. This affords a specimen of what might have been expected if the other ships had carried that sail which was necessary to enable them to come up with the enemy. It has been proved by Captain Inman, that when I desired him to drive away a frigate that was reconnoitring us, he was apprehensive of his masts going by the board, though he did not think it a time to make a signal of inability. Another consequence of attempting to renew the action would have been the capture of the Windsor Castle and the prizes; for, independent of the Rochefort squadron, the enemy had ships on the weather bow, to take advantage of those ships that separated from our squadron. By pursuing that line of conduct which I did, I preserved the victory I had gained, in defiance of the hostile squadrons. Had I attempted to renew the engagement, I should have sustained a loss in the want of frigates. The advantages of having frigates and light ships upon such an occasion are so well known to you, that it would be superfluous in me to point them out. Permit me to say a word or two on the subject of the superiority of the enemy in point of numbers. I am far from encouraging the idea that an engagement ought not to be risked where the enemy are superior. I know the gallantry, bravery, and heroic spirit of British sailors too well to entertain such a thought for a moment. My own conduct, I trust, sufficiently proves that I am influenced by no such sentiment; but I deprecate the idea that an engagement must be continued by a Commanding Officer as long as he can continue it, even though he should put at hazard the advantages he has before gained. I maintain, that to encourage such an idea, would one day prove fatal to the Officers, and dangerous to the country. The necessity of continuing an engagement must always depend on its own circumstances, and the discretion of the Officer who commands, subject to that responsibility which attaches to the situation in which he is placed. Circumstanced as I was, it appeared to me to be impracticable to force the enemy to action with such advantage as would justify me, even if I had nothing to apprehend but the opposing squadron. But when I reflected, that sixteen sail were at Ferrol, who might have come out to the assistance of the combined fleet, or that the blockade of Ferrol being no longer continued, they might be pushing to England, the invasion of which was an event daily expected, I felt, that by renewing the action I should run too great a hazard, and put my fleet in a state of danger, which I could not have been justified for doing. I therefore thought it best to keep my squadron together, and not to force the enemy to a second engagement, till a more favourable opportunity. At the same time, conceiving that their object was to join the ships at Ferrol, I determined to prevent them; I kept within them and Ferrol, and also kept between them and the Windsor Castle, meaning, if I found an opportunity, to attack them afterwards. That this was my determination, will be proved by a witness, to whom I communicated my having formed this resolution. I will prove that I acted upon it during the two days, keeping the squadron in sight, and never avoiding an engagement with the enemy—on the contrary, whenever the enemy showed a disposition to engage, I held my wind, and, no doubt, if they had persevered, they would have met with a proper reception—if ever they did entertain any such intention, they abandoned it.—During the whole of the 23d the enemy had the wind, and at the close of the day they were at a distance of four leagues. At day-break on the 24th, the enemy's fleet were six leagues to the West, and to be seen only from the mast-head; the wind was in our favour, though but very light breezes, and I doubt whether I could have overtaken them—certainly I could not, without separating the squadron, and as they would not renew the action when the wind was in their favour, I could hardly expect that they would when it was in ours. I could not have prevented them from making signals to the fleet at Ferrol. I therefore did not think the opportunity afforded of overtaking them by the state of the wind sufficient ground to induce me to alter my opinion. At six o'clock they were entirely out of sight; on the 25th we continued our course East and by North, and having accompanied the Windsor Castle and prizes so far to the North, that I thought them safe from the combined as well as the Rochefort squadron, I parted, and said I should go back to Cape Finisterre, in hopes of seeing Lord Nelson; if I did not, that I should proceed off Ferrol, to see if any favourable opportunity should offer of attacking the enemy to advantage. I arrived at the place of rendezvous previously directed by the Commander in Chief, but did not find Lord Nelson. At length the combined squadrons were enabled to get into Ferrol and Corunna, and I joined the Commander in Chief off Ushant. I have thus given a faithful narrative of my proceedings until my joining in the North Seas, a period of 5 months, during which I was perpetually at sea; and here, having trespassed so much on your patience, my narrative might close; but the Court will, I trust, permit me to add one fact, as it will show that the Commander in Chief approved my conduct, and that he expressed his approbation, which certainly he would not have done if he had thought I had ill discharged my trust. He had before that transmitted to me the approbation of the Admiralty of my conduct, and only four days afterwards he put under my command twenty sail, desiring me to cruise in search of the combined fleet, and to use my utmost endeavours to intercept them. I immediately sailed in pursuance of his order. The combined squadron had left Ferrol, and I was in time to enable Admiral Collingwood to secure them in Cadiz. At this time nothing of blame had reached my ears. Thinking that I had well and successfully exerted myself in the service of my country, it did not suggest itself to my mind that any fault could be found with me. The congratulations I received were flattering. The Court are in possession of the letter which I received from the Admiralty, and the approbation expressed by the Commander in Chief. The latter was the most solid proof that could be given of the manner in which his orders had been executed; and I flattered myself that I should have been honoured by my Sovereign, and that my brave associates would have had the reward they had so well merited. The Court will judge what were my feelings, what my disappointment, to find myself traduced and falsified in the newspapers. Even the most moderate accused me of playing with the feelings of the public. I felt that the manner of publishing the account of the victory in the Gazette might have given occasion for the aspersions against me; for you will observe, that instead of being published as an extract of my dispatch, it was published as a copy, and concluded with the passage, "When I have put the squadron to rights, I shall endeavour to renew the action," omitting altogether the subsequent part of the letter. Here I must protest against the slightest censure on the Admiralty. They, doubtless, were anxious to give the public the earliest intimation of the victory, and did not think it necessary to give any account of the Rochefort and Ferrol squadrons. If they had done so, the public would not have drawn the conclusion they did, nor would the public have been so sanguine in their expectations, if the letter had been published as an extract, because they would have imagined there was something else in the letter which the Admiralty thought proper to conceal. If the Admiralty had been aware of this, sure I am, from the readiness with which they gave me a copy of my letter, they would have avoided putting me in the unfortunate situation in which I am placed. In availing myself of the liberty of defending my own character and conduct, I shall be careful not to state any thing prejudicial to the public. I shall rather run the risk of suffering by the concealment of that which ought not to be published. I think it can be attended with no bad consequences to state that passage in my letter, the omission of which I complain. It is this—"At the same time it will behove me to be on my guard against the combined squadrons in Ferrol and Rochefort; therefore I may find it necessary to make a junction with the Commander in Chief off Ushant." Had this part of my letter been published, I beg leave to ask whether the public would have been so sanguine as they have been?—Assuredly they would not; nor should I have had occasion to give you this trouble. I stated, that the enemy had sent off one of their crippled ships to Ferrol, and that on the morning of the 23d there appeared to be two ships less in the combined fleet than on the preceding day. The Court will, I trust, think I do not unnecessarily trespass on their time further to mention another public letter. I owe it to Admiral Stirling and to myself to say, that I took the earliest opportunity of supplying the omission of his name in my letter to the Admiralty, an omission which was only to be attributed to the illness of my Secretary, and that I afterwards gave him that share of approbation which was due to his merit. It would be improper to comment on the different reports which have been circulated; but there is one, which is so entirely destitute of foundation, that the Court will forgive me if I call it to their attention. It has been asserted and reported, that I said to Lieutenant Nicholson, when he left me with the dispatch, that I had written to the Lords Commissioners, saying that I had it in my power to bring the combined fleet to action, and that I was determined to do so. If this had been so, Lieutenant Nicholson would have been called. His not being called, gives additional weight to my declaration, that I never did send such message—that I do most solemnly declare. The enemy were at the time out of sight, and it was impossible to renew the action. He was, therefore, not warranted in affirming that, or in making any such representation, as from me. I am aware these observations will not vary the question—they will not, I trust, be deemed wholly irrelevant, but, on the contrary, will justify me for having desired an opportunity of exculpating myself to the public, and removing the imputations against me. The opportunity has been offered, and I hope the explanation will be satisfactory. The question resolves itself into two branches: first, Whether I could have renewed the engagement with advantage? and, secondly, Whether it was prudent not to renew it, and I did not wisely exercise my discretion? On the first, you have heard the evidence for the prosecution. The result is, that on the 23d July it was impossible to bring the enemy to action unless they thought proper to renew it, and that on the 24th I had no chance of overtaking them without separating my squadron. In addition to that evidence, I shall trouble you with very little. I shall prove the damages the different ships had sustained, with the additional circumstance, that it was not, from the state of the weather, possible to take the people out of the captured ships; and here I have to lament the absence of Captain Prouse, but I trust I shall be able to prove these matters without his assistance, as his arrival is so extremely uncertain. You will take into your consideration the questions, Whether the enemy would have staid till I came up with them? Whether I should have separated myself from the disabled part of my squadron and you must know, there is a material difference between renewing an attack with a willing and an unwilling enemy. It has been said that I meant to renew the action, by the signal to ask if any of the ships wanted to lie by. My reason for that signal was, that I might form my line to the best advantage, in case the enemy was inclined to renew the action. At this time the Windsor Castle was in tow of the Dragon, and the Malta was to leeward; and although I might have formed a line, it would have been impossible to have made an attack. That the signal was not understood, is evident; for Captain Inman has said, that he did not think it a time to make a signal of inability in sight of an enemy. The Court will recollect that I was at that time in possession of the return of the damages of each ship. The answer in the negative to my signal, expressed only the sentiments of the individual, and the Court will give me credit for every disposition to encourage that ardour in the officers and seamen, and their readiness at all times to meet the enemy, which easily accounts for their unwillingness to give signals of inability. Mr. President; with the rank and character I hold, I think I should not have been justified, if, to this feeling of bravery and courage, I had put the British squadron to hazard, the preservation of which was of so much importance to the country. A question has been put to Captain Inman, to know whether I asked him for the situation of the enemy. With respect to the fact stated by Captain Durham—when he made the signal, I had formed my plan, and to have desired him to keep the enemy in sight would only have had the effect of separating him from me. I best knew my own intentions. The signal I made was No. 77, to bring to, and not the signal to keep the enemy in sight. In forming an idea of the second question, namely, the renewing of the engagement, the Court will forgive me if I refer to my situation. I had but fourteen sail without frigates, the enemy had eighteen with many frigates. I could not hope to succeed without receiving great damage; I had no friendly port to go to; and had the Ferrol and Rochefort squadrons come out, I must have fallen an easy prey. They might have gone to Ireland. Had I been defeated, the enemy would have acquired spirit, and it is impossible to say what the consequence might have been. The question is great and momentous. It affects every officer who may be placed in a situation of command. Miserable must be their conduct, if they are to be censured for a fair and honest discharge of their duty, and the due exercise of their discretion. I have ever felt that I have exercised mine wisely, and for the advantage of the service and the country. Were I placed under similar circumstances again, I should act in a similar manner, unless this Court, putting themselves in my situation, shall tell me I have acted erroneously; but this I trust they will not do. If I may be allowed to look at subsequent events, I might say, that by the conduct I adopted, I was enabled to pursue the combined squadron into Cadiz, by which I laid the foundation of that splendid victory which engages the attention of the country. By being placed under the necessity of demanding this inquiry, I have been prevented from sharing in the glories of that day; and, believe me, that has been no small part of my sufferings *(the gallant Admiral turned round, and wiped a tear from his eye)*. The judgment of this Court will, I hope, reinstate me in society, and restore to me unsullied that fair fame and reputation which have been so cruelly attacked.

The first branch of evidence consisted wholly of written documents, which were laid upon the table, but not read. They were the original correspondence between Lord Gardner and Admiral Calder—the letters and orders of Lord Cornwallis—the orders of the Admiralty, desiring the Admiral to be on his guard against the Rochefort and Ferrol squadrons—the orders of Lord Nelson to the Commanders in the Tagus—the Gazette account of the action of the 23d—the Admiral's letter, with the unpublished paragraph, and several other letters between the Admiral and other Commanders.

Captain Allen Hyde Gardner, of the Hero, was first called and examined by Sir Robert Calder, having first verified his report of the damages done to his ship.

Q. Did the enemy ever chase, or make any attempt to force me to action, on the 23d of July last?—A. No.

Q. Could I have forced them to action on that day?—A. Not if they chose to avoid it.

Q. If I had gone towards the enemy on the 24th, could I have overtaken them, if they had chosen to avoid me, without approaching so near the shore as to enable them to communicate by signal by land?—A. I am not acquainted with the relative sailing of the two fleets, but I am of opinion they could have communicated with the shore before they could have been brought to action, had they wished so to do.

Q. Was the British fleet always kept by me between that of the enemy and the Port of Ferrol, as long as the enemy were in sight?—A. The British squadron was always nearer the Port of Ferrol than that of the enemy.

Q. Was your mast in danger by carrying sail when you was sent by me to Admiral Cornwallis, on our return to Ushant?—A. In carrying sail to accomplish that duty, which was only performed on Sir Robert Calder's appearing in sight of Admiral Cornwallis's fleet, the fore-mast of the Hero was in danger of going over the side.

Cross-examined by Mr. Bicknell.

Q. When was the report made; was it during the time the combined fleets were in sight?—A. I think about the 24th the combined fleets were in sight.

Q. From the manner in which you have described the state of the fore-mast of the Hero, at the time you joined Admiral Cornwallis, what do you suppose would have been the consequence, had the Vice-Admiral found it necessary to carry sail in pursuit of the enemy after the action?—A. I think the fore-mast, particularly on the 24th, when there was a considerable degree of swell, had we carried sail, must have gone by the board, from its having appeared to be in such danger after we had fished it to the utmost of our means.

Q. What masts of the Hero were found necessary to be, and were taken out, when the Hero's defects were made good in port, upon her coming in for that purpose after the action?—A. The fore-mast and main-mast were taken out, and replaced by new ones.

Q. As the British fleet was always nearer to the shore than the enemy, while in sight, in what way could they have approached the shore, to communicate with it, before some part of the British fleet, not disabled, could have closed with that part of the enemy that were disabled?—A. When I said the shore, I meant any space of it, between Cape Finisterre and Ferrol, by which means their wishes might be communicated to the latter place.

Q. What distance did you ever think yourself at any time, while you was in sight of the French fleet, from any part of the shore?—A. On the 24th we were, by our account, 38 leagues N. W. from Ferrol, the wind then N. E.

Re-examined by Admiral Calder.

Q. Can you recollect whether you sent any report of damages by the Frisk or Nile, on the night between the 22d and 23d?—A. Yes, I did; I told the Lieutenant of the Nile nearly what appeared before the Court.

Q. In what you said to the Lieutenant, did you lay any stress on the state of the two lower masts?—A. No, only that they were badly wounded.

Re-examined by Mr. Bicknell.

Q. As you have said, that you are not acquainted with the relative sailing of the two fleets, on what ground do you form your opinion, that the enemy could have reached near enough to shore to have communication with Ferrol, before you could have fetched?—A. From their being fifteen or sixteen miles distance from us at the time, and the enemy's line of battle ships were found generally to sail as well as ours.

Q. Did you receive any message or information, after the action of the 22d of July, from the Vice-Admiral, that it was his intention to renew the engagement; and through what channel?—A. Lieutenant Fennel, of the Nile, told me he was sent on board to know the damages sustained, and that the Admiral meant to renew the action in the morning. This was immediately after the action.

Q. When did you receive this?—A. Between two and three o'clock of the 23d.

Admiral Calder.—I admit, I have stated in my defence that I hoped to renew the action in the morning.

The admission was put in as evidence.

Examined by Sir Robert Calder.

Q. Did the enemy appear to you to have sustained any considerble damage in their masts and yards?—A. No; I only observed one main-top-sail-yard gone in the whole squadron; we were too far to observe their sails.

Captain Arthur Kaye Legge, of the Repulse.

Q. Is that the report yon made to me of the damages received by you on the 22d?—A. Yes, if that is the second report I sent in.

The report was read; it stated considerable damages.

Q. Did you make a similar report on the night of the 22d?—A. I did not then know that the bowsprit had been wounded; I only specified that the rigging had been cut, and sails; the officer of the Frisk came on board so soon after the action, as I was the next ship to the Admiral, that I had no report made to me of the damages. My first report was transmitted to the Admiralty.

Admiral Calder.—All the first or rough reports were sent to the Admiralty.

Q. Was you employed in fishing your bowsprit, and of course your masts, all the 23d July?—A. No, the bowsprit was not considered to be so badly wounded as to occasion its being fished, till after it was sprung on the evening of the 25th; the people were occasionally employed on the 23d, in knotting and splicing, and repairing the rigging and sails. The fore-top-sail, I think the main-top-sail, was repaired in the night; the fore-top-sail was badly torn.

Q. Did you make the signal to me, on the 25th, of the bowsprit being sprung?—A. Yes.

Q. Was not that the first time we had carried much sail after the action?—A. I do not think that any sail had been carried before that, and the Repulse was under her three top-sails, a fore-top-mast-stay-sail, and mizen-stay-sail.

Q. Did you, about the same time, observe the Malta make the signal of having sprung her fore-yard?—A. Yes, I think her main-yard—her lower yard.

Q. Was the squadron brought to on the occasion?—A. Yes, on the occasion of the Repulse making the signal, having occasion to lie by.

Q. How long was it before the Repulse made the signal that she was ready to proceed on service?—A. The Repulse made the signal for having sprung her bowsprit about seven o'clock in the evening of the 25th, when we were obliged to let every thing fly to save the mast, and made the signal of her being ready to make sail, as soon as signals could be distinguished, at day-light in the morning of the 26th.

Q. Did the enemy ever chase, or make any attempt to bring me to action on the 23d of July?—A. Never, always kept running down to windward.

Q. Could I have forced them to action on that day?—A. I think not.

Q. Did the enemy appear to you to have sustained any considerable damages in their masts and yards?—A. No, I could only distinguish one ship, with, I think, her main-top-sail-yard down. Some others might have their sails clued up to repair.

Q. If I had gone towards the enemy, could I have overtaken them, if they had chosen to avoid coming to action, without preventing their approaching the shore between Ferrol and Cape Finisterre, and communicating, by land, signals with Ferrol?—A. I should think, if they avoided an action, you could not.

Q. Was the British fleet always between that of the enemy and the port of Ferrol, as long as the enemy were in sight?—A. I should think they were, till the 24th; but not the latter part of the time when we saw them, they then stood to the southward.

Q. When we parted with them, could they have fetched Ferrol?—A. As well as I recollect, I should think not.

By the Court.—As you have stated to the Court, that you did not discover your bowsprit to have been sprung before the evening of the 25th, do you apprehend, if you had been obliged to carry sail upon the Repulse, in pursuit of the enemy, that the bowsprit would have borne it?—A. The bowsprit was not sprung till the evening of the 25th, and as I then went under three top-sails and fore-sail, I should suppose it was not equal to carry much sail upon it at any time after the action.

Q. Was there not much sea going on the 24th?—A. A heavy sea, and almost calm; the ship rolling very much.

Q. All the day?—A. After a breeze sprung up, the ships did not roll.

Q. What time was that?—A. About nine or ten o'clock in the morning.

Captain Charles Boyle sworn.

Verified the report of the damage his ship, the Windsor Castle, had sustained.

Examined by Sir Robert Calder.

Q. Did I hail you myself very soon after the action ceased, when you was passing close to windward of the Prince of Wales?—A. Certainly.

Q. What did I say to you?—A. You asked me if my fore-top-mast would be got up very soon, and actively, without loss of time.

Q. What was your answer?—A. Every exertion should be made on my part.

Q. What was my reply?—A. The Admiral did not doubt it.

Q. Was your ship in a state to have worked to windward, either in line of battle or order of sailing, so as to have forced the enemy to action either on the 23d or 24th of July?—A. No.

Q. Did you receive a messsage from me, saying, that I should constantly regulate my sailing by yours and the crippled ships, and that I should keep between you and the enemy for their protection?—A. Yes.

Q. Did I do so?—A. Yes.

Q. Did you see the whole, or only part of our squadron, on the morning of the 23d, at day-light?—A. Saw only part.

Q. What distance were you from them?—A. I could not immediately specify; but to the best of my belief, about four or five miles.

Q. Could you have made a junction with the squadron if I had not edged down?—A. It was impossible, in the state the Windsor Castle was in.

Q. How far were the Malta and frigates to leeward of you on the morning of the 23d?—A. I conceived ourselves to be pretty nigh between the squadron, and the Malta, Thunderer, frigates, and prizes.

Q. Could I have forced the enemy to action on the 23d?—A. Not the whole squadron; we could not have been taken there without being towed.

Q. When did I part company with you?—A. On the 25th, between five and six o'clock.

Q. Did you receive any orders from me to regulate your conduct by, when I should have parted company with you? A. Yes.

Q. Have you my letter?—A. I have not; I gave it to the Commander in Chief.

(The Orders were produced.)

Q. Considering your crippled state, and the relative situation of the two fleets, could the Windsor Castle have been towed up to the enemy, so as to have renewed the action either on the 23d or 24th?—A. On the 23d, taking the day from day-light until the evening, the Windsor Castle could have set but very little sail, the fishing of the lower yards, bending a new fore sail and main-sail, fishing the main-top-sail-yard, knotting all her stays, the whole of them and rigging, she could have made but little sail; therefore the powers of a 74 acting upon a body like the Windsor Castle, this Court will judge how far she was likely to be carried up to an enemy directly to windward. On the 24th the Windsor Castle was enabled to carry more sail; we had got up a jury fore-top-mast, a top-gallant-mast for a fore-top-mast, and were in a better state; at that time, if taken in tow, we could have kept our station in the line, but could not have been carried to windward fast enough to approach an enemy that might be inclined to evade an action.

Q. I beg Captain Boyle would state to the Court what impediment there was to his getting up a proper fore-top-mast on the 24th.—A. The fore-top-mast was shot away between the cap and the tressel-trees, therefore took the cap with it, carried away all the larboard side of the top and cross-trees, and when the spare cap was got up, to go over the mast-head, there was not sufficient time to fit the cross-trees and top on the larboard side, so as to have supported the proper fore-top-mast; besides, the fore-mast was wounded in such a way, that we could not, without taking much time, have fished it to be able to have carried proper top-sails, had we been able to rig the jury-cross-trees, which we had not time to do.

Captain William Lechmere

Verified his report of the damages of his ship, the Thunderer.

Q. Did the enemy ever chase, or make any attempt to bring me to action, on the 23d of July?—A. No.

Q. Could I have forced the enemy to action on the 23d of July, if they had chosen to avoid it?—A. No.

Q. Did the enemy appear to you to have sustained any considerable damage in their masts and yards?—A. None in their masts; they shifted a top-sail-yard or two, which I believe was the utmost.

Q. Was the British fleet always kept between that of the enemy and the port of Ferrol, as long as the enemy were in sight?—A. Till the afternoon of the 24th we were always nearer Ferrol than the enemy.

Q. Could they (the enemy) have fetched Ferrol?—A. No, the wind was E.N.E. It is impossible they could.

Q. If I had gone towards the enemy on the 24th, could I have overtaken them, if they had chosen to avoid me, without approaching so near the shore, between Ferrol and Cape Finisterre, so as to enable them to communicate, by signals by land, with Ferrol?—A. No.

Captain William Brown sworn,

He proved the report of the damages to his ship, the Ajax.

The Court asked the Vice-Admiral if he meant to examine Captain Brown to the same points?—He said, yes. Upon which the Court said, it did not conceive it necessary to examine Captain Brown, or any other witness, to the same points.

Captain Harvey

Was called to verify his report of the damages sustained by his ship, the Agamemnon.

Captain William Cummings,

Of the Prince of Wales, was next called.

Examined by Sir Robert Calder.

Q. *As you were near my person during the greater part of the action, was there any part of my conduct that exhibited fear or a want of zeal for His Majesty's service?* —A. MOST CERTAINLY NOT.

By the Court.—Q. What number of British ships appeared to you, on the morning of the 24th, to be incapable of sailing in order of battle, or in order of sailing? —A. I imagine the whole, except the Windsor Castle, might be formed in line of battle.

Q. If the Windsor Castle had been taken in tow, considering the relative situation of the two fleets, could the British squadron have renewed the action on the 24th, the enemy declining so to do?—A. Certainly not.

Q. Did the Vice-Admiral decline the action, either on the 23d or 24th, if the enemy had been inclined to renew it?—A. He did not.

Admiral Calder.—" Mr. President, I consider Captain Cummings the only person competent to speak to this question put to him by me, or I should have had no difficulty in putting the same question to every Captain in the fleet."

Captain Edward Griffiths, of the Dragon.

Q. Do you know of signal posts being erected along shore, between Cape Ortegal and Cape Finisterre, and to Ferrol?—A. Yes.

Q. Did you reconnoitre the port of Ferrol about the 29th of July?—A. On the 29th of July I did.

Q. Had the combined squadrons then arrived there?—A. No.

Q. Do you remember one being blown off the coast by south-westerly winds on the 1st of August?—A. It blew a hard gale of wind from the south-west on the 1st, not directly off the coast, but close along shore, which would blow us more along shore than off.

Q. When did we return there?—A. I cannot recollect the day precisely; I should think we made land about two days after.

Q. Had the combined fleets taken the opportunity of our being blown off to get in, and of how many did they then consist?—A. Yes, they must have got in during our absence, as I saw a fleet afterwards at anchor off Corunna, and they consisted of 13 sail of the line, four frigates, and a brig; at the same time saw the squadron in Ferrol that had been there for many months.

Q. Is that your report?—A. It is.

(It was produced and laid on the table,)

By the Court.—Had you not the Windsor Castle in tow after the action of the 22d?—A. Yes.

Q. Under what sail was the Windsor Castle when you took her in tow?—A. I cannot say precisely, but she had very little; no sails forward but a jib from the boom to the fore-mast end, and some small after sail. This was the morning of the 23d.

Q. At what rate did you then tow her, and what sail had you then set?—A. As well as I recollect, only single reefed top-sails and stay-sail. I don't suppose we could at any time on the 23d have exceeded two knots.

Q. Could the Windsor Castle have been put in a condition by the evening of the 24th to have made it practicable for you to have towed her so as to have sailed in order of battle in the rear of a fleet, to have pursued an enemy with any probability of coming up with them, if they were not inclined to battle? —A. I should think not, the Windsor Castle being at the best of times but a dull sailing ship: if the enemy were inclined to avoid a battle, certainly not.

Captain Charles Elphinstone Fleming sworn.

Q. Did you take one of the prizes in tow after the action?—A. Yes, the el Firme.

Q. In what state was the prize when you took her in tow?—A. Her rudder disabled, many of her ports blown off, and she made so much water through the shot holes, that we could just keep her free.

Q. Were you able to have towed her up to the squadron, if I had not edged up to you?—A. No, the Egyptienne's rudder was gone, and the prizes were disabled, so that we could make very little way.

Q. Did you continue her in tow till you parted from the squadron?—A. No.

Q. Did the swell of the sea prevent your getting up jury-masts?—A. Yes, there was a very heavy swell, which prevented the boats going alongside her, and prevented our getting up jury-masts.

Q. Did the prize the Syrius, in tow, also lose her masts?—A. Yes, all her masts were gone, except the fore-mast, which was not fit to carry sail.

Q. Could you have taken the prisoners and wounded men out of the prizes in order to destroy them, if necessary?—A. I intended to do so, to let them sink, as there was so much difficulty to get the Spaniards to the pumps.

Q. How long was you at Rochefort before you sailed with Admiral Stirling?—A. I do not recollect the exact time; I came in June and left in July.

Q. What was the force of the enemy in that port?—A. Five sail of the line and five or six frigates, I do not recollect which, and three or four brigs.

Q. When did they sail?—A. I do not know; I heard they sailed the day after. I was told by a French prisoner I took, l'Acteon, a French corvette, the Captain of which informed me, he had sailed with the Rochefort squadron the day after Admiral Stirling left that port in October last.

Lieutenant Thomas Warren sworn.

Q. Was you my Signal Lieutenant in the month of July last?—A. Yes.

Q. Did you observe the enemy's ships on the morning of the 23d?—A. I did.

Q. Did you perceive they had a smaller number of ships on the morning of the 23d than they had on the 22d, the day of the action, besides the two prizes we had taken from them?—A. I did.

Q. Did you observe any of the enemy's ships advance from their weather bow?—A. I did; four sail of the line, besides frigates, were separated from the fleet, apparently in good order.

Q. Did they appear to have sustained material damage in their masts and yards?—A. Nothing of consequence.

Q. What was the signal made to the Defiance on the morning of the 24th?—A. No. 77, to bring to.

Q. What is the number of the signal made to reconnoitre the enemy?—A. 19.

Q. Was that number made to the Defiance on that day?

Court.—Was any signal made to the Defiance to look out between the British fleet and that of the enemy, or to watch their motions, previous to that signal for her to bring to?—A. No, none.

Q. Do you know by what accident the Defiance came in that situation?—A. Being the sternmost ship of the weather line a signal was made to bring her to, as one of the enemy's frigates was coming up a-stern to reconnoitre us; previous to which a signal was made to the Dragon to reconnoitre.

Q. Was any signal made after that to call in the Defiance to join the fleet, before he made the signal to the Vice-Admiral to ask if he should any longer keep sight of the enemy?—A. None, except that of answering her signal.

Q. Did the four sail of the line on the weather bow appear to be part of the fleet you engaged, or were they fresh ships that had not been in the action?—A. I conceived them to be part of the fleet with which we had been engaged.

Q. What was the number of the enemy's line of battle ships at that time?—A. 18.

Q. Was the signal which was made to Captain Durham to bring to repeated by Admiral Stirling before it was answered?—A. I did not see it.

[It was here proposed by Mr. Bicknell to call back Captain Durham, to explain his evidence, but Admiral Calder saying that he conceived his mistaking the signal to be accidental, it was deemed unnecessary.]

Mr. John Sutor, Chaplain to the Phœnix.

Admiral Calder.—I call this witness to show my apprehensions of the Rochefort and Ferrol squadrons, which I have mentioned in my defence to-day, and that I expressed them at the time. If the Court think this unnecessary, I have no farther trouble to give them. I mean this, that I may not be supposed to have taken up the ground since the 23d,

The Court thought it evidence proper to be received.

Q. Do you remember my sending to you a copy of the duplicate of my account of the action, in consequence of the illness of my Secretary —A. I do.

Q When?—A. On the 24th of July last.

Q. Did I say any thing respecting my further intention?—A. You observed, that from accounts you received of the danger of the different ships, it would be very imprudent in you to attempt to force the enemy to renew the action; that the damages were very considerable, and that if you had it in your power to renew the action, you must abandon the captured ships and the Windsor Castle.

Q. Did I make any and what observations of the probability of the Rochefort squadron being at sea?—A. You told me you fully expected they were, as the wind was fair for sailing at the time Admiral Stirling left the blockade.

Q. Did I say any thing of the French squadron?—A. You observed, it was very probable they would be at sea, as they would have been apprised of the combined squadron being returned from the West Indies, and that the wind had been fair for their sailing many days subsequent to your leaving the blockade of Ferrol.

Sir Pobert Calder.—I have no further trouble to give the Court, I have no other witness to call.

The Court adjourned till ten to-morrow.

FOURTH DAY, DEC. 26.

The Court assembled, pursuant to adjournment, at ten o'clock precisely, and a prodigious number of persons, anxious to hear the result of so important a trial, were on board the Prince at an early hour. The President and Members of the Court began their deliberations soon after 10—the door was locked, and a sentry placed to guard it. The day was wearing away, and they had not come to any determination.—It was near 4 o'clock, when many thought another adjournment would take place, that the Court was opened and Admiral Calder called. The rush for admittance was similar to that which sometimes takes place in the gallery of the House of Commons. When every thing was ready, there was the most profound silence, a sort of awful attention.

The Judge Advocate read the following Sentence of the Court:—

" At a Court Martial assembled on board His Majesty's ship Prince of Wales, in Portsmouth harbour, on the 23d day of December, 1805, and continued by adjournment from day to day, until the 26th day of the same month,

Pursuant to an order from the Right Honourable the Lords Commissioners of the Admiralty, dated the 15th day of November last past, and directed to the President, setting forth, that Sir Robert Calder, Bart., Vice-Admiral of the Blue, had, by his letter to their Lordships' Secretary, dated the 13th day of September last, requested, for the reasons therein mentioned, that an inquiry may be made into his the said Vice-Admiral's conduct, on the 23d day of July last, the day after the engagement with the combined fleets of France and Spain, or upon the whole or such part thereof (when in presence of the enemy), as should appear for the good of His Majesty's service, and for enabling him to give his reasons publickly for his conduct on that occasion.

And that their Lordships thought fit, in compliance with the Vice-Admiral's request, and for the reasons mentioned in his said letter, that a Court Martial should be assembled, for the purpose above mentioned, and also for inquiring into the whole of the said Vice-Admiral's conduct and proceedings, on the said 23d day of July, and into his subsequent conduct and proceedings, until he finally lost sight of the enemy's ships; and to try him for not having done his utmost to renew the said engagement, and to take and destroy every ship of the enemy, which it was his duty to engage, the Court proceeded to inquire into the conduct and proceedings of the said Vice-Admiral Sir Robert Calder, with His Majesty's squadron under his command, on the said 23d day of July last, and also into his subsequent conduct and proceedings, until he finally lost sight of the enemy's fleet, and to try him for not having done his utmost to renew the said engagement, and to take or destroy every ship of the enemy, which it was his duty to engage, and having heard the evidence produced in support of the charge, and by the said Vice-Admiral Sir Robert Calder, Bart. in his defence, and what he had to alledge in support thereof, and having maturely and deliberately weighed and considered the whole, the Court is of opinion, that the charge of not having done his utmost to renew the said engagement, and to take or destroy every ship of the enemy, has been proved against the said Vice-Admiral Calder; that it appears that his conduct has not been actuated either by cowardice or disaffection, but has arisen solely from error in judgment, and is highly censurable, and doth adjudge him to be severely reprimanded, and the said Vice-Admiral Sir Robert Calder is hereby severely reprimanded accordingly.

"(Signed) GEORGE MONTAGU.

J. HOLLOWAY,	R. S. ROWLEY,
E. THORNBOROUGH,	I. COFFIN,
J. SUTTON,	J. BISSETT,
R. D. OLIVER,	J. IRWIN,
J. A. WOOD,	J. SEATER,
T. B. CAPEL,	J. LARMOUR.

M. GREETHAM. Jun.
Deputy Judge Advocate of the Fleet."

Promotions and Appointments.

Rear-Admiral George Martin, to be second in command at Portsmouth, instead of Sir Isaac Coffin, who has obtained twelve months' leave of absence; Rear-Admiral George Murray, to command the Dungeness squadron; Captain Oldham, to the Ville de Paris; Lord W. Stuart, to the Lavina; Captain M'Kinley, to the Quebec; Captain Curry, to the Roebuck; Captain J. Ross Farquharson (late Ross) from the Africa, to the Gibraltar; Captain Lechmere, to the Prince; Honourable Captain Dundas, to the Euryalus; Captain J. Dunbar, to the Astrea; Captain Carthew, to the Crescent; Captain J. F. Douglas, to the Bellona; Captain Bligh (son of Admiral Bligh), to the Pylades; Mr. William Brewer, to be Purser of the Dasher; Alexander M'Lean, Esq., to be Secretary to the Transport Board, for that part of the business relative to the sick and wounded office, which by an order of Council is attached to that Board.

Captain J. C. Searle, to the Monarch; Captain R. Jackson, to the Edgar; Captain G. R. Collier, to the Minerva; Captain Fielding, to the Revolutionaire; Captain Downman, of the Diomede, to the Diadem, bearing Sir Home Popham's broad pendant; Captain Lake, of the Childers, to the Surinam; Captain H. Laroche, of the Kangaroo, is promoted to a Post Captain, and appointed to the Blanche; Captain T. Searle, is appointed to the Thunderer; Lieutenant Ellison, Admiral Montagu's first Lieutenant, and Lieutenant Charlton, Admiral Rowley's first Lieutenant, are promoted to Commanders; Captain W. Beauchamp, to the Dedaigneuse; Captain G. Heathcote, to the Sir E Hughes.

Mr. W. Walker (2,) is appointed Surgeon of the dock-yard at Portsmouth, in the room of Dr. Fidge, who retires.

List of the Commanders who have been promoted to the rank of Post Captain, and of the Lieutenants who have been advanced to the rank of Commander:—*To be Post Captains*—Captains Rosenhagen, Ramsey, Carteret, Vaughan, Rodney, M'Leod, Mason, Ommaney, J. Sykes, Impey, Heywood, Kent, H. Laroche, Hancock, Duff, Snell, Duncan, Bushby, Mackey, Hodgeson, J. L. Popham, Watson, Henniker, Pellew, Foster, Johnstone, Curtis, Lewis, Brown, Carden, Kerr, Shippard, Scott, Henderson, Smith, Bowen.—*To be Commanders*—Lieutenants Tucker, Ellis, Packwood, Balfour, Hopkins, Hunt, Balderstone, Maxwell, Stevenson, Bowes, Hon. G. Waldegrave, Valentine, Parker, Rogers, Bradshaw, Palmer, Steward, Markland, Charlton, Perry, Lysaught, Dickinson, Ryder, Gordon, Palmer, Hodge, Garland, King (1), Walpole, Forrest, King, Hycks,

Handfield, Stodart, Honey, Sheriff Adye, Hollinworth, Rogers, Winter, Warwick. Lake, Raitt, Prowse, Hope, James Mein.

Captain Nicholls is appointed Comptroller of the Navy, in the room of Sir Andrew Hamond, who has retired. Admiral Vashon and Captain W. A. Otway, are appointed Commissioners of Naval Inquiry, in the room of Sir C. Pole and Captain Nicholls.

Captain J. Bowen, to be Captain of the Channel Fleet; Captain Western, to command the Hibernia; Sir John Gore, to the Revenge; Hon. Captain Bouverie, to the Medusa; Captain Burn, to the Albicore; Captain R. B. Campbell, to the Cygnet; Captain Mounsey, to the Rosario; Captain Palmer, to the Nautilus; Captain Raitt, to the Scout; Captain Sutton, to the Oberon; Captain Dilkes, to the Hazard; Captain G. Reynolds, to the sea fencibles at Deal; Captain S. Bateman, to the sea fencibles at Dublin; Captain J. Wolley, to the Africa; Captain T. Innis, to the Childers; Captain J. Thompson, to the Fly; Captain Tower, to the Camilla; Captain Gordon, to the Moselle; the Rev. Mr. Parker, to be Secretary to Earl St. Vincent.

BIRTH.

On the 15th of February, at Godalming, Surrey, the lady of Captain S. J. Ballard, Royal Navy, of a son.

MARRIAGE.

On the 28th of January, was married, Mr. T. Shoveller, of Portsea, Surgeon in the Navy, to Miss King, of Titchfield.

OBITUARY.

On the 5th of December died, at the Hospital at Gibraltar, Captain Norman, of the Royal Marines, who was wounded on board the Mars, in the action of Trafalgar.

Captain Richardson, of His Majesty's ship Utile, whilst on a cruise in the North Seas. This gentleman was one of the Lieutenants of the Royal George when she sunk.

(From the Portsmouth papers of the 10th February.)

The following affecting case has been communicated to us by an officer, with a desire that we would solicit the benefactions of those who can feel for the distressed. We most willingly give it insertion, and inform our readers, the naval ones more particularly, that the smallest donation will be received at the banks of Messrs. Griffiths and Co. Messrs. Grant and Co. and by the Printer:—Lieutenant Dobson, of the Royal Navy, lately arrived from England, to command one of His Majesty's gun-boats at Dublin. He brought an amiable wife and two children in distressed circumstances. He retired with his family to reside on board his vessel.—Accustomed to the comforts of a gentlewoman, his wife was seized with a fever, was removed to lodgings, and died on the 20th of December. Agonised at this sudden, severe, and premature deprivation, he was soon bereft of reason, and expired on the 26th of the same month. He was about 30 years of age, and had served his country faithfully.—She was delicate, beautiful, and not twenty-two. Their children, a boy about three years old, and a girl about three months, have no means of even temporary support, but from those who have hearts to *feel*, and means to *give*. Rear-Admiral Wolsely, No. 2, Kildare-street, can vouch for the truth of the above.

On the 4th of February, Mrs. Mosberry, wife of R. Mosberry, Esq., of His Majesty's dock-yard, at Portsmouth.

On the 27th of January, Lieutenant Billinghurst, of the Royal Navy, at the signal station, Isle of Wight, who had served His Majesty 44 years; he was a man of strict honor, and is much regretted.

On the 11th of February, Mrs. Rankin, wife of J. Rankin, Esq., of His Majesty's dock-yard here.

Miss Hardy, eldest daughter of the late Admiral Sir C. Hardy.

At Bath, Mrs. Birchall, wife of Captain Birchall, of the Navy.

SIR EDWD. BERRY,

Captain R.N.

Published 31st March 1808, by J. Gold, 103, Shoe Lane, Fleet Street.

BIOGRAPHICAL MEMOIR OF

CAPTAIN SIR EDWARD BERRY, KNT.

"A THOUSAND CHIEFS HIS GALLANT COURSE PURSUE."
CAREY.

THE circumstance of Sir Edward Berry having participated in the perils and glory of three of the engagements in which the immortal Nelson was concerned, affords a sufficient motive for introducing him to the notice of our readers.

This gallant officer was born in the year 1766. His education was liberal; but fortune had not blessed his birth with independence, and he was left to search for that competence which, when honourably acquired, confers consequence and obtains respect. His father was a respectable member of the mercantile community in London; but dying before he had realized an adequate provision for his family, a young widow, and seven children, were left with but very slender means of support. But, though suddenly bereaved of a parent, and deprived of the flattering prospects of wealth, the offspring of Mr. Berry were not destitute of friends. Titus, his younger son, was bred to the profession of a Surgeon, and is now in extensive practice. Of five daughters, one died young, two are married, and two, we believe, still remain single.

Edward, the subject of the present memoir, evinced an early predilection for the naval service; and, favoured by circumstances, he was, when very young, initiated in that profession, to which his talents and his courage have done so much credit. The Rev. Mr. Titus Berry, his uncle, had been the master of an academy at Norwich, where the late Lord Mulgrave received part of his education. Under the auspices of that nobleman, Edward had therefore the good fortune to commence his nautical career, about the year 1779, when under the age of fourteen. His first voyage was to the East Indies, in the Burford, of 70 guns.

We are not aware of any particular service in which Mr. Berry was employed, in the earlier part of his progress; but during the time that Lord Spencer presided at the Admiralty, he distinguished himself by spiritedly boarding a ship of war, which had been grappled; an act of heroism and honour for which he was rewarded with a Lieutenant's commission. Shortly after this, in Lord Howe's engagement of the 1st of June, 1794, he had a farther opportunity of signalizing himself; by the intrepid bravery of his conduct, for which he obtained the notice and approbation of his superior officers.

Mr. Berry's very conspicuous merit attracted the observation of Earl St. Vincent and Commodore Nelson, two of the first officers of the age, with whom he had the satisfaction of forming a lasting and honourable friendship. By Lord Nelson, whose skill in selecting of officers, and in appreciating their talents, was equalled only by his own consummate professional excellence, he was particularly distinguished. He served under him as first Lieutenant, in the Captain, on the memorable 14th of February, 1797; and, by his extraordinary activity in boarding the San Nicholas and San Josef, both of which yielded to the superior prowess of Nelson, he acquired the honest eulogium of every officer in the fleet. Lieutenant Berry was the first man who jumped into the mizen chains of the San Nicholas, whither he was followed by a party of seamen and marines destined for the service. When Commodore Nelson reached the quarter-deck, he found his Lieutenant in possession of the poop, and one of his men hauling down the Spanish ensign. The Commodore, having secured the San Nicholas, gave the word for boarding the San Josef, when Lieutenant Berry assisted him into the main-chains of the latter ship, and had afterwards the satisfaction of attending him on the quarter-deck, at the moment of his receiving the sword from the Spanish Commander. The assistance which he afforded, and the spirit which he displayed, throughout the whole of this important encounter, greatly endeared him to his superiors in naval rank, and fixed him so firmly in the friendship of the gallant Commodore, that their mutual attachment terminated but with the lamented death of the latter*.

In the course of the year 1797 Mr. Berry was made Post, and appeared at Court with his friend Sir Horatio Nelson. When His Majesty was condoling with that Hero on the loss of his arm, which had been shattered at the attack upon Santa Cruz, Sir Horatio pointed to Captain Berry, observing, that *he had still his right arm left!*

In 1798, Captain Berry was appointed to the Vanguard, the flag-ship of Admiral Nelson, in the squadron detached by Earl St. Vincent into the Mediterranean. The proceedings of the squadron subsequently to its sailing from Gibraltar, comprehending the battle of the Nile, have been so amply related in the first Volume of our Chronicle†, that it would be wholly superfluous again to notice them at large. Notwithstanding the excessive damage which the Vanguard received in the squall by which she was overtaken; and notwithstanding the unfriendly reception which she experienced at St. Pierre's, the Admiral determined not to remove his flag; and Captain Berry, by an uncommon exertion of those resources, which British seamen generally possess within themselves, soon refitted his ship, while at anchor in St. Pierre's Road, and put to sea again in tolerable condition.

In the action of the Nile, which shortly followed, he had a full opportunity of displaying his abilities and gallantry. In the heat of the action, when Admiral Nelson was wounded in the head, Captain Berry caught him in his arms, and caused him to be immediately conveyed to the cock-pit. No sooner did he perceive that the Spartiate was dismasted, than he sent Lieutenant Galway, with a party of marines, to take possession of her; and on that officer's returning with the French Captain's sword, Captain Berry immediately delivered it to Admiral Nelson, below. From time to time he apprised the Admiral of the progress of the action; and when l'Orient took fire, he exerted

* For a variety of details, relative to the engagement of the 14th of February, the reader is referred to Vol. II, page 500; and to Vol. III, page 173, *et seq.*

† *Vide* page 43, *et seq.* *Vide* also Vol. III, page 181, *et seq.*

himself to the utmost in endeavouring to preserve the lives of her unfortunate crew. Indeed, to the promptitude of his conduct may be attributed the early dispatch of boats from the Vanguard and other ships, by which upwards of seventy Frenchmen were saved.

Soon after the action, Captain Berry was sent to England with the official dispatches, in the Leander, of 50 guns, Captain Thompson *. It will be recollected that, on her passage, the Leander had the misfortune to fall in with a French ship (le Genereux) of very superior force; but, disdaining to yield without a contest, the Leander resolutely maintained an engagement with her for several hours, till she was so completely crippled, that farther resistance became ineffectual and hopeless, and she was compelled to surrender. This action was perhaps one of the most bloody, upon a small scale, that was fought during last war. Captain Berry, who had fully coincided with Captain Thompson as to the propriety of fighting, found at one time six of the ship's company fall around him; and at the same moment received a wound from part of a man's skull, which was driven through his arm. This compelled him to retire, for the purpose of having his wound dressed. The prisoners were carried into Corfu, and afterwards marched to Trieste, whence, at the close of the year, they were exchanged.

On his return, Captain Berry was received by his countrymen with great applause: the honour of knighthood was conferred on him †; the Corporation of London having previously voted him their thanks and the freedom of the city. For this civic compliment, he expressed his acknowledgments, in the following letter to Sir William Anderson, then Lord Mayor:—

SIR, *Kensington, April 23, 1799.*

I HAVE this instant had the honour of receiving your favour of the 16th of October last; which, I conclude, has been travelling in quest of me since that period.

* *Vide* NAVAL CHRONICLE, Vol. XIV, page 6.

† December 12, 1798.

Permit me, Sir, to return you, and the Court of Common Council of the City of London, my warmest thanks and most grateful acknowledgments, for the very high compliments I am honoured with.

Believe me, Sir, I esteem it as the highest mark of my country's approbation, to gain which is most gratifying: at the same time I have to assure you, that, under the flag of Rear-Admiral Lord Nelson, I only obeyed his Lordship's commands.

I have the honour to be
Your very faithful and obedient Servant,
E. BERRY.

On Captain Berry's paying a visit to Guildhall, on the 8th of August following, he was presented with the freedom of the city, in a gold box, pursuant to the vote passed in the preceding year.

Shortly after this period, Sir Edward proceeded to the Mediterranean, as Captain of the Foudroyant, of 80 guns, Lord Nelson's flag-ship. The health of his Lordship requiring some relief from the toils of service, Sir Edward landed him at Sicily.

The Foudroyant was subsequently stationed off Malta, with a squadron of ships of war under the command of Captain Manley Dixon, for the purpose of preventing succours being thrown in, or any of the enemy's vessels escaping out of the ports. On the night of the 30th of March, 1800, Captain Dixon, in order to observe the enemy's motions more narrowly, directed Captain Blackwood, in the Penelope, to stand close in to the Valette. About midnight an enemy's ship was descried by him; a circumstance of which Captain Dixon was immediately apprised by the Minorca brig, Captain Miller; Captain Blackwood also making the necessary signals, and giving chase himself. The remaining ships of the squadron, which were at anchor, instantly cut or slipped their cables, and went in pursuit, under a press of sail, guided solely by the cannonading of the Penelope. At day-break, the Lion, Captain Dixon's ship, had arrived within gun-shot of the chase, and the Penelope was observed to be within musket shot, raking her; the efforts of her well-directed fire, during the night, having carried away her main and mizen-top-masts and main-yard. The enemy appeared to be in great confusion, being reduced to her head-sails, going with the wind on the quarter. The Lion ran close alongside; the yard-arms of both ships being just clear, when a destructive broadside of three round shot in each gun was poured in, luffing up across the bow, when the enemy's jib-boom passed between the main and mizen shrouds. After a short interval, the boom was carried away, and the ships were disentangled. Captain Dixon's object was to prevent being boarded, or being exposed to the powerful broadside of the enemy; he therefore maintained his position across her bow, firing to great advantage; while his opponent could only return with her bow chasers and musketry, the fire of which was prodigious, she being full of troops.

About fifty minutes after the commencement of the action, the Foudroyant came up under a press of canvas, and ran so close alongside, that her spare anchor was but just clear of the enemy's mizen chains. Sir Edward hailed her Commander, and ordered him to strike; but the Frenchman, instead of complying with the order, brandished a sword over his head, in token of defiance; and, discharging a musket at Sir Edward, poured in a tremendous broadside, which nearly unrigged the Foudroyant. The guns of the latter, however, being prepared with three round shots in each, returned the compliment with interest. A second broadside from the Foudroyant brought down her adversary's main and mizen-masts; and at the same time shivered to tatters her own fore-top-mast, jib-boom, sprit-sail, main-top-sail-yard, stay-sails, fore-sail, and main-sail. In this state it was difficult to get her to fall off, so as to maintain her position. The combatants therefore separated for a few minutes; and Sir Edward, calling his men from the main-deck, cut away part of the wreck, and succeeded in rendering his ship again obedient to the helm. He once more laid her alongside her determined opponent, who had nailed her colours to the stump of the mast, and displayed her flag on a pole over them. Sir Edward then re-commenced a heavy and well-directed fire, his men having got into a system of firing every gun two or three times a minute, with the utmost regularity. Musketry was occasionally used, when the Foudroyant was very nearly on board the enemy; but towards the close of the action, her mizen-mast being almost in two, Sir Edward called the marines from the poop, and put them to the great guns, by which means many lives were saved. At a few minutes past eight A. M. the enemy's foremast was shot away; and, becoming a mere log, she struck her colours. She proved to be le Guilliaume Tell, of 86 guns, and 1000 men, bearing the flag of Rear-Admiral Decres, the only remaining ship of the French fleet which had escaped from the battle of the Nile.

During the action, Sir Edward Berry was slightly wounded, but not so as to induce him to quit the deck, where he displayed the utmost gallantry, activity, and presence of mind.

In the course of this engagement, so honourable to both of the contending parties, the Foudroyant expended one hundred and sixty-two barrels of powder, twelve hundred 32-pound shot, twelve hundred and forty 24-pound ditto, one hundred 18-pound ditto, and two hundred 12-pound ditto. Her total loss was eight men killed, and sixty-one wounded. She was greatly damaged; but by the unremitting vigilance of her gallant Commander, she was soon refitted and again ready for sea*.

In the month of June following, Sir Edward brought the Royal Family of Naples from Palermo to Leghorn, on board the Foudroyant; and before they left her, Her Majesty, the amiable but ill-fated sister of the lamented Marie Antoinette of France, presented him with a gold box, set with diamonds, and a diamond ring.

His engagement with the Guilliaume Tell was the last opportunity which Sir Edward had of supporting the honour of the British flag during the late contest; and since the commence-

---

* For farther particulars of the above action, *vide* Captain Dixon's Gazette letter, NAVAL CHRONICLE, Vol. III, page 500; the French Admiral's account, Vol. IV, page 233; and critical remarks, page 317. For a view of the action, *vide* also Vol. IV, page 233.

ment of the present war, until last summer, he remained unemployed. He was then appointed to the Agamemnon, of 64 guns; in which ship he was present at the glorious battle of Trafalgar.

Previously to that action, he is stated, on the authority of the public newspapers, to have had the following extraordinary escape from capture:—

From the most authentic documents (say they) we have this intelligence: That on the morning of the 10th of October, at half past three, off Cape Finisterre, Sir Edward Berry, in the Agamemnon, discovered eight sail to windward; at four, one of them bore down towards the Agamemnon. The private night signal was made, but not answered. Sir Edward therefore kept his course, S. by W. full, and with all sail set except studding sails. At day-light the private signal was made, but not answered. The first ship that bore down was soon discovered to be a three-decker, with five ships of the line, two frigates and a brig, evidently French. The three-decker was within gun-shot at day-break, and crowded all sail to get alongside the Agamemnon, as did the 80-gun ship, which was on her lee quarter. There being a butt of water before the breast of each gun, Sir Edward ordered them all to be started, and the casks thrown overboard, to be clear for battle. At nine the Agamemnon gained upon the three-decker, but the 80-gun ship neared the Agamemnon. Sir Edward determined not to keep away, and could not tack without the certainty of a broadside from the three-decker, and being raked by the 80-gun ship when in stays, he therefore kept the ship steady in her course, furling the top-gallant-sails, and hauling down the stay-sails in the squalls, and setting them occasionally. At ten the 80-gun ship gained upon the Agamemnon, he therefore ordered the weather-quarter boat to be cut away, and ran out the stern chasers. At eleven the French Admiral relinquished the chase, and called in the 80-gun ship, when each hoisted the colours of their nation; and soon after Sir Edward came within signal of l'Aimable frigate, the Hon. Captain Bouverie, to whom he communicated what had happened; but this extraordinary manœuvre will be more fully explained when Sir Edward Berry's letter to his glorious Chief shall be published. The chase continued the space of 70 miles by the log.

No letter, of the nature alluded to, has yet appeared.

In the succeeding action, of the 21st of October, the Agamemnon was engaged in the van division of the fleet. Sir Edward, there cannot be a doubt, fulfilled his duty to the utmost possible extent; but it does not appear that his ship had any opportunity of particularly distinguishing herself. Her loss amounted to only two killed and seven wounded.

Previously to Sir Edward's leaving England for the Mediterranean last war, he married, in 1799, the daughter of Dr. Foster, of Norwich.—Mrs. Berry, Sir Edward's mother, entered into a second marriage with Mr. Godfrey, the late celebrated chymist, of Southampton-street; but has been several years again a widow. Enjoying a jointure of 500*l.* a year, from Mr. Godfrey, she lives in great respectability at Kensington Gravel Pits.

Sir Edward, we believe, is also in very easy circumstances. He had an uncle, who early in life went to India; and, having realized a considerable fortune, at his death he bequeathed the greater part of it to his nephews and nieces; so as to place the whole family in possession of a comfortable state of independence.

Sir Edward Berry, in the Agamemnon, is at present stationed with the North Sea Squadron off the Texel.

NAVAL ANECDOTES, COMMERCIAL HINTS, RECOLLECTIONS, &c.

NANTES IN GURGITE VASTO.

RECENT INSTANCE OF BRITISH HEROISM.

THE Spanish lugger, Barbarossa, arrived at Whitehaven on the 8th of February, under the command of Mr. Patterson, from St. Andero, a Spanish port in the province of Biscay, which place she left about three o'clock in the morning of the preceding Sunday, but whence she had been intended to sail (under the command of Captain Pedro de Orovmandia) for La Vera Cruz, in the Gulf of Mexico, New Spain. Her destination was altered in the following manner:—Twenty-six English prisoners were confined in a castle near the place where the Barbarossa was fitting out.

They formed the resolution of attempting to liberate themselves, and of trying to make their passage home in her. When the time arrived for carrying their project into execution, the majority of them shrunk from a design which was to be attended with so much danger. Eleven of them, however, persevered; four of these belonged to Whitehaven, viz. Mr. Patterson, who had been Mate of the Curwen, Captain Shippard, of Workington, (captured some time ago,) the Carpenter of the same, and two others. Between two and three in the morning of Sunday, the 2d, they effected their escape out of prison, boarded the lugger, cut her out, passed two strong batteries, (by one of which they were hailed,) and got out to sea; the next day they lost two of their masts in a heavy gale of wind; but pursuing their course with great resolution, and certainly with singular success, they arrived safe at Whitehaven as stated above. Her cargo cost in Spain not less than 25,000*l.* sterling, exclusive of the vessel, which, at a very moderate estimate, may be set down at 800*l.* The Barbarossa, after delivering her cargo, it appears, was to proceed to the West Indies, equipped with ten carriage guns, and seventy men, to cruise against the English.

ACCOUNT OF THE ROCHEFORT SQUADRON.

BY the arrival of Captain Radford, from Teneriffe, from which place he made his escape, we have been put in possession of some very interesting details relative to the proceedings of the Rochefort squadron.

Captain Radford sailed in the Mary and Ellen, from Guernsey, on the 16th of July, and on the 22d of the same month fell in with the Rochefort, *alias* the *invisible* squadron, as it has been termed in the City, from the adroitness with which it has steered clear of our squadrons sent in pursuit of it.

The Mary and Ellen, notwithstanding her endeavours, could not escape from the enemy. There was attached to the squadron a remarkable fast sailing brig, named le Cerf, from which, in almost every kind of weather, nothing could escape. As soon as the Mary and Ellen was taken possession of, and her crew put on board the squadron, she was burnt. She was the first prize the squadron had taken on its second cruise, and had not been more than six days at sea. The Commodore made no secret of informing Captain Radford, that he had sailed from Rochefort for the special purpose of joining the combined fleets, of whose intended arrival in the Mediterranean he had been apprised; and that it was his intention to burn, sink, or destroy, every vessel (no matter of what nation) that he could capture, to prevent all intelligence of his squadron from transpiring. In every respect he kept his word, except in the instance of an American ship bound to Bourdeaux. This ship was chased for upwards of seven hours, before the squadron could come up with her; when the Commodore ordered the American Captain on board his ship, and asked him, in the most insulting tone, how he had dared to give him so much trouble? The Captain replied, that he had only obeyed the instructions of his owner, which were, to make the best of his way to market with his goods, as other vessels had sailed with similar freights. After some further threats, the American was suffered to proceed.

Whilst Captain Radford was on board the squadron, the enemy took and destroyed forty vessels, sailing under neutral flags: five of them were Americans, 25 Swedes, and several Danes and Prussians. The Spaniards were not spared; they burnt two ships of that nation, laden with corn, passing from one of the Canary islands to another. They fell in with a Prussian East Indiaman, homeward-bound, and thinking her to be too valuable a prize to destroy, they took her in tow. In the course of the night, it blew a gale of wind, and being very dark, the Prussian embraced the opportunity, by cutting the rope which had her in tow, and was fortunate enough to escape.

One morning, at day-break, the squadron was thrown into confusion, by perceiving, in the midst of it, an English 74-gun ship: instead of giving her battle, each ship made the best of her way from her; the Commodore alledging for his conduct, that he had no doubt but the English 74 was the van ship of Lord Nelson's fleet, who had come amongst them for the purpose of a decoy. It was, in the course of this cruise, that they fell in with a convoy from England, and destroyed several ships. They also destroyed the Goldfinch and Brothers, from Tobago to London, and Sparrow, from Newfoundland, bound to the Mediterranean. When the squadron fell in with the Calcutta and her convoy, that ship made a most gallant defence; she entirely disabled a frigate, after a broadside or two; and it was not until she was overpowered by two 74's, that she gave up the contest; one of them was very roughly handled, and lost, in killed and wounded, 30 men—the Calcutta lost nine. In the mean time, the convoy escaped; which was a matter of great anxiety and concern to the Commodore. Having been now a considerable time at sea, and searched in vain for the combined fleets, it was resolved that they should attempt to get into Cadiz.

Le Cerf was accordingly dispatched to reconnoitre, and soon brought back intelligence, that an English squadron was off the port. They next tried Ferrol, but had the mortification to find that port also blockaded. It was then resolved to proceed to Brest or Rochefort; but these ports being both strictly watched by our ships, the enemy was again foiled, and obliged to put off to sea. A second attempt was made at Cadiz, but was attended with no better success. Having on board a number of discontented prisoners, and being reduced to the scanty allowance of half a pint of water per day for each man, they at length determined to make Teneriffe, where they arrived about the latter end of November.

The American Consul, as well as the Prussian and others, came on board the squadron the moment they were apprised that subjects of their several nations were prisoners, to demand their liberty. The only satisfaction given by the Commodore was, that if he had done wrong, he would answer for it on his arrival in France.

By this time Captain Radford had ingratiated himself into the favour of the several officers, and was the only Englishman allowed the honour of dining on shore with them. On the evening advancing, the party grew merry, Captain Radford was permitted to the door, and availing himself of the opportunity, he escaped, under cover of the night, to the town of Oratavie, where he remained concealed until he procured a passage on board a Spanish coaster, bound to the island of Lazaretto, from which place he came home in the ship America, belonging to the United States.

LORD NELSON.

MR. CHARNOCK, in his recently-published *Memoirs* of Lord Viscount Nelson, relates the following anecdote of that illustrious Officer:—

When a Captain, his ship, which had been detached from the fleet on some particular service, rejoined the fleet, needing no inconsiderable refitment and recruit of stores, as well as provisions, ere it could be again pronounced in a fit condition to put to sea. The Commander in Chief, after having received the report, is said to have taken his barge, and proceeding to the ship in question, hailed her, and inquiring for Captain Nelson, told him he should expect his ship to be ready by day-light the ensuing morning. In the ordinary routine of service, many days, at least, would have been necessary for the purpose of re-equipment. Captain Nelson was struck with the magnitude of the task imposed on him, and answered, without giving himself time to recollect, "that it was impossible." His superior officer, with rather unwarranted peevishness, replied, "I don't care for that, I'll have it done." Captain Nelson put an end to the conversation, by answering with the greatest spirit, and still more laconically, "then it shall be done," and quitted the stern gallery without adding another word.

LORD NELSON'S ITALIAN TITLE.

FOR the following information on this subject, we are also indebted to Mr. Charnock's work:—

The Editor of a new edition of *The British Peerage* having, on the suggestion of a learned friend, taken the liberty of writing to his Lordship, (then cruising in the Mediterranean,) transmitted him the following remark on the origin of his title:—"When the King of the Two Sicilies conferred the additional title of Bronte upon that gallant Lord, as a reward for the protection which his fleet afforded to his dominions, he, perhaps, was not aware of its appropriate meaning. It is the *Greek word* for *thunder*. The name of the individual Cyclops, who, in poetic fable, is described as forging the *thunder* of Jupiter, was Bronte. His residence was of course at Ætna, in the island of Sicily.

To this intimation, his Lordship, with his usual affability and attention, immediately returned the following polite answer:—

SIR, *Victory, at Sea, Oct.* 13, 1804.

I am favoured with your letter of August 22. Your observation, with regard to the Dukedom of Bronte, in Sicily, I take to be perfectly just; and I cannot therefore have any objection to your making what use of it you think proper. I will not fail sending the Gazette to Rome by the first opportunity; and, desiring you will believe me thankful for your kind wishes, I remain your most obedient humble servant,

Mr. J. Debrett. NELSON AND BRONTE.

The paper alluded to in the gallant Nobleman's letter, was *The Calcutta Gazette Extraordinary*, of February 27, 1803, containing the speech of the Marquis Wellesley, in the College of Fort William, in Bengal, on distributing the prize-medals and honorary rewards to those young gentlemen who had excelled in oriental learning. It was addressed to the very learned society of the *De Propaganda Fide*, at Rome, who have enriched the world with many valuable oriental works.

LORD NELSON'S PRAYER.

THE following fine composition, so honourable to its heroic author, was written, we are informed, about an hour before the commencement of the battle of Trafalgar:—

May the Great God, whom I worship, grant to my Country, and for the benefit of Europe, a great and glorious Victory! and may no misconduct in any one tarnish it! And may humanity, after Victory, be the predominant feature in the British Fleet!—For myself, individually, I commit my life to Him who made me; and may his blessing light upon my endeavours for serving my Country faithfully!—To Him I resign myself, and the JUST CAUSE *which is entrusted to me to defend!*—

AMEN—AMEN—AMEN!

Victory, Oct. 21, 1805—in sight of the combined fleets of France and Spain—distant about ten miles.

The original of the above, in the hand-writing of Lord Nelson, is said to be in the possession of Sir William Scott.—Devotion itself acquires new attractions from so unaffected an apostrophe, poured forth at so interesting a moment; and his country, from this additional evidence of his virtues, will increase that reverence which is due to his memory.

CAPTAIN WRIGHT.

THE following account of the dreadful sufferings of this gallant and lamented officer, is extracted from a volume of letters, just published, from a gentleman at Paris to a nobleman at London; entitled, *The Secret History of the Court and Cabinet of St. Cloud.*—

From the last time that this officer (Captain Wright) had appeared before the criminal tribunal which condemned Georges and Moreau, his fate was determined on by our government. His firmness offended, and his patriotism displeased; and as he seemed to possess the confidence of his own government, it was judged that he was in its secrets; it was therefore resolved, that if he refused to become a traitor he should perish a victim. Desmarets, Fouché's private Secretary, who is also the Secretary of the secret and *haute* police, therefore ordered him to another private interrogatory. Here he was offered a considerable sum of money, and the rank of an Admiral in our service, if he would divulge what he knew of the plans of his government, of its connections with the discontented of this country, and of its means of keeping up a correspondence with them. He replied, as might have been expected, with indignation to such offers, and to such proposals; but as they were frequently renewed with new allurements, he concluded with remaining silent, giving no answer at all. He was then told that the torture should soon restore him his voice; and some select *gens-d'armes* seized him, and laid him on the rack, where he uttered no complaint, not even a sigh, though instruments the most diabolical were employed, and pains the most acute must have been endured. When threatened that he should expire in torments, he said, "I do not fear to die, because my country will avenge my murder, while my God receives my soul!" During the two first days that he was stretched on the rack, his left arm and right leg were broken, and his nails torn from the toes of both his feet; he then passed into the hands of a Surgeon, and was under his care for five weeks; but before he was perfectly cured, he was carried to another private interrogatory, at which, besides Desmarets, Fouche and Real were present.

The minister of police now informed him, that from the mutilated state of his body, and from what he had gone through, he must be convinced, that it was not the intention of the French government ever to restore him to his native country, where he might relate occurrences which the *policy* of th French required to be buried in oblivion; he therefore had no choice, between serving the Emperor of the French, or perishing within the walls of the prison where he was confined. He replied, that he was resigned to his destiny, and would die as he had lived, faithful to his king and to his country!

The man in the full possession of his mental qualities and corporeal strength, is in most cases very different from that unfortunate being, whose mind is enervated by sufferings, and whose body is weakened by wants. For five months Captain Wright had seen only gaolers, spies, tyrants, executioners, fetters, racks, and other tortures; and for five weeks, his food had been bread, and his drink water. The man, who thus situated and thus perplexed, preserves his native dignity and innate sentiments, is more worthy of monuments, statues, or altars, than either the legislator, the victor, or the saint.

This interrogatory was the last undergone by Captain Wright. He was then again stretched on the rack; and what is called by our regenerators the *infernal* torments, were inflicted on him. After being pinched with red hot irons, all over his body, brandy mixed with gunpowder was infused in the numerous wounds, and set fire to several times, until nearly burned to the bone. In the convulsions, the consequence of these terrible sufferings, he is said to have bit off a part of his tongue; though, as before, no groan was heard. As life still remained, he was again put under the care of his former Surgeon; but as he was exceedingly exhausted, a spy, in the dress of a protestant clergyman, presented himself, as if to read prayers to him. Of this offer he accepted; but when this man began to put some invidious questions, he cast on him a look of contempt, and never spoke to him more. At last seeing no means to obtain any information from him, a Marmaluke last week strangled him in his bed. Thus expired a Hero, whose fate has excited more compassion, and whose character has received more admiration here, than any of our great *men* who have fallen fighting for our Emperor. Captain Wright has diffused new rays of renown and glory on the British name from his tomb as well as from his dungeon.

You have certainly a right to call me to an account for all the particulars I have related of this scandalous and abominable transaction; and though I cannot absolutely guarantee the truth of the narration, I am perfectly satisfied of it myself, and I hope to explain myself to your satisfaction. Your unfortunate countryman was attended by, and under the care of, a Surgeon of the name of Vangoord, who gained his confidence, and was worthy of it, though employed in that infamous gaol. Either from disgust of life, or from attachment to Captain Wright, he survived him only twelve hours, during which he wrote the shocking details I have given you, and sent them to three of the members of the Foreign diplomatic corps, with a prayer to have them forwarded to Sir W. Sidney Smith, or to Mr. Windham, that those his friends might be informed, that, to his last moment, Captain Wright was worthy of their protection and kindness. From one of these ministers I have obtained the original, in Vangoord's own hand-writing.

I know that Buonaparté and Talleyrand promised the release of Captain Wright to the Spanish Ambassador; but at that time he had already suffered once on the rack; and this liberality on their part was merely a trick to impose upon the credulity of the Spaniard, or to get rid of his importunities: had it been otherwise,

Captain Wright, like Sir George Rumbold, would himself have been the first to announce in your country the recovery of his liberty.

HEROIC CONDUCT OF MR. SPRATT, MATE OF THE DEFIANCE.

THE following extraordinary instance of bravery is recorded in the *Gibraltar Chronicle* of January the 11th:—

IN the late glorious action with the combined fleets, His Majesty's ship Defiance, commanded by P. C. Durham, had engaged a French 80-gun ship, within pistol-shot. Mr. Spratt, Mate of the Defiance, from his great activity, had been honoured with the command of the boarders, and likewise promised an opportunity to signalize himself. This brave young officer, in the midst of the action, asked his gallant Captain permission to board, who immediately ordered the helm a-weather, and the boarders to be ready; but this true son of Neptune, fearing the ship would not close, and unwilling to lose so glorious an opportunity, requested of the men who could swim, to follow him. He plunged into the water, swam to the enemy's stern, and entered the gun-room port alone, by the assistance of the rudder chains. His men either misunderstood, or did not hear him, in the clamour of the battle; but our hero made his way courageously through the different decks, and was soon after seen on the enemy's poop, with his hat on the point of his cutlass, calling the boarders to his assistance, who were then anxiously waiting for the ships to close. He attempted to haul down the French colours, but was attacked by several grenadiers, whom he repulsed with success. The ships being pretty close, several of our tars got over, who bent their vengeance on an officer. He cried for mercy, and threw himself at our hero's feet, who saved his life. He had scarcely performed this piece of service, when a musket was levelled at his breast, but so close, that he fortunately struck it downward; receiving, however, the shot through his leg, which was severely fractured. He afterwards fought two of the enemy on his knees, who were soon dispatched by some of the brave tars by whom he was so gallantly supported. The ship soon after struck, and proved to be l'Aigle. This young officer is in the navy hospital; and, we are happy to hear, in a fair way of doing well.

PORTSMOUTH CHURCH.

THE ship at the top of the steeple of Portsmouth church has been taken down and repaired. There having been various reports of its dimensions, we give the following as an accurate statement:—From the stem to the taffrail, 3 feet 5½ inches; the width of the deck, 10½ inches; and the depth of her hull, 14½ inches. She is entirely of copper, and has been new gilt. On the fane of her fore-mast, is the date of her being first placed on the steeple, 1710; the figures being pierced through the fane. The names S. Hawkins, and J. Norris, Churchwardens, with the date, August 17th, 1805, are now stamped on the vessel; and also the names G. Belfour, who new gilt the ship, and J. Hill, who repaired the copper-work. The fane of the fore-mast, and the whole body of the ship, traverse with the wind.

NATIVES OF OWHYHEE.

IT is a curious fact, that the natives of Owhyhee, where Captain Cook lost his life, have, since the æra of the well-known voyage of Captain Vancouver, made astonishing advances to dexterity and skill in our most useful European arts. Tama-hama, the King, is another Peter the Great. Captain Vancouver laid down the keel of his first vessel in 1792. He is now master of more than twenty vessels (some even copper bottomed,) of different sizes, from twenty-five to fifty tons. He encourages Europeans to settle in the island, provided they be industrious, and are acquainted with the arts which may be of use to him. He has a company of body-guards, whom he makes to imitate the European discipline. He has a palace built in the fashion of Europe, of brick, with glass windows. His subjects have learned to make trading voyages as far as the north-west coast of America. He has accumulated larger stores of fire-arms, gunpowder, hardware, and cloth of different sorts, than he has occasion to consume; and it is a truth, however surprising it may appear, that he and his subjects already meditate the design of a trade with China, to be carried on in vessels of their own construction, navigated by their own people. The population of Owhyhee, and the other Sandwich isles, has increased considerably since they were first discovered. On the contrary, that of Otaheite has, in between thirty and forty years, been diminished by dissoluteness, idleness, child-murder, small-pox, and disease, from 200,000 souls to little more than 5000!!

ADMIRAL LANGARA.

ABOUT the middle of January, died at Madrid, the celebrated Admiral and Captain-General of the Spanish Navy, Don Juan de Langara. In consequence of his disregard of his private interest, he died poor, and his widow was in the greatest embarrassment how to provide a funeral adequate to his rank.—The Prince of the Peace being informed of this, wrote a letter to Madame de Langara, in which he expressed his regret at the decease of such a meritorious officer, and, at the same time, informed her he would defray the expenses of the funeral, which was conducted with the utmost magnificence.

CORRESPONDENCE.

MR. EDITOR,

HAVING for years observed with pleasure the interest the NAVAL CHRONICLE invariably evinces in the cause of the "Nation's best Hope," I beg leave to submit the following remarks, for the perusal of your readers, hoping they may catch the eye of those who have it in their power to redress the grievances complained of by a class of officers not unworthy of the solicitude of their country, I mean the Post Captains and Commanders of the British Navy. In the first place, it will hardly be necessary to state, that, with few exceptions, these officers have attained their rank by long and laborious service in the subordinate stations of the Navy; but I will not dwell on their merits or claims, they are known and acknowledged by the country at large; and it is not, I am convinced, the wish of their countrymen, that those whom they look up to as the defenders of every thing most dear to Britons, should many of them feel distress, and silently suffer from want of pecuniary aid, when it is in the power of their country to relieve them. The majority of the Post Captains receive 8s. per day half-pay; Commanders, 6s. 6d. This, I contend, is not sufficient to support them as gentlemen, not to call in question their rank in society; nor is it, in any sense of the word, a remuneration for the important services that body of men daily render their country. I am now, Sir, come to that part of my letter which principally induced me to address you. When a Captain is appointed to a command, either abroad, or at a port in England, he is under the necessity of bearing every expense, both of joining his ship, and also of providing himself with every thing needful for his intended voyage or cruise: he is, according to the custom of the service, obliged to ask at least *three* of his officers every day to partake of his table, and occasionally to afford comfort to the sick. To defray these necessary expenses, he is not allowed one shilling in addition to his pay; which, in the largest frigate, falls short of 300 pounds per annum; and in the smallest, considerably short of 200. In the higher classes, the pay is better proportioned to these expenses; but in any, it is inadequate. I speak from experience, when I say that Captains are not unfrequently obliged to borrow money, to enable them to fit out their ships, often on disadvantageous terms, relying on the chance of making captures for repayment, which I may venture to assert, falls not to the lot of one in ten of the number employed.

A POOR POST CAPTAIN.

MR. EDITOR,

THE importance of the art of navigation to this island, in times of peace as well as of war, is generally acknowledged; yet perhaps it may be doubted, whether it have been encouraged here in a degree suitable to its importance. I am aware of the rewards which have been offered, by certain acts of parliament, for the discovery of the longitude at sea, &c.; yet more might certainly have been done to excite emulation among men of science. In support of this assertion, were it necessary, I might enumerate the prizes which, from time to time, have been given by foreign academies for improvements in navigation and astronomy, and recount the learned tracts which have been produced in consequence of such encouragement; but I shall at present wave the subject.

In all civilised nations, arts and sciences have been considered as forming a part of the education of the great, and as being particularly under their patronage. Amongst the men of rank in this country, in former ages, are to be found the names of Napier, Bacon, Boyle, Newton, Macclesfield, and Stanhope; men who excelled in science themselves, and who patronised it in others. May I then be allowed to suggest to the higher classes of society, the propriety of subscribing a few hundred pounds for the purpose of defraying the expense of printing such scientific tracts, as are not easily to be met with, and are not likely to be undertaken by any bookseller or publisher, from the improbability of their meeting so extensive a sale as might answer the purpose of trade.

These ideas occurred to me on the recent perusal of the *Scriptores Logarithmici*, published some time ago by Baron Maseres. The preface to the fourth volume of that work appears to be written with so benevolent a design, and points out to the great, objects so worthy of their attention, that, as I wish it to be more generally known, it will afford me much pleasure to see it noticed in the NAVAL CHRONICLE.

The passage alluded to, begins in page 9 of the preface, where, speaking of Dr. James Wilson's *Historical Dissertation on the Rise and Progress of the Modern Art of Navigation*, the Baron says:—

It is full of curious historical matter, and has suggested to my mind a wish that some person of affluence, fond of the subject of navigation, and who should have been indebted to it, perhaps for his rank or fortune, would cause a collection of all the authors on that subject, whose works are mentioned in this dissertation, to be made, and reprinted in a handsome manner in a set of quarto volumes of the size of these volumes of the *Scriptores Logarithmici*. Such collections of learned tracts on particular subjects, under various titles suited to the several subjects of which they treated, would be very convenient in the present state of science, which is extended to such a variety of subjects, and dispersed in such a number of different books, that it is very difficult and very expensive for a person, fond of any particular branch of science, to procure himself all the books that relate to it. Besides the collection called the *Scriptores Nautici*, relating to navigation, there might be a collection called *Scriptores Statici*, relating to the doctrine of *staticks*, or bodies at rest that form an equilibrium, or counterpoise to each other; under which head all the books of merit that treat of the *lever*, the *inclined plane*, and the other mechanical powers, would be comprized, and those that treat of the catenary curve, and of the partial immersion and the positions of bodies floating in liquids of greater specific gravity than themselves, and of many other curious subjects of the like nature. And there might be another collection called *Scriptores Phoronomici*, relating to the doctrines of bodies in motion; under which head would be comprized Galileo's Mechanical Dialogues, of which the third and fourth contain the doctrine of the fall of heavy bodies to the earth, with the law of their acceleration, and of their motion on inclined planes, and of the motion of the pendulum in circular arches, and of the motion of projectiles, which (abstracting from the resistance of the air,) would describe paraboles; and under the same head would be comprised Mr. Huygens's track on the motions of perfectly elastic bodies striking against each other; and his admirable treatise *de Horologio Oscillatorio*, or on the motion of a pendulum clock, and his tract on central forces; and all Sir Isaac Newton's most profound, but very difficult work, called the *Principia; or, Mathematical Principles of Natural Philosophy*, with the several commentators on it, and Herman's *Phoronomia*, and Euler's work *de Metu*. Another collection might relate to the finding the centres of gravity of different bodies; which is, I believe, a more subtle and difficult subject than is generally supposed. This collection might be called *Scriptores Centrobarici*. And another collection might consist of all the writers on opticks, under the title of *Scriptores Optici*. This collection should comprise the work of Euclid, or that which has been ascribed to him on this subject; and those of Athazen, and Vilellio, and Roger Bacon, (the learned English monk,) and *Antonio de Dominis*, and Willebrond Snell, and des Cartes, and Huygens's Dioptricks, and his treatise *de Lumine*, and other works of his on the subject of Opticks; and James Gregory's *Optica Promota*, and Dr. Barrow's *Lectiones Opticæ*, and Sir Isaac Newton's *Lectiones Opticæ*, and his treatise on *Opticks*, or Experiments on Light and Colours; and Molineux's Dioptricks, and Dr. Smith's Complete System of Opticks, and Harris's Opticks, and many papers in the Philosophical Transactions relating to the same subject. If such separate collections of authors were published, every person who was devoted to any particular branch of these sciences, (and no man can attend to all of them, or even to many of them, with any great prospect of becoming masters of them,) might buy the collection which related to his particular branch at a moderate expense.

CAUSES OF THE NAVAL SUPERIORITY OF ENGLAND.

MR. EDITOR,

THE naval superiority of England is felt and acknowledged by all nations, and has excited the admiration even of her enemies. Her fleets, attaining the zenith of nautical skill, have performed actions which will be read by posterity with astonishment; and it may not be uninteresting to inquire into some of the causes that have so decidedly secured to her the Empire of the Ocean.

Surrounded by the sea, and depending for her very existence, as an independent nation, upon maritime resources, England, at an early period, attended to the formation of a navy. During the administration of Cromwell, the English name became terrible at sea; and the Dutch, who till then had been considered invincible, received most decisive defeats. From that period, the English seamen have entertained a thorough contempt for their foes, and the latter have always engaged them with reluctance. A people renowned for skill, valour, and repeated successes, have to contend with dispirited antagonists; and, in this respect, the English have constantly had the vantage ground.

A strict attention to discipline has at all times characterised the British navy. "The power and effect of every great body depends upon the manner in which it is put in motion;" and Britain is principally indebted for her victories to the matchless œconomy of her naval system. Orders are obeyed with a promptitude which must be seen to be appreciated, and which facilitates operations, that a disorganised enemy can never execute. On the other hand, the French marine constantly in disorder, became, in consequence of the romantic ideas which the revolution had diffused over the minds of the mariners, unmanageable. It was, however, supposed that those ideas which had rendered the French armies respectable on the land, would also scatter the naval enemies of the republic. Their squadrons, which, under the *grand Monarque*, were unable to contend with those of England, were now to wrest from her, for ever, the Sovereignty of the Main. The battle of the first of June was, however, the triumph of discipline and subordination, and terminated in the complete humiliation of the republican flag.

As the political furor subsided, the leaders of the French people, roused by their many losses, began to see the necessity of reforming their almost ruined marine. Buonaparte was among the first to notice the pernicious effects of the revolutionary doctrines, which had destroyed every useful distinction of rank, and which had taught the French seamen to put themselves on a level with their commanders. In an interview with the Admirals and Captains of the Toulon fleet, he addressed them in these words :—"*The losses of the French navy should not excite surprize. Its officers have not had sufficient authority to cause themselves to be respected.—On land, an undisciplined army may sometimes be victorious; at sea, never.*"—But it is not on a sudden that unruly bodies of men can be brought to that degree of order which may entitle them to be esteemed *disciplined.* It is also much more difficult to cause an unorganized navy to act with effect, than to arrange an army.—The latter may be formed in a year or two, and if repulsed, may be rallied and recruited: but seamen are not to be raised on the emergency of the moment; they are nursed in the cradle of a tempestuous sea from their infancy, and, from that tender state, are familiarized to dangers and death. At the time when the First Consul began the work of reformation, the prime mariners of France were pining in English prisons, and his conscripts were very indifferent substitutes; whatever discipline, therefore, he might institute, would be of trivial service. The ships of the republic had also remained for a long season inactive: and inactivity is still more hurtful to the naval than to the land service: those ships had also been beaten, and disgraced. With the English, there had been a course of loyalty, discipline, skill, activity, and continued victory. The latter rushed into battle assured of conquest: the former considered combat and defeat as the same thing.

At the revolution, too many of the naval commanders quitted the French service; and if to the defection of these be added the many, who, for their loyalty perished, "*Quem neque pauperies, neque mors, neque vincula terrent,*" we may well suppose that it was no easy matter for Buonaparté to organize his disordered marine.

The French fleets have also been suffered to leave port, not only deranged as to subordination, but deficient in equipment. While British vessels are prepared for war, in a manner which no nation yet has rivalled, those of France enter on the ocean destitute of the stores necessary to the waging of successful war. In the battle of the 1st of June, the superiority of British equipment was manifest. The anchor of the Brunswick having hooked that of le Vengeur, both ships necessarily fell alongside each other.

In this situation, the crew of the former finding it impossible to *ram home* their ammunition, by reason of their *wooden rammers* coming in contact with the sides of their opponent, had recourse to the rope rammers, with which every British ship is furnished, and very easily effected their purpose. The French seamen had no such resource, and le Vengeur soon after sunk.

[To be continued.]

AN HONOURABLE ACCOMMODATION OF OUR DIFFERENCES WITH THE DEY AND REGENCY OF ALGIERS.

[Extract of a letter from His Majesty's ship Superb.]

Maddalena Bay, Sardinia, January 16, 1805.

ON the 28th of December, having received on board a Mr. Cartwright, lately from England, we parted from our squadron, then off Cape San Sebastiano; and at day-break of the 3d inst. arrived off Algiers. The Rev. Dr. Scott, Chaplain of the Victory, and the Rev. Mr. Evans, of the Superb, (both conversant in the Italian language,) went ashore with Lieutenant Butler early in the forenoon, and were soon conducted into the presence of the Dey. After the usual salutation of shaking hands, (a privilege allowed to none but British subjects,) Dr. Scott proceeded to read to him Lord Nelson's letter, which was in Italian: it was further explained either in the Turkish or in the Morisco language, by Mr. Busnach, a very opulent merchant, chief of the Jewish inhabitants, and possessed of great influence at Algiers. His Highness the Dey expressed his satisfaction in the strongest terms at our having brought with us a Consul: but, on hearing that part of the letter which stated the conditions on which alone he could ever be landed, he not only vehemently protested he would never comply with them, but even advanced in opposition, a claim on his part; which, as far as I can learn, was never insisted on when we were there in January and June last. Mr. Evans, on this, returned on board, in order to communicate to Captain Keats the result of the audience; and on the following morning he went ashore again with further instructions—but all tending invariably (if we may judge from the final issue of the embassy) to the unconditional attainment of the demands already delivered in. Dr. Scott, in the mean time, had been very actively and usefully engaged in impressing on the minds of the Ministers, that nothing else than absolute compliance with the ultimatum proposed, could ensure a continuance of that amity which had so long prevailed between His Britannic Majesty and the Kingdom of Algiers. On the 5th Captain Keats landed, and had an audience of the Dey. I am inclined to believe that it was a *tempestuous* one—but that it finally had a good effect. On the morrow, he returned to the charge; and, after a long and violent consultation in full Divan, it was at length determined that his demands ought to be complied with. That night he was under the necessity of remaining on shore. Here I must observe, that Mr. Mountford, Secretary to Colonel Lear, the American Consul, (then at Malta respecting their affairs with Tripoli,) had on the 3d made an offer of his house and table as long as the Superb should remain off Algiers; his friendly and hospitable invitation was gladly and thankfully received: it appearing by no means politically advisable to open the English house. Our terms having now been fully acknowledged to be equitable and honourable, and a perfect compliance with them having been promised, no further cause of complaint seemed to exist:—But a serious and unexpected obstacle intervened at the very moment that the primary and principal object of the Embassy was about to be attained by us. The consequence was, that Captain Keats, after a spirited remonstrance, instantly returned on board. Nearly at that time, having by means of signals, made by one of our boats ashore, received favourable intelligence, the wind also favouring us, we came to an anchor, and were saluted with 21 guns; which compliment we immediately returned. On the morning of the 8th all impediments were removed; and the indispensable demands, first proposed, being now unconditionally acceded to and carried into effect, Mr. Cartwright landed about noon, and was received with the usual marks of distinction—but with unusual joy; for the inhabitants—Turks, Moors, and Jews, dread above all things a war with England. He was presented by Captain Keats to the Dey, who received him in a very gracious and friendly manner. The English Consular house was then thrown open, and thus was Mr. Cartwright most honourably established at Algiers.

On the 11th, having taken in a plentiful supply of fresh provisions and vegetables, &c., Captain Keats had his audience of leave; and in the evening we left the bay. The wind proving favourable, we joined our brave Commander in Chief and the squadron, early on the 15th, at this anchorage. I cannot conclude without expressing my full conviction, that this happy termination of our differences with Algiers, is principally to be attributed to the zeal, judgment, and intrepidity of Captain Keats; the whole tenor of whose conduct was such as to extort professions of respect and esteem even from the Ministers he treated with, at the very moment that they were reluctantly complying with his demands. Calling to mind the very tenacious and irritable disposition of the Dey, biassed by pecuniary considerations, inflamed also by the sly insinuations and artful intrigues of a designing faction, at the head of which is the representative of Buonaparté; powerful at the time; but whose strength is *now* no more:—If you consider these, I say, and the many other obstacles we had to contend against, you will admit that we have accomplished a task Herculean.

The Superb, you will remember, is the ship that, in the awful and memorable night of the 12th of July, 1801, (having been sent a-head by the Admiral, the gallant Sir James Saumarez,) singly opened her fire on the rear of the combined enemy, and caused the destruction of the Real Carlos and San Hermenegildo, of 112 guns each; after which she chased, fought, and captured le Saint Antoine, of equal force with herself. *There* we had an opportunity of maintaining the honour of the British flag; and we have now been the means of hoisting it again at Algiers, with increased respect and dignity. After an absence of nearly four years, we now naturally look with anxious hopes to that happy period which will recall us to the bosom of our friends and relatives, to our dear fire-side, in the favoured abode of happiness and liberty.

MR. EDITOR,

THE following is an extract of a letter written by an officer of the Bellerophon:—

(From Mr. Mottley's Portsmouth Paper.)

Bellerophon, off the Start, Dec. 2, 1805.

I HAD the pleasure of writing to my aunt from off Cadiz, on the 21st of September, just after the entry of the combined fleets into that place. I am happy to convey you now the intelligence of their entire defeat; which, though I was confident would take place whenever they mustered courage enough to come out, yet I scarcely expected they would so soon have given us an opportunity of again showing the superiority of the British Navy. You will doubtless have already seen a much better account of the action than I can possibly give you; but as I hope what few particulars I have been able to obtain, will not prove unacceptable to you, I sit down to give you the best account in my power.—

The combined fleet, after their action with Sir R. Calder, put into Vigo, and leaving there three of their disabled ships, sailed again for Ferrol, off which they were joined by fourteen sail of the line, and proceeded with the whole of their fleet, consisting of twenty-nine sail of the line, to Cadiz, where they arrived on the 20th of August. Admiral Collingwood, with four sail of the line, was cruising off the port when they hove in sight, and would most probably have been taken had they attempted to pursue him, which luckily they did not. The Bellerophon, and three more sail of the line, which were up the Straits, joined Admiral Collingwood on the 23d, and Sir R. Calder's squadron on the 31st. Our fleet then consisted of twenty-six sail of the line, and we immediately resumed the blockade of Cadiz with the greatest severity, till Lord Nelson joined and took the command on the 29th of September. His plan being to give the enemy an opportunity of coming out, he only left a squadron of frigates cruising off the harbour, whilst the fleet continued cruising to the N.W., frequently out of sight of land. As we knew the enemy, who were now reinforced by five sail of the line in Cadiz, had positive orders to put to sea, and retrieve their character, after their action with Sir R. Calder, we were in momentary expectation of their coming out, and every ship that was perceived coming from the in-shore squadron was expected to convey the welcome intelligence. Every one was in the highest spirits; and so confident were our people of success, that on the very morning of the action, when we were bearing down on a superior fleet, they were employed in fixing the number of their prizes, and pitching upon that which should fall to the lot of each of our ships: ours, by the calculation of the oldest sailors on board, was to have been the Santissima Trinidada, the Spanish four-decker; and I dare say we were far from being the only ship in the fleet that had fixed upon her. We were not long kept in that state of anxiety and suspense, which you will naturally suppose every one in our situation must have felt, for about nine o'clock in the morning of the 19th of October, the Mars was observed firing guns and making signals for the enemy's fleet being getting under weigh. The Admiral immediately made signal for a general chase, and to clear for action, which was obeyed with the greatest alacrity, and in ten minutes the whole fleet was under all sail, steering for the Straits, which was supposed to be the enemy's destination, for the purpose of forming a junction with the Carthagena and Toulon squadrons. The Bellerophon, Belleisle, Leviathan, Orion, and Polyphemus, soon showed their superiority of sailing, and got far a-head of the rest of the fleet: at day-light in the morning we were in sight of the Rock of Gibraltar, but, on a frigate's making signal for the enemy's fleet bearing N.E., wore, and again formed the order of sailing: the day was unfavourable and weather squally, so that we did not get sight of the enemy, though our small vessels formed a chain betwixt them and us. In the following night we got so close to them as to perceive plainly their signals, and every one was in the most anxious state of suspense, till day-light the next morning (21st,) when the enemy was plainly discerned about seven miles to leeward of us, and about five leagues from Cape Trafalgar. Every advantage was on their side; they had thirty-three sail of the line, whilst we had only twenty-seven: they were full of seamen and troops, and had a friendly port under their lee; whilst we had to beat off shore after the action, and might certainly have expected some of our disabled ships would have drifted on shore, but nothing was an obstacle to the Hero of Aboukir, and he immediately made signal to bear down upon the enemy in two columns, himself in the Victory leading the starboard division, Admiral Collingwood in the Royal Sovereign the larboard one, in which the Bellerophon was the fifth ship; no signal was ever obeyed with more promptitude; one would have thought that the people were preparing for a festival, rather than a combat; and no dissatisfaction was expressed, except at the state of the weather, which was calm, and prevented our nearing the enemy till ten o'clock, when a light breeze springing up, we came up with them fast. They were in the mean time employed in forming a close and well-imagined, though, till now, unexampled order of battle; but which, had their plan of defence been as well executed as it was contrived, would have rendered our victory much more dearly bought than it has been: they were formed in a double line, thus—

1 2 3

4 5 6

French and Spaniards alternately, and it was their intention on our breaking the line (which manœuvre they expected we should as usual put in execution) astern of No. 4, for No. 2 to make sail, that the British ship in hauling up should fall on board of her, while No. 5 should bear up and rake her, and No. 1 would bring her broadside to bear on her starboard bow.—Luckily, this manœuvre only succeeded with the Tonnant and Bellerophon, which were among the ships that suffered most. A few moments before the action commenced, Lord Nelson conveyed the following sentence by telegraph, to the fleet—"England expects every man will do his duty!" The loud and repeated cheering with which this was received, was a convincing proof that such an injunction was needless.

At noon precisely the action commenced by the Fougeux and Monarca opening fire on the Royal Sovereign. Now follows an extract from our log:—"12 10 Royal Sovereign opened fire on the enemy's centre.—12 13 answered 16 general.—12 20 Royal Sovereign, at the head of the larboard division, broke the enemy's line astern of a Spanish three-decker, and engaged her to leeward, being followed by the Mars, Belleisle, and Tonnant, who engaged their respective opponents.—12 25 opened our fire on the enemy.—12 28 Victory, at the head of the starboard division, opened her fire on the enemy.—12 30 engaging both sides in passing through the enemy's line, astern of a Spanish two-decker (El Monarca.)—12 35 fell on board the French two-deck ship l'Aigle, whilst hauling to the wind, our fore-yard locking with her main one, kept up a brisk fire both on her, on our starboard bow, and a Spanish two-decker (El Monarca) on the larboard bow, at the same time receiving and returning fire with a Spanish two-decker (Bahama) on the larboard quarter, and receiving the fire of a Spanish two-decker (St. Juan Nepomuceno) athwart our stern, and a French two-decker (la Swiftsure) on the starboard quarter: the action soon after became general. At one the main and mizen-top-masts fell over the starboard side, main-top-sail and top-gallant-sail caught fire.—1 5 the Master, and 1 11 the Captain fell, still foul of l'Aigle, and keeping up a brisk fire from the main and lower decks; quarter-deck, poop, and forecastle being nearly cleared by the enemy's musketry, chiefly from troops on board l'Aigle.—1 20 the jib-boom was shot away.—1 40 l'Aigle dropt astern under a raking fire from us as she fell off, our ship at this time quite unmanagable from braces, bowlines, &c. shot away.—1 45 l'Aigle was engaged by the Defiance.—2 5 she struck.—On the smoke clearing up, observed several of the enemy's ships had struck.—Fired several shot at El Monarca, our first opponent, when she struck.—3 sent an officer and party of men to take possession of her.—3 6 the ship being ungovernable, and in danger of falling on board of Tonnant, Temeraire, and prizes, made 318 to Sirius, out boats and sent them a-head to tow, towed and swept the ship clear of them; received prisoners from our prizes.—4 5 answered 101.—4 10 opened our fire on five French ships making off to windward, the sternmost of which was cut off, and struck to the Minotaur.—5 7 the firing ceased, thirteen sail of the enemy's ships making off to leeward, four of their line to windward.—5 20 answered 99 general.—5 30 took possession of El Bahama, Spanish 74.—Sunset, one of the prizes sunk, another blew up." Thus far our log; but it will not be amiss to mention, that whilst engaged with the five ships in this situation, l'Aigle twice attempted to board us, and hove several grenades into our lower deck, which burst and wounded several of our people most dreadfully, she likewise set fire to our fore chains; our fire was so hot, that we soon drove them from the lower deck, after which our people took the coins out, and elevated their guns, so as to tear her decks and sides to pieces: when she got clear of us, she did not return a single shot whilst we raked her, her starboard quarter was entirely beaten in, and, as we afterwards learnt, 400 men *hors de combat*, so that she was an easy conquest for the Defiance, a fresh ship: we were well matched, she being the best manned ship in the Combined, and we in the British fleet. Unfortunately situated as we were, I have no doubt she would have struck, had we been able to follow and engage her for a quarter of an hour longer; but had we been fairly alongside of her, half an hour would have decided the contest; for I must say I was astonished at the coolness and undaunted bravery displayed by our gallant and veteran crew, when surrounded by five enemy's ships, and for a length of time unassisted by any of ours. Our loss, as might be expected, was considerable, and fell chiefly on our prime seamen, who were foremost in distinguishing themselves; twenty-eight, including the Captain, Master, and a Midshipman, were killed outright; and 127, including the Captain of Marines, who had eight balls in his body, and his right arm shot off, before he quitted the deck; Boatswain, and five Midshipmen, were badly wounded, and about forty more slightly, so as not to be incapable of duty; nineteen of the wounded had already died before we left Gibraltar. I consider myself as very fortunate in having escaped unhurt, as our class suffered so severely. Our second Lieutenant, myself, and eight men, formed the party that took possession of the Monarca: we remained till the morning without further assistance, or we should most probably have saved her, though she had suffered much more than ourselves; we kept possession of her however for four days, in the most dreadful weather, when having rolled away all our masts, and being in danger of immediately sinking or running on shore, we were fortunately saved by the Leviathan, with all but about 150 prisoners, who were afraid of getting into the boats. I can assure you I felt not the least fear of death during the action, which I attribute to the general confidence of victory which I saw all around me; but in the prize, when I was in danger of, and had time to reflect upon the approach of death, either from the rising of the Spaniards upon so small a number as we were composed of, or what latterly appeared inevitable from the violence of the storm, I was most certainly afraid; and at one time, when the ship made three feet water in ten minutes, when our people were almost all lying drunk upon deck, when the Spaniards, completely worn out with fatigue, would no longer work at the only chain pump left serviceable; when I saw the fear of death so strongly depicted on the countenances of all around me, I wrapped myself up in a union jack, and lay down upon deck for a short time, quietly awaiting the approach of death; but the love of life soon after again roused me, and after great exertions on the part of the British and Spanish officers, who had joined together for the mutual preservation of their lives, we got the ship before the wind, determined to run her on shore: this was at midnight, but at day-light in the morning, the weather being more moderate, and having again gained upon the water, we hauled our wind, perceiving a three-decker (El Rayo) dismasted, but with Spanish colours up, close to leeward of us: the Leviathan, the first British ship we had seen for the last thirty hours, seeing this, bore down, and firing a shot a-head of us, the Rayo struck without returning a gun.

PHILOSOPHICAL PAPERS.

Extracts from a Book entitled, "Naval Speculations and Maritime Politics; being a Modest and Brief Discourse of the Royal Navy of England, and of its Œconomy and Government." By HENRY MAYDMAN. 1691.

[Continued from Vol. XIV, page 135.]

FIFTHLY; The Master Attendant is an officer of business and trust, for transporting of ships in and out of the harbour, taking care for laying the ships (all that enter the port) at safe moorings; that they damnifie not each other, do not break loose, &c.; to take care to unstore, ungun, unrigg, and unballast them; and bring them to and from the dock, and heave them into the dock, and out, provide ballast, and all manner of rigging, cables, sails, anchors, and cordage, for them; suitable and answerable stores for their voyage: and on their returns again to survey the Boatswain's remains, and take care for the laying them up for preservation; the Clerk of the Survey being the Surveyor's instrument, for surveying the stores of as well the Boatswain's stores, under the Master Builder's oversight, passing their accounts by the vouchers signed by the Builders and Master Attendant, of their remains; and of the Captains, their expense at sea. The Master Attendant also commands and directs the labourers of the yard; orders the cutting and making of rigging at the rigging house, appoints and directs the ordinary; that is, the Boatswain's servants, and extraordinary men, born on the ships in harbour; and takes notice of the respective persons under his command, of their either neglect or attending their duty: all which he performs by his substitutes, as by the Boatswains of ships for the ordinary, and when he detaches labourers to work on float, to clear ships, heave ballast, &c. And for the labourers, the Boatswain of the yard, although warranted, works them; yet subordinate to the Master Attendant: the said Yard-Boatswain also directs the teams of draught horses, for drawing of timber, &c., and heaving it out of vessels by labourers; also all manner of stores received in, and cleaning of the docks and yards, providing of shovels, pickaxes, hand-spikes, ropes, blocks, and all instruments to do the said work, and for heaving in and out ships at the docks. The Master Attendant also appoints Pilots for carrying ships in and out of harbour, and signs their bills for it; as also the huyes and lighters hired for carrying of ballast. His business is of large extent, and he ought to be a man of good knowledge, as of the practice of the navy, so as of the shoals and tides of the harbour; a man of care, industry, courage, temperance, justice, and honesty; and well encouraged and supported in his commands: so ought also the Check, Builders, &c. in their respective stations, by the Commissioner of the place, and also of the Board: whereas if he be void of knowledge, great damages will ensue to ships in their transportations and ridings, he not being acquainted with the shoals, and setting of tides, and the lyings of moreings in the harbour: the elder Boatswains indeed may be his guide, who officiate under him; but they will be apt to be cross, and think they are wronged of their birth-right, whose opinion I cannot condemn: neither can I think it either just, expedient, or safe, to the King's service, to put a stranger who never served, nor knew the practice of the navy, over the heads of able men, who have spent their whole days in the said service;

and therefore I cannot forbear to say here, as I have elsewhere said, in the preferment and encouragement of Clerks: for it is hard measure, that a man shall be neglected, and put by preferment, not for any inability, but that he hath not made interest enough, or is not willing to down with his dust; although he has served his life long, and is a man of much experience and merit; which sort of men, as I have elsewhere said, are modest, and backward to offer to buy (as I there called it) their fetters.

One thing I have forgotten to hint, before the which perhaps may not be unfitly applied here; it being an observation I have made in the Navy, viz. That it is the opinion and practice of many, not the best officers, that they will bid the highest rate for advancement; concluding, that when attained they are arrived into the Land of *Canaan*, (viz. Rest,) but not of promise to them; but was promised, perhaps, to more meritorious men, but that their money and interest came short: yet of rest they are resolved to make it; concluding, that their profits being increased, their cares should be abated: and therefore they do resolve to live quiet and secure, and act that part that shall procure them that; and let the world go round, if their policy fail not, their sleep shall be sound; and let the inferior be industrious and full of cares: but I think it is altogether unsuitable to the mind of a good man or christian, a good officer, or liegeman to his King and Country; and also should think, the higher his office the more his cares; not only in the sight of good men, but required by God: for the sword of justice was never designed by him to be put into the hands of one who will sheath it, and play the truant; wherefore I am well assured, that it would contribute to the welfare and promotion of the glory and strength of the Navy and Nation, and be most agreeable to the dictates of God Almighty, to let justice be plentifully administered through the whole series of the affair; that the least member thereof may gather enough for the expense of his family, of that heavenly dew of manna, which is the emanations of Heaven upon man; and he that hath justice in him, hath (although but weakly) one of the cardinal attributes of God. I will end this paragraph with a declamation against the injustice of some years past; to dispose of the places of the biggest ships, unto young uncapable men, that never served in the affair; nor, I believe, never will, when need requires it; but like the drones in the bee-hive, live at home, and spend the honey, and the public service serve only them: nay, one employment hath not been enough, but two or three of the best; I mean, of the middle stations of the Navy; I say, two or more have been one man's share, and deserving men, of good and approved abilities, and of long standing and service, have been put by, or only continued in their low and beginning station; and by consequence must veil to children and pupils in business, if they will have bread.

But I return to my Master Attendant, who if he be not a man of novel inventions, and break the practices of the yards, and do not be put upon through his weakness, and ignorance of his authority, and right of command, by any malevolent and turbulent Boatswain, that acts under him; and who tells him, that it is not the duty of the ordinary to heave out the provisions left in the ships; for they are not the King's, but the Purser's; and so cause the wheels to stand still, and the docks to stand void, as I have before hinted, and so damnifie the service considerably, and also the officer: I say, he ought also to have courage, and stand on his right of commanding men out of ships, to clear others, as the necessity of the service requires, and the Commissioner of the place directs; although there be a Captain that denies his men to do it, except they be paid for it; I say he ought to bid hard up to the positive point, and there to leave it, and the damages thereof, at the Captains or Commissioners doors. So that you see, that the vertue of courage must not be wanting; for if it be, he cannot perform the service well. Also justice and honesty he ought to be well stockt with; otherwise he will be tempted to connive with the Boatswain's embezzlements, and sign over large expenses; and he may be tempted to sign over large ballast-bills: and again, he may abuse and hinder many other good officers in their servants, under the pretence of uprightness to the King's business; and pour out his favours upon his creatures: I say, this officer ought to be endued with very good vertues, or else he may, instead of doing much service to the affair, do very much disservice, &c.

Sixthly, The Clerk of the Survey is an officer presented thereto by the Surveyor, but warranted by the Admiralty; who keeps the account of all stores received into the yard by the Store-keeper; surveys them at their entrance; and is one that signs the bills for them to the Navy-board. He surveys all remains of stores at the returns of ships from sea; of Boatswains, and Carpenters, and passes their accounts. He signs vouchers to Store-keepers for sea stores, with the Master-Attendant, and Builders, with whom, and the Store-keepers, his business interferes very much; and his affair or duty being in a less compass, and without the reach of much disquiet, or trouble, he may be the more happy, if he be a man of that temper, to use it so. His business being retired, and within himself, his temptations to dishonesty are the more and more recluse and private, having opportunities thereby to cause him to fall, and break his trust; and therefore had need be a man endowed with honest and just principles: also, he ought to be of good knowledge in the nature of stores, and a ready Clerk for accounts. Mostly, the Surveyor takes great care to present a fit and experienced Clerk, otherwise it would distract his office aloft; and, commonly, he presents one that has served before, in some under-clerkship of the same office; which is a sort of justice I wish were practised throughout the Navy. I am sure he is the more safe and quiet in his business; and, no doubt, the better dispatches are made therein, by people apt and known to the business, without tricks, projects, or new fangles for lucre. I know no office in the Navy of that quantity, that transacts their business with dispatch, with so little notice or perturbation, and are so very sedate and quiet; undoubtedly, the more happy themselves, and those that negotiate with them; and the services of the King in that affair go, or at least run, in the strait channel, without meanders and turnings.

Naval Reform.

THE SIXTH REPORT OF THE COMMISSIONERS OF NAVAL INQUIRY.

[Continued from page 157.]

IN May, 1801*, some regulations were established, by order of His Majesty in Council, for the better government of the dock-yards; grounded on the report made in 1788 by the Commissioners appointed by

---

* *The Examination of Mr. Thomas Netherton, First Clerk to the Clerk of the Check of His Majesty's Yard at Plymouth; taken upon Oath the 29th of August*, 1803.

How long have you been a clerk to the clerk of the check of this dock-yard, and how long in your present situation?—I have been in the office since the 7th November, 1761; and I was made first clerk, I think, in March 1785.

What instructions has the clerk of the check for his guidance, in the performance of his several duties?—To the best of my recollection I never saw the instructions given to the late clerk of the check at the time of his appointment, but I have understood them to be of a date prior to the year 1700. At the visitation of Lord Howe, when first Lord of the Admiralty, those instructions were

an Act of Parliament passed in the twenty-fifth year of his present Majesty's reign, to inquire into the fees and emoluments of the public Offices.

---

said to have been delivered to the Board, and an expectation entertained that new instructions would speedily be given, as the old ones were in many instances obsolete; but some years after printed instructions were sent to the officers, which I have understood were copies of the former.

Is there any general abstract in the clerk of the check's office of the warrants of the Navy Board, which contain instructions for the regulation of his conduct? —No.

Can the clerk of the check readily and distinctly, by reference to the books and papers in his office, collect the instructions and intentions of the Navy Board on every particular branch of his duty?—I consider he cannot, without looking over the orders issued from the first establishment of this dock-yard, which are very voluminous.

Under what instructions do the clerks in the clerk of the check's office act?—To the best of my recollection the instructions given to the clerks respecting their duties were verbal; but since the appointment of the present clerk of the check, written instructions to the several clerks were drawn up by his direction, and entered in a book, and lodged in the office for their guidance.

Has it been usual for the clerk of the check to allot different duties to the clerks in his office, sometimes employing them on one service and sometimes on another?—The present clerk of the check has done so.

When were the present rates of daily pay for the artificers and labourers of this yard established?—This yard was first established in January 1691; but there is a book in the clerk of the check's office, by which the artificers and labourers employed in the King's service appear to have been paid for the month of December 1690, in which the builder is borne at the rate of two shillings and a penny a day; the foremen or quartermen at two shillings and twopence, the joiners at one shilling and eightpence a day, the oakum boys at eightpence a day, and the others at the same rate as at present: the shipwrights two shillings and a penny, the pitch-heaters one shilling and sixpence, and the labourers one shilling and twopence a day, with the same rate of pay for extra as at present, excepting the shipwrights, who had then eightpence a tide, for which they now receive seven pence halfpenny.

When were the artificers of this yard first employed by task and job, and what directions have been given by the Navy Board from time to time on that subject? —The shipwrights were first employed by task work in the building of new ships in the year 1775, for which they were paid according to a scheme of prices fixed by the Navy Board, by their warrant of 22d March, 1775. This scheme was altered, by their warrants of 22d August, 1775; 3d May, 1776; and 7th January, 1784.—On the first institution of task work, the men continued to work by task but a short time, being dissatisfied with the original scheme of prices, as no provision was made therein for the payment of labour on materials which might prove defective; they in consequence struck work, and were discharged from the King's service on the 29th June, 1775, but on the 21st August following were re-entered, with an option of working either task or day work.—The task work was renewed in 1788, and the shipwrights have been so employed on new work at different times, at the discretion of the Navy Board, ever since.

The principal objects of these regulations were, the establishment of a system for the better management and conversion of timber; the

The first scheme for task work for the mast-makers was dated the 2d September, 1790, and the mast-makers employed on task work were governed by the rates contained in that order until the 21st February, 1799, when a new scheme was established by the Navy Board, which has been acted upon ever since.—The scheme of task for the boat-builders for building new boats was established 7th November, 1794, which has been acted on ever since.—The scheme of prices for the shipwrights employed in the capstern house, was dated 27th April, 1795, and for those employed in the top house and stocking anchors on the 16th May following, by which they have since continued to work. The shipwrights employed by task on new ships have only been permitted to work the single day hours, except on particular occasions, such as bringing to hot plank, and works of a like kind; and although they have in general been paid according to the amount of their earnings, those earnings have in some instances been restricted to double day's pay. The employment of the shipwrights by job work, in the repairs of ships, was first established by the Navy Board's warrant of 3d December, 1783, which directs that no job shall be undertaken until a valuation for the work was settled by the master shipwright and his assistants, in conjunction with the clerk of the check, which valuation was to be submitted for their approbation. On the 3d January, 1802, a scheme of prices for job work was established by the Navy Board; and for such works only as were not included in that scheme, a valuation was to be proposed by the officers to the Navy Board for their approbation. The warrant for employing the workmen by job, was not acted upon in this yard till the year 1788, the men objecting to work by the piece; and the earnings of the shipwrights were restricted to two tides in the summer and one tide in the winter, in addition to their common day's pay. This rate and mode of working was continued till May 1790, when job work was discontinued, and the workmen were directed to work as much extra as possible. On the 23d September, 1790, directions were given to work such job and task as could be performed by daylight, till 11th January, 1791, when the armament being at an end, all working by job was discontinued. By warrant, 13th January, 1791, the shipwrights were directed to be employed by job, single day, and two tides in the common working hours of the yard, in the summer months, and single day in the winter. In consequence of an application from the men to the Admiralty, to be allowed to work extra, or to be granted such relief as might be thought proper, Commissioner Fanshawe, on the 23d February, 1792, directed the men to be acquainted that they would be allowed to work two tides extra in the summer months. On 6th January, 1793, directions were given by the Navy Board to employ the shipwrights by job double days in the single day hours, and to discontinue sending the propositions of the work to be performed, and the prices to be allowed, which had been usual, confiding in the officers that they would take care the men performed work equal to the double day's pay. On the 7th of October, 1794, the Navy Board directed that propositions for the value of the work should be sent to the Board for their approbation, either prior to the work being performed, or at the end of every month; that task and job should be wrought only in the common working hours of the yard; that shipwrights, whether in houses or on board ships, should be employed at the rate of double days by task and job; those not capable of working by task and job, to be employed at the rate of two tides extra by day work. This warrant continued in force till March, 1803; in November, abolition of the fees, perquisites, and emoluments, formerly received by the officers and clerks; and of the long established privilege enjoyed by the

1798, the workmen were directed to be employed, by the Navy Board's warrant, two tides extra after bell ringing, which continued till January, 1801, when it was increased to one night extra after bell ringing. The mast-makers have been employed by job, on the authority of the Navy Board's warrant of 31st January, 1791, 12th October, 1793, and 18th December, 1795; but no certificates of the jobs performed, as well as I can recollect, were sent to the clerk of the check's office, but the men were paid the same rate of earnings as the other shipwrights, in consequence of a note from the master shipwright to the clerk of the check, that they were to be employed upon the masts and yards of ships fitting, at the rate of double days by job, and at two tides or one night extra, when the other shipwrights worked at that rate. The boat-builders were employed from October 1794, to the 13th March, 1795, at the rate of two tides extra by day work, when the Navy Board directed the boat-builders to be employed by job, according to a scheme of prices then transmitted; the officers taking care to estimate the nature of the repairs, so that the workmen should be paid in proportion to their exertion, and the public service thereby benefitted. On the 10th October, 1801, directions were given by the Navy Board to employ all the artificers at the rate of double days during the winter, as the daylight would no longer allow their working extra; and the Navy Board, by their warrant of 12th March, 1803, directed, that the artificers should be employed as much extra as possible, to get the ships ready which were fitting for sea. As the orders respecting task and job work directed that such work should be performed in the single day hours, the Navy Board's warrant of November, 1798, to work two tides extra after bell-ringing, was understood to mean, that this extra should be independent of the job work performed in the common working hours, and the same construction was put on the Board's warrant of 8th January, 1801, for working one night extra after bell-ringing, it being considered, that such extra was intended as an inducement to the men to exert themselves as much as possible, in consideration of the additional wages they would receive; but new officers having been appointed to the yard previous to March 1803, the question was asked, Whether the workmen were to be paid extra allowance for the hours they were employed after bell-ringing, or whether the whole of the men's earnings should be paid for at the prices allowed for job work? and the Navy Board directed, that they should be paid at the prices of job work for the whole of the work performed, without restricting the amount of their earnings.

What were the earnings of the artificers previous to their being employed by task and job?—In the seven years' war, ending in November, 1762, the artificers were generally employed at the rate of two tides extra, for which they worked three hours beyond the working hours of the yard, and on particular emergencies one night extra, for which they worked five hours, and in like manner during the American war. In the peace from 1762 to April 1764, they were employed and paid at the rate of single days; and from 1764 to December 1770, they were employed at the rate of one tide extra during the summer months, for which they worked an hour and an half beyond the usual time, excepting in the year 1765, when they were employed at that rate only from the 2d of August to the 30th September. In the armament of 1770, from December 1770 to February 1771, the artificers were paid at the rate of two for one, for which they worked the extra hours. From 1771 to the commencement of the American war, they were

workmen of carrying chips out of the yard, which had grown into a serious abuse.

---

employed one tide extra during the summer months. From 1783 to 1788, when the job work commenced, they were likewise employed one tide extra during the summer months.

Were the several schemes for job and task work sent to the clerk of the check, for his guidance in setting off the earnings of the artificers?—Yes, the several schemes for job and task work, which I have before stated, are lodged in the clerk of the check's office.

Have the earnings of the artificers and labourers during the late war, been in general set off agreeably thereto by task and job notes, sent to the clerk of the check from the master shipwright, or have they in general been paid by a note from the master shipwright, that their earnings were to be set off as two for one, or two for one and two tides, or three for one, agreeably to the extra allowed to be worked by the Navy Board?—The earnings of the shipwrights employed by task work, have been set off by a note or certificate from the master shipwright of the quantity of work performed, valued at the rate prescribed by the Navy Board's warrants; the earnings of the boat-builders, when employed by job, have been set off by a certificate from the master shipwright, that the value of the work performed, rated according to the prices prescribed by the Navy Board, was equivalent to double days work. For the general employment of the shipwrights by job work, no scheme of prices was fixed by the Navy Board till the 2d of January, 1802; but prices for the several works were proposed by the officers in general, some time after the performance of the work, to the Navy Board for their approbation; and the Navy Board in consequence either approved or reduced the prices, as they thought proper, and directed the clerk of the check to set off the earnings of the men accordingly. But as the waiting for the directions of the Board would, in many instances, have delayed the making up of the pay-books of the yard, the shipwrights employed by job were set off without any regard to the reduction which might be made in the prices by the Navy Board, at the rate of double days, upon a general note from the master shipwright that they were to be so employed, conformably to the Navy Board's warrant of the 7th October, 1794; but no certificate that work was done equivalent thereto, was transmitted by the master shipwright to the clerk of the check's office, except for works performed between January 1793, and October 1794, when the propositions for job work were not sent to the Navy Board, and any extra directed by the Navy Board, in addition to the two for one by job in the common working hours of the yard, was set off in the same manner.

When were the job notes and certificates of the work actually performed by the shipwrights, agreeably to the Navy Board's order, first sent by the master shipwright to the clerk of the check's office?—For Lady Quarter 1802.

Was it before or after the removal of the late master shipwright?—It was about one month before the removal of the late master shipwright.

How long has it been the practice for one of the assistants and foremen to sign certificates of the actual performance of the shipwrights work by job?—The job notes sent to the clerk of the check's office have been signed by one of the assistants, as well as the master shipwright, since the appointment of Mr. Tucker; and since the 1st February last, he has required one of the assistants and foremen to sign a certificate at the foot of the note, that the works have been actually performed.

In lieu of the multifarious emoluments of the officers and clerks, arising from fees and perquisites, permanent annual salaries were allotted to them,

---

Ought not such job notes, by the Navy Board's directions, to have been sent to the clerk of the check's office, from the first introduction of job work in 1788?—I consider they should.

Did the clerk of the check call upon the master shipwright for notes, for the employment of the shipwrights by job, to authorize him to set off their earnings?—I do not recollect that he did.

Did the clerk of the check make any representation to the Navy Board, that the master shipwright did not furnish him with notes of the earnings of the shipwrights by job?—He did not. The master shipwright having sent him a note, stating at what rate the men were to be paid, agreeably to the Navy Board's order.

Do you apprehend that any job notes were actually made out, of the work performed by the shipwrights prior to Lady Quarter 1802?—Accounts of the work said to be performed by job were sent to the Navy Board, agreeably to the form prescribed by their warrant of the 20th November, 1788; but as such accounts did not specify the times between which the work was performed, it was no guidance to ascertain the earnings of the people.

Was there any account made out, or check kept, prior to Lady Quarter, 1802, by which it could be ascertained that the shipwrights actually performed as much work by the scheme of prices for job, as would entitle them to two days' pay for one?—I have always understood that such an account was kept in the department of the foreman of the shipwrights, except from January 1793 to October 1794.

By whom was the account of work performed collected?—I cannot speak positively.

At what rate were the men working in Lady Quarter, 1802, when certificates of the work actually performed were first sent to the clerk of the check's office?—Double days in the single day hours, and no extra.

Was the amount of the earnings by such job notes, equal to two days' pay for one?—(a.) In several instances they were not, and the earnings were set off according to the notes.

Were they paid agreeably to such earnings?—(b.) No. In consideration of the men's representation of the shortness of their pay, and the officers reporting that they had been employed in working up old materials, the Navy Board directed the men at the dock side to be paid two for one.

THOMAS NETHERTON.

Ewan Law.
John Ford.
Henry Nicholls.
William Mackworth Praed.

The Examination of Mr. Thomas Netherton, continued 30th August, 1803.

Was the amount of the propositions of job work made to the Navy Board, at any time compared with the earnings set off on the pay books?—No; they could not be compared, as the propositions did not specify the time in which the work had been performed.

proportioned to the responsibility and labour of their situations; and an allowance in money was given to the workmen for the loss of the chips,

---

If the propositions had mentioned the time between which the work had been performed, could not the earnings of the men have been duly checked?—Certainly, while the men were only employed on double days; but when the men were employed two for one by job in the common working hours, and two tides, or one night extra after bell-ringing, those propositions could be no guidance, as the men continued to work on the same job in the extra hours, although they were paid separately for staying such extra hours.

Were any directions given by the Navy Board that the work performed in the extra hours should be valued as job work?—Not till April, 1803.

How have the quartermen of the yard, whose gangs have been employed upon task work, been paid?—They have been paid in proportion to the earnings of the working men; their daily pay being one-fifth more.

As the Navy Board's warrant of the 23d March, 1775, directed that they should only be set off two tides in addition to their common day's pay, when employed on task work, when was such order first deviated from?—The Board's warrant of 13th March, 1784, directed that they should be allowed equal earnings with the men, not exceeding one night extra; and the warrant of 22d May 1797, directed them to be allowed the general extra of the shipwrights employed by task or job.

Have the shipwrights, generally employed in the mast and boat-houses, been selected from the working gangs, on account of their age and infirmity, and in consequence of their not being able to perform so good a day's work as the rest of the men?—A great part of them were.

Were they paid as much wages during the late war as the most efficient shipwrights?—The men in the masthouse employed by job, were paid the same earnings as the most efficient men at the dock side; but not so much as the men in the task companies, when they were employed by task.

Were they not paid as much as the men belonging to the task companies, when such companies were not working task?—Yes, they were.

By what authority were the shipwrights, working in the masthouses, employed by job, double days in the single day hours?—By the Navy Board's warrant of October 1794.

Was there ever any scheme of prices for job work for the mastmakers sent to this yard, or have propositions for the work performed, with the prices to be paid, been sent to the Navy Board?—Prices for certain articles by job were fixed by the Navy Board's warrants of 31st January, 1791, 12th October, 1793, and 18th December, 1795.

Previous to the establishment of job work, when the shipwrights were permitted to earn as much as they could by task, what was the general average of their daily earnings?—The general average of their daily earnings by task, when it was first established in 1775, was three shillings and tenpence halfpenny; their earnings by task, when not restricted, have since varied from four shillings and twopence to six shillings and sixpence per day.

Can you account for the average earnings of the shipwrights by task having increased so much?—Yes, I can in some measure. It having been directed, after the first establishment of task in 1775, that the price of the different articles of work should be increased or reduced, in the proportion as the tonnage of the shipbuilding was more or less than the tonnage specified for each class of ships according to the following table, which is paid to them weekly by the clerk

---

in the scheme of 1775, and the tonnage of His Majesty's ships having been very much increased from 1775 to 1788, when task work on new ships was resumed in this yard, I conceive this circumstance was in a great measure the occasion of the increase in the men's earnings. The men, on resuming task work, were likewise allowed for their workmanship on any timber, &c. that was found unfit for use during the time of working on it, or after it had been wrought.

What is the general average of the daily earnings of the shipwrights, now that they are permitted to earn as much as they can by job work?—From the 12th to the 31st of March, the average amounted to seven shillings and ninepence a day, exclusive of chip and lodging money.

Can you account for the earnings of the shipwrights employed by job exceeding the earnings of those employed by task?—Men employed by task were confined to the common working hours, and those employed by job, from 12th to 31st March, were employed five hours each day in addition to the common working hours.

Do you consider the employment of the artificers and labourers by job during the late war, to have been an ideal system to give the men greater wages?—I consider the system of job work to have been intended as an encouragement to the men, and in lieu of an increase of wages; and that the men exerted themselves much more after the system of job was established than they had generally done before.

THOMAS NETHERTON.

Ewan Law.
John Ford.
Henry Nicholls.
William Mackworth Praed.

The Examination of Mr. Thomas Netherton, continued 31st August, 1803.

Was the warrant of the Navy Board of 7th of October, 1794, directing the workmen of this yard to be allowed two days' pay by job, for working in the common hours of the day, tantamount to doubling the pay of the efficient men?—I consider it to have been so.

Has that order been acted upon ever since?—It was acted upon to the 12th March, 1803, since which the men have been permitted to earn as much as they can by task or job.

Had any order, previous to the 7th of October, 1794, been given by the Navy Board for increasing the price of the labour of the workmen performed in the common working hours of the yard?—Yes; the warrant for working the shipwrights by task work, dated 22d March, 1775, which restricted their time of working to the common day hours, and allowed them to earn what they could according to the scheme of task; and the warrant of 3d December, 1783, directing the men to be employed by job work in the common day hours, limiting their earnings to two tides additional in summer time, and one tide during the winter months.

As all the artificers of the yard are now paid by job, how are the shipwrights attending the caulkers to let in graving pieces, and the timber tasters, and other artificers employed on similar services, where no account of their work can posof the check, through the medium of the quartermen and foremen in the different branches.

DESCRIPTION OF WORKMEN.	Rate per Day.
To shipwrights	*Sixpence.*
To apprentices of shipwrights, during the first four years of their apprenticeship	*Fourpence.*
To do., for the last three years of their apprenticeship	*Sixpence.*
To caulkers, joiners, house carpenters, and sawyers	*Fourpence.*
To the apprentices of caulkers, joiners, and house carpenters, during the first four years of their apprenticeship	*Twopence.*
To do., during the last three years of their apprenticeship	*Fourpence.*
To scavelmen and labourers	*Threepence.*

The allowance in lieu of chips has been extended by the Navy Board to other classes of workmen, as will appear by the establishment of the yard.

sibly be taken, paid?—The shipwrights employed to square for the caulkers, are and have been paid at the same rate of earnings as the caulkers with whom they work, by warrant of the Navy Board of the 5th January, 1784.—The timber tasters, when the labourers have been employed by task work in loading and unloading timber, &c. have been paid at the same rate of task work as the labourers, and have been permitted, after the labourers left work, to work the extra hours with other shipwrights employed in the capstern and top house.—Other artificers employed on similar services, where no account of their work can possibly be taken, have usually been paid at the rate of earnings of the class to which they belonged, which has been confirmed, with a few exceptions, by the Navy Board's warrant of 21st May, 1803.

In the propositions for shipwrights' jobs transmitted to the Navy Board, have any other workmen, or have teams of horses, been stated as a part of the estimated expense?—With respect to the shipwrights, they have been stated to have been employed with them; but I have always understood that their wages were not considered as a part of the value of the work performed. With respect to the bricklayers and masons, the earnings of the labourers and horses employed with them were included in the value of the job.

When workmen were employed on similar jobs, and propositions were made without the addition of labourers and horses, were the works then estimated at the same price?—I have understood they were.

What do you apprehend was intended by including labourers and teams of horses in the propositions of shipwrights to be employed by job?—To bear the number of men and teams of horses mentioned in that proposition, at the same rate of extra pay as the shipwrights employed on the job.

[To be continued.]

PLATE CC.

THIS View of Goree, by Mr. Pocock, will remind our readers of the re-capture of that Island by Captain E. S. Dickson, on the 9th of March, 1804; after it had remained in possession of

the French from the 18th of January in the same year *, when it had been taken by an expedition from Cayenne. A very ample account of the reduction of this Settlement by Admiral Keppel †, appeared in our Biographical Memoir of the Hon. Admiral Digby.

Sabat informs us, that Goree was given up to the Dutch in 1617, by Biram, King of Cape Verde. In 1663 it was taken by the English under Commodore Holmes; and the next year was re-taken by De Ruyter. It surrendered to a French squadron under the Comte d'Estrees, in 1677. The Dutch made some attempts in 1679 to recover it, but were repulsed. According to Batbot, the forts of Goree were taken on the 4th of February, 1692, by Mr. Booker, the English General at Gambra; and retaken by the French in 1693.

In that excellent collection of voyages which goes by the name of Astley's ‡, we learn, that Goree derived its name, either from being so called by the Dutch on account of its good Road, or from a town in Zealand of the same appellation. It lies N.N.W. and S.S.E. within cannon shot of the western coast of Africa. This Island is famous for the observations that were made there in 1682, by Messieurs des Hayes, Varin, and du Gloss, Members of the Royal Academy of Sciences, who were sent thither by Louis the fourteenth.

The variation of the needle at Goree is uncertain; differing in different parts even of this little Island from one to fourteen degrees; but always declining to the N.W. The cause of this has been ascribed to some mines of iron, the marks of which appear in several stones like iron-dross; as also, to a spring of mineral water. The pilots find no variation in the Road of Goree. The highest and lowest tides have been observed to flow on a day or two after the full, and after the change of the moon. The difference of the tides is about five feet, rarely rising one or two feet higher, except in winds blowing off the sea.

This Island, in latitude 14° 40′ N., and longitude 17° 25′ W., is only a barren rock, a mile long, and a furlong broad. But from its being so near Cape Verd, it seems a very convenient place for trade. The fort stands on the northern part, which is high and steep. A small spring hardly supplies half the garrison with water. To come into the Road, get the N.E. point of the Island, which is a low point of white sand, a sail's breadth open of Cape Manvel, and anchor at half a league from the Island, in ten fathoms and a half, coarse sand and coral.

* Nav. Chron. Vol. XII, page 61. † Vol. XI, page 90. ‡ Four Volumes in quarto.

ADDENDA

TO

THE BIOGRAPHICAL MEMOIR

OF THE LATE RIGHT HONOURABLE

HORATIO LORD VISCOUNT NELSON, K.B.

AND DUKE OF BRONTE;

VICE-ADMIRAL OF THE WHITE SQUADRON.

(Concluded from page 152.)

THE undermentioned is a list that has been handed to us, of the Naval Officers who attended the funeral from the Admiralty to St. Paul's.

Capt. Sir Samuel Hood, K.B.
—— Fred. Belton
Lieut. James Wallace
Capt. Burlton
Lieut. Purchase, of the Defence
Rear-Admiral Bertie
Lieut. L. B. Reeves } Victory
—— J. G. Peake } Victory
—— Ballard
Rear-Adm. Sir Edmund Nagle, Knt.
Capt. John Hayes
—— Lumley
—— Whyte.
—— S. Scudamore Heming
Lieut. Crofton } Marines.
—— Morgan } Marines.
—— Cowperthwaite } Marines.
—— Bate } Marines.
—— Goltwaltz } Marines.
—— Campbell } Marines.
Capt. John Tower
—— Watkins
—— Edward Williams
—— Thomas Wolley
—— Thomas Cooke
—— J. Walton
—— H. Stacpole
—— J. W. Trotter
—— Dalling
—— D. Scott, (Bellerophon)
—— Sir Rupert George
—— George Pearson
—— William Kent
Lieut. Richard Crawford
—— Henry Hargrave
—— James Milne
—— Wm. Colliers Barker
Capt. Lodington, Marines
—— Thomas Surcombe
Lieut. Fisher
—— John Murray Wegg
Capt. Richard Lee
—— James Green
—— Galway
—— Towry
—— William Browne
—— Toker
—— Henry Cox, Marines
—— H. E. R. Baker
Lieut. Geo. Antrim
Capt. Andrews
—— Edward O'Bryan
—— William Waller
—— William Mounsey
—— Edward Lloyd Graham
—— Abdy
Vice-Admiral Ed. Edwards
Capt. Hon. Hen. Bennett
—— H. Tarnall
Rear-Admiral Sir Isaac Coffin
Capt. Sir Edward Hamilton
—— Burn, Royal Marines
Lieut. Steele, ditto
Capt. Thomas Boys
—— Alexander Skene
—— John Broughton
—— T. Sherman, Marines
—— Thompson, do.
—— John Smith
—— William Richardson
—— Tremenheere, Marines
Lieut. Charles Jones
Capt. Richard Williams
—— Thomas Surridge
Lieut. Joseph Coome, Marines
—— James Tithall, do.
—— William Field
—— John Read

Capt Walter Tremenheere
—— William Price Curnby
—— Richard Carruthers
Lieut. William Somerville
Adm. Sir John Orde
Capt. Alexander
—— Archibald Duff
—— Charles Dilkes
—— Isaac Smith
—— John Hatley
—— A. S Burrows
—— Sir Francis Laforey
—— James Nicolson
—— Kennedy
Adm. Charles Chamberlayne
Capt. Humphries
—— John Boyle
—— Richbell
Lieut. Jones
—— Thomas Wing
Capt. E. Rotheram, Royal Sovereign
Lieut. Janverin, Defence
Capt. Samuel Sutton
—— Hardy, Victory
Adm. Murray
Lieut. Henry Thomas Hardacre
Capt. Robert Lambert
—— James Oswald
—— Henry Samuel Butt
—— Henry Stuart
—— John Temple
—— T. O. G. Skinner
Lieut. John Bowen
—— Thomas Wilkins
—— Robert Dunham
—— Williams
—— King } Victory
—— Bligh } Victory
—— Yule
—— Pascoe
—— Browne
—— Hills
Capt. A. Tinling
—— James Dunbar
Lieut. Thomas Hughes
Capt. Courtenay Boyle
—— Richards
—— Vincent
—— Percival, Royal Marines
—— Cotterell
—— Guyot
—— Alexander Mackenzie

Capt. Durham, Defiance
—— Hallard
—— Haywood
—— D. Miller
Rear-Admiral Wells
Capt. John Tower
Hon. Capt. H. Blackwood, Euryalus
Capt. Moorsom, Revenge
—— Ballar
—— Farquhar
—— Cartier
—— Yeo
—— Thomas Stanes
—— W. Pierrepont
Lt. Col. Berkeley } Royal Marines
Lieut. Lawson } Royal Marines
Adm. Sir Peter Parker, Bart.
—— Viscount Hood
—— Sir Charles M. Pole
—— Bligh
—— Lord Radstock
—— Caldwell
Vice-Admiral Whitshed
—— Taylor
—— Stanhope
—— Savage
Rear-Admiral T. Drury
—— Eliab Harvey
—— Aylmer
—— Domett
—— Waymouth
—— Peacock
Lieut. Edmund Hanning Thomas
Capt. William Green
—— William Roberts
Lieut. J. W. Bazaljette
Capt. William Hotham
—— J. K. Shepherd
—— William Ponsonby
—— Cunningham
—— Robert Jackson
—— Sir W. H. Douglas
—— G. Murray
Adm. Sir Roger Curtis, Bart.
Vice-Admiral C. P. Hamilton
Rear-Admiral Thomas West
—— John Markham
—— Edmund Bowater
—— Wells
Vice-Admiral Nugent
Hon. Capt. Gardner
Capt. Maxwell

So early as three and four o'clock, on the morning of Thursday, thousands of people were in motion, lest they should not reach the places whence they intended to witness, what may almost be termed the apotheosis of Lord Nelson.

An hour before day-light, the drums of the respective volunteer *corps*, in every part of the metropolis, beat to arms. The summons was quickly obeyed; and, soon after, the troops lined the streets, from the Admiralty to St. Paul's, agreeably to the orders which had been issued. By day-break, the Life Guards also were mounted at their post in Hyde Park; and in St. James's Park were drawn up all the regiments of cavalry and infantry, quartered within a hundred miles of London, who had served in the glorious campaigns in Egypt, after the ever-memorable victory of the Nile. There was also a detachment of flying artillery, with twelve field-pieces and their ammunition tumbrils.

Between eight and nine o'clock, eight mourning coaches and four brought the Heralds and Pursuivants of Arms from their college to the Admiralty. No carriages, but those which were connected with the procession, (the carriages of Foreign Ambassadors excepted,) were permitted to pass through the Strand, Fleet-street, or Ludgate-hill.

The remainder of the procession followed, as nearly as might be, in the order which had been presented. The chief deviation was, that, to afford the spectators a more complete view of the coffin, it appeared on the car, stripped of its pall, on a platform covered with black cloth, festooned with velvet richly fringed, and decorated with escutcheons on each side, between which were inscribed the words *Trinidad* and *Bucentaur*. The car stopped for some moments, immediately opposite to the statue of King Charles, at Charing-cross. Every hat was off, every sound was hushed, and the most awful silence prevailed.

The whole moved on in solemn pace, through the Strand to Temple-bar Gate, where the Lord Mayor of London, attended by the Aldermen and Sheriffs, and the Deputation from the Common Council, were waiting to receive them. As the procession advanced within the City, the six carriages of the Deputation from the Common Council fell in between the Deputation of the Great Commercial Companies of London and the Physicians of the Deceased, who were in a mourning coach; a conductor on horseback having been appointed to indicate the station. The carriages of the Aldermen and Sheriffs fell in between the Knights Bachelors and the Masters in Chancery. The Lord Mayor rode from Temple-bar to St. Paul's on horseback, uncovered, and carrying in his hand the City sword.

His Royal Highness the Duke of York and his Staff, with the Colonels of Volunteers, followed the funeral car on horseback.

On the arrival of the procession at St. Paul's, the cavalry marched off to their barracks: the Scotch regiments drew up in the area fronting the church, and marched into the western-gate, and so remained. The forty-eight Greenwich Pensioners, with forty-eight Seamen and twelve Marines, from the Victory, entered the western-gate, ascended the steps, and divided in a line on each side under the great western portico, and the remainder of the procession entered the church, dividing on each side, and taking the rank and stations assigned them.

When the funeral car reached the great entrance, it was drawn up without the western gate. The body was taken from the car, covered with the pall, and borne by twelve Seamen from the Victory, and was received within the gate by the Supporters and Pall-bearers, who had previously alighted for its reception.

The procession entered at the great western gate.

The noble cathedral of St. Paul had been thrown open for the reception of visitors, at the early hour of seven in the morning. Such, however, was the anxiety of the public to witness the solemnities of the day, that many suffered from the pressure before the opportunity for admission was afforded. A very short time elapsed after the doors were opened, before the principal part of the seats were occupied; and the interest was so deep, that no uneasiness whatever appeared to be produced by the time which it became necessary to wait, exposed to a great severity of cold. From seven o'clock till one, the company sat still, and not a symptom of impatience was discoverable.

A few minutes after one o'clock, the approach of the procession was announced, and the great western door was thrown open. At half after one General Sir D. Dundas marched in at the head of the grenadier companies of the 21st and 31st foot, and the 79th and 92d Highland regiments, amounting altogether to about 300 men. These troops moved in slow time by single files, and formed lines on each side of the way assigned for the procession from the western gate, along the aisle, the dome, and on to the gate of the choir. Having turned to the front, they, after some preliminary manœuvres, were ordered to rest on their arms reversed; and in this position they remained until the whole ceremony was concluded. The appearance of this fine body of men considerably augmented the interest of the scene. Upon any other occasion, the manly, soldier-like figures, which the Highland grenadiers presented, would have been deservedly the objects of particular notice and admiration. The 92d were placed at the eastward of the aisle; the 79th under the dome, and the other companies took the western extremity. Previously to the introduction of these companies, a great part of 200 men belonging to the West London regiment of Militia, were employed in the body of the church to guard particular seats, and to prevent any part of the crowd from getting into those places which were set apart for the accommodation of those nobility, &c. who were expected in the procession. The whole of the Militia were placed under the command of the Dean, who had parties of them stationed at the several doors of the church, in order to prevent pressure or riot.

Some time had elapsed before the regiments to which the flank companies belonged had filed off to make way for the procession. The part of it which entered the church did not appear until two o'clock. It was preceded by some Marshal's men to clear the way. They were followed by two naval Captains, the first bearing the standard, the other the guidon. These Captains were Benyon and Laforet. Each was supported by two Lieutenants. Of the different degrees of rank, the Gentlemen and Esquires led the way;—and among them were several of the most respectable men belonging to the commercial community. The Aldermen of London went in on the north side of the procession, and took their station opposite to the box assigned for their accommodation. His Royal Highness the Prince of Wales, accompanied by the Dukes of Clarence and Cumberland, and conducted by the Dean, walked through the church to the choir, where they remained for a short time, and then returned to join the procession. His Royal Highness the Prince of Wales took his place in the procession immediately after the Lord President of the Council (Earl Camden), and was followed by the Dukes of York, Clarence, Kent, Cumberland, Sussex, and Cambridge. The Lord Mayor and his suite were next to the Royal Dukes. His Lordship wore a large black silk gown, provided for the occasion, highly fringed with gold lace, several rows of which were on the arms and round the collar.

The most interesting part of the cavalcade—that which was certainly best calculated to make a strong impression upon the minds of the spectators, was the exhibition made by the brave Seamen of the Victory, who bore two Union Jacks, and the St. George's Ensign, belonging to that ship. These colours were perforated in various places by the effects of the shot of the enemy. Several parts of the ensign were, literally, shattered. These parts were particularly exposed to view, and the effect which such a display was calculated to produce may be more easily conceived than described.

Immediately on the van of the procession entering the great western door, the organ commenced. The Minor Canons, Vicars Choral of the Cathedral, assisted by the Choristers from the Chapel Royal, and the Minor Canons and Vicars Choral belonging to the church of St. Peter, Westminster; together with some Gentlemen from Windsor, amounting together to upwards of 100, sung as the procession moved from the west door to the choir the following Anthems, which were set to music by Dr. Croft:—

I am the resurrection and the life, saith the Lord: he that believeth in me, though he were dead, yet shall he live. And whosoever liveth and believeth in me, shall never die. *St. John*, xi. 25, 26.

I know that my Redeemer liveth, and that he shall stand at the latter day upon the earth. And though after my skin, worms destroy this body; yet in my flesh shall I see God: whom I shall see for myself, and mine eyes shall behold, and not another. *Job*, xix. 25, 26, 27.

We brought nothing into this world, and it is certain we can carry nothing out. The Lord gave, and the Lord hath taken away; blessed be the name of the Lord. 1 *Tim.* vi. 7. *Job*, i. 21.

The procession passed through the enclosed place in the centre of the dome, and of course over the grave, on its way to the choir. Although the first part entered the church about two o'clock, the whole did not reach the choir till four. It remained in the choir during the performance of evening service, in the course of which the following Anthems, &c. were sung:—

Dixi Custodiam, *Psalm* xxxix.

I said, I will take heed to my ways: that I offend not in my tongue.

I will keep my mouth as it were with a bridle: while the ungodly is in my sight.

I held my tongue, and spake nothing: I kept silence, yea, even from good words; but it was pain and grief to me.

My heart was hot within me; and while I was thus musing, the fire kindled: and at the last I spake with my tongue.

Lord, let me know mine end, and the number of my days: that I may be certified how long I have to live.

Behold, thou hast made my days as it were a span long: and mine age is even as nothing in respect of thee; and verily every man living is altogether vanity.

For man walketh in a vain shadow, and disquieteth himself in vain: he heapeth up riches, and cannot tell who shall gather them.

And now, Lord, what is my hope: truly my hope is even in thee.

Deliver me from all mine offences: and make me not a rebuke unto the foolish.

I became dumb, and opened not my mouth: for it was thy doing.

Take thy plague away from me: I am even consumed by means of thy heavy hand.

When thou with rebukes dost chasten man for sin, thou makest his beauty to consume away, like as it were a moth fretting a garment: every man therefore is but vanity.

Hear my prayer, O Lord, and with thine ears consider my calling: hold not thy peace at my tears.

For I am a stranger with thee: and a sojourner, as all my fathers were.

O spare me a little, that I may recover my strength: before I go hence, and be no more seen.

Glory be to the Father, and to the Son: and to the Holy Ghost;

As it was in the beginning, is now, and ever shall be: world without end. *Amen.*

Domine, refugium. *Psalm* xc.

Lord, thou hast been our refuge: from one generation to another.

Before the mountains were brought forth, or ever the earth and the world were made: thou art God from everlasting, and world without end.

Thou turnest man to destruction: again, thou sayest, Come again, ye children of men

For a thousand years in thy sight are but as yesterday: seeing that is past as a watch in the night.

As soon as thou scatterest them, they are even as a sleep: and fade away suddenly like the grass.

In the morning it is green, and groweth up: but in the evening it is cut down, dried up, and withered.

For we consume away in thy displeasure: and are afraid at thy wrathful indignation.

Thou hast set our misdeeds before thee: and our secret sins in the light of thy countenance.

For when thou art angry, all our days are gone: we bring our years to an end, as it were a tale that is told.

The days of our age are threescore years and ten; and though men be so strong, that they come to fourscore years; yet is their strength then but labour and sorrow; so soon passeth it away, and we are gone.

But who regardeth the power of thy wrath: for even thereafter as a man feareth, so is thy displeasure.

So teach us to number our days: that we may apply our hearts unto wisdom.

Turn thee again, O Lord, at the last: and be gracious unto thy servants.

O satisfy us with thy mercy, and that soon: so shall we rejoice and be glad all the days of our life.

Comfort us again, now after the time that thou hast plagued us: and for the years wherein we have suffered adversity.

Shew thy servants thy work: and their children thy glory.

And the glorious Majesty of the Lord our God be upon us: prosper thou the work of our hands upon us, O prosper thou our handy work.

Glory be to the Father, and to the Son; and to the Holy Ghost;

As it was in the beginning, is now, and ever shall be: world without end. *Amen.*

Magnificat (*or the Song of the blessed Virgin Mary,*) *St. Luke*, i. 46.

My soul doth magnify the Lord: and my spirit hath rejoiced in God my Saviour.

For he hath regarded: the lowness of his hand-maiden.

For behold, from henceforth: all generations shall call me blessed.

For he that is mighty hath magnified me: and holy is his Name.

And his mercy is on them that fear him: throughout all generations.

He hath shewed strength with his arm: he hath scattered the proud in the imagination of their hearts.

He hath put down the mighty from their seat: and hath exalted the humble and meek.

He hath filled the hungry with good things: and the rich he hath sent empty away.

He remembering his mercy, hath holpen his servant Israel: as he promised to our forefathers, Abraham and his seed for ever.

Glory be to the Father, and to the Son: and to the Holy Ghost;

As it was in the beginning, is now, and ever shall be: world without end. *Amen.*

Anthem. *Psalm* xxxix.

CHORUS.

5. Lord, let me know my end, and the number of my days: that I may be certified how long I have to live.

6. Thou hast made my days as it were a span long: and mine age is nothing in respect of Thee, and verily every man living is altogether vanity.

TREBLES.

7. For man walketh in a vain shadow, and disquieteth himself in vain: he heapeth up riches, and cannot tell who shall gather them.

CHORUS.

8. And now, Lord, what is my hope? truly my hope is even in Thee.

13. Hear my prayer, O Lord, and with thine ear consider my calling: hold not thy peace at my tears.

15. O spare me a little, that I may recover my strength: before I go hence, and be no more seen.

During the performance of the service in the choir, the evening approached, and lights became necessary. Arrangements had been made for the purpose, and, as soon as it was found requisite, a number of torches were lighted up in the choir, both below, and in the galleries. At the same time, the vast space under the dome was illuminated, (for the first time since its construction,) to a sufficient degree for the solemn purposes of the occasion, by a temporary lanthorn, consisting of an octagonal framing of wood, boarded on the outside, and finished at top by eight angles, and at bottom by a smaller octagon. This was painted black, and upon it were disposed about 130 patent lamps. It was suspended by a rope from the centre of the lanthorn; and, when drawn up, it gave as much light as was wanted in the church. There were some other lights placed in the aisles, but these were of no great consequence. The grand central light, though inferior to the celebrated annual illuminated crucifix of St. Peter's, had a most impressive and grand effect, and contributed greatly to the grandeur of a spectacle in which the burial of one of the first of Warriors and of Heroes was graced by the appearance of all the Princes of the Blood, of many of the first nobility of the land, and of an unexampled number of the subjects of His Majesty in general.

A bier, covered with black velvet, and ornamented with gold fringe and tassels, was placed in the choir, for the reception of the coffin, during the service which was performed there.

About five o'clock, the procession returned from the choir to the grave, in an inverted order, the rear, in proceeding to the choir, forming the van on its return.—On reaching the dome, the Dukes of York, Kent, Sussex, and Cambridge, filed off to the Royal box, where, however, they remained but a short time before they proceeded to the enclosure which surrounded the grave.—The Lord Mayor and Aldermen repaired to their box, where they remained till the ceremony of interment was over.—The officers of the navy and army, who assisted in the procession, continued in the body of the church.

The Dean (Bishop of Lincoln), and the Residentiary (Bishop of Chester), with two Prebends, ascended a desk which had been constructed for the solemn occasion.

On the return of the coffin from the choir, a grand funeral canopy of state was born over it by six Admirals. It was composed of black velvet, supported by six small pillars covered with the same material, and crowned by six plumes of black ostrich feathers; the vallens were fringed with black, and decorated with devices of festoons and symbols of his Lordship's victories, and his arms, crest, and coronet, in gold.

When the coffin was brought to the centre of the dome, it was placed on a platform sufficiently elevated to be visible from every part of the church.—The state canopy was then withdrawn, and the pall taken off. The carpet and cushion on which the trophies were deposited, were laid by the Gentleman Usher who carried them, on a table placed near the grave, and behind the place which was occupied by the Chief Mourner.—The coronet and cushion, borne by Clarencieux King of Arms, was laid on the body.

The Chief Mourner and his Supporters placed themselves at the head of the grave, and the Assistant Mourners, with the Relations of the Deceased, near to them.

During the return of the corpse from the choir to the place

of interment, a solemn dirge was performed on the organ; after which was sung the following

ANTHEM.

Man that is born of a woman, hath but a short time to live, and is full of misery. He cometh up, and is cut down like a flower: he fleeth as it were a shadow, and never continueth in one stay.

In the midst of life we are in death: of whom may we seek for succour, but of thee, O Lord, who for our sins are justly displeased?

Yet, O Lord God most holy, O Lord most mighty, O holy and most merciful Saviour, deliver us not into the bitter pains of eternal death.

Thou knowest, Lord, the secrets of our hearts: shut not thy merciful ears to our prayer; but spare us, Lord most holy, O God most mighty, O holy and merciful Saviour, thou most worthy judge eternal, suffer us not at our last hour, for any pains of death, to fall from thee.

Then the officiating Minister said,

Forasmuch as it hath pleased Almighty God, of his great mercy, to take unto himself the soul of our dear brother here departed, we therefore commit his body to the ground; earth to earth, ashes to ashes, dust to dust; in sure and certain hope of the resurrection to eternal life, through our Lord Jesus Christ, who shall change our vile body, that it may be like unto his glorious body, according to the mighty working, whereby he is able to subdue all things to himself.

After which was sung by the whole Choir,

I heard a voice from heaven saying unto me, Write, from henceforth blessed are the dead, which die in the Lord: even so saith the spirit; for they rest from their labours. *Rev.* xiv. 13.

Concluding Anthem.

Verse. His body is buried in peace.
Chorus. But his name liveth evermore.

Precisely at thirty-three minutes and a half past five o'clock, the coffin was lowered into the grave, by balance weight, secret machinery having been constructed expressly for the purpose.

The funeral service having been concluded in the most solemn and impressive manner, Sir Isaac Heard, Garter King at Arms, proclaimed the style and titles of the deceased Lord, in nearly the following words:—

Thus it hath pleased Almighty God to take, out of this transitory life, unto his divine mercy, the Most Noble Lord Horatio Nelson, Viscount and Baron Nelson of the Nile, and of Burnham Thorpe, in the County of Norfolk, Baron Nelson of the Nile, and of Hilborough, in the same County; Knight of the Most Honourable Order of the Bath; Vice-Admiral of the White Squadron of the Fleet, and Commander in Chief of His Majesty's Ships and Vessels in the Mediterranean:

also Duke of Bronte in Sicily; Knight Grand Cross of the Sicilian Order of St. Ferdinand and of Merit; Member of the Ottoman Order of the Crescent; Knight Grand Commander of the Order of St. Joachim; and the Hero who, in the moment of victory, fell covered with immortal glory!—Let us humbly trust, that he is now raised to bliss ineffable, and to a glorious immortality!

The Comptroller, Treasurer, and Steward of his Lordship's household then broke their staves, and gave the pieces to Garter, who threw them into the grave, in which also the flags of the Victory, furled up by the sailors, were deposited.—These brave fellows, however, desirous of retaining some memorials of their great and favourite Commander, had torn off a considerable part of the largest flag, of which most of them obtained a portion.

The ceremony was finally concluded a little before six o'clock, but the church was not entirely vacated till past nine.

The procession left the church in nearly its original order, but gradually separated, according as its respective members retired after the fatigues of the day.

Thus terminated one of the most impressive and most splendid solemnities that ever took place in this country, or perhaps in Europe.

The funeral car, which attracted so much notice in the procession, was designed by, and executed under the direction of the Rev. Mr. M'Quin, a particular friend of Sir Isaac Heard.—It was modelled, at the ends, in imitation of the hull of the Victory. Its head, towards the horses, was ornamented with a figure of Fame. The stern, carved and painted in the naval style, with the word "Victory," in yellow raised letters on the lanthorn over the poop. The sides were decorated with escutcheons, three on each. Between them, two on each side, were represented four scrolls, surrounded by branches and wreaths of palm and laurel, and bearing the names of the four principal French and Spanish men of war, which had been taken or destroyed by the deceased Hero; viz. the San Josef, l'Orient, Trinidad, and Bucentaure. The body of the car consisted of three platforms, each elevated above the other. On the third was the coffin, placed, as on the quarter-deck, with its head towards the stern, with an English Jack pendant over the poop, and lowered half staff. There was an awning over the whole; consisting of an elegant canopy, supported by four pillars, in the form of palm trees, and partly covered with black velvet. The corners and sides were decorated with black ostrich feathers, and festooned with black velvet, richly fringed. It was at first intended, that the fringe should be gold; but it was afterwards considered, that it would give too gaudy an appearance to the solemn vehicle, and therefore black fringe was adopted every where instead of it.—Immediately above the festoons, in the front, was inscribed, in gold, the word NILE, at one end: on one side, the following motto—"*Hoste devicto, requievit:*" behind, the word TRAFALGAR; and, on the other side, the motto—"*Palmam qui meruit ferat.*" The carriage was drawn by six led horses, in elegant furniture.

It is a curious circumstance, that, after the construction of the car, necessity required it to be twice altered. In the first instance, it was discovered to be too high to pass under the arch at Temple-bar; and after this had been remedied, it was found to be too wide to enter the gates of the Admiralty.

During the Friday and Saturday after the procession, the car was exhibited to the populace, in the King's Mews, Charing-cross.

The preservation of this truly magnificent carriage. in the construction and embellishment of which the sum of 700*l.* is said to have been expended, being desirable, the following letter was dispatched from the Admiralty to Greenwich Hospital:—

SIR, *Admiralty Office, Jan.* 11.

My Lords Commissioners of the Admiralty being desirous that the Funeral Car, which yesterday conveyed the remains of the late Vice-Admiral Lord Viscount Nelson, K. B. from hence to St. Paul's Cathedral for interment, should be deposited in the Royal Hospital for Seamen at Greenwich, to perpetuate the memory of the Deceased, I have their Lordships' commands to desire that you will acquaint the Directors therewith, and request their acceptance of the said Car, for the purpose above mentioned, directions having been given for its being conveyed to the Hospital to-morrow, and delivered into the charge of such person as may be appointed to receive it.

I am, Sir, your very humble servant,

WILLIAM MARSDEN.

John Dyer, Esq. Secretary,
Greenwich Hospital.

In consequence of the above, the Car was, on Sunday morning, conveyed to Greenwich Hospital, drawn by six of the King's black horses, with three postillions in the royal liveries, attended by a coachman on horseback, and escorted by a strong detachment of the Royal Westminster Volunteers, accompanied by a part of the band of that corps. It arrived on the Green, where it was received by Lord Hood, about noon; and, at one o'clock, it was deposited in the Painted Chamber.

Having thus attempted to describe the last obsequies of our beloved and lamented Hero, we leave his honoured remains to the enviable repose of the virtuous.

NAVAL LITERATURE.

Biographical Memoirs of LORD VISCOUNT NELSON, *&c. &c. &c., with Observations, critical and explanatory. By* JOHN CHARNOCK, *Esq., F. S. A., Author of the Biographia Navalis, and the History of Marine Architecture, &c. &c.* 8vo. pp. 608. 1806.

IN taking up a book, there is always a pleasure in knowing the qualifications of the author, and what were his motives for writing it. To most of our readers Mr. Charnock's name and labours are well known; and when it was understood, that he was preparing a life of Lord Nelson for the press, the public attention was directed towards it, expecting to find a more complete work than any which had hitherto appeared on the subject. The following information, respecting the origin of the present performance, will not, we presume, be unacceptable:—

An enthusiastic attachment to the naval service, says the writer, and all that relates to it, has been, from his childhood, his ruling passion. It has led him in more instances than one, to devote his pen to the illustration of its mechanical œconomy, and to the biography of many of its numberless heroes. With a disposition so inclined, and habits so fixed, it became his fortune to gain some personal knowledge of the great man whose memory he now seeks to consecrate; and that occasional intercourse took place in the house of the late Captain William Locker, Lieutenant-Governor of Greenwich Hospital, with whom the author may presume to boast of many years' strict intimacy and friendship, and whose high character in public service, and in private life, are above his powers of praise. That excellent officer, as we shall see, was in a manner Lord Nelson's professional father. By him a thousand traits and anecdotes were communicated in that exquisite manner of simplicity and feeling which belonged almost peculiarly to himself. By him the present work was suggested, even during the life of his Lordship, almost in the form of a request: certain materials, whose value will speak for them in the course of the ensuing pages, have been since supplied by his estimable family. Thus, with an original bias to the subject, some aid of private intelligence relative to it; and, perhaps above all, pushed on to the undertaking by the late prodigious conclusion of the Hero's triumph, have promoted the author's presumption in devoting his feeble powers to their celebration.

The author farther informs us, that he "claims little merit beyond that which of right belongs to a faithful collector and reporter of much authentic intelligence, that had been before widely scattered under the public eye. He hopes, by this faithful miniature representation of Lord Nelson, to correct the defects and mistakes of such miserable sketches as have already appeared, and to furnish an outline to those who may, in future, be inclined to amplify on a subject which affords such boundless space."—As a *collector*, Mr. Charnock is unquestionably entitled to ample credit; but we must be permitted to observe, that, in common with his rival biographers, he is chiefly indebted to *The* NAVAL CHRONICLE for the mass of his information. Unlike his fellow-labourers, however, who in the art of literary piracy have eminently distinguished themselves, Mr. Charnock, with a spirit of candour and liberality, which reflects high credit on his character, has acknowledged the source whence he has derived his materials.

In observing, that Mr. Charnock is chiefly indebted to our Publication for his particulars respecting the late Lord Nelson, we allude to the general memoirs of his Lordship's life. To the Appendix, occupying nearly seventy closely printed pages, and containing between forty and fifty letters from Lord Nelson to his friend William Locker, Esq., late Lieutenant-Governor of Greenwich Hospital, several of them illustrative of those memoirs, we have no claim. For them, the public are wholly indebted to Mr. Charnock. They stamp an exclusive value upon his book, which must render it acceptable to every admirer of our departed Hero.

For the gratification of our readers, at a future period we shall probably take the liberty of extracting some of those letters, but, at present, our limits will not permit.

From his own work, *The* BIOGRAPHIA NAVALIS, to which we have frequently had occasion to refer, and from *The* NAVAL CHRONICLE, Mr. Charnock has formed a number of interesting sketches, relating to living and deceased officers. These he has thrown into the form of notes, giving his book the air of an agreeable Miscellany, well calculated to relieve the tedium of a long cruise.

In point of matter, Charnock's memoirs of Lord Nelson will be found exceedingly cheap.

The Post Captain, or the Wooden Walls well manned; comprehending a View of Naval Society and Manners. 8vo. pp. 300. 1806.

WE fear that this Volume, which is not without its merit, has been made up to impose on the credulity of the naval profession, and more particularly of the public in general; by having Dr. Moore's name *pasted* on its back. Had it been really the production of the author of *Zeluco,* we would gladly have eked out a seven shilling piece from our half-pay to purchase it. But *Mr. Thomas Tegg,* the publisher, ought not in these hard times to hang out false colours, to get off his crudities.

Every page abounds in sea terms, sometimes delivered like a seaman: but there is also a vast deal, which betrays the slang of a land lubber, such as we meet with at masquerades, from cocknies dressed in sailors' jackets and trowsers. As a view of Naval Manners, the volume is very imperfect: this requires the hand of a Master. For, strange as it may seem, nothing is so little understood in this country as the real character of its mariners. The following chapter is one of the best:—

He scorns the wanton's eye that lustful roves,
No nymph can move him but the girl he loves.

AUTHOR.

"Let this day," cried Captain Brilliant, as he walked towards Temple-bar, arm-in-arm with his Lieutenant: "let the events of this day, Echo, be recorded in the log-book of your life."

"Bestow your charity, my noble sea officers," cried a one-legged sailor to our heroes.—"Bestow your charity upon poor Jack, who is hove to under a stormy-stay-sail!"

"Here, shipmate!" cried Brilliant, "is half a crown for you."

"Here I come, Sir," cried Jack, redoubling his agility—"here I crowd all the sail I have left!"

"And there's another half crown," said Echo.—"Luff, boy! Luff! and catch it in your hat."

"God Almighty bless you both!" cried Jack. "I could tell you were seamen by the peak of your mizens. I might have begged of the red jackets till all was blue again! Huzza! huzza! huzza!"

As our heroes passed along the Strand, they were accosted by a hundred gay ladies, who asked them if they were good-natured.

"Devil take me!" exclaimed Echo, "if I know which way my ship heads: but there is not a girl in the Strand that I would touch with my gloves on."

"That will do for the marines," said Captain Brilliant.

"Last night, Sir, at this hour, I would have steered into the midst of the grand fleet. I would in a very short time have brought some ship to action; but now I luff up, I bear away to keep clear of them."

"You are in love, Echo. Hoa! the Sophonisba ahoy!"

"I will send to-morrow for a taylor: I will bend a new suit of sails."

"In love, by all that's true!"

"I will *fumigate* my pocket-handkerchief with lavender and *bergamyhot*."

"In love, or I am not here!"

"I will improve myself in flute-playing."

"In love, to a certainty."

"I will have my hanger new mounted."

"In love, there's no doubt!"

"I will have my teeth cleaned by a dentist."

"In love, as sure as the devil's in London!"

At Piccadilly these heroes took a coach and proceeded to Chelsea; Captain Brilliant sleeping the whole way, and Echo singing, as he looked towards the moon,

I saw her faint, or else 'twas fancy!

The twentieth Chapter, which contains an account of Mr. Keith's captivity among the American Indians, apparently a true narrative, is detailed with considerable interest. We can only insert the beginning of it, as a fragment:—

And their attention gain'd, with serpent tongue
Organic, or impulse of vocal air,
His fraudulent temptation—

MILTON.

In the month of August 1795, I proceeded down the Ohio river, in a large boat, with a young wife, to whom I had been married a twelvemonth, and a child of three months old that she carried in her arms.

I was transporting my family and effects from Dog's Town to Fishing Creek, where I had purchased a mill, which stood hard by the Falls.

We felt some little regret on leaving our old abode. There is a certain attachment to place and things, by which a town, a house, or a tree, have an influence over the mind. Log's Town is not an enviable place of residence. Yet I doubt whether Baron Trenk left his dungeon without some degree of pensiveness.

Our feet clung to the threshold of the door of our old house. My wife gazed with wildness at the locust tree, under whose shade she had so often sat with me, and listened to the mocking-bird's song; and I saw a tear fall from her eye upon the child that slept at her bosom.

A couple of negroes, Jack and Cuffey, rowed our canoe, and I undertook to steer her. Towards evening we had reached a broad part of the Ohio; the current ran strong in our favour; and there was less occasion for rowing, than to keep the canoe in the middle of the river.

The moon, in solemn majesty, was rising from the woods; the fire-fly was on the wing, and the banks of the Ohio echoed with the incessant and melancholy cry of the whip-poor-will.

"Mossa Keith!" cried the negro Cuffey, "something not aright. Something scare whip-poor-will. She cry like a mother that lose her pickniny."

I could not forbear smiling at the superstition of the fellow: but my wife drew nearer to me, and hugged the babe closer to her breast.

In a few minutes more, the most lamentable cries that ever were uttered assailed our ears. My wife screamed with affright, and the arms of the rowers were suspended.

I instantly put my fusil upon the whole cock, and kept the canoe in the middle of the stream, ordering at the same time the negroes to pull away.

I directed my eye towards the spot from whence the noise proceeded; and, being recovered from my emotion, could discern a white man, kneeling at the bank of the river, supplicating me, with every gesture and attitude that wretchedness could dictate, to take him into the boat.

I called to Jack and Cuffey to lie upon their oars. The poor wretch repeated his cries. "Oh! take him on board!" exclaimed my wife. "His cries pierce my heart."

I steered towards the shore, and told the stranger to get on board.

"Alas!" faultered the man, "I have not strength left to move. For five days I have been without food, save now and then an acorn. Oh! leave me not to perish; but help me, I beseech you."

I ordered the negroes to lift the man on board; but they had scarce jumped on shore, when a dozen of Indians rushed from a wood, yelling out the most diabolical screeches and notes, and surrounded us in a twinkling.

The white man who had thus decoyed us to the shore was a prisoner to the Indians, and was employed by them, under the penalty of death, to ensnare the incautious passenger down the river, by his piercing cries, and lamentable exclamations. Two captives they had dispatched with their war-clubs for refusing to perform the office.

I was quickly disarmed by the Indians; and Cuffey, in his attempt to flee into the woods, was overtaken by a young war-captain, and tomahawked on the spot. Thus fell the best negro I ever owned, and for whom I had often refused three hundred dollars.

When the Indians had plundered the canoe of my effects, they wantonly set fire to her, and burned her to the water's edge. The canoe had cost me ninety dollars, and was almost without an equal.

Having loaded three horses with plunder, the Indians dragged us to their flying camp, about a mile in the woods, where we found several women and girls stewing venison for supper in a loblolly-pot.

Perceiving the tenderness I felt towards my wife, they were under no fear that I should attempt to escape; but entertaining suspicions of negro Jack, they secured him during the night in a very effectual manner. They cut down a sapling the size of a man's thigh, and having made notches in it to receive the negro's legs, placed over each a pole, which they crossed with stakes driven on each side into the ground, and in the crotchets of the stakes placed other poles, or rides. This confined the prisoner on his back: and, for their greater security, they put a thong of leather round his neck and fastened it to a tree.

I made a bed for Fanny and myself, by strewing branches on the ground; and obtained, after much entreaty, a blanket for a covering. It may reasonably be expected that in this melancholy condition sleep was a stranger to our eyelids.

The next morning, the Indians painted my wife red and black, and Jack with the same colour; but I was smutted over with black only. By this mark I knew they had devoted me to death; but I carefully concealed my suspicion from my wife.

With the rising sun we jogged forward towards the mountains. The company consisted of twelve Indian warriors, six squaws, three boys of twelve years, five children in arms; my wife and her child, myself, negro Jack, and Richard Edwards, the white man, who had decoyed us on shore. To this group must be superadded the three horses, loaded with the plunder of my boat.

It was a beautiful sun-rising. All nature seemed refreshed; and the dew fell drop by drop from the trees of the forest.

The wild turkeys were calling to each other from the lofty branches of the oak; the cardinal was expanding his golden plumage to the sun; the wood-pecker was sticking his beak at the worms in the bark; and the mocking songster, with faint carol, was hailing the return of day.

We had not proceeded a mile, when an Indian picked up the scalp of a white man, which he presented to Namasket, the chief of the party.

I could perceive the roses fly the cheek of Fanny, on beholding this spectacle.

Proceeding onward, I eased my wife of the child, and carried it myself. When it was froward, the mother would take him, and give him the breast.

One of the Indian women, who had no milk in her breast, wanted my wife to suckle her child. This I would not suffer. Upon which Squanto, the husband, (the fellow who tomahawked Cuffey,) was so incensed, that he not only insulted Fanny, but filled the child's mouth with sand.

I could not contain myself. I snatched a tomahawk from the hand of an Indian, who stood next to me and called to Squanto to defend himself. He made a vigorous onset at me with his war-club. I evaded it by jumping on one side, and with the tomahawk I struck him a blow on the head, which instantly deprived him of life.

On seeing Squanto fall, several of the Indians discovered great rage, and approached to dispatch me. A mighty strife ensued among them. Some would kill me; others would prevent it: and thus one Indian was striving with another.

Fanny had clung to me, determined to share my fate. I loved her with all the feelings of a man. And it was not without secret satisfaction, that I reflected the immortal part of us would both visit the other world together. I therefore suffered her to cling to me, and called to the Indians,—"*Tapoy! Tapoy! Pe quish a con gau mowon! manitowwhi gau no mun iss e to ta!*"—"Indians! Indians! Strike us all three! Let us all die together.

The hand of our destiny interposed to save us. Namasket was disposed in our favour; in which disposition he was confirmed by the cries of a beautiful Indian girl, whom he had but very lately married.

His voice restrained the arms and fury of the Indians. A kind of debate was held: a grave was dug, the dead Indian interred, and a quantity of stones piled over the spot.

NAVAL HISTORY OF THE PRESENT YEAR, 1806.

(*February—March.*)

RETROSPECTIVE AND MISCELLANEOUS.

THE Victory of Sir John Duckworth will again inform the imperial manufacturer of lies and calumny, that the English are not skulking, as he was pleased to assert, *behind their dirty Channel.* The colonial adventures of this Usurper have thus cost him near thirty ships of the line within the last six months. The squadron first chased by Admiral Duckworth, is conjectured to have been that which is under the command of Prince Jerome.

Of the British squadron which accomplished the late gallant achievement, the Canopus was formerly the French ship le Franklin, Rear-Admiral Blanquet, taken by Lord Nelson in the battle of Aboukir; the Donegal was formerly the French ship le Hoche, one of the French squadron dispatched for the invasion of Ireland, and taken off the coast of Donegal by Sir John Borlase Warren in 1798; and the Agamemnon is Lord Nelson's old ship, which that gallant and lamented Hero went to visit at Portsmouth, when he last sailed from that port from England, previous to the great battle of Trafalgar, in which he fell. The Agamemnon was commanded by Sir Edward Berry, who was his Lordship's Captain in the Vanguard, in the battle of Aboukir. Of the other gallant Chiefs who distinguished themselves upon this occasion, the Hon. Captain Stopford is thir son of the Earl of Courtown, and the Hon. A. Cochrane is youngest son of the Earl of Dundonald. Lieutenant Seymour, who was so severely wounded in the action off St. Domingo, is the son of the late Lord Hugh Seymour. His wound was by a grape shot, which penetrated the jaw, and tore away part of his teeth.

Sir John, it is well known, was detached by Lord Collingwood in quest of a French squadron known to be at sea, and was actually in sight of one near the Cape de Verd Islands, but lost them. He proceeded to the West Indies, however, and arriving in the Leeward Islands, received no tidings of the enemy. He then dispatched the Powerful, Captain Plampin, one of the ships under his command, to the East Indies, to announce that an enemy's squadron was out, and his then unsuccessful chase. In the Leeward Islands he was joined by Admiral Cochrane, in the Northumberland; and by the Atlas, Captain Pym. Happily, he at last received information that the enemy were in St. Domingo bay, and thither he proceeded. He arrived in time to catch the enemy, who, apprised of his approach, were under weigh for a position where they would have been under the protection of Fort Ocoa; but they were intercepted and brought to action in the most masterly manner. With the result our readers are acquainted. It is mentioned, that on seeing the enemy Sir J. Duckworth gave out a telegraphic signal to his fleet, "THIS IS GLORIOUS," alluding to the enemy's fleet in a situation to be engaged, which was equivalent to a victory, and therefore hailed by the whole squadron. The enemy, considering his inferiority (for even equal numbers must, after so many defeats, be counted inferiority,) behaved bravely, as their loss demonstrates. Sir John Duckworth, however, reprobates the conduct of the Captain of the Diomède, which ship ran on shore after she had struck, and the Agamemnon, therefore, had ceased firing. This proceeding is unquestionably repugnant to the laws of war; and those who escaped are, according to precedent, liable to be considered prisoners.

The service which Admiral Duckworth has performed for his country, is such as might have been expected from him, when we reflect on the school in which he was qualified for naval eminence. He served as Lieutenant to Earl St. Vincent. In the action of the 1st of June he commanded the Orion; and it was Lord St. Vincent's wish that he should be second in command in the Channel fleet.

To compare the contest off Domingo with the noble triumphs of Nelson, would be invidious and absurd; the least praise that can be bestowed upon it, and the highest applause, are summed up in very few words: The French fleet was discovered, brought to action with the utmost promptitude, and after an encounter more memorable on account of the superior skill and adroitness displayed by the British officers and seamen, than of the ensanguined fury with which it was fought, completely captured, or annihilated.

What greater achievement can be expected from men? Our enemies will perhaps plead in their justification that we have conquered with a superior force; a circumstance, which though it takes nothing from the success, materially diminishes the glory of the event. In replication to this plea, we cannot refrain from the just opportunity they afford us, much as it may gall a wound yet scarcely healed, of bringing to their recollection the events which took place, during an encounter between a French fleet, consisting of thirty sail, thirteen of which were of the line, and a British squadron, of rather inferior force to that under the orders of Mon. le Seigle, commanded by that gallant, and truly valuable officer, the present Admiral Cornwallis. Half the enemy's fleet tacked in shore, in the afternoon of the 16th of June, 1795, and a change of the wind brought those ships to windward of the British ships, so that on the morning of the 17th, at daylight, the enemy were seen on both quarters of the Vice-Admiral's squadron. At nine o'clock one of their headmost ships began firing on the Mars, the sternmost of the British line; and the rest of their fleet, as they came up, in succession commenced, to use Mr. Cornwallis's own terms, " a blazing fire," which continued, at intervals, during the whole day, but without effecting any injury to the British ships, or, consequently, affording any advantage to the enemy. The Mars having fallen a little to leeward towards the close of the day, the enemy, as their last effort, appeared to threaten rather a serious attack on that ship; but on the Vice-Admiral's bearing up to support her, they abandoned their intention; and, notwithstanding their wonderful superiority, began to draw off, insomuch that, by sunset, the whole of the enemy's fleet having tacked, left the British to pursue their course unmolested. Thus did this brave man acquire the honour of having defended himself with success, and brought off entire, as well as uninjured, the squadron he commanded, in defiance of the utmost efforts of an enemy, whose fleet consisted of thirteen ships of the line, fourteen frigates, and three smaller vessels.

The squadron of Mr. Cornwallis was inferior to that of le Seigle, inasmuch as though the number of ships was equal, the ship which bore the French flag was infinitely superior in her dimensions, her weight of metal, and the number of guns she mounted, to the Royal Sovereign, which, though a first rate, is by no means the largest, or stoutest ship in the British service: there were moreover, in the French St. Domingo squadron, two ships mounting 84 guns each, while those under Mr. Cornwallis, the Triumph, Mars, Brunswick, and Bellerophon, were only of 74 guns each. We will not insult a defeated, and prostrate enemy, by stating the inference naturally to be drawn; we shall content ourselves with saying,—*So much for the boasted skill of French officers and of French seamen in naval tactics.* Were we inclined to insult, we might parodize on the insolent expression attributed, though we believe falsely, to Buonaparté, during the last campaign, " That a British Admiral can derive little honour from the defeat of any French officer we at present know of, employed in the service of that country."

An erroneous idea went abroad on the appointment of Mr. Grey to the head of the Board, which we feel it our duty to contradict. Mr. Grey, in his present high and illustrious station, stands alone, uncontrouled by any one. Neither Lord St. Vincent's system, nor any other system, can possibly be forced on Mr. Grey's independent mind; which never did, nor ever will submit to be fettered: and in this respect he is zealously supported by Sir Charles Pole.

Admiral Sir J. B. Warren's fleet, according to dispatches received by the Sprightly cutter, arrived off Madeira on the 15th of February, and continued cruising there on the twentieth: its force consists of seven sail of the line, two brigs, and a cutter.

According to letters from Rochfort, one of our small cruisers, on the 15th of

March, stood close into that harbour, disguised as a neutral ship, and distinctly counted five sail of the line and four frigates, and several armed vessels, ready for sea, at single anchor, with their sails bent; a corvette stood out to speak our cruiser, on which she directly up quarter-cloths, and blazed away at her so briskly, that the enemy found it necessary to bear away under the batteries, which opened their fire, but without damage to the vessel which reconnoitered. She returned to Rear-Admiral Thornborough, who was all well at the date of the above letters, with five sail of the line and two frigates, ready to meet the enemy, if he feels bold enough to come out.

Letters on Service,

Copied verbatim from the London Gazette.

[Continued from page 162.]

ADMIRALTY-OFFICE, FEBRUARY 8, 1806.

Copy of a Letter from the Hon. W. Cornwallis, Admiral of the Red, &c. to W. Marsden, Esq.; dated Ville de Paris, off Ushant, the 20th January, 1806.

SIR,

I HAVE the honour to enclose, for the information of the Lords Commissioners of the Admiralty, a letter from Lieutenant Thomas Nesbitt, commanding His Majesty's gun-brig the Growler, acquainting me of his having, on the 28th instant, captured the French lugger privateer Voltigeur, of St. Maloes.

I have the honour to be, &c.
W. CORNWALLIS.

His Majesty's Gun-Brig Growler, off Brest, January 30, 1806.

SIR,

I beg leave to inform you, that, on the morning of the 28th instant, when running for this station, in pursuance of your orders, His Majesty's gun-brig under my command captured le Voltigeur lugger privateer, of St. Maloes, pierced for 14 guns, but having only six nine-pounders on board, with a complement of sixty-six men; out one day, but had not taken any thing.

I have the honour to remain, &c.
T. NESBITT. Lieut. and Commander.

To the Honourable William Cornwallis, Admiral of the Red, &c.

Copy of another Letter from Admiral the Hon. W. Cornwallis to W. Marsden, Esq.: dated on board the Ville de Paris, in Cawsand Bay, the 5th of February, 1806.

SIR,

I have the honour to enclose, for the information of the Lords Commissioners of the Admiralty, a letter I have received from Lieutenant Thomas Swain, of His Majesty's gun-brig Attack, acquainting me of his having captured the French privateer therein mentioned.

I have the honour to be, &c.
W. CORNWALLIS.

His Majesty's Brig Attack, at Sea, 29th January, 1806.

SIR,

I beg leave to inform you, that his Majesty's gun-brig Growler, in company with the Attack, at day-light on the 28th instant, fell in with and captured the

French lugger privateer Voltigeur, of 14 guns and seventy men. Having learnt from them that another lugger, then in sight, was also an enemy's privateer of a similar description, nothing was left undone to come up with her; and, after a circular chase of nine hours, I got alongside, and captured her. She proves to be le Sorcier, of and from St. Maloes, with sixty men and 14 guns, ten of which they had thrown overboard during the chase, commanded by Guilliaume Françoise Neele: out two days, and had taken nothing, but was to cruise for two months. I feel pleased that two such vessels should fall into our possession, as they might have done much mischief to our western commerce.

I have the honour to be, &c.

THOMAS SWAIN.

Copy of a Letter from Vice-Admiral Lord Collingwood, Commander in Chief of His Majesty's Ships and Vessels in the Mediterranean, to W. Marsden, Esq.; dated on board the Queen, at Sea, the 21st of January, 1806.

SIR,

I enclose, for the information of the Lords Commissioners of the Admiralty, a report of captures between the 17th of November last and the 9th instant.

I am, &c.

COLLINGWOOD.

A Return of Vessels captured and detained by the Squadron under the Command of the Right Honourable Lord Collingwood, Vice-Admiral of the Blue, and Commander in Chief in the Mediterranean, &c. between the 17th November 1805, and January 1806.

Prussian ship Minerva, of 1 gun, 6 men, and 200 tons burthen, from Barcelona bound to Embden, laden with brandy: detained by the Thunder bomb, November 17, 1805.

Swedish ship St. Jean, of 2 guns, 8 men, and 150 tons burthen, from Vigo bound to Stralsund; laden with cocoa and fish: detained off Malaga, by ditto, November 27, 1805.

Sicilian ship la Divine Providence, of 9 men and 50 tons burthen, from Palermo bound to Genoa; laden with sundries: detained by the Morgiana, December 1, 1805.

French privateer Andromeda, of 4 guns and 43 men: captured by the Spider, December 10, 1805.

Danish ship Vildanden, of 8 men and 72 tons burthen, from Barcelona bound to Copenhagen: detained by the Thunder bomb, December 19, 1805.

Danish ship Sophia, of 1 gun, 10 men, and 200 tons burthen; laden with nuts, &c., from Altona bound to Salo: detained by ditto, same date.

Ragusan ship Terpsichore, of 280 tons, from the Isle of France bound to Leghorn; laden with sugar, coffee, &c.: detained by the Childers, December 24, 1805.

Moorish ship Mitica, of 4 men and 20 tons, from Oran bound to Algesiras; laden with sundries: detained by the Martin, January 5, 1806.

Portuguese ship San Antonio, of 4 men and 35 tons, from Tetuan bound to Malaga; laden with sundries: detained by ditto, January 9, 1805.

Portuguese ship Carmen, of 4 men and 25 tons burthen, from Cadiz bound to Malaga; laden with glass: detained by ditto, same date.

COLLINGWOOD.

FEBRUARY 11.

Copy of a Letter from Admiral the Rt. Hon. Lord Gardner to W. Marsden, Esq.; dated on board His Majesty's Ship the Dryad, in Cork Harbour, Feb. 5, 1806.

SIR,

His Majesty's ship Druid arrived here early this morning; and I have the pleasure to enclose, for their Lordships' information, copy of a letter, dated at sea, 2d instant, from Captain P. B. V. Broke, giving an account of his having captured the French ship privateer Prince Murat, having on board eighteen 6-pounders, and 127 men; five days at sea; from l'Orient, and had not made any captures.

I have the honour to be, &c.

GARDNER.

MY LORD, *Druid, at Sea, February 2, 1806.*

I have the pleasure to inform you, that His Majesty's ship under my command captured this morning, after a chase of ninety miles, the Prince Murat French ship privateer, of 18 guns, six-pounders, and 127 men, commanded by Monsieur Rine Murin, out five days from l'Orient, and had made no captures. She is a coppered ship, and a fast sailer. I have sent her to Plymouth; and have the honour to be, &c.

The Rt. Hon. Admiral Lord Gardner,
Admiral of the White, &c. P. V. B. BROKE.

FEBRUARY 18.

Copy of a Letter from Vice-Admiral Dacres, Commander in Chief of His Majesty's Ships and Vessels at Jamaica, to William Marsden, Esq.; dated at Port Royal, December 19, 1805.

SIR,

I enclose you a copy of a letter I have received from Captain Macdonnell, of the Bacchante, acquainting me of his having captured the Spanish privateer schooner dos Azares.

I am, &c. J. R. DACRES.

SIR, *His Majesty's Ship Bacchante, at Sea, 18th Nov. 1805.*

I have the honour of informing you, that, in cruising off the north east end, to protect the ships bound to this side of the island, we discovered a schooner under the land. Knowing our misfortune of not sailing well, I stood off, and was chased by her until she found her mistake, on which I tacked, and made all sail; and, after a chase of seven hours, we run alongside and boarded the Spanish privateer schooner the les dos Azares, Captain Ealletam Garcia, of thirty-six men, out four days from Cuba, and had taken nothing; armed with two three-pounders, and in all respects perfectly prepared for boarding. Three of the privateer's crew are badly wounded.

I have the honour to be, &c.

RANDALL MACDONNELL.

To James Richard Dacres, Esq., Rear-Admiral
of the Red, Commander in Chief.

Copy of another Letter from Vice-Admiral Dacres, to W. Marsden, Esq.; dated at Port Royal, December 25, 1805.

SIR,

I transmit herewith, for the information of their Lordships, the copy of a letter from Captain Coghlan, acquainting me of the capture of the Bellona schooner privateer by His Majesty's sloop Renard.

I am, &c. J. R. DACRES.

His Majesty's Sloop Renard, Port Royal Harbour,
SIR, *November 21, 1805.*

I have the pleasure to acquaint you with the capture of the French privateer schooner Bellona, on the 11th ultimo, by this ship, after a long chase and some firing, at the north side of St. Domingo. She has four carriage guns, and fifty men; was seven days from Barracona, had taken one American brig. She is only four months old, and is considered the fastest sailer out of Cuba.

I have the honour to be, &c.

JEREMIAH COGHLAN.

To J. R. Dacres, Esq., Rear-Admiral of the
Red, and Commander in Chief.

GAZETTE EXTRAORDINARY.

FEBRUARY 27.

Copy of a Letter received this day by Captain Downman, from Sir Home Popham, K.M., Captain of His Majesty's Ship Diadem, to W. Marsden, Esq.; dated on board the said Ship, in Table Bay, the 13th January 1806.

SIR,

When I address you, for the information of the Lords Commissioners of the Admiralty, on an occasion of such public interest and importance as the capture of the Cape of Good Hope, which is now in possession of His Majesty's troops under that renowned General Sir David Baird, I consider it unnecessary to trouble their Lordships with a detailed account of the proceedings of the fleet from St. Salvador, which, however, will be conveyed in another dispatch.

On the 3d inst. we made Table Land; and, on the 4th, in the evening, we reached our preconcerted anchorage to the westward of Robben Island, though too late to do any thing but take a superficial view of Blue Berg Bay, where it was proposed to land the main body of the army, making, however, a demonstration off Green Point, with the Leda frigate, and the transports containing the 24th regiment, which was certainly well executed by Captain Honyman. On the 5th, at three o'clock in the morning, the troops were put in the boats, and assembled alongside of l'Espoir, but the surf ran so high, that a landing was deemed totally impracticable, and consequently the troops returned to their ships; and I immediately accompanied the General on board l'Espoir, for the purpose of making a close examination of the whole coast from Craig's Tower to Lospard's Bay; on no part of which did it appear possible to land a single boat without extreme danger.

To the evil consequences of delay in commencing operations on an enemy's coast, was to be added the very alarming possibility that some reinforcement might arrive by one of the various squadrons in motion when we left Europe; and therefore the General and myself were induced to consider, that however difficult the task might be of advancing from Saldanha Bay, yet it was an object of very great moment to accomplish a safe and speedy landing for the troops; and the instant the decision was made, the Diomede, with the transports of the 38th regiment, the cavalry ships, and a proportion of artillery, under the orders of Brigadier General Beresford, sailed for Saldanha, preceded by Captain King in l'Espoir, having on board Captain Smyth of the Engineers, (an officer well acquainted with the country,) with a view of seizing the Postmaster, and as many cattle as possible, antecedent to the arrival of the advanced division of the fleet. Soon after the Diomede weighed the westerly wind began to abate, and on the 6th in the morning the officers examining the beach reported that the surf had considerably subsided during the night, which indeed was so evident from the Diadem when she stood in shore, that I requested Sir David Baird to permit General Fergusson, and Colonel Brownrigg, the Quarter-master General, to attend the officer on his second examination, that their feelings might in some measure be balanced against those of professional men, and to satisfy the army that no measure, in which its safety was so intimately connected, should be determined on without due and proper deliberation. In the mean time the Diadem, Leda, and Encounter, were placed in a situation to render the most effectual assistance; and the 71st and 72d regiments, with two field pieces and a howitzer ready mounted, in the boats of the Raisonable and Belliqueux, rendezvoused alongside the two former ships, manifesting the most ardent desire for the signal from General Fergusson. At this moment the Protector joined the squadron; and Captain Rowley, who was well acquainted with the anchorage, volunteered his services to place her to the northward, so as to cross the fire of the Encounter, and more effectually cover the landing of the troops. Captain Downman at the same time went in shore with a light transport brig, drawing only six feet, to run her on the beach as a break-water, if it would in any degree facilitate the debarkation of the troops. —At half past twelve, the Encounter conveyed, by signal, General Fergusson's opinion, that a landing might be effected, and the joy that was manifest in the countenance of every officer, heightened the characteristic ardour of the troops;

and under an anxiety, probably, to be first on shore, induced them to urge the boats to extend their line of beach further than was prudent, and occasioned the loss of one boat, with a party of the 93d regiment. I report this event to their Lordships with the most unfeigned regret; and it is doubly painful to me, because, from all the efforts of an enemy posted on an advantageous height, the army had only two men wounded in landing. This circumstance must fully prove how well the covering vessels were placed, and how ably their guns were served; and I trust my Country will acquit me of not having applied every expedient that could be devised to prevent the occurrence of an accident which I so sincerely deplore. The surf increased considerably towards the close of the evening, and about eight o'clock the landing of any more troops was stopped, but recommenced in the morning, when all the men and prisoners, which the General judged necessary to take, were disembarked without a moment's loss of time.—Conceiving that a detachment of the squadron might be of service at the head of the Bay, I proceeded there with the Leda, Encounter, and Protector, and a division of transports; and I understand, from firing occasionally that evening over the bank towards the Salt Pan, that the enemy was obliged to move from an eligible situation which he had before occupied. On the following morning we discovered the British army advancing, with an unparalleled rapidity, over a heavy country, defended by a numerous train of well served artillery; and as I conceived a few fresh troops might be applied to advantage, I desired Capt. Downman to land with the marines of the squadron, and two field pieces, to await the arrival of Sir David Baird, at Reit Valley, whom I very soon after had the pleasure of personally congratulating on the victory he had obtained over a General of such high military fame as General Jansens. When the army was in motion to take up its position at Craig's Tower, and while I was proceeding up the Bay to anchor in the most convenient place for landing the battering train, a flag of truce was discovered coming towards the Diadem, by which I received the letter, No. 1, from the Commandant of the Town and Castle; and the next day, in conjunction with Sir David Baird, the Capitulation No. 2, was accepted, and at six a royal salute was fired from the squadron, on His Majesty's colours being once more hoisted on the Castle. Although their Lordships will perceive by the detailed account of our transactions here, and the accompanying plan of the different dispositions which were made, that no brilliant service fell to the lot of the squadron I have the honour to command, yet it is what I owe every officer and seamen to state, that under the most laborious duty I ever experienced, their zeal never abated. To Captain Rowley I feel personally indebted for his readiness on every occasion; and I have no doubt but the highest satisfaction will be expressed of the conduct of Captain Byng, who commanded the marine battalion, by an authority far exceeding mine. And I enclose, for their Lordships information, a copy of the report he made me on the conduct of the officers serving in that battalion; to which, exclusive of those belonging to the squadron, are added Captain Hardinge, of the Salsette, and several other officers, now on their passage to India to join their ships. Captain Butterfield and Lieutenant Cochrane, of the transports, were on all occasions ready to forward the service, and we are particularly indebted to Captains Cameron, Christopher, and Moring, of the Honourable Company's ships Duchess of Gordon, Sir William Pulteney, and Comet, who particularly exerted themselves in assisting the troops through the surf. It is impossible for me to transmit any returns of the stores taken, by this opportunity, or of the state of the Bato, of 68 guns, in Seamen's Bay; but it is, however, so strongly reported, that the enemy has not completely succeeded in his attempt to burn her; that I have sent Captain Percy to take possession of her, and, if possible, to move her into safety, as the enemy has totally abandoned her. Captain Downman, of the Diadem, will have the honour of delivering this dispatch to their Lordships, and from the intelligent manner in which I am satisfied he will explain every movement, and the causes by which I have been actuated, I trust he will require no further recommendation to their Lordship's protection. I cannot, however, conclude this letter without assuring their Lordships, that I know no instance where a stronger degree of confidence and unanimity has been exemplified between the two professions, than on the present occasion; and I humbly hope this circumstance, coupled with the meritorious and successful issue of Sir David Baird's military dispositions, will recommend this armament to His Majesty's most gracious favour and protection.

I have the honour to be, Sir,

Your most obedient humble servant,

HOME POPHAM.

SIR, *His Majesty's Ship Belliqueux, Table Bay, 11th Jan.* 1806.

After the public orders issued by General Sir David Baird, I feel it unnecessary to trouble you with any further report on the conduct of the marine brigade than to send you a copy of it. I never witnessed more zeal and determined spirit than was universally prevalent; and I take the liberty of annexing the names of all the volunteer* officers; and I return my thanks to them, as well as those officers from the Indiamen, so ably led by Captain Edmeads, of the William Pitt, to whom I am particularly indebted for his exexertions.

I have the honour to be, &c.

To Sir Home Popham, K. M., Commodore, &c. GEORGE BYNG.

MARCH 1.

Copy of a Letter from Captain Sir Home Popham, of His Majesty's Ship Diadem, to W. Marsden, Esq.; dated in Table Bay, January 13, 1806.

SIR,

I have the honour to transmit you copies of two letters, which I yesterday received from Captain Donnelly, who had been detached to procure intelligence; and, in justice to an officer of such merit, I cannot omit expressing my regret that I was deprived of the benefit of his exertions in the various duties which have been lately carried on at this place.

I have the honour to be, &c.

HOME POPHAM.

His Majesty's Ship Narcissus, Cape Mount, Coast of Africa,

SIR, *N. E. Five Leagues, October* 30, 1805.

Proceeding on the secret service which you did me the honour of charging me with, I fell in with the Columbus Guinea-ship yesterday, the Master of which, Mr. Callow, informed me a brig and schooner, French privateers, were infesting this coast, and had captured the Horatio Nelson, the stoutest ship coming out this season, after a severe action.

I immediately disguised the ship I command, and edged in shore, in the hope of meeting them, directing the Columbus to proceed on her voyage down the coast. At ten o'clock this morning we descried the above-mentioned privateers, and the Horatio Nelson in chase of the Columbus; and, as we perceived them coming fast up with her, we stood towards them completely disguised, and cut them off from her. In passing, I directed her Master still to keep running away. When the privateers saw us separate, they wore, and stood towards us. When we approached within pistol-shot, they commenced a fire, assisted by the Horatio Nelson, which carried twenty nine-pounders, and two twelve-pounders. We were obliged to fire upon them, and did them much damage, before the largest struck. When we got possession, we immediately pursued the Horatio Nelson, in preference to the schooner.

In the mean time the Columbus wore, and stood towards the Horatio Nelson, and exchanged broadsides as they passed; and she afterwards wore, and kept firing at her, until we arrived up with her, when she struck.

I have given her in possession of Mr. Callow, Master of the Columbus, who behaved very well on the occasion, in order to her being sent to Cape Massarida, where her late Master and part of the crew are; and I rejoice this nest of thieves

* Captain Harding, Lieutenants Pigot, Graham, Sutherland, Mingay, Carew, and Pearce.

(for they have plundered from all nations) is destroyed, particularly as we spoke many valuable vessels just coming on the coast. The schooner escaped with only a few men on board, as her crew were sent on board the Horatio Nelson, which was fitted for cruising.

I have the honour to be, &c.

Commodore Sir Home Popham, K. M. ROSS DONNELLY.
&c. &c. &c.

P. S. The brig we captured is named le Prudent, of four twelve-pounders, eight six-pounders, and seventy men.

His Majesty's Ship Narcissus, off the Cape of Good Hope,
SIR, *Christmas Day*, 1805.

Yesterday afternoon, while we were anxiously looking out in the ship I command, for the squadron and convoy under your orders, we discovered a ship coming from the land about Table Bay, in chase, steering down before the wind; she approached within eight or nine miles, and then hauled her wind from us. We instantly pursued, and kept her in view until half past nine at night, when the weather became so thick, we lost sight of her.

Judging, however, from her fast sailing, she was a ship of war, and would most likely push back for the Cape Town to give intelligence of our being on the coast, I plyed to windward all night to cut her off, and at day-light had the pleasure of seeing her at a considerable distance to windward. At nine o'clock we neared her fast, and fearing she would make in for the shore, I used every endeavour to prevent it, but without effect, as she was still to windward of us; and after various manœuvres to escape close to the surf along shore, and both keeping up a partial fire, we compelled her to run a-ground.

Soon after we observed her three masts and bowsprit go by the board, and her boats went adrift.

In such a distressed situation, with a heavy swell and surf setting on the beach, we forbore firing at her, although she vauntingly displayed the colours, which (considering her force,) she deprived herself the power of protecting; and I very much fear the greatest part of the crew will be lost.

Immediately after this event, we captured a Dutch sloop, bound with naval stores from the Cape Town to a line of battle ship lying at Simon's-Bay.

The people on board informed us, the vessel we ran on shore was a French ship of two and thirty thirty-two pounders (short guns) and 250 men, and had just sailed from Table Bay; that she had on board the ordnance, &c. of l'Atalante French frigate lately lost there, and was bound with them to the Mauritius, where ordnance stores were wanted to fit other ships.

I remain with great respect, &c.

To Commodore Sir Home Popham. ROSS DONNELLY.

Copy of a Letter from Captain Lobb, of His Majesty's Ship Pomone, to W. Marsden, Esq.; dated off Lisbon, February 10, 1806.

SIR,

I have the honour to acquaint you, for the information of the Lords Commissioners of the Admiralty, that the boats of His Majesty's ship under my command captured, off Lisbon, the 25th ultimo, El Bengador Spanish lugger privateer, with one gun, and twenty-eight men; she had been six weeks from Bayonne.

The Maid of the Mill, William Dearing, Master, from Newfoundland, was retaken at the same time, the only capture the lugger had made. I sent her to Lisbon, the port she was bound to; and the privateer was destroyed.

You will be pleased to communicate the enclosed to their Lordships.

I have the honour to be, &c.

W. G. LOBB.

SIR, *His Majesty's Ship Curieux, at Sea, Feb.* 6, 1806.

I beg to acquaint you, that yesterday His Majesty's sloop Curieux, under my command, fell in with, twenty-four leagues west of Lisbon, and captured, after a chase of four hours, the Baltidore Spanish lugger privateer, mounting six carriage guns, and forty-seven men. She had been from Ferrol one month, and had captured the Good Intent, from Lisbon bound to London.

I have the honour to be, &c.

William Granville Lobb, Esq.; Captain of His Majesty's Ship Pomone. J. JOHNSTONE.

List of Two Brigs recaptured by His Majesty's Sloop Star, John Simpson, Esq. Commander, off Villa de Conde, January 24, 1806.

Brig Adventure, belonging to Pool, from Newfoundland, bound to Oporto, laden with fish, under convoy of His Majesty's Ship Mercury.

Brig Argo, belonging to Teignmouth, from Newfoundland bound to Lisbon, laden with fish, under convoy of His Majesty's ship Mercury.

N. B. Made the signal to the Mercury for the Good Intent being in sight which she recaptured.

J. SIMPSON, Captain.

MARCH 4.

Copy of a Letter from the Hon. Rear-Admiral Cochrane, Commander in Chief of His Majesty's Ships and Vessels at the Leeward Islands, to W. Marsden, Esq; dated on board the Jason, at Barbadoes, the 24th December, 1805.

SIR,

I enclose the Copy of a letter I received from Captain N. D. Cochrane, of His Majesty's sloop Kingfisher, giving an account of the capture of a French privateer of 14 guns; and I am happy to acquaint you, for the information of the Lords Commissioners of the Admiralty, that her prize has been recaptured by His Majesty's sloop Melville. I have the honour to be, &c.

A. COCHRANE.

Kingfisher, December 18, 1805. *Barbadoes bearing N. by W., distant* 13 *or* 14 *leagues.*

SIR,

I beg leave to inform you, that on the 16th inst., at half-past seven, A.M., I had the good fortune to come up with and capture after a chase of twelve hours, l'Elizabeth French privateer schooner from Guadaloupe, armed with ten long sixes and four nine-pounder carronades, and sailed with a complement of 102 officers and men, eleven of which had been sent away in a prize, the Cambrian, from Cork bound to Jamaica, laden with coals, having parted from the Fisguard's convoy on the 29th of October.

L'Elizabeth has been a great annoyance to the trade in this country, and has often escaped from our cruisers by her superior sailing; is a fine vessel, well armed and equipped, and, in my opinion, admirably calculated for His Majesty's service. I have the honour to be, &c.

N. D. COCHRANE.

Rear-Admiral the Hon. Alexander Cochrane, Commander in Chief, &c.

Copy of another Letter from the Hon. Rear-Admiral Cochrane, to W. Marsden, Esq.; dated on board the Northumberland, off Martinique, December 31, 1805.

SIR,

I have the honour to enclose, for the information of the Lords Commissioners of the Admiralty, a list of vessels captured by the squadron under my command.

I am, &c. A. COCHRANE.

List of Ships and Vessels captured by the Squadron under the Command of the Hon. A. Cochrane, Rear-Admiral of the White, &c. &c. &c., from the 2d of April to the 31st December, 1805.

French schooner privateer l'Empereur, of 12 guns and 80 men, from Martinique on a cruise: taken by the Eagle, April 2, 1805.

Spanish schooner privateer Fama, of 4 guns and 60 men, from Vigo, on a cruise: taken by the Circe, March 1, 1805.

French schooner privateer la Desirée, of 10 guns and 80 men, from Guadaloupe, on a cruise: taken by the Barbadoes, April 8, 1805.

French schooner privateer la Constance, of 10 guns and 75 men, on a cruise: taken by the Circe, June 21, 1805.

Spanish schooner privateer la Damas, of 4 guns and 65 men, from Cumana bound to Demerary: taken by the Kingfisher, May 11, 1805.

French schooner privateer le Temprebort, of 4 guns and 35 men, from St. Domingo, on a cruise: taken by the Unicorn, May 4, 1805.

Spanish schooner privateer la Justicia, of 4 guns and 95 men, from Cumana, on a cruise: taken by the Cyane, May 16, 1805.

French schooner privateer la Josefine, of 2 guns and 35 men, from St. Pierre, on a cruise; taken by the Ramillies and Illustrious, July 7, 1805.

Spanish schooner Casualidad, from Puerto Cavello bound to Old Spain, laden with cocoa: taken by l'Epervier, May 25, 1805.

English ship Heroine, from London, laden with dry goods: retaken by l'Eclair, April 5, 1805.

Spanish brig Santo Christe, from Spain, bound to the Havana, laden with brandy: taken by the Alligator, June 24, 1805.

A Spanish schooner, name unknown, from Margaritta, bound to Oronoko, laden with salt: taken by the Trinidad, May 3, 1805.

A French sloop privateer, name unknown, of 1 gun and 25 men, from Cumana, on a cruise: taken by ditto, May 31, 1805.

French schooner privateer la Petite Aricere, of 4 guns and 35 men, on a cruise. taken by the Grenada, July 24, 1805.

French schooner privateer Teaser, of 7 guns and 51 men, from Guadaloupe, on a cruise: taken by the Osprey, May 17, 1805.

French national vessel Cyane, of 18 guns and 170 men, from Martinique on a cruise: taken by the Princess Charlotte, October 4, 1805.

French national vessel Naiad, of 18 guns and 195 men, from Martinique, on a cruise: taken by the Jason, October 13, 1805.

Spanish schooner Three Schooners: taken by ditto, same date.

French felucca privateer San Benite, of 1 gun and 18 men, on a cruise: taken by the Netley, October 4, 1805.

Spanish ship Notre Dame del Carmen, from the Havana, bound to Cadiz, laden with cocoa: taken by the Unicorn, October 15, 1805.

An English ship, name unknown, laden with slaves, &c.: retaken by the Pheasant, December, 1805.

French schooner privateer Elizabeth, of 12 guns and 102 men, from Guadaloupe, on a cruise: taken by the Kingfisher, December 16, 1805.

A Spanish polacre, name unknown, from Cadiz, bound to Vera Cruz, laden with merchandise: taken by the Hyena and Kingfisher, same date.

English ship Clio, laden with merchandise, one of the Cork convoy: retaken by the Pheasant, same date.

English ship Cambrian, laden with coals, one of the Cork convoy: recaptured by the Melville, same date.

English ship Sir C. Hamilton, from the coast of Guinea, bound to Surinam, laden with 327 slaves, three ton of ivory, gunpowder, and dry goods: retaken by the Alligator.

ALEX. COCHRANE.

MARCH 10.

Copy of a Letter from Admiral Montagu, Commander in Chief of His Majesty's Ships and Vessels at Portsmouth, to W. Marsden, Esq.; dated the 9th Inst.

SIR,

I beg you will be pleased to lay before the Lords Commissioners of the Admiralty the enclosed letter from Lieutenant Shells, of the Forward gun-vessel, acquainting me of his having fallen in with and captured la Rancune French lugger privateer, off Dunnose. I have the honour to be, &c.

GEO. MONTAGU.

His Majesty's Gun-brig Forward, at Sea,
SIR, *February 7, 1806.*

I beg leave to inform you, that at three A.M., Dunnose bearing N.E. by E. six or seven leagues, we fell in with a French lugger privateer, which, after a chase of half an hour, and a short firing, we captured. She proves to be la Rancune, of Cherbourg, Captain Foliot; out of Cherbourg twelve hours, but had taken nothing. She is pierced for twelve guns, had only four mounted with swivels and small arms. Two of the enemy are wounded, one dangerously.

I have the honour to be, &c.

To George Montagu, Esq., Admiral of the White, &c. DAN. SHEILS.

MARCH 22.

Copy of a Letter from the Earl of St. Vincent, K.B., Admiral and Commander in Chief of His Majesty's Fleet employed, and to be employed, in the Channel, Soundings, or wherever else His Majesty's Service shall require, to W. Marsden, Esq.; dated on board the Hibernia, in Falmouth Harbour, the 19th Instant.

SIR,

I have the honour to transmit, for the information of the Lords Commissioners of the Admiralty, the enclosed copy of a letter from Captain Paget; and have great pleasure in expressing my admiration of the gallant exploit therein recorded.

I am, &c.

ST. VINCENT.

MY LORD, *Egyptienne, off Cape Finisterre, 9th March, 1806.*

I have the honour to inform your Lordship, that having received intelligence of a large French privateer being in the harbour of Muros, I decided on seizing the first opportunity of gaining possession of her; I accordingly anchored His Majesty's ship under my command off that port last night, and immediately sent the boats away to endeavour to cut her out, in which, I am happy to acquaint your Lordship, they succeeded, though she was moored close to the beach, and under the protection of two batteries, which kept up an incessant fire, till she was towed clear of their range.

This vessel, which appears to be perfectly adapted for His Majesty's service, proves to be l'Alcide, of Bourdeaux, a frigate built ship, pierced for 34 guns, only two years old, and had, when last at sea, a complement of 240 men. This affair, so honourable to those who achieved it, was conducted by Captain Handfield, who was ably supported by Lieutenants Alleyn and Garthwaite, of the marines, the petty officers and boats' crews.

To account for that enterprising zealous officer, Captain Handfield, being in the Egyptienne, I have to inform your Lordship, that not having received an official communication of his promotion previous to our sailing, he volunteered, remaining in the ship as first Lieutenant during the cruise.

I have the honour to be, &c.

The Earl of St. Vincent, Admiral of the Red, and Commander in Chief, &c. &c. &c. CHARLES PAGET.

GAZETTE EXTRAORDINARY.

MARCH 24.

Dispatches, of which the following are copies, from Vice-Admiral Sir John Thomas Duckworth, K. B., commanding a squadron of His Majesty's Ships, addressed to W. Marsden, Esq.; and brought to England by Captain Nathaniel Day Cochrane, were yesterday received at the Admiralty:—

Superb, to Leeward of the Town of St. Domingue
SIR, *about 12 Leagues, Feb. 7, 1806.*

As I feel it highly momentous for His Majesty's service, that the Lords Commissioners of the Admiralty should have the earliest information of the movements of the squadron under my command, and as I have no other vessel than the Kingfisher that I feel justified in dispatching, I hope neither their Lordships nor Vice-Admiral Lord Collingwood will deem me defective in my duty towards his Lordship by addressing you on the happy event of yesterday; and as you will receive my letter of the 3d instant herewith, I shall only say, I lost not a moment in getting through the Mona Passage, and on the 5th in the afternoon was joined by the Magicienne, with a further corroboration from various vessels spoken, of an enemy's force of ten sail of the line, with as many frigates and corvettes, being in these seas; I therefore continued under easy sail for the night, in my approach off the town of St. Domingue, having given orders to Captain Dunn, of the Acasta, whose zeal and activity I have experienced for a series of years, to make sail with the Magicienne, Captain M'Kenzie, two hours before day-light, to reconnoitre; when at six o'clock the Acasta, to our great joy, made the signal for two of the enemy's frigates; and before seven, for nine sail at anchor; at half past that they were getting under weigh: the squadron under my command then in close order with all sail set; and the Superb, bearing my flag, leading, and approaching fast, so as to discover before eight o'clock that the enemy were in a compact line, under all sail, going before the wind for Cape Nisao, to windward of Ocoa Bay; and as they consisted of only five sail of the line, two frigates, and a corvette, (which hereafter will be named,) I concluded, from the information I was in possession of, that they were endeavouring to form a junction with their remaining force, and in consequence shaped my course to render abortive such intention, which was completely effected by a little after nine, so as to make an action certain. I therefore telegraphed the squadron, that the principal object of attack would be the Admiral and his seconds; and at three quarters past nine, for the ships to take stations for their mutual support, and engage the enemy as they got up; and a few minutes after, to engage as close as possible, when, at a short period after ten, the Superb closed upon the bow of the Alexander, the leading ship, and commenced the action; but after three broadsides, she sheered off: the signal was now made for closer action, and we were enabled to attack the Admiral in the Imperial, (formerly le Vengeur,) the fire of which had been heavy on the Northumberland, bearing the Honourable Rear-Admiral Cochrane's flag. By this time, the movement of the Alexander had thrown her among the lee division, which Rear-Admiral Louis happily availed himself of, and the action became general, and continued with great severity till half past eleven; when the French Admiral, much shattered, and completely beat, hauled direct for the land, and not being a mile off, at twenty minutes before noon ran on shore; his foremast then only standing, which fell directly on her striking; at which time the Superb being only in seventeen fathom water, was forced to haul off to avoid the same evil; but not long after, the Diomede, of 84 guns, pushed on shore near his Admiral, when all his masts went; and I think it a duty I owe to character and my country to add, from the information of Sir Edward Berry, after she had struck, and the Agamemnon desisted from firing into her, from the Captain taking off his hat, and making every token of surrender; and Captain Dunn assures me, both ensign and pendant were down;—to comment on which, I leave to the world. About fifty minutes after eleven, the firing ceased; and upon the smoke clearing away, I found le Brave, bearing a Commodore's pendant, the Alexander, and le Jupitre, in our possession.

When I contemplate on the result of this action, when five sail of the line had surrendered, or were apparently destroyed in less than two hours, I cannot, though bound to pay every tribute to the noble and gallant efforts of the Honourable Rear-Admiral Cochrane, Rear-Admiral Louis, the Captains, Officers, Seamen, and Royal Marines, under my command, be vain enough to suppose that, without the aiding hand of Providence, such result could have been effected, and with a loss so comparatively small; and though I shall ever sympathize with the connections of those that fell, the reflection on the cause will, I hope, afford much consolation.

To speak individually to the conduct of any one, would be injurious to all; for all were equally animated with the same zealous ardour in support of their King and Country. Yet, possessed of these feelings, I cannot be silent, without injustice, to the firm and manly support for which I was indebted to Captain Keats, and the effect that the system of discipline and good order in which I found the Superb, must ever produce; and the pre-eminence of the British Seaman could never be more highly conspicuous than in this contest.

After the action, the water being too deep to anchor in the Bay of St. Domingue, it was requisite to bring to with the prizes, to repair the damages, put the ships in a manageable state, and shift the prisoners, which took me till this afternoon; when I detached the Honourable Captain Stopford in the Spencer, with the Donegal and Atlas, which latter had lost her bowsprit, with the prizes to Jamaica; and being anxious, with Rear-Admiral Cochrane, that he should return to his command, where his services must be wanted, a jury main-mast is fitting to the Northumberland, under this island, to enable her to get to windward, when I shall order the Agamemnon, which is staying by her, to accompany the Rear-Admiral to his station; and I am now proceeding with the Canopus, Rear-Admiral Louis, Acasta, and Magicienne, off St. Domingue, to make certain of the Imperial and Diomede being completely wrecked, after which, I shall repair to Jamaica.

Having recited the transactions of this glorious combat, which will fairly add another sprig of laurel to our Naval History, and assist in promoting our Country's good,

I am, Sir, &c. J. T. DUCKWORTH.

SIR, *Superb, off St. Domingue, Feb. 7, 1806.*

For the information of the Lords Commissioners of the Admiralty, I send you herewith a list of the killed and wounded in the squadron under my command during the action of yesterday; but as it was hastily collected, should I find any errors, they shall be amended by a subsequent opportunity. You will also have the French Captain's statement of their loss in the captured ships; and I can venture to say, the French Admiral's will not be in a less proportion; and the striking of the Diomede implies she did not escape the irresistible fire of His Majesty's ships. A copy of my public thanks given to the Admirals, Captains, &c. for having so gallantly performed their duty in this truly decisive action, I request you will lay before their Lordships.

I am, Sir, &c.

To W. Marsden, Esq. &c. Admiralty. J. T. DUCKWORTH.

BRITISH LINE.

WEATHER DIVISION.	*Guns.*	LEE DIVISION.	*Guns.*
Superb	74	Canopus	84
Northumberland	74	Donegal	74
Spencer	74	Atlas	74
Agamemnon	64		

Frigates.—Acasta, Magicienne, Kingfisher, Epervier.

FRENCH LINE.

L'Alexandre, of 84 guns; 300 killed and wounded.—Taken.

L'Imperial, of 120 guns; number of killed and wounded not known, but certainly many.—On shore, and completely wrecked.

Le Diomede, of 84 guns; number of killed and wounded not known, but certainly many.—On shore, and completely wrecked.

Le Jupitre, of 74 guns; 200 killed and wounded.—Taken.

Le Brave, of 74 guns; 260 killed and wounded.—Taken.

Frigates.—La Felicité; escaped.—La Comète; escaped.

Corvette.—La Diligence; escaped.

Imperial	Contre-Amiral le Siegle. Capitaine le Pigot.
Alexandre	——— Garreau.
Brave	——— Condé.
Diomede	——— Henry.
Jupitre	——— Laiguel.

An Abstract of the Killed and Wounded on board the respective Ships of the Squadron under the Command of Vice-Admiral Sir John Thomas Duckworth, K. B., in the Action of the 6th of February, 1806, in the Bay of the Town of St. Domingue.

SUPERB.

Seamen killed.—John Brookbank, Thomas Phenne, Isaac Legard.
Marines killed.—Thomas Kenry, William Morgan, Clement Alcock.
Total.—6 killed.

Officers wounded.—Charles Patriarch, Lieutenant, badly; William Pickering, Master, badly; Charles Wallington, Thomas Jackson, Joseph Bullen, James Willcox, Midshipmen; all slightly.

Seamen wounded.—Thomas Richards, John Willson, Alexander Macdonald, all dangerously; Nathaniel Hasset, John Nightengale, James Cotte, James Willson, William Jones, Philip Jones, all badly; David Davis, Henry Walker, William Moody, T. Grills, John Wallbrook, John Henderson, John Badcock, John Neil, Bayan Swiney, James Clegg, Andrew Rawn, William Henry Leaver, John Handy (boy), James English, Patrick Murphy, Thomas Tyler, George Rock, John Reading, Andrew M'Donald, John Williams, Michael Mileday, R. Longo, Thomas Ryar, Philip Brooks, William Moffatt, Jos. Lothain, George Browne, John Haylor, Jos. Legg, Andrew M'Kearkin, George Scott, all slightly.
Total.—40 wounded.

Royal Marines wounded.—James Quarman, dangerously; Samuel Paradice, John Keimar, both badly; Thomas Getting, James Thomas, Thomas Warmwood, John Donough, Daniel Roberts, A. Osser, all slightly.
Total.—9 wounded.

Recapitulation.—No Officers killed; 7 Officers wounded; 3 Seamen killed; 40 Seamen wounded; 3 Royal Marines killed; 9 Royal Marines wounded.
Total.—6 killed, and 56 wounded.—62.

NORTHUMBERLAND.

Officer killed.—David Ridgeway, Midshipman.

Seamen killed.—James Driscole, Robert Hollis, George Ugler, John Humphries, Alexander Tosh, Richard Ashman, John Muir, Thomas Rowe, John Gardner, Kenneth M'Kenzie, Thomas Smith (2), John Coutee, William Shortman, John Kennedy, James Morrison, William Robinson, John Waters, John Naseby.

Marine killed.—Jacob Seaford.

Admiral's Cook killed.—Alexander Sapenack.

Officers wounded.—George F. Seymour, Lieutenant, badly; William Millard, C. W. Selwyn, Midshipmen, badly; Henry Stokes, ——— Comer, P. Peacock, Midshipmen, slightly; Jeremiah Laurence, Supernumerary Midshipman, badly; Daniel Sheridan, Boatswain's Mate, badly; Louis Lape, French Pilot, badly.

Seamen wounded.—Thomas Hoskins, George Martin, William Western, James Rogers, Manuel Say, John Chester, James Scott, Michael Atkinson, Thomas M'Carty, Alexander M'Cloudy, John Laurence, John Davy, Lewis Grant, Robert Hunter, William Cody, John Cullam, Thomas Kenyon, Joseph Bell, Peter Johnson, Thomas Grampus, William Watson, John George, Robert Willson, Michael Hunt, Peter Kelly, John Casey, H. Jacobs, all badly; John Rowan, William Duncan, Robert White, Michael Landy, Daniel Connell, Henry Roach, Michael Perrith, Godfrey Hyer, John Holmes, Baptiste Belville, Hedrick Aubert, Thomas Evans, Michael Manning, John Bowre, Alexander Law, Calvin Swift, Edward Teale (boy), Charles Hardy, all slightly.

Secretary's Clerks wounded.— ——— Thomas, badly; Jeremiah Honey, slightly.

Quarter Master wounded.—George Lamb, slightly.

Boatswain's Mates wounded.—James Maxwell, John Ellender, slightly.

Sergeant of Marines wounded.—Thomas Jones, badly.

Private Marines wounded.—Jos. Sparkes, Edward Davis, Thomas Jones, John Pullen, Thomas Hodgets, William Williams, John Palmer, William Cannon, John M'Gowan, John Adams, James Rogers, all badly; William Clerk, F. Davis, Thomas Lynch, Francis Murphy, George Bishop, John Saville, all slightly.

Retinue wounded.—James Ward, John Fullam, slightly.

Recapitulation.—1 Petty Officer killed; 13 Officers wounded; 19 Seamen killed; 48 Seamen wounded; 1 Marine killed; 18 Marines wounded.
Total.—21 killed, and 79 wounded.—100.

CANOPUS.

(Return of Names not sent.)

8 killed, 15 badly wounded, 7 slightly wounded.—Total, 30 killed and wounded.

SPENCER.

(Return of Names not sent.)

14 Seamen killed; 40 Seamen wounded; 3 Marines killed; 6 Marines wounded.

Name of Officer killed.—Martin Oates, Boatswain.

Names of Officers wounded.—Honourable Robert Stopford, Captain, slightly; James Harris, Lieutenant, slightly; James Cuthberson, Lieutenant of Marines, badly; William Neame, Midshipman, slightly.

Recapitulation.—1 Officer killed; 4 Officers wounded; 14 Seamen killed; 40 Seamen wounded; 3 Marines killed; 6 Marines wounded.
Total—18 killed, and 50 wounded.—68.

DONEGAL.

Officer killed.—Charles H. Kynaston, Midshipman.

Seamen killed.—William Upham, Jeremiah Wakely, William Bickhuss, Andrew Vinburgh, Mervan Richardson, Benito Lodrigues, Lennard Mason.

Private Marines killed.—William Moore, Patrick Kenesick, Edward Trippurst, John Millichamp.

Officers wounded.—Mr. John Airey, Master, Mr. ——— Rudall, Mr. ——— Ogieun, Mr. ——— Acton, all badly.

Seamen and Marines wounded.—John Owens, Peregrine Brighton, John Hutchson, James Elliot, David Perkins, Richard Curtis, Thomas Willson, Joseph Williams, James Herriott, Thomas Murray, John Chadwick, John Butcher, all badly; Thomas Hughes, Joseph Stanby, Thomas Dacres, William Telly, Thomas Cooper, Richard Lewis, Henry Moore, Robert Casie, Daniel Blaney, James Othew, John Masson, James Rees, John Cussens, John Owen, William Jones, Thomas M'Clay, Henry Shedley.

Recapitulation.—1 Petty Officer killed; 4 Officers wounded; 7 Seamen killed; 33 Seamen and Marines wounded; 4 Marines killed; Marines wounded *.
Total.—12 killed, and 33 wounded.—45.

ATLAS.

Seamen killed.—John Ross, John Neville, John Graves, William Bond, John Williamson, John Brown, Nicholas Bokman.

Marine killed.—Samuel Chambers.

Master wounded.—Mr. William Mowbray.

Boatswain wounded.—Mr. Stephen Spargo.

Seamen wounded.—Michael Redman, Joshua Barbou, John Henley, Thomas M'Bride, Samuel Chubb, William Robinson.

* In the Return, whether Seaman or Marine wounded, is not expressed.

Recapitulation.—No Officer killed; 2 Officers wounded; 7 Seamen killed; 9 Seamen wounded; 1 Marine wounded.

Total.—8 killed, and 11 wounded, (four of which badly, names not expressed.)-19.

AGAMEMNON.

Seaman killed.—James Cavanagh.

Boatswain's Mate wounded.—Richard Busto.

Seamen wounded.—John Morgan, Alexander M'Farlane, Robert Bocock, Eman Joseph.

Sergeant of Marines wounded.—William Norton.

Corporal of Marines wounded.—Roger Sturgeon.

Private of Marines wounded.—B. Kellen, Timothy Rielly, John Robertson, Nicholas Cooke, William Cole, J. Hallett.

Recapitulation.—1 Seaman killed; 5 Seamen wounded; 8 Marines wounded.

Total.—1 killed, and 13 wounded.—14.

General Abstract of Killed and Wounded.

Superb.—6 killed and 56 wounded.—62.
Northumberland.—21 killed and 79 wounded.—100.
Canopus.—8 killed and 22 wounded.—30.
Spencer.—18 killed and 50 wounded.—68.
Donegal.—12 killed and 33 wounded.—45.
Atlas.—8 killed and 11 wounded.—19.
Agamemnon.—1 killed and 13 wounded.—14.
Total.—74 killed and 264 wounded.
Grand Total of British killed and wounded—338.

J. T. DUCKWORTH.

Superb, off St. Domingue, Feb. 7, 1806.

As it is impossible for language to convey an adequate sense of my feelings to the Honourable Rear-Admiral Cochrane, for the noble support rendered me by the Northumberland, or to Rear-Admiral Louis, and the Captains of the squadron under my command, for the bravery and judgment displayed in the service of their King and Country, by effecting a complete victory in as short a period as our naval annals can produce, I therefore can only, with a heart impressed by the highest sense of admiration and approbation, beg to offer to the Honourable Rear-Admiral Cochrane, Rear-Admiral Louis, the Captains, Officers, and Seamen, and to the Officers, Non-commissioned Officers, and Privates of the Royal Marines, my warmest thanks; and I desire that the Captains will convey those my sentiments of admiration and approbation, with thanks, in the most gratifying manner, to the Officers, Seamen, and Royal Marines, as a proof of my high sense of their services in the battle of yesterday.

To the Hon. Rear-Admiral Cochrane, Rear-Admiral Louis, the Captains, Officers, Seamen, and Royal Marines.

J. T. DUCKWORTH.

Superb, to Leeward of the Town of St. Domingue, February 8, 1806.

SIR,

Having, in a letter of about two hours since, acquainted you of my intentions to fire the Imperial and Diomede, I have the satisfaction now to say, that Captain Dunn, who I had employed on that service, has rescued all the prisoners from perishing through a tremendous sea, and completed the whole of the service highly to my satisfaction and his own honour, which I am to desire you will state to the Lords Commissioners of the Admiralty; and I am, Sir, yours, &c.

J. T. DUCKWORTH.

To W. Marsden, Esq., &c. Admiralty.

NAVAL HISTORY OF THE PRESENT YEAR, 1806.

(February—March.)

RETROSPECTIVE AND MISCELLANEOUS.

[Continued from page 245.]

AN occurrence is said to have taken place at a small village in Staffordshire, which perhaps may occasion some inquiry.—A man who had lived there some years upon a comfortable annuity, has declared upon his death-bed, that he was hired to set fire to His Majesty's ship the Boyne, of 98 guns, which ship the public may remember to have been burnt at Spithead, upon her return from the West-Indies, where she had borne the flag of Sir John Jervis (now Lord St. Vincent), who, in consequence of this misfortune, lost all his baggage and papers. The man, however, has left some documents, which may, perhaps, throw some light upon this mysterious affair.

The Lords Commissioners of the Admiralty have directed their Solicitor to prosecute Mr. Chivers, of the Arethusa from London to Surinam, in consequence of a letter from Captain Bolton, of His Majesty's ship Fisgard, under whose convoy the Arethusa sailed from Cork, on the 16th of October last, stating, that he had disobeyed signals, and conducted himself on other occasions in a very outrageous and improper manner.

The ship Isabella, lately stranded on the Horse Sand, has been weighed by persons under the direction of Mr. Heather, merchant, at Portsmouth, and brought to a place close to the harbour to be broken up: she is upwards of 600 tons burthen.

The French have already begun to consider of plans for turning the maritime resources of Venice to their advantage. Preparations, it is said, are making for constructing ships of war in the arsenals. Timber for building them, as well as seamen for navigating them, are expected to be found in Dalmatia. The last time the French had possession of Venice, they destroyed several hulls of ships in the arsenal, which they could not remove, on delivering up the place to the Austrian government.

February 15.—The Patriotic Fund at Lloyd's amounted to 147,300*l.*, of which 100,600*l.* were collected at places of divine worship.

Portsmouth, Feb. 18.—This morning the Alexandria, fir-built frigate, was launched at this Dock-yard. The launch gave great pleasure to a vast concourse of people: not the smallest mishap of any kind occurred. Commissioner Sir Charles Saxton, and a great number of naval officers, were present. A sloop is to be laid down on the same slip, to be called the Brazen.

The Surgeon of the Petterell sloop of war has been tried at Jamaica by a Court-Martial, for neglect of duty to a wounded seaman on board, found guilty, and sentenced to twelve months' imprisonment in the Marshalsea, and to be rendered incapable of ever officiating again in his Majesty's service.

Letters from Gibraltar, dated the 1st March, brought by the Townshend packet, state, that Mr. Cartwright, His Majesty's Agent and Consul-General at Algiers, landed at Gibraltar the 27th February, from the Niger frigate.

Mr. Cartwright, after trying in vain every means in his power to procure satisfaction to various demands, consistent with the treaties between our government and the regency, finding it impossible to avert the daily insults which the Dey and his Agents offered to the British legation and subjects, intimated that he intended to depart, and demanded his passports; which were granted to him without difficulty.

It appears from the above statement, that a war between this country and Algiers is inevitable.

March 18.—At two o'clock, a Privy Council was held at the council office in the Treasury, which was attended by the Lord Chancellor, Sir Wm. Scott (Judge of the Admiralty Court), Mr. Grey (First Lord of the Admiralty), the Master of the Rolls, Lord Minto, the Attorney General, and Mr. Wickham. Sir Stephen Cotterell and Mr. Fawkener attended as Clerks to the Council.—The business for which the Council was assembled was to investigate a charge of a most heinous nature against Lieutenant S———— ————, of the royal navy, on suspicion of assisting in the wilful murder of Nicholas, Smith, and Dause, three seamen under his command, in the East Indies. The Council sat upon this extraordinary business till six o'clock.—These three men are said to have been flogged to death, under circumstances of peculiar horror, and without the previous sentence of a Court Martial. We do not think it just or prudent, on *ex parte* evidence, to enter into the details. On the return of the witnesses to England they gave information of the transaction.

The Gazette of the same date contains the offer of a reward of 200*l.* for the apprehension of Lieutenant George Rutherford, who stands charged with the murder of three seamen of His Majesty's ship Trident, while Commander of that ship at Butcher's Island, near Bombay, in the East Indies, in March, 1801; and who escaped from the Salvador del Mundo, at Plymouth, on the 12th inst. by jumping overboard.

Between six and seven o'clock, on the morning of the 19th of March, a small lugger-rigged French fishing-boat, bearing a white flag, appeared off Dover, about two leagues to the N. E. It was evident, from the course of the tide, that she could not make Dover for some time; but, as she had been perceived from the Downs, the Venus frigate, Captain Matson, was soon after seen standing round the South Foreland, and the French boat made towards her. A French naval officer delivered to Captain Matson a packet of dispatches, who gave him a receipt for them, and the boat, with the officer, was ordered to return immediately to the French coast. Admiral Holloway, the commanding officer in the Downs, forwarded the dispatches by express, and they reached town, yesterday, between two and three.

As to the purport of this communication a laudable secresy is observed. The official mode of speaking of it is to say, that it was addressed to the Transport Board, and relates probably to an exchange of prisoners. But, from the circumstance of Mr. Fox's having had a very long audience of His Majesty, in the afternoon, and from the language of the French papers, we have no doubt, that the dispatches contained some offer to commence a negociation for peace. It is said that the French naval officer, who came over in the flag of truce, was Captain Majendie, who, it will be recollected, was Admiral Villeneuve's first Captain, and who was allowed to depart for France about two months since, for the purpose of negociating a cartel for the exchange of prisoners of war.—Mons. Bomquete, a French pilot, who was in the boat, says that Boulogne is become a King's port; no merchant vessels, privateers, or even prizes, are permitted to enter, unless loaded with ordnance or military stores; there has been a very large bason made to hold the flotilla, and which contains 17 feet water at high water, and the port is said to contain ten at low water; a large harbour is also made at Wymill and at Vimereux, with immense fortifications to defend them, and the flotilla is again equipping. The dispatches are supposed to relate to an exchange of prisoners; but those who brought them knew nothing of the contents, about which no rumour had transpired, as they were sent off as soon as received. It is rather curious that this French boat should look out for an English cruiser to deliver the dispatches to all night without success, while the sea *swarms* with French privateers!

The Moniteur notices the capture of the Cape of Good Hope in a manner that indicates great dissatisfaction with the Dutch. The Governor of the Cape is stated to have refused a reinforcement of 2000 men from the Isle of France, and the Dutch ships in the eastern seas are stated to have done nothing for the common cause. These reflections against the Dutch will probably lead to some interference with their Government, calculated to render it more actively subservient to the Court of St. Cloud. The attacks of foreign settlements is represented as an abandonment of the Continent.

Extract from the Exposé, presented by the Minister M. de Champagney, March 6.

"If you cast your eyes on our ports, you will see that exertions are making on both seas, to render them more accessible, more commodious, and more secure. Basons are digging at Antwerp; sluices and canals are forming at Antwerp, Dieppe, Ostend, Dunkirk, and Havre. At Honfleur, Bourdeaux, Nice, Hulinguen, Belleisle, Ajaccio, and Bastia, quays are constructed, and jetties or moles lengthened or rebuilt. All these different kinds of works are carrying on at Rochelle. The cleansing of the ports of Cette and Marseilles is continued, and that of Oleron is enlarging. The ports of Dielette and Casteret are prepared in such a manner as to be capable of receiving a great number of vessels and gun-boats, which will alarm the inhabitants of the English islands of Jersey and Guernsey, as those at Boulogne menace Dover and London. The soundings taken at Brun have afforded satisfactory results; the Rhone will have a port. Engineers have examined what improvements it is possible to make in that of Genoa. Six millions eight hundred and fifty thousand francs have been expended on the military ports. This sum has been principally applied in the excavations, the jetties of the mole, the construction of the outer port and bason, and the foundation of the new port Buonaparte, which, destined to complete this beautiful maritime creation, and worthy of his name, will be, on the channel, the terror of England; at Boulogne, the bason and the sluice, the completion of the works which constitute the whole of the port, and the construction of the establishments by which it is surrounded; at Ambleteuse, the works necessary for deepening the port, the elevation of the jetty, which protects it from the sand driven against it by the west winds, the line-walls, and the buildings; at Brest, the formation of an artificial island, the excavations in the rock, the hospitals, the magazines, the arsenal, the barracks, and the completion of the batteries; at Antwerp, the continuation of the rapid works which are to form the arsenal of our marine on the North Sea, the erection of quays and work-shops; in the Road of Rochefort, the jetties on which Boyard is to be erected, and the operations of every kind required by this difficult construction.

"Eleven other ports have constantly had works in activity; Ostend, for the completion of the batteries, and the formation of a marine hospital; Dunkirk, for cleansing and repairs; Etaples for the establishment of a powder magazine; Havre, for the maintenance of its establishments; l'Orient, for the erection of an armoury, and the repairs of its buildings; Rochefort, for the repair of the quays, the enclosure of the arsenal, &c.; Toulon, for the construction of the general magazine which was burned, the building for the great masts, and the works for raising four vessels by which it was obstructed. This port, one of the most beautiful works of art and nature, recovered from its disasters, will soon be free from every vestige of them: the same hand which took it from the enemy will restore it to its former prosperity.

"It is the will of the Emperor, as well as the desire of the whole nation, to augment our navy; and, as we lost some ships in the late engagements, it is a new motive for redoubling our ardour. A great number of our cruisers are scouring the seas, and have attacked the commerce of our enemies in the remotest regions. Our whole flotilla shall shortly revive by the return to its banks of the conquerors of Ulm and Austerlitz. But all those warlike measures shall be nothing more than measures tending to peace, and even a moderate peace, in which we shall secure the pledge of not being surprised and seized upon under the most vain and perfidious pretences; it were otherwise better to endure still the miseries of war, rather than make a peace which would expose us to new losses, and afford fresh aliment to the bad faith and avarice of our enemies."

The Egyptienne frigate, Hon. Capt. Paget, has sent into Plymouth a beautiful French frigate almost new, which her boats cut out in a most gallant manner close in with the Isle de Rhé. She is called the Alcide, and has made but one voyage; she is pierced for 28 guns on the main deck, and 10 guns on the quarter and forecastle; she was refitting for sea. Lieutenant Hadfield commanded the boats by which she was cut out.

The Colpoys brig, Lieutenant Usher, has had a most gallant action with a ship of superior force off Ferrol almost under the batteries. The enemy were forced to run ashore, where the vessel bilged and sunk: the crew were saved.

At the Court of Common Council, held on the 20th of March, at Guildhall, a letter from Lord Barrington, enclosing a petition in behalf of several seamen prisoners, confined in the citadel of Valenciennes, in France, were read, and referred to the Committee for General Purposes, to consider the best mode of promoting and affording relief to our fellow subjects who are prisoners in France, who are to report theron.

Motions of thanks to Sir J. T. Duckworth, and the Officers, &c. under his command, have been voted by both Houses of Parliament.

Promotions and Appointments.

The King has been pleased to grant to the Right Hon. Richard Brinsley Sheridan, the office of Treasurer of His Majesty's Navy.

Captain Burrowes is appointed to the Tonnant, at Portsmouth; Captain Pipon, to the Rose; Captain Oliver (late first Lieutenant of the Phœnix), to the Ariel; Lieutenant King, of the Diadem, is promoted to the rank of Post Captain, and appointed Sir Home Popham's Captain; Captain Edmonds, of l'Espoir, is promoted, and appointed to the Diomede; Lieutenant Hope, of the Narcissus, is promoted to be a Commander, and to the command of l'Espoir.

Portsmouth, March 8.—This day, at twelve o'clock, the Right Hon. the Earl of St. Vincent arrived at Sir George Prevost, the Lieutenant-Governor's house. His Lordship immediately called upon Admiral Montagu, and then went to the Dock-yard, to pay his respects to Commissioner Sir Charles Saxton. After examining the various improvements in the Dock-yard, in company with Sir Charles Saxton, Admiral Montagu, Admiral Martin, and the Rev. Mr. Parker, his Secretary, his Lordship embarked, at three o'clock, from the King's Stairs, in the Dock-yard, and went on board the Hibernia of 100 guns, at Spithead. His Lordship was cheered by the fleet at Spithead, the yards being manned on his approach. His Lordship's flag, the Union at the main-top-mast head, was hoisted soon after twelve o'clock, and saluted by Admiral Montagu's ship.—The Captains of the ships at the port will pay their respects to his Lordship to-morrow, on board the Hibernia. His Lordship does not come on shore again. The Hibernia will sail to-morrow, if the wind continues fair.

Doctor Baird, Inspector of Hospitals for the Western District, goes with Lord St. Vincent, to examine into the state of the health of the seamen in the Channel fleet.

Captain Lukin is appointed to the Thunderer; Captain Mansell, to la Sophie; Captain A. M. M'Kenzie, to the Combatant: Captain Warwick Lake, to the Valorous; Captain Cooke, to the Dauntless; Captain Yarker, to the Julia; Captain Stewart, to the Avon; Captain Worth, to the Helena; Captain Sheriff, to the Curieux.

Captain Forbes, of the Merlin, is appointed to the Racehorse, at this port, the largest sloop in the service. This meritorious and brave officer has been wounded seven times in action; three of the wounds he received in his body.

Captain William Hellard is appointed to the command, *pro tempore*, of the Renown. He was first Lieutenant of the Defiance, in the action of Trafalgar. Captain Thicknesse is appointed to the Hecla; Captain Trollope, to the Electa; Captain T. Brown (1st), is appointed to the Tonnant, at this port, which is fitting for Admiral E. Harvey's flag, for the Mediterranean. Captain J. Agassey, to the Rattler; Captain Parkinson, to the Merlin.

Vice-Admiral Berkeley, in addition to his being made Inspector of the Sea Fencibles, is appointed to superintend the raising of men for His Majesty's fleets, and to inspect the signal stations along the coast; Captain H. Pigot, to the Alligator; Captain J. Stewart, to the Sea Horse; Captain Wingates, to the Zebra; Lieutenant Lord J. Townsend, to la Ville de Milan; Captain Killwick, to the Howe store ship, which is fitting at Woolwich for the Cape of Good Hope; Captain Owen, of the Immortalite, to the rank of Commodore, and to command the Clyde; Captain Crofton, to the Snake; and Henry Grant, Esq., to be private Secretary to Mr. Grey

Captain Sir Thomas Masterman Hardy, Bart., who so nobly fought in the Victory, off Trafalgar, is appointed to the command of the Sampson, of 64 guns, at Portsmouth.

MARRIAGES.

On the 1st of March, by the Rev. J. G. Bussel, Mr. Patrick Kane, Purser of His Majesty's ship Lavina, to Miss Jenkinson, of Portsmouth.

At St. Mary-le-bone Church, Captain J. S. Rainier, of the Royal Navy, to Miss E. Deare, one of the daughters of P. Deare, Esq., of Nottingham-place.

Captain Ryves, of the Royal Navy, of Shroton-house, to Miss E. Graham, daughter of R. Graham, Esq., of Chelsea College.

OBITUARY.

In the West Indies, Captain Brownrigg, of His Majesty's ship Dart, and Captain Orde, of His Majesty's ship Nimrod.

Lately, in the prime of life, Lieutenant Baker, of His Majesty's ship Cerberus, and brother of the brave Captain Baker, late of the Phœnix. He had the acting command of the Cerberus during Captain Selby's absence, and went on shore at Guernsey rather indisposed, where he died in a few hours.

Near Prees, Shropshire, Mr. John Benbow, clock and watch maker, at the advanced age of 107. He was of the same family as the famous Admiral Benbow; was universally esteemed for his integrity and ingenuity; and what is very surprising, he executed the most intricate branches of his profession till within a few years of his death, and retained his mental faculties unimpaired to his latest moments. He lived in three centuries; and a son, a grand-son, and several great grand-children, resided with him at the time of his decease. He was remarkable for sobriety, early rising, and retiring soon to rest; the liquor to which he was most partial was treacle beer.

Lately, at Portsmouth, Captain Hall, aged 91. He was Surgeon's Mate of the Centurion; and went round the world with Lord Anson, in the year 1740, when the Manilla galeon, Nostra Signora de Cabadonga, was taken. She was the richest prize ever taken, having near a million and a half of dollars on board, and was larger, and of more force, than the Centurion. Mr. Hall came home Surgeon of her. It was after this voyage, which lasted three years and nine months, that Lord Anson, when he landed here, on the Point, fell upon his knees, and offered an ejaculatory prayer to Him who had preserved him from such imminent dangers! Captain Fortescue is the only person living who went on that voyage.

Lately, at Ipplepen, Captain Kendall, of the Navy.

Lately, at the Blossoms Inn, of a deep decline, Captain U. Jennings, of the Royal Navy, at Portsmouth.

Admiral Langara died at Madrid, in January.

At Naples, on the 21st of January, in his 85th year, Henry Ellis, Esq. early in life distinguished by an attempt to discover a North West passage; afterwards, at different periods, Governor of Georgia and Nova Scotia; a Member (perhaps the oldest) of the Royal Society, as well as of several learned Continental Societies.

In the Hospital at Mill Prison, Plymouth, Monsieur du Bois, Captain of the French ship le Duguay Trouin, of 74 guns, in consequence of the wounds he received in Sir Richard Strachan's action.

Captain George Duff

BIOGRAPHICAL MEMOIR

OF THE LATE

CAPTAIN GEORGE DUFF,

WHO FELL IN THE ACTION OFF TRAFALGAR.

——— MY SON, AVENGE MY DEATH!
AND, ON THAT OCEAN WHERE THY FATHER LIES,
PROVE THYSELF WORTHY OF TRAFALGAR'S DAY.

THIS Officer, born in 1764, was the son of the late James Duff, Esq. of Banff, a younger brother of the family of Hatton, in the County of Aberdeen, and nearly related to the Earl of Fife. His mother was a daughter of Mr. Skene, of Rubislaw, in the same county, an amiable woman, of delicate health, who died six weeks after she had brought this son into the world.

Few persons, whose instinctive genius point to a particular profession, have ever shown a more early predilection than the subject of this memoir did, for the Navy. When only a boy, he in hours of play was always found, either among the shipping in the harbour of Banff*, about half a mile from the town, or in boats on the Doveran, which skirts its lower streets, and runs into the sea, near to which was his father's house. As a boy he was sprightly, active, and enterprising; and so bent towards the Navy, that seeing his father was averse from his going to sea, he endeavoured, when about nine years of age, to escape; by concealing himself on board a small merchant vessel, in which he actually sailed to a neighbouring port. The Master, upon finding him on board, sent him back to his father, who then became sensible that his son's inclination could not be counteracted, and wisely agreed to his going into the Royal Navy. He had been educated at home by a private tutor, who was now directed to turn the whole attention of his pupil towards studies most connected with his intended pro-

* At the mouth of the River Doveran. This harbour is neither large, nor good, and is often stopped by shifting sands, after storms.

fession; and he was immediately rated in a ship of war, and two years afterwards was sent to join that experienced and distinguished officer, his grand-uncle, Commodore (afterwards Admiral) Robert Duff*, who commanded at Gibraltar, with his flag on board the Panther, of 60 guns, in September, 1777. It is to be regretted that we cannot trace this zealous and active youth throughout the first period of his interesting career. He was always remarkably modest and reserved in whatever regarded himself; but we have heard him mention, when asked, in how many battles he had fought? that he had been in thirteen engagements before he was sixteen years of age. This was during the American war, in the Mediterranean, and in the West Indies; and we know, that in consequence of his gallant services, he was at that early age made a Lieutenant. He was at the taking of the Spanish Admiral Langara, and his squadron of five sail of the line, off Cadiz, in the beginning of 1780, and went from thence with Sir George Rodney's fleet to the West Indies. Mr. Duff was probably at that time a Lieutenant in the Montagu, of 74 guns, for in October, that year, he served in her when she was blown out of St. Lucia in the great hurricane, totally dismasted, thrown upon her beam ends, and in the greatest danger of being lost. Upon that occasion his manly exertions were said to have been very conspicuous, and by the falling of one of the masts he unfortunately got a contusion on his right leg, which was healed with great difficulty, and was often troublesome to him during the rest of his life, particularly in tropical climates.

The Montagu having miraculously outlived the hurricane, was rigged with jury-masts, and got back with great difficulty to St. Lucia. She was there refitted, and Lieutenant Duff continued to serve in her, in the various encounters which our fleet had with the French till the glorious 12th of April, 1782; when the Count de Grasse, their Commander in Chief, in the Ville de Paris, of 110 guns, the largest ship in the world, and four other ships of the line, were taken and brought to Jamaica by our victorious fleet.

* This officer died Vice-Admiral of the Red, at Queen's Ferry, on his return to his native country, June 6, 1787. He was made Post, October 23, 1746, and appointed to the Anglesea.

Lieutenant Duff, some time after his arrival in the harbour of Port Royal, and as soon as his duty would permit, knowing that Captain Dirom was in that island, inquired for, and visited him at Spanish town: the Captain was at that time Adjutant-General in Jamaica; and although he could have no idea, that in the course of ten years they should become so nearly connected, he had then a great regard for Lieutenant Duff, whom he had known from childhood. After presenting his friend to Major-General Archibald Campbell, the Governor, and enforcing the professional merit of the young hero; the General had the goodness to introduce him to Sir George Rodney, then on a visit at his country house, near Spanish town. Sir George received the nephew of his friend Admiral Duff in the most favourable manner, and upon knowing his services, put him on his list for promotion. This introduction to the Commander in Chief, which to an ardent and aspiring mind seemed so promising of success, did not avail Lieutenant Duff; as Sir George soon afterwards quitted his command and returned home: having upon a change of Ministry been unfortunately recalled, before the news of his splendid victory had reached England.

Although disappointed, during the American war, in his well-founded hopes of promotion, Lieutenant Duff persevered in his profession, and continued upon foreign service. The Camilla sloop of war, commanded by Captain Hutt, in which Mr. Duff was first Lieutenant, being ordered in June 1784, to take home General Campbell, his family and suite; the General was enabled, during the voyage, to observe how deserving our hero was of the notice which he had taken of him in Jamaica; and the kind attentions which the Lieutenant showed to the General's family, and in particular to his friend Captain Dirom, more than amply repayed the civilities which the former had met with from them on shore. The Camilla reached Portsmouth in six weeks, and soon afterwards returned to Jamaica, where Lieutenant Duff served in different ships. He was first Lieutenant of the Europa, of 50 guns, when Captain (now Rear-Admiral) Vashon was appointed to that ship; who found her crew in so excellent a state of discipline, as gained Lieutenant Duff the esteem both of his Captain, and of Commodore (now Admiral Lord) Gardner, who at that time commanded upon the Jamaica station.

So long a period of service in the West Indies, during which Lieutenant Duff was often obliged to subsist chiefly on salted provisions, at length affected his health, and particularly the wound in his leg, which broke out, and had a very alarming appearance: insomuch, that in 1787 it became absolutely necessary for him to return to England. On his arrival there, he proceeded to Scotland by sea, to his father at Banff; where his native air, a change of diet, and the society of friends to whom he was warmly attached, soon effected the restoration of his health.

In 1790, Lieutenant Duff, then employed upon the home service, was recommended by the Duke and Duchess of Gordon in the handsomest and strongest manner, to the protection of the Right Hon. Henry Dundas, Minister for Scotland, the liberal patron of merit. Mr. Dundas, since created Viscount Melville, then filled the office of Treasurer of the Navy, and upon knowing the services of Lieutenant Duff, was pleased to prefer his claims in such terms to the Board of Admiralty, that he was immediately appointed Captain and Commander of the Martin sloop of war, upon the coast of Scotland.

Soon after his promotion, Captain Duff married Miss Sophia Dirom, second daughter of Alexander Dirom, Esq. of Muiresk, to whom he had been from childhood attached; and fixed the residence of his family at Edinburgh.

Upon the breaking out of the last war, in the beginning of 1793, the same influence was again most kindly exerted for Captain Duff's further promotion; and he was one of the very few Masters and Commanders, who were appointed Post Captains by the Earl of Chatham; to whom he had the honour to have been personally known, when his Lordship, then a Captain in the army, went out to Gibraltar in the ship in which Mr. Duff served, during the former war. At his Lordship's desire, Captain Duff soon after relinquished the command of a frigate, then fitting out for him; in which at so early a period of the war he would probably have made his fortune, in order to go upon an expedition to the West Indies, as Captain of the Duke, of 90 guns, bearing the flag of the Hon. Commodore Murray. This ship led the attack on the batteries at Martinico; and, at the close of the action, after silencing the battery to which she had been opposed, the powder magazine had but just been secured, when she was struck by lightning, her main-mast shivered to pieces, and her hull so damaged, that it was necessary to send her home to be repaired.

The further attack upon Martinico having been deferred, the Commodore returned to England in the Duke. He expressed the highest esteem for Captain Duff; and reported his conduct to have been so meritorious, that he was immediately appointed to the command of the Ambuscade frigate, of 32 guns, and two years afterwards to the Glenmore, of 38 guns. In these ships he served in the North Seas, and upon the coast of Ireland, until 1801; when, upon a general promotion in the Navy, he was appointed to the Vengeance, of 74 guns, belonging to the Channel fleet.

This ship, after having been detached to the Baltic to reinforce the fleet that attacked Copenhagen, became one of the squadron under Rear-Admiral Campbell; which, after cruising for some time off Rochefort, was sent to Bantry Bay for the protection of that part of Ireland. Upon this station they continued until the signature of the preliminaries of peace; when, instead of returning to their homes, to which, after so long a war, the officers and men anxiously looked forward, they were ordered to Jamaica, to watch the movements of the armament sent from France, to attempt the recovery of the French part of the island of St. Domingo from the usurped government of the Blacks.

Captain Duff had no opportunity in the course of the last war, either of further signalizing himself, or of materially improving his fortune; but he was always active and vigilant, and though strict in discipline, had the happiness of being respected and beloved by the officers and men of every ship which was under his command. On the trials at Portsmouth, it came out in evidence, that when the ringleaders of the mutiny, which arose in the squadron in Bantry Bay, sounded the crew of the Vengeance, they found them so attached to their Captain, that they could not be moved. That ship, there is reason to believe, was the only one in which no mutinous spirit broke out; and upon the squadron coming to Portsmouth, previous to their sailing for the West Indies, her crew was indulged with leave to come on shore by turns, while all the others were confined to their ships.

Not more than eighteen months had elapsed, after Captain Duff had returned from the West Indies, to the bosom of his family and friends, when the present war broke out. He again solicited employment: and a general invasion of these united kingdoms being threatened by the French and their allies, he, in the mean time, without pay or emolument, assisted the General, and staff officers, in examining the coasts of the Frith of Forth, with which he was well acquainted, and in making arrangements for its defence. His steady patron, the Duke of Gordon, with his excellent son the Marquis of Huntley, seconded his application to be again called into active service; and General, the Earl of Moira, Commander of the forces in Scotland, by whom he had been appointed to the command of a division of the craft which had been voluntarily offered for the defence of the Frith of Forth, generously and unsolicited, wrote to Earl St. Vincent, then first Lord of the Admiralty, in Captain Duff's behalf.

Upon the general promotion in the Navy which took place in April 1804, Captain Duff was appointed to the command of the Mars, of 74 guns, and immediately proceeded to join her off Ferrol. He cruised off that port, and successively off Rochefort and Brest, as one of the Channel fleet, until in May last, he was detached to Cadiz, under Vice-Admiral Collingwood; whose small squadron of four ships of the line, afterwards increased to eight, continued to keep their station off that port, unawed by the arrival of the combined fleet.

Vice-Admiral Lord Nelson having, in the end of September, returned from England to resume the command upon that most important station, made a disposition of his increased force into two divisions, one of which was to be led by himself, and the other by Vice-Admiral Collingwood. Rear-Admiral Louis having been detached to the Mediterranean with seven sail of the line; Captain Duff had the honour, upon his departure, though there were senior Captains in the fleet, to be appointed to command the advance, or inshore squadron, of four sail of the line; by the recommendation, no doubt, of Vice-Admiral Collingwood, who selected the Mars as second to himself, in his division.

The squadron commanded by Captain Duff was stationed midway between our frigates, which cruised close to the harbour of Cadiz, and our fleet, which kept out of sight of the port. From the time the enemy's fleet began to come out on the 19th, he was almost constantly employed repeating signals from the frigates to the fleet: he followed, and kept sight of the enemy on the 20th, and continued making signals with colours by day, and blue lights at night, until the memorable morning of the 21st; when, it being certain that the enemy's fleet could not escape, the signal was made for his squadron to return, and take their places in the order of battle. The signal was then made for the Mars to lead the lee division of our fleet, and to break the enemy's line. Captain Duff, knowing that his ship sailed ill, ordered every stitch of canvas to be instantly set; and in the meantime, while bearing down upon the enemy, went through his ship to see that every thing was in readiness for action. He spoke to his officers and men in every part of the ship; and, among other directions for their conduct, strictly enjoined them not to waste their fire, *as he would take care to lay them close enough to the enemy*. The Mars, notwithstanding every exertion, was passed by the Royal Sovereign, bearing the flag of Vice-Admiral Collingwood; then the Belleisle also shot a-head, and they were in action a few minutes before the Mars: each ship breaking through a different part of the enemy's line.

The wind, which had been light, then became more uncertain, and prevented the rest of the ships from closing immediately with the enemy: so that the few who were first engaged, were in a manner surrounded, and had for some time to maintain a most severe conflict. There was a French ship on each side of the Mars; and a Spanish ship, a first rate, on her bow; and a fourth ship also within range of shot. The ship on her starboard quarter, the Fougueux, was soon disabled, and it was thought she had struck, but her colours had only been shot away, as she had never ceased to fire. The Captain of marines on the poop, seeing that the Fougueux in dropping to leeward, was getting into a position which would enable her to rake the Mars, and that she was preparing to do so, came down to the quarter-deck to mention it to Captain Duff. The want of wind rendered it impossible to alter the position of the Mars, nor could it with safety be attempted, in regard to the enemy's other ships: Captain Duff therefore said to the Captain of marines, "Do you think our guns would bear on her?" He answered, "I think not, but I cannot see for smoke."—"Then," replied the Captain, "we must point our guns at the ships on which they can bear. I shall go and look; but the men below may see better, as there will be less smoke."—Captain Duff went to the end of the quarter-deck to look over the side; and then told his Aid-de-camp, Mr. Arbuthnot, to go below, and order the guns to be pointed more aft, meaning against the Fougueux. He had scarcely turned round to go with these orders when the Fougueux raked the Mars. A cannon shot killed Captain Duff, and two seamen who were immediately behind him: the ball struck the Captain on the breast, and carried off his head; his body fell on the gangway, where it was covered with a spare colour, an union jack, until after the action.

The battle now raged in its utmost fury, and both fleets were enveloped in smoke. The carnage on both sides, particularly on that of the enemy, was immense: and about the same time that the gallant Duff fell in the Mars, being one hour and five minutes after the commencement of the action, Captain Cooke, the companion of his youth, was killed in the Bellerophon, and their Commander in Chief, the illustrious Lord Nelson, was mortally wounded on board the Victory.

The Mars continued engaged during the whole of the action, frequently with fresh ships; but suffered from none so severely as she had done from the Fougueux, which continued to drift to leeward, until she was engaged by others of our ships, and finally captured by the Temeraire.

On board the Mars, besides Captain Duff, there were killed in the action, Mr. Alexander Duff, Master's Mate, acting Lieutenant, Messrs. Corbyn and Morgan, Midshipmen, and 25 seamen and marines. The wounded amounted to near 16 officers, 5 petty officers, and 60 seamen and marines: in all 98 killed and wounded. Among the latter was the gallant Captain of marines, Norman, who afterwards died of his wounds.

When the battle had ceased, and it was generally known in the Mars that their gallant Captain was killed, there was scarcely a dry eye among the crew. Every one felt that he had lost his friend and benefactor; and they all exclaimed, "We never shall again have such a Commander!"

Captain Duff was a man of fine stature, strong and well made, above six feet in height, and had a manly, open, benevolent countenance. During thirty years service he had not been four years unemployed, and that was about twenty months after his return from the West Indies in 1787; and not quite two years after the last war. Although he went early to sea, he lost no opportunity of improving himself in the theory, as well as in the practice of his profession; and acted the part of an instructor, and father, to the numerous young men who were under his command. By his beloved wife he had five children; of whom a boy and two girls remain, together with their disconsolate mother, to mourn their father's death. His son, thirteen years of age, had joined him as a Midshipman on the 19th of September last, and soon after his arrival on board the Mars, wrote exultingly to his mother, that his father's ship had been put in the post of honour next to Vice-Admiral Collingwood, in his division of the fleet. This spirited youth, who has commenced his career in so interesting a manner, was, after the glorious victory of Trafalgar, removed by Admiral, now Lord

Collingwood, with the kindest attention, from on board the Mars, to the Euryalus frigate; which soon afterwards was sent with dispatches to England. The Hon. Captain Blackwood, the distinguished officer who commands that ship, has undertaken in the handsomest manner to continue to take charge of the son of his respected friend the late Captain Duff; than whom he has been pleased to say, "His Majesty's service could not boast of a better, or more gallant officer." We can add with the greatest truth, that he was also a tender husband, an affectionate parent, a dutiful son, and a sincere friend!

The first Lieutenant of the Mars, Mr. Hennah, who, after his gallant Captain fell, emulated his conduct in fighting the ship with admirable skill and intrepidity, took the first opportunity of leisure, after the battle, and the subsequent storm, to write the following letter to Mrs. Duff:

His Majesty's Ship Mars, off Cadiz. Oct. 27, 1805.

MADAM,

I BELIEVE that a more unpleasant task, than what is now imposed upon me, can scarcely fall to the lot of a person, whose feelings are not more immediately connected by the nearer ties of kindred: but from a sense of duty, (as first Lieutenant of the Mars,) as being myself the husband of a beloved partner, and the father of children; out of the pure respect and esteem to the memory of our late gallant Captain, I should consider myself guilty of a base neglect, should you only be informed of the melancholy circumstances attending the late glorious, though unfortunate victory to many, by a public gazette. The consequences of such an event, while it may occasion the rejoicings of the nation, will in every instance be attended with the deepest regrets of a few.

Alas! Madam, how unfortunate shall I think myself, should this be the first intimation you may have of the irreparable loss you have met with! what apology can I make for entering on a subject so tender and so fraught with sorrow, but to recommend an humble reliance on this great truth, that the ways of Providence, although sometimes inscrutable, are always for the best.

By this, Madam, you are in all probability acquainted with the purport of my letter. Amongst the number of heroes who fell on the ever-memorable 21st inst. in defence of their King and Country; after gloriously discharging his duty to both; our meritorious and much respected Commander, Captain George Duff, is honourably classed: his fate was instantaneous; and he resigned his soul into the hands of the Almighty, without a moment's pain.

Poor Norwich is very well. Captain Blackwood has taken him on board the Euryalus, with the other young gentlemen that came with him, and their schoolmaster.

The whole of the Captain's papers and effects are sealed up, and will be kept in a place of security until proper persons are appointed to examine them. Meanwhile, Madam, I beg leave to assure you of my readiness to give you any information, or render you any service in my power.

And am, Madam, with the greatest respect,
Your most obedient and most humble servant,
WILLIAM HENNAH.

The same opportunity brought also the following letter to Mrs. Duff, from Rear-Admiral the Earl of Northesk:—

Britannia, off Cape Spartel, Nov. 6, 1805.

MADAM,

IT is with the greatest grief I have to inform you, that my much-lamented and dear friend Captain Duff fell in the action of the 21st, in the arms of victory, covered with glory. I well know what you, his family, and relatives, must feel on this melancholy occasion. But my dear Madam, the consideration of the sorrows of this life, and the glories of the next, is our best support.

I have directed Mr. Hennah, the first Lieutenant of the Mars, to take every possible care of what is on board, but the ship is now at Gibraltar.

I am, Madam, with great regard,
Your obedient humble servant,
NORTHESK.

Among the numerous letters of condolence addressed to Mrs. Duff and her family, on this melancholy occasion, by their relations and friends at home, the following extract is particularly interesting, being from the Rev. Mr. David Milne, Minister of the Gospel at Edinkillie, in the county of Moray; who was tutor to Captain Duff for several years before he went to sea.

I have every cause to lament the loss, our country at large, and yourself in particular, have sustained in the valiant and amiable Captain Duff. I had the honour to know him in his earliest days, and ever found his mind possessed of the finest dispositions, and always pointing to that element on which he so gloriously fell. I rejoice to find his country is so sensible of his merit that a monument is voted for him, with others, at the public charge.

In order to illustrate the character which we have given of this most amiable man, and excellent officer, whose life may be offered as an inestimable pattern to society at large, as well as to his profession, we shall annex some extracts from his letters. They are addressed to his brother-in-law, and to his wife; but chiefly to the latter: who from motives of delicacy has with the greatest difficulty been prevailed upon to permit them to meet the public eye; and Mrs. Duff could only have been induced to do so, by the consideration that their contents will do further honour to the memory of her beloved and lamented husband.

Captain Duff was in the practice of writing from day to day to his wife, and dispatching his letters as opportunities occurred. In this manner, his correspondence with her, had it been preserved, would have been very voluminous: but each time on his return home, he always asked for his letters, and destroyed them: thinking they were too bulky, and not of importance to be preserved. Thus it is only during his last absence, that we are enabled to give such extracts; with which two are included from the Captain's son to his mother; one just after he joined his father, and the other after his honourable death.

Extracts from the Letters of Captain Duff, of the Mars, to his family; from the time he left them in May 1804, to the time of his death, the 21st of October, 1805.

(No. I.)

To his Brother-in-law, Colonel Dirom, Deputy Quarter-Master-General in North Britain.

MY DEAR FRIEND, *Burton, Westmoreland, 7th May,* 1804.

I HAVE frequently had to thank you for your kindness and attention, but never more than lately, since I have been ordered away. I beg my best wishes to all your family, and I hope you will make Sophia* keep up her spirits.

* Mrs. Duff.

(No. II.)

Captain Duff to his Wife.

Plymouth Dock, May 25, 1804.

I AM glad to find our little George is better, and that you have got into your own house. Many happy days I hope we shall enjoy in it together, and I trust the prospect is not very distant; I think the Russians seem now in earnest, and that the Emperor of the Gauls will not long enjoy his new dignity.

Sir Edward Pellew goes to India, and Cochrane is to have the command of the ships off Ferrol. He will be my Commander, and will I am sure be a pleasant one.

Indefatigable, at Sea, 2d June.

IT was a month yesterday since I left my dearest wife and little ones—I hope ere many more that some good fellow will have made Buonaparte quiet, as I fear till he is so we shall have no peace.

(No. III.)

To the same.

Mars, off Ferrol, June 5.

WE fell in with the squadron on Sunday evening late, and yesterday I took the command of this ship, which is a very fine one indeed, if she could but sail. Our good friend Cochrane is quite well. We all dined with him yesterday; and until we get a little to rights, I shall continue to mess with him. Say to my father, that I have just arrived there, and will write to him by the next opportunity. The Spaniards are very civil to our ships, and there is no idea of a war with them.

(No. IV.)

To Colonel Dirom.

Mars, off Ferrol, June 5.

I HAVE at last got to my ship, which is a fine one, but sails very ill. However, I hope the Admiralty will allow her to be docked by and bye, and then she may sail better. The French have five sail of the line here and one frigate, a Dutch one; but all in such order, that I suppose they will never come out while we have two ships to oppose them.

(No. V.)

To his Wife.

June 10.

I UNDERSTAND that the Spaniards have sent very heavy complaints against the French squadron lying in Ferrol. They have been circulating seditious books, and endeavouring to make the people discontented with their government.

June 13

My old Mars is certainly a very fine ship; and if I could only persuade her to sail a little better, and could get a few good men, being now above *seventy* short of complement, I would not wish for a better ship. The ward-room officers seem to be pleasant good people, and I have no doubt we shall go on very well together. We have got a famous party of marines, and with them and the officers we can keep the Johnnies in very good order, if they should ever want it, which at present they do not.

(No. VI.)

To the same.

June 17.

AS the French officers and seamen are all on double pay while they remain in Ferrol, (being on foreign service, and not yet able to return to a port in France,) they will not be in any hurry to come out to be taken possession of by us, which they know must be their fate.

(No. VII.)

To the same.

July 4.

WE have plenty of good provisions, our men never taste a piece of salt meat, and they have plenty of fresh water and fruit. We take it by turns to be the look-out ship, and I suppose I shall be a fortnight at least at anchor after this week. We go on shore whenever we please, excepting to Ferrol, and I have generally walked three or four hours every day, when the weather would allow it. My leg is perfectly well*, as we have not gone so far to the south as to affect it.

July 10.

The night before we came inshore the French line-of-battle ship escaped from Corunna to Ferrol! I wish it had not happened during my look-out; but we are all much better pleased she has got there, as it was impossible to prevent them from going there if they wished it: but now they are shut up, so that they cannot get out without our seeing them.

(No. VIII.)

To the same.

July 15.

YESTERDAY was a great day with the Frenchmen, being the coronation of their Emperor. They saluted at sunrise, at noon,

* A hurt which he received in the great hurricane, in October 1780, in the West Indies.

and at sunset; and all their ships were finely dressed out with colours; but I hear they do not much like the dignity he has assumed. Yesterday they say was likewise the day they were to land in England; if so, not a few of their heads will be broken by this time; but they will take a little longer to consider before they set out.

(No. IX.)

To the same.

July 16.

I AM told this afternoon that some misunderstanding has taken place between the Spaniards and the Americans; which is very probable, as the Americans have got so near the kingdom of Mexico, and which they will have possession of before half this century is out.

(No. X.)

Captain Duff to Brigadier-General Dirom.

Plymouth Dock, August 18.

I CONGRATULATE you most sincerely on your promotion, and I hope you may long enjoy all your good things in health and happiness. It is not yet determined what they mean to do with our ship. I think she must go into dock; but it is not certain whether that may be here or at Portsmouth. Many thanks for your attention to Norwich *. I hope, poor fellow, he will do well: he has not much to look forward to but what he must make for himself.

(No. XI.)

Captain Duff to his Wife.

September 7.

SINCE I wrote you last, the Mars has got a great deal done to her. She is new coppered, has got a false keel, and every thing I have asked is to be done; so that I am in great hopes I shall be able to show some of my friends how handsomely her stern is painted,

Mars, off the Start, October 10, 1804.

I have just returned from the Admiral, and have got my orders to go to Rochfort and join Admiral Collingwood.

(No. XII.)

To the same.

October 23.

WE have had a severe gale of wind to-day from the westward. The French could not have wished for better weather to get out, if they had a mind to try their luck.

---

* Captain Duff's son.

October 26.

I have not yet seen my Admiral. I suppose the wind has blown him off his station, but I hope to-morrow we may meet, and the sooner the better. He is one of the old school, a steady officer, and good seaman.

(No. XIII.)

Captain Duff to Brigadier-General Dirom.

Cawsand Bay, October 9.

I GO to-morrow morning to join the fleet, which is at present in Torbay. I am glad to find that our new Admiralty have allowed the ships to come in when the weather is bad. It will save many pounds and many lives during the winter.

(No. XIV.)

Captain Duff to his Wife.

October 28.

I HAVE at last fallen in with my Admiral, and have had the happiness to receive your letter of the 12th inst. I am sorry to hear such bad accounts of my father. I fear he has much failed, and that I have not much chance of seeing him again*.

(No. XV.)

To the same.

October 30.

I WENT on board my Admiral yesterday to dinner, without being invited; and left the first Lieutenant here to take my place. I had a note from my old friend Gardner, who is here in the Hero, saying the Admiral would be glad to see me, as he dined there, so I went, and found *as usual* a very hearty and friendly welcome. We have with us the Dreadnought, Queen, Hero, Warrior, and Mars, with the Doris and some small craft inshore.

October 31.

No news, only a very blowing disagreeable day, of which we may expect many before the winter is over. However, I think my

* Captain Duff's father died at Banff, much respected, on the 19th of November, 1805, in the 76th year of his age. He was twice married, and had a number of children. The Captain was one of three (two sons and a daughter) by the first marriage. His brother was several years older than him, and died when finishing his education as a merchant, in Holland. One of his half-brothers, Fife Duff, a very active fine young man, was a Midshipman with him in the Ambuscade and Glenmore frigates, but was unfortunately seized with a putrid fever at Plymouth Dock, where he died in 1801. Several of the Captain's sisters, but none of his brothers, are now alive.

ship seems to sail pretty well, and I have every hope of her improving daily.

November 2.

The Tonnant has joined us this afternoon, but it blows so hard that we have not yet got our letters by her. Our good Admiral takes very good care of us; and should it come on to blow very hard, we have a fine anchorage off Quiberon Bay open for us. I have never been there yet, but my pilot is well acquainted with this coast, and is a very sober good man.

(No. XVI.)

To the same.

November 8.

WE have a cold blowing day, and it looks like a gale of wind. However, we have a good comfortable ship under foot. I should not have liked to have been sent here before she was docked, as, from her bad working and sailing, she was not safe on a lee shore.

November 9.

You cannot imagine how gay we are to be to-night. About a week ago I received a petition from the gentlemen of the cockpit, requesting to be allowed to perform the tragedy of Douglas, with the pantomime of Harlequin and the Miller; and last night a ticket was sent to me, with a bill of the play. The performance to commence at 5 o'clock. What think you of all these fine doings? It is an innocent amusement, much better than being idle and drinking.

November 10.

This is a proper gloomy November day, but not much wind. I went to the theatre last night, and I can assure you it was no bad performance. Between the play and the farce we had a most excellent Irish song, from one of the sailors. The music indeed was very good, and the entertainment for the night concluded with God save the King. The whole was over a quarter before eight o'clock. They had several scenes not badly painted. The ladies' dresses were not very fine, but did credit to their invention. Lady Randolph was all in black, made out of silk handkerchiefs; and I believe Anne's dress was made of sheets: but upon the whole they looked remarkably well.

November 11.

Just going to bed. We have had a very rolling day, and blowing a gale, but I think it is now going off. As yet I have not benefited much from my Parson; for every Sunday except one, since he joined, we have had a gale of wind, and could not have prayers.

November 17.

We have had two very fine days. Yesterday I went on board the Admiral, and met Gardner and Jervis. The former pressed us to stay, and we all dined with him. Jervis, who is the last from the fleet off Brest, says we are to be relieved every six or seven weeks.

(No. XVII.)

To the same.

November 23.

WE have had a fine day, and we Captains have all been on board the Admiral to make our bow. He wanted us much to dine with him; but I was very glad to get off, as it is too late in the season to dine out of the ship at sea. Indeed *even here I like home* much better than any other place. I am just going to bed, as I expect to rouse out at twelve, if not sooner, to wear ship; so God bless you all!

December 2.

WE have still our good easterly wind, which I hope may continue for these six weeks, or till I be relieved; as we have fine smooth water, and now and then we get a little fish, with our trowl: we have as yet tried it only once, and that for a short time; when I got a very good turbot for my share.

We have had two very good sermons from our Chaplain, last Sunday and to-day, and he reads the prayers very well.

(No. XVIII.)

To the same.

Mars, January 24, 1805.

WE fell in with the Colossus this morning, and have now bore up with a fair wind for Ushant, where I suppose we shall meet Admiral Cornwallis to-morrow. The Rochfort squadron has of course got out, and it is supposed to have gone to Brest. I think it the best thing that could happen, as we shall have only one port instead of two to watch. It was quite a farce to say, that our squadron was blockading the ships in Rochfort; we were only running great risk with our own: for I was always convinced that the French might have got out any day they pleased, without our ever seeing them. They must however have passed very near us in the night, from the situation we were in, and the place where they were seen; and had we met, I think we should have given a good account of them.

January 31.

Poor Captain Jervis, of the Tonnant, and some of his boat's crew, were drowned on Saturday last in going on board the San

Josef. I am very sorry for him indeed, as he was a particular friend of mine, and a very good fellow. He was heir to Lord St. Vincent's title and fortune.

(No. XIX.)

To the same.

February 11.

WE left Torbay this afternoon, and were joined this day by Sir Robert Calder and his squadron.—I suppose they must have gone to look into l'Orient, for the ships which got away from Rochfort. Where they have got to, is as yet not known; but we shall hear of them somewhere by and by; perhaps in the East or West Indies, where they may do much mischief.

(No. XX.)

To the same.

March 27.

THE French fleet have got out of Brest Harbour, and are anchored in Bertheaume Bay. We were within four or five miles of them, our inshore ships just out of gun-shot. We are all clear for action, but it depends entirely upon them to come to it, or not. If they do, I trust we shall be victorious, and have a lasting peace. They are at present four sail of the line more than us; but if we do our duty, I think we shall give a very good account of them. Should I unfortunately fall, I hope that our friends will take care of you and our dear little ones. I have done all, my dearest Sophia, to make you and them comfortable, that our small funds would allow; but I am sorry to say, they are very small indeed. I regret much you never would allow me to speak of making a settlement, nor would look at the one I had made.

(No. XXI.)

To the same.

May 6.

I HAVE been paying my respects to-day to Admiral Collingwood. He is the senior officer ordered to be ready for foreign service, and a fine steady good officer he is. I do not know one I would so soon go on service with; but he is still of my opinion, that it is a matter of precaution, having so many sail of the line ready to follow the enemy wherever he may go, and by no means clear that we should ever leave the fleet.

I long much to be with you all, and to see our young Miss Anne*. We are now very old married folks: this day 14 years was the first time I could claim you as my *own*, and we have

* Born since his departure.

had very little of one another's society since we have been married. This war must soon have an end, when I hope to remain with you altogether; for we are now become rather an old couple, and do not wish for a change: Indeed I do not think it ever was our wish, I may say, since we first knew each other. I frequently recollect with pleasure our playing together when at school, at my father's. In short, it requires every thing here to keep one's spirits up, so far from those we love.

May 7.

I have no news to tell my ever dearest Sophia; but as a ship from England has been in sight all day, I take her to be the Bellerophon, our old friend Cooke, and I hope to have some letters by him from you. He is one of my oldest friends in the service, and was, till the other day, Captain of the guard-ship at Plymouth; but he was no sooner appointed to the Bellerophon, than he was ordered to fit for foreign service*. If we go to the Mediterranean, I shall be very glad to have so good and old a friend of the party. God bless you all, and good night.

(No. XXII.)

To the same.

May 10.

I SENT away my journal yesterday to my dearest Sophia: we were afterwards joined by my old friend Cooke, in the Bellerophon, who brought me out some ducks and fowls; and Baylis, in the Windsor Castle, who brought me some vegetables, &c. Sir John Orde and his squadron parted from us last night, I suppose for England.

I have taken a prize to-day! about two o'clock a cask went close to us, and as I could easily get into my station again, I sent after it, when at last we got it on board with a good deal of trouble. It proved I think to be a hogshead of claret; which from the state of, and the number of barnicles upon, the cask, must have been at least several years in the water. The wine is quite sound, and I hope when settled will turn out well. I wish it was in Castle Street such as it is; of course it is very thick at present, but a little time will let us know what our prize is.

May 11.

The Admiral about six o'clock this evening made our signal; the

* Captain Cooke, after the most gallant conduct, fell about the same time as his friend Captain Duff, in the battle of Trafalgar. The enemy were attempting to board, when he was struck with a grape shot in the breast, and fell upon the deck. His men were going to carry him below, when he exclaimed, "*Let me die in peace!*"

Ramillies, the Tonnant, Bellerophon, Illustrious, Minotaur, and Colossus; to close to Admiral Collingwood, and put ourselves under his orders. Before sunset Admiral Collingwood bore up, and made the signal for his division to rendezvous in Cawsand Bay.

Plymouth Dock, May 13.

We came in here yesterday, but, as I was almost the rear ship, too late for the post. It is now nearly past time again, and I have not been off my legs since six o'clock; so that I have only time to say I am perfectly well, and the general opinion is, that we are going to the Mediterranean, as Lord Nelson will be obliged to follow, or has already followed the ships from Cadiz.

(No. XXIII.)

To the same.

Mars, at Sea, May 24.

ON Tuesday morning, after we were under weigh, I finished my letter to my ever dearest Sophia, and sent it on board the Montagu, which was lying in Cawsand Bay, to be forwarded to the post office. The next morning we joined the fleet under Lord Gardner, and stood very close into Brest, that the French should see our force; which consisted of 31 sail of the line, besides frigates: and I suppose we should have left the fleet that night, but a frigate, I believe la Loire, joined us, and made the signal that she had been chased by five line-of-battle ships. Upon this our Admiral was called on board the Commander in Chief. Admiral Collingwood, in the Dreadnought, with the Ramillies, Tonnant, Colossus, Achille, Illustrious, Bellerophon, Minotaur, Mars, and the Endymion frigate, bore up to the westward. As there was no communication unless by signal, I could not write; but from the course we are steering there is little doubt we are going off Cadiz.

Sunday evening, May 26.

I went on board our Admiral to-day, as it was calm, and like a good boy staid there to church, as I have no Parson here. I find it was la Loire that joined the fleet. She fell in with the Rochfort squadron on their return from the West Indies, so that I hope we shall now have no chance of going there. This evening we saw five sail, and I believe one of them is the Royal Sovereign, our good friend Sir Richard Bickerton.

June 2.

On Monday morning I went on board the Admiral, and met our good old friend Sir Richard; and as he had a brig with him, that he was going to send to England, I wrote you a few lines by her.

which will convince you that our destination is Cadiz; and I have great hopes that we may pick up something after all. Sir Richard is well, but has not seen his wife since January, 1804. I was very glad I had a fine piece of roasting beef remaining; which, with some vegetables, and a little nice butter, I sent to the worthy Baronet. He is gone to join Sir Robert Calder off Ferrol.

June 9.

Yesterday morning we got sight of Cadiz, and are now close in. We see, I think, only three ships of the line at anchor in the bay. We were joined yesterday morning by the Acasta, Seahorse, two other frigates, and two brigs, which have been cruising off here. The Ramillies and Illustrious have parted company with us: and from the course they were steering, when we saw them last, I have little doubt are going to the West Indies.

I have heard that the Spaniards expect a line-of-battle ship and a frigate home with money; so we must keep a good look out for them. I hope therefore to be able to desire you to look out for a country house, and to order a carriage to be built for us.

(No. XXIV.)

To the same.

Mars, off Cadiz, June 14.

WE were very unlucky in not getting here a few days sooner, as one of the Spanish line-of-battle ships, I believe the Gloriosa, an 80 gun ship, came out to try how they could manage; and our frigate, the Lively, teased and drew her off from the shore, and she has not yet been able to return. We have had a line-of-battle ship and a frigate working out for her, but we fear she has gone to Teneriffe.

June 23.

Yesterday our friend Sir Richard Bickerton joined us in the Queen, from Ferrol. I went on board our Admiral to see him, and staid to dine with them. He is gone up the Mediterranean, and has got from our squadron the Tonnant, the Bellerophon, and the Minotaur. I wished much to have gone with him, but my Admiral had the picking of the ships, and seems to like the old Mars to remain with himself. I could not be better than with either Admiral, as they are both very kind and civil to me, and I could not ask to go with Sir Richard for fear of offending Admiral Collingwood; as his keeping me here is certainly a compliment, and I now become the senior Captain with him.

June 27.

I dined on Tuesday with our Admiral, on a turtle I had shot

with my gun a day or two before, and sent to him; and very good it was.

(No. XXV.)

To the same.

July 6.

THE day before yesterday I boarded the ship with General Moreau, his wife and family. I should have liked much to have gone on board myself to have seen him, but I did not think it right.

(No. XXVI.)

To the same.

August 22.

I JOINED the squadron yesterday. The combined fleet came off Cadiz the day before, and chased our ships away. I was then in Tangier, and being informed of it by one of our frigates, which was going to Sir Richard Bickerton, I returned immediately. I had luckily got plenty of bullocks for ourselves and the squadron, and as much vegetables as I wanted for myself.

(No. XXVII.)

To the same.

August 26.

ON Friday we were joined by the Queen, Tonnant, Bellerophon, Minotaur, and two frigates; but I am sorry to find our friend Sir Richard Bickerton is left behind sick at Gibraltar, and is going home by the first opportunity. Admiral Knight succeeds him in the command of the squadron.

August 27.

The enemy are still snug in port. They have not been joined by the ships from Carthagena, so that I think it likely they may go up the Mediterranean.

August 31.

We were joined yesterday by Sir Robert Calder, with 18 ships of the line, and we now consist of 26. Our friends in Cadiz will not therefore come out again for some time. We expect to be joined every day by Lord Nelson with one or two ships, so that we shall have more than we want.

I went on board Admiral Louis last night, where I found Pultney Malcolm, and his brother: they made many kind inquiries about you all, and desired to be particularly remembered to you: he has now the Donnegal, a very fine ship indeed. He has gone inshore with Admiral Louis to watch Cadiz; I may not therefore see him again for some time, as my Admiral has taken me close to himself.—He is a very fine fellow, and stuck very close to the combined fleet with his little squadron.

(No. XXVIII.)

To the same.

September 1.

I SENT away a letter yesterday to my ever dearest Sophia, by the Latona. As we are now so large a fleet, we shall have more frequent opportunities to England, and I shall begin another: but I am very anxious to hear how you all do, as I have as yet had no answer to any I wrote you since we sailed, which is now a very long time. I mentioned in my last that Pultney Malcolm was here. He is gone inshore with Admiral Louis, to get the combined fleet out, as we do not show our reinforcement, in hopes they may be tempted to come out; but I fear they will hear of it, and remain quietly at anchor.

September 7.

On the 3d I went on board the Britannia, to see my old friend Lord Northesk, and found him just finishing a letter to his wife; so I sat down and wrote a few lines to go by the same opportunity, which was a brig to Faro, a port in Portugal, whence the letters will be sent to Lisbon, and by the packet to England.

September 9.

We are just going to Tetuan for water, and perhaps to Gibraltar, with the Conqueror. I suppose I shall be gone for at least a week.

(No. XXIX.)

To the same.

September 23.

MY dearest Sophia will readily believe how much I rejoiced on Saturday last to see our boy. He is very well, and has not been in the least sick. All the rest are also well, though they have been sick during the passage. It was very fortunate my meeting with the Aurora, as I was ordered by the Admiral to speak a frigate off the Gut, before I went to Tangier; and in doing so, I fell in with our boy, and got him out, otherwise it might have been some weeks before he had joined me. I have for the present taken him into the cabin to mess, and sleep. He seems very well pleased with his choice of a profession, and I hope will continue so. I had the pleasure of receiving by the Aurora, yours of the 27th July, 2d and 12th of August, but I was informed a week before of Norwich's coming. It is very odd, that on Sunday before he joined, our Captain of marines*, who is a very pleasant fellow, told me when I went down to dine in the ward-room, that he seldom dreamt, but

* Captain Norman, who since died of his wounds.

he could not resist telling me his dream of last night, that my son had arrived, and that he was taking him all over the ship to show it to him. So when Master Norwich made his appearance, the dream came into my head immediately.

(No. XXX.)

To the same.

September 28.

I WAS called away yesterday, and now sit down again to write my ever dearest wife a few more lines, and to thank her for her picture; though I must own I am not at all pleased with it, as I don't think it does you any justice, nor do I think I should ever have taken it for you, if I had not been told it was intended for you. I think the one done by Smith* was better.

October 1.

On Saturday night we were joined by Lord Nelson with the Victory, Ajax, Thunderer, and the Euryalus; when I had the happiness of receiving yours, my ever dearest wife, of the 8th September, and the papers up to the 7th. Many, many thanks! I dined with his Lordship yesterday, and had a very merry dinner; he certainly is the pleasantest Admiral I ever served under. I hope the Austrians and Russians will make quick work with Buonaparte, and let us get to our homes once more; when I expect to be an Admiral before I am called upon again.

(No. XXXI.)

Captain Duff to Brigadier-General Dirom.

October 1.

MANY thanks, my very good friend, for your letter, and for your kindness to all at home. You would hear from Sophia that our youngsters joined me about ten days ago. I was luckily coming from Gibraltar.

I understand from good authority, that on the 13th ult. a dispatch came from Buonaparte, by way of Madrid, desiring the combined fleet to put to sea; but after a council of war from sunrise to sun-set, they returned for answer, that it would not be proper their going to sea with our present fleet in the offing. Since that time we have been joined by Lord Nelson.

My best wishes attend you and yours; and if you can offer my best respects and thanks to Lord Moira, for his kindness to me, you will much oblige your most sincere friend,

GEORGE DUFF.

---

* Probably the artist at Edinburgh.

(No. XXXII.)

Extract of a Letter from Mr. Norwich Duff to his Mother, dated His Majesty's Ship Mars, October 1, 1805.

MY DEAR MOTHER,

I TAKE the opportunity of the Nimble cutter brig going to England to write you, as I should not wish to lose a single opportunity. I received your kind letter of the 25th August yesterday, and the next day one from John Dirom*. Although I liked the Aurora very much, yet I like the Mars twenty times better. We had a very pleasant voyage in the Aurora, though a very long one, on account of a very large convoy, and contrary winds. I was not the least sick during the whole voyage. Lord Nelson joined us on Thursday, with the Victory, which we left at Spithead. We lead the lee line of the fleet, which is the next best post to the Admiral.

(No. XXXIII.)

Captain Duff to his Wife.

MY DEAREST SOPHIA, *Mars. October* 7, 1805.

I HAVE but just time to tell you that Norwich and all of us are well. The Admiral has for some days past detached me with three sail of the line under my command, as the advance squadron; and just called me in to give me some wine, when I found the Bittern sloop of war is going to Lisbon, and I do not like to lose the opportunity. I will begin you another letter to-morrow, but since *I am Commodore*, I have not much time during the day, and am ready for my nap as soon as I can in the evening. I hope our dear little ones are well, and that our mother and sisters, &c. are so likewise. With every good wish and love to you and them, I ever am, my dearest Sophia, your own

GEORGE DUFF.

(No. XXXIV.)

To the same.

Mars, off Cadiz, October 8, 1805.

I WROTE my dearest Sophia a few lines yesterday by the Bittern; but as I left the fleet immediately, I do not know whether the Defiance brought us any letters or not. We are detached only three or four leagues from the fleet, and always in sight of it. At present our squadron consists of the Mars, Defence, Colossus,

* The General's oldest son, ten years old.

and Ajax. I suppose as soon as Admiral Louis returns from Gibraltar, where he is now gone to water, &c., he will take the command of the advance squadron, and *deprive me of my honours.*

October 10.

I am just returned from dining with Brown, of the Ajax, *one of my squadron.* He is a very old acquaintance of mine, ever since 1780, when we were in the West Indies together, and have met frequently since on service. I am sorry the rain has begun to night, as it will spoil my fine work, having been employed for this week past to paint the ship *à la Nelson*, which most of the fleet are doing. He is so good and pleasant a man, that we all wish to do what he likes, without any kind of orders. I have been myself very lucky with most of my Admirals; but I really think the present the pleasantest I have met with: even this little detachment is a kind thing to me, there being so many senior officers to me in the fleet, as it shows his attention and wish to bring me forward; but I believe I have to thank my old friend Collingwood for it, as he was on board the Victory when I was sent for.

(No. XXXV.)

Captain Duff to Mrs. Duff, dated Mars, off Cadiz, October 17, 1805.

I SENT away my letter to my ever dearest Sophia on Sunday, by the Prince of Wales. I am sorry to find there have been two opinions of Sir Robert Calder's conduct, when in sight of the enemy. I regret it very much, as he is a very worthy gallant officer. As the situation of the enemy's fleet, and the orders he was under, were known only to himself, I am very glad to find a court martial is to take place; I hope it will completely clear him.

Lieutenant Capples, one of our marine officers, a very good man, being ordered home in the Prince of Wales, I have sent by him the moorish plaid, or whatever you may call it, and have desired him to do the best he can to get it to you, which I am sure he will do*.

On Sunday I got your letter of the 22d August, by Lisbon: it was rather long in coming, but as I wish to hear from my dearest wife every opportunity, you may as well now and then send a letter that way.

* Mrs. Duff was very anxious to receive this last present from her beloved husband, which had not reached her before the accounts of his death, but has been since carefully delivered by Mr. Capples, when he came to Edinburgh.

From all accounts, we shall have war on the Continent, but I think the hotter war the sooner peace. As to ship, station, Admiral, &c. I cannot be better off. We have been long told that a promotion is to take place; but I will never believe it till I see it in the Gazette, as I cannot see how they can make one, when we have so many on the Admirals' list already; if they take in the same number as they have usually done, in two promotions I shall be very near, if not in it; but I have so many great men near me, they will get the marines. I should have no objection to a few years of them in peace without the flag; but my chance is little indeed. However, I have this comfort to say, that few have served more than me, for whatever may fall to my lot.

October 18.

I now re-commence my letter of yesterday. The only news I have since heard, is that Sir Richard Strachan, with six sail of the line, was in sight of the French squadron from Rochfort, which has been cruising off Cape Finisterre for a long time: if he gets up with them, he will I hope give a good account of them.

You ask me about Lord Nelson, and how I like him. I have already answered that question, as every person must do that ever served under him. When we want any thing we shall go to Gibraltar, as there is a dock-yard and stores there, and I suppose we shall remain off here till the combined fleet gives us the slip. This place is easy to blockade during the summer, but *no place* can be blockaded in the winter; and although every look-out possible will be kept, I have little doubt of their getting off, if they wish it, during the winter.

Captain Duff having the command of the advance or inshore squadron, and the enemy's fleet having begun to come out on the 19th, his time appears to have been so completely occupied, that he did not continue his letter to his wife, as usual, on the 19th and 20th.—The following few lines, written on a separate half sheet of paper, and sealed with a wafer, were however found along with his other unfinished letters, in his writing box.

(No. XXXVI.)

To the same.

MY DEAREST SOPHIA, *Monday morning, Oct.* 21, 1805.

I HAVE just time to tell you we are going into action with the combined fleet. I hope and trust in God that we shall all behave as becomes us, and that I may yet have the happiness of taking my beloved wife and children in my arms. Norwich is quite well, and happy. I have however ordered him off the quarter-deck.

Yours ever, and most truly,

GEORGE DUFF.

Captain Duff's son, and three other boys who went out with him, were stationed on the lower deck during the action, where, their schoolmaster writes, they behaved like *young Nelsons.*

(No. XXXVII.)

Extract from Mr. Norwich Duff's Letter to his Mother, written after the Battle of Trafalgar, but without date.

MY DEAR MAMMA,

YOU cannot possibly imagine how unwilling I am to begin this melancholy letter. However, as you must unavoidably hear of the fate of dear Papa, I write you these few lines to request you to bear it as patiently as you can. He died like a Hero, having gallantly led his ship into action, and his memory will ever be dear to his King, his Country, and his Friends. It was about fifteen minutes past twelve in the afternoon of the 21st of October, when the engagement began, and it was not finished till five. Many a brave Hero sacrificed his life upon that occasion to his King and his Country. You will hear that Lord Viscount Nelson was wounded in the commencement of the engagement, and only survived long enough to learn that the victory was ours.—"*Then,*" said that brave Hero, "*I die happy, since I die victorious,*" and in a few minutes expired.

We are now all on board the Euryalus, with the Hon. Captain Blackwood, and, in compliance with the wish of Admiral Collingwood, are now on our way to England, that we may have an opportunity of more readily knowing your wishes respecting our future conduct. Captain Blackwood has indeed been very polite and kind to me; and has requested Mr. Dalrymple to let my uncle know, that on account of his acquaintance with my Papa, he will feel very happy in keeping me on board his ship.

My dear Mamma, I have again to request you to endeavour to make yourself as happy and as easy as possible. It has been the will of Heaven, and it is our duty to submit.

Believe me your obedient and affectionate Son,

N. DUFF.

NAVAL ANECDOTES, COMMERCAL HINTS, RECOLLECTIONS, &c.

NANTES IN GURGITE VASTO.

CAPTURE OF THE BRUNSWICK INDIAMAN.

MR. PEARS, Purser of the Honourable Company's ship Brunswick, arrived at the India House December 7, 1805, with the melancholy intelligence of that ship having been captured by Rear-Admiral Linois, in the Marengo, accompanied by la Belle Poule frigate, on the 11th July last, off Point de Galle. This ship separated from the homeward-bound China fleet in February last for Bombay, in consequence of her springing a leak, and after very great exertions in keeping her afloat, arrived there, making nearly six feet water per hour. After receiving the necessary repairs, she sailed from Bombay for China on the 1st July, with three country ships, two of which parted company on the 4th, in very dark, blowing, squally weather. On the 11th, the Sarah, Captain M'Intosh, being the only ship then in company with the Brunswick, they fell in with the French squadron, to which, after an ineffectual attempt at resistance, the Brunswick surrendered: the Sarah being considerably to windward, made for the land, closely pursued by the frigate, and soon after ran upon the breakers, with all sails set, when she immediately hoisted a signal of distress, and from the report made by the Captain of la Belle Poule, upon his return, she must be totally lost. Captain Grant and the officers of the Brunswick were sent on board le Marengo, who continued her cruise to the south; and on the 6th of August, in lat. 20°, long. 80° 30′ E. they fell in with an outward-bound India fleet, consisting of eleven sail, about four P.M., they were standing to the north, and when first discovered, it being thick, hazy weather, were not more than three or four miles distant. Every thing was immediately cleared for action, and the Brunswick's officers and men sent below. The action commenced about thirty minutes past five, P.M., and continued without intermission nearly half an hour. The Admiral bore up to leeward of the fleet, and continued receiving and returning their fire until they had passed them all, when having received several shot from one which they supposed to be a man of war, they continued under a press of sail, and kept hauling out to windward all night, still keeping in sight of the fleet. The Brunswick, which was then in company, separated from the fleet at the beginning of the action, and standing to the south, was soon out of sight. At daylight the English fleet was perceived about four miles astern to leeward; all hove to in line-of-battle, expecting the attack of the French Admiral, who had then shortened sail under his top-sails and fore-sails. About seven A.M. the Marengo bore up to reconnoitre and ascertain the force of the English, when having ran about a mile and a half to leeward, she again hauled her wind, the English still preserving the same line as before. The Admiral and his Captains now held a consultation, the result of which was, that they thought the English force too much for them, and the idea of a farther attack was immediately abandoned. About two P.M. the English man of war set his top-gallant-sails, the fleet also made more sail, and kept edging to leeward, the French ships still keeping upon a wind, under easy sail; about sunset the merchantmen were nearly six miles to leeward. At nine P.M. the Marengo tacked and stood to the south, and we saw no more of the fleet.—There were eleven sail, one of which appeared to be a 74-gun ship, five to be large China ships, and five to be Bengal ships, which the French officers said were full of troops. The damage sustained by the Marengo were three men wounded, a shot through the fish of the main-mast, one struck the fore-yard, one through the poop, several shots through her sails, and the ship's sides full of musket balls. La Belle Poule—two men wounded, cross jack-yard carried away in the slings, hulled in two places under the chess-trees, and the fore-sail so much cut as to be obliged to shift it. The French ships now made sail for the Cape of Good Hope, and arrived in Simon's Bay on the 13th of September, where they found the Bato, of 64 guns, but in a completely dismantled state, having no ship's company on board. The officers and men from the Brunswick were immediately landed, and Admiral Linois gave permission to Captain Grant, Mr. Pears, and two Midshipmen, to take their passage to Europe on board a Danish ship which was upon the point of sailing for Copenhagen.

Two days before Captain Grant sailed, a ship was seen coming into the Bay, making signals of distress, and firing guns for assistance; she proved to be the Brunswick, who had lost three anchors the preceding night, and, for want of timely aid from the French men of war, was driving fast upon the beach, where she soon went on shore about a mile from Simon's Town: in a few hours part of her false keel and sheathing were thrown upon the beach by the surf which was breaking over, and when the Dane sailed, had upwards of twelve feet water in her hold.

The officers and seamen of the Brunswick were expected to leave the Cape in a few days, in a cartel brig hired for the purpose of carrying them to St. Helena.

The Dannibroog touched at St. Helena on the 7th of October, at which time the Hon. Company's ships Worcester and Skelton Castle had arrived, and were detained for convoy. On the 5th of November spoke His Majesty's brig Teignmouth, with five ships in company, which they supposed to be the Tottenham, Lord Eldon, and three Whalers. The Danish ship Wilhelmine Teresa was also in sight of the fleet. Lat. 22° 28′ N., long. 30°.

Mr. Pears adds, "Not knowing of the importance of an accurate statement of the forces at the Cape, I merely inquired their number, and was informed there were about five thousand men, principally Dutch. The inhabitants appeared very favourably disposed towards the English, but had no expectation of a visit from them.

PIRATES.

India.

IT appears that the pirates, who have long infested the river from Canton to Macao, have lately increased to such a degree as to render the passage of boats between these places not a little dangerous. They had even the audacity to attack an American vessel going up the river; but though the number of their small vessels was very great, they were repulsed with loss. They are in greatest force near the foot of the west branch of the river, and retire with their booty, and evade pursuit in the innumerable canals with which that part of the country is intersected. A very strong proof of their strength is, that while formerly they were accustomed to put all their prisoners to death in the cruelest manner, they now almost uniformly ransom the vessels, retaining hostages for the due performance of the agreement. Besides the two vessels which the Portuguese are obliged to keep at Macao for protecting the trade of the river, the government has been forced to fit out several armed vessels to act against the pirates, and have purchased some ships from the Europeans, for the same purpose. The increase of these disorders is undoubtedly very much owing to the distracted state of many of the provinces of China. In some of them, particularly to the northward, the country is in a state of open revolt. The attention of the government is thus drawn off from the management of the southern districts, where great disorders in consequence prevail.

Apostrophe to the Shade of NELSON, *By* JOHN THELWALL, *Professor of the Science and Practice of Elocution. Extracted from his Trident of Albion,* 8vo.

WHAT grasp of mind can comprehend—what power of language can do justice, to the invincible spirit, the fertility of invention and resource, under every circumstance of difficulty and danger, displayed by this great Commander?—to that rapidity of conception—that promptitude of thought, which perceived the bearings of every exigency; and devised and adopted, on the instant, the plans of attack, manœuvre, and operation, which the circumstances, however unexpected, might require?—to that collected boldness, and impetuous hardihood, which realised in action every project which his boundless science and fertile genius had devised?—and, above all, to that rapidity of evolution, from post to post, from sea to sea, from pole almost to pole, which seemed, as it were, to control the very elements; and, like the motion and operations of lightning, gave an appearance of omnipresence to his resistless courage?

Eulogy has no metaphor that can do justice to this splendid career; and panegyric itself must borrow its language from the simple pages of historical record, if it would paint, even in an individual instance, the enterprising activity of his fiery spirit; when, yet in a subordinate situation, in the conflict of doubtful battle, he seized the moment of critical conjuncture; and, attacking, with his single, smaller vessel, the well-seconded force of a superior foe, he passed, sword in hand, from his own deck, up the towering sides of his enemy; overpowered the desperate resistance of its crew; and then made the mastered vessel, a step, as it were, from which, with equal impetuosity and success, he passed to another of still superior magnitude, and overwhelmed all opposition with a courage, which appeared to be supernatural.

But this was only a prelude to those splendid achievements, in every part of which he displayed an equal mixture of enthusiasm and presence of mind. To him, wounds, hardships, sufferings, privations, and mutilations, presented no obstructions in the career of duty. "Victory, or Westminster Abbey!—*A glorious life, or an honourable tomb*," seem to have been regarded, almost as equal blessings; and the loss of limbs, and the abridgement of the powers of exterior sense, appear only to have concentrated the patriotic fire that burned within, and to have increased the valour and comprehension of his soul.

And can we remember, without emotions of gratitude, the benefits which this comprehension and this valour have conferred upon his country! whose fate it is, perhaps, too much to say, *that he has averted*—(since the danger may yet return;—and since, even in the last extremities, "come what come may," Britons may surely rely on the energies of their united valour!) but whose shores he has, at any rate, for a while, preserved from the impending ravages of invasion. And can we, while we taste (though but for a while) the renovated blessing of security, forget, that he who conferred that blessing is no more to be a participator of its enjoyments!

Upon such a subject, grief might, assuredly, be eloquent; and the voice of lamentation might be heard in every street.

But no—Heroic Spirit! Not such are the tears that should embalm thy memory; not such is the mourning with which thy obsequies should be accompanied. Let effeminate sorrow melt over the pale victims of affliction and disease! Let the dirges of lamentation resound over the grave of virgin loveliness cropped in its vernal bloom; but the tomb of the Hero is the temple of his triumph; and the trophies that adorn it are the altars on which compatriot youths should offer up their vows of emulation. Yes! thou heroic Spirit! if, yet conscious to the transactions of this fragile world, thou hoverest, with patriotic solicitude, over the country thou hast so bravely defended—Yes, thou wilt exclaim, "By other actions acknowledge my services and estimate my loss, than by tears and lamentations! by other offerings consecrate my memory than by the dirges of desponding sorrow. Proclaim your admiration, by imitating my example; and with pen of adamant, engrave upon your hearts the language of my last injunction. Landsmen, as well as seamen, may yet be summoned to the exertions and the sacrifices it demands. Even yet, upon your coasts you may be called upon to repel the invader;—and, if you should, keep then in your recollections—*What England expects of every individual;* and write your remembrances of me with your swords!"

We hear thee, patriotic spirit!—We receive thy awful admonitions—not into our ears, but into our hearts:—those hearts, from which we breathe, with determined unanimity, the fervent, the inviolable vow, "To assert as thou hast asserted, even in death, the independence of our country; and to prove, under all extremities, that we are not forgetful of the injunctions, or the example, of the Heroic Martyr of Trafalgar.

MR. EDITOR,

THE following was found among the papers of the late Captain George Clarke. Lorenzo Doria came on board his ship as a common sailor. S. S.

Lorenzo Doria, an immediate descendant of the celebrated House of Doria of Genoa, is at present, from revolutionary causes in servitude.

He is of an excellent disposition, has conducted himself with the greatest propriety whilst on board His Majesty's ship under my command, and is sixteen years of age.

(Signed) GEORGE CLARKE.

(Signed) LORENZO DORIA.

Braakel, Chatham, May 5, 1804.

FROM MICHAUX'S TRAVELS IN THE UNITED STATES.

THE navigation of the Ohio and the Mississippi is so much in use, that the distance from Pittsburg to New Orleans is now known with great precision: it is fixed at 2100 miles. The carrying boats generally require, in the spring, from forty-five to fifty days to perform this passage, which two or three persons in a light vessel (piroque) can accomplish in twenty or twenty-five days.

It is not perhaps known to many people in Europe, that vessels of a considerable tonnage are built at Pittsburg on the Ohio. One of the principal dock-yards is on the Monongahela, two hundred toises from the last houses in the town. The timbers employed in their construction are the white oak, quercus alba; the red oak, quercus rubra; the black oak, quercus tinctoria; a species of walnut, juglans pignut; the cluster cherry-tree, cerasus virginiana; and a species of pine, which is used for masts, and also for such parts of the vessel as require a lighter wood. All these woods being in the vicinity, the expenses of construction are less considerable than in the ports of the Atlantic States. The cordage is fabricated at Redstone, or at Lexington, where two good ropewalks are established, which also supply the ships built at Marietta and Louisoille. When I was at Pittsburg in July 1802, there was a three-masted vessel on the stocks, of two hundred and fifty tons burthen, and a galliot of ninety, which were nearly finished. These vessels were to go down to New Orleans in the following spring, with a cargo of the productions of the country, and, before reaching the ocean, would make a voyage of near 2200 miles. There is not a doubt but that, hereafter, vessels will be constructed two hundred leagues above the mouth of the Missouri, fifty above that of the Illinois river, and also in the Mississippi, two hundred leagues above the place where these rivers join it: that is to say, six hundred and fifty leagues from the sea; for in the space mentioned, their depths are as great as that of the Ohio at Pittsburg; and it would be wrong to suppose, that, in time, the vast countries watered by these rivers will not be sufficiently populous to execute such enterprises. The rapid population of the three new western States, in circumstances infinitely less favourable, warrant this opinion. These States, in which, thirty years ago, there were scarcely three thousand inhabitants, have at present more than four hundred thousand; and among all the plantations, which on the roads are seldom more than four or five miles asunder, it is very common to find one, even of the most flourishing, of which the proprietor may not be asked, with confidence, from whence he emigrated; or in the trivial language of the Americans, *From what part of the world are you come?* as if these west and fertile regions were intended to be the point of concentration, and common country of all the inhabitants of the Globe.

NEWLY DISCOVERED ISLAND.

CAPTAIN CROOKER, in the ship Nancy, of Boston, on his late passage from Europe to Canton, made a new discovery of an island lying in the Pacific Ocean, as will appear from the following extract from his journal:—" Thursday, 20th December, 1804, variable winds, mostly from N.E. with squalls and calms, steered N.N.W. At 1 P.M. we very unexpectedly discovered from the poop-deck an island bearing N.E. by N. ¼ N. distant about 11 leagues. At 6 do. it bore N.E. about 7 leagues to the nearest shore. It appeared to be about 12 or 13 miles long from N.N.W. to S.S.E. It is quite high land, with some considerable mountains in the middle, and I presume may be seen off the deck at the distance of 15 leagues in clear weather. Its latitude I make, from good observations of the sun's altitude, to be 5 degrees 12 minutes; and from an observation of a star's altitude, when the island was seen E. of us, to be 5° 11′ N.; and its longitude from two sets of distances of moon and star, taken when about 50 miles from it, to be 162° 58′ E. of Greenwich. Having no such island laid down in any of my charts, (India pilot,) I conclude it must be a new discovery, and as such I name it Strong's Island, in compliment to Caleb Strong, Esq., Governor of the Commonwealth of Massachussetts."

Captain Swaine, of Nantucket, about two years since, on a voyage to India, discovered an island not laid down in any chart, the latitude and longitude of which was not published. Captain Swaine, it is hoped, will make the mention desired, that it may be determined whether it was the same island seen by Captain Crooker or not. The publication of discoveries made by navigators, and their detection of errors in charts, is of great utility, and worthy of prompt imitation.

CORRESPONDENCE.

MR. EDITOR, *Charlestown, October 14.*

YESTERDAY arrived the British sloop of war, Peterell, Captain Lamborne. This vessel is one of the convoy of the Jamaica fleet, which left that island early in September.

Saturday afternoon, off North Edisto, the Peterell was engaged by a French privateer schooner, called the Superb, Captain Domonique, of 14 guns, and 150 men, which has been cruising off this port, for some days past, with an intention of taking the Two Friends.

The privateer ran alongside, and attempted to board, when a broadside from the Peterell was poured into her, which made great havoc among her crew. The action lasted about twenty minutes, when the Frenchmen sheered off, and set all sail to ecape. The Peterell gave chase, which was continued for some hours; but by the superior sailing of the privateer, she got the weather gage of the ship, and escaped. Lieutenant Maitland, and one man of the Peterell were killed in the skirmish, and four men wounded. When the privateer attempted to board, one man more forward than the rest sprang into one of the port-holes, and is now a prisoner on board the Peterell. He says that from 30 to 40 were killed on board the schooner before he left her. They took the Peterell for a guineaman, nor did they discover their mistake until they had got alongside, when they found her to be a vessel of war. One of the officers attempted to haul down their colours, but the Captain instantly blew out his brains. The privateer received much injury in the action, had her larboard bow beat in, and it is supposed, should she meet with any bad weather, she must inevitably sink; it is therefore probable she will go into Savannah, and have the necessary repairs done to her. They may as well repair this privateer, as give provisions, water, &c. to the one which captured M'Neal. Fortunately for Captain M'Neal, the Petcrell left the convoy to see her safe in, as the privateer knew the Two Friends, and was determined to take her. The remains of Lieutenant Maitland were brought up to town this morning, and interred in the burying-ground of St. Philip's Church. A detachment of marines, and a number of sailors belonging to the ship, preceded the corpse, which was followed by the officers of the ship, and the British Consul, as mourners, and a number of respectable merchants and citizens closed the procession. At the grave, the funeral honours usually paid upon such occasions were performed by the marines in such a manner as to do credit to the most veteran troops.

Five days after the action, the privateer brought to the ship Rolla, Hutchison, of Charleston, from Liverpool, about 100 miles eastward of the bar, and forced Captain Hutchison on board with his papers, where he was immediately surrounded by upwards of 18 of the crew, who, after many violent threats, were proceeding to deprive him of his papers, and threatening to send his ship to Curacoa; but Captain Hutchison producing papers accompanied with certificates from the American Consul at Liverpool, that his cargo was American property, he was allowed to proceed. Captain Hutchison found that they had not omitted supplying themselves with stores, articles of clothing, &c.

Extract of a Letter from an Officer on board the ARETHUSA *Frigate, dated Barbadoes, January* 13, 1806.

AFTER a very perilous, although speedy passage, we have arrived in Carlisle Bay with a part of our convoy.—We sailed from Cove on the 12th Dec. with a convoy of 23 ships, having the Wasp sloop of war and the Boadicea in company. On the 16th, when in lat. 46° 8′ N., long. 12° 14 W., we fell in with a squadron of the enemy's ships, (supposed to be the Rochfort,) consisting of five sail of the line, (one a three decker,) and three frigates; besides having nine sail so far to leeward that we could not make them out, but from subsequent information that we have gained, we suppose these nine sail to have been part of the African convoy under the Lark sloop, which they had captured some little time before; the Lark escaped. Early on the morning of the 16th, when we perfectly made them out, we made the signal for the convoy to disperse:—17 sail stood on to the S.W., the men of war and six sail tacked and stood to the N.W. The whole of the French squadron chased them, and during the whole day never detached any ships after the 17 sail that stood on to the S.W. —The Boadicea and Wasp, with the merchantmen, I think, if the enemy had continued the chase all night, might have stood a bad chance of being taken. But the Arethusa, contrary to all our expectations, seemed to fly: we could play round the whole of them. At night fall the enemy left off chasing, and tacked to the S. W. Captain Brisbane immediately ordered the Wasp to Rochfort, Ferrol, Cadiz, and Gibraltar, to give the requisite information to the respective Commanders on these stations, and ordered the Boadicea to keep sight of the enemy wherever they went; and if they fell in with any men of war, to send them to Admiral Cornwallis directly. At 12 o'clock that night we steered W. with the six sail of the convoy, and by day-light the next day, to our utter astonishment, we again discovered the enemy in chase of us with all sail set, but yet at a very great distance: they chased us for a few hours, and then left it off, as a hopeless effort. Shortly after we fell in with the Active frigate, and sent her also to watch the motions of the enemy, and dispatched the Boadicea directly to Admiral Cornwallis. By these precautions that we have taken, we have not only saved all our convoy, (not one of them has been taken,) but I trust in God that all the French ships are, before this time, in possession of some of our cruisers. On the 23d ultimo we fell in with Sir John Thomas Duckworth and six sail of the line, with two frigates, near Madeira, and gave him the information detailed above. They had been to Teneriffe after the very squadron we had met with, and learned that they had been actually there, and had taken part of the Lark's convoy, and left Teneriffe only two days before the British squadron arrived there. On our passage out we fell in with two more of our convoy, and learned from them that not a ship had been taken: and upon our anchoring here this day, we, to our great surprise, found Sir J. T. Duckworth and his squadron at anchor. An old messmate of mine, belonging to the Canopus, one of his squadron, has just come on board to see me, and informed me that two days after they spoke us (the 25th ultimo,) they fell in with six sail of the line and a frigate, and chased them for two days, but lost them at last in thick weather. As the squadron was short of water, they bore up to protect us, thinking that the enemy were in pursuit of us. They have not since been heard of, and Sir John sails again to-morrow for England. I have been thus particular, because I have literally nothing else to say. I have not been on shore here, as we are to proceed to Jamaica with that part of the convoy which is bound there, and Jamaica is our station. Although the weather is now excessively hot, I have felt no inconvenience further than perspiring profusely, which I conceive to be very salutary.

MR. EDITOR,

THE following singular Letter appeared in the Gentleman's Magazine for January (page 36). I am unable to comprehend its drift: perhaps some of your Correspondents may.

Q.

MR. URBAN, *Jan.* 9.

WHEN the British Admiral, during the American war, was ordered to retreat before the combined Spaniards and French in our own channel, the ships accordingly ran up to the eastward; yes, ran away, Mr. Urban; the seventy-fours having the fire-ships in tow. In that disgraceful scene a Boatswain's Mate stept over the ship's bows, and lashed a double hammock fast round the figure head of the late king. "What are you doing there?" says the Lieutenant on the forecastle;—"Only securing his peepers," says Jack.—"Peepers! d—mn you, what do you mean?" bawls the Boatswain.—"Why, we arn't ordered to break the old boy's heart, are we? I'm sure if he was once to turn, and see this day's work, not all the patience in Heaven would hold him a minute longer."

The crew of one of our capital ships are just now as indignant as our friend the Boatswain's Mate; and I feel commissioned to acquaint your readers with some particulars not recorded (in Vol. XXXI, page 617,) merely to show, that great and unequalled as the whole profession and life of Lord Nelson has been, there existed, at all times, Captains of his own stamp, who never threw away a shot.

When the Bellona, in 1761, was closing with the Courageux, the French had begun to fire, and there appeared some impatience amongst the people on the main deck to return it: but Faulknor, our gallant Captain Faulknor, (and all of that name since have proved of the same metal,) leaned forward over the barricade—"*My Boys*," said he, "*hold hard, I'll tell you when to fire: let us see the white of their eyes first, and take my word for it, they will never stand the singeing of their whiskers.*"

This was emphatic language to sailors, often heard before, and often since; but never on so great an occasion, as from our departed Hero on board the Victory off Trafalgar.

Mr. Urban, you have already given the result *. We knocked up the Courageux in less than an hour; and added a most useful seventy-four to the British Navy; while Captain Logi , in the Brilliant, beat off the two French frigates, which never dared to come near her.

The glory of the ship alluded to, may suffer eclipse by mismanagement, but her acquired honours can never be taken away. The spirit of a Douglas will renew her greatness, and keep her steady in any course that may lead to battle. Methinks every original beam, knee, stancheon, and carline, creaked out disappointment, when that unexplained application of the rudder turned the good ship from the track of the enemy. *Sub judice lis est.* All the country requires a knowledge of this business; and if no better account is received from Plymouth, one may be reckoned upon from me.

J. H.

MR. EDITOR, *St. John's, Newfoundland, Nov. 24, 1805.*

OUR passage to this dreary place has furnished a singular instance of Divine protection; sufficient, I imagine, to convince the most stubborn atheist, if such a monster really exists, of the existence of a God.

We sailed from St. Helens, 21st May, 1805, for Newfoundland, and on the fifth of June crossed the Flemish Cap, or False Bank. On the sixth, after being foggy for near twenty-four hours, it cleared up, and we saw a large island of ice; we were in latitude 47° 30′ N., longitude 47° 30′ W., more than two hundred miles from the land. In the evening it came on foggy again: and about two o'clock, in the middle watch, having passed several small pieces of ice, and thinking that they d noted a proximity to a large island, the Captain ordered the ship to be hove-to on the starboard

* Our readers will find some new and interesting particulars relative to this celebrated event, in the first memoir of our next Volume.

tack, as the fog was come on very thick, and the ship was going about seven knots under her top-sails.

About ten minutes after the ship had been hove-to, a monstrous island of ice was discovered by the Captain, close to us, on the lee bow—Our ship had just fallen off. By his direction the main-top-sail was filled—the spanker hoisted, and the ship hove in stays. The island was by this time so near, that the same wave washed against it and our sides; and the daylight coming on, displayed our dreadful situation in all its horrors. Never before did I witness so terrific a scene! The Ice Island was at least 300 feet high; and so close, that it towered over our mast heads; the sea breaking over it with a tremendous roar.

When the ship came-to, we found we should just weather it on the tack we were on: the helm was righted, and as it was perfectly steep, we cleared it! If like many we afterwards saw, it had possessed any projecting pieces, our ship must inevitably have been dashed to pieces; and in all probability every soul lost, as we were quite alone.

After this providential escape, the weather held clear for a few hours, when we found ourselves surrounded by a number of Ice Islands. So that whenever it came on foggy, which it frequently did, and so thick we could scarce see the bowsprit end, we were in danger of instant destruction, and therefore either hauled to the wind, instead of making the best of a fair wind, or kept on our course with the yards braced up. In one middle watch we counted fifteen islands. Being unable to avail ourselves of the fair wind, we did not make St. John's till the 9th; and every time the fog cleared away, we saw a number of islands all round us, some more than three quarters of a mile long, and all upwards of 300 feet high, and as hard as rock. After making St. John's, it came on so thick we were obliged to stand off under a close reefed main-top-sail and fore-sail, and the wind being easterly, the harder it blew the thicker the fog was, and we did not get in till the 11th. There were so many islands of ice off the harbour's mouth, that it was difficult to find a passage, and some lay aground in 90 fathoms. They are frequently seen to go right in the wind's eye at the rate of three knots an hour, carried by a current, which is not felt on the surface of the water. To give you an idea of their bulk, it is computed that they always float seven-eights *under* water. The oldest inhabitant at Newfoundland does not remember so much ice as has been seen this year.

MR. EDITOR,

CONCEIVING that some of the recent proceedings of the American Senate, relative to the impressing of seamen, and the non-importation of British commodities, demand the serious attention of our legislature, I am induced, through the meduim of your widely-extended publication, to offer a few remarks on these subjects.

The impressing of seamen belonging to the United States, by British cruisers, has long been matter of complaint on the part of the Americans; and, from the difficulty which exists, in distinguishing the natives of England from those of America, it is possible that they may have some cause for dissatisfaction. The Americans assert, that they have remonstrated with the British government on the subject, and that their remonstrances have not been attended to. There is some difficulty in believing this. At all events, the sanguinary measures which have been proposed by some of the Members of Congress, are wholly without an excuse.

It appears, from the American papers, that on the 20th of January, a Bill was brought forward in the Senate of the United States, by a Mr. Wright, a Member for Maryland, entitled, "*A Bill for the Protection and Indemnification of American Seamen.*" I shall not trouble you with the detailed provisions of this instrument. It will suffice to state, that it goes to enact, that all persons who shall impress seamen from on board an American vessel, shall be adjudged "PIRATES and FELONS," and, on conviction, shall suffer DEATH! that, in case any one shall thus attempt to impress, the person on whom the attempt shall be made shall be entitled to a bounty of two hundred dollars for *killing* or *destroying* the offender; and that every impressed seaman, on board a foreign ship, shall be entitled to sixty dollars per month for his services while on board: all of which sums so paid, *to be taken fram any private money due from citizens of the United States to citizens of the offending power.*

Setting aside the vindictive and sanguinary nature of such a Bill, it contains more serious matter of comment than may at first strike the eye. On consideration, it will be found to amount to a distinct declaration, that no officer of a British ship must take British-born seamen out of any vessel *carrying the American flag*, under the penalty of being treated as a pirate and a felon, and suffering death! Thus, if every man in the British Navy were induced by Americans to desert and enter into their service, we must not claim them as British subjects, because they may have been naturalised by the President of the United States of America.

Another view, which the framer of such a measure must unquestionably have had, is that of holding out an invitation to our seamen to desert, and promising them protection and reward. Such doctrines, so openly and so vindictively avowed, call for immediate and decisive notice.

The remonstrance which Mr. Monro, the American Minister resident at the British Court, has presented, is far more sensible, temperate, and even conciliating. "The United States," says he, "are aware, from the similarity in the person, in the manners, and above all, the identity of the language, which is common to the people of both nations, that the subject is a difficult one. They are equally aware," he continues, "that to Great Britain also it is a delicate one, and they have been willing, in seeking an arrangement of this important interest, to give a proof, by the mode, of their very sincere desire to cherish the relations of friendship with her."

The discussions on this subject have been followed up by a resolution, brought forward in the House of Representatives, prohibiting the importation of all goods or merchandise, of the growth, product, or manufacture of Great Britain, or of any of the colonies or dependencies thereof, into the United States. The alledged causes for this resolution are, our impressing citizens of the United States, and compelling them to serve on board our ships of war; and seizing and condemning vessels belonging to citizens of the United States, not contraband of war, and not proceeding to places besieged or blockaded, under the pretext of their being engaged in time of war, in a trade with our enemies, which was not allowed in time of peace.

Notwithstanding this resolution, the injustice of which is evident at the first glance, it is notorious, that the American flag is frequently hired out to our enemy, for a small sum, to be used for the double purpose of relieving that enemy from the calamities of war, and of enabling him to carry on war upon us with better effect; and the identical American merchants, who are so furiously clamouring against the injustice of our Navy, are in the daily habit of committing the grossest crimes, in order to rob that Navy of the prizes which should be the reward of its toil and courage.

With respect to any warlike attempts, on the part of America,

Serres del.
Hall sc.

against this country, notwithstanding her boastings and insults, the very idea is ludicrous; for, according to the last official statement of her naval force, presented on the 30th of January, she is only in possession of eleven frigates, four brigs, two schooners, two bombs, and a few gun-boats; a great part even of this force being unfit for service.

Whether the Bill which I have first alluded to, has finally passed into a law, is not yet known in this country. It is sincerely to be hoped, notwithstanding the infuriated spirit of some individual members of the Congress, that the American government will be found to entertain a greater respect for justice, than to stain its annals by a consent to a measure so repugnant to every honourable feeling.

Every well-wisher of his country, both in England and America, must regret that the citizens of the latter power should weakly suffer themselves to be led away by the suggestions of French emissaries, who swarm throughout the United States, and who are indefatigably employed in exciting discontent, and fomenting differences. Their natural sense ought to inform them, that these men, as well as their employers, would gladly witness the destruction of both nations, in the selfish hope of establishing a commerce amidst their general ruin. I am, &c.

AN ENEMY TO CRUELTY, OPPRESSION, AND INJUSTICE.

PLATE CCII.

THE details of naval encounters officially published by government, being confined almost solely to those actions which have been fought and conducted by officers bearing His Majesty's commission, a variety of contests in the *petite guerre*, sustained by persons commanding private ships and vessels fitted for war, pass unrewarded by the honest applause of their countrymen, merely on account of their want of publicity. Without intending the most distant slight on the exertions of those brave and able men, who have so unremittingly displayed their talents in the service of their country as officers of the Royal Navy, we hope we may stand excused in saying, that actions have been fought by various ships and vessels, the property of private individuals, which would have reflected the highest honour on the best disciplined, and best conducted ship of war belonging to the public service. We know of no one, that has evinced more gallantry, more professional ability, or nautical skill, than that which was displayed in the rencounter of which we are about to give a plain but truly interesting detail, extracted purely from the minutes taken either during the action itself, or immediately subsequent to it.

Narrative of the Proceedings on board the Armed Lugger, ARISTOCRAT, *commanded by Captain* WILKINS, *on the 15th of July,* 1795.

AT five A.M. we took on board eight Frenchmen, together with Mons. Prejant, from off the coast of France, where the greater part of them had been employed on secret service. They informed us, that orders had been received at St. Maloes, directing the superintendant of that port to send out every armed vessel, capable of putting to sea, for the purpose of either taking, or at least driving us off the coast. To this account we at first paid but very little attention; but one of the persons who reached us, having most solemnly asserted he had himself ran from one of the vessels in question, at ten P. M., on the preceding day; and added to that assurance a declaration equally serious, that his son commanded another of the flotilla intended for the service in question, we considered the information too important to be totally neglected; and accordingly made every effort in our power to work up to the island of Choze. The wind being to the northward and westward, and a flood tide running, we stood off shore with our larboard tacks on board, and discovered soon afterwards to the westward of us a large cutter, bearing down directly before the wind. We then tacked to the southward, and ran in shore; and on a second tack we made to the northward, we fetched the island of Choze; we then came to an anchor, intending, if we were permitted to do it without interruption, to lay there during the remainder of the tide. The cutter, which we had discovered in the morning, kept on her course, till she reached within gun-shot of us, when she immediately began to engage. Every thing being properly prepared on board the Aristocrat, under the expectation of the attack, we immediately slipped our cable, and put the lugger under all the sail she could possibly crowd, in chase of the enemy. A brisk and constant fire was spiritedly maintained on both sides; but the distance from the shore being short, the cutter got under the guns of a strong battery, and the Aristocrat was under the necessity of giving up farther pursuit. We immediately stood into the offing to the northward, and presently afterwards saw a flotilla, consisting of several armed vessels, coming down before the wind, toward Choze; at the same time, the cutter first chased, stood out under an easy sail, and worked to the westward, keeping a respectful and proper distance from us, out of gun-shot. Finding we had no means of avoiding an action with the whole of the enemy's force, which had by this time reached the island of Choze, and was lying too, ready to receive us, the Frenchmen on board manifested the strongest agitation and alarm, at the apprehended risk they ran of suffering an ignominious death, provided they fell into the hands of their pursuers.

I (Captain Wilkins) assured them they might rest extremely easy, that they should not be made prisoners: and I gave them this assurance under the positive determination I had formed, that if the enemy's flotilla so far succeeded in the attempt of laying us on board, in such force as to render escape impossible, that I would fire the powder-room, which contained, exclusive of that intended for the use of the lugger herself, 125 barrels, which we had been ordered to land, if possible, in France. When we came within gun-shot of the brig which lay most to the eastward, she immediately opened her fire on us: this circumstance took place at half past ten A.M., and the salute was instantly returned by the Aristocrat; not only so far as regarded herself, but also the cutter first chased, which had by this time got up so close alongside to leeward, that we must have ran her on board, if she had not put her helm to starboard, for the express purpose of avoiding us.

The fire now became general, and very heavy;—the Aristocrat lay in the very centre of the enemy's squadron;—the shouts of *Vive la Republique* issuing from every vessel belonging to the flotilla, were loud and incessant: at the same time the huzzas on board the Aristocrat were no less violent and animated. The French Commodore lay nearly in the centre of his squadron, bearing a distinguishing pendant. His ship, which was called the Societé Populaire, mounted eighteen 18-pounders; and as though considering our capture an event of absolute certainty, he had actually hoisted out his boats, in order that as little delay as possible might take place in the removal of our people when made prisoners on board his own ship, and the other vessels under his orders.

Finding we should be under the necessity of passing within pistol-shot of the Commodore, I considered it most prudent to reserve our fire till we approached him as close as possible. Having acted in conformity with this resolution, we had very soon the satisfaction of finding the enemy must have received considerable damage: he showed no inclination to press the encounter; and the Aristocrat having shot a little a-head, after sustaining very little injury in this spirited and unequal action *, stood on with her starboard tacks on board, for the Diligence, a brig mounting twelve 18-pounders, and the Rondell, a vessel of the same description, carrying fourteen 6-pounders, which lay prepared, and ready to receive us. Being under the disagreeable necessity of passing directly between these vessels; and being consequently obliged to luff up for one, and bear away for the other, in orde to give our fire the greater effect, we unfortunately fell to leeward; and had to sustain not only the attack of the two brigs just mentioned, but also that of nearly the whole of the enemy's squadron, which kept an incessant and galling fire on us.

In this manner did we continue engaged, till we had stood within gun-shot of a large fort belonging to the enemy, situated at the entrance of St. Maloes harbour: we accordingly tacked at two P.M., to the northward, being at that time too, actually surrounded by all the enemy's vessels. The fire continued on both sides without the smallest interruption; but we had at length the satisfaction of perceiving that a cutter, which had very materially annoyed us, was water-logged: she left off chase, and immediately ran for St. Maloes. At four P.M. we tacked, and stood to the southward; the whole of the French coast being all this time lined with people, who were in the most earnest expectation of beholding the surrender of the Aristocrat.

The engagement was maintained, some very trivial intervals excepted, with as much fury as ever; the Aristocrat having tacked every two hours alternately to the northward and southward, till half past ten o'clock; by which time she had worked well up to windward. Finding the tide had now shifted in shore, we tacked off Cape Frechel, under the bows of the Diligence, which was at that time the headmost of the enemy's squadron. We exchanged several broadsides with this vessel; but having by this time gained the weather-gage of the whole flotilla, and the night coming on dark, we soon lost sight of the enemy; and having stood on till we discovered the Minques rocks, we there came to anchor, the people being completely exhausted, having been in action, almost incessantly, for the space of nearly eighteen hours.

* See the plate.

List of the Squadron which we engaged.

Societé Populaire,	ship, ...	18	18-pounders.
La Diligence	brig, ...	12	do. do.
La Brave	ditto	4	36-ditto.
La Rondell	ditto	14	6-ditto.
La Furette......	ditto	12	4-ditto.
L'Harmonie	ditto	4	24-ditto.
Le Terreur	cutter....	10	4-ditto.
Le Marat	ditto	10	4-ditto.
La Furette.....	lugger....	3	24-ditto.

The Aristocrat mounted four 6-pounders, and 8 fours.

N.B. Mr. J. Richardson was sent by the Prince de Bouillon with a flag of truce into St. Maloes. From him we received authentic information, that the enemy's squadron received very considerable damage in the engagement. On board the Societé Populaire the slaughter was not only prodigious, but five of her guns were dismounted, her hull much damaged, her sails and rigging shot to pieces; the Diligence had five men killed, and several wounded; one of the cutters was so disabled, that when she got into St. Maloes, she had seven feet water in her hold. We were certain indeed, before we gained the intelligence just mentioned, that the injury sustained by the enemy must have been excessive, since we were for several hours incessantly engaged within pistol shot.

Captain Wilkins at present commands a small schooner*, called the Princess Charlotte, mounting six carronades, employed as an hired tender, intended to be attached to the command of Sir Sidney Smith. This is the only provision, public or private, that has been hitherto made for him. He commanded the Aristocrat five or six years, both before and subsequent to the action just described; but never was in the

* In order to account properly to the reader for the apparent temerity of Captain Wilkins, in threatening to blow up his vessel, rather than submit to become a prisoner, it is necessary to state that the government (as it was called) of France, on account of the mischief the Aristocrat had effected, by the introduction of casual supplies, &c. to the insurgents in la Vendée, had publicly offered a reward of 2000*l*., as a national act, to any person who should capture Captain Wilkins. After such conduct, he certainly had every reason to expect he would be compelled to undergo indignities before his death did take place, far worse than even death itself.

Royal Navy, being employed only as the Master of his own vessel, which was hired, or chartered by government. The Aristocrat was, towards the conclusion of the war, taken into dock, repaired by Mr. Wilkins at a very considerable expense, and, at the express stipulation of government, converted into a brig. When refitted, and sent to sea a second time, a Lieutenant in the Navy was put on board to command her, and Mr. Wilkins consequently became destitute of employment; in which state he remained till the gallant Sir Sidney, as the friend and patron of neglected merit, procured him the appointment he now holds.

The ingenious Mr. Serres has judiciously chosen, as the subject of his sketch, that interesting period of the encounter, when the Aristocrat, having disabled and passed the Societé Populaire, stood on to engage the Diligence and Rondell.

Naval Reform.

THE SIXTH REPORT OF THE COMMISSIONERS OF NAVAL INQUIRY.

[Continued from page 220.]

AS the business of a dock-yard is of a complicated nature, and as we conceive the detail will be better understood by branching it into as many heads as the subject will admit, we shall therefore pursue that course in our reports; and shall commence with,

The Mode of employing and paying the several Classes of ARTIFICERS *and* LABOURERS.

The number of artificers and labourers, borne on the books of His Majesty's dock and rope yards at Plymouth on the 6th of September, 1803,

How have the caulkers been employed and paid during the late war, and how are they employed and paid at present?—The caulkers have been and are employed by stint on new work, and job on old work, and have attended, except in cases of new work, on ships' wales and bottoms, the same hours as the shipwrights, which I have before stated, and have been paid at the same rate of earnings, by a note from the master shipwright, and a certificate thereon from the master caulker or foreman, that the quantity of work had been performed, to

was two thousand four hundred and ninety-six. The annual amount of the wages paid to the workmen, and for the hire of the teams employed, in the years 1758, 1780, and from 1793 to 1802, has been as follows:—

Year.	Amount of Workmen's Wages.		
	£.	s.	d.
1758......	73,904	8	0
1780......	109,771	8	0
1793......	135,592	15	5
1794......	143,079	19	8
1795......	144,511	8	9
1796......	152,462	18	5
1797......	176,974	13	11
1798......	167,369	19	0
1799......	189,003	10	11
1800......	200,050	9	1
1801......	206,064	8	3
1802......	132,205	16	6

entitle them to the extra they were allowed to work, which is stated in the note. When employed by stint on new work on ships' wales and bottoms, if their work is performed by certain hours limited by the master shipwright, they leave the yard when the work is done. The caulkers' schemes of job and stint, dated 6th May, 1773, and the 5th December, 1783, differ from the mode of payment of other artificers when employed by job and task, who, to earn a double day's pay, do twice the quantity of work required of them for a single day's pay, whereas the caulkers earn a double day's pay, doing less than twice the quantity of work required of them to earn a single day's pay, as follows:—

	For a Single Day.	One Tide.	Two Tides.	The Double Day.
For caulking a Seam of Plank 3 inches in thickness, they are required to perform.....Feet	30	7½	15	25
Do....of ten inches..........	13	3	6	10

How have the joiners, house carpenters, bricklayers, and masons, been employed and paid during the late war, and how are they employed and paid at present?—Joiners have been employed by task, agreeably to the Navy Board's warrants of 2d June, 1774, 22d March, 1775, the 13th June, 1785, and 22d February, 1786, and by job work during the late war. The propositions for task and job have been transmitted to the Navy Board at the beginning of each month, and a certificate of their monthly earnings, signed by the master shipwright, was sent to the clerk of the check and to the Navy Board, in the form prescribed. The house carpenters, bricklayers, and masons, have been employed by task or piece work at different times since the year 1765, whenever large works in their respective branches of business, and the prices to be paid for the same, could be proposed to the Navy Board for their approbation. The house carpenters,

The principal classes of artificers employed in the yard are,

SHIPWRIGHTS,	BRICKLAYERS and MASONS,
CAULKERS,	SAILMAKERS,
JOINERS,	RIGGERS,
HOUSE CARPENTERS,	and
SMITHS,	ROPEMAKERS.

The whole of the workmen, except the three latter classes, are employed under the direction and superintendance of the master shipwright; the

---

bricklayers, and masons, have been employed by job, being proposed monthly, the same as for the joiner's task.

Were the propositions sent to the Board at the beginning of each month for the employment of the joiners, house carpenters, bricklayers, and masons, regularly acted on?—In many cases they could not, other works intervening which required to be immediately attended to.

In the return made to the Navy Board at the end of each month, of the work performed, was any deviation from the proposition noticed?—Never, to the best of my recollection.

By what authority did the clerk of the check set off the earnings of the men employed on jobs, not proposed to the board at the beginning of the month?—By a certificate from the master shipwright, stating that work was performed to that value.

Was it possible that the proposition for works to be performed by job, sent in the beginning of the month, could include all the works that might be requisite to be performed in the course of that month?—In many instances not.

With whom did the propositions for the employment of the joiners, house carpenters, bricklayers, and Masons, by job, and the prices to be paid, originate?—With the masters of the several branches, who represented the work to be performed, and the price to be paid, to the master shipwright for his approbation.

Did the wages and emolument of such persons during the late war, by the employment of their apprentices, depend on the amount of the prices so proposed?—Yes, until 1st July, 1801, when the new regulations of the yard took place.

Are there any classes of artificers now employed in this yard by job, who estimate the amount and value of their own work?—The blockmakers, cooper, brazier, locksmiths, and plumbers, usually make out their accounts of work performed and the value thereof, and which are examined and corrected by the master shipwright, and monthly certificates of their earnings sent to the clerk of the check's office, signed by the master shipwright and one of the men of each branch.

Can the master shipwright possibly be acquainted with all the works performed by such persons in their several branches?—I conceive he cannot. The present master shipwright investigates the prices to be allowed very closely; but, I conceive, the quantity of work performed is ascertained by the workmen, who sign the note previous to the master shipwright.

When were such persons first employed on job work, and how were they before paid?—The plumber and brazier were first employed by job, by the Navy Board's warrant of 30th March, 1796; the blockmakers, locksmith, and cooper, in consequence of the Board's warrant of 10th October, 1801, were first employed by job in December following. They were formerly employed such extra as the service required by day work, and were paid at the established rate.

Do the earnings of such persons, whilst they continue to be paid by job, very

sailmakers and riggers are under the master attendant; and the ropemakers are considered as a separate establishment, under the direction of officers specifically appointed for the purpose.

The vacancies for artificers and labourers are filled up by the nomination of the officers having the direction of them, subject to the approbation of the Commissioner; they are examined by the surgeon of the yard previous to their entry, to ascertain that they have no bodily infirmities; and each artificer is tried as to his professional skill and ability, by the foreman of the shipwrights or master workmen.

---

much depend upon the account they may choose to render of their own work?—Certainly.

Do you conceive it would be more advantageous to government to employ such persons by the day instead of by job?—Yes; I think it would.

How have the smiths been employed and paid during the late war, and how are they now employed and paid?—The common working day of the smiths is from six o'clock in the morning till six o'clock in the evening in the summer, and from six in the morning till dusk in the winter, and for a day's extra they remain in the yard beyond that time three hours. They have been, and are now employed as much extra as the service required, not exceeding three days' pay in one, except on anchor work, when they have been employed such further extra as the heat required.

How have the sawyers been employed and paid during the late war, and how are they now employed and paid?—The sawyers have been employed by contract, and paid according to the rates directed by the Navy Board. The work performed by the sawyers is ascertained by a shipwright appointed for that purpose.

How have the sailmakers been employed and paid during the late war, and how are they now employed and paid?—They were employed by task during the late war, according to the scheme established 17th May, 1764, and are now employed by task, agreeably to rates established in 1802, and their earnings are set off by a certificate from the master sailmaker to the clerk of the check, of the quantity of work performed by each man.

How are the riggers, riggers' labourers, scavelmen, and the labourers of the yard, employed and paid, and how have they been employed and paid during the late war?—The riggers and riggers' labourers during the late war, were employed extra as the service required, and paid for the same at the established rates; but were not employed by job work until the warrant of the Navy Board of 24th October, 1801, for which they are paid at the rate of double days in the single day hours, upon a certificate from the master attendant that they have performed work equivalent thereto; and they have been allowed extra since April last, of one or two tides, as the daylight would admit, for which they have been paid at the usual rate of fourpence a tide. Scavelmen, during the late war, when employed with the shipwrights, have been set off the same rate of working as the shipwrights. They are now paid by certificate from the master shipwright; those who work the single day hours at the rate of double days, and those who work four hours extra time at the rate of double days and two tides. The yard labourers are now, and have been employed by task not exceeding double days, except in particular instances in landing, preparing for survey, and stowing away stores, agreeably to a scheme dated the 3d April, 1758, to which alterations and

The common hours of labour in this yard have been regulated according to the different seasons of the year:—

From the 2d of December to the 1st of February, they are from seven o'clock in the morning till dusk in the evening:

From the 2d of February to the 1st of March, from half-past six o'clock in the morning to six in the evening, if the day-light will permit:

From the 2d of March to the 1st of October, from six in the morning to six in the evening:

From the 2d of October to the 1st of December, from a quarter past six in the morning to six in the evening, or as long as the daylight will permit:

The workmen have likewise a stipulated time for dinner, which varies also according to the seasons of the year; being two hours in summer, one hour and a half in spring and autumn, and one hour in winter.

The artificers and labourers are mustered by the clerk of the check, or some of his clerks, in general by the first and third; the workmen being

---

additions have been made by warrant of 2d September, 1772. Those employed with the shipwrights were set off the same rate of working as the shipwrights. Those labourers, at present not employed on task work, are paid at such rate of earnings as is certified by the master shipwright to the clerk of the check, that they have deserved, not exceeding double days pay in the single day hours. Those who work four hours extra time, are paid at the rate of double days and two tides.

Has the Navy Board's warrant of the 24th October, 1801, been constantly acted upon, so as to give the riggers and riggers' labourers double days pay for working in the single day hours?—Yes.

Had there been any order previous thereto, which gave to the riggers or their labourers more than the established rate of daily pay for working in the single day hours?—None, that I know of.

How have the extra men belonging to the ordinary been paid during the late war, and how are they now paid?—They are and have been paid at the rate of one pound four shillings a lunar month, and allowed provisions at the rate of extra petty warrant.

Do they ever receive extra pay?—Those employed on board the Navy transports have been allowed the increased wages of able seamen, and the full allowance of provisions, and are allowed voyage money for each trip to and from the eastern yards; but those employed in the general service of the port have no allowance of extra. The extra men employed in the commissioner's clerks of the check and surveying master's boats, when going on board ships in the Sound and Cawsand Bay, were allowed one day's provisions in addition to their ordinary ration, which has been discontinued since the last visitation of the Admiralty Board.

THOMAS NETHERTON.

Ewan Law.
John Ford.
Henry Nicholls.
William Mackworth Praed.

divided, and borne upon separate books, in order that they may be called at the same time in different parts of the yard, to save time in mustering.

When the workmen are allowed to leave the yard to dine, they are mustered three times a day; on their coming to work in the morning, on their returning from dinner, and again when they quit work in the evening; but when they are employed extra, and remain at work during their dinner time, they are mustered only in the morning and afternoon.

It has been * stated to us, that the workmen are allowed in winter from

---

* *The Examination of Mr. Thomas Netherton, continued 1st September*, 1803.

Is there any actual or implied contract entered into by the artificers and labourers at the time of their admission, with respect to forfeitures for non-attendance, or any other circumstance?—None, that I know of.

Is there any fee paid by the artificers and labourers on their entry, or for making out the quarterly certificate of the amount of the earnings?—There has been none to my knowledge, since the late regulations which took place on the 1st July last.

How often are the artificers and labourers mustered or called, and by whom?—The artificers and labourers are mustered at coming to work in the morning, and when they go out of the yard to dinner; they are mustered on their return, and on leaving the yard in the evening, by the first and third clerks, and by the other clerks in the office occasionally. The first clerk musters the shipwrights, quarter boys, blockmakers, caulkers, pitchheaters, and oakum boys, and the apprentices of those classes; the third clerk musters the rest of the artificers, the teams, and the labourers.

When do the musters commence, and what time does it take to muster the artificers and labourers?—The musters commence from ten to fifteen minutes in winter, and from five to ten minutes in summer, after the time appointed for the men's coming into the yard; and the musters occupy from twenty-five to thirty minutes.

How are the persons who may be present or absent at the muster, distinguished on the check book?—The mode of checking those absent, is by a dot above or below the line against the men's names on the check book; a dot above denotes their having been absent at the morning muster, and below at the afternoon muster. Those present at the respective musters, have a cross line drawn against their names; the following is an example:—

Absent morning and afternoon.........................

Present at the respective musters.........................

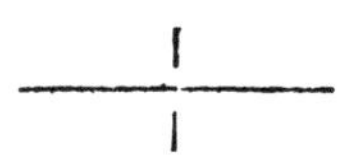

At morning muster only.........................

At afternoon muster only.........................

Have the muster books been kept locked up after mustering?—Generally they have, when not in use.

ten to fifteen, and in summer from five to ten minutes for assembling, beyond the time prescribed for their coming into the yard; and that the mustering takes up from twenty-five to thirty minutes.—Allowing the time

---

May the checks be removed by drawing a line over the dots, so as not to leave a trace of their having been checked?—It may be done.

Has the amount of the men's earnings by days, nights, tides, and half tides, been set off on the check book by characters above and below the musters, and carried from thence to the pay book?—Yes.

Do you think such mode of setting off the musters and earnings of the men would be liable to great abuse, if there should be a clerk in the clerk of the check's office inclined to give the men more wages than they had actually earned?—Certainly it might.

Do you know of any instances of such abuse, or attempts at such abuse, in this yard?—I do not know of any now; it has been practised; but, to the best of my belief, it has not existed since the enforcing of the late regulations, by the respective clerks taking the oaths, and giving the bonds required of them, in the month of October, 1801.

Were instances of taking off the checks upon the muster books of the yard frequent, prior to the enforcing of the late regulations in 1801?—If a man had lost a day or two in a quarter or half a year, the check has been taken off.

Do you know of any instances in which the earnings of the artificers and labourers have been set off on the muster and pay books beyond their actual earnings?—In the instances of apprentices and stationed men they have.

Were instances of setting off the earnings of such persons beyond their actual earnings frequent previous to the enforcing of the regulations in 1801?—I consider they were.

Has it been usual for any of the officers to employ the labourers or other persons belonging to the yard on their private affairs?—It has.

Were such persons always mustered?—Generally.

Does such practice now exist?—Not to my knowledge.

When was such practice discontinued?—To the best of my recollection at the commencement of the new regulations in July 1801; but it had been considerably reduced since the appointment of Commissioner Fanshawe.

Are there any artificers and labourers belonging to this dock-yard, who now receive pay and are not regularly mustered?—None.

Is there a daily report made, and by whom, of the persons who may absent themselves from the yard?—There is not a daily report made of persons who absent themselves; but a report is made daily to the Commissioner of such persons who are not present when called, but afterwards appear, and are not permitted to go to work; and likewise of persons who have permission to pass the gate, with the reason of such permission assigned.

After what period are men discharged who absent themselves from their duty without leave?—Usually six successive days, which is the time directed by the Navy Board; a return being then made to the Commissioner.

Is there any penalty or forfeiture attached to persons absenting themselves without leave?—No; but they do not receive wages for the time they are absent.

Does the surgeon of the yard furnish the check office with a list of the persons who may be sick, or incapable of performing their duty, and at what period?—The

so lost to be upon an average only half an hour, and the number of men belonging to the dock-yard to be two thousand one hundred and ninety, as it stood on the 6th of September 1803, there would be a loss of time in

---

surgeon of the yard furnishes the office with a list of the persons hurt in the service twice a week, and at intermediate times in cases of accident, but he takes no notice of the men sick; the men hurt are not put on the surgeon's note, without producing a certificate from the officer under whom they were employed at the time of receiving the injury.

Is the pay of such persons as may be hurt in the service continued to them, and for what period?—The single days pay is continued to them during the time they are on the surgeon's note.

Have you reason to believe that it has been a practice for men who have been sick, and not hurt in the service, to receive their pay by a note from the surgeon?—I have no reason to believe that it has been a practice lately: since Mr. Shephard has officiated as surgeon of the yard, he has, I believe, put a stop to it.

Have you any reason to believe that men have received extra wages when upon the surgeon's notes?—They never have to my knowledge.

How do you ascertain and distinguish in mustering those who are sick from those who absent themselves without leave?—From the officer under whom they work, or some of the men stating they are sick, and they are distinguished in the muster book by an S under the check.

When the men are answered for as being sick, does the surgeon visit them to see that they are so?—Not that I know of; he has no account of those said to be sick from the check office.

When men have been absent by sickness, have they ever been allowed to receive their pay during their absence?—They are not now, but in some instances they have been, before the late regulations.

Were such instances frequent prior to the establishment of the late regulations in July 1801?—They were not frequent.

What officers grant leave of absence to the artificers and labourers of the yard?—The master shipwright and master attendant grant leave of absence by note, which, if approved, is signed by the Commissioner.

Has their pay ever been continued to them when absent on leave?—Not to my knowledge, except when persons have occasional leave for a short time in the course of the day.

Are copies of the muster or call books sent to the Navy Board, and at what periods?—They never have been sent to my knowledge.

Is there any return of the musters of the yard made to the Navy Board?—None; but a weekly account of the numbers borne is sent.

Are there any artificers and labourers now employed in the yard, not on the list for superannuation, nor on the surgeon's note, who receive only single day's pay?—Yes, one caulker, one joiner, one house carpenter, and one labourer, who are infirm men, and the clerk of the chapel.

Are there any persons now employed in the yard, who only work during the common working hours, that receive less than double days pay?—I do not recollect any others than those before-mentioned, the men on the surgeon's note, and on the list for superannuation.

What is the amount of the pay and allowances per day of the scavelmen and

the course of the year by the morning and noon musters, equal to the employment of thirty-four thousand two hundred and seventy-three men for

---

labourers of this yard?—They were generally allowed, from the 12th to the 31st of March last, double days for working the single day hours, making the pay of the scavelmen three shillings, and of the labourers two shillings and fourpence a day, exclusive of threepence a day for chip money. In Midsummer quarter those employed the single day hours only, were allowed double days pay; and those employed four or five extra hours were paid at the rate of double days and two tides, making the pay of the scavelmen three shillings and eightpence, and of the labourers three shillings, exclusive of the chip money.

What is the price of labour in this neighbourhood?—I should suppose those employed in and about the town of Dock, about two shillings a day, and those in the country from one shilling and sixpence to two shillings a day.

Have there been any instances in this yard of artificers having been paid according to the prices allowed for job work, when employed upon task or new work?—Never to my knowledge.

Do you know what merchant shipwrights are paid by the day in this neighbourhood?—I am informed from three shillings and sixpence to four shillings a day, exclusive of drink money occasionally.

Has it ever been a practice in the clerk of the check's office in this port, to make application to the executive officers for job or task notes or certificates, in order to increase the wages of the artificers or labourers?—Never to my knowledge.

Who makes out the pay books of the yard?—The first and third clerks make out the pay books for the persons whom they respectively muster.

By whom are the pay books examined, and by whom are they signed?—The pay books are examined by some other clerk in the office, and signed by the clerk of the check.

Has the clerk of the check received all the vouchers necessarry to enable him to set off the earnings of the men for the quarter ending 30th June last?—He has not.

Do you conceive it to be possible, after the pay books are made out, that any person can go through all the calculations of the earnings of the men, necessary to examine and check the pay book previous to the usual time of its being paid upon?—I conceive it to be impossible, from the variety of services the men have been employed upon during the quarter, for each of which a distinct rate and amount of earnings must be calculated.

Do you apprehend it will be necessary to pay the artificers and labourers of the yard, on the calculation of their earnings, as it may be first set off on the pay book, before the calculations are checked?—I conceive it will not be paid before the calculations are checked.

How long do you apprehend the payment of the yard will be delayed beyond the usual period, in order that the pay book may undergo the necessary examination?—It will depend on the time we receive the job notes from the master shipwright's office, the greater part of which for that quarter are not yet received at the clerk of the check's office.

Have there been any instances in which the pay of men has been set off on the pay books, which to your knowledge they have not earned?—Only in the instances I have before stated.

a day; and the value of the labour so lost, estimating the pay of the workmen on an average at three shillings per day, is five thousand one hundred and forty pounds nineteen shillings.

How often is the yard paid, and for what periods?—Quarterly, and one quarter usually in arrear.

Are the pay books, and the several vouchers from which they are made out, sent to the Navy Board for examination previous to their being paid upon? —No.

Has the correctness of the amount of the earnings of the artificers and labourers of this yard, set off on the pay books during the late war, depended wholly on yourself and the other clerks in the clerk of the check's office?—Yes, I consider it has, as far as relates to the setting off the earnings from the several vouchers.

Have the vouchers, from which the earnings of the men have been set off on pay books, been regularly preserved?—Many notes and vouchers are missing.

To what circumstance is that owing?—Formerly, when the notes were few, they were regularly indorsed, and put away; but as the notes multiplied exceedingly of late years, they were only filed, in consequence of which some of the notes have been lost, but none of them intentionally mislaid or destroyed to the best of my belief. On my proposition to the present clerk of the check, the notes for extra work, and for employment of artificers, are now written in books.

How often have the men on the list for superannuation been mustered?—In general, when not on the surgeon's notes, daily.

What work have they in general performed, and what pay have they received? —I have generally understood light work in houses, and they have been only paid single day's pay.

Have there been any instances of men on the list for superannuation being paid extra wages?—None to the best of my recollection.

How long have you known a person to be continued on the list for superannuation before he has been superannuated?—In the instance of Thomas Davies, joiner, from the 1st October, 1797, to the 27th June, 1800, and several persons from 1st July, 1798, to the 27th June, 1800.

Whose duty is it to represent to the Navy Board the artificers and labourers, who, from age and infirmity, may be incapable of performing their duty?—The master shipwright and master attendant in their respective departments.

Has it ever been customary to muster the artificers and labourers in the presence of the officers of the yard, in order to see what men are fit for service, and who are objects for superannuation or discharge?—It has in some instances been done by the commissioner and officers of the yard, but not of late years: The commissioner attends the payment of the workmen quarterly, which is tantamount to a muster.

Upon a reduction of the number of artificers and labourers, has it been usual to select and discharge the idle, disorderly, and inefficient men?—The idle and disorderly men were usually first selected; and if a further number was necessary, those last entered were discharged, except in the discharge in November last, when the idle, disorderly, and inefficient men were discharged, without regard to their length of service; but those inefficient men who had good characters have been since superannuated.

[To be continued.]

CORRECT RELATION OF SHIPWRECKS.

[Continued from Vol. XIV, page 256.]

No. XIV.

Again the dismal prospect opens round,
The wreck, the shore, the dying, and the drown'd.

FALCONER.

IN our fourth volume, page 441, we inserted a short account of the melancholy loss of the CHARLES BARING West Indiaman; but that, being neither so circumstantial, nor so perfect as we could have wished, we have thought it not inexpedient to give the following more ample detail of that disaster, with which we have been lately furnished.

THE ship, Charles Baring, John Aris, Commander, sailed from Port Royal, in the Island of Jamaica, bound to London, on the evening of the 6th of September 1800; on the 8th she weathered the east end of the island, and on the following day made Navasa, as well as Hispaniola, otherwise St. Domingo: from this time till the 17th, the wind continued in general from the eastward, with light breezes, and remarkable fine weather for the season; on the 18th the ship cleared the windward passage, but the wind still continuing easterly, very little progress was made in the voyage during the remainder of the month. Nothing however very material occurred till the 5th of October, when a heavy gale of wind came on, which continued three days; during this time the cross-jack-yard, and the main-top-gallant-mast were carried away, and the main-top-sail split; but these were nevertheless disasters, comparatively trivial, to what might have been expected from the violence of the tempest. To these ostensible and manifest injuries, must however be added one, infinitely more dangerous, though not perhaps so conspicuous to a casual observer:—the frame of the ship, though originally by no means weak, had been violently shaken, by the tremendous swell which she had encountered during the preceding days; the vessel in question had originally been a Spanish corvette, captured by the English, and sold into the service of the merchants: ill constructed for such an occupation in the first instance, she became, when laden, still less capable of sustaining the rude shocks of those waves through which she had been necessitated to pass. Although there was no absolute leak so violent as to threaten immediate destruction, yet the seams of the vessel had opened so considerably by her working, that the quantity of water admitted through them in various places became in a few days truly alarming. On the 15th, in the morning, the situation of the crew became still more desperate, from the increased quantity of water, which found its way into the hold. So rapidly were the symptoms of the approaching disaster augmented, that ere night the constant labour of one pump was hardly able with the greatest exertions to keep the water under. By the 17th matters still became more desperate, and unremitted labour at both pumps became indispensably necessary. On the 20th, notwithstanding every exertion of the crew, the water gained on both pumps; and on the 21st, at five A. M., it was found, on sounding the pump well, that the ship had five feet water in her hold. Every effort had been previously made, without success, to discover some particular leak, which being reduced, might not only render the labour of the crew less intolerable, but afford some prospect of saving the vessel. The Captain, who, completely exhausted with incessant fatigue, had been under the necessity of lying down about an hour before the well was sounded, was immediately informed of the desperate situation in whch the vessel was; he accordingly ordered the gun-deck to be instantly scuttled on each side the main-mast, for the purpose of getting at the pump-well. This preliminary measure being effected, he caused two casks to be prepared for the purpose of bailing; a head was taken out of each, they were then slung, and the proper tackles fixed to them, for the purpose of hoisting and lowering them; a man was then stationed to attend each cask in the pump-well, where it was tilted over, and of course filled in an instant; six men being stationed above to each tackle fall, the casks were hoisted up with the greatest expedition, and a few seconds only intervened between the deliveries of the water, so that the ship was freed from more than a ton every minute, in addition to that which was discharged by both pumps, which were kept constantly at work: so serviceable was that measure, that by noon on the same day, the Captain and the crew had the inexpressible satisfaction to find their exertions had gained on the leaks nearly three feet. The joy however with which these glad tidings were received, and which manifested the most happy effects on the countenances of every individual, was unfortunately of very short duration. The coffee and cocoa in the hold got loose, and was carried by the stream of water into the well in such quantities, as almost entirely to choak the pumps, and render them useless. So grievously was this disaster felt, that the water gained very considerably during the night. At eight, A. M. on the 22d, the Captain ordered the guns to be thrown overboard, in the hopes of easing the ship: this necessary service was in a great measure executed merely by the passengers, whose active and reiterated exertions during the whole of the melancholy scene, merited the highest applause. At six P. M. the pumps became completely choaked, and useless; the depth of water in the hold had increased to seven feet, and was then rapidly gaining; the hands that had through necessity been compelled to quit the pumps, were ordered to heave as much of the cargo out of the fore-hold overboard, as could be got at; the ship being found to settle very much by the head. At two A. M. on the 23d the water had reached the orlop-deck beams; but at six A. M. the exertions of those employed in clearing the fore-hold had been so effectual, as to permit two other casks to be worked down the fore-hatchway, in the same manner as had been before practised, and still continued to be unremittingly persevered in, in the midships, or main-hold. A glimmering of hope now began for a short time to show itself; but alas! even this faint alleviation of sorrow and distress was but of short duration. The water was in some small degree indeed diminished, but at four P. M. the wind, which, though violent, had blown from a favourable quarter, for the preceding ten days, changed suddenly to the north east, with every appearance of the most unpropitious weather. At eight P. M. the Captain was under the necessity of ordering the ship to be hove to; at twelve o'clock the wind had risen to an hurricane, and the ship was laid on her beam ends: in this situation every effort became useless, for the water delivered from the casks upon the gun-deck, returned immediately back again into the hold, there being no passage for it through the scuppers. From this perilous situation, the preservation of the vessel was considered impossible; the people too were so jaded, from their unremitted exertions for the space of nine days and nights, that death almost instantaneous, which appeared surrounding them on every side, seemed rather as a welcome relief, from farther toil, than as an event replete with horror and distress. The gale still continued to increase, and the vessel long ere morning, was expected to founder every moment. At dawn of day, as an aggravation, if such were possible, of misery, the main-mast went over the side, and it was with the utmost difficulty that it was cut clear. No prospect now presented itself of saving the lives of any of the crew, except by means of a small long boat, and the jolly boat, which were not competent to contain more than half the number of persons on board. The preservation indeed of the smallest remnant, can only be attributed to one of those extraordinary interventions of divine Providence, which human adoration can never sufficiently revere. The instant the boats were hoisted out, the first care of Captain Aris was to cause four ladies, who were passengers on board, to be put into the largest, an operation of some difficulty, under the existing circumstances, but which was fortunately accomplished through his great exertions without accident, notwithstanding every time the boat approached the vessel, it was in danger of being overset by the very heavy swell, which was then running. A compass, a quadrant, a top-gallant royal, some water, and provisions, were afterwards conveyed into the boat, which was immediately veered astern. Captain Aris now addressed the people without agitation, he pointed out to them how impossible it was for the boats to save all, and the only expedient he could contrive for their farther assistance, was, that they should set to work, and form a species of raft, or catamaran, of cotton bags, spars, &c., on which it was possible they might keep themselves afloat till they were fortunate enough to fall in with some vessel capable of taking them up: Captain Aris added, that the boats should continue with them, for the purpose of supplying them with provisions and necessaries; he insisted at the same time, no person should quit the ship, until he himself did, and that he was determined to remain on board, either until she sunk, or till the raft was finished. To these orders, and in these regulations, the whole crew unanimously conformed, and acquiesced. They agreed to remain with him to the last moment, and to fulfil his commands with all possible promptitude: they accordingly immediately began to construct the proposed raft. We feel it difficult on this occasion to point out whether the greatest portion of praise was due to the Commander (Captain Aris) for the consummate coolness, intrepidity, and judgment which he displayed in the midst of immediately impending danger, or the strict principles of subordination manifested by the crew throughout the whole of the trying scene, and their promptitude in obeying all commands issued to them. Such conduct in both parties can scarcely receive adequate applause and veneration. To such men, and to such men only, can the art of navigating ships be safely confided.

A very short time before the ship actually foundered, a gentleman named Bennet, being one of the passengers, who had, together with the ladies already mentioned, got safe into the long-boat, called to Captain Aris, and pressed him in the most urgent manner to quit the ship, for he was positive she was then in the very act of sinking; Captain Aris, replied, "*Never! I will not quit her while she floats.*" Mr. Bennet spiritedly and affectionately replied, he would wait five minutes longer, and if the vessel did not founder within that time, he would return on board and share the same fate with him. By this time, the construction of the raft rapidly advanced; the labour of a single hour longer would have completed it; all persons on board however became apprised of their fate; the vessel foundered; the scene now became dreadful, and terrific in the extreme; every person that could swim, attempted to reach the boat, which was by this time at some distance from the ship; the rope having been cut by those who had first reached her, in order to prevent her going down in the same vortex with her, as would inevitably have proved the case, had not such measure been pursued. Some succeeded; others perished in the attempt; many appeared floating about on cotton bags, spars, &c., while a few hesitating to quit the ship, while the smallest portion of her remained above water to sustain them, waited their inevitable doom in silence, and increased if possible a mutual horror, by casting an anxious and supplicating look on their comrades in the boat, who possessed not the smallest possibility of rendering them any assistance whatever. At this awful moment, Captain Aris, who, true to his former professions, had continued with his vessel to the last, jumped into the sea, and with the greatest difficulty reached the boat, into which he was taken by the exertions of Mr. Bennet.

The situation of the survivors was but little less horrible, than that in which their comrades were seen but the instant before; the death of the former it was true they had been the melancholy witnesses of; but their own was considered also inevitable; it was supposed an impossiblity the boat could continue long supported above the surface of the water; there were on board her twenty-eight persons, a number doubling that which she was calculated to carry, in a moderate sea, and which consequently caused her to sink so deep, that she could scarcely be said to be suspended in the water.

The gale continued with unremitting violence; the sea ran mountains high; and as a prelude to the complete destruction of the whole, the jolly-boat, after being driven by a sea, which forced her with such violence against the rudder of the long-boat, as to carry it away, was sunk, together with two of the crew, which were all that were then on board her. The long-boat being so deep, the utmost exertions were necessary, to keep her free; part of almost every sea forcing its way into her, particularly if they chanced to be at the head of it, when it broke; in about an hour after the ship had sunk, Abraham Day, the man who was then employed in steering the boat with an oar, called out, a sea was following that would overwhelm it: the words were scarcely uttered, when the tremendous stroke was felt. As the immediate forerunner of their dissolution, "Lord have mercy on us!" became the unanimous exclamation. The boat, and all the unfortunate persons it contained, were literally buried in it; and some moments elapsed, ere they could distinguish each other. The boat was completely filled; the water ran over each gunwale; so that not an instant was to be lost in throwing every thing overboard, that could lighten her. The provisions, and the cask of fresh water, were immediately abandoned to the waves; the future prospect of a lingering death being preferred, owing to the natural clinging hope of life, to one more instantaneous. Fortunately, two or three buckets had been thrown into the boat; by the active use of which, and the aid of hats, which were incessantly employed in the same species of service, the water was bailed out, and the boat freed in a few minutes. Had, however, another sea followed, all must inevitably have perished. Captain Aris immediately observed, as though prophetically, that as Providence had spared them, when apparently so near the brink of eternity, his hopes revived; and he trusted that same Providence had decreed their future preservation.

Words could however hardly point out a situation more desperate than that to which these unfortunate persons were now reduced; they were almost totally destitute of water, being prudentially restricted to an allowance of two wine glasses only to each person in the twenty-four hours. The small portion of bread which they had on board, was damaged, and completely soaked through with the salt water, and there was no probability of their being able to make any land. The boat, notwithstanding every article that could possibly be spared had been thrown overboard, still continued so deep, that it was impossible to keep her in any other situation than before the wind and sea; an attempt towards any direct and specific course could not be even thought of; so that the miserable bark was of necessity abandoned totally to the mercy of the winds and of the waves.

In this dreadful condition did these unfortunate persons continue, without the means of contriving the smallest shelter, though constantly wet, and exposed to a violent gale, which blew extremely cold from the north-east, for the space of three nights and two days, when they were most providentially met with, and taken up by the American brig Harriett, belonging to New York, bound to Bristol. Words want sufficient energy to do justice to the humanity and benevolence which these hitherto unfortunate persons experienced both from the Captain and his crew: they themselves had, through the extraordinary length of their passage, been, through necessity, reduced to short allowance the day before; but notwithstanding their hospitality, in consequence of the number of their guests, appeared so violently to accelerate their own distress, if not their destruction, the most perfect philanthropy beamed in every eye; and the heart of the host, if the term be allowed, appeared to expand in as great a degree at the pleasure of relieving wants, as that of the guests could, with gratitude, at having them palliated. On the 6th of November, the brig happily reached Kinsale, in Ireland, where the greater part of the fortunate survivors were immediately landed.

We cannot conclude this short narrative without observing, first, that notwithstanding the hardships of various kinds experienced by the survivors, as well before they quitted the ship, as afterwards, one person only (General le Grand, a French General, a passenger) fell a victim to them; and secondly, that however great the general distress might be, of the persons who had quitted the ship, it was considerably aggravated by the peculiar situation of Madame Beauvais, and her two daughters, who experienced the inexpressible anguish of witnessing the dissolution of a most affectionate father, and a most tender husband. This gentleman, unable to make these much loved relatives hear his last words, drew his sword, and waving it three times over his head, took this method of bidding them an eternal farewell. By the ship's account she was in latitude 42° 30′, longitude 40°, when she foundered.

Names of the Persons saved in the Boat.

Captain John Aris; General le Grand, who died two days after we got on board the brig; Madame le Grand; Madame Beauvais; two Misses Beauvais; Captain Fitzmaurice; Mrs. Fitzmaurice; Thomas Bennet, Esq.; James Gatty, 2d Mate; George Darbish, Boatswain; Richard Jackson, Carpenter; John Jones, Gunner; Thomas Blayadine, Cook; George Rose, Gunner's Mate; twelve seamen, and one soldier.—Total, 28.

Lost.

General Beauvais; Mr. Murray, late Master of the Surprize frigate; M. de la Font, Doctor; Mr. Holloway, Chief Mate; two servants of Generals le Grand and Beauvais; ten seamen, and eleven soldiers.—Total, 27.

NAVAL LITERATURE.

An Essay on the Construction of the Sails of Ships and Vessels, with Plans and Descriptions of the Patent Sails, showing the many Dangers that may be avoided, and the Advantages derived from adopting the improved Sails, &c. By Captain MALCOLM COWAN, *of the Royal Navy.* 4to. pp. 12, with a Plate.

THIS little pamphlet contains a few short remarks on the defects of sails, as hitherto constructed; and adds thereto a very plain and concise description of the new invention, and of the various advantages that may be expected to result from the use and adoption of it. No person acquainted with the nature of maritime pursuits will hesitate for a moment in perfectly acquiescing with the opinion of the author, as to the magnitude and the importance of the subject. The constant and melancholy experience of years, and of ages, has incontrovertibly established the fact; and interest, as well as humanity, most imperiously demand that all possible attention, and candid investigation, in respect to the merits of the ingenious contriver, should be paid to him. The lives, as well as the property of thousands, would be rendered, by the success of his project, infinitely less subject to danger and destruction, than the imperfect art of navigating vessels in former years has proved them to be; and Captain Cowan, as well as Mr. Greathead, will have the satisfaction of passing through life with that most grateful of all consolations, the reflection, "*that he who preserves the existence of a single Roman citizen, deserves better from his country, than he who has contributed to the destruction of an hundred of its enemies.*"

We lament the want of sufficient room, to give a more extensive extract from this interesting little memoir. The following, however, will be found to convey no very imperfect idea of the arguments in favour of the invention. or, at least, of the necessity of some material alteration in the mode of sail-making, as hitherto practised.

"Ships are driven on shore every winter by hundreds, that might, with proper sails, have escaped all danger. The loss of one sail, in many situations, is followed by the inevitable loss of the ship and crew. Sails are often split in hauling up to reef, and it may be necessary to reef a sail that is worn, to preserve it from splitting; hence the necessity of their being constructed to reef without starting tack or sheet.

Many ships have been lost by not having time, or drift, to haul their courses up, to reef them on the yard, by which they risk their splitting; a circumstance which alone must convince the seaman of the utility of having sails that can be reefed without taking their effect off the ship.

Many dangers may be avoided, by carrying sail with safety to the masts and yards. A ship can carry top-gallant-sails that reef at the foot, with safety, when other ships must furl theirs; an evident advantage in many situations.

The top-sails of ships, with one or two reefs at the foot, can be reefed in a minute by one seaman, at each lower yard-arm, while they remain set with the top-gallant-sails over them, by only settling the hallyards; by which a ship in squally weather, on many occasions, would have a great advantage, particularly in chase, &c.; and when caught by a sudden shift of wind on a lee shore, or obliged to haul suddenly to the wind from sailing large.

The facility with which sails that reef at the foot can at all times be managed, would enable ships to make quicker voyages; and prevent them often, when weakly manned, from detaining fleets; by the difficulty and danger of carrying sail being entirely removed; and enable merchant ships to be navigated with fewer hands, which would be a considerable saving of expense, and a great advantage in time of war in particular, when men are so scarce.

If the sails were made with horizontal cloths and seams, the sails would stand better, particularly in a gale of wind; as the strongest direction of the cloth and seams would be opposed to the greatest force of the wind, which acts horizontally; and should the sail split in that direction, it would still remain full, and be less liable to blow away altogether, which is generally the case when a sail splits in a vertical direction. Storm stay-sails set purposely with the cloths horizontal, have proved this beyond a doubt.

Many seamen are lost every winter, by falling overboard from the yards while reefing the sails; as it is more dangerous, and requires longer time to perform in a gale of wind, than furling the sails, which is not so often necessary as reefing.

Ships may sometimes avoid a lee-shore, by carrying a timely press of sail; and when in that perilous situation, in a gale of wind, the safety of the ship may solely depend on the sails being kept set; though it may be necessary to reduce them, either to save them, or ease the ship. The common sails require to be hauled up, to be reefed, at the risk of splitting them, at a time, perhaps, when the ship is in imminent danger, from the want of sea room; and the best seamen of the crew must be sent on the yards, when they possibly may be much wanted on deck.

Whole fleets are often caught by a sudden shift of wind, on a lee-shore, thrown into confusion, and obliged immediately to reef their sails, at the same time the ships may require the whole of their crews on deck, to attend the working of the ship, to keep clear of each other; particularly when it happens in the night time, with the wind squally and variable.

When ships from foreign voyages enter the English or Irish channels in the winter time, when the days are short and the nights long. with weak or disabled crews, or men not accustomed to cold or frost, such as Lascars, negroes, &c.; it is with the greatest difficulty they can be prevailed on to go aloft; but should they get on a lee-shore, which all ships are liable to, and with an helpless crew, nothing can exceed the horror of their situation, should they not be able to proportion their sail to the wind in time to save the ship."

On the origin of the invention, the author thus briefly expresses himself:—

The origin of the invention of the patent sails was in a gale of wind, on a lee-shore, in which a line of battle ship was exposed for many hours to the danger of being totally lost, with all her crew, by the splitting of her sails, and the utter impossibility of reefing them. No human means then known, were left untried to save the ship; and when to all appearance every hope had vanished, and silent horror and resignation prevailed throughout, the obvious defects, and the erroneous construction of the sails for centuries past, became apparent. Fortunately for the world, Providence interposed, and, by a shift of wind, saved the ship and the invention from being buried in eternal oblivion, for the preservation of thousands, in ages to come.

We shall conclude with the following extracts, from authentic documents in the possession of the patentee; which may serve to convince those who have hesitated to adopt the patent sails, as to their utility, on the opinion of some of the most skilful and experienced officers of His Majesty's Navy.

On the 12th of March, in a very strong gale of wind from E.N.E., I had occasion to reef the courses: they were reefed in two minutes, with very few seamen, and without the least fret or chafing. They have many advantages over the old construction, particularly on a lee-shore, when weakly manned, as they can be reefed without starting tack or sheet, or a single man going aloft.

And I find the sail to haul up by far more snug, than the old way; and in my opinion I cannot perceive any objection against it.

My officers and men, from seeing them reefed in the gale, are quite delighted with them, now they perceive their utility.

Depend upon it, no seaman can start an objection, when they have seen them reefed in a gale of wind. It blew excessively hard, and we shipped several very heavy seas.

I think them particularly calculated for narrow-seas and lee-shores.

The day after we sailed for Plymouth, we bent our courses; and during our cruise we had frequent opportunities of trying your reef. The officers could not too much admire such an excellent invention, which, ere long, I have no doubt, will be generally adopted. To the merchant service it is of the greatest consequence; for it is so plain a thing, that the utility of it must strike any person that has ever been at sea.

I have shown my plan to the most distinguished officers, they highly approve of it: in fact, every person who has seen it is of the same opinion, and do not find one objection against it.

It is a plan I should adopt were I afloat again, and had the means of obtaining the sails.

I can reef the sails in two minutes; and it is much approved of by all my officers.

To the mode of reefing the courses by the foot, I am happy to give you my decided approbation; as you are enabled to reef a course without losing the effect of the sail, requires but a few men to take in the reef, and it is done in a shorter time than could possibly be expected; and I hope it may be adopted generally throughout the service.

On the foregoing subject there can be but one opinion; nor can that opinion be otherwise than favourable both to the invention and the inventor. We shall dismiss it for the present, owing, as we have already premised, to our want of sufficient room to amplify as we could wish. Considering it, however, as a desideratum of the highest importance, we shall at our first leisure return again to the charge, and state the numerous advantages expected, as the result of the invention; and add thereto such comments as may most forcibly strike us.

CHRONOLOGICAL SKETCH

OF THE

MOST REMARKABLE NAVAL EVENTS

OF THE YEAR 1805.

JANUARY.

7. A FRENCH messenger, with dispatches for the British Government, arrived in the Downs, having been received on board the Tickler gun-brig from a flag of truce which came out of Boulogne. This messenger was the bearer of the overtures after noticed in His Majesty's speech to Parliament.

8. Copies of the Spanish Declaration of War against this country received in London.

11. Letters of marque and reprisal issued against Spain.

12. The Doris frigate, Captain Campbell, lost near Quiberon Bay.

15. A French squadron sailed from Toulon, and some of the ships returned to that port, while others went into Spanish ports.

24. Counter Declaration of the British Government against Spain, and the Powers connected with the negotiation, laid before Parliament.

31. The London Wet Docks at Wapping opened, the tide admitted, and a brig introduced from the River Thames.

FEBRUARY.

4. The Acheron bomb and Arrow schooner, having a fleet of merchantmen under convoy, captured by two frigates belonging to the French squadron, which sailed from Toulon on the 15th of January. Almost the whole of the convoy, however, escaped.

6. Loss of the Abergavenny Indiaman, wrecked off the Shambles; the Captain, and nearly 300 of the crew and passengers, being drowned.

12. Debates in both houses of Parliament on the Spanish war.

17. His Majesty's ship Cleopatra taken in the West Indies by the Ville de Milan, a large French frigate. On the 23d, the Lea der fell in with the Ville de Milan, took her, and recaptured the Cleopatra.

21. A French squadron, which had sailed from Rochfort, landed troops in Dominica, and made an attack on that island, but were repulsed by General Pre-

vost. They afterwards visited other West India islands, levied contributions, and returned to France.

MARCH.

12. Intelligence received of the Centurion, of 50 guns, having beat off a French squadron, consisting of the Marengo, of 80 guns, Admiral Linois, and two strong frigates, in Vizagapatam roads.

18. The Tenth Report of the Naval Commissioners, on which the motions respecting Lord Melville, &c. were founded.

30. A fleet of 11 sail of the line, with troops on board, sailed from Toulon, and proceeded down the Mediterranean.

APRIL.

8. In the House of Commons, Mr. Whitbread moved a series of resolutions, founded on the Tenth Report of the Naval Commissioners, and censuring the conduct of Lord Melville. On the division, the numbers on each side were equal, viz. 216; and the Speaker gave his casting vote for the resolutions. The resolutions were presented in an address to His Majesty; and Lord Melville afterwards resigned his office of First Lord of the Admiralty.

9. The fleet from Toulon passed the Straits of Gibraltar, and formed a junction with the Spanish and French ships in Cadiz, from which the combined squadrons soon after sailed for the West Indies.

18. A meeting of the Livery of London, to consider the abuses brought to light by the publication of the Tenth Report of the Naval Commissioners, &c. This meeting was followed by a number of others on the same subject, in various parts of the country.

19. The expedition under the command of Sir James Craig sailed from Spithead.

24. Nine vessels belonging to the enemy's flotilla captured by our cruisers off Cape Grisnez.

26. A long debate in the House of Commons upon Mr. Whitbread's motion for a farther inquiry into the Tenth Report of the Naval Commissioners.—Mr. Pitt moved an amendment upon the motion, which was carried by a majority of 78.

30. Lord Barham appointed First Lord of the Admiralty.

MAY.

1. Toulon fleet effects a junction with that of Ferrol. Sir John Orde abandons the blockade of Cadiz.

6. In the House of Commons, Mr. Whitbread having moved an address to the King, praying His Majesty to erase the name of Lord Melville from the list of the Privy Council, Mr. Pitt intimated that His Majesty had already been advised to take that step.

26. A grand ceremony on the completion of the New Docks at Wapping, and two vessels in the Oporto trade, and several Spanish prizes, introduced with great pomp from the Thames.

JUNE.

4. A strong Spanish fort in Muros Bay gallantly stormed and taken by 50 (officers included) of the crew of the Loire frigate, under the command of the first Lieutenant, Mr. Yeo.

12. Defence delivered by Lord Melville in the House of Commons.

13. Mr. Whitbread's motion for the impeachment of Lord Melville negatived. Mr. Bond's motion for a criminal prosecution against Lord Melville carried.

25. On the motion of Mr. Leycester, the resolution for the criminal prosecution of Lord Melville was rescinded, and a resolution for impeaching his Lordship adopted.

26. Mr. Whitbread appeared at the bar of the House of Lords, accompanied by a great number of members of the House, and impeached Lord Melville of high crimes and misdemeanors.

JULY.

1. Intelligence received of the arrival of the combined fleets in the West Indies; and letters posted at Lloyd's announced that they entered Port Royal Martinique, on the 14th of May.

8. Captain Bettesworth, of the Curieux, arrived at the Admiralty with dispatches from Lord Nelson, respecting the combined fleets in the West Indies; in consequence of which, a bulletin was published by the Admiralty.

9. Mr. Whitbread presented particular articles of impeachment at the bar of the House of Lords.

— An Admiralty bulletin announced the arrival of Lord Nelson in the West Indies, and of the combined fleet having been seen on the 20th of May, on its return to Europe.

17. An attack made by the Immortalité frigate and the gun-brigs off Boulogne, on a division of the hostile French flotilla coming from Dunkirk; in which a number of the enemy's vessels were sunk and driven on shore, and some taken.

19. The Blanche frigate captured, after a most gallant defence, by an enemy's squadron in the West Indies.—Soon after the Blanche struck, she sunk.

22. Sir Robert Calder, with 15 sail of the line, fell in, off Ferrol, with the combined fleets of the enemy, consisting of 20 sail of the line; and after an action, which lasted more than four hours, captured two sail of the enemy, both Spanish ships of the line, viz. the St. Rafael and Firma.

— A bulletin from the Admiralty gave information of the combined fleets having (on the 7th of June, the day after they left Martinique,) captured the Antigua convoy. In consequence of some of our frigates appearing, the enemy afterwards burnt their prizes.

AUGUST.

10. The Didon French frigate, of 44 guns, captured by the Phœnix, of 36 guns, in lat. 43. 16. N., long. 12. 14. W.

14. The Prince of Wales packet was taken, in lat. 43., long. 13., by le Prince de Paix, of 24 long nine-pounders and 220 men, after a chase of 34 hours, and sent for Vigo; but was recaptured by the Poulette, just as she was going into the harbour.

— A bulletin from the Admiralty announced that the combined fleets had got into Ferrol. The first port they made, after the battle with Sir R. Calder, was Vigo, which they entered on the 27th of July. They afterwards stood for Ferrol, which they entered on the 5th or 6th of August.

— The combined fleet, consisting of 27 or 28 sail of the line and several frigates, entered the harbour of Cadiz.

21. Lord Nelson, after his chase of the combined fleets, arrived in London, and was followed by crowds in the streets.

— The Brest fleet came out, and anchored in Camaret Bay; but being attacked by Admiral Cornwallis, retreated into the inner harbour. The enemy consisted of three three-deckers and eighteen two-deckers, whilst the British fleet was only 17 sail of the line,

23. A bulletin from the Admiralty announced that the combined French and Spanish fleets, consisting of 27 or 28 sail of the line, had been seen on the 13th, outside of the harbour of Ferrol, steering W.N.W.

26. The junction between Sir Robert Calder and Admiral Collingwood took place, off Cadiz.

— Sir William Sidney Smith attempted to burn the Boulogne flotilla with the fire machines called *Carcasses*.

SEPTEMBER.

1. The Dutch transports in the Texel began to disembark their troops, which marched directly for Nimeguen. Admiral de Winter also struck his flag.

2. By accounts received this day from India, information was had, that, on the 19th of December, at night, was launched from the Dock-yard at Bombay, a beautiful frigate, named the Pitt, being the first ever built in India for His Majesty's service.

4. The pay of the Lieutenants of the British Navy was raised to 8s. per day, and that of the Masters to 12l. per month.

5. The East India fleet came into the Downs, having on board property belonging to the East India Company to the amount of 9,700,000l., private property about 4,600,000 , and the duty to Government amounting to 5,600,000l.

15. Lord Nelson sailed in the Victory, accompanied with the Euryalus frigate, from Portsmouth, to take the command of the fleet off Cadiz.

The Calcutta man of war was captured by a French squadron in lat. 49. 40., long. 11. 40.

29. Lord Nelson arrived off Cadiz.

OCTOBER.

15. A boat was launched from the harbour of Boulogne, and, drifting with the tide, was taken up by the Immortalité frigate, containing the following bulletin:—" Ulm has surrendered to the French army, and the Austrian army is annihilated !"

16. The first embarkation of troops for Hanover took place at Ramsgate.

— A sloop of 300 tons was blown up opposite Walmer Castle, by a newly-invented Catamaran.

19. An official note was stuck up at Lloyd's, communicating the agreeable intelligence that the blockade of the Weser and Elbe was removed, in consequence of the evacuation of Hanover by the enemy.

21. Lord Nelson engaged the combined fleets of France and Spain off Cape Trafalgar, about 60 miles eastward of Cadiz; and after a dreadful conflict of four hours, sunk or destroyed 20 sail, made the French Commander in Chief, Admiral Villeneuve, and two Spanish Admirals, prisoners: one Spanish Admiral was killed, and another badly wounded. The British force consisted of 27 sail of the line (including three 64's). The enemy had 33 sail of the line; 18 French, and 15 Spanish. The ever-to-be lamented Nelson, whose flag was hoisted on board the Victory, fell at the close of the engagement, and was succeeded by Rear-Admiral (now Lord) Collingwood.

24. The Ocean, rated a 98, but pierced for 128 guns, besides carronades, was launched.

27. Exemption granted by His Majesty to neutral ships, from the blockade of Cadiz and St. Lucar, provided they did not carry into, or bring from those ports any warlike or naval stores.

NOVEMBER.

1. The gallant Captain Wright died in the Temple prison at Paris.

4. Commodore Sir Richard Strachan fought and captured four French sail of the line, with an equal number of British ships; Cape Ortegal then bearing N.E. 5 leagues. This was part of the combined fleet which escaped undamaged from off Trafalgar.

21. The Lord Mayor, Aldermen, &c. proceeded from Guildhall to St. James's, with an Address to His Majesty, on the late victory.

25. A forged letter sent from the Dutch coast, in the name of Admiral Kirk-

hert, to our squadron cruising off Holland, in which it was stated that the Emperor of Austria and Buonaparté had signed a treaty of peace.

27. *London Gazette.—Summary of the Killed and Wounded in the Action off Cape Trafalgar:—*

KILLED.		WOUNDED.	
Officers	21	Officers	41
Petty Officers	15	Petty Officers	57
Seamen	283	Seamen	870
Marines	104	Marines	196
Total	423	Total	1164

DECEMBER.

4. The Victory arrived at Portsmouth with the remains of Lord Nelson.

5. A General Thanksgiving for the splendid victory of Trafalgar.

7. Intelligence received at the India House of the capture of the Brunswick Indiaman, by the French Admiral Linois, on the 11th of July.

14. A French squadron of seven sail of the line and four frigates seen at sea, and supposed to have escaped from Brest.

23. The trial of Sir Robert Calder commenced at Portsmouth, on board the Prince of Wales. It terminated on the 26th, when he was reprimanded.

NAVAL HISTORY OF THE PRESENT YEAR, 1806.

(*March—April.*)

RETROSPECTIVE AND MISCELLANEOUS.

ON Friday, the 25th of April, Lord Howick submitted an estimate to the House of Commons, for augmenting the pay of the Officers and Seamen in His Majesty's Navy, agreeably to the following scale, to commence from the 1st of May, 1806.

	s.	d.	
To Admirals of the Fleet, an increase of	10	0	a Day.
Admirals	7	0	——
Vice-Admirals	5	0	——
Rear-Admirals	3	6	——
Captains of ships above third rates	4	0	——
——— of ships above sixth rates	3	0	——
Warrant Officers, an increase of pay of	6	0	a Month.
Petty Officers (whose numbers are also to be considerably augmented)	5	0	——
Chaplains not to receive an increase of salary for their duty as such; but, with the office, the yearly salary of 20l., hitherto appropriated to the Schoolmaster.			
Masters and Surgeons having had an increase of pay last year, are not included in the present increase.			
Captains of the Top and of the Forecastle, an increase of...	9	6	a Month.
Able Seamen, an increase of 1s. a week, or	4	0	——
Ordinary Seamen 6d. a week, or	2	0	——
Landmen not to receive any increase; the prospect of being rated as Able Seamen being a sufficient stimulus			

Lord Howick observed, that with respect to the pensioners of Greenwich Hospital, who, by age or infirmity, were incapable of farther service, he should, by gradations, propose an advance as far as one shilling per day. He farther proposed, that one shilling in the pound should be deducted from all prize money, to go to the military chest at Chatham; and he had reason to believe, that His Majesty would make a grant of one shilling in the pound from all *droits* of Admiralty, for the same purpose.

Upon the subject of the negociations between Great Britain and France, the following article appeared in the *Amsterdam Courant*:—

" According to all accounts, it seems that France has made proposals of Peace to England, but nothing further is known. The British Cabinet have held two Councils upon the subject of these proposals, which were made by M. Talleyrand to Mr. Fox, and also through Baron Jacobi, the Prussian Minister."

That the course which Prussia has been so far degraded, as to adopt by the direction of Buonaparté, will embarrass our commerce considerably there can be no doubt. But we trust that the enterprize of our Merchants will be able to elude this unheard of armed confederacy against our trade. If the Ports of Denmark were left to us, the attempt would soon be defeated; but we see little reason to hope that Buonaparté will suffer so direct a facility of thwarting his views to remain; and it is to be feared that Denmark must do what Prussia is forced to do; for to the latter we cannot ascribe a hostile mind. Her cowardice, her pusillanimity, perhaps her necessity, alone consents.

On the 22d of March, Admiral Verhuel, the Dutch Secretary for the Marine, arrived from Paris, and immediately waited on the Grand Pensionary. Admiral Verhuel had been consulting with the French Government respecting the naval campaign. On the 19th, Admiral de Winter passed through Brussels, on his way to the Hague, and it is conjectured that the Batavian sea forces will be actually employed.

It appears that so late as the 6th of this month, the King of Prussia had taken no measure for seizing upon the British vessels in the ports within the circle from which, agreeably to the proclamation of Count Schulenburgh, of the 28th ult., British vessels were in future to be excluded. A vessel, the Omnium, Marshall, has arrived in the river, which left Bremen on the 6th. The Prussian government seem to have calculated upon the tame acquiescence of our Ministers in the hostile measures they had resolved to adopt. The answer of Count Hardenberg to the Merchants of Berlin, and on their application to know whether they had reason to apprehend hostilities on the part of this country, in consequence of the occupation of Hanover, shows that no retaliation on our part was dreaded. The blockade of the Elbe, Weser, and the detention of Prussian vessels, must, therefore, have excited the utmost surprise at Berlin.

As the connection between France and Prussia leaves little room to think that the retaliation to which we have resorted will, in the first instance at least, produce a change of determination, it is expected that matters will proceed to open hostility. Prussia has already done to us the utmost injury within her power to inflict; but the extension of the principle we have already adopted, to the ports of the Baltic, which, with the co-operation of Sweden and Russia, could easily be effected, must completely put a stop to all her foreign trade. Indeed, while it is supposed that Buonaparté will insist upon shutting the Sound against us, which he cannot do, it is clear that we can easily do it against his ally, the King of Prussia, by suffering no vessel bound to a Prussian port to enter the Baltic. A few vessels stationed near the mouth of the Sound could effect that object.

Dowining street, April 8, 1806.

The King has been pleased to cause it to be signified by the Right Honourable Charles James Fox, His Majesty's Principal Secretary of State for Foreign Affairs, to the Ministers of Neutral Powers residing at this Court, that the necessary measures have been taken, by His Majesty's command, for the blockade of the entrance of the Rivers Ems, Weser, Elbe, and Trave; and that, from this time, all the measures authorised by the law of Nations, and the respective treaties between His Majesty and the different Neutral Powers, will be adopted and executed with respect to all vessels which may attempt to violate the said blockade.

The French are labouring with the greatest activity at Venice, in the equipment of a fleet. Orders have been given for building there ten ships of the line. The rich arsenal of Venice, and the forests of Dalmatia, furnish every thing necessary for their completion.

Letters on Service,

Copied verbatim from the LONDON GAZETTE.

[Continued from page 259.]

ADMIRALTY-OFFICE, MARCH 27, 1806.

Copy of a Letter from Vice-Admiral Dacres, Commander in Chief of His Majesty's Ships and Vessels at Jamaica, to William Marden, Esq.; dated at Port Royal, the 13th of January, 1806.

SIR,

IT is with pleasure I transmit, for the information of the Lords Commissioners of the Admiralty, the copy of a letter which I have received from Captain Hall, of the Malabar, enclosing one from Captain M'Kenzie, of the Wolfe, whose conduct on this occasion I feel highly meritorious. Their Lordships, always ready to reward merit, will, I am sure, show their approbation of Captain M'Kenzie's zeal and activity. I am, &c.

J. R. DACRES.

His Majesty's Ship Malabar, off Port Azaracleres, Island of Cuba, Jan. 2, 1806.

SIR,

I have the greatest satisfaction in having it in my power to acquaint you, that His Majesty's ship under my command, and His Majesty's sloop Wolfe, have this day captured le Regulateur and le Napoleon, two of the largest French schooner privateers out of St. Jago, protected by a double reef of rocks. Captain M'Kenzie, whose vigilance deserves every praise, saw one of them go in this morning. On coming off the port, I sent the Master to sound for anchorage, who found a passage on the reef, through which the Wolfe was successfully conducted, and most ably anchored within musket-shot of the enemy, attended by the boats of both ships manned and armed. Le Regulateur was armed with a brass eighteen pounder, four six-pounders, and manned with eighty men. Le Napoleon was armed with one long nine-pounder, two twelve-pounder carronades, and two four-pounders, and manned with sixty-six men; and it is but justice to say they were well defended, the action continuing, without intermission, an hour and three-quarters, when the survivors of the crews abandoned them, and landed in the woods, four only being made prisoners, one of whom is mortally wounded. They were then towed without the reefs, when the Regulateur (a remarkable fine schooner) sunk, and I am sorry to say Thomas Smith, a marine belonging to His

Majesty's ship under my command, went down in her: except this man, I have not sustained any loss. The officers, seamen, and marines of the Malabar discharged their duty most perfectly to my satisfaction. Mr. Thomas Fotheringham, the Master, deserves particular praise for having, in the shortest time, examined the passage, so that the Wolfe could be taken in, a circumstance the enemy had not the least idea could be attempted, and without which the conquest, had it been effected, must have been attended with very serious loss; it is, therefore, attributable to the gallant, cool, and able manner in which the Wolfe was conducted and fought, and which, I beg leave to offer my opinion, merits the fullest acknowledgments to Captain M'Kenzie, and likewise to his officers and ship's company.

I beg leave to enclose a copy of Captain M'Kenzie's letter to me on the occasion, with his report of killed and wounded on board the Wolfe.

I have the honour to be, &c.

To James Richard Dacres, Esq., Rear Admiral of the Red, Commander in Chief. ROBERT HALL.

His Majesty's Sloop Wolfe, Port Azarades 2d of January, 1806.

SIR,

I have the honour to acquaint you, in compliance with your orders, I proceeded with His Majesty's ship under my command, to cover the boats destined for the attack of the two French privateers in this port; but, on approaching, I found them moored in so advantageous a situation, and so well prepared, I thought it would be imprudent to allow them to proceed. I, therefore, stood in six fathoms water, within a quarter of a mile of the enemy, and opened my fire, which was continued for one hour and three-quarters, when I perceived the enemy were quitting the vessels; the boats were then ordered to proceed and take possession. They proved to be le Regulateur and Napoleon schooners; the former, a most beautiful vessel, mounting one long eighteen, and four six-pounders, brass, with eighty men: the other, a very fine vessel, also with one long nine, two twelve-pound carronades, two fours, and sixty-six men. It gives me infinite satisfaction to bear testimony to the cool and determined bravery displayed by every officer and man I had the honour to command; nor can I omit expressing my warmest thanks to Mr. T. Fotheringham (Master of the Malabar), for the very judicious manner in which he conducted the ship to anchor; and also the officers and crew of the Malabar's launch and jolly boat, who volunteered their services at the guns. I have a most heartfelt satisfaction in having so small a list of killed and wounded to subjoin. The loss of the enemy could not be ascertained; but, from the appearance of the decks, it must have been great. I am sorry to add the Regulateur sunk a short time after being in our possession, by which two unfortunate wounded Frenchmen were lost.

I have the honour to remain, &c.

Robert Hall, Esq., Captain of His Majesty's Ship Malabar. G. C. M'KENZIE.

Killed and Wounded on board His Majesty's Sloop Wolfe, January 2, 1806.

Killed.

Joseph Taylor and Samuel M'Mackin, Seamen.

Wounded.

Alexander M'Dowal and Frederick Ranckin, seamen; Robert Sallinger, marine; Benito Blanche (prisoner), dangerously.

Total—2 killed, and 4 wounded.

APRIL 1.

Copy of a Letter from Vice-Admiral Lord Collingwood, Commander in Chief of His Majesty's Ships and Vessels in the Mediterranean, to William Marsden, Esq.; dated on board the Queen, at Sea, the 28th of February, 1806.

SIR,

Having received information that the French frigates in the port of Cadiz were eady to put sea, the Hydra and Mozelle were kept close off the port for the purpose of watching them narrowly; the squadron about ten leagues off, until the 23d, when a strong Levant wind began, (which still continues to blow) and had, on the 26th, driven the squadron as far to the westward as Cape St. Mary. On the 27th, at nine in the morning, I received a report from the Mozelle, that four French frigates and a brig had put to sea at nine o'clock the evening before, and steered to the Westward. I immediately informed the Captains of the Tigre, Orion, and Unité, of the circumstance, by Telegraph, and directed them to chase to the N. W.

The Hydra cut the brig off from her consorts, and took her. She is very large, has ports for twenty guns, and mounts eighteen nine-pounders, with one hundred and thirty men. I enclose a copy of a letter from Captain Munday, stating his having captured her. I am, &c.

COLLINGWOOD.

MY LORD, *His Majesty's Ship Hydra.*

I have the honour to represent, that, at a quarter after nine, P.M., Cadiz Light-House bearing east three miles, and standing in shore with a strong easterly wind, we discovered the enemy's squadron of frigates already outside of us, the Mozelle making the signal for them at the same moment. I immediately bore up, intending to steer on a parallel with the enemy, in order to watch their movements, and had the satisfaction to find we gained on them; at eleven, seeing they steered a steady course, I commenced firing alarm guns, and throwing up rockets, and ordered Captain Carden (whose attention and assistance has been very great during the short time he has been under my orders,) to steer west by north, in order to give your lordship the intelligence.

At thirty minutes after two we found we had closed the squadron considerably, in consequence of their having altered their course a point to the westward; and on observing one of them to be much astern of the rest, I thought it very possible to cut her off, and, after a chase of two hours, succeeded: in coming up with her she fired a broadside at our rigging, and surrendered.

I find her to be le Furet French man of war brig, commanded by Monsieur Demay, (Lieutenant de vaisseau,) mounting eighteen long nine-pounders, but pierced for twenty guns, only four years old, and of the largest dimensions, and stored and victualled for five months, of all species.

I have the honour to be, &c.

To the Rt. Hon. Lord Collingwood, G. MUNDY.
Commander in Chief, &c.

Copy of a Letter from Admiral Montagu, Commander in Chief of His Majesty's Ships at Portsmouth, to Wm. Marsden, Esq.; dated 29th of March, 1806.

SIR,

Be pleased to inform my Lords Commissioners of the Admiralty, that the Greyhound revenue-cutter, commanded by Mr. Richard Wilkinson, arrived here this afternoon, having taken, off the Berry Head, and sent into Weymouth, la Princesse Caroline de Granville, French Lugger privateer, commanded by Louis Colar, carrying six brass four-pounder guns, swivels, and small arms, and rowing eighteen oars. She had been out three days from Granville, and was manned with thirty-eight men. I have the honour to be, &c.

GEO. MONTAGUE.

APRIL 7.

Copy of a Letter from the Earl of St. Vincent, K.B., Admiral and Commander in Chief of His Majesty's Fleet employed in the Channel, Soundings, &c., to Wm. Marsden, Esq.; dated on board His Majesty's Ship the Hibernia, off Ushant, April 1, 1806.

SIR,

I enclose, for the information of the Lords Commissioners of the Admiralty, a copy of a letter which I, this day, received from Lieutenant T. Usher, commanding His Majesty's armed brig the Colpoys, I am, &c.

ST. VINCNET.

Colpoys Hired Brig, Plymouth,
March 30, 1806.

MY LORD,

I have the honour to acquaint your Lordship, that, cruising in His Majesty's brig Colpoys, under my command, agreeably to the orders of Admiral Cornwallis, on the 21st of this month, we chased three Spanish luggers into the port of Avillas; and as we had a fine commanding breeze, I determined on following them in, notwithstanding the fire of a six-gun battery, under which they ran, but which I considered the Colpoys as competent to silence. For this purpose we prepared for anchoring with springs; and on arriving within the range of the enemy's guns, and before our carronades could be worked with effect, the wind died away. To draw the fire from the brig, and in order to lose no time in effecting my object, the two boats were immediately manned with volunteers, and, after pushing through a heavy fire of grape from the battery, and the musketry of a party of soldiers, which had been sent on board the vessels to defend them, I succeeded with six men, in the headmost boat, in boarding and carrying them, the enemy jumping over one side as we entered on the other; thirteen of them fell into our hands: the second boat, which pulled heavy, came up afterwards, and we succeeded in bringing them off. Notwithstanding the heavy fire of the enemy's battery of twenty-four-pounders, two men only received any hurt; one of them, I am sorry to add, a dangerous wound, though, I hope, not mortal.

I have felt it a duty I owe to the steady courage and perseverance of the Master, Mates, and crew of the Colpoys, to detail to your Lordship the circumstances of this little enterprize, as they have uniformly shown the same determination in my support in other affairs the Colpoys has been engaged in since I have had the honour to command them. I annex, in the margin, for your Lordship's information, the names of the captured vessels,

I have, &c.

Rt. Hon. Earl of St. Vincent, &c. THOMAS USHER.

Mames of the captured Vessels.

El Santa Buena Ventura, of two guns, laden with flax and steel.
San Antonio, of two guns, laden with flax and steel.
San Real, in Ballast, and sent away with eleven prisoners.

Wounded.

Thomas Ash (severely) and John Robinson.

APRIL 11.

Copy of a Letter from Captain John Davie, late Commander of His Majesty's Sloop Favourite, to Wm. Marsden, Esq., dated on board the Trio Cartel, Falmouth, April 8, 1806.

SIR,

I have the honour to enclose a copy of my letter to Captain Maxwell, of His Majesty's ship Arab, giving an account of the capture of a French privateer by His Majesty's late sloop the Favourite, under my command.

I am, Sir, &c. JOHN DAVIE.

His Majesty's Sloop Favourite, off the Tris Pongas, Dec. 28, 1805.

SIR,

I have the honour to acquaint you, that, in obedience to your orders of the 18th instant, I proceeded in His Majesty's sloop, under my command, to the islands des Loss, where I was informed, that the privateer you sent me in pursuit of was at anchor in the river of Pongas. I immediately shaped a course for that place; and, when within a few leagues of it, two sail were discovered, which Mr. Wilson (who volunteered to be our Pilot) affirmed were vessels which had been captured by her. Conceiving it to be my duty, I instantly made all sail, and gave chase to them. Owing to the shallowness of the water, and incorrectness of the charts, we did not reach the entrance of the river till this afternoon, when we discovered the privateer under sail, and working out. She allowed us to approach within half gun-shot, when she attempted to get away. I immediately commenced a fire from the bow-guns, which soon induced her to shorten sail, and, to my surprise, haul athwart, and rake us. I did not choose to alter the ship's course, because it would have prevented my getting so near as I intended; but, when within our own length, I luffed up, and gave her our broadside. The Captain had the temerity to continue engaging us for twenty minutes, which cost him and ten others their lives, and twenty-five men badly wounded; whilst I am happy to say, that Lieutenant Odlum, of the Royal African corps, (a passenger,) is the only person hurt on board of us, and he is slightly wounded. On taking possession, she proved to be le General Blanchard privateer, mounting sixteen guns, and manned with one hundred and thirty French and Spaniards.

I cannot do sufficient justice to the zeal and perseverance displayed by Lieutenants Parsons and Ingram, Mr. Soady, the Master, as well as all the other officers, seamen, and marines, under my command, in a tedious chase of three days, obliged, principally, to sweep and tow the ship, where we had never more than three fathoms water; and regret, very sincerely, that their bravery and good conduct was not directed against a vessel of greater force.

I have the honour to be, &c.

Keith Maxwell, Esq., Captain of His Majesty's Ship Arab, &c. JOHN DAVIE.

APRIL 15.

Copy of a Letter from Vice-Admiral Sir J. T. Duckworth, K.B., to Wm. Marsden, Esq.; dated Superb, Port Royal, Jamaica, Feb. 16, 1806.

SIR,

Captain Henry, of the French ship Diomede, which ran on shore, and I afterwards ordered to be burnt, being, with his officers, among the prisoners rescued the afternoon of the 9th, before that event took place, he approached to offer Captain Keats his sword, which he, from the report which had been made to me by Sir Edward Berry, and, except in the act of hailing, confirmed by Captain Dunn, that the ship had struck before she ran on shore, it was disdainfully refused. This of course made explanation necessary on my side; and I acquainted Captain Henry that I had marked his dishonourable conduct in my public letter; when feeling, as he appeared to do, like a man of honour, and referring to his officers and ship's company, they gave the strongest testimony that the pendant was always flying though the ensign was shot away; and this, from strict investigation since my arrival here, appears to be the case; and as Sir Edward Berry is not present to refer to, and the Commodore in the Brave allows he hailed the Agamemnon, and what has been recited passed between them, I have no doubt that the Diomede has been mistaken for the Brave, by her ensign being down; I, therefore, Sir, feeling that character is much more valuable than life, am to beg the heavy charge on Captain Henry may be done away in such manner as in their Lordships' judgment may appear most proper. I am, &c.

J. T. DUCKWORTH.

Copy of a Letter from Vice-Admiral Dacres, Commander in Chief of His Majesty's Ships and Vessels at Jamaica, to Wm. Marsden, Esq.; dated on board His Majesty's Ship Shark, Port Royal, February 9, 1806.

SIR,

I have the pleasure to enclose, for the information of the Lords Commissioners of the Admiralty, the copy of a letter received from Captain Dashwood, of His Majesty's ship Franchise, giving an account of the behaviour of Lieutenants Fleming and Douglas, and Lieutenant Mends, of the marines, of that ship, with the boats' crews, who, in so determined a manner, cut out of the bay of Campeachy His Catholic Majesty's brig Raposa, against such superior force and opposition. I trust their Lordships will think their conduct worthy of their approbation.

I am, &c.

JAS. R. DACRES.

His Majesty's Ship Franchise, at anchor, off Campeachy, January 7, 1806.

SIR,

Having received information from a neutral, that several Spanish vessels had very lately arrived in the bay of Campeachy, and conceiving it practicable, from the local knowledge I had of that place, that they might be cut out without running much risk; I have presumed in consequence to extend the limits of the orders with which you honoured me, and proceeded to this anchorage; and although I am well aware of the great responsibility, yet, as it was undertaken solely with a view of forwarding the King's service, by distressing his enemies, so I have the vanity to hope it will be sanctioned with your high approbation.

I have, therefore, the honour to report that I, last evening, anchored the Franchise in quarter less four fathoms, a-breast the town of Campeachy; and as it was impossible, from the shallowness of the water, to approach nearer to the shore than five leagues, I dispatched the senior officer, Lieutenant John Fleming, accompanied by Lieutenant P. J. Douglas, the third; Lieutenant Mends of the marines, and Messrs. Daly, Lamb, Chalmers, and Hamilton, Midshipmen, in three boats, with orders to scour the bay, and bring off such of the enemy's vessels as they might fall in with. But from the distance they had to row, joined to the darkness of the night, and the uncertainty of their position, it was four o'clock in the morning before they could possibly arrive, long after the rising of the moon, which unfortunately gave the enemy warning of their approach, and ample time for preparation, even to the tricing up of their boarding nettings, and projecting sweeps to prevent the boats from coming alongside; and although the alarm was thus given from one end of the bay to the other, and instantly communicated to the castle on shore, yet nothing could damp the ardour and gallantry of the officers and crew who had volunteered on this (as it ultimately proved) hazardous service, for that instant two of His Catholic Majesty's brigs, one of twenty guns, and one hundred and eighty men; the other of twelve guns and ninety men, accompanied by an armed schooner of eight, and supported by seven gun-boats of two guns each, slipped their cables, and commenced a most severe and heavy cannonading on the three boats, which must soon have annihilated them, had not Lieutenant Fleming, with great presence of mind, and unchecked ardour, most boldly dashed on, and instantly laid the nearest brig on board. He was so quickly supported by his friend, Lieutenant Douglas, in the barge, and Mr. Lamb, in the pinnace, that they carried her in ten minutes, notwithstanding the very powerful resistance they met with. The whole of this little flotilla pursued them for some distance, keeping up a constant fire of guns and musketry, which was so smartly returned both by the brig and boats, that they soon retired to their former position, leaving Lieutenant Fleming in quiet possession of his prize, which proved to be the Spanish monarch's brig Raposo, pierced for sixteen, but only twelve guns mounted, exclusive of cohorns, swivels, and numerous small arms, with a complement of ninety men, but only seventy-five actually on board; the Captain, Don Joaquin de la Cheva, with the senior Lieutenant, the civil officers, and a boat's crew, being absent on shore. She appears almost a new vessel, coppered, sails well, and, in my humble judgment, admirably calculated for His Majesty's service. It is with the most heartfelt satisfaction I have to announce, that this service was performed without the loss of a single man, and only seven slightly wounded. But I lament to say, that that pleasure is, in a great measure, damped by the great effusion of blood on the part of the enemy, they having had an officer and four men killed, many jumped overboard and were drowned, and the Commanding Officer and twenty-five wounded; many of whom, I am sorry to add, are, in the Surgeon's opinion, mortally. I have, therefore, from motives of humanity, sent the whole of them on shore with a flag of truce, where the brave, but unfortunate, wounded can be better taken care of, which, I trust, you will approve. Lieutenant Fleming speaks in the highest terms of approbation of the prompt and gallant support he met with from Lieutenants Douglas and Mends, as well as the other officers and crew under his orders. Indeed there was not a man on board but was anxious to be of the party; and I am sorry I could not indulge Lieutenant T. J. Peschell, the second; but his presence was absolutely necessary on board.

To an officer of your discriminating judgment, I trust I shall stand excused if I take the liberty of recommending Lieutenant Fleming to your notice for his meritorious conduct on this occasion. He appears to me to be an officer of distinguished merit and bravery, and I understood he was highly respected by his late Captain, the good, the amiable, and my gallant predecessor, the Honourable John Murray. I have the honour to be, &c.

C. DASHWOOD.

To James Richard Dacres, Esq., Commander in Chief, &c.

APRIL 15.

Copy of a Letter from Vice-Admiral Dacres, Commander in Chief of His Majesty's Ships and Vessels at Jamaica, to Wm. Marsden, Esq.; dated on board His Majesty's Sloop Shark, Port-Royal, February 9, 1806.

SIR,

His Majesty's ship Magicienne (Penguin in company,) having captured the Spanish packet el Carmen, I enclose you a copy of Captain Mackenzie's letter for their Lordships' information. I am, &c.

JAMES R. DACRES.

His Majesty's Ship Magicienne, Mona Passage, February 4, 1806.

SIR,

On the 25th ultimo His Majesty's ship, under my command, captured, after a chase of twelve hours, el Carmen Spanish packet, commanded by an officer of the same rank as a Commander in the British Navy; she is pierced for fourteen guns, but had only two mounted, and eighteen men; the Penguin sloop was in company. I have the honour to be, &c.

James Richard Dacres, Esq., Commander in Chief, &c. ADAM MACKENZIE.

APRIL 22, 1806.

Copy of a Letter from the Earl of St. Vincent, K.B., Admiral and Commander in Chief of His Majesty's Fleet employed in the Channel, Soundings, &c., to Wm. Marsden, Esq.; dated on board His Majesty's Ship the Hibernia, off Ushant, April 14, 1806.

SIR,

I, yesterday, received from Vice-Admiral Thornbrough the letter, with its enclosure, from Captain Lord Cochrane, of which copies are herewith transmitted, for the information of my Lords Commissioners of the Admiralty. The gallant and successful exertions of the Pallas, therein detailed, reflect very high honour on her Captain, officers, and crew, and call for my warmest admiration.

I am, &c. ST. VINCENT.

Prince of Wales, off Rochfort, 9th April, 1806.

MY LORD,

I have the honour to transmit to your Lordship a copy of a letter I have this day received from Captain Lord Cochrane, of His Majesty's ship Pallas, under my orders. It will not be necessary for me, my Lord, to comment on the intrepidity and good conduct displayed by Lord Cochrane, his officers, and men, in the execution of a very hazardous enterprise in the Garronne; a river the most difficult, perhaps, in its navigation of any on this coast; the complete success that attended it, as well as the destruction of the vessels of war mentioned in the said letter, on the coast of Arcassore, bespeaks their merits more fully than is in my power to do; to which may be fairly added, that nothing can evince more clearly the high state of discipline of the crew of the Pallas, than the humanity shown by them to the enemy in the conflict.

I have the honour to be, &c.

The Earl of St. Vincent, &c. EDWARD THORNBROUGH.

His Majesty's Ship Pallas, off Chasseron, 8th April, 1806.

SIR,

Having received information, which proves correct, of the situation of the corvettes in the river of Bourdeaux; a little after dark, on the evening of the 5th, the Pallas was anchored close to the Shoal of Cordovan; and it gives me satisfaction to relate, that, about three o'clock, the national corvette la Tapageuse, of fourteen long twelve-pounders and ninety-five men, which had the guard, was boarded, carried, and cut out, about twenty miles above the shoals, within two heavy batteries, in spite of all resistance, by the first Lieutenant Mr. Haswell, Mr

Sutherland the Master, Messrs. Perkyns, Crawford, and Thompson, together with the Quarter-Masters, and such of the seamen, the serjeant, and marines, as were fortunate enough to find place in the boats.

The tide of flood ran strong at day-light; la Tapageuse made sail; a general alarm was given; a sloop of war followed, and an action continued, often within hail, till, by the same bravery by which the Tapageuse was carried, the sloop of war, which had been before saved by the rapidity of the current alone, after about an hour's firing, was compelled to sheer off, having suffered as much in the hull as the Tapageuse in the rigging.

The conduct of the officers and men will be justly appreciated. With confidence I shall now beg leave to recommend them to the notice of the Lords Commissioners of the Admiralty.

It is necessary to add, that the same morning, when at anchor, waiting for the boats, (which, by-the-bye, did not return till this morning,) three ships were observed bearing down towards the Pallas, making many signals: they were soon perceived to be enemies. In a few minutes the anchor was weighed, and, with the remainder of the officers and crew, we chased, drove on shore, and wrecked, one national twenty-four-gun ship, one of twenty-two-guns, and la Malicieuse, a beautiful corvette of eighteen guns: their masts went by the board, and they were involved in a sheet of spray.

All in this ship showed good zeal for His Majesty's service. The warrant officers, and Mr. Tattual, Midshipman, supplied the place of those commissioned. The absence of Lieutenant Mapleton is to be regretted; he would have gloried in the expedition with the boats. The assistance rendered by Mr. Drummond of the Royal Marines, was such as might have been expected.

Subjoined is a list of the wounded, together with the vessels captured and destroyed since the 26th ultimo. I am, Sir, &c.

Vice-Admiral Thornbrough, &c. COCHRANE.

Killed.—None:

Wounded.

Michael Molley, both arms off.
Henry Crookman, in the arm.
John M'Donald, in the back.

Vessels taken or destroyed.

Le Dessaix, chasse marée—taken.
L'Isle Daix, ditto—taken.
La Pomone, brig—taken.
A large brig—burnt.
A chasse marée—wrecked.

National Ships.

La Tapageuse, of 14 guns and 95 men—taken
La Malicieuse, of 18 guns—wrecked.
Imperial, ship, of 24 guns—wrecked.
Imperial, ship, of 22 guns—wrecked.

COCHRANE.

Copy of a Letter from Admiral Lord Gardner, Commander in Chief of His Majesty's Ships and Vessels at Cork, to Wm. Marsden, Esq.; dated on board the Trent, Cork Harbour, April 16, 1806.

SIR,

Enclosed I have the honour of transmitting, for the information of the Lords Commissioners of the Admiralty, a letter from Captain Brace, of His Majesty's ship Virginie, giving an account of his having, on the 9th instant, in lat. 46 deg. 49 min. N., long. 10 deg. 25 min. W., captured the Spanish schooner privateer Vengador, mounting 14 guns, and having a complement of eighty-two men.

I understand from Lieutenant Powell, who is arrived in charge of the above privateer, that she is out twelve days from Bourdeaux, and had not made any captures during that period. I have the honour to be, &c.

GARDNER.

His Majesty's Ship Virginie, at Sea, 9th April, 1806,
lat. 46 deg. 49 min. N., long. 10 deg. 25 min. W.

MY LORD,

I have the honour to acquaint your Lordship, that at six P.M. I captured a fast sailing Spanish schooner privateer, called the Vengador, mounting fourteen guns, with a crew of eighty-two men. I have the honour to be, &c.

C. BRACE.

To the Rt. Hon. Lord Gardner, Admiral of the White, Commander in Chief, &c.

APRIL 23, 1806.

Copy of a Letter from Admiral Young, Commander in Chief of His Majesty's Ships and Vessels at Plymouth, to William Marsden, Esq.; dated on board His Majesty's Ship Salvador del Mundo, Hamoaze, April 21, 1806.

SIR,

I transmit you herewith, for the information of the Lords Commissioners of the Admiralty, a letter which I have received from the Commander of the Hind revenue cutter, giving an account of his having captured the French privateer brig l'Intrepide, of 14 guns, and which he brought in this morning.

I have the satisfaction to add, that the John, one of the brigs taken by this privateer, has been recaptured by the Confiance, and is arrived here.

I have the honour to be, &c.

W. YOUNG.

Hind Revenue Cutter, Catwater, Port of Plymouth,
April 21, 1806.

SIR,

I beg you will be pleased to acquaint my Lords Commissioners of the Admiralty, that on Wednesday the 16th inst. having received information at Scilly that a vessel had been captured off that island by a French brig privateer, of 14 guns, I immediately got under weigh, and proceeded to sea; and on Friday the 18th, had the satisfaction of falling in with her, Scilly bearing N.N.E. three leagues; she hoisted American colours, and allowed us to approach; fired a broadside into us, and a volley of musketry; then, with a crowd of sail, she attempted to get off, depending on her superior sailing; but, after a chase from nine A.M. till twelve, and a running fight from twelve to three, she struck to the Hind revenue cutter under my command, and proves to be l'Intrepide, of St. Maloes, of fourteen guns, eight of which had been previously put into the hold, Joseph Boursin, Commander, who, with two of the enemy, were killed, and two are dangerously wounded. She has been out twenty days, and has captured four vessels.

I have every reason to hope that neither of them can, as yet, have got into any French port, by what I can learn from those who belonged to them, and who were taken in the Intrepide. She is a new vessel, and was returning from her second cruise: she has, and would have been, a great annoyance to our trade, being a very fast-sailing vessel.

On board of the Hind we have none killed or wounded; nor any damage, other than the rigging and sails being cut. I cannot do sufficient justice to the zeal and steady conduct of Mr. Pitt, Chief Mate, and the officers and men under my command. I have the honour to be, &c.

THO. MURRAY ALLAN.

Brig Mary, M'Arthur, Master, from Ireland, a light transport, retaken and sent into Scilly.

Admiral Young, &c.

APRIL 26.

Copy of a Letter from Rear-Admiral the Hon. Alexander Cochrane, K.B., Commander in Chief of His Majesty's Ships and Vessels at the Leeward Islands, to William Marsden, Esq.; dated on board the Northumberland, Carlisle Bay, Barbadoes, 7th March, 1806.

SIR,

I enclose, for the information of the Lords Commissioners of the Admiralty, the copy of a letter from Captain Smith, of His Majesty's sloop Woolverine, giving an account of the capture of a privateer: also the copy of a letter from Lieutenant Barker, commanding the Grenada, acquainting me of his capturing a French letter of marque.

Captain Younghusband, of His Majesty's ship Heureux, has also sent in here two schooner privateers, which he has lately captured, but I have not yet received his official account thereof. I have the honour to be, &c.

ALEX. COCHRANE.

His Majesty's Sloop Woolverine, 60 leagues to windward of Barbadoes, Jan. 31, 1806.

SIR,

I have the honour to inform you, that this morning I captured the French schooner privateer Petite Confiance, after a long chase. She had one large gun mounted, (her two others having been thrown overboard in chase,) and fifty men; a month out from Guadaloupe, and has taken nothing.

I have the honour to be, &c.

Rear-Admiral Cochrane, &c. J. SMITH.

His Majesty's Brig Grenada, St. George's Bay, Grenada, February 18, 1806.

SIR,

I HAVE the satisfaction to acquaint you, that, on the 15th instant, the Pearl Rock, Martinique, bearing east, distant four or five leagues, at four A. M. I discovered a suspicious vessel to the southward, to which I immediately gave chase; at seven o'clock I fired a shot at her, which she returned, and hoisted French colours, and a close action ensued. In consequence of light winds, and my being to leeward of the enemy, I dropt a-stern several times, which prolonged the action considerably, the smoke from the guns taking the wind out of our sails. At thirty minutes past eleven the enemy struck his colours, and found her to be the French schooner letter of marque, Princess Murat, having on board two forty-two pounders, one nine-pounder, with several swivels and blunderbusses, and fifty-two men; out from Martinique twelve hours, and bound to St. Domingo, laden with dry goods, noyeau, &c.

I am sorry to add, Mr. Atkins the Master, a brave and good officer, who has served several years with me, is severely wounded, but, I trust, will speedily recover; and one boy, who died a few hours after the action.

The enemy had three men killed, and 7 wounded.—I beg leave to observe, that the enemy's guns were mounted in such a manner, as to enable them all to bear, at the same time, in any direction, which made them very superior in weight of metal.

The enemy's masts and rigging were so much crippled, that on the night of the 16th both masts went by the board. The Grenada has suffered much in rigging; both top-masts being quite disabled, main-boom shot away; both lower masts damaged, and sails cut to pieces, with the heavy showers of grape and canister from the forty-two pounders.

The conduct of Mr. Malone, Sub-Lieutenant, Mr. Atkins the Master, Mr. Briggs, Midshipman, (who has just served his time,) the petty officers, seamen, and a party of the 60th regiment, serving as marines, I cannot sufficiently extol their coolness, and strict attention to my directions during the action, being such as are so truly characteristic in the British seaman.

I have the honour to be, &c.

JOHN BARKER.

The Honorable A. Cochrane, Rear-Admiral of the White, Commander in Chief, &c. &c. &c. Leeward Islands.

Copy of a Letter from Captain George Younghusband, Commander of His Majesty's Ship Heureux, to William Marsden, Esq.; dated in Carlisle Bay, Barbadoes, 28th February 1806.

SIR,

Admiral Cochrane not being at present on the spot, I beg leave to enclose to you a letter, (for the information of my Lords Commissioners of the Admiralty,) informing him of the capture of two of the enemy's schooners on the 16th and 17th instant.

I have the honour to be, &c.

GEORGE YOUNGHUSBAND.

His Majesty's Ship Heureux, Barbadoes, W. by N. 60 Miles, Feb. 18, 1806.

SIR,

I have the honour to acquaint you, that on the 16th instant I fell in with, and, after a short chase, captured la Bellone French privateer, mounting fourteen nine-pounders, and having on board one hundred and seventeen men.

The Bellone had on board eight thousand dollars, being her owner's share of a prize they had carried into Cayane.

I have likewise the pleasure to add, that I yesterday captured, after an eight hours' chase, la Bocune French privateer schooner, mounting three guns, and having on board sixty men.

I have the honour to be, &c.

Rear-Admiral Cochrane. G. YOUNGHUSBAND.

Promotions and Appointments.

Rear-Admiral Eliab Harvey has hoisted his flag on board the Tonnant, of 80 guns, and sailed to join the Channel fleet.

Captain Bedford is appointed to the Kent; Captain Garrett, to the Prince of Wales; Captain Luken, to the Gibraltar; Captain Spranger, to the Warrior; Captain M. Seymour, to the Amethyst; Captain N. D. Cochrane, to be a Post Captain; and Lieutenant Salmon, to the Clinker gun-vessel.

Lieutenant Gilchrist is appointed to the el Corso, receiving-ship at Gravesend, under the command of Captain Mottley.

Mr. Gobble, late of the Victory, is appointed Purser of l'Espoir sloop, Captain Hope, which is fitting for foreign service, at Spithead.

N. P. Rothery, Esq. is appointed by the Right Hon. the Lords Commissioners of the Admiralty to take possession of all Prussian vessels that may arrive.

Captain Gosselin is appointed to the Audacious; Captain J. A. Wood, to the Latona; Captain R. Piercy, to la Belette; Captain Rains, to the Sea Fencibles at Ramsgate.

Vice-Admiral the Hon. George Cranfield Berkeley is appointed Commander in Chief at Halifax.

Rear-Admiral Sir Thomas Trowbridge is appointed Commander in Chief at the Cape of Good Hope.

Lieutenant Daly, who brought the last dispatches from the Cape of Good Hope, and Lieutenant R. Fowler, are promoted to be Commanders.

Captain Hopkins is appointed to the Satellite sloop, at Sheerness; and Lieutenant Fleming, to the Richmond gun-vessel.

Captain Halkett is appointed to the Ganges; Captain B. Clement, to the Goelan, at Jamaica; Lieutenant Mitchell, son of the late Admiral Sir Andrew Mitchell, is promoted to be a Commander.

BIRTHS.

Lately, at the Admiral's House, Portugal-street, Grosvenor-square, the Hon. Mrs. Berkeley, of a son.

On the 12th March, the wife of Mr. Simpson, Surgeon of His Majesty's ship Arethusa, of a son, at his house in George-street, Stonehouse, near Plymouth.

Lately, the wife of Robert Elmore, a fisherman, at Narrow Wall, Lambeth, near the Old Barge House, of two boys and a girl, who, with the mother, are likely to do well.

MARRIAGES.

At Bungay, Captain Sutton, of the Royal Navy, to Miss Ives, daughter of the Rev. J. Ives.

Captain Digby, of the Royal Navy, to Viscountess Andover, daughter of T. Coke, Esq., of Norfolk, M.P.

OBITUARY.

Lately, at Freshwater, in the Isle of Wight, Miss Hamond, sister of Sir Andrew Snape Hamond, Bart.

March 29. At Portsea, James Peers, Esq., formerly Deputy Comptroller of the Customs at Portsmouth.

Lately, at Haslar Hospital, Lieutenant Furness, late of His Majesty's ship Illustrious.

April 1. At Ramsgate, Captain Harry Furnall, of the Royal Navy, nephew of Sir Harry Neale, and Commander of the Sea Fencibles at Margate.

Lately, at Sierre Leone, on the coast of Africa, Captain W. Day, of the Royal Navy.

7. At Newlands, near Lymington, in the prime of life, Capt. Whitby, of the Royal Navy, who lately resigned the command of his Majesty's ship Gibraltar, through ill health. He was a very excellent officer, and an intimate companion of the brave Admiral Cornwallis, at whose seat he died.—Captain Whitby was the eldest son of the Rev. Thomas Whitby, of Cresswell-hall, near Stafford. He was admitted into the Royal Navy at the age of 12 years: from which period, a short interval only excepted, he was continually engaged for twenty years in the active duties of his profession, till about the 20th of March last, when indisposition, from unwearied and unremitted attention, compelled him to solicit, from the Lords of the Admiralty, a short leave of absence from the Gibraltar of 80 guns; to which ship, from the Ville de Paris, he had been recently appointed. This indisposition, which at first excited no serious apprehension, assumed, after the lapse of some days, a more formidable aspect; and so rapid and overwhelming was its progress, that notwithstanding every effort of medical skill, it soon subdued a very useful and valuable life. So true it is, "that in the midst of life we are in death."—Into the Minerva frigate, then bearing the flag of the Hon. Admiral Cornwallis, his patron and friend, Captain W. was made Post, in 1793. Of his professional skill, zeal for the naval service, and constant attention to even the most minute parts of his duty, there is very ample testimony from those who, from situation, are the most competent judges. His loyalty to his Sovereign, and his attachment to his Country and its dearest interests, were ardent and sincere. The powers of the mind, which he was cultivating with assiduous care, were such, that few subjects to which he applied his attention steadily, could elude their grasp. To speculate upon the product of such powers, thus cultivating, is now, alas! as useless as it is vain: equally useless too it is to lament the loss of one naval character, however considerable, when every British naval officer, and every seaman, is a Hero. The family, however, and relations, friends, and acquaintances of such a young man, may be allowed to mourn and lament their loss; though at the awful dispensation of Providence they dare not, because they are forbidden, to murmur.

At Bermuda, where he went for the recovery of his health, Vice-Admiral Sir Andrew Mitchell, K.B., and Commander in Chief on the Halifax station. He was made a Post Captain in 1778; a Rear-Admiral in 1795; and a Vice-Admiral in 1797.

ERRATA

IN THE BIOGRAPHICAL MEMOIR OF SIR EDWARD BERRY.

"A Friend of Sir Edward Berry" has informed us, that Mrs. Godfrey, the mother of that officer, has been dead upwards of two years; and that her jointure, as Mrs. Godfrey, was only 200l. *per annum*, instead of 500l.

Sir Edward Berry's surviving sisters are *all* married.

For Lord Spencer, page 178, line 3, *read* Lord Chatham.

Subsequently to the battle of Trafalgar, Sir Edward, we believe, was some time stationed off the Texel; but of this we are not certain. He afterwards proceeded to the West Indies; and, as appears from Vice-Admiral Sir J. T. Duckworth's gazette letter, was present in the action off St. Domingo, on the 6th of February 1806. In this engagement, the Agamemnon, Sir Edward's ship, had one seaman killed, and five seamen and eight marines wounded.

THE RIGHT HON.BLE LORD COLLINGWOOD

Vice Admiral of the Red Squadron

Published 31st May 1806, by J. Gold, 103, Shoe Lane, Fleet Street.

BIOGRAPHICAL MEMOIR

OF

CUTHBERT LORD COLLINGWOOD,

VICE-ADMIRAL OF THE RED,

And Commander in Chief of the Mediterranean Fleet.

"Full many a gem of purest ray serene
The dark unfathom'd caves of Ocean bear;
Full many a flower is born to blush unseen,
And waste its sweetness on the desert air."

Gray.

IT is not the character of the British nation to withhold from its brave defenders the fair fame to which their heroic deeds have led: and if it has been left until now to enrol among our naval worthies the noble Admiral who is the subject of the present memoir, it is to be placed to an account highly honourable to our country, and to the service in which his talents have been employed. "His life," to use his own modest language, so like to all his other sentiments, "had been a continual service at sea, but unmarked by any of those extraordinary events or brilliant scenes which hold men up to particular attention, and distinguish them from those officers who are zealous and anxious for the public service:"—one among the number of those meritorious officers who are both able and zealous for the public service, but whose good fortune it had not yet been to be brought forward into the more conspicuous sphere of public notice, or to have had the opportunity for which they pant to display their talents in their country's service, and swell the pages of our naval annals with triumphs and achievements of their own. Many are the Howes, the Hoods, the Duncans, the St. Vincents, and the Nelsons, who are not yet known to that public whose loud applauses are lavished upon those distinguished ornaments of the profession, who have already done that for their country which these will one day do. Such is the height to which the naval character of the nation hath risen, and so progressive have been the stages of its glory, that it is not in the ordinary services or successes of the profession that the merits of a Commander are discerned. Accustomed to such brilliant successes, and such great examples of talent and ardour, we scarce feel the news of a single capture which has been made with no less honour to the Commander than the prouder triumph of a fleet; nor in the splendid victory of the squadron do we appreciate the services of the individuals who have contributed to acquire it; much less do we discover in the character of those who only want the opportunity to display them, those talents, which though not yet brought into action, are ready to share in the honours of their profession whenever the occasion may arise to call them into notice.

But though the public eye is only to be attracted by great and splendid victories, which neither the rank nor the good fortune of these has yet afforded them the opportunity to achieve, let not the ardour of their aspiring minds be checked by denying to them the praises which belong to their merits, and the hope that they may one day vie with the noble examples that they have to stimulate their exertions. Though like the stately oak which is cut down to build the floating batteries that have been the stages of their glory, the heroes of the present day must yield to the stroke which severs them from the stations they adorn, another and another still succeeds to supply their place, as the advancing growth of the forest furnishes to our Navy the constant succession which every year requires.—

> " Tall oaks for future Navies grow,
> Fair Albion's best defence."
>
> WATTS.

> " So generations in their course decay,
> So flourish these when those are past away."
>
> POPE.—ILIAD.

And deep as the wound, and painful as our sufferings are, when age or glory deprives us of the services of one of our illustrious chiefs, another is found to supply the loss.—

> " Like leaves on trees the race of man is found,
> Now green in youth, now withering on the ground;
> Another race the following spring supplies,
> They fall successive, and successive rise."
>
> POPE.—ILIAD.

And never shall there be wanting a succession of able and active Commanders to call forth and direct the native and irresistible courage of our British tars against the enemy that shall presume to insult our shores, or to dispute the empire of the seas.

Cast but an eye upon the long list of Admirals, Captains, and Commanders, nay why should the subalterns be overlooked, those future heroes whose early promise has pointed them out to their superiors in the more confined sphere of action in which their services have had to range. Their ripening talents and rising fame have not been undistinguished in the subordinate ranks of the profession; and why should we be disposed to doubt that their services will rise with their rank, and the opportunities which they may have to display their maturer talents at a future time? Honoured with the notice and the patronage of those distinguished characters who have trodden the path of glory, and set them the bright examples which they follow, they come recommended to us by the best judges of their merit, and from a school in which they have already gained the prizes which must encourage them to become the candidates for future fame. These are the seeds of a future harvest selected by those who were best able to appreciate their worth. These are the choice selections of those experienced veterans to whom we look for the defence of our country, and the future glory of the British flag; who saw in the early bud and the opening blossom what we may rest assured will one day or other confirm their hope and approve their choice. It is sufficient not merely to keep our spirits from sinking under the loss of one of our heroes, but to raise our highest expectations, that they who are to be our future Nelsons have been the pupils of our past. Never will they forget under whose tuition they were formed, nor cease to emulate the heroic deeds of those who were their patrons and examples in early life, the ornaments of their day, the revered names to which their country looked up with confidence while they lived, and remember with grateful affection in their graves. The lessons, the examples, the achievements of those under whom they served, will live in their remembrance, and be a constant spur to stimulate them to deeds of like renown.

Burning for the glory which these have attained, they will never cease to seek the opportunity of like distinction; and whenever the occasion shall arise, what they have seen in others will be both the pledge and model of what they will do themselves.

And if in the rising race of naval heroes we have this good ground of confidence, that they will keep up the honour of the British flag, what may we not expect from the matured talents and tried abilities of those who have been the companions, the sharers, the leaders in those victories which are already the subjects of our pride—the Collingwoods, the Strachans, the Duckworths, and, not to run through the list of those brave and experienced officers who have already distinguished themselves in the service, numbers of others who are not yet known to the public eye, nor otherwise recognized than in those services which have contributed to the mass of our naval glory, and swelled the amount of that sum which constitutes our national pride.

Among the number of those brave defenders of whom we have known but little, and to whom the public has been much indebted without the opportunity of acknowledging the services which have contributed to exalt our Navy to the proud eminence it has attained, we embrace with peculiar pleasure the occasion which presents itself to select the name of Collingwood for the subject of our present memoir.

Cuthbert Collingwood was born at Newcastle-upon-Tyne; and though it is not in the long train of ancestors that we trace his descent to high birth and honours not his own, his parents were respectable, and though not in opulent circumstances, were able to give him the advantage of an education, that has enabled him to become the founder of his own fortune, and the architect of his own fame. The *res angusta domi*, instead of deducting from his present dignity, might be the subject of an honest pride; and those circumstances which a false shame might wish to conceal, have been frequently the occasion to call forth virtues which else had been never known. The filial affections and duties which shone forth in his character at a time when every little that he could save from his own slender income to add to the comforts of his family was of consequence to himself, would, if it concerned us to follow him into the privacy of domestic anecdote, do him no less honour as a man, than his public character, with which only we have to do, will ever redound to his praise in the line of his profession. He had a younger brother (Wilfred) also in the Navy, who attained the rank of Captain, and died in the West Indies: and he has another brother (John) in the Customs, and two sisters now living in Newcastle.

Cuthbert, at a very early age, indicated the bent of his genius and inclination to a maritime life, and after six or seven years' education at the grammar school, under the care of the Rev. Mr. Moises, he entered in the year 1761 into the service, under the protection and patronage of his maternal uncle, Captain (afterwards Admiral) Braithwaite*, who had at that time the command of the Shannon frigate, into which he was made Post on the 6th of April, 1761; to whose regard for him, and the interest which he took in his improvement in all the branches of nautical science, he owed the foundation that was laid for his future advancement in the line of his profession. With him he served many years. We find him a Midshipman in the Gibraltar in 1766, and from 1767 to 1772, Master's Mate in the Liverpool; when he was taken into the Lenox, Captain (now Admiral) Roddam, whose connexion and regard for the family, and high opinion of the merit of these young men, led him to take both him and his brother Wilfred under his protection, and to interest himself in their promotion. By this brave and discerning officer he was recommended to Vice-Admiral Graves, and afterwards to Vice-Admiral Sir Peter Parker.

He had been now thirteen years in the service without promotion, so little did his prospects at first setting out in life keep pace with his merit, or forebode the honours to which he has since arrived! On the 27th of February, 1774, he went in the Preston, under the command of Vice-Admiral

* Richard Braithwaite, Esq., Admiral of the Blue, died at Maize Hill, Greenwich, June 28, 1805, in his 80th year.—See NAVAL CHRONICLE, Vol. XIV, page 86.

Graves, to America, and the following year was promoted to the rank of fourth Lieutenant in the Somerset, on the day of the battle at Bunker's Hill, where he was sent with a party of seamen to supply the army with what was necessary in that line of service. The Vice-Admiral being recalled, and succeeded upon that station by Vice-Admiral Shuldham, sailed for England on the 1st of February, 1776. In the same year Lieutenant Collingwood was sent to Jamaica in the Hornet sloop, and soon after the Lowestoffe came to the same station, of which Lord Nelson was at that time second Lieutenant, and with whom he had been before in habits of great friendship. His friend Nelson had entered the service some years later than himself, but was made Lieutenant in the Lowestoffe, Captain Locker, in 1777. Here their friendship was renewed; and upon the arrival of Vice-Admiral Sir Peter Parker to take the command upon that station, they found in him a common patron, who, while his country was receiving the benefit of his own services, was laying the foundation for those future benefits which were to be derived from these promising objects of his patronage and protection: and here began that succession of fortune which seems to have continued to the last; when he, whom the subject of our present memoir had so often succeeded in the early stages of his promotion, resigned the command of his victorious fleet into the hands of a well-tried friend, whom he knew to be a fit successor in this last and triumphant stage of his glory, as he had been before in the earlier stages of his fortune. For it is deserving of remark, that whenever the one got a step in rank, the other succeeded to the station which his friend had left; first in the Lowestoffe, in which, upon the promotion of Lieutenant Nelson into the Admiral's own ship, the Bristol, Lieutenant Collingwood succeeded to the Lowestoffe; and when the former was advanced in 1778, from the Badger to the rank of Post Captain in the Hinchinbrooke, the latter was made Master and Commander in the Badger: and again upon his promotion to a larger ship, Captain Collingwood was made Post in the Hinchinbrooke.

In this ship Captain Collingwood was employed in the

spring of 1780, upon an expedition to the Spanish main, where it was proposed, by the river San Juan and the lake Nicaragua and Leon, to pass by a navigation of boats into the South Sea. The plan was formed without a sufficient knowledge of the country, which presented difficulties that were not to be surmounted by human skill or perseverance. The river was difficult to proceed on from the rapidity of the current and the several falls over the rocks, which intercepted the navigation, and the climate was deadly. No constitution could resist its effects. At the port of San Juan, Captain Collingwood joined the Hinchinbrooke, and took the command; but Captain Nelson, who was promoted to a larger ship, had received the infection of the climate before he went from the port, and had a fever from which he could get no relief until he quitted his ship and returned to England. And even there it was long before he recovered from the effects of a sickly climate, and the severe services to which he had been exposed. Captain Collingwood, by the strength of a better constitution, resisted many attacks, and survived most of his ship's company, having buried in four months no less than 180 out of the 200 which composed it. The climate was alike fatal to the other ships employed on this expedition, which suffered in the same or still greater proportion. The men on board the transports all died, and some of the ships having none left to man them, sunk in the harbour; but transport ships were not wanted, for the troops they brought were no more. They had fallen not by the hands of an enemy, but sunk under the contagion of the climate.

From this dreadful scene, that Providence which had hitherto preserved his life to be the future instrument of good to his country, and to the cause of humanity which he was born to serve, at length happily released him. He quitted this station in the August of 1780, and in the following December was appointed to the command of the Pelican, of 24 guns; but his continuance in this ship was but of short duration; for on the 1st of August in the following year, so fatal to the West India Islands, in a violent hurricane, and in the midst of a most tempestuous night, she was wrecked upon the Morant Quay. Here again Providence interposed to preserve his own and the lives of his ship's company; for the next day, not without extreme difficulty and peril, by the help of rafts made of the small and broken yards, they got on shore; and upon those small sandy hills, with little food or water, remained ten days, until a boat went to Jamaica, and the Diamond frigate was sent to their relief.

Thus rescued from a perilous situation, it was not long before an opportunity presented itself to resume his station in the service of his country. He was appointed next to the command of the Sampson, of 64 guns, in which ship he served to the peace of 1783, when she was paid off, and he was appointed to the Mediator, and sent to the West Indies, where he again met his friend Nelson, who at that time commanded the Boreas frigate upon the same station. The friendship which subsisted between these two young men, who were hereafter to make so conspicuous a figure upon the great theatre of naval glory, appears from the letters which were written during this period by the latter, to his friend Captain Locker, and which have been lately published in the appendix to his life*. In one of which, dated on board the Boreas, September 24, 1784, he says, "Collingwood is at Grenada, which is a great loss to me, for there is nobody that I can make a confidant of." In another, dated November 23, "Collingwood desires me to say he will write you soon such a letter that you will think it a history of the West Indies. What an amiable good man he is!" Again, March 16, 1785, St. Kitts,—"What a charming good man! He is a valuable member of society." Off Martinique, March 5, 1786, he writes, "This station has not been over pleasant: had it not been for Collingwood, it would have been the most disagreeable I ever saw."

In this ship, and upon this station, he remained until the latter end of 1786, when upon his return to England, and the ship being paid off, he took the opportunity to visit his native country, and renew his acquaintance with his family and friends,

* Charnock's Biographical Memoirs of Lord Viscount Nelson.

whom he had left at an early age, and had been so long separated from them, that until this period he had been almost a stranger to them.

In this retirement, and the society of his friends, after a service of five and twenty years, he continued to enjoy himself in Northumberland until the year 1790, when, on the expected rupture with Spain on account of the seizure of our ships at Nootka Sound, he was again called into employ in the armament then fitting out, and appointed to the Mermaid, of 32 guns, under the command of Admiral Cornish, in the West Indies: but the dispute with Spain being adjusted without hostilities, and no prospect of immediate employment again at sea appearing, he once more returned to his native country, and in this interval of repose formed a connexion with a lady of great personal merit, and of a family highly respectable. The lady whom he married was Sarah, the eldest of the two daughters of John Erasmus Blackett, Esq., one of the Aldermen of Newcastle, and brother of the late Sir Edward Blackett, Baronet, of Matson, in Northumberland, and of the Reverend Henry Blackett, the present venerable and worthy Rector of Boldon, in the county of Durham. By this lady he has two daughters; the elder, Sarah, thirteen years of age; and Mary Patience, the younger, twelve; both living with their mother at Morpeth, the place of his Lordship's residence, if residence it can be called to him, who has hitherto had it so little in his power to set his foot on shore, or consider any spot but as a place to cast his anchor for a time, till the service of his country should again call him to pursue the track of glory, on his own element.

It was not long permitted him to enjoy the repose of private and domestic life. From the endearments of a connexion so happily formed, and from the social circle of his friends, to whom his own amiable and virtuous character could not fail to attach him, he was, on the breaking out of the war with France in 1793, called to the command of the Prince, Rear-Admiral Bowyer's flag-ship, with whom he served in this ship, and afterwards in the Barfleur, until the engagement of the 1st of June, 1794. In this action he distinguished himself with great bravery, and the ship which he commanded is known to have had its full share in the glory of the day; though it has been the subject of conversation with the public, and was, we believe, the source of some painful feelings at the moment in the Captain's own mind, that no notice was taken of his services upon this occasion, nor his name once mentioned in the official dispatches of Lord Howe to the Admiralty. These misapprehensions too frequently arise from a want of attention to the circumstances on the part of others, and that nice sense of honour in the party concerned, which, however laudable in itself, is too apt to be wounded by jealousies of its own creation, or the busy suggestions of others, ever ready to awake that suspicion which is so painful to the subject, and often most injurious to the public service. Perhaps Lord Collingwood, if he were now to review the circumstances of the case, and to consider how difficult he has found it himself to do justice to the merits of those under his own command, without hurting the feelings of others, alike jealous of honour, and alive to the slightest appearance of neglect, might see the conduct of Lord Howe in a different light from what it appeared to him at the time.

In his Lordship's first dispatch, dated the 2d of June, he particularizes Rear-Admiral Bowyer, as one that had lost his leg in the engagement, and he adds, "Though I shall have on the subject of these different actions with the enemy, distinguished examples hereafter to report, I presume the determined bravery of the several ranks of officers, and the ship's companies employed under my authority, will have already been sufficiently denoted by the effect of their spirited exertions, and I trust I shall be excused for postponing the more detailed narrative of the other transactions of the fleet thereon, for being communicated at a future opportunity." And in his supplementary letter to the Admiralty, (June 21,) he very carefully guards against the too jealous feelings of his officers, by noticing the impossibility of doing full justice to their merits on such occasions. "The Commander of a fleet, their Lordships know, is unavoidably so confined in his view of the occurrences in time of battle, as to be little capable of rendering personal testimony to the meritorious services of officers who have profited in a greater extent by the opportunities to distinguish themselves on such occasions. To discharge this part of my duty, *reports were called for from the flag officers of the fleet,* for supplying the defects of my observance under the limited circumstances above-mentioned. Those officers therefore who have such particular claim to my attention, are the Admirals Graves, Sir Alexander Hood, the Rear-Admirals *Bowyer*, Gardner, and Pasley, Captain Lord Hugh Seymour, &c."

The Admiral, whose flag-ship Captain Collingwood commanded, is here particularly noticed as one of those who had particular claim to attention, and surely the Captain must have his share in the intended praise. And if in the number of those commanders whose merits were to be discovered by the reports of the Admirals in whose squadrons they were, his name is not to be found, it will be remembered from whom the Commander in Chief collected his intelligence; and that if any omission there were, it must be his own Admiral, and not the Commander in Chief, on whom the blame must rest, in not having distinguished his Captain among those who were entitled to peculiar praise: if it be not rather to be accounted for in another way, and that in the state in which the wounded Admiral then was, it devolved upon his Captain to make the report; and Captain Collingwood, every one knows, would be more likely to suppress than bring forward any thing that might seem to redound to his own praise.

On His Majesty's visit to the fleet on their return to Spithead, Admiral Bowyer, though unable to receive in person from his Sovereign the gold chain and medal appended, was honoured with this distinguishing mark of approbation; and if there were any omission, or any delay, in the communication of the honour intended in the presentation of medals to the several Captains, it may be ascribed to any other cause rather than to design or disrespect on the part of the Commander in Chief. The absence of Captain Collingwood, no longer the commander of the Barfleur, and probably no longer under his Lordship's command, might have rendered it impracticable to present the medal to him when he conferred it upon the several other Captains; and to "the *soldier jealous of honour*" as to the subject of jealousy in other cases, "*trifles light as air are proofs as strong as holy writ.*" The smallest delay which might arise from distant station, accident, or any other cause, might, with an impression already upon his mind too favourable to such a suspicion, be construed into design; though nothing could be more improbable than that a man of Lord Howe's discernment, and without a motive, without the smallest ground of previous dislike, but on the contrary, with an high opinion of the merit of Captain Collingwood, should have intended a slight upon his character, which no other person in the fleet would, he must be well assured, for a single instant entertain. Certain it however is, that this was a subject of offence to Captain Collingwood, and many letters of explanation passed between them; but to no purpose. Whatever might be the conciliatory conduct and language of the Commander in Chief, the Captain continued inflexibly to refuse the proffered honour; and if we cannot admit the premises, we must at least admire the spirit which dictated the conclusion, that he could never condescend to wear that distinction of which he was not thought worthy by his Commander in Chief: but would wait till he should have done something that might entitle him to the honour of wearing it. Well has his subsequent conduct confirmed his former merit, and proved his title to that and still higher honours!

Rear-Admiral Bowyer's flag, in consequence of his honourable wound in this day's action, no longer flying on board the Barfleur, Captain Collingwood was appointed to the command of the Hector, on the 7th of August, 1794, and afterwards to the Excellent, in which he was employed in the blockade of Toulon, and in this ship he had the honour to acquire fresh laurels in the brilliant victory off the Cape of St. Vincent's, on the 14th of February, 1797. In this day's engagement, which will ever stand pre-eminent among the many occasions on which the British flag has maintained its wonted superiority, in spite of numbers, rate, or weight of metal, the Excellent took a distinguished part. To the penetrating genius, the quick discernment the enterprising spirit, and never failing resources of a Nelson, combining with the rare and matchless powers of his mind, the most active personal exertions; with the consummate skill of the most able and experienced Commander, the daring hardihood of a common seaman; not the public only, but the companions and witnesses of his intrepidity and skill, have always ascribed the successful manœuvre by which 15 ships of inferior force were able to dispute the day with 27 of the Spanish line, and 7 of these of the first rate; and not only to contend, but to carry off four of them as the prizes and triumphs of their superior gallantry and skill.

What the brave Nelson did upon that occasion is too well known to be here recounted; but while we contemplate with astonishment what the French would call the *prodigies of valour*, that he effected by his wonderful genius, and the actual services of his own ship, we do not forget the obligations which their country owes to every man who bore a part in a contest perhaps the most unequal, and a victory, all circumstances considered, the most extraordinary, that our naval history can furnish. So great and splendid have been the successive triumphs of our Navy, that one has chased the other out of remembrance, and we are apt to overlook the past, or at least the most striking features of former victories, in contemplating the subsequent and more recent successes with which our naval contests have been crowned.

> " *What's the newest* victory?"
> " *That of an hour's age doth hiss the speaker,*
> *Each minute teams a new one.*"
>
> SHAKSPEARE.

But great and extraordinary as the triumphs are which British skill and prowess have since achieved, never can the honour of our Navy rise higher than on this glorious day: and if we had nothing else to immortalize the fame of our present hero, it would be a monument that would last as long as time should suffer a record to remain, that the name of Collingwood was among the foremost of the brave and triumphant heroes of this day. We mean not to detract from the merit of the companions of his victory. Where every man did his duty, and every man must have done it to the full extent of human powers, it might seem invidious to dwell upon the particular merits of any one who bore a part in this glorious victory; but justice to the merits of a brave and distinguished officer compels us to put in our claim to a peculiar share of that praise which must belong to Captain Collingwood.

So well did the Hero of the Nile know his value, that when the ship which Captain Collingwood commanded was sent to reinforce this squadron, he exclaimed with great joy and confidence in the talents and bravery of her Captain, "See here comes the Excellent, which is as good as two added to our number." And the support which he in particular this day received from this ship, he gratefully acknowledged in the following laconic note of thanks:—

"*Dear Collingwood! A friend in need is a friend indeed.*" And in a short detail of the transactions of his own ship, sent home, as it since appears from one of his letters to Captain Locker*, to be, if he approved, inserted in the papers, we have this best of all authorities, from the best of all judges, Commodore Nelson's own account of what his friend Collingwood did on that memorable day. "At this time the Salvador del Mundo and San Isidro dropped astern, and were fired into in a masterly style by the Excellent, Captain Collingwood, who compelled the San Isidro to hoist English colours; and I thought the large ship Salvador del Mundo had also struck; but Captain Collingwood disdaining the parade of taking possession of a vanquished enemy, most gallantly pushed up with every sail set to save his old friend and messmate, who was to appearance in a crippled state. The Barfleur being a-head, the Culloden crippled and astern, the Excellent ranged up within two feet of the San Nicholas, giving a most tremendous fire. The San Nicholas luffing up, the San Joseph fell on board her, and the Excellent passing on for the Santissima Trinidada, the Captain resumed her station a-head of them, and close alongside."

* Published in the Appendix to Charnock's Biographical Memoirs of Lord Nelson, page 67.

We have traced the brave and meritorious subject of our memoir in two of the great naval victories which this revolutionary war produced. It did not fall to his lot to have any share in the subsequent battle of the Nile; nor had he the good fortune to be placed in a station where any further opportunity was afforded to display his talents during the remainder of the war. He continued in the command of the Excellent, under the flag of Lord St. Vincent, till January, 1799, when his ship was paid off: and on the 14th of February, in the same year, on the promotion of flag officers, he was raised to the rank of Rear-Admiral of the White; and on the 12th of May following, hoisted his flag on board the Triumph, one of the ships under the command of Lord Bridport on the Channel station.

In the month of June 1800 he shifted his flag to the Barfleur, on the same station; and in 1801 was promoted to the rank of Rear-Admiral of the Red, in which ship, and upon the same service, he continued to the end of the war, without any opportunity of doing more than effectually blockading the enemies' fleet in their own port, while they were proudly vaunting of their preparations for invading us: a service not less important to the honour, the interest, and the security of the nation, than those more brilliant achievements which dazzle the public eye, and meet the popular sentiment, which counts only upon victories, and estimates the talents and services of our naval heroes, rather by their good fortune than by their merits; by the number of their prizes than by their judicious arrangements, and patient endurance of toil and peril in the prevention of mischief, and the execution of plans that furnish no opportunities to display the more shining talents and services which are the subjects of popular admiration and applause. In the estimation of the statesman, and the opinion of those who form their judgment by another standard than that of success, the brave and persevering Cornwallis, patient of toil, and unwearied in the execution of an arduous trust, will be ranked with the conquerors of the Nile and Trafalgar; and though to the feelings of himself, and the companions of a laborious and mortifying service, may be wanting those gratifications which have fallen to the lot of others more fortunately placed, and their praises are not resounded in the senate or the public prints; though no illuminations or titles reward their merits while they live, or monuments record their services after death, those services will live in the grateful remembrance of all who know how to appreciate the security they have enjoyed; and the pages of history will hand down to posterity the names to whom we owe the proud honour of displaying the British flag from day to day upon the coasts of the enemy, at the very time that they were holding forth the terrors of invasion to alarm the fears of the nation, and lead us to expect them on our own.

In this state of inaction, in which there was little else left for our Navy to do, was the subject of this memoir for some time placed, until the peace, or truce, took place; when in all the confidence of integrity, which a nation, conscious of its own sincerity, is too apt to place in the pacific dispositions and professions of its enemies, our Navy was fast dismantling, and our naval heroes retiring from the fatigues of war to visit their native soil, to enjoy the repose of a short respite from the toils and perils of war, and to refresh themselves for the contest which they would so soon be called to renew.

The Barfleur, among others, returned to Spithead on the 6th of May, 1802, and Rear-Admiral Collingwood had now an opportunity to visit his family and friends in Northumberland. But here it was not to be expected that he could long remain. The sore that was so hastily and superficially healed, could not but soon break out again, and call for all the energies of the nation to meet the more virulent and dangerous appearance that it had now assumed.

Not one short year had elapsed when the King's message to Parliament (March 8, 1803,) announced the appearance of a new war; and on the commencement of hostilities, Admiral Collingwood was again called into service. On the promotion of Admirals on the 23d of April, 1804, he was made Vice-Admiral of the Blue, and resumed his former station off Brest. The close blockade which Admiral Cornwallis kept up requiring a constant succession of ships, the Vice-Admiral shifted his flag from ship to ship as occasion required, by which he was always upon his station in a ship fit for service, without the necessity of quitting his station and returning to port for victualling or repairs. On this station he remained, patiently enduring with his brave Commander in Chief and his squadron all the hardships of war without the honour, all the toils and dangers of a tempestuous and perilous service, and all the mortifications which bravery must endure when disappointed of its opportunity to add to its own, and the honour of the British flag, the glory of annihilating this as it had done almost every other of the fleets of the enemy.

From this station the Vice-Admiral was called in May 1805, to a more active service, having been detached with a reinforcement of ships to the blockading fleet at Ferrol and Cadiz. Here the opportunity was presented for the exercise of much skill and talent, to effect the object with a force so inadequate to the service, that it seems almost incredible that he should have been able to succeed in blocking up the French and Spanish fleets as he at one time did, off Cadiz, with only four sail under his command.

Perhaps it would be difficult to fix upon a period, or a part of the character of Lord Collingwood, which called for powers of a more peculiar kind, or displayed his talents to more advantage, than the period and the service in which he was now employed. Left with only four ships of the line, to keep in nearly four times the number, that he should have been able with these to block up the port of Cadiz, and confine their fleet in their own harbour, is an instance of genius and address that is scarcely to be parallelled in the pages of our naval history. It appears almost impossible so to have divided his little force as to deceive the enemy, and effect the object of his service: but this he did. With two of his ships close in as usual to watch the motions of the enemy, and make signals to the other two, who were so disposed, and at a distance from one another, as to repeat those signals from one to the other, and again to other ships that were supposed to receive and answer them, he continued to delude the enemy, and led them to conclude that these were only part of a larger force that was not in sight, and by this *ruse de guerre* he kept them in, and not only secured his own ships, but effected an important service to his country, by preventing the execution of any plan that the enemy might have had in contemplation, and keeping them together for the glory of a future day.

On the return of Lord Nelson in the month of September he resumed the command, and Vice-Admiral Collingwood was his second; and the Commander in Chief knew he should be well seconded in such a character. Arrangements were made, and such a disposition of the force under his command as might draw the combined fleets out and bring them to action. In a letter to a friend, dated the 3d of October, Lord Nelson wrote that the enemy were still in port, and that something must be done to bring them to battle. "In less than a fortnight," he adds, "expect to hear from me, or of me, for who can foresee the fate of battle*?"

At length the opportunity offered. The plan that was laid to lure them out succeeded. Admiral Louis having been detached with four sail of the line to attend a convoy to a certain distance up the Mediterranean, and the rest of the fleet so disposed as to lead the enemy to believe it to be not so strong as it was, Admiral Villeneuve was tempted to venture out with 33 ships under his command, (18 French and 15 Spanish,) in the hope of doing something to retrieve the honour of their flag, and restore his falling credit with Buonaparte. On the 19th of October Lord Nelson received the joyful intelligence from the ships that were left to watch their motions, that the combined fleet had put to sea, and as they sailed with light westerly winds, his Lordship concluding their destination to be the Mediterranean, made all sail for the Straits with the fleet under his command, consisting of 27 ships, three of which were sixty-four's. Here he learnt from Captain Blackwood that they had not yet passed the Straits, and on the 21st, at day-light, had the satisfaction to

* Letter to a friend, dated off Cadiz. *Vide* NAVAL CHRONICLE, Vol. XV, page 37.

discover them six or seven miles to the eastward, and immediately made the signal for the fleet to bear up in two columns. It fell to the lot of Vice-Admiral Collingwood, in the Royal Sovereign, to lead his column into action, and first to break through the enemy's line; which he did in a style that commanded the admiration of both fleets, and drew from Lord Nelson this warm and honourable testimony to the skill and bravery of the partner of his glory, "Look at that noble fellow! Observe the style in which he carries his ship into action!" While the Vice-Admiral, with equal justice to the spirit and valour of his friend, was enjoying the proud honour of his situation, and saying to those about him, "What would Nelson give to be in our situation!"

The action began at 12 o'clock: at fifteen minutes past one, it appears by the log-book of the Victory, that Lord Nelson received the fatal wound, and at 3 P.M., many of the ships having struck their colours, gave way. Admiral Gravina, the Spanish Commander, with 10 ships, besides frigates, stood towards Cadiz: and the British fleet were left with 19 ships of the enemy, as the trophies of their victory; two of them first rates, with three flag officers, of which the Commander in Chief (Villeneuve) was one. One of the prizes, the Achille, a French 74, took fire and blew up.

The circumstances of this splendid victory are too recent and fresh in the remembrance of our readers, to need the recital in this place of those particulars which heighten the glory of this action, and do honour to the several ships on which it fell to bear a more conspicuous part in the service of this proud day. They will be found in Lord Collingwood's dispatches, and in various other places of our CHRONICLE, in which we have had, and shall have frequent occasions to recur to this engagement. What he did we must not expect to hear from himself; but the severe loss in his own ship is the best proof of the share which the Royal Sovereign had in this victory. The returns were, three officers, two petty officers, twenty-nine seamen, and thirteen marines, killed; and three officers, five petty officers, seventy seamen, and ten marines, wounded.—Total, 141. Nor need we upon this occasion renew the painful sensations which every reader will have felt in the death of that great man, whose ever-to be-lamented fall, in the midst of victory, added to the share which had already fallen to his brave second in command, the honour of completing the triumph which he did not himself live to enjoy.

On the death of Lord Nelson, the command of his conquering fleet and the completion of the victory devolved upon Vice-Admiral Collingwood, who, as he had so often done in the early part of his life, now for the last time succeeded him, in an arduous moment, and most difficult service. He had succeeded him as Lieutenant: he had followed him in the ship in which he was promoted to the rank of Master and Commander: he had been made Post into the Hinchinbrooke, upon his friend's removal into a larger ship; and now at last, to close the scene, he succeeded him as Commander in Chief. The tender concern that he expressed upon this occasion, is no less honourable to the feelings of friendship, than his whole conduct, throughout the trying difficulties that devolved upon him, redounds to his character as a seaman. In his letter to the Admiralty he says, "I have not only to lament in common with the British Navy and the British Nation, in the fall of the Commander in Chief, the loss of a Hero whose name will be immortal, and his memory ever dear to his country; but my heart is rent with the most poignant grief for the death of a friend, to whom, by many years intimacy, and a perfect knowledge of the virtues of his mind, which inspired ideas superior to the common race of men, I was bound by the strongest ties of affection; a grief to which even the glorious occasion on which he fell does not bring that consolation which perhaps it ought." And nothing can better prove the sincerity of his attachment, than his immediate care to provide for those whom he knew to be the objects of his Lordship's good opinion, and the intended objects of his promotion; one of whom that had already passed as Lieutenant, the writer of this is able from his own knowledge, and a grateful remembrance of the circumstance, to state, was sent for on the morning after the victory, and consoled in the loss of his patron by that preferment, which if he had survived to retain the power that had fallen into the hands of his successor, he had the best of all grounds to expect from himself.

Having conquered one enemy, and acquired all the glory that ambition itself could wish for, now commenced another scene, in which new perils and difficulties were to be encountered, and powers of another kind were to be displayed: and if the trying situation in which he was placed was attended with mortifications and disappointments that were enough to damp the spirits of a conqueror, it will be remembered that the elements were the enemy with which he had now to combat; those elements to which the French government, in their usual stile of bombast and falsehood, ascribe their loss*, but which unhappily interposed, not to deduct from their disgraceful defeat, but to deprive their conquerors of the well-earned fruits of their victory, and their country of the benefit of a numerous fleet, that their valour had made their own.

The Royal Sovereign had lost her masts in the action; none remained but the tottering foremast, which went in the subsequent gales. In this state of his own ship the Vice-Admiral had been obliged to call the Euryalus to make his signals while the battle lasted, and after the action he shifted his own flag into this frigate. Many other of his ships were dismasted, all shattered, in thirteen fathoms water, off the shoals of Trafalgar; and when he made signal to prepare to anchor, few of the ships had an anchor to let go, their cables being shot. Here was occasion for all his powers, and perhaps much as we have to be the subject of admiration and gratitude in the action itself, we have more to admire, and to call forth our grateful feelings to Providence, and to this active and experienced officer, as the instrument in the hand of Providence, in the subsequent services and exertions which saved the whole of our own triumphant fleet, and so many of the ships and lives of the enemy from the imminent peril of their situation. Justly does he ascribe the

* "*Through the elements we have lost some ships*, after an engagement imprudently commenced." Speech of the Emperor on the opening of the Legislative Body, March 2.

success of those exertions to the interposition of that same good Providence which aided them through such a day, and preserved them in the night, by the wind shifting a few points, and drifting the ships off the land, except four of the captured dismasted ships, which were then at anchor off Trafalgar, and he hoped would ride safe till these gales were over *.

Difficulties upon difficulties still arose to mortify his feelings, and call forth all his exertions. In his next official letter he tells their Lordships that a continued series of misfortunes had attended him, but they were "of a kind that human prudence could not possibly provide against, or his skill prevent." Unfavourable as the weather was, 13 or 14 of the captured ships were towed off to the westward, where he ordered them to rendezvous round the Royal Sovereign, in tow by the Neptune; but on the 23d the gale increased, and the sea ran so high that many of them broke the tow rope, and drifted far to leeward before they were got hold of again; and some of them taking advantage of the dark and boisterous night, got before the wind, drifted upon the shore, and sunk.

In the afternoon of that day the remnant of the combined fleet which had not been much engaged, stood up to leeward of his shattered and straggling prizes, which obliged him to collect a force out of his least injured ships, and form to leeward for their defence, and the bad weather continuing, had determined him to destroy all the leewardmost, that could be cleared of the men. The Trinidada was cleared and sunk, and four others. The Redoubtable sunk astern of the Swiftsure while in tow. The Saint Anna he had no doubt was sunk, her side being almost entirely beat in; and such was the shattered condition of the whole of them, that unless the weather moderated. he doubted whether he should be able to carry a ship of them into port.

* Official letter of the 22d October. And the Editor of the *British Flag Triumphant*, in a note to his prefatory address, says, "I have been assured by a Captain in the Navy, who acted a most distinguished part upon that glorious day, that there was a moment when the danger was so imminent, that had not the wind providentially shifted a few points, the greater part of our fleet must inevitably have perished, in spite of all the skill and energy so signally manifested by the illustrious Collingwood."—Page 9.

In his next official letter (the 28th) he gives a still more deplorable account of his situation, which "had been the most critical, and their employment the most arduous that ever a fleet was engaged in." By the extraordinary exertions, however, that were made for their preservation, four 74 gun-ships (three of them Spanish and one French) were saved and sent into Gibraltar. Of the remainder, nine were wrecked, three burnt, and three sunk. Two others were taken, but got into Cadiz in the gale. Four others which had got off to the southward were afterwards taken by the squadron under Sir Richard Strachan. So that out of the 33 ships, of which the combined fleet consisted, there were only 10 left, and many of these in such a shattered state, as to be little likely to be further serviceable.

A more complete victory never was obtained; but greatly would it have added to the joy of the nation, and gratified the feelings of the brave Admiral, and the companions of his glory, if he could have succeeded in sending the whole of the captured ships into port, to have remained as so many lasting monuments of their victory, and so much added strength to the British Navy: but the strength of the enemy is no less diminished by their destruction; and though it is painful to humanity to remember the cause, their Navy is for ever deprived of the services of the numerous crews, which all the humane exertions of their conquerors could not rescue from the fate to which their ships were destined *.

The humanity of the Vice-Admiral, who truly fulfilled the prayer of his noble friend and predecessor, *that humanity after victory might be the predominant feature in the British fleet* †, was no less conspicuous in his attention to the sufferings of the wounded prisoners. To alleviate those sufferings as much as possible, he wrote to the Governor of Cadiz, proposing to give them up to the care of their own hospitals, on his sending boats

* Upwards of 100 of our gallant seamen perished in their generous efforts to save the prisoners out of the different prizes; and Captain Malcolm, and his ship's company, in the Donnegal, at the imminent hazard of being totally lost, rescued hundreds of the enemy from a watery grave. *Gibraltar Chronicle*, Nov. 9, 1805.

† Entry in his Diary on the morning of the engagement.

for their conveyance, and giving receipts for the number, with an acknowledgment of their being prisoners; and an engagement that they should not serve again by sea or land till they should be regularly exchanged: a proposal that was received with becoming thankfulness on the part of the Governor, and with the strongest expressions of gratitude by the whole country; and it is but justice to the Spanish nation to acknowledge, that an offer was made in return by the Marquis of Solano, of the use of their hospitals for our wounded seamen, pledging at the same time the honour of Spain for their being carefully attended.

Indeed the whole of Lord Collingwood's conduct upon this occasion, whether we consider him as a seaman or a christian, an able commander or as a private friend, skilful and brave in action, or cool and collected in the trying scenes of difficulty and danger which followed; no less firm in adversity than free from pride in the hour of victory, as humane as he is brave, and good as he is great, must impress us very strongly in his favour, and lead us to look with the fullest confidence to such a character as most happily formed to be the successor of our departed Hero;"—" worthy (as that great man said of Sir John Jervis, his Commander) of such a fleet, for he knows how to use it in the most beneficial manner*." In saying this we mean not to detract from the merits of other great and gallant men. We have already admitted, and our pride and confidence are gratified in the reflection, that there are numbers in succession waiting only for the wind and tide of fortune to bring their talents into action.

Were we disposed, in our esteem of this distinguished character, to pay a compliment to his merits that might be considered as more exclusive, it would be the pious gratitude of his feelings, and his confidence in God, that we should hold up as the discriminating feature to distinguish between him and other men. Numerous as we have allowed are the able and the brave; but seldom have we found the man in whom both these characters were united, (Nelson always excepted,) who in the pride of con-

* Letter to Captain Locker, November 5, 1796

quest, and amidst all the vanity that it is calculated to feed, not forgetting in whose hands it is to prosper or to defeat the highest talents, and the utmost strength of man, could lay aside all the pride of the conqueror, and ascribe his successes unto God. This in a most eminent degree Lord Collingwood did. Scarce was the battle over, when the arrangement was made for a day of thanksgiving throughout the fleet, to that Providence to whom he did not think it beneath a conqueror to own that he was indebted for the brilliant success with which the day had terminated. So much to the honour of this illustrious and virtuous character is the general order that he issued on this occasion, that though it has already appeared in a former volume, we should not do justice to the pious feelings which it expresses, if we did not in this place bring it to the recollection of our readers, as one of the traits which must ever redound to his own praise, while he so justly ascribes his success to a higher power, to whom the glory of it must belong.

The Almighty God, whose arm is strength, having of his great mercy been pleased to crown the exertions of His Majesty's fleet with success, in giving them a complete victory over their enemies on the 21st of this month; and that all praise and thanksgiving may be offered up to the throne of grace, for the great benefit to our country and to mankind, I have thought proper that a day should be appointed of general humiliation before God, and thanksgiving for his merciful goodness, imploring forgiveness of sins, a continuation of his divine mercy, and his constant aid to us in the defence of our country's liberties and laws, and without which the utmost efforts of man are nought: and direct therefore that be appointed for this holy purpose.

Given on board the Euryalus, off Cape Trafalgar, October 22, 1805.

C. COLLINGWOOD.

In this, as we have before had occasion to observe, "an example is furnished both to commanders and men of every rank and description, whether naval or military, to look unto God for strength, and to ascribe their successes to him who ruleth alike the ragings of the sea and the events of war; and great as the benefit of this unexampled victory will be to our own country, and in our own day, the benefit of that example of devout and religious praise, which the relation of this event, both in the language and spirit which it breathes, will extend to other countries and future times, may be greater in a moral point of view than it is even in a political *."

The pious gratitude of the Commander in Chief upon this occasion, as in the victory of the Nile, could not fail to make a suitable impression, not only upon the feelings of our own seamen, but upon the prisoners, both officers and men, from whom it must have drawn the same involuntary tribute of admiration which they paid upon the former occasion, when they saw their conquerors engaged in the same solemn act of praise and thanksgiving for the victory which had then been obtained, "that it was no wonder we could preserve such order and discipline, when we could impress the minds of our men with such sentiments, after a victory so great, and at a moment of such seeming confusion †."

Lord Nelson, imbibing from his early education those principles which were to be the ground of his confidence upon all occasions, felt the comfort and advantage of them to the closing moment of his life; and his successor, alike trained in the school of virtue, felt the same confidence in the hour of difficulty and need: and the pious reference of his glorious victory, and his subsequent escape from the perils which he had to combat, to that Almighty Power, "whose arm is strength," proves that the lessons of his youth had not been forgotten, but matured and confirmed by the experience and events of future years. "They who go down to the sea in ships, and occupy their business in great waters, these men see the the works of the Lord, and his wonders in the deep ‡." In both these characters we see the effect exemplified; and as the venerable father of the former,

---

* Extract from a Sermon on the occasion. NAVAL CHRONICLE, Vol. XV, page 32.

† Gentleman's Magazine. January, 1799.

‡ Psalm cvii, 23, 24.

when congratulated by a Right Reverend Prelate * on his having lived to see the eminence which his son had attained, replied, "I rejoice still more that he has proved himself to be what he always was from his earliest youth, a sincere christian;" so may the tutor † of our surviving Hero, alike venerable in years, and rejoicing as he must do in the successes and honours of his pupil, still more rejoice to see that he retains the early principles of his youth; those principles which are so conspicuous both in his language and conduct, and which did not escape the notice of his Sovereign. Reluctant as it may be to the feelings of this venerable divine, to take to himself any share in the praise which is justly ascribed to those early principles which were laid in the mind of this distinguished character, we trust that he will suffer his own private feelings in this instance to yield to the public wish, and that neither he, nor the noble Lord, to whom it did so much honour to communicate that which he conceived would give pleasure to his old and respected master, will be offended, if we present to our readers the congratulatory letter which conveyed the compliment that His Majesty condescended to pay him on the occasion.

DEAR SIR,

I CANNOT forbear congratulating you, whilst we are all congratulating our country, upon the services which your former scholar, and my old schoolfellow, Lord Collingwood, has done the country, and the honour he has done himself. I can sincerely assure you, that my satisfactions upon the late events have been materially increased by a notion I entertain that you would receive some pleasure in recollecting that he had been educated under you. My gracious Master the King, observing the other day that Collingwood's was an excellent letter, added immediately, "He was however bred at the same school as the Chancellor." I told him that I was confident the Admiral would refer to you all the merit he had, either in expressing himself so well as to his language, or in expressing sentiments which do him so much honour as a vir-

* Dr. O'Beirne, Bishop of Waterford. Thanksgiving sermon on the victory.

† The Rev. Mr. Moises, formerly master of the school at Newcastle, under whose care Lord Collingwood was between six and seven years.

tuous and pious man. God bless you, my dear Sir, and believe me with the most sincere and affectionate regard and respect,

Your faithful friend and servant,

ELDON.

Though the mind of this learned and truly primitive divine is too well stored with sources of its own, to need the addition of reflected praise of any kind, and such are the mental and bodily powers which he retains, that he is able still to add to the accumulation of more than fourscore years*; yet must such a letter have been a comfort to his aged mind, and yielded all the pleasure which his grateful scholar so kindly wished it to convey.

In recording the memoirs of Lord Collingwood, we have considered it to be due to his character, not to overlook a feature so prominent and distinguishing, and at the same time so worthy of imitation in all future heroes. And if it will operate as an example to the rising generation, who are following in the same path of glory, but are too apt to be deterred by the laugh of their companions, and examples of another kind, from considering the attainments of virtue among the ornaments of their profession—if it will lead them to consider that there is nothing discreditable to the character of a brave and enterprizing officer, in being at the same time a pious and good man—if from such a pattern they may take courage to be at once virtuous and intrepid, ornaments to religion as well as to their profession, friends to virtue, and as such, the best friends and defenders of their country, we shall not think we have dwelt too long upon the subject, if we add to the testimonies which we have already so abundantly adduced, one more honourable proof which we are able to give of his virtuous character, and that from his

* In a visit which was lately paid to this venerable father of our church, by a neighbouring clergyman, he was found reading, without spectacles, the Homilies of Chrysostom, in the original language; and it is a circumstance gratifying to the feelings of humanity, that this ornament of religion, literature and human nature, is able in his 85th year to read any author, sacred or classical, with as much facility as at any period of his life. Long may he continue to enjoy the *mens sana in corpore sano*, and the pleasure of having lived to see three of his scholars at the head of their several professions; two of them honoured with the peerage, and the third (Sir William Scott) no less eminent in his line!

earliest youth, and upon the authority of one who knew him on his entrance into life, and was the patron of his merit, and a Captain under whom he served; who has passed through all the stages of the same profession, and is now, if not at the very head of the list, only preceded by one other of the early patrons of our distinguished subject, the brave veteran Admiral Roddam.

While we congratulate this venerable seaman, high in rank and character as venerable in years, whose own name has been enrolled among our naval worthies*, and who is now in the enjoyment of his health and faculties at the age of fourscore years and more, on his having lived to see the proof of his discernment, and the honours to which his countryman has arrived, we indulge a pleasure, which our readers will equally feel with ourselves, in transcribing from a letter written by this gallant veteran, subsequent to the victory of Trafalgar, the honourable testimony which he bears to the early promise, and the private worth, of the subject of our memoir. "His private worth equals the splendour of his well-known public value. He is in every respect a great and good man: and in every circumstance, both professionally and other wise, he has fully proved himself deserving of the high opinion I early formed of him, and which I always hoped would in time render him as much approved by his country as he was valued by me."

His own great merit, rather than interest or friends, has, under Providence, at length brought him into that notice, and that high sphere of action, in which the opportunity has been afforded to display his talents to advantage, and to call forth the well-earned praises and admiration of his country; and we trust the time is not far distant when he will have further occasion to add to his own, and the honour of the nation, by gathering up the fragments that remain of the broken Navy of our enemies. But in proportion to what has been already done, it must not be forgotten that less remains to do †. If we expect that his shall

---

* NAVAL CHRONICLE, Vol. IX, page 253.

† In little more than six months we have taken and destroyed no less than 30 ships of the line; 2 by Sir Robert Calder, 19 in the action off Trafalgar; 4 by Sir Richard Strachan, and 5 in the West Indies, by Admiral Duckworth.

rise one above the other like the glories of his predecessor, and that where Nelson left off he is to begin the climax which shall exalt him to an equal height beyond the present, we do him not justice. Not so much to humble that pride which might savour of presumption, as to do justice to the merits of our present and future heroes, we should remember how little is left for them to do. When shall the boasted armaments of our enemy again present a fleet of three and thirty sail to afford another harvest like the glorious and abundant harvest of Trafalgar? All that does remain for British skill and British gallantry to effect will be effected; and should the opportunity again occur, it will not pass by without bringing once more into our view those talents of which the public have already had such noble specimens. Lord Collingwood has been an active and a faithful servant of the public through a long course of years; and though, like many others, little known beyond the line of his profession, his country has been receiving the benefit of his services for five and forty years, with little intermission from the privations and hardships of a life at sea, having had, as we have seen, but a few years out of all that time to himself, and the enjoyment of his friends. As he writes himself, in a letter which is now before us, dated the 7th of January last, before he could know what his country would do for his family:—"Since the year 1793, I have been only one year at home. To my own children I am scarcely known; yet, while I have health and strength to serve my country, I consider that health and strength due to it: and if I serve it successfully, as I have ever done faithfully, my children will not want friends."

In this confidence he has not been disappointed. His children will not want friends. His country is not ungrateful. It is not the character of the British nation to

"Pay a life of hardships with a line."

The same grateful feelings, so honourable to the character of the nation, and so encouraging to the rising race of heroes, which have attended the departed Nelson to his grave, which have affectionately mourned over his ashes, which have decreed monuments to his memory, and entailed estates upon his posterity, that his name may be had in everlasting remembrance, have not been unmindful of the partner of his glory, or the brave seamen who have contributed to immortalize their names. In grateful acknowledgment of the services of the latter, the abundant subscriptions that have been poured into the Patriotic Fund for the wounded, and the widows and orphans of the deceased, will ever remain a monument of national gratitude, highly honourable to the country, and encouraging to the brave seamen who shall hereafter be employed to fight its battles. And for the former, he has been promoted in rank, has been honoured by his Sovereign with the peerage, and his country has added to these distinguished honours the more solid rewards which his services had well entitled him to expect. On the 9th of November, when the rank of Rear-Admiral of the Red was restored in the Navy, he was advanced from the Blue to the rank of Vice-Admiral of the Red. On the same day His Majesty was graciously pleased to confer upon him and his heirs male, the title of Baron Collingwood, of Caldburne and Hethpoole, in the county of Northumberland: and the two Houses of Parliament, in addition to their vote of thanks, concurred in a grant of two thousand pounds a year for his own life, and the lives of his two succeeding male heirs, which upon finding that he had only two daughters, was afterwards changed into pensions upon them.

And in conferring the benefit, a just eulogium was passed upon the noble Admiral, by the Minister who introduced the motion, prefacing it with that due tribute of praise which was in every one's mouth, and vibrated in every rejoicing heart; but which received an additional lustre from the testimony which had been borne to his merits by one whose opinion is decisive upon such questions, and who had anticipated all that his grateful country has since experienced, but which he himself, alas! did not survive to witness, and record with his own discriminating and judicious praise. The satisfaction which he expressed on the appointment of the Vice-Admiral as his second, and his perfect confidence in the talents and zeal of such an able and active coadjutor, is worth a thousand of the compliments that we might pay; and if the praise that we have attempted to confer, could be supposed to want any confirmation, we have only to refer to such an authority to substantiate all that we have said.

To the grateful remuneration of his services, which his country has not been backward to confer, we have now the satisfaction to add a very handsome addition to his good fortune, which he has since received, through a private channel, in the bequest of an estate by one of the same name, but very distantly, if at all related, the late Edward Collingwood, Esq., of Chirton, near North Shields. This estate*, which would have been a proper appendage to the title, will, like the title itself, be probably lost to his family, in default of a male heir to inherit it: but though the estate is entailed, and will, if he should leave no son, go into another channel, and his title will be extinct, his name and his services will never be forgotten. Long may he live himself to enjoy his well-earned honours and rewards; and if, before he retires to reap the fruits of his labours in those domestic and social comforts which it has hitherto been so little in his power to enjoy, there remain for him, like his illustrious predecessor, higher honours and further proofs of his gallantry to display, the occasion is all that we have to wish him; fully confident in the powers which he has already had the opportunity to display, in his zeal for the service, in his own strong attachment to his King and Country, in the strong abhorrence with which, in common with every friend to religion, order, and justice, he sees the usurpation of tyranny and injustice in other countries, and his strong desire to be one of the instruments in the hand of Providence to humble the pride, and check the progress of that dangerous enemy to the peace and independence of all nations, which leaves us no choice but that of victorious warfare or illusive peace. He is one of those,

* About £.1400 per annum, with the house and half the library: the other half to be selected by Spencer Stanhope's third son, to whom the bulk of his fortune now, and the remainder, with the rest of the library, which is very valuable, eventually goes.

who, if they can do more than preserve the liberties and rights of our own nation, will do this; and teach the proud tyrant, that however he may trample upon the rights of other nations, and spread desolation and oppression every where else, the empire of the seas is still our own. The land we live in shall still be free, proudly defended by its wooden walls, and those brave warriors who are emulous to share with the heroes that have gone before them the glory of maintaining the superiority of the British flag, and the independence and prosperity of the British nation. We know enough of Lord Collingwood to be assured of this, that he will not rest upon any past services or successes, if more it be in his power to do.

"Nilque putans actum dum quid superesset agendum."

We cannot conclude our memoir of this noble and distinguished officer, with a higher compliment to his talents or his gallantry, than the eulogy that was pronounced in the House of Lords by one who is himself both a judge of merit and a distinguished character in the line of his profession*, "that he only wants the opportunity to prove himself

A SECOND NELSON."

NAVAL ANECDOTES, COMMERCIAL HINTS, RECOLLECTIONS, &c.

NANTES IN GURGITE VASTO.

SOME PARTICULARS RESPECTING ADMIRAL DUCKWORTH.

THIS gallant officer, who has recently distinguished himself by the destruction of Lesseigue's squadron in the West Indies, is the son of a clergyman, and descended of an old and highly respectable family. He was Midshipman on board the Kent when her aftermost magazine blew up. From this miraculous escape it would appear as if Heaven had rescued him for the glory of his country. He was then appointed Lieutenant, and went on the coast of America with the brave Captain Fielding, in the Diamond, where he became a thorough seaman. He was made Lieutenant

* Lord Hood.

of the Princess Royal, on the West India station; after which he was appointed Master and Commander of the Rover sloop of war; he was then posted into the Terrible, of 74 guns, whence he was raised to the rank of Admiral's Captain of the Princess Royal, Admiral Rowley. In all these gradations his merit was conspicuous on many occasions, and not a few presented themselves in the different periods of his nautical life.

French Account of the late Action in the West Indies, between Vice-Admiral Sir J. T. DUCKWORTH, *K.B., and Vice-Admiral* LESSEIGUES.

[FROM THE MONITEUR.]

Paris, March 30.

HIS Excellency the Minister of Marine has received the following dispatch from Captain Cocault, Commandant of His Majesty's corvette la Diligente, dated Port Louis Road, March 26:—

SIR,

Scarcely at anchor in this road, it is with regret that I seize the occasion to give you an account of the misfortunes which the vessels under Vice-Admiral Lesseigues have sustained, and of which the corvette I have the honour to command formed a part.

We left Brest on the 13th of December, the wind blowing pretty fresh from the N.E., to the number of fifteen ships of the line, six frigates, and four corvettes.

On the 24th we separated in several squadrons, and I was ordered to put myself under the command of Vice-Admiral Lesseigues.

On the 25th, the winds continuing N.N.E., we made sail to the westward, when we discovered a convoy of upwards of 30 sail to the windward*. The Commandant made the signal to haul our wind and give chase, but after a pursuit of eight hours, despairing of being able to come up with them, in consequence of their position, and the great distance they kept, he collected the squadron, and continued his voyage.

On the 4th Nivose, lat. 44°, long. 24° from the meridian of Paris, we experienced a dreadful storm, the wind north. All the vessels suffered much; the Jupiter lost her main-top-mast, and the Diomede made a great deal of water.

The Alexandre and le Brave separated from us on the 5th,

* This was probably the Arethusa frigate and convoy.—Vide extract of a letter from an officer on board the Arethusa, page 302.

when Vice-Admiral Lesseigue's division was reduced to three ships of the line, two frigates, and a corvette.

We discovered the Azores on the 2d of January, and on the 19th we were in sight of St. Domingo.

On the 20th, in the morning, I had orders to take the lead of the division, for the purpose of mooring in the road of St. Domingo, but the calms I met with were the cause of all the vessels arriving and coming to their moorings at the same time; viz. at two in the afternoon.

The Admiral immediately gave orders for the disembarkation of the troops, to the number of sixteen or eighteen hundred men, with ammunition and other necessaries for the colony. This was completed on the 21st, and on disembarking we were convinced of the satisfaction the colony would feel upon receiving this reinforcement; the colony, however, was in a very good condition, and enjoyed perfect tranquillity.

On the following days the vessels were employed in taking in water, and repairing the damages occasioned by the bad weather. On the 29th the Alexandre joined the vessels in the road, and on the same day I was ordered out upon observation to the windward, and, favoured by the breezes from shore, was upon the point of fixing my cruise off the isles of Javna.

On the 5th of February, conformably to my instructions, I took my course to St. Domingo, and being off the road at six in the morning, I discovered several sail to the E.N.E., which I immediately knew to be an enemy's squadron. I then distinguished in this squadron *nine ships of the line* and *several frigates*, and immediately made the signal of an enemy of superior force to our squadron. At half-past six the Admiral answered my signals; and in nearing his moorings, I perceived on board his vessel the signal for slipping his cables. At seven o'clock the four ships of the line, and the two frigates, were under sail, with a very light wind; while the enemy's *nine* ships of the line and frigates were favoured by the shifting of the breeze from the north to the eastward.

At a quarter before nine o'clock, the Commandant made a signal for forming the line, and at the same time to carry all sail, and prepare for action. The enemy, however, continued to gain upon us considerably.

At ten o'clock the headmost ship of the enemy's line was engaged with the Alexandre, and in a quarter of an hour afterwards the fight was general. The quickness of the firing, and the thick smoke which concealed the vessels, prevented us from distinguishing any object. Being to the windward of our squadron, and at no great distance from the shore, I received a part of the enemy's fire, which was directed against our headmost ships; and at last, to avoid going on shore, I found myself obliged to crowd sail, and go before the wind: the frigates, la Comète and la Felicité practised the same manœuvre.

At half-past eleven o'clock, the smoke having in some measure dispersed, I discovered one of our ships dismasted, and on fire, and surrounded by *several* of the English vessels; the rest, notwithstanding their inferiority, maintained the contest with *great fury*; but at half-past one, overpowered by the enemy's superior numbers, they had run aground. *Our frigates*, which had previously approached the scene of action, now found it *convenient* to haul their wind, and I thought it proper to follow their example; but *fearing* that our retreat should be cut off, we stood out to sea. However, we had in the mean while approached near enough to observe the state of both squadrons: three of our ships seemed to be grounded near the batteries; the whole were dismasted, and in the enemy's possession. *Two* English ships lay near our own that were ashore, *as bare as sheer-hulks*, *all* their masts and rigging shot away; they had fired signals of *distress*, and the frigates seemed busy in saving the crews: *two other* English ships, dismasted at the same time, were in the offing, and in a *distressed* situation; and the *rest* of the enemy's squadron seemed to have suffered considerably.

The French ships that were aground had their colours flying, and seemed to us to have hoisted out their boats for the purpose of putting their people on shore. Our ships had displayed a singular share of courage and resolution. The behaviour of the crews left us no doubt that, with an *equal* force, the enemy would have been *crushed*. If the squadron had been able to get to windward, and clear the coast, I am persuaded it would have had the *advantage* of the enemy, and been able to *escape*. Until this unhappy affair our cruise had all the success desired: our misfortunes arose from our remaining too long in the road. Our corvette being chased by the enemy's frigates was obliged to bear away. After having passed to the west of the island of St. Domingo, we entered the English Channel on the 24th of February. In the night between the 9th and 10th of March, lat. 38°, long. 40°, we met with a violent gale from the S.W., and I lost sight of the frigates la Comète and la Felicité, with whom I kept company after leaving

St. Domingo; not being able to hear any thing of them after the late gale, I neglected no means for hastening my return to France.

On the 25th of March, at day-break, I discovered the Isles de Glenau, and on the 26th I moored in the road of Port Louis, from whence I have the honour to transmit these unpleasant details. I have the honour to offer your Excellency the assurance of my respect.

COCAULT.

PATRIOTIC FUND.

Lloyd's, March 25, 1806.

AT a General Meeting of the Committee, held this day,

Read from the London Gazette Extraordinary of the 24th instant, letters from Vice-Admiral Sir John Thomas Duckworth, K.B., commanding a squadron of His Majesty's ships, addressed to William Marsden, Esq., relating an engagement with a French squadron at St. Domingo, on the 6th of February, in which all the enemy's line-of-battle ships were captured or destroyed.

Resolved, That a Vase, of the value of four hundred pounds, ornamented with emblematical devices, and an appropriate inscription, be presented to Vice-Admiral Sir John Thomas Duckworth, K.B.

Resolved, That a Vase, of the value of three hundred pounds, with an appropriate inscription, be presented to Rear-Admiral the Hon. Alexander Cochrane.

Resolved, That a Vase, of the value of three hundred pounds, with an appropriate inscription, be presented to Rear-Admiral Thomas Louis.

Resolved, That a Sword of the value of one hundred pounds, or a Vase of the same value, (at their option,) be presented to each of the Captains and Commanders of His Majesty's ships, who contributed to that brilliant and decisive victory.

Resolved, That the Sum of one hundred pounds be presented to each of the Lieutenants of His Majesty's Navy, Captains of Royal Marines, and other Officers, in the second class of His Majesty's proclamation for the distribution of prize-money, who was severely wounded; and the Sum of fifty pounds to each Officer of the same rank, who was slightly wounded.

Resolved, That the Sum of fifty pounds be presented to each of the Officers in the third class, who was severely wounded; and the Sum of thirty pounds to each Officer of the same rank, who was slightly wounded.

Resolved, That the Sum of forty pounds be presented to each of the Officers in the fourth class, who was severely wounded; and the Sum of twenty-five pounds to each Officer of the same rank, who was slightly wounded.

Resolved, That the Sum of forty pounds be presented to every Seaman or Marine, whose wounds may be attended with disability or loss of limb; the Sum of twenty pounds to each Seaman or Marine severely wounded; and the Sum of ten pounds to each Seaman or Marine slightly wounded.

Resolved, That Relief be afforded to the Widows, Orphans, Parents, and Relatives, depending for support on the Officers, Petty Officers, Seamen or Marines, who fell in the engagement, as soon as their respective situations shall be made known to the Committee.

J. P. WELSFORD, Secretary.

THE LIFE OF A SAILOR.

CAPTAIN THOMAS BARWISE, of the ship Cumberland, of Whitehaven, (a native of Lousey, in Abbey-Holm,) in the course of twenty-six years has made five voyages to Waterford, three to France, one to Gibraltar, two to Greenland, one to the East Indies, five to America, and fifteen to Jamaica!—Captain Barwise is only forty-two years of age, *eighteen* of which (and since he was of the age of sixteen years) he has *lived at sea.*—It is further worthy of remark, that he never lost an apprentice, nor one man, in nine voyages to Jamaica; and that of the twenty-six years of his seafaring life, he was three years in the King's service, and has been twenty years in the employ of the house to which he was an apprentice.

MARITIME LAW OF AMERICA.

[Extract from a Law of the United States of America, approved March 3, 1805.]

SEC. 6.—*And be it further enacted,* That whensoever any officer of an armed vessel, commissioned *by any foreign power,* shall on the high seas commit any trespass or tort, or any spoliation, on board any vessel of the United States, or any unlawful interruption or vexation of trading vessels actually coming to or going from the United States, it shall be lawful for the President of the United States, on satisfactory proof of the facts, by proclamation, to interdict the entrance of the said officer, and of any armed vessel by him commanded, within the limits of the United States. And if at any time after such proclamation made *he* shall be found within the limits of the United States, he shall be liable therefore to be arrested, indicted, and punished by fine and imprisonment in any Court of the United States, having competent jurisdiction; and it shall be a part of the sentence, that he shall, within such time after the payment of his fine and the expiration of his term of imprisonment, as the Court shall direct, leave the United States, never to return. And if he shall return within the limits of the United States after the passing of such sentence, or be found therein, after the period limited by the Court as aforesaid, he shall again be liable to be indicted, fined, and imprisoned, at the discretion of the Court.

GREAT UTILITY OF ICE.

IT is a fact, though not generally known, that ice, if excluded from the open air, will keep for ages; and that, though ever so old, upon being exposed to the open air, it will produce as pure, soft, and wholesome water, as it would have done on the day when it was congealed. In latitudes where plenty of ice is to be found, where then is the utility or propriety of ships coming so often into harbour for water, when ice hoisted at any time will serve the purpose much better, be attended with less trouble and expense, and be found less cumbrous either in ships of war or merchantmen? In the trackless paths of ocean, where no fresh water is found, ice may be used for quenching of thirst, invigorating exhausted strength, and enlivening drooping spirits; as, in its formation, every particle of salt is excluded. The durability, and other valuable qualities of ice, are of equal, if not of greater importance, to seafaring people as to those who dwell upon land.

FRENCH PRISONERS.

IT has been suggested by an intelligent writer, that suitable accommodations should be provided in one of the small islands close to the main land, in some of the northern parts of the kingdom, where any number of them might be guarded by a single armed vessel. They might be daily supplied with provisions from the main land; but, in case of blowing weather, a fortnight's store might be always kept on the island. They could neither escape nor procure arms; and, if they were even to make themselves masters of the island, they might very soon be starved into submission. They might be permitted to enjoy a greater degree of indulgence than in our prisons in the interior; and with considerably less expense, and no danger to the state. Such of them as had trades or professions might be allowed, as far as the nature of the situation would admit, to exercise them. Free access might also be permitted to such as wished to visit them, subject to necessary forms and regulations. Such an establishment would be at once economical and humane. It would be very bad policy to deliver up the French seamen, who fall into our hands, otherwise than in exchange for English seamen, since this would be gratuitously enabling them to man their ships of war, or to fit out privateers to molest our commerce; and because, in the course of a few years of war, the number of the enemy's seamen that may fall into our hands and cannot be exchanged, will, in all probability, be very considerable.

NAVAL ENGAGEMENT.

MR. EDITOR,

AS a matter of curiosity, the following description of a naval engagement, which took place in the year 1340, cannot be otherwise than acceptable to your readers; and, as it tends to prove, that between the English and French battle and victory are nearly synonimous terms, it merits more extensive circulation than it is likely to obtain, by being confined to the old chronicles of Froissart, from which it is here extracted.

I am, &c. N. P. D.

Edward and his whole Navy sailed from the Thames the day before the eve of St. John the Baptist, 1340, and made strait for Sluys.

Sir Hugh Quiriel, Sir Peter Bahucet, and Barbenoir, were at that time lying between Blanckenburg and Sluys, with upwards of 120 large vessels, without counting others; these were manned with about 40,000 men, Genoese and Picards, including mariners. By the orders of the King of France they were there at anchor, waiting the return of the King of England, to dispute his passage.

When the King's fleet was almost got to Sluys, they saw so many masts standing before it, that they looked like a wood. The King asked the Commander of his ship what they could be; who answered, that he imagined they must be that armament of Normans which the King of France kept at sea, and which had so frequently done him much damage, had burnt his good town of Southampton, and taken his large ship the Christopher.

The King replied, "I have for a long time wished to meet with them, and now, please God and St. George, we will fight them; for, in truth, they have done me so much mischief, that I will be revenged on them, if it be possible."

The King then drew up all his vessels, placing the strongest in front, and on the wings the archers. Between every two vessels with archers, there was one of men at arms. He stationed some detached vessels as a reserve, full of archers, to assist and help such as might be damaged.

When the King of England and his Marshals had properly divided the fleet, they hoisted the sails, to have the wind on their quarter, as the sun shone full in their faces, which they considered might be a disadvantage to them, and stretched out a little, so that at last they got the wind as they wished.

The Normans, who saw them tack, could not help wondering why they did so, and said they took good care to turn about, for they were afraid of meeting with them; they perceived however by his banner, that the King was on board, which gave them great joy, as they were eager to fight with him; so they put their vessels in proper order, for they were expert and gallant men on the seas. They filled the Christopher, the large ship which they had taken the year before from the English, with trumpets, and other warlike instruments, and ordered her to fall upon the English.

The battle then began very fiercely; archers and cross-bowmen shot with all their might at each other, and the men at arms engaged hand to hand. In order to be more successful, they had large grapnels, and iron hooks, with chains, which they flung from ship to ship, to moor them to each other. There were many valiant deeds performed, many prisoners made, and many rescues.

The Christopher, which led the van, was re-captured by the English, and all in her taken or killed. There were then great shouts and cries, and the English manned her again with archers, and sent her to fight against the Genoese.

This battle was very murderous and horrible. Combats at sea are more destructive and obstinate than upon land, for it is not possible to retreat or flee—every one must abide his fortune, and exert his prowess and valour.

Sir Hugh Quiriel and his companions were bold and determined men, had done much mischief to the English at sea, and destroyed many of their ships; this combat, therefore, lasted from early in the morning until noon, and the English were hard pressed, for their enemies were four to one, and the greater part men who had been used to the sea.

The King, who was in the flower of his youth, showed himself on that day a gallant Knight; as did the Earls of Derby, Pembroke, Hereford, Huntingdon, Northampton, and Gloucester; the Lord Reginald Cobham, Lord Felton, Lord Bradeston, Sir Richard Stafford, the Lord Percy, Sir Walter Manny, Sir Henry de Flanders, Sir John Beauchamp, Sir John Chandos, the Lord Delaware, Lucie Lord Malton, and the Lord Robert d'Artois, now called the Earl of Richmond. I cannot remember all the names of those who behaved so valiantly in the combat; but they did so well, that, with some assistance from Bruges and those parts of the country, the French were completely defeated, and all the Normans and the others were killed or drowned, so that not one of them escaped. This was soon known all over Flanders; and when it came to the two armies before Thin l'Evêque, the Hainaulters were as much rejoiced as their enemies were dismayed.

TEMPERATURE OF THE SEA.

M. PIRON has lately communicated to the French National Institute, a memoir on the temperature of the sea; an interesting subject, capable of being applied to various useful purposes, and which has accordingly engaged the attention of a considerable number of philosophical observers. His general facts are, 1. The mean temperature of the sea at its surface is commonly more elevated than that of the air. 2. It is higher the nearer to the continents and large islands. 3. At a distance from the shore, in deep seas, the water is colder below than at its surface; and the more the greater the depth. All the observations seem to show, that in the abyses of the ocean, as well as on the summits of mountains, even under the equator, eternal frost prevails. 4. A similar cold is observed in extensive lakes, and even within the earth at great depths; but it appears to be less sudden. 5. These results concur in proving, that the temperature within the earth is not every where the same and equal to $93\frac{3}{4}$°, as has been long thought (about 50° Fahr.)

NEW INVENTED ICE PRAAM.

A MECHANIC of Copenhagen has made a model of a praam, intended to conduct, without danger, ships of the largest dimensions across the ice. The model has been examined by the most celebrated engineers on the continent, and promises to be of great service to the Danish marine.

EXPENSES OF THE COMMISSION FOR NAVAL REVISION.

A MOTION having been made in the House of Commons, for an account of the items of the 20,000*l.* charged in the Naval Estimates, as having been appropriated to the Board of Naval Revision, great surprise was expressed by Mr. Whitbread, at so large a sum being disbursed on account of this Commission, when that of Naval Inquiry had, after three years of the most laborious investigation, occasioned an expenditure of little more than 5000*l.* The following is extracted from the statement of the Commissioners of Naval Revision on the subject:—

Office of Naval Revision, 5th September, 1805.

An Estimate of the Money that will be wanted for defraying the Expense of the Commission, appointed by His Majesty, for revising and digesting the Civil Affairs of the Navy:—

For the year 1805.........10,000*l.*
For the year 1806.........10,000*l.*
—————20,000*l.*

BARHAM, WM. DOMETT,
ROGER CURTIS, AMBROSE SERLE.

Copy of a Letter from the Commissioners for Revising the Civil Concerns of the Navy, to the Lords Commissioners of the Admiralty.

Office for Revising, &c. the Civil Affairs of His Majesty's Navy, March 4, 1806.

MY LORDS,

Mr. Marsden informs us, by his letter dated 28th ult., that the Lords Commissioners of the Admiralty having observed in the Naval Estimates, an increased charge of 20,000*l.*, at the rate of 10,000*l.* per annum, occasioned by the expense attending the business of the Commissioners for revising the civil concerns of the Navy; and their Lordships not being able, from the general statement that has been laid before them, to form any opinion as to the propriety of disbursements to so large an amount, he is directed to request, that, as far as may be done without inconvenience, and with as little delay as possible, we would acquaint him, for your Lordships' information, with the particular items of which that sum is composed.

We have to state to your Lordships, that, on the 31st of July last, Lord Barham informed us, that, in a conference with the late Chancellor of the Exchequer, it was determined that the expenses attending the Board of Revision, being Naval, should form a part of the Naval Estimates; and we understood this was confirmed by a letter from the Treasury to the Board of Admiralty, dated the 16th of August last.

Lord Barham further informed us, that, at the same conference, Mr. Pitt authorized him to acquaint us, that in making up the estimate of the expenses of our Board, the salaries of the Commissioners were to be stated at 1500*l.*, and the salary of the Secretary at 800*l.* per annum.

We were afterwards called upon, by a letter from your Lordships' Board, dated the 22d of August last, to transmit to the Admiralty the amount of the expenses attending the business of our commission, that the same might be provided for in the Naval Estimate; in answer to which, we sent, in our letter, dated 5th September last, the Estimate referred to; being

For the year 1805........10,000*l.*
For the year 1806........10,000*l.*
————20,000*l.*

proceeding on a supposition that the business committed to us would be brought to a conclusion in two years.

The items, of which those sums are composed, consist of the salaries of the Commissioners, of the Secretary, and of the Clerks employed under them, with house or office rent, and various contingent expenses of no considerable amount, but of which an accurate account is of course kept by us.

We have the honour to be,
My Lords,
Your Lordships' most obedient humble servants,
BARHAM, WM. DOMETT,
JOHN FORDYCE, AMBROSE SERLE.
ROGER CURTIS,

The Right Hon. the Lords Commissioners of the Admiralty.

ANECDOTE OF LORD RODNEY.

THE name of Rodney is so justly dear to the British Navy, that every particular respecting him must be acceptable. The subjoined anecdote, relating to one of his most memorable achievements, is extracted from the *Memoirs of Richard Cumberland,* recently published:—

It happened to me, says Mr. Cumberland, to be present and sitting next to Admiral Rodney at table, when the thought seemed first to occur to him of breaking the French line, by passing through it in the heat of action. It was at Lord George Germain's house, at Stoneland, after dinner, when having asked a number of questions about manœuvering of columns; and the effect of charging with them on a line of infantry, he proceeded to arrange a parcel of cherry stones, which he had collected from the table, and forming them as two fleets, drawn up and opposed to each other, he at once arrested our attention, which had not been very generally engaged by his preparatory inquiries, by declaring he was determined so to pierce the enemy's line of battle, (arranging his manœuvre at the same time on the table,) if ever it was his fortune to bring them into action. I dare say this passed with some as mere rhapsody, and all seemed to regard it as a very perilous and doubtful experiment; but landmen's doubts and difficulties made no impression on the Admiral, who having seized the idea, held it fast, and in his eager animated way, went on manœuvring his cherry stones, and throwing the enemy's representatives into such utter confusion, that already in possession of that victory in imagination, which in reality he lived to gain, he concluded his process, by swearing that he would lay the French Admiral's flag at his Sovereign's feet; a promise which he actually pledged to His Majesty in his closet, and faithfully and gloriously performed.

That he carried this projected manœuvre into operation, and that the effect of it was successfully decisive, all the world knows. My friend Sir Charles Douglas, Captain of the fleet, confessed to me that he himself had been adverse to the experiment, and, in discussing it with the Admiral, had stated his objections; to these he got no other answer, but that "his counsel was not called for, he required obedience only, he did not want advice." Sir Charles also told me, that whilst this project was in operation, (the battle then raging,) his own attention being occupied by the gallant defence made by the Glorieux against the ships that were pouring their fire into her, upon his crying out, "Behold, Sir George, the Greeks and Trojans contending for the body of Patroclus." The Admiral, then pacing the quarter-deck in great agitation, finding the experiment of his manœuvre, which, in the instance of one ship, had unavoidably miscarried, peevishly exclaimed, "Damn the Greeks! and damn the Trojans! I have other things to think of." When in a few minutes after, his supporting ship having led through the French line in a gallant style, turning with a smile of joy to Sir Charles Douglas, he cried out, "Now, my dear friend, I am at the service of your Greeks and Trojans, and the whole of

Homer's Iliad, or as much of it as you please; for the enemy is in confusion, and your victory is secure." This anecdote, correctly as I relate it, I had from that gallant officer, Sir Charles Douglas, untimely lost to his country, whose candour scorned to rob his Admiral of one leaf of his laurels; and who disclaiming all share in this manœuvre, nay confessing he had objected to it, did, in the most pointed and decided terms, again and again repeat his honourable attestations of the courage and conduct of his commanding officer on that memorable day.

NAUTICAL CLOCK.

A NAUTICAL clock was lately stolen from the observatory of Colonel Beaufoy, at Hackney Wick, which was a very extraordinary piece of mechanism. It had four hands, the first of which pointed at the number of yards a ship sails; the second showed the hundreds of yards, from 100 to 2000; the third specified the number of miles, from one to ten; and the fourth the tens of miles, from 10 to 100. This curious machine was put in motion by a log-line, and the whole was considered as an invention of the greatest importance to navigators.

CAPTAIN HENNAH.

MR. EDITOR,

IN perusing the memoirs of the late gallant Captain George Duff, contained in the last number of the Naval Chronicle, it was impossible not to admire the excellent letter from his no less gallant first Lieutenant (now Captain) Hennah, who has expressed himself as a truly *christian* Hero. We were discussing this subject at our club a few evenings since, when a shipmate of Captain Hennah's bore ample and honourable testimony to the merits of that gentleman; in whom are united the skill and bravery of a British officer, the feelings of a father, and the principles of a most worthy christian. The whole ship's crew were so thoroughly convinced of this, that it was with the greatest difficulty he could restrain their joint application to Admiral Collingwood, to have their first Lieutenant appointed Captain of the Mars, immediately after the ever-memorable battle of Trafalgar. He could not, however, refuse their second request, in a letter, of which I now send you a copy, and which,

I doubt not, will obtain an early insertion in our favourite publication, the Naval Chronicle. I must now crave Captain Hennah's pardon for taking this liberty without his consent, which his modesty would have prevented me from obtaining; but he will recollect, as a friend to discipline, that I must obey my orders; for I am, Sir, his hearty well-wisher, and your humble servant,

JACK TAR,
Secretary to the Club.

Portsea, May 14, 1806.

(COPY.)

To WILLIAM HENNAH, *Esq., commanding His Majesty's Ship* MARS.

SIR, *October* 24, 1805.

WITH the greatest respect we beg leave to inform you the general wish of the ship's company of His Majesty's ship Mars, for your humane and good conduct since your commencement in the ship, and especially since the death of our gallant Captain, George Duff, Esq. For your great and noble actions, we return you our sincere thanks, and hope you will not take it amiss in our applying to have you continued as our Commander; also be pleased to accept of a present of a sword, for your great exertions on the 21st of October, 1805, on the ship's arrival in England.

Signed, for the ship's company of His Majesty's ship Mars,

Joseph Glover, Master at Arms.
Patrick Mahony, Ship's Carpenter.
John Myers, do. acting.
William Johnston, Boatswain's Mate.
William Drake, do.
William Brucklye, do.
William Ansly, do.
William Tettaman, do.
Thomas Williams, do.
J. M'Donnel, Captain of the Forecastle.
D. M'Kenzie, Quarter Master.
John Jones, do.
A. Stephens, Captain of the Forecastle.
James Crummetty, Quarter Master.
William M'Clean, Gunner's Mate.
Robert Coates, Quarter Master.
William Lang, do.
John Pearson, do.
William Davies, do.
Hugh Beck, Ship's Cook.
William Webb, Gunner's Mate.
John Anderson, Quarter Master.
William Bradford, Purser's Steward.

Those brave fellows have, I understand, subscribed between one and two hundred pounds, for the purchase of the sword.

POWERFUL INCENTIVES TO VICTORY.

THE following is an extract of a letter from an officer of distinction, belonging to the squadron under Vice-Admiral

Duckworth, dated on board His Majesty's ship Superb, south of St. Domingo, Thursday evening, Feb. 6, 1806:—

Captain Keats, before we began, suspended to the mizen-stay a portrait of our beloved Hero (Nelson). There it remained unhurt, but was completely covered (so was Captain Keats himself) with the blood and brains of poor Brookbank, one of our Boatswain's Mates. Two or three minutes before the work of death began, officers' hats off on the quarter-deck, our band played "God save the King!" then came, "Off she goes!" and next, "Nelson of the Nile!"—Never was enthusiasm greater than ours, and to it we went with heart and hand.

JUST REFLECTIONS ON THE DEATH OF LORD NELSON.

THE following apostrophe, on the events of Lord Nelson's last victory, is extracted from a letter written by a lady of distinction in Ireland:—

Never was there, indeed, an event so mournfully, and so triumphantly important to England, as the battle of Trafalgar: the sentiment of lamenting the individual more than rejoicing in the victory, shows the humanity and affection of the people of England. But their good sense, upon reflection, will dwell on the conquest only, because no death at a future moment could have been more glorious, and might have been less so. The public would never have sent him on another expedition; his health was not equal to another effort; and he might have yielded to the natural, but less imposing effects of mere worldly honours. Whereas, he now begins his immortal career, having nothing left to achieve upon earth; and bequeathing to the English fleet a legacy, which they alone are able to improve. Had I been his wife, or his mother, I would rather have wept him dead, than seen him languish on a less splendid day.

"In such a DEATH there is no STING,
"In such a GRAVE is everlasting VICTORY."

PLATE CCIV.

THE annexed view of "The Royal Academy, established in His Majesty's dock-yard at Portsmouth, for educating young gentlemen to the sea service," is from a design of Mr.

Royal Naval Academy Portsmouth.

John Theophilus Lee, (son of the late Captain John Lee, of the Royal Navy,) who was a pupil at that academy in the years 1800, 1801, and 1802.

As an accompaniment to the plate, we are persuaded, that many readers of the Naval Chronicle will be much gratified by a copy of the *Rules and Orders* of an institution, from which many of our ablest officers have derived a portion of their knowledge. We therefore subjoin the following, as sanctioned by the Admiralty Board, on the 1st of November, 1773.—

RULES AND ORDERS, &c.

ARTICLE I.

NONE shall be admitted into the academy, but the sons of noblemen or gentlemen, who shall not be under twelve years of age, nor above fifteen, at the time of their admission; except fifteen young gentlemen, the sons of commissioned officers of His Majesty's fleet, who are to be educated at the public expense, and may, by His Majesty's order in council, dated the 8th of October, 1773, be admitted at the age of eleven years, but not above fourteen; the same to be certified by the minister or churchwardens, from the register-book of the parish where they were baptized.

II. No scholar shall be admitted into the academy until he has been examined by the head master in presence of the governor, who are to judge whether he has made such a progress in his education, as may, in their opinion, qualify him to enter upon the plan of education appointed for the academy; and until he produces a certificate of his morals and good behaviour from the master or person under whom he was last taught.

III. The Lord High Admiral, or Lords Commissioners of the Admiralty for the time being, shall appoint the masters, ushers, and scholars, and may at any time dismiss such as they shall judge deserve it.

IV. The commissioner of His Majesty's Navy for the time being at the dock-yard at Portsmouth, shall be the governor of the academy; and the masters, ushers, and scholars, shall be obedient to, and observe his directions.

V. The master of the academy is to reside in the apartment allotted for him in the building, and to have government over the teachers, ushers, and scholars, who are all to observe and obey his orders.

VI. The teachers and ushers are to be accommodated with lodgings in the building, if there is room, which they are to furnish at their own expense.

VII. The scholars are to lodge in separate chambers, and all to board with the master, who is to be paid by each of those who are admitted into the academy upon the original establishment, the sum of twenty-five pounds a year and no more, and who is to be paid the like allowance, by bills signed by the Navy Board upon the Treasurer of His Majesty's Navy, for each of the fifteen sons of sea officers before mentioned: in consideration of which, he is to keep them a decent and proper table, and to find them in washing, fire, candles, towels, table and bed-linen, and the necessary utensils of the house.

VIII. The master is to keep a register of the names of the scholars, wherein he is to set down the days of their first appearance, the times they are absent, and the day of their discharge.

IX. The master is to treat all the scholars with equal care and attention, and to see that the other teachers and ushers do the like; there being no preference or distinction to be suffered among the scholars, either in boarding, lodging, schooling, or otherwise, but all to be upon an equal foot, except the encouragement due to such as shall distinguish themselves from their fellows, in application to their studies.

X. No scholar shall be allowed to keep a servant, but content himself with the attendance provided by the master.

XI. Every scholar is to be provided yearly, at his own expense, with a new suit of blue clothes against His Majesty's birth-day, conformable to a pattern suit lodged with the master, except the sons of sea officers before described, who are to be allowed, by the Navy Board, five pounds a year each, to provide the same.

XII. The master is to take care, that all the scholars go neat and decent in their apparel, and that they show due respect to the commission officers of the Navy, and to the officers of the yard, whenever they meet with them.

XIII. It being intended, that the scholars be instructed in writing, arithmetick, drawing, navigation, gunnery, fortification, and other useful parts of the mathematicks; and also in the French language, dancing, fencing, and the exercise of the firelock; and a master, together with a competent number of qualified teachers and ushers being appointed for that purpose, the said master is to settle a plan for a regular and orderly course in their several studies, and from time to time to vary it as he shall find necessary; which he is to lay before the Lords Commissioners of the Admiralty for their consent and approbation.

XIV. The hours of teaching shall be the same as are appointed for the shipwrights working; excepting that the scholars shall be allowed half an hour for breakfast, and an hour and an half for dinner; and no times of intermission or holidays are to be allowed, except such as are observed in the dock-yard, and except Saturday in the afternoon.

XV. On Sundays, and other days of public worship, the scholars are constantly to go to church, accompanied by the master and teachers.

XVI. There will be provided, at His Majesty's expense, a complete set of arms and accoutrements for every scholar, which the fencing master is to keep in his custody, until they are delivered out to the scholars.

XVII. Such scholars as have been a year in the academy, are to be taught to fence, and perform the exercise of the firelock, at such hours as shall be settled in the general plan of teaching; and the fencing master is to deliver to each scholar a complete set of arms and accoutrements, which they are to keep in their possession during their continuance in the academy.

XVIII. The fencing master is to see that the arms and accoutrements be always kept clean and in good order, by the person appointed for that purpose.

XIX. If any of the scholars shall lose or spoil their arms or accoutrements, the master is to provide others for them, at the expense of their parents or relations, and to give them due correction.

XX. When any of the scholars are drawn out to practise the exercise of the firelock, whether singly or in company, they are to be dressed in their blue clothes, with their swords by their sides; but the governor may dispense with the blue clothes when he thinks proper.

XXI. The commissioner is frequently to go in to the scholars, and inspect into the studies and behaviour of the scholars, and the methods used by the masters and teachers in instructing them; and shall represent his observations, as well of the forwardness and improvement of the former, as of the diligence and attendance of the latter, to the secretary of the Admiralty.

XXII. No scholar to be permitted to go out of the dock-yard without leave from the commissioner, having first obtained the approbation of the master in writing to apply for such leave; and, in case of transgression, the commissioner is to cause him to be punished in such manner as he judges proper; and, upon a repetition of the fault, to acquaint the secretary of the Admiralty therewith, in order to his being dismissed.

XXIII. The scholars are to be punished for their faults, during the first year of their being in the academy, by the rod, by imposition of task, or by confinement, at the discretion of the head master; and for more heinous offences, by expulsion, by order of the Lord High Admiral, or Lords Commissioners of the Admiralty for the time being.

XXIV. The scholars, after having been a year at the academy, and having received their accoutrements, swords, and firelocks, are to be punished for their faults, by imposition of task, or by confinement, at the discretion of the head master, or by confinement with a sentinel at the door, at the discretion of the governor; and for more heinous offences, by being mulcted of a part of the time which is allowed to be included in the time of service, necessary to qualify them to be Lieutenants in the Royal Navy; or by expulsion, by order of the Lord High Admiral, or Lords Commissioners for the time being.

XXV. If any scholar shall be expelled from the academy, he shall never afterwards be admitted to serve in the Royal Navy.

XXVI. Upon application from the parents or guardians of any of the scholars to the commissioner, he may give them leave, either at Christmas or Whitsuntide, to be absent for three weeks to visit their friends. If any scholar shall absent himself at other times of the year, even though it be by leave, or shall exceed the time allowed him at Christmas or Whitsuntide, such time of absence shall not be included in the time of service necessary to qualify him for a Lieutenant. But if the absence be without leave, he shall be dismissed or punished in such other manner as the Lord High Admiral, or the Lords Commissioners of the Admiralty for the time being, shall direct.

XXVII. The master is to certify the names of such of the scholars as have been a year in the academy, to the commissioner; after which time they are to be excused from going to school two afternoons in the week; and the commissioner shall direct one of the master's attendants, to carry them, one of the said afternoons, into the rigging-house, and to show them the manner of preparing and fitting the rigging of ships; as also into the store-houses and sail-lofts; and likewise to take them afloat when any works are doing that are fit for their knowledge, and even to employ them in such works as are proper for them.

XXVIII. The commissioner is likewise to direct the master shipwright, another of the said afternoons, to instruct them in the knowledge of the proportions and use of all the parts that compose a ship, and in such other matters relating thereto, as he shall judge proper.

XXIX. The commissioner may likewise appoint any ship or vessel in ordinary, of the smallest rate, to be placed as near the dock-yard as may be, and order the scholars to rig and unrig her frequently, under the inspection of one of the master's attendants, or boatswain of the yard: he may also cause two guns to be placed in her, with their furniture, and some powder and shot, and order one of the most experienced gunners of the ships in ordinary to exercise and instruct them in the use of cannon.

XXX. No scholar is to remain in the academy above three years, nor less than two years, except the sons of sea officers under the above description, who shall not remain less than three, but may be permitted to continue five years therein, unless they shall sooner have gone through the plan of learning, and their parents or guardians shall desire to have them sent to sea, or unless they shall have attained the age of seventeen; beyond which age they are not to remain in the academy, but shall be sent to sea. And as it is intended to send every year a part of the scholars, who have been longest there, to sea, the commissioner of the Navy is to advise with the master and other teachers of the academy, and the officers of the yard; and from their reports, and his own observation, to send annually, the first week in March, to the secretary of the Admiralty, a distinct account of the qualifications of each of the said scholars, what proficiency they have made in their several studies, and of their genius and inclinations to the sea service.

XXXI. When any scholars are drawn out of the academy to be sent to sea, the master is to give each of them a certificate of the time he has spent in the academy, from the day of his appearance to his discharge, taking care to deduct the times he may have been absent, (except three weeks at Christmas or Whitsuntide,) and also the times which are ordered to be abated in punishment of faults committed in the academy, and to express the same in the certificate.

XXXII. When a scholar is appointed to go to sea, he is to leave his arms and accoutrements in the academy, under the care of the fencing master.

XXXIII. When any scholars are ordered to serve on board His Majesty's ships, the vacancies in the academy shall be filled up, and the established number of each class always kept complete.

XXXIV. The scholars in His Majesty's ships shall be kept to the duty of seamen, but have the privilege of walking on the quarter-deck, and shall be allotted a proper place to lie in, without setting up any cabins for them; and they shall be rated on the ship's books with the title of "Volunteers by order," and receive able seaman's pay.

XXXV. The Captain shall oblige the volunteers to keep journals, and to draw the appearances of head-lands, coasts, bays, and such like; and the master, boatswain, and schoolmaster, shall instruct them in all parts of learning that may qualify them for the duty of able seamen and midshipmen.

XXXVI. After two years' service at sea, the Captain of the ship shall rate them midshipmen ordinary, or midshipmen if they are qualified for it.

XXXVII. Volunteers, who have been educated in the academy, shall have free liberty, whilst their ships are at Portsmouth, to frequent the school, and to be instructed both there and in the yard *gratis*, in the same manner as when they were scholars, but without any other charge to His Majesty.

XXXVIII. If the ships, which any volunteers serve in, return to Spithead from a foreign voyage, the said volunteers are strictly charged to go to the master of the academy, and show him their journals, which the said master is to inspect, and also to examine the said volunteers, and represent to the secretary of the Admiralty how he finds they have improved themselves in seamanship.

XXXIX. The Captain is, without partiality, to give the volunteers, at the end of their service in the ship, such certificates of their sobriety, obedience, diligence, and skill in the profession of a seaman, as they shall deserve; and also of the length of time they have served with him, either as volunteers or midshipmen ordinary.

XL. When a volunteer by order is paid off, upon his bringing to the Admiralty a certificate from his Captain of his good behaviour, the Lord High Admiral, or Lords Commissioners of the Admiralty, may give an order (if he desires it) for his having the free use of the academy *gratis*, and to be instructed there, and in the yard, as the scholars are, but without any other charge to His Majesty.

XLI. Volunteers, educated in the academy, and sent from thence by order of the Lord High Admiral, or Commissioners of the Admiralty, to serve in His Majesty's ships, shall be qualified, in point of time, for Lieutenants, after so many years' service at sea, as, together with the time specified in the certificate given them upon their leaving the academy, (not exceeding three years for the sons of sea officers before mentioned,) shall complete the term of six years, provided they have served two years thereof as mates, midshipmen, or midshipmen ordinary in His Majesty's ships, and are not under twenty years of age; but they shall pass the usual examination of their abilities, before they can be preferred.

CORRESPONDENCE.

MR. EDITOR,

THE following is an extract of a letter from a Midshipman of the Ramillies, one of Sir J. B. Warren's squadron, to his parents in London.

The Prize, Marengo, Praya Bay, St. Jago, April 3, 1806.

DEAR PARENTS,

NOT having an opportunity of writing to you before, since I left England, I have now to inform you that we have been cruising for some time off the Cape de Verde Islands; and I have the pleasure to say, that on the morning of the 13th March, the Admiral had information given him by the Locust gun-brig, that two of the enemies' ships were to windward. He immediately made signal for the whole squadron to tack; which was done accordingly, and we kept standing on till daylight under a press of sail. It was the middle watch, I was on duty. At 4 o'clock all hands were called: we waited with impatience until daylight appeared, then we saw from the mast-head the London engaging a French line-of-battle ship and a frigate; the signal was instantly made for a general chase; our little ship being a prime sailer, came up first to the combatants, when the French frigate made sail, and endeavoured to get away from her companion, but the Amazon frigate, of 36 guns, who had all the time stuck close to her, followed her, and as she passed the enemies' line-of-battle ship, poured a broadside into her, as an *English salute* on such occasions: in a short time she came up with the French frigate, which after a sharp engagement at last struck to the Amazon; she proves to be the Belle Poule, of 40 guns, and one of Admiral Linois' squadron. By this time we were coming very near to the London and her opponent; we beat to quarters, and double shotted our guns, and as we were about passing the London, who had most nobly sustained a severe conflict, she bore up a little and fired another broadside into the enemy; then cheered us as we passed; we returned the compliment, and immediately got between the French ship and them. The enemy fired but one shot at us in that situation, which we did not return, as our orders were not to fire until we came *within pistol shot;* and when we had just attained our proper distance, I have the honour to say, she immediately struck to us, seeing all further resistance vain; the last broadside from the London having made such havock amongst her men, as having killed or wounded above twenty by that fire alone: we immediately lowered our boat, and our first Lieutenant went on board, who took possession, and hailed us. The ship taken was the Marengo, Admiral Linois, from the East Indies, who was then on board, and severely wounded in the leg, and his first Captain having lost his right arm. The total number of the killed and wounded on board the enemy I believe to be about 150: I am sorry to say a number are dangerously so, and dying fast. After remaining a short time on board the Marengo, our first Lieutenant returned to our ship, and ordered a Mr. James, another Midshipman, and myself, to go on board the prize with 40 men, from our ship; the same number has been taken from every ship in the fleet, and the first Lieutenant of Admiral Warren's ship is acting Captain. We are all in good health, and extremely happy together, and we are now laying at the Island of St. Jago, taking in fresh provisions and water. We have this moment I am writing received orders to weigh, and get under sail, but where we are bound to I know not; but I hope soon to see you all well and happy in old England.

W. A. B.

MR. EDITOR,

ENCOURAGED by the polite attention you have paid to several of my former communications, induces me to forward you the enclosed. It was the subject of a leisure hour, and it is probable may prove entertaining to some of your readers. I have taken some care to make the lists as perfect as possible, but should any errors have crept in, I shall esteem it a favour to have them corrected.

Your well-wisher,

A.

Great Queen Street, Lincoln's Inn Fields,
May 15, 1806.

A List of English Admirals slain in Battle, or taken Prisoners by the Enemy; collected from the earliest Periods.

Admiral Sir Thomas Knevet; blown up in action with the French fleet 1512
Admiral Sir Edward Howard; slain in action with do. near Brest 1513
Admiral Sir Richard Granville; slain in action with the Spanish fleet 1591
Rear-Admiral Peck; slain in battle with the Dutch fleet ...1652
Admiral Deane; slain ....do.........do.-...........1653
Rear-Admiral Sampson; .....do..........do............1665
Vice-Admiral Lawson; ......do..........do............1665
Vice-Admiral Sir W. Berkeley; ....do.....do.......1666
Admiral Sir G. Ayscue; taken prisoner by the Dutch fleet..1666
Rear-Admiral Kinnes; killed in battle with do. 1666
Admiral the Earl of Sandwich; killed.....do.....do.......1672
Rear-Admiral Sir Fletcher Holles; slain..do.....do.......1672
Admiral Sir Edward Spragge; slain.......do.....do.......1673
Rear-Admiral Carter; killed in battle off la Hogue.........1692
Rear-Admiral Benbow; died of his wounds in the action with du Casse 1702
Admiral Lord Viscount Nelson; slain in action with the French and Spanish fleets off Cape Trafalgar............1805

A List of French Admirals killed or taken Prisoners by the English; from the most early Time.

Admiral Buhnchet; slain in action with the English fleet under Edward III. 1340
Admiral de Kernel; taken prisoner ....do....do..........1340
The Admiral of Bourbon; taken prisoner by the English fleet under the Earl of Huntingdon.........................1417
Admiral Primanget; blown up in action with the English fleet off Brest..1512
Rear-Admiral M. de Belleisle; slain at the battle of Malaga 1704
Admiral de Pontis; taken prisoner by Sir J. Leake's squadron off Gibraltar...................................1705
Admiral Count de St. Paul; slain in battle with an English convoy 1705
Admiral de la Jonquierre; taken by Admirals Anson and Warren's fleet...1747

Admiral Marquis d'Albert; taken by Admiral Hawke's squadron 1747

Admiral Marquis du Quesne; taken prisoner by Admiral Osborne's squadron in the Mediterranean................1757

Admiral de la Clue; died of his wounds received in action with Admiral Boscawen's fleet........................1759

Rear-Admiral Count de Vergen; killed in battle with Admiral Hawke..1759

Admiral Count de Grasse; taken prisoner by Lord Rodney 1780

Admiral Brueys; slain at the battle of the Nile............1798

Rear-Admiral Blanquet du Chely; taken prisoner at do....1798

Rear-Admiral Perre; taken prisoner by Lord Keith's fleet..1799

Rear-Admiral Decres; taken do. by the William Tell 1800

Admiral Villeneuve; taken prisoner by Lord Nelson at the battle of Trafalgar.................................1805

Rear-Admiral Magon; killed in action at do. 1805

Rear-Admiral Dumanoir le Pelley; taken by Sir R. Strachan's squadron 1805

Rear-Admiral Linois; taken by Sir John Warren's do.....1806

A List of Dutch Admirals killed or taken Prisoners by the English; from the most early Date.

Admiral de Galen; killed in battle with an English squadron in the Mediterranean 1653

Admiral Martin Van Tromp; slain in battle with Admiral Blake's fleet..1653

Rear-Admiral Floriz; taken prisoner ....do...........1653

Lieutenant-Admiral Opdam; killed in battle with the Duke of York's fleet 1665

Lieutenant-Admiral Rortenair; killed .....do.....do.....1665

Admiral Stellingweif; killed ....do.....do.....1665

Lieutenant-Admiral John Evertzen; taken prisoner in 1653, and afterwards slain in an engagement with Admiral Monk's fleet.......................................1666

Lieutenant-Admiral Cornelius Evertzen; slain ..do...do...1666

Vice-Admiral Vander Hulst; slain......do....do........1666

Rear-Admiral Staghonwer; slain ....do.....do.......1666

Lieutenant-Admiral Tierke Hiddes de Huries; slain..do..do. 1666

Vice-Admiral Ronders; killed in action with Admiral Monk's fleet 1666

Rear-Admiral de Horn; killed ....do............1666

Rear-Admiral Van Saan; slain ....do............1666

Vice-Admiral Bankert; taken prisoner in action with Admiral Monk's fleet 1666
Lieutenant-Admiral de Gent; slain in battle with the English fleet under the Duke of York 1672
Vice-Admiral Schaam; slain........do..........do.......1673
Rear-Admiral Ulug; slain.........do..........do.......1673
Vice-Admiral de Liefede; killed in action with the English fleet under Prince Rupert...............................1673
Vice-Admiral Sweers; killed ......do..........do.......1673
Vice-Admiral John Frederickson; slain in action with an English squadron near Bombay 1672
Rear-Admiral Van Ness; taken prisoner by Sir J. Holmes' squadron 1671
Rear-Admiral Van Binkes; taken prisoner by Lord Rodney 1781
Vice-Admiral Curl; killed in an engagement with an English squadron 1781
Rear-Admiral Lucas; taken prisoner by Sir George R. Elphinstone's fleet...................................1796
Admiral de Winter; taken prisoner by Lord Duncan, off Camperdown 1797
Vice-Admiral Reyntejies; taken prisoner by do., and afterwards died of his wounds 1797
Rear-Admiral Munier; taken prisoner by Lord Duncan....1797
Rear-Admiral Story; taken prisoner by Admiral Mitchell..1799

Spanish Admirals killed or taken Prisoners by the English; from the earliest Period.

Admiral Don Pedro de Valdes; taken prisoner by the English fleet under Lord Howard, in the Channel.............1588
Admiral Don Hugo de Moncada; taken....do.....do.....1588
Admiral Don Miguel de Oquendo; taken ..do.....do.....1588
Vice-Admiral Siriago; taken prisoner by Sir Richard Levison's squadron, off Ireland 1601
Admiral Mair; taken prisoner by Sir George Byng, off Scilly..1718
Admiral Don Antonio de Castenetta; taken prisoner by do. 1718
Rear-Admiral Don Chacon; taken prisoner by do...........1718
Admiral Don Blass; taken prisoner at Carthagena 1741
Admiral Don Geranimo Montero; taken prisoner by Lord Anson in the Acapulco prize 1744
Admiral Don Juan de Langara; taken prisoner by Lord Rodney...1780

Rear-Admiral Don Francisco Xavier Winthuysen; slain in battle with Lord St. Vincent's fleet 1797

Rear-Admiral Don Sebastian Ruiz d'Apodaca; taken prisoner at Trinidada, after burning his squadron 1797

Rear-Admiral Don Bustamanta; taken prisoner in la Medée frigate 1804

Admiral Gravina; died of his wounds received in battle with the British fleet off Trafalgar 1805

Vice-Admiral Don Ignatio Maria d'Aliva; taken prisoner off Trafalgar 1805

Rear-Admiral Don Balthazar Hidalgo Cisneros; taken prisoner do. 1805

Total.

English Admirals, slain, &c.			16
French	do.	do.	21
Dutch	do.	do.	29
Spanish	do.	do.	16
			82

MR. EDITOR,

THE following is an extract of a letter from an Officer on board His Majesty's ship Arethusa, to his relation in London, dated at sea, April 9, 1806:—

I HAVE just time to acquaint you that we are now on our return from a successful cruise, having taken no fewer than ten prizes in the course of nine weeks. We have three of them now in company—five we lost in bad weather, after taking out three of their cargoes, and saving the people.—It is impossible for me to estimate the amount of prize-money, but I trust it will be tolerable. Most luckily the homeward-bound packet is now in sight, and I have just finished a hasty letter to ———. I have enjoyed very good health, and indeed so have all our ship's company; and as we are now in the way of making money, I trust we shall continue.—Long before you receive this you must have heard of Admiral Duckworth's brilliant business with the French squadron. We were at sea, at a great distance, when it took place, and have only heard of it as yet through the medium of neutrals; but as soon as we arrive, we will learn all the particulars at Jamaica, where we expect to be in the course of a week at most.

T. S.

EXTRACT of a letter from a Midshipman on board the Marengo, dated Spithead, May 15, 1806, to his Parents in London.

DEAR PARENTS,

HAVING wrote you from the Island of St. Jago on the 3d of April last, informing you of the capture of this ship by the London, one of Sir J. B. Warren's squadron, at which time we were getting under weigh for England; nothing particular happened until the 23d, when it began to blow one of the heaviest gales of wind (for the time it lasted) that seamen ever experienced, which, with the crippled state of our ship, rendered our situation still more dangerous. Imagine our condition at that time, with a crazy ship, having been three years in the East Indies, three times on shore during her stay there, and had received no repairs since she first left Europe; besides, in the engagement she had with the London, she was so severely handled, that the whole of her upper works were shook to pieces; the carpenters indeed from the different ships of the fleet came on board, and plugged the shot holes, as well as our situation (being at sea) would admit of: in this shattered state had we to encounter the furious storm that followed, which my ability can give but a faint description of; nevertheless, for your information, I will endeavour to relate it as it came upon us:—About nine o'clock in the morning the atmosphere appeared thick and black, and clouds hanging very heavy over our heads; we saw the threatening storm approaching by degrees, and made the best preparation in our power to meet it.—At eleven o'clock it blew excessively hard, and rained violently; sent top-gallant-masts and yards down, the sea running mountains high, and the ship labouring heavy; in this perilous situation we remained the whole day, dreading the approach of night: at five P.M. the Admiral made the signal for each ship to carry a light during the night, and to repeat every signal made by him: at six not one of the squadron in sight of us, and our ship became totally unmanageable to the most able seamanship, and still the storm appeared to increase with redoubled fury: thus were we left to ourselves in this hopeless and forlorn condition, conscious of the unfortunate state of our ship, and dreading every moment some unforeseen accident: at seven our mizen-top-mast was blown away close to the mizen-cap; this we thought but a trifle, to what we were in momentary, but fearless expectation of meeting with: we soon cut the rigging away, and overboard it went; then all hands were called, as the ship was making three feet water per hour: we kept constantly pumping, until the moment arrived, when, with a tremendous crash, the once high, lofty, and towering main-mast, with the mizen, fell, and like the once first city in the world, never to rise again; nothing now appeared before our eyes but the tottering foremast, which in a few minutes fell down also. At this moment it appeared that certain destruction would follow; judge then of the helpless condition of 330 poor unhappy mortals, left destitute of aid, in the midst of the ocean, struggling for life, and every next moment expecting a watery grave; here you will imagine our misfortunes complete, but still we were doomed to experience others, for the pumps we were keeping the ship clear with went overboard with the main-mast; we had then recourse to the chain pumps, which we sent some men down to, and to our sorrow they reported they were choaked; however, it was our last resource, and every endeavour was used to get them to work, which was happily accomplished in a short time. Wonderful are the exertions of man when his life is in danger; but certain death appals even the stoutest heart; when the lofty main-mast fell, (and with it almost all our hopes,) the hardiest seaman with the stoutest heart stood for a while motionless, like a marble statue, until still more imminent danger recalled our wandering senses, when a cry became general for axes, tomahawks, and such other implements as could assist us in cutting away as fast as possible the rigging from the ship; the mast still hanging about her, was striking her with great violence; the foremast was under the lee bow, the main-mast under the quarter, and the mizen-mast under the counter, striking the rudder. In this perilous condition she lay for above half an hour, and every roll the ship took the waves brought the mast against her, and would in time have knocked her to pieces; but by a perseverance and courage truly characteristic of a British seaman, the ship was at length extricated from them, a sight I beheld with all imaginable pleasure. But this great work was not entirely completed until daylight the next morning; for although we had got rid of this great evil, we were still in the utmost danger, and momentary expectation of the lower deck guns breaking loose, which if that had happened, our destruction would have been inevitable; but, thank God! he was pleased to ordain it otherwise. After the masts fell we became a perfect log upon the water, the sea running a tremendous height, and we expecting every minute to be swallowed up in the gulf of darkness: picture for a moment in your own mind the complicated dangers that we were then exposed to, and you will feel sincerely for the unhappy sufferers. I assure you that it has made a serious impression on my mind, and has taught me with what pleasure and resignation a man can make up his thoughts to resign his last breath from this world of troubles; we had five men drowned, and twenty wounded by the falling of the masts; but after all these dangers, thank God we have survived the whole, and brought her under jury masts to Spithead, with the Belle Poule frigate, her companion, and the rest of the fleet safe.

W. A. B.

Naval Reform.

THE SIXTH REPORT OF THE COMMISSIONERS OF NAVAL INQUIRY.

[Continued from page 323.]

WE are therefore of opinion, that the public would derive considerable advantage were the workmen mustered in five or six divisions by different clerks, at the same time, instead of two.

When the workmen during the late war were paid for working the whole of their dinner time, they were allowed half an hour to eat their dinners, which were brought into the yard: this apparent overpayment is stated by

---

What are the common working hours of this yard at different seasons of the year, which constitute a day's work?—From 1st December to 2d February, from seven o'clock in the morning to as long as the daylight will permit in the evening. From the 2d February to 1st March, from half-past six in the morning to six in the evening, if the daylight will permit. From 1st March to 1st October from six in the morning to six in the evening. From the 1st October to 1st December, from a quarter past six o'clock in the morning to six in the evening, or as long as the daylight will permit. They are allowed for dinner time, from the 2d February to 22d April inclusive, and from 24th August to 31st October, one hour and a half. From 23d April to 23d August, two hours; and from 1st November to 1st February, one hour. They are likewise permitted, by the usage of the yard, to have half an hour to eat their breakfasts, although there is no order for it.

Are they the same at all His Majesty's yards?—I do not know.

Into what divisions of time was the extra worked by the artificers and labourers of the yard made, and what was the rate of pay for such divisions?—The extra hours were originally divided into tides and nights; one hour and a half for a tide, and five hours for a night; for the latter the same pay is allowed as for a day's work, and for the former something less than the third of a day's work. Workmen employed afloat, when those of the same class working ashore left the yard at the usual dinner time, were allowed half a tide for continuing on board the ship.

the officers to have been counterbalanced by the time saved, which would otherwise have been lost in mustering, had they quitted the yard: so that

---

Where the men have worked their dinner time, were they allowed any time for eating their dinners?—They have been allowed sufficient time just to eat their dinners.

Were they paid for the whole of the time allowed for dinner?—Yes.

What allowance have the men for working on Sundays, and sleeping on board His Majesty's ships?—One night in addition to their earnings on each service.

What authority did the clerk of the check, during the late war, require for setting off the extra to artificers for sleeping on board His Majesty's ships?—A note from the master shipwright or master attendant.

Have men ever been paid such extra when they did not sleep on board ships? —I believe they have in many instances, especially the officers' apprentices.

How were the artificers employed on board His Majesty's ships victualled?—By a note from the clerk of the check, addressed to the Purser of the ship.

Were they always entered on the ship's books?—No.

When the artificers were not put on the ship's books, how was the Purser allowed for the provisions issued to them?—By a certificate from the clerk of the check, stating the number of days they were victualled.

What allowances have the artificers when they are working by job on board His Majesty's ships, for the time lost in passing to and from them?—They were allowed in the months of November, December, and January last, in cases where their earnings fell short of double days, a sum not exceeding ninepence a day, to bring up their earnings to that amount.

Have the artificers and labourers of the yard been ever mulcted of their pay, by whom, and under what circumstances?—They have been mulcted of their pay occasionally for absenting themselves from their work, loitering in the top house, and for doing their work inefficiently, on the representation of the master shipwright or master attendant to the commissioner; and in cases of embezzlement, thrice the value of the articles embezzled, of small amount, was charged against their wages, until the passing of the late act for punishing offences in a summary way.

Have you reason to believe the several schemes of job and task work are fair and equitable, and that the artificers can earn, by equal exertion, as much when employed on one article of job or task as another?—I cannot form a competent judgment.

Have any persons been appointed quartermen or foremen in this yard who could not write?—Not to my knowledge.

Have the persons appointed quartermen in this yard been capable of keeping the accounts required of them?—I believe not always.

By whom are the several notes for job and task work directed to be signed?—The propositions for job were directed to be signed by the master shipwright and his assistants, and the clerk of the check. The notes to the clerk of the check were formerly signed by the master shipwright, and the initials of the name of the person making up the account likewise; since Christmas quarter, 1801, the job notes have been signed by the master shipwright, and a certificate of the work being duly performed is now annexed, signed by the assistant, and master or foreman of the class of workmen employed.

Do you conceive that all the persons who certify the work stated in job and

the above calculation equally holds good, whether the men were, or were not mustered in the middle of the day. In the evening the muster does not

---

task notes to have been performed, actually measure and inspect such work?—I believe not.

Are the artificers and labourers of this yard so frequently broken off by the docking of ships and other circumstances, as to render it very difficult, if not impossible, to ascertain the value of their work, and to pay them equitably for their labour by job?—They are; and I consider it, in many instances, to be impossible to pay them equitably for their labour by job.

Is the present system of employing all the artificers and labourers of this yard by job so complicated, and the schemes of prices for the different works so incomplete, as to be likely to produce much inconvenience, and an increased expense to the public service?—I consider it to be so.

Who received the wages of the apprentices to the officers of this yard prior to the late regulation respecting apprentices?—The persons to whom they were bound.

How were they generally employed?—The apprentices to the principal officers were generally employed in the mould loft and cabins, working at their tools only occasionally; those to the quartermen and workmen, generally with their masters.

Have you ever known any of the apprentices to the officers borne out in different jobs on the same day?—No.

What is the highest rate of earnings which you have known to be set off to the officers' apprentices?—The highest rate of earnings of the people they were stated to be employed with.

As you have stated that the apprentices of officers have been generally employed in the mould loft, occasionally working at their tools; has it been a general practice to bear out such apprentices as were employed by task or job?—Yes.

Was it usual to move the officers' apprentices from one gang to another, in order to give them greater extra?—It was not the practice, excepting with respect to the caulkers' apprentices, who have been removed in many instances.

Were any applications made for its being done?—Application was made, but it was objected to by the late clerk of the check.

THOMAS NETHERTON.

Ewan Law.
John Ford.
Henry Nicholls.
Wm. Mackworth Praed.

The Examination of Mr. Thomas Netherton, continued 2d September, 1803.

Have all the original books, by which the artificers and labourers of this yard have been mustered since the year 1790, been regularly preserved?—It was the practice to muster by rough call books, which being copied into the fair books, have not been kept; but it is now the practice to muster by the fair book, which is kept.

Have the books of the clerk of the check's office been regularly kept at the office, or have they been occasionally removed from the yard?—The books of

take place until after the bell has rung for the men to leave work, and consequently the time taken up in mustering is not lost to the public.

---

the clerk of the check's office have, in some instances, been removed from the yard, in case of the sickness of clerks, and occasionally to bring up arrears.

What books have been so taken from the yard?—I cannot exactly say what books; the receipt books have never been taken out of the yard to my knowledge.

Have any of the clerks in this yard, during the late war, received, directly or indirectly, any present, fee, gratuity, or reward, for taking off the checks of any of the artificers or labourers, or for otherwise setting off on the pay books, wages beyond the amount of their actual earnings?—There has been paid to the first and third clerks respectively, by the artificers, &c., a fee for the quarterly notes, certifying the amount of their wages for the quarter in arrear; but on no other occasion that I know of.

What were the usual fees paid by the artificers and labourers for such quarterly notes, prior to the abolition of fees?—The foreman and officers having apprentices, except the master shipwright, have generally given from half a guinea to a guinea a quarter, and the quartermen from three shillings and sixpence to half a guinea, for themselves and apprentices; the artificers from one shilling to two shillings and sixpence, and a shilling for their apprentices; and the labourers, I have understood, paid a shilling: the whole of such fees were optional, and in a few cases they were not paid.

What was the annual average amount of such fees received by you as first clerk?—I have never at any time kept an account of them; but as far as I can judge, the annual average never exceeded three hundred pounds per annum.

What was the amount of the other emoluments of your situation as first clerk to the clerk of the check?—I should suppose about fifty pounds a year, arising from the usual fee for the entry of the artificers: a fee quarterly from the contractor, for painters' work; of two guineas and fees, for copies of officers' warrants belonging to the ordinary, and filling up indentures of apprentices to officers of the ships in ordinary.

Were the teams of horses during the late war mustered, and their earnings set off on the muster book, in the same manner as the workmen and their earnings?—Yes.

Were they paid at the same rate of job and extra as the workmen?—Yes, in instances where the master shipwright sent notes for their being employed with the persons working job or extra, but not otherwise, to the best of my knowledge.

Do you apprehend that any of the checks against the teams of horses have been taken off from the muster books?—Not to my knowledge.

Have you any reason to believe that, during the late war, the contractors for horses have received more for their employment than they have actually earned, agreeably to the contract, and the several warrants of the Navy Board?—They did not to my knowledge.

Do you apprehend that any clerk or other person in the yard has received any present, fee, gratuity, or reward, at any time, from the contractors for horses, in consideration of their being paid a greater sum for the employment of their horses than they actually earned?—Not to my knowledge.

Has the clerk of the check of this yard ever received from the Navy Board a general index of their standing orders, with their dates arranged under the several

At the times of mustering, if any of the men do not answer on being called, they are checked, or noted absent on the book, by dots placed against their names, thus $\frac{\cdot\ \text{Morning}}{\cdot\ \text{Evening}}$; and the mark denoting them present, or entitled to their pay for the day, is drawn through the line thus $\frac{\mid\ \text{Morning}}{\mid\ \text{Evening}}$. By this mode of setting off the musters, the means of abuse are easy, as the check can be removed almost beyond the power of detection, merely by drawing a line over the dots.

---

heads of his duties, to enable him the more readily to refer to their instructions?—An abstract of the dates of the Navy standing orders to 31st December, 1784, arranged under the proper heads, was sent by the Navy Board the 29th of March, 1785; and it was mentioned in the warrant of that date, that, after a general collection of the standing orders then preparing should be completed, the substance and dates of all such general warrants as should be thereafter issued, should be sent, so that they might be added in their place under the proper heads, and afford an easy reference to the original warrants, when the abstract should be in any degree doubtful; but no such general collection has been received here, nor have the substance and dates of the general warrants issued since that period been sent.

Are the job notes by which the artificers and labourers of this yard are paid, transmitted to the Navy Board for their approbation?—Propositions for job work, not contained in the different schedules of prices, are sent; but the notes or certificates by which the men are set off, are not sent.

Are they returned to this yard when approved or altered?—The propositions are not returned when approved or altered, except in some recent instances for joiners and house carpenters' work, but the Navy Board give directions to set off the men's earnings according to the propositions received, or with alterations, as the case may be.

What proof is there that the job notes sent to the clerk of the check's office are made out in conformity to the propositions sent to the Navy Board?—The signature of the master shipwright, in whose office a copy of the proposition sent to the Navy Board is kept.

THOMAS NETHERTON.

Ewan Law.
John Ford.
Henry Nicholls.
Wm. Mackworth Praed.

The Examination of Mr. Thomas Netherton; continued 3d September, 1803.

As the shipwrights are now said to be paid by job according to the work they may perform, how are they paid when broken off from their work for a portion of a day, and employed in docking and undocking ships, or other occasional work, in the common working hours of the yard?—If they are employed for a part of a day, I do not know that they are paid any thing for it.

If they had been paid any thing for it, must you not have known it by setting off the earnings of the men upon the pay book?—I should know it, if any notice of such employment were made on the job note, but I should not know it if it were covered by an addition being made to the quantity of work bonâ fide per-

In the course of our inquiry, it appeared that this abuse had existed previous to the regulations before alluded to, established in May 1801, when the clerks, whose particular duty it was to muster the workmen, were in the practice of receiving fees quarterly from the men, for notes, certify-

---

formed on the job they were taken from, as a compensation for the time they were employed on such other service.

Must not the amount of the wages to be set off on the pay books of the yard, since the employment of all the artificers, and most of the labourers, by job, be much more subject to error than when they were employed by day work?—Certainly.

Are they not more particularly liable to error from the short time allowed for making out the pay books, owing to the delay in the delivery of the vouchers of the earnings of the men to the clerk of the check?—In some measure they are, from the little time allowed to examine them, and the number of hours the clerks are obliged to employ themselves, without intermission, in making the very intricate calculations which are required to ascertain the amount of each man's earnings.

THOMAS NETHERTON.

Ewan Law.
John Ford.
Henry Nicholls.
Wm. Mackworth Praed.

The further Examination of Mr. Thomas Netherton; taken upon Oath 27th September, 1803.

From the introduction of job work for the shipwrights in 1788, to the 2d of January, 1802, were the shipwrights paid by a general note from the master shipwright to the clerk of the check, without any regard to the propositions sent to the Navy Board?—They were, without any other reference to the proposition than to observe if it were stated to be for double days, excepting from the 8th January, 1793, to the 7th October, 1794, during which time the propositions were dispensed with, and certificates sent to the clerk of the check by the master shipwright, that the men's earnings amounted to two for one.

When were job notes for the shipwrights first sent to the clerk of the check?—To the best of my recollection in February 1802, for those employed at the dock side.

Could the clerk of the check before that period, by any documents which passed through his office, have set of the actual earnings of the men by job on the pay books?—There was no document furnished by which he could, when job work became general, in January 1793.

When was the rate of pay directed by the Navy Board first compared with the earnings of the men by job, and their wages set off on the pay books accordingly?—From 1st January 1802.

By what direction, or to what circumstance was it owing, that job notes for the shipwrights were first sent to the clerk of the check in January 1802?—The warrant which accompanied the schedule of prices for the shipwrights' work by job, directed that the men's earnings on the articles therein mentioned, should be computed at the prices set against the same, and that only the value of the articles not mentioned in the schedule were to be proposed to the Board for their

ing the amount of their wages, upon the credit of which many of them were in the practice of borrowing money; these fees varied in amount from one shilling to five shillings on each note, according to the class and wages of the party.

---

approval: in consequence thereof, notes were made for the articles contained in the schedule, and on the same note the value of the articles reported to the Board was added, to enable the clerk of the check to ascertain the whole amount of the men's earnings.

To what circumstance was it owing that in January 1802, when the alteration was made in the propositions sent to the Navy Board, that the wages of the shipwrights were then set off according to the proposition or job note, instead of the former practice of setting them off by a general note?—The Board's warrant of October 1801, directing the artificers to be employed double days in the winter months, was considered as a full authority for setting them off at that rate, without regard to the amount of the work performed, or sending propositions to the Board; but when the Board's warrant accompanying the schedule, was received, it was understood, that however loosely the accounts of job had been made up during the war, that from that period due attention should be paid in observing that the amount of works performed was equivalent to the wages set off, which wages were not to exceed double days.

Have notes for the earnings of the shipwrights by task been regularly sent to the clerk of the check's office since the introduction of task work?—To the best of my recollection they have.

Do you know of any instances where shipwrights employed by task have been allowed extra?—To the best of my recollection they have not.

THOMAS NETHERTON.

Ewan Law.
Henry Nicholls.
Wm. Mackworth Praed.

The further Examination of Mr. Thomas Netherton; taken upon Oath the 28th October, 1803.

Did the Navy Board, by warrant to the clerk of the check, approve of the following prices, and direct them to be set off accordingly on the books of the yard; viz.

For the Canopus in October 1801:
Stages to make to the Channels 6 No. at £.10 .... £.60 0 0
For the Tonnant in September 1802:
Stages to make to the Channels 6 No. at 10*s*. 3 0 0

The former was approved by the Navy Board's warrant of the 22d October, 1801; and the latter by warrant of 6th November, 1802.

When do you apprehend the shipwrights of this yard will be paid for the quarter ending the 30th June last?—On Monday next.

How much later will that be than you have ever known the yard to be paid?—The payment for Christmas quarter last was delayed until the 11th of April following: for Lady quarter until the 20th July: in no other instances have I known the pay of the yard delayed on account of the pay books not being completed.

Although these fees were represented to have been given for the quarterly notes, yet we are inclined to believe that they have operated with the clerks in the removal of the checks; for since that inducement was removed, the practice, as it has been stated to us, has been discontinued.

We are however of opinion, that the recurrence of this abuse would be prevented, if the clerks were to deliver to the Commissioner, immediately after mustering, a list of the men who had not answered to their names, by which lists the muster books should be examined previous to the pay books being made out from them.

[To be continued.]

Have any of the job notes for the quarter ending 30th September last, been delivered to the clerk of the check?—Part of the job notes for the month of July were received at the office in the course of this week.

Do you apprehend the payment for the quarter ending 30th September, will be delayed longer after the usual time of paying, than it is likely to be delayed for the quarter ending 30th June last?—This will depend principally on the time the job notes are received at the clerk of the check's office, and in some measure on the assistance granted: if two additional clerks be entered for the purpose, (agreeably to Mr. Pering's letter to Commissioner Fanshawe of yesterday,) and the job notes for the quarter ending in September are delivered in a fortnight or three weeks, the books may be completed about the middle of January.

Are the artificers at present employed in the Sound and Cawsand Bay to be paid by job or by day work?—The artificers at present employed in the Sound and Cawsand Bay are working by job.

What do you apprehend will be the annual expense to the public, of the clerks and other persons employed in making out accounts, in consequence of employing the artificers and labourers by job?—About one thousand and forty pounds a year.

THOMAS NETHERTON.

Ewan Law.
John Ford.
Henry Nicholls.

Alterations and Additions made by Desire of the Examinant, the 16*th Day of February* 1804, *to the Answers given by him on the* 29*th of August* 1803.

(a) Yes; but in Michaelmas and Christmas quarters 1802, the earnings of the shipwrights fell short of two for one, and they were set off according to the notes.

(b) They were but for the months of September, October, November, and December 1802? They were not. In consideration of the men's representation of the shortness of their pay, and the officers reporting that they had been employed in working up old materials, and on iron fastened ships, the Navy Board directed the men at the dock side to be paid two for one in those months.

THOMAS NETHERTON.

Naval Poetry.

The heart's remote recesses to explore,
And touch its Springs, when Prose avail'd no more.

FALCONER.

EXTRACTS

FROM

DR. YOUNG'S REFLECTIONS

On the Public Situation of the Kingdom in 1745, addressed to the Duke of Newcastle.

BRITAIN!—that word pronounc'd is an alarm;
It warms the blood, though frozen in our veins;
Awakes the soul, and sends her to the field,
Enamour'd of the glorious face of Death.
Britain!—there's noble magic in the sound.
O what illustrious images arise!
Embattled, round me, blaze the pomps of War!
By sea, by land, at home, in foreign climes,
What full-blown laurels on our Fathers' brows!
Ye radiant trophies, and imperial spoils!
High beats the pulse: the noble pulse of war
Beats to that ancient measure, that grand march,
Which then prevail'd, when Britain highest soar'd,
And every battle paid for Heroes slain.
In military garb, and sudden arms,
Up starts Old Britain; crosiers are laid by;
Trade wields the sword, and agriculture leaves
Her half-turn'd furrow: other harvests fire
A nobler avarice, avarice of renown!
And laurels are the growth of every field.
In distant courts is our commotion felt;
And less like Gods sit monarchs on their thrones.
What arm can want or sinews, or success,
Which, lifted from an honest heart, descends
With all the weight of British wrath——
Or Death, or Victory, must be resolv'd;
To dream of mercy, O how tame! how mad!
One that has suck'd in malice with his milk,

Malice to Britain, Liberty, and Truth:
Less savage was his brother-robber's nurse,
The howling nurse of plundering Romulus.
Hail to the brave! be Britain Britain still,
Britain! high favour'd of indulgent Heav'n!
Nature's anointed Empress of the deep!
The nurse of merchants who can purchase crowns:
Supreme in Commerce! that exuberant source
Of wealth, the nerve of war; of wealth, the blood,
The circling current in a nation's veins,
To set high bloom on the fair face of Peace.
This once so celebrated seat of power,
From which escap'd the mighty Cæsar triumph'd;
Of Gallic lilies this eternal blast;
This terror of Armadas! . . .
This small Isle wide-realm'd Monarchs eye with awe!
Which says to their ambition's foaming waves,
"Thus far, nor farther!"—Let her hold, in life,
Nought dear disjoin'd from freedom and renown;
Renown, our ancestors' great legacy,
To be transmitted to their latest sons.
——————— This sacred Isle,
Cut from the Continent, that world of slaves;
This temple built by Heaven's peculiar care
In a recess from the contagious world,
With Ocean pour'd around it for its guard,
And dedicated long to Liberty,
That health, that strength, that bloom of civil life!
This temple of still more divine; of Faith
Sifted from errors, purify'd by flames,
Like gold, to take anew Truth's heavenly stamp,
And, rising both in lustre and in weight,
With her bless'd master's unmaim'd image shine.
Would'st thou, whose hand is at the helm, the bark,
The shaken bark of Britain, should outride
The present blast, and ev'ry future storm?
Give it that ballast which alone has weight
With Him, whom wind, and waves, and war obey.
Persist. Are others subtle? thou be wise:
Above the Florentine's court-science raise,
Stand forth a patriot of the moral world,
The pattern, and the patron of the just:

Thus strengthen Britain's military strength,
Give its own terror to the sword she draws.
Ask you, "What mean I?"—The most obvious truth,
Armies and fleets alone ne'er won the day.
When our proud arms are once disarm'd, disarm'd
Of aid from Him by whom the mighty fall;
Emasculated, then, most manly might,
Or, tho' the might remains, it nought avails.
Then wither'd weakness foils the sinewy arm
Of man's meridian, and high hearted power.
O Britain! often rescued, often crown'd
Beyond thy merit, and most sanguine hopes,
With all that's great in war, or sweet in peace,
Know from what source thy signal blessings flow!
Though bless'd with spirits ardent in the field,
Though cover'd various Oceans with thy fleets,
Though fenc'd with rocks, and moated by the main,
Thy trust repose in a far stronger guard;
In Him, who thee, though naked, could defend,
Though weak, could strengthen; ruin'd, could restore.
How oft, to tell what arm defends thine Isle,
To guard her welfare, and yet check her pride,
Have the winds snatch'd the victory from war;
Or, rather, won the day, when war despair'd!
How oft has providential succour aw'd,
Aw'd while it bless'd us, conscious of our guilt;
Struck dead all confidence in human aid,
And, while we triumph'd, made us tremble too! . . .
For know, my Lord, 'tis writ in adamant,
'Tis fixt, as is the basis of the world,
Whose kingdoms stand or fall by the decree.
—*What saw these eyes, surpriz'd?*—Yet why surpriz'd?
For aid Divine the crisis seem'd to call;
And how divine was the monition given!
—As late I walk'd the night in troubled thought,
My peace disturb'd by rumours from the north,
While thunder o'er my head, portentous roll'd,
As giving signal of some strange event,
And Ocean groan'd beneath for her he lov'd,
Albion the Fair! so long his Empire's Queen,
Whose reign is, now, contested by her foes;

On hêr white cliffs, (a tablet broad and bright,
Strongly reflecting the pale lunar ray,)
By Fate's own iron pen I saw it writ,
And thus the Title ran :—

THE STATESMAN'S CREED.

Ye States! and Empires! nor of Empires least,
Though least in size; hear Britain!—Thou whose lot,
Whose final lot, is in the balance laid!
Irresolutely play the doubtful scales,
Nor know'st thou which will win. Know then from me,
As govern'd well or ill, States sink or rise:
State Ministers, as upright or corrupt,
Are balm, or poison, in a Nation's veins,
Health, or distemper; hasten or retard
The period of her pride, her day of doom;
And though, for reasons obvious to the wise,
Just Providence deals otherwise with men,
Yet believe Britons! nor too late believe,
'Tis fix'd—by Fate irrevocably fix'd,
Virtue and Vice, are Empire's Life and Death.

IMITATION OF HORACE, BOOK XVI, ODE 2.

BY MR. HASTINGS,

ON HIS PASSAGE FROM BENGAL TO ENGLAND.

FOR ease the harass'd seaman prays,
When equinoctial tempests raise
The Cape's surrounding wave;
When hanging o'er the reef he hears
The cracking mast, and sees or fears,
Beneath, his wat'ry grave.

For ease the slow Mahratta spoils,
And hardier Sic erratic toils,
While both their ease forego;
For ease, which neither gold can buy,
Nor robes, nor gems, which oft belie
The cover'd heart, bestow;

For neither gold, nor gems combin'd,
Can heal the soul, or suff'ring mind:
Lo! where their owner lies;
Perch'd on his couch distemper breathes,
And care, like smoke, in turbid wreaths
Round the gay ceiling flies.

He who enjoys, nor covets more,
The lands his father held before,
Is of true bliss possess'd:
Let but his mind unfetter'd tread
Far as the paths of knowledge lead,
And wise, as well as blest.

No fears his peace of mind annoy,
Lest printed lies his fame destroy,
Which labour'd years have won;
Nor pack'd committees break his rest,
Nor av'rice sends him forth in quest
Of climes beneath the sun.

Short is our span; then why engage
In schemes, for which man's transient age
Was ne'er by fate design'd?
Why slight the gifts of nature's hand,
What wand'rer from his native land
E'er left himself behind?

The restless thought, the wayward will,
And discontent, attend him still,
Nor quit him while he lives;
At sea, care follows in the wind,
At land, it mounts the pad behind,
Or with the post-boy drives.

He who would happy live to-day,
Must laugh the present ills away,
Nor think of woes to come;
For come they will, or soon or late,
Since mix'd at best is man's estate,
By Heaven's eternal doom.

To ripen'd age Clive liv'd renown'd,
With lacks enrich'd, with honours crown'd,
His valour's well-earn'd meed;
Too long, alas! he liv'd to hate
His envied lot, and died too late
From life's oppression freed.

An early death was Elliott's doom,
I saw his op'ning virtues bloom,
And manly sense unfold;
Too soon to fade! I bade the stone
Record his name 'midst hordes unknown,
Unknowing what it told.

To thee, perhaps, the fates may give,
I wish they may, in health to live,
Herds, flocks, and fruitful fields;
Thy vacant hours in mirth to shine,
With these the muse already thine,
Her present bounties yields.

For me, O sho e! I only claim
To merit, not to seek for fame,
The good and just to please:
A state above the fear of want,
Domestic love, Heaven's choicest grant,
Health, leisure, peace, and ease.

NAVAL HISTORY OF THE PRESENT YEAR, 1806.

(*April—May.*)

RETROSPECTIVE AND MISCELLANEOUS.

THE capture of the Marengo, with Admiral Linois, and the Belle Poule (2), and the assassination of the brave Villeneuve, form the principal events we have to record: for the trial of Lord Melville, owing to the regulations that were enacted, must not yet come under our notice.—Respecting the murder of poor Villeneuve, Mr. R. Yorke makes the following remarks, in his Political Review: "In Holland it is generally whispered and believed, that Napoleon Buonaparté was the author of the tragical catastrophe. I did indeed expect, when I had made up my mind to investigate the fact, that the Prefect of the Department would have proved to be one of the cut-throats who figured upon the bloody theatre of the French revolution; and consequently that he would be a proper instrument for the perpetration of any deed which the French Tyrant might dictate. It happens, however, that the Prefect of the Department, of which Rennes is the capital, is no less a person than the once celebrated M. Mounier, a man whose life has not been stained by any of those crimes for which the Ruler of France and his accomplices are notorious. Neither are the Sub-prefect nor the members of the executive power in that department at all remarkable for their revolutionary conduct. We must therefore reject every idea of casting suspicion upon them, while we are in possession of no better evidence than what has been furnished by the minor Parisian journals. There are, however, whole troops of men retained by Buonaparté, for the purpose of executing those secret orders of his government, the deep ingenuity of which he dare not publicly avow. Among these may be ranked the *gens d'armes*, those infernal agents of his police, who are scattered over the surface of France with the view of maintaining tranquillity and subordination. It is well known at Paris, that this description of persons infuse terror and suspicion wherever they go; and the distinguished favour with which they are treated and received by the Sovereign, confirm the general opinion that they are the executioners employed to bereave of life those unhappy victims of the Tyrant's wrath, whose sudden death, or disappearance, is so often the subject of remark in the French papers. I conclude, therefore, that Admiral Villeneuve was put to death by some of these assassins, in virtue of orders from Fouche, the Minister of Police, or through the intervention of Barrère, the secret Police-agent of the court of St. Cloud.

"The attitude in which the deceased Admiral was discovered, is a presumptive proof that he was murdered. He is stated to have given himself five stabs with a knife, and to have been found *resting on the handle, with the blade entirely fixed in his body*. A position scarcely possible for a dying man to have continued in; and therefore he must have been placed in that situation by his murderers, after they had effected their purpose

"The time and manner of his death afford fresh subjects for the deepest suspicions. He was on his return to Paris, to justify himself in the presence of his master, by whom he had been calumniated; and to vindicate his conduct in the eyes of his countrymen. The honour of a military man having been injured by the cowardly aspersion of the wretch whom he had served with fidelity, it was natural that Admiral Villeneuve should be desirous to remove that foul blot upon his character, before he could form the resolution to destroy himself."

Vice-Admiral Knight, whose health has for some time been in a very precarious state, returns home from Gibraltar at his own express solicitation.

A pamphlet, styled *An Inquiry into the State of the Nation*, written by a Mr. B——, under the direction of Lord Holland, has been much read; admired by its own party, but deservedly reprobated by all independent men. It abounds with curious facts, and acute remarks; but the former ought not to have been disclosed, and the latter are impolitic. The following extract towards the close (page 205) will show the drift of this Inquiry:—

"We have now taken a general survey of the relations of England with foreign Powers, and have viewed in detail *the hopelessness of her situation*, if she still persists in building upon the chance of an immediate resistance to the influence of France. Very few words are required, to deduce from the investigation which has just been closed, the lessons of political conduct pointed out by the experience of the past, and by the actual state of affairs. That the high, unbending, unaccommodating tone, which we have been accustomed to hold all over the world, and which the personal behaviour of our foreign ministers has generally rendered still more unpalatable, is in the extreme foolish at all times, and particularly unfit for the present aspect of things, needs not be proved by a single argument, or illustrated by one example."

The American papers give us the following intelligence:—Miranda's expedition occupies, almost exclusively, the public attention. His object is generally believed to be to revolutionize South America; a project for which he is eminently qualified. The American government were not, it is asserted, acquainted with Miranda's intentions.

A New York paper says:—"We have great satisfaction in communicating to the public the following pleasing information, inasmuch as it completely clears the government of all criminal connivance at, or participation in, the late mysterious expedition under Miranda. A letter is received in town from General Dearborn, Secretary at War, in which he peremptorily declares, that neither the administration, nor any of the heads of departments individually, have any knowledge of the destination of the Leander; that on this subject neither Mr. Jefferson nor Mr. Madison ever had any conferences and communications with General Miranda; that it was not until after she had sailed, that they were advised of her being destined on a hostile voyage; and that on receiving this advice, suits were immediately instituted against the parties concerned, and that too before any representations were made to them by any foreign minister or agent."

Miranda's sailing is known at the Havana, and measures have been taken to frustrate his designs.

Colonel William Smith, Surveyor of the Port of New York, has been removed from office, in consequence of his secret connection with Miranda. We have not heard of the appointment of a successor.—*Aurora.*

Letters on Service,

Copied verbatim from the LONDON GAZETTE.

[Continued from page 351.]

ADMIRALTY-OFFICE, APRIL 5, 1806.

Copy of a Letter from the Earl of St. Vincent, K. B., Admiral and Commander in Chief of His Majesty's Fleet employed in the Channel, Soundings, &c., to William Marsden, Esq.; dated on board the Hibernia, off Ushant, the 30th March, 1806.

SIR,

I HAVE great pleasure in forwarding to you, for the information of the Admiralty, the very modest relation of a neat action performed by Captain Loring, of the Niobe, who has just joined with the corvette his prize; and as the Crescent has many defects which require looking into, I have directed Captain Carthew to receive the prisoners on board that ship, and to proceed with the prize to Plymouth Sound.

I am, &c. ST. VINCEET.

MY LORD, *His Majesty's Ship Niobe, March* 30, 1806, *at Sea.*

His Majesty's frigate under my command, on the 28th instant, at ten in the morning, gave chase to three French frigates and a brig standing out of l'Orient, in the hopes of getting an opportunity of attacking some of them separately; and at ten at night came up with, and took possession of the sternmost, the national corvette le Néarque, of sixteen guns and ninety-seven men; had sailed from l'Orient on the same morning, victualled and stored for five months.

I have the honour to be, &c.

J. W. LORING.

The Earl of St. Vincent, K. B. &c.

APRIL 29.

Copy of a Letter from Vice-Admiral Lord Collingwood, Commander in Chief of His Majesty's Ships in the Mediterranean, to William Marsden, Esq.; dated on board His Majesty's Ship, Queen, off Cadiz, the 20th March, 1806.

SIR,

I enclose, for the information of the Lords Commissioners of the Admiralty a copy of a letter which I have this day received from Lieutenant Stockham, commanding His Majesty's ship the Thunderer, giving account of his having captured, on the 12th instant, the Spanish schooner privateer Santo Christo del Paldo, of fourteen guns and sixty-seven men; and of his recapturing a Danish brig on the same day, which had previously been detained by the privateer.

I am, &c. COLLINGWOOD.

His Majesty's Ship Thunderer, off Cadiz,
MY LORD, *March* 20, 1806.

I have the satisfaction to inform your Lordship, that at daylight in the morning of the 12th instant, in lat. 41. deg. 53, min. north, long. 15 deg. 27 min. west, I discovered three strange sail on my lee bow, one of which appeared suspicious. I made all sail possible, and, after five hour's chase, captured her. She proved to be a Spanish schooner privateer, mounting fourteen long guns, viz. ten sixes, and four four pounders, name Santo Christo del Paldo, Jean Gonzales, commander, sixty-seven men; from Bayonne, out fifteen days, sails fast. Hull, rigging, and sails quite new; victualled for four months; had captured a Swedish brig the Pomone, Maenous Sandalons, Master, belonging to Gottenburgh, last from Gibraltar, bound to Liverpool with a cargo of currants; also a galliot, name Louisa et Emelia, Jean Peter Johnson, Master, belonging to Hamburgh, last from Lisbon, bound to Cherbourg, laden with cotton and hides; and a Danish brig, Grunstad, which vessel I recaptured at seven the same evening, and sent a petty officer in her to England; her cargo was lintseed, fruit, &c.

The privateer is seventy-five tons, Spanish measurement.

I have the honour to be, &c.
JOHN STOCKHAM.

Right Honourable Lord Collingwood, &c. &c. &c.

MAY 3.

Copy of a Letter from the Honourable Rear-Admiral Cochrane, Commander in Chief of His Majesty's Ships and Vessels at the Leeward Islands, to William Marsden, Esq.; dated at Barbadoes, the 16th March, 1806.

SIR,

I send, for the information of the Lords Commissioners of the Admiralty, copies of two letters I have received from that active officer Captain Younghusband, of His Majesty's ship Heureux, giving an account of the capture of a French privateer, a Spanish letter of marque, and a Spanish merchant brig:—also the copy of a letter from Captain Collier, of His Majesty's sloop Wolverene, stating the capture of a French national armed schooner; and an extract of a letter from acting Lieutenant Briarley, of His Majesty's armed brig Steady, giving an account of his taking possession of a row boat privateer, and recapturing her three small prizes. I have the honour to be, &c.

ALEX. COCHRANE.

His Majesty's Ship Heureux, N. E. End of
SIR, *Trinidad 4 miles, Jan.* 15, 1806.

I have the honour of informing you, that I yesterday captured the Spanish letter of marque Amelia, of eight six-pounders and forty men, from Corunna to Chamana, with a valuable cargo of dry goods and wine.

I have further to inform you, that the Heureux and Kingsfisher captured, on the 28th of last month, the Spanish merchant brig Solidad, from Cadiz to Vera Cruz, laden with brandy and wine.

I have the honour to be, &c.
Rear-Admiral Cochrane. G. YOUNGHUSBAND.

SIR, *Heureux, Barbadoes, March 10, 1806.*

I have the honour to inform you, that, on the 8th instant, I fell in with and captured the French privateer ship le Huron, mounting sixteen eighteen pounder carronades and two long nines, and having on board 130 men. Upon the Heureux's coming alongside le Huron she opened a smart fire, which was soon silenced; by which act of rashness her Captain, second Lieutenant, and two men, were killed, and seven seamen wounded.

I have the honour to be, &c.

G. YOUNGHUSBAND.

Rear-Admiral Cochrane, &c. &c.

SIR, *His Majesty's Brig Wolverene, 12th March, 1806.*

I have the honour to inform you, that His Majesty's brig under my command, after a chase of fifteen hours, captured the French national schooner le Tremeuse, carrying two nine-pound carronades, one long six-pounder, and fifty-three men; twelve days from Guadaloupe, and had not captured any thing.

I have the honour to be, &c.

F. A. COLLIER.

Honorable A. Cochrane, Rear-Admiral of the White.

Extract of a Letter from Lieutenant Briarley, commanding His Majesty's Armed Brig Steady, 24th of December, 1805.

In consequence of a request from his Excellency the Governor of Trinadad, I proceeded to Pardo Bay, on the Spanish coast, in the Brilliant schooner, attended by a launch, and took possession of the Vacuna, a small row boat privateer, and a schooner and two sloops which she had captured, their crews having deserted them on our appearance.

Copy of another Letter from the Honourable Rear-Admiral Cochrane, to William Marsden, Esq., dated at Barbadoes, March 22, 1806.

SIR,

I send for the information of the Lords Commissioners of the Admiralty, copy of a letter from Captain Sir Edward Berry, of the Agamemnon, stating the capture of a privateer by that ship and the Heureux.

I have the honor to be, &c.

ALEX. COCHRANE.

SIR, *Agamemnon, at Sea, March 30, 1806.*

esterday at noon, Barbadoes bearing south 72 deg. west, distant fifty-six miles, two strange sail were seen to windward, steering large. We soon discovered one of them to be His Majesty's ship Heureux, in chase of an enemy's schooner. Being to leeward, I was happy in having it in my power to assist the Heureux, by preventing the chase getting before the wind, though she endeavoured to cross us. The Agamemnon gained very fast on her to leeward, as did the Héureux to windward. Both ships got alongside of her at half past seven P. M., when the Heureux took possession. She proves to be the Dame Ernouf, of sixteen long sixes, (thrown overboard in the chase,) and one twelve-pounder, with a complement of 115 men; had been out fourteen days from Guadaloupe, without making any capture.

I have the honour to be, &c.

EDW. BERRY.

Rear-Admiral the Hon. A. Cochrane.

Copy of a Letter from Rear-Admiral Sir James Saumarez, Bart. and K. B. to William Marsden, Esq.; dated at Guernsey, the 27th April, 1806.

SIR,

Herewith I enclose, for the information of the Lords Commissioners of the Admiralty, a letter I have received from Lieutenant Charles Shackleton, of the Rebuff gun-brig, acquainting me with the capture of the Sorciere lugger privateer, belonging to St. Maloes. She surrendered to the Mayflower privateer, of

Guernsey, which joined in the chase, and, from her fast sailing, came up with her: great praise is due to Mr. James Laine, her commander, for his activity and exertions on this occasion.

The Sorcière is a remarkable fast sailer, and has done immense injury to our trade, particularly off the coast of Ireland, and in the Bristol Channel.

I am, &c. J. SAUMAREZ.

His Majesty's Gun-Vessel Rebuff, Guernsey Road,
SIR, *April 27, 1806.*

I have to inform you, that on the 26th instant, at eight A M. Guernsey bearing S. E. distant seven leagues, I fell in with a French lugger privateer, to which I gave chase; at two o'clock a cutter privateer joined in pursuit from to windward, and to which she surrendered at half past four, after a chase of near nine hours.

She proves to be the Sorcière of sixteen guns and forty-six men, belonging to St. Maloes, out four days, but had made no captures.

I am, &c. C. SHACKLETON.

To Sir James Saumarez, Bart. K. B. &c. Guernsey.

MAY 6.

Copy of a Letter from Sir John Borlase Warren, Bart. and K. B., Vice-Admiral of the Blue, &c. &c. &c. to William Marsden, Esq.; dated on board His Majesty's Ship Foudroyant, at Sea, the 14th of March, 1806.

SIR,

I request you will communicate to their Lordships, that, at half past three A. M. on the 13th of March, His Majesty's ship the London, which I had stationed to windward of the squadron, having wore, and made the signal for some strange sails, I directed the squadron to wear likewise upon the larboard tack, the wind being at W. S. W.; and, as daylight appeared, made the signal for a general chase; soon afterwards the London was observed in action with a large ship and a frigate, and continued supporting a running fire with those ships which were endeavouring to escape, until half past seven, when the Amazon, being the advanced ship, pursued also and engaged the frigate, which was attempting to bear away. The remainder of the squadron approaching fast upon the enemy, (and the action having continued from before daylight until forty-three minutes after nine A. M.,) the line of battle ship, bearing the flag of a Rear-Admiral, struck; and, at fifty-three minutes past the above hour, the frigate also followed her example, when an officer came on board the Foudroyant with Admiral Linois sword, and informed me that the ships which had surrendered to His Majesty's colours were the Marengo, of 80 guns, 740 men, and the Belle Poule, of 40 guns, eighteen-pounders, and 320 men, returning to France from the East Indies: these ships being the remainder of the French squadron which had committed so much depredation upon the British commerce in the Eastern world.

I have much satisfaction in stating the meritorious and gallant conduct of Captains Sir Harry Neale and William Parker, supported by the zeal and bravery of the officers and crews of their respective ships, who claim my warmest thanks and acknowledgments; and whose exertions, I hope, will recommend them to their Lordships' particular notice and favour.

I cannot, however, avoid regretting that the force of the enemy did not afford to the officers and men of the other ships of the squadron, who showed the most earnest desire to have closed with the enemy, an opportunity of displaying that valour and attachment to their King and country, which, I am confident, they will be happy to evince upon some future and more favourable occasion.

I have enclosed a list of the killed and wounded on board His Majesty's ships, as well as their defects; and have likewise forwarded a particular statement of the ships captured, together with an account of the loss sustained by the enemy, being the most correct that could be ascertained from the rolle d'equipage. Rear-Admiral Linois is among the wounded, as well as several other officers.

I have the honour to be, &c.

JOHN BORLASE WARREN.

Foudroyant, at Sea, March 13, 1806.

A Return of the Killed and Wounded on board His Majesty's Ships London and Amazon, belonging to the Squadron under the Command of Vice-Admiral Sir J. B. Warren, Bart. K. B., &c. at the Capture of the Marengo and Belle Poule, on the 13th March, 1806.

Killed on board His Majesty's Ship London.

Mr. William Rooke, Midshipman; James Murphy, Henry Van Fleylen, John Lay, James Slyde, seamen; William Bryan, boy; John Moore, landman; William Griffith, William Jummers, Thomas Toole, private marines.

Dangerously wounded.

Patrick Fitzpatrick, Quarter Gunner; John Dulforce, able seaman; Francis Costello, John Burges, Francis Sutton, William Brazil, ordinary seamen; John O'Brien, William Brown (1), Thomas Waterson, Jos. Skelton, landmen; William Roberts (2); Richard Hodges, Jonathan Hurcombe, John Shepherd, Bryan Rilley, privates, royal marines.

Slightly wounded.

Richard Poole, Thomas Cox, William Bruce, privates, royal marines.

Officers wounded.

Mr. William Faddy, Lieutenant, dangerously; Mr. J. W. Watson, Midshipman, slightly.

H. NEALE.

Killed on board His Majesty's Ship Amazon.

Mr. Richard Seymour, first Lieutenant; Mr. Edward Prior, second Lieutenant, royal marines; William Gundy, able seaman; George Royal, private marine.

Wounded.

George Marcus, Quarter Master, severely; William Lane, ordinary seaman, severely; John Fox, ship's corporal, slightly; Richard Brown and Jonan. Curtis, able seamen, slightly; Horter Leander, ordinary seaman, slightly.

W. PARKER.

Foudroyant, at Sea, March 14, 1806.

A List of Ships belonging to the French Government, captured on the 13th March, 1806, by a Squadron under the Command of Vice-Admiral Sir John Borlase Warren, Bart., K. B., &c.

Marengo, 80 guns, 740 men, Rear-Admiral Linois, Vrignaud, first Captain, Chasseriau, second Captain.

Belle Poule, 40 guns, eighteen-pounders, 320 men, Bruillac, Captain.

J. B. WARREN.

Foudroyant, at Sea, March 13, 1806.

A Return of the Killed and Wounded on board the Marengo and Belle Poule, in the Action on the 13th March, 1806.

Marengo and Belle Poule.—Sixty-five killed, and eighty wounded.

J. B. WARREN.

Copy of a Letter from Admiral Lord Gardner to William Marsden, Esq.; dated at Cork, the 28th April, 1806.

SIR,

Enclosed, I transmit, for their Lordships' information, copy of a letter delivered to me this day by Captain Maitland, of His Majesty's ship Loire, giving an account of the capture, by that ship, on the 22d instant, of the Princess of Peace, Spanish schooner privateer, which vessel arrived here this morning with the Loire.

I have the honour to be, &c.

GARDNER.

MY LORD, *Loire, at Sea, April 23, 1806.*

I have to inform you, that His Majesty's ship Loire, yesterday evening, in lat. 48 deg. 30 min. long. 12 deg. 20 min., captured the Princess of Peace, a very fine new Spanish privateer schooner, pierced for 14 guns, though only carrying one large twenty-four pounder, and sixty-three men; she had been out of passage five days, on her first cruise, without having taken any thing.

I have the honour to be, &c.

Right Honourable Lord Gardner, &c. F. L. MAITLAND.

Copy of a Letter from Captain G. R. Collier, Commander of His Majesty's Ship the Minerva, to Wm. Marsden, Esq.; dated off Cape Finisterre, April 26, 1806.

SIR,

I have the honor to enclose a copy of my letter, of this day's date, to Eliab Harvey, Esq., Rear-Admiral of the Blue. I am, &c.

G. R. COLLIER.

SIR, *Minerva, off Cape Finisterre, April 26, 1806.*

I have the honor to inform you, that, waiting in Finisterre Bay for moderate weather, and the junction of His Majesty's gun brig Conflict, Lieutenant J. B. Batt, to cut out some small craft lying under the town, a French privateer lugger rounded the Cape, and immediately wore, and stood to sea. At eleven P. M., after a chase of near sixty miles, she was boarded by Lieutenant Batt, and proved to be the French lugger Finisterre, of 14 guns, and fifty-two men, commanded by Mons. Michelle Denré; left Corunna that morning, had made no capture, and intended cruising off Oporto for British convoys.

I have great pleasure in stating the very active conduct of Lieutenant Batt, of the Conflict, to whom I feel principally indebted for the capture of the privateer.

I have the honour to be, &c.

To Eliab Harvey, Esq., Rear-Admiral of the Blue, &c. GEORGE R. COLLIER, Captain.

MAY 10.

Copy of a Letter from the Earl of St. Vincent, K.B., Admiral and Commander in Chief of His Majesty's Fleet, &c., to Wm. Marsden, Esq.; dated on board His Majesty's Ship the Hibernia, off Ushant, the 3d May, 1806.

SIR,

I this day received the enclosed copy of a letter from Lieutenant Usher, of the Colpoys hired brig, containing his account of the capturing two chasse marees in the river Donillan. I am, &c.

ST. VINCENT.

MY LORD, *Colpoys Hired Brig, off the Glenans, April 25, 1806.*

I have the honor to acquaint your Lordship, that on the 19th instant, standing along shore between the Glenans and Isle Groer, with the Attack in company, I perceived two chasse marees at anchor in the entrance of the river Donillan, and which, upon our approach, quitted their anchorage and ran up the river. Finding it necessary to silence a two gun battery before the boats could get to them, I landed with twelve men from each brig, and, after a short skirmish, got possession of, and nailed up the guns (twelve-pounders); I afterwards brought the vessels down the river, and destroyed the signal post of Donillan. I am happy to acquaint your Lordship that the only damage we sustained was having some of our standing running rigging and sails cut.

I have to acknowledge the support I received from Lieutenant Swaine by his well directed fire upon the enemy's guns during the time we were reconnoitring the river and beach. I feel much obliged to Mr. Wood, Assistant Surgeon of the Growler, who volunteered his services, and attended the party that landed.

I have the honor to remain, &c.

THOMAS USHER.

Names of the captured Vessels.

Vincent Gabriel.——Murie Francaise.

To the Right Hon. Earl St. Vincent, Commander in Chief.

Copy of a Letter from Michael Novella, Commander of the Felicity Private Ship of War, of 12 guns, to Wm. Marsden, Esq.; dated at Gibraltar, the 1st March, 1806.

SIR,

I beg leave to inform you, that during my last cruise to the westward, I made the following captures, viz.

The French privateer Josefina, of one eighteen-pounder, and two nine-pounder carronades, and thirty-seven men.

Two Spanish gun-boats, Nos. 12 and 15, commanded by Lieutenants of the Navy, mounting each one twenty-four pounder, one thirty-six pounder carronade, and two swivels, and forty-five men

And His Majesty's late lugger Experiment, mounting four four-pounders, and manned with thirty men. I have the honour to be, &c.

his
MICHAEL ✕ NOVELLA.
Mark.

MAY 13.

Copy of a Letter from William Young, Esq., Admiral of the Blue, and Commander in Chief of His Majesty's Ships and Vessels at Plymouth, to Wm. Marsden, Esq.; dated on board the Salvador del Mundo, in Hamoaze, the 10th May, 1806.

SIR,

I herewith transmit, for the information of the Lords Commissioners of the Admiralty, a copy of a letter from Captain Broke, of His Majesty's ship the Druid, to Admiral Lord Gardner, acquainting his Lordship of the capture of the French brig Corvette le Pandour. I have the honour to be, &c.

W. YOUNG.

MY LORD, *Druid, Plymouth Sound, May 9, 1806.*

I have the honor to inform you, that on the 1st instant I fell in with a French brig corvette, which, after a run of 160 miles, we chased into the squadron of Rear-Admiral Stirling; where she was brought-to at eleven o'clock P. M. She proved to be le Pandour, of 18 guns, six-pounders, (two of which were thrown overboard during the chase,) and 114 men, commanded by M. Malingre, Capitaine de Vaisseau, from Senegal bound to France.

Rear-Admiral Stirling has ordered me to take possession of her. I have brought her into this anchorage, and have the honor to be, &c.

P. B. V. BROKE.

To the Right Hon. Alan Lord Gardner, &c. Cork.

MAY 17.

Copy of a Letter from Vice-Admiral Lord Collingwood, Commander in Chief of His Majesty's Ships and Vessels in the Mediterranean, to William Marsden, Esq.; dated on board His Majesty's Ship Queen, off Cadiz, the 19th of April, 1806.

SIR,

I have the satisfaction to acquaint you, for the Lords Commissioners of the Admiralty, that His Majesty's ship the Renommée, Captain Sir Thomas Livingstone, (one of the ships stationed off Carthagena, for the purpose of watching the enemy's squadron,) on the 4th instant, captured the Spanish brig of war the Vigilante; for the particulars of which, I refer you, Sir, to the enclosed copy of Captain Sir Thomas Livingstone's letter. I am, &c.

COLLINGWOOD.

His Majesty's Ship Renommée, at Anchor, Europa Point,
MY LORD, *W. N. W. one Mile, 5th April, 1806.*

I informed your Lordship by the Nautilus, that on the 3d instant, two Spanish ships of the line, a frigate and brig, came out of the Port of Carthagena, having under their protection a few small coasters, and that the ships of the line and frigate chased us to the southward, while the brig and convoy steered along shore to the westward, the wind being north easterly.

Finding that the Renommée had left the Spanish ships a great distance a-stern, I made sail as soon as it was dark for Cape de Gatte, in the hope of cutting off the brig, and in this I was not disappointed, for at two A. M. on the 4th instant, we saw the brig anchor under Fort Callertes, distant from it about two cables' length.

I was prevented, by baffling winds, from getting up to her for three quarters of an hour, but when we did get up, her fire was soon silenced, and she was in our possession at half past three; the batteries on the shore began to fire as soon as we were within reach, and continued doing it till we were out of their range. There were two gun-boats with the brig, that fired a few shot at first, but they soon ceased, and I believe ran on the beach. The brig was in the act of warping on shore when we commenced firing, but fortunately we cut the warp, and thereby prevented her getting on shore. I am happy to say in this affair we sustained little or no damage, and had only two men wounded.

The brig proved to be the Vigilante, belonging to His Catholic Majesty, commanded by Teniento de Navio Don Joseph Julian, mounting 18 guns, viz. twelve twelve-pounders, long guns, and six twenty-four pounders, shorter, with a crew of 109 men, and is well calculated for His Majesty's service.

She had one man killed and three wounded in the fray; her mainmast went overboard soon after we took possession, and the foremast was nearly sharing the same fate; I therefore took her in tow, and bore up for this anchorage, where I arrived this day; and was the more induced to take this measure, as, upon our appearance off Cape de Gatte, all the beacons towards Carthagena were fired, and I did not know how near the ships which had chased us the day before might be: I hope, therefore, your Lordship will approve of my having so done.

I have reason to be well satisfied with my officers and crew on this occasion; their steady and well-directed fire did them great credit.

As soon as the prisoners are landed, &c. I shall return to my station.

I have the honour to be, &c.

To the Rt. Hon. Lord Collingwood, &c. THO. LIVINGSTONE.

Copy of a Letter from Commodore Sir Home Popham to William Marsden, Esq.; dated on board His Majesty's Ship Diadem, Table-Bay, March 4, 1806.

SIR,

I beg you will do me the honour to inform my Lords Commissioners of the Admiralty, that, at nine this morning a ship was discovered coming from the southward under a press of sail, and, soon after, two more; one of which the station on the Lion Rump reported to be of the line, and an enemy's ship, upon which I directed the Diomede and Leda to slip, and keep on the edge of the South Easter, which had partially set in on the east side of the bay.

At eleven the headmost ship hoisted French colours, and stood towards the Diadem; and, by this time, I was satisfied, from the judicious manœuvres of the ships in the offing, that they could be no other than the Raisonable and Narcissus.

At twelve the French frigate passed within hail of the Diadem, when we changed our colours from Dutch to English, and directed her to strike, which she very properly did immediately, and I sent the Honourable Captain Percy, who was serving with me as a volunteer, to take possession of her. She proved to be la Volontaire; is nearly eleven hundred tons, and mounts 46 guns, with a complement of 360 men on board.

I congratulate their Lordships that, by this capture, detachments of the Queen's and 54th regiments, consisting of 217 men, who were taken in two transports in the Bay of Biscay, are restored to His Majesty's service.

I have the honor to be, &c.

HOME POPHAM.

MAY 20.

Copy of a Letter from Vice-Admiral Lord Collingwood, Commander in Chief of His Majesty's Ships and Vessels in the Mediterranean, to W. Marsden, Esq.; dated on board the Ocean, off Cadiz, 30th April, 1806.

SIR,

I enclose, for the information of the Lords Commissioners of the Admiralty, a letter from Captain Mundy, of His Majesty's ship the Hydra, giving an account of his having captured the Spanish national schooner Argonauta, on the morning of the 28th instant, after a long chase.

I am, &c. COLLINGWOOD.

His Majesty's Ship Hydra, at Sea,
28th April, 1806.

MY LORD.

I have the honour to inform you, His Catholic Majesty's schooner Argonauta, commanded by Lieutenant Don Josef de Mendivil, and destined for Buenos

Ayres, with dispatches, was captured this morning by His Majesty's ship under my command, (after a chase of 230 miles, in lat. 34 deg. 9 min N., and long 9 deg. 29 min. W.

She is a remarkable fine vessel of her kind, having originally carried ten six-pounders and two eights, all of which, however, were taken out previous to her proceeding across the Atlantic on the above service; at the time of capture having only four sixes mounted on stocks, and a complement of 20 officers and men. She is coppered, and well found in every sort of store, and appears perfectly adapted for His Majesty's service.

I have the honcur to be, &c.

G. MUNDY.

To the Right Hon. Lord Collingwood,
Commander in Chief, &c.

Copy of a Letter from Vice-Admiral Dacres, Commander in Chief of His Majesty's Ships and Vessels at Jamaica, to Wm. Marsden, Esq.; dated at Port-Royal, March 27, 1806.

SIR,

I have the honour to enclose, for the information of the Lords Commissioners of the Admiralty, the copy of a letter I have received from Captain Waller, of the Serpent, detailing the capture of one of His Catholic Majesty's guarda costas, by the boats of that sloop, in a very gallant manner.

I am, &c. J. R. DACRES.

His Majesty's Sloop Serpent, Port Royal Harbour, Jamaica, March 6, 1806.

SIR,

I have the honour to inform you, that, on the 28th of November last, being off the Island of Bonecće, at five P. M. two sail appeared in the N. E. quarter. As they were far to windward, and night approaching, I judged, by commencing a chase at that time, there was but little prospect of keeping sight of them after close of day, I therefore continued with the ship in the same situation as when first seen till dusk, and then bore up; made all sail for Truxillo Bay, the entrance of which we reached before eleven o'clock the same night. I was induced to believe, by the direction they were steering, added to other circumstances, this was their destination. At two in the morning of the 29th, these vessels were seen rounding the east point forming Truxillo Bay, but hauling so close to the land that they were scarcely to be discerned. Experiencing a strong current, at the same time setting the ship out, and the wind also in that direction, which they avoided in shore. I found, under these great disadvantages, there was no probability of acting against them with effect without the boats, so they were instantly dispatched under the orders of Mr. William Patfull, the second Lieutenant, and Mr. Charles Trace, Master's-Mate, in the launch, and the cutter with Mr. Samuel Nisbett, Midshipman, and Mr. Thomas Scriven, the Purser, all of whom came forward in a very handsome manner, offering their services, as well as every man employed on this occasion. We had made them out before night; one to be a felucca, the other felucca rigged forward, but having a schooner sail aft, which convinced me they were enemy's armed vessels; I therefore directed the boats to act together, and attempt the largest first. On approaching her they received a heavy discharge from great guns and small arms, but their exertions soon caused them to board and carry their object: which proved to be a schooner built vessel and guarda costa, called the St. Christo Vil Pano, bearing the colours and belonging to His Catholic Majesty, from the Havannah, mounting one long traversing eighteen pounder, two four-pounders, four brass three-pounders, small arms, &c. and forty men, commanded by Don Juan Christovel Tierro, who, and twenty-five others, escaped by jumping overboard and swimming on shore: Lieutenant Patfull, with the launch alone, lost no time in pursuing the other, but am sorry to say, she eluded his vigilance under cover of the night, by lowering her sails, then sweeping round the opposite side of the bay close to Lukes Keys; and at daylight was nearly under the fort Truxillo; a Spanish felucca privateer mounting one four-pounder and forty men; she had accidentally joined the captured vessel off Cape Antonio five days before. I feel much pleasure in saying this service was performed without the loss of a man; and great credit is due to Lieutenant Patfull, not only for his judgment in laying the boats on board, the gallant manner he led them on, but for his active exertion respecting the pursuit; the other officers and men employed under his orders, highly merit my warmest acknowledgments, all of whom I take the liberty of recommending to your notice.

I have the honour to be, &c.

J. WALLER.

To J. R. Dacres, Esq., Vice-Admiral of the White, &c.

Copy of a Letter from Rear-Admiral the Honourable Sir Alexander Cochrane, Bart. Commander in Chief of His Majesty's Ships and Vessels at the Leeward Islands, to William Marsden, Esq. dated at Barbadoes, the 30th March, 1806.

SIR,

I enclose, for the information of the Lords Commissioners of the Admiralty, copy of a letter from Sir Edward Berry, Captain of His Majesty's ship Agamemnon, giving an account of the capture, by that ship and the Carysfort, of la Lutine, a very fine brig corvette of eighteen guns and one hundred men, from l'Orient, with dispatches for Martinique.

I have the honour to be, &c.

ALEX. COCHRANE.

SIR, *His Majesty's Ship Agamemnon, at Sea, March 24, 1806.*

I have the honour to acquaint you, that this morning at daylight, (Martinique bearing S. 81 deg. W. distance 170 miles,) two sail were seen to windward, evidently a frigate in chase of a brig, steering large under a press of sail. Captain M'Kenzie, of the Carysfort, soon made himself known to me by signal, and that the chase was an enemy; the Carysfort having been in chase thirty hours, and by the greatest perseverance and attention kept sight of her the whole night, the enemy manœuvring in a masterly style the whole time. At half past seven, finding she could not cross us, she surrendered, and proved to be the French national brig la Lutine, Monsieur Crocquet Dechauteurs, commander, from l'Orient, bound to Martinique, out thirty-three days, and had not made any capture; she is a remarkably fine vessel, quite new, mounts eighteen guns, two of which were thrown overboard in the chase, is well appointed in every respect; sails uncommonly fast, and is, in my opinion, well calculated for His Majesty's service.

I have, &c. E. BERRY, Captain.

The Honorable A. Cochrane, Rear-Admiral of the White, &c. Barbadoes.

MAY 24.

Copy of a Letter from Admiral Lord Gardner, to Wm. Marsden, Esq.; dated on board the Trent, in Cork Harbour, the 15th Instant.

SIR,

I enclose, for their Lordships' information, copy of a letter I received this morning from Captain Moubray, of the Active, giving an account of the capture by that ship of the French schooner les Amis, a letter of marque, bound from Bourdeaux to Cayenne.

I am, Sir, &c. GARDNER.

MY LORD, *Active, at Sea, April 27, 1806.*

I do myself the honour to acquaint your Lordship, that His Majesty's ship under my command has this day captured the French schooner les Amis, a letter of marque of four six-pounders and twenty men, belonging to Cayenne, and bound thither with a cargo of wine and various merchandize from Bourdeaux.

I have the honor to be, &c.

R. H. MOUBRAY.

Right Hon. Admiral Lord Gardner.

Promotions and Appointments.

Captain Ryder, of Portsea, is appointed to the Gorgon, of 44 guns; and Captain Thicknesse to the Sheldrake, a new sloop, at Portsmouth.

Captain Cuming is appointed to the Sampson; Captain Ommanney, to the Isis; Captain Wainwright, to the Chiffonne; Hon. Captain Boyle, to the Royal William; Captain Strutt, to the Skylark sloop; J. Backie, Esq. to be Purser of the Hon. Admiral Berkeley's flag-ship; and Lieutenant Bremar is appointed to the Diana.

Captain Vincent, who so nobly and gallantly defended the Arrow in the Mediterranean, and for which he was made a Post Captain, is appointed to the Brilliant; Captain Lobb, to the Captain, of 74 guns; Captain Barrie, to the Pomona; Sir T. Hardy, to the Triumph; Captain Bennet, to the Fame; Captain J. Langharne, to the Iris; Captain Lord Cochrane, to the Shannon; Captain Lye, to the Terpsichore; Hon. Captain Bennet, to the Croccodile; Captain Humphries, to the Leander, (the Hon. Admiral Berkeley's flag-ship); Captain de Stark, to the Avon; Captain T. Baker, who bravely fought and captured la Didon, to the Tribune, *vice* Captain Bennet, who has taken the command of the Fame; Captain M'Kinley, to the Lively; Captain Lord Falkland, to the Quebec; Captain Farquhar, who gallantly defended the Acheron, to the Ariadne; Captain Stanfell, to the Scorpion; Captain Miller, to the Pallas; Lieutenant Meik, son of Dr. Meik, Physician to Portsmouth Garrison, to the Captain.

Mr. Maddock, Clerk in the Clerk of the Check's office, at the Dock Yard, Portsmouth, is made a Purser, and appointed to the Saracen.

BIRTH.

May 20. At Tingrith House, in Bedfordshire, the lady of Captain Whyte, of the Royal Navy, of a son.

MARRIAGES.

Lately, S. Hemphill, Esq. of the Navy, to Miss C. Palmer, of Southampton.

May 15. Captain Burdett, of the Navy, to Miss Browne, only daughter of Colonel Browne, of Glennagary, county of Dublin.

22. Captain Colby, of the Navy, to Mrs. Costin, late of Bedford.

OBITUARY.

April 15. At his house, George-street, Stonehouse, Plymouth, the infant son of Thomas Simpson, Esq., Surgeon of His Majesty's ship Arethusa.

24. At Great Yarmouth, Mrs. Langford, aged 21, the wife of Captain Langford, of the Royal Marines.

Lately, at Haslar Hospital, aged 21, Lieutenant Billinghurst, of the Royal Marines, son of Lieutenant Billinghurst, who died lately at one of the signal posts in the Isle of Wight. He was buried in Portsmouth Garrison Chapel, on Thursday, with military honours.

Lately, at Portsea, ——— Covey, cook of one of the ships in ordinary at Portsmouth, who lost both his legs on board the Venerable, Lord Duncan's flag ship, in the glorious action off Camperdown. The following trait in this brave man's character, is related by Dr. Duncan, Chaplain of the Venerable:—"You are not," says the Doctor, "to imagine I was circumscribed to the narrow bounds of my clerical office. In the day of blood I was on triple duty; alternately acting as Sailor, Chaplain, and Surgeon's Assistant, when the battle might too truly be said to bleed in every vein. I was now called to minister to the recoverable, now the irrecoverable. A marine of the name of Covey was brought down to the surgery, deprived of both his legs; and it was necessary, some hours after, to amputate still higher. 'I suppose,' says Covey, 'those d—d scissars will finish the business of the bullet, master Mate?'—'Indeed, my brave fellow,' cried the Surgeon, 'there is some fear of it.'—'Well, never mind,' cried Covey, 'I've lost my legs, to be sure, and mayhap may lose my life; but we beat the Dutch! d—n me, we have beat the Dutch! this blessed day my legs have been shot off, so I'll even have another cheer for it—huzza! huzza!'" This anecdote plainly shows that Covey was naturally a brave man. He used often to tell the circumstance with tears in his eyes; for what the pangs of that distressing moment could not produce, his subsequent reflections, and new manner of life, did. He was awful as a swearer, as he afterwards felt and acknowledged; but long before his death, his oaths were turned into praises, and his last words were—Hallelujah! Hallelujah!

RIGHT HON.BLE WILL.M  EARL of NORTHESK, K.B.

Rear Admiral of the Red Squadron

Publish'd 30 June 1806 by J. Gold 103 Shoe Lane Fleet Street

BIOGRAPHICAL MEMOIR

OF THE

RIGHT HON. WILLIAM EARL OF NORTHESK, K.B.

REAR-ADMIRAL OF THE RED SQUADRON,

And one of the three Flag Officers who commanded the British Fleet in the ever-memorable Battle of Trafalgar.

"THOUGH TRAIN'D IN BOISTEROUS ELEMENTS, HIS MIND
WAS YET BY SOFT HUMANITY REFIN'D;
EACH JOY OF WEDDED LOVE AT HOME HE KNEW;
ABROAD,—CONFESS'D THE FATHER OF HIS CREW;
BRAVE, LIBERAL, JUST;—THE CALM DOMESTIC SCENE
HAD O'ER HIS TEMPER BREATH'D A GAY SERENE."

UNDER how plain, and apparently common an exterior, is the brilliancy of the diamond concealed, till the hand of the polisher unveils its native lustre! it then bursts upon the eye with unthought of splendour, and reaches its just level in the scale of general estimation.

With public characters the case is often similar. Their intrinsic value frequently remains long unnoticed, or unknown; till opportunity, the file of merit, elicits their latent brightness, and suddenly presents them to public admiration and esteem.

This observation is strongly exemplified in the instance of the noble Admiral, of whose family and memoirs we are about to offer to our readers a brief, but correct sketch. He has devoted almost the whole of his life to the naval service of his country, in which he has attained distinguished rank. His professional conduct has been marked by a steady zeal, and uniform correctness: he has preserved the "noiseless tenor of his way," attended by silent respect; and if he has not displayed the dazzling coruscations of a comet, he has at least moved with mild, equable, unsullied lustre, through his prescribed orbit. The glorious and unparalleled victory of Trafalgar has recently attracted towards him the eyes, and the hearts of his grateful country; and has taught her to anticipate from his courage and talents, future laurels, and reiterated triumphs.

The family of this noble and gallant officer has been settled for some centuries in the county of Angus, in Scotland. His ancestors came originally from Hungary, about the year 1200, in the reign of William, from his great valour surnamed THE LION, at which time the family name was de Bolinhord: but remaining on the estate of CARNEGIE, they adopted *that* as the family name, agreeably to the custom of the age and country.

In the reign of King Charles the First, the eldest of four brothers was created Earl of Southesk, and Lord Carnegie; and the second was advanced to the dignities of Lord Inglis Maldie, and Lord Lour; which titles he afterwards exchanged for those of Earl of Northesk, and Lord Rosehill. In consequence of the attachment of this family to that amiable, but unfortunate Prince, they were fined by Oliver Cromwell 10,000*l*. They were afterwards equally remarkable for their support of the revolution, and for their steady loyalty to the House of Hanover. In the rebellion in 1715, when the family mansion house was taken possession of by the Old Pretender, the Countess of Northesk was obliged to seek refuge in the Castle of Edinburgh, where she was delivered of the late George, Earl of Northesk, (named after His Majesty, King George the First, who was one of his sponsors by proxy). He died in 1792, having served with a considerable degree of credit in the Royal Navy, and attained the rank of Admiral of the White Squadron of His Majesty's Fleet.

The subject of these memoirs was his third son, by the Lady Anne Leslie, daughter of Alexander, Earl of Leven and Melville; and was born about the year 1760. Being early destined for the sea service, he embarked in the year 1771, with the Honourable Captain Barrington, in the Albion. He next served with Captain Macbride, in the Southampton, and Captain Stair Douglas, in the Squirrel; was made acting Lieutenant in the Nonsuch, and confirmed by Lord Howe* in 1777, into

* The memoir of this officer appeared in Vol. I of the NAVAL CHRONICLE.

the Apollo. He afterwards served with Admirals Sir John Lockhart Ross*, and Lord Rodney*; and by the latter was made a Commander after the action of the 18th April, 1780, (in which he served as a Lieutenant in the Admiral's ship;) and promoted to the Blast fire-ship. He was advanced to the rank of Post Captain in April 1782, and was appointed to the command of the Eustatius, in which he was present at the reduction of the island of that name. From this ship he was removed into the Enterprize frigate, in which he returned to England, and was paid off at the peace in 1783.—In 1788 he succeeded his elder brother, as Lord Rosehill; and in 1790, on the Russian armament, was appointed to the command of His Majesty's ship Heroine, of 32 guns; but was paid off when the apprehension of a war with that Power ceased.

In 1792, on the demise of his father, his Lordship succeeded to the title and estate; and in January 1793, he commissioned His Majesty's ship Beaulieu, of 40 guns, and went to the Leeward Islands; whence he returned with convoy in the Andromeda, which was shortly after put out of commission.

In 1796 Lord Northesk was elected one of the sixteen representatives of the peerage of Scotland, in the Parliament of Great Britain, and Governor of the British Linen Company. He was in the same year appointed to the command of His Majesty's ship Monmouth, of 64 guns; and employed in the North Sea, under the orders of the late Lord Viscount Duncan; until in May 1797, the spirit of disaffection which had originated in the Channel fleet, unfortunately spread to that squadron; and the Monmouth was one of the ships brought to the Nore. On this occasion, Lord Northesk, after having been several days confined, was required by Parker, and his committee of delegates, (as an officer, of whose humanity, and general estimation in the service, as a friend to the seamen, they expressed the highest sense,) to present a letter to the King, containing a statement of their alledged grievances. With *this* his Lordship reluctantly complied, having previously declared, " that from the nature of

* The memoirs of these officers appeared in Vols. VI and I of the NAVAL CHRONICLE.

their demands, he could give them no encouragement to expect success." The subsequent events of that temporary delirium among our seamen are sufficiently known. After the trials were over, Lord Northesk resigned the command of the Monmouth, and remained unemployed till the year 1800, when he was appointed to His Majesty's ship Prince, of 98 guns, in the Channel fleet, under the command of his illustrious relative, the Earl of St. Vincent; in which ship he continued till the peace in 1802, when he again returned from active service; and the same year his Lordship was re-elected one of the sixteen Peers of Scotland.

On the renewal of hostilities with the French republic in 1803, his Lordship was among the foremost to offer his services, and was immediately appointed to His Majesty's ship Britannia, of 100 guns. In her he served in the Channel, under the command of the Hon. Admiral Cornwallis, till May 1804, when he was promoted to the rank of Rear-Admiral of the White. In the following month he hoisted his flag in the same ship, and continued to serve in her on her former station, in the arduous blockade of Brest, during the trying and tempestuous winter of 1804; and till August in the following year; when he was detached with a squadron, under the orders of Vice-Admiral Sir Robert Calder, to reinforce Vice-Admiral Collingwood off Cadiz.

In the glorious and decisive Battle of Trafalgar, on the ever-memorable twenty-first of October, the Britannia had the honour to bear his Lordship's flag; and took a distinguished share in achieving the victory. Previously to that great event, it had been directed by the Commander in Chief, in consequence of her heavy rate of sailing, *that the Britannia should constantly take a position to windward of him;* and, on the morning of that glorious day, he ordered by signal, *that she should assume a station as most convenient, without regard to the order of battle;* and afterwards sent verbal directions to Lord Northesk, by the Captain of the Sirius, *to break through the enemy's line astern of the fourteenth ship.* This was effected in the most masterly and gallant manner; though the Britannia was severely galled in bearing down, by a raking fire from several of the enemy. On passing through the line, and hauling up, she was the fourth ship of the van division in action, (the Victory, Temeraire, and Neptune, alone preceding her,) and, in a short space of time, completely dismasted a French ship of 80 guns, who waved a white handkerchief in token of submission*. She afterwards singly engaged, and kept at bay, three of the enemy's van ships, that were attempting to double upon Lord Nelson's flag-ship; the Victory at that time already warmly engaged with two of the enemy, and much disabled. During the whole continuance of this long and bloody conflict, the noble Admiral zealously emulated the conduct of his illustrious leader, displaying the most heroic courage, tempered by the coolest judgment and presence of mind; and was ably seconded in his exertions by his gallant Captain, Charles Bullen. Nor was his conduct after the action less meritorious; while his skill and promptitude were equally conspicuous, in the arduous task of

* After fully describing the gallant conduct of the Victory, Temeraire, and Neptune, the author of the poem entitled *The Battle of Trafalgar*, (Doctor Halloran, late Chaplain and Secretary to Lord Northesk,) thus particularizes the achievements of the Britannia, in which he served:—

"Nor less Britannia, from each blazing side,
On the fierce foe her missile thunders plied;
On her tall mast brave Northesk's flag uprear'd,
An angry meteor to their view appeared;
Whose sanguine cross, unfurl'd by Zephyr's breath,
Glar'd on their fleet, destruction, blood, and death!
High on her deck her noble Chieftain stood,
To guide her progress through the scene of blood;
While valiant Bullen, press'd with martial fire,
His zeal to second, and her crew inspire;
Each emulous to lead her on to fame,
And prove her worthy of her glorious name!
Now, bursting through the centre of the foes,
On either side such storms of shot she throws;
Dismay, confusion, seize their scatt'ring fleet,
Who urge on terror's wings their swift retreat!
Yet, from the torrent of incessant fire,
With headlong speed, while num'rous foes retire;
The mighty Bucentaur dismasted lay,
And to the victors fell, a sinking prey;
While, o'er her stern the crew a signal wav'd,
And from their gen'rous foe forbearance crav'd."

securing the captured ships. And, when the order was given for destroying the prizes, after removing from them the *British Seamen,* his zeal in that truly dangerous service, in a tempestuous sea, and heavy gale of wind, was exceeded only by his exemplary humanity. Though urgent signals were made, and *repeated,* "to expedite their destruction;" his Lordship would on no account suffer l'Intrepide, the nearest of the captured ships to the Britannia, to be scuttled or burned, till his boats, at the imminent hazard of their brave seamen's lives, had rescued from the devoted prize, all her wounded men, and the whole of her surviving crew.

His Majesty, in testimony of his approbation of his eminent services, has honoured his Lordship with the Red Riband; and both Houses of Parliament, the Corporation of London, and of several other Cities and public Companies, have concurred in voting him their thanks. Every mark of royal approbation is certainly honourable; and though the Red Riband has not usually been conferred on Peers, *previously such,* yet as a military order, it may not be an unappropriate distinction for his Lordship. What may be his feelings, or private sentiments on the subject, the writer of these memoirs cannot pretend to develope. But

"Nullius addictus jurare in verba magistri,"

he must, for *himself,* take the liberty to profess, as his decided opinion, "that his Lordship's services remained too long unnoticed, and ultimately have received a very frigid, and inadequate reward." He by no means wishes to institute invidious comparisons; or, in the smallest degree, to detract from the eminent merits of another most gallant and distinguished officer. Yet he conceives it must be obvious, "that while a *private Captain,* commanding a detached squadron, for having captured four previously-beaten ships, *with a superior force,* has received the same distinction as his Lordship, "the Order of the Bath," accompanied by more *solid considerations,* a "*Flag Officer,*" the second surviving Hero of the incomparable Battle of Trafalgar, has been most unequally remunerated, for the highly distinguished part he bore, in achieving, *with inferior numbers*, that most brilliant of all British victories. His grateful country, however, must participate his Lordship's proud consciousness, that his merits and services shed around his character a brighter and more permanent lustre, than any which ribands or stars can confer on his person; or which can emanate from human distinctions.

Lord Northesk is now in his 47th year: in person, above the middle size, robust, and well made; with a manly, open countenance, strongly indicative of his leading traits of character, great firmness, tempered by equal mildness and humanity. As an officer, he is scrupulously correct; and a warm supporter of the discipline of the service; though so averse from unnecessary rigour, that when a private Captain, the writer has known him devote hours together to the patient investigation of *truth*, before he would consent to inflict punishment. He is, consequently, much beloved by his officers and men; to whom he is endeared equally by this strict impartiality of conduct, as by his general urbanity, and friendliness of disposition. He possesses a strong and correct judgment, with a cool discriminating mind; and if he display not that brilliancy of talents, which dazzles; or that superiority of genius, which distinguishes a "*favored few*," he at least exhibits a sound understanding; and (which is the most valuable of all the senses; or, as the poet says, "fairly worth the *seven*,") "*plain solid sense*."

In private life, and in his domestic relations, no man can be more fortunate than his Lordship; possessing the warmest esteem of his friends, and the fondest affection of his family. Great therefore has been the sacrifice of comfort and happiness, which he has for many years made to the duties of his profession. He married in 1787, Miss Ricketts, niece of the Earl of St. Vincent, and sister of the late gallant and lamented Captain Jervis. By this lady he has been blessed with two sons, and four daughters, to whom their amiable parent, withdrawing from the glare of public life, has performed her maternal duties in a manner truly honourable and exemplary. In her neighbourhood (Rosehill, near Winchester) she is beloved and venerated as the friend and patron of the distressed; to whose wants and comforts she administers with constant, but unostentatious liberality. The eldest son*, Lord Rosehill, emulating the example of his illustrious father, and grandfather, has already made his debût in the naval service, under one of its bravest and ablest officers, Sir Thomas Troubridge; and is *now* in the East Indies. Judging from his early disposition and talents, we may venture to indulge the pleasing anticipation, that he will live to achieve future victories for his country, and to add more honours to the noble houses of Northesk and St. Vincent.

"Dum pater Æneas, et avunculus excitat Hector."

* Our readers will, we trust, excuse us for quoting the annexed reference to this promising young nobleman, from the "*Battle of Trafalgar.*"

"Yet mourn not, Britain! with unceasing grief,
Your fallen Warriors, or their matchless Chief;
But, with your sorrows blend a conscious pride,
That, crown'd with glory, in your cause they died.
See too, exulting in your conqu'ring fleet,
What youthful hearts with emulation beat;
To climb the zenith of bright glory's Sun,
And win such wreaths as gallant NELSON won!
'Mongst these brave youths, their country's rising prop,
Her present solace, and her future hope;
Urg'd by his father's, and his grandsire's fame,
With joy the Muse beholds her ROSEHILL's name!
And, if her vision, with prophetic glance,
Can pierce futurity's opaque expanse;
She sees for thee, thy happier fates entwine
A fortune, worthy thy illustrious line!
Sees, in long series, gallant deeds prepare
For thee, dear youth, a second Trafalgar!
Sees Britain hail, repair'd, her Hero's loss,
And ROSEHILL rise, what godlike NELSON was."

Since the preceding memoir was written, the noble Admiral has had the honour of being invested by His Majesty with the Order of the Bath. The followiug is the official account of the ceremony:—

Queen's Palace, Thursday, June 5, 1806.

Ceremonial of the knighthood and investiture of the Right Honourable William Earl of Northesk, Rear-Admiral of the red squadron of His Majesty's fleet, Knight of the most honourable Order of the Bath.

The Knights and Officers of the Order, attending in their mantles, collars, &c. proceeded into the Sovereign's presence, making the usual reverences, in the following order:—

The gentleman usher of the order, in his mantle, chain, and badge, bearing the red rod.

Deputy bath king of arms, in the mantle, chain, and badge, with the sceptre of bath, bearing the riband and badge of the order on a crimson velvet cushion.

The genealogist, in his mantle, chain, and badge.

KNIGHTS COMPANIONS:

Sir David Dundas.

Sir John Thomas Duckworth. Sir Thomas Trigger.

Lord Hutchinson.

Sir John Colpoys.

Sir Alured Clarke.

Right Honourable Sir Joseph Banks, Bart.

Lord Keith.

Lord Henley.

Lord de Blaquiere.

The dean of Westminster, dean of the order, in his mantle, chain, and badge.

His Royal Highness the Duke of York and Albany, first and principal companion.

Then, by His Majesty's command, Rear-Admiral William Earl of Northesk was introduced into the presence, between Sir David Dundas and Sir John Thomas Duckworth, the two junior knights companions present, preceded by the gentleman usher of the order, with reverences as before.

The sword of state was thereupon delivered to the Sovereign by Lord de Blaquiere, the second knight in seniority present; and Rear-Admiral William Earl of Northesk, kneeling, was knighted therewith. Then His Royal Highness the Duke of York, the senior knight, presented the riband and badge to the Sovereign, and His Majesty put them over the new knight's right shoulder, who, being thus invested, had the honour to kiss the Sovereign's hand, and withdrew, and the procession returned to the privy chamber in the order as aforesaid.

NAVAL ANECDOTES, COMMERCIAL HINTS, RECOLLECTIONS, &c.

NANTES IN GURGITE VASTO.

ADDITIONAL PARTICULARS OF ADMIRAL DUCKWORTH'S ENGAGEMENT WITH THE FRENCH SQUADRON IN THE WEST INDIES.

THE following particulars are given in a letter from a naval officer, on board His Majesty's ship Superb, dated Port Royal, Jamaica, Feb. 17, 1806:—

After leaving Lord Collingwood, we fell in with a French squadron on the 25th December, off the Canaries, which we now know was commanded by Jerome Buonaparté. You cannot conceive the joy expressed by every one on board; every individual thought himself a king, and expected that day to have been one of the happiest Christmases they ever spent; but from the very bad sailing of several ships of the fleet, Jerome had the good luck to escape, and the joy of the squadron was turned into melancholy, which had not altogether worn off, until we found the squadron at St. Domingo. I can give you very little idea of the exultation expressed by every countenance, when they were certain of bringing them to action. The scene was truly grand, particularly when you consider the feelings on board the two squadrons; the one making every exertion to get away, and determined to run the gauntlet in order to escape; the other straining every nerve to prevent their flight. They were at this time going before the wind, and we were endeavouring to cross them, in order to prevent the possibility of their escape, which fortunately, from the superior sailing of the Superb, we were enabled to effect. The enemy brought their two largest ships together, (l'Alexandre the headmost, and l'Imperiale,) seemingly with a view to quiet the fire of the English Admiral in the Superb, before any of the other ships could come up; but in this they were disappointed, for the second broadside from the Superb fortunately did such execution on board the enemy's headmost ship, l'Alexandre, that she became quite unmanageable, and lost her station. The three-decker was by this time within pistol-shot of the Superb, and apparently reserving her fire for us; but at this critical moment Admiral Cochrane, in the Northumberland, came up. and notwithstanding the small distance betwixt the Superb and l'Imperiale, he gallantly placed her between us, and received the whole broadside of the largest, and esteemed the finest ship in the French Navy: several of the shot passed quite through the Northumberland into the Superb. The action then became general, and, as you must be already informed, terminated most honourably for the British Navy; for although the enemy were only a little inferior, yet, according to the most accurate calculation, they were entirely annihilated in the short space of one hour.

ANOTHER BRITISH GAME COCK.

THE following is an extract from another letter, written, it is believed, by the same officer as the preceding, on the Superb's passage from Jamaica:—

Having before given you some additional particulars of the action of St. Domingo, I must now beg leave to relate an anecdote of an English game cock. You must know, then, that on the Superb's poop-deck was a large wooden fabric, forming an oblong hollow square, and so constructed, that the upper apartments served for marine arms, and the lower for poultry: now, it happened in the very hottest of the battle, whilst we were closely engaged with the three-decker (l'Imperiale), that a 42-pounder double-headed shot broke through this useful compound structure, destroying no less than 27 stand of arms, as it since appeared, and making terrible havoc among the feathered race: splinters, bayonets, and broken muskets, &c. prevailed in all directions. When lo! from the midst of this "confusion worse confounded," up sprung this gallant cock, till then "unknown to fame," and perched on the spanker boom, crowing exultingly.—Another shot cutting the boom in two close at his feet, now drove him from his post. Indignantly retreating a few paces aft on the broken poop, again he fixed his stand; and thence, ever and anon, was heard his clarion voice to sound amid the "din of war." This appears strange, you will say, and yet it is not altogether singular. A circumstance nearly similar, I have heard, took place in the Marlborough, on the memorable 1st of June, 1794; I say nearly similar, because in that instance the bold bird was *sound*, though not *safe*—whereas *our* little hero was found, on examination, to have received many severe contusions, and to have lost an eye, ere he extricated himself from the melancholy ruins of his fallen house, and the sad wreck of his mangled messmates. Hardly had the battle ceased, when some of the brave men whose dangers he had thus shared, introduced him to our notice, with an earnest request to save him from the dire hand of our poulterer. Soon we saw him caressed by all, and decorated with rings and ribands. *Never* is he to die the death so common to his kind—and this he seems to know: for so perfectly tame is he become, that he will perch and crow on one's arm, feed from the hand, and even admit, without fear, of being fondled like the gentlest lap-dog. So much for our favourite bold chanticleer.

MOCK GALLANTRY OF THE FRENCH.

WHILST the Topaze French frigate, which lately escaped from Lisbon to France, lay at the former place, her officers frequently fell in company with the officers of the Falmouth packets, who sometimes inquired when they meant to sail? To this the Frenchmen usually answered, "That their honour did not require them to face three English frigates which they knew to be waiting for them; but that they should not hesitate to encounter any one English frigate, and a brig or sloop of war into the bargain—*aye, and capture both of them.*" At last some wag stuck up an advertisement in Lisbon, offering to contract with any person who would engage to carry the Topaze overland to France! Though this did not drive Captain Baudin to sea, it prevented his officers appearing on shore so often as formerly; and at last, the absence of the Pomone, the only ship that had ever watched him, encouraged him to run.

DREADFUL MASSACRE.

THE subjoined account of the massacre of the officers and crew of the ship Atahualpa, is copied from a New York paper, to which it was sent by Captain Isaacs, of the Montezuma:—

The ship Atahualpa had been lying at anchor in Sturgis Cove, up Mill Bank Sound, three days. The natives had, during that time, been remarkably civil. On the 12th of June, 1805, they came off in several canoes, and desired Captain Porter to purchase their skins; and about 10 o'clock, Calete, the chief of one of their tribes, desired Captain Porter to look over the side and see the number of skins in his canoe. Captain Porter was complying, but was obliged to bend over the rail, when the chief threw his coat over his head, stabbed him twice between his shoulders, threw him overboard, and gave the signal for a general attack.

Mr. John Hill, the chief Mate, was shot through the body, but ran below, got his musket, returned on deck, shot the chief, and gave him his mortal wound.

John Goodwin, the second Mate, shot dead.

John G. Rackstraw was daggered, and died immediately.

Lyman Plummer was daggered, and lived until the ship was got out, when he requested the surviving crew to take care of the ship, and find Captain Brown.

Isaac Summers, cooper, Luther and Samuel Lapham, Peter Spooner, seamen, and John Williams, cook, were all killed. The cook defended himself bravely as long as his hot water lasted, but that being expended, they cut him down with an axe. Three seamen, one Sandwich Islander, and a Kodiac Indian, were dangerously wounded. Five more of the crew were slightly wounded; and three men and a Sandwich Islander were all that escaped unhurt.

These four at length bravely rushed through the crowd of Indians, got below, and finding a few muskets loaded, fired them through the loop-holes in the break of the forecastle, which terrified the natives, and many jumped overboard. The four men then regained the deck, and after fighting some time with a few Indians who seemed determined to hold their prize, killed or drove all overboard. One canoe was now seen under the bows, endeavouring to cut the cable; but a swivel was brought from the after-part of the ship, and discharged at them; ten were killed by the swivel, and one by a musket-shot, so only one was left alive in the canoe.

The crew lost their jacket knives, by plunging them into the skulls of the Indians, from whence they were unable to draw them out. After the decks were cleared, the topsails were loosed, when the ship swung her head off shore, the cable was cut, and after some time beating, was able to get out of the Sound. Two days after were off Newatta; the wind coming a-head, shaped a course northward.

June 13.—Deposited the bodies of our murdered shipmates in the deep.

CAPTAIN WRIGHT.

THE late Captain Wright, whose sufferings have excited so much interest in this country, is said to have written the annexed letter, while confined in the Temple at Paris, to Mr. Wallis, his first Lieutenant, who was at the same time prisoner in Verdun depôt:—

MY DEAR WALLIS,

In order to intrude but little on the translator* in office, and favour an early delivery of my letter, I send this time merely a short one, in acknowledgment of your kind perseverance, which procured me the pleasure of receiving yours of the 29th of August, a few days ago. Accept of my best thanks for your congratulations on my promotion, which, however, is become indifferent to me, farther than it demonstrates the justice and liberality of government, of which I never entertained a doubt. I beg you to bear in mind, that I have every proper feeling upon the subject, and that the handsome manner in which it has been conferred, has not escaped my observation, or failed to have due weight upon me, although it has been in my contemplation to resign my commission, through an official channel here, in order to relieve government from the embarrassment my extraordinary situation must have placed it under, and to prevent a practice, which I forbear to characterize, from bearing on any other victim on either side; but I felt, upon further reflection, that although I was willing to forego its protection, yet no act of mine, thus situated, could absolve my government from the performance of its duty to a British subject. I rejoice to hear that you are under the jurisdiction of a liberal-minded military man, for I was under some anxiety as to the regime you might be subject to. I think I had already prepared you to expect benevolence from individuals, where they might be at liberty to exercise that right. I doubt not you will make use of the instance under your own eye, to obliterate from the young minds of my poor boys † unfavourable impressions, to which they may have already yielded. I rejoice also to hear, at length, that you are near those dear boys, in whose progress my whole solicitude centres. Give them my best wishes, and refresh their memories with what has been so often impressed upon them. I must have no idleness, no indecorous boyish tricks, no habits of riot or inebriety, no deviation from the truth, no adoption of prejudice, no tendency to exaggeration, no indiscriminate censure or proscription *en masse*, but a liberal,

---

* Is the Secretary, who translates the letters of prisoners into French, for the inspection of the officer commanding the depôt.

† Three of his young Midshipmen; one his own nephew, aged 15, who was sent to Metz military prison for having a small piece of line in his trunk, at the time of his being in the citadel, which could only be for the purpose of playing with; one a nephew of the gallant Sir W. S. Smith; and the other a young boy, whose relations I have not a perfect knowledge of.

gentlemanly conduct, and a steady, persevering assiduity, which will alone surmount the difficulties that are before them. Remind them often of their distinction, of the precious leisure they have upon their hands. Let the main-spring of their actions be the character of my dear country, &c. Remind them often how much I expect from them.

If Mr. Travin's son * be with you, let him partake of all the advantages I propose securing to my own three boys, but with such delicacy as will hurt neither his own nor his parent's feelings. In the mean time, apply to my authority wherever the pecuniary means are obtainable, which, in the course of our correspondence, should it continue, I shall especially appropriate.

I am not unaware, my dear Wallis, that I am thus imposing a difficult task, and laying a heavy burden upon you; but I am sure you will undertake it with pleasure.

Give my best respects to all my officers individually, and tell the Doctor I take it for granted he makes good use of his leisure. I recommend him to walk the public hospitals, if there be any in the neighbourhood, and to follow up chemistry with ardour.

I shall be very glad to hear from any of my officers, when they are in a scribbling mood. If it be possible, let my servant King attend on the boys, and tell him I have begged of you to take care of them.

Is poor Mr. Brown† recovered? The last I heard of him was before your departure hence. Pray give an account nominally of all my people. Poor old Sampson, I suppose you know, is no more. Is that poor being ‡, whose wishes death seemed unwilling to accomplish, still living?—I have a little cat that has just taken the caprice of lying along my paper, and purs to me, so you may perceive that I am not without amiable society; and I must tell you, for the comfort of any other little amiable creature who may weep for my misfortunes, that I can bear them, however great or multiplied; but that I am less ill off than people at a distance (whose apprehensions magnify evil) are aware of, for I have within a few months obtained the facility of procuring books, and subscribing to the *Moniteur*, whose fables and prejudices I assure you I am not in the least danger of adopting. Now fare you well, and believe me, most faithfully and unfeignedly, your friend.

P. S. Tell me, particularly, what all the boys have done; tell them I continually think of them.—Adieu!

---

* One of his warrant officers, whose son was also on board.

† Mr. Wright's Clerk.

‡ One of the crew, who had been long sickly.

THE FRENCH HEROES OF TRAFALGAR.

THE *Moniteur* of May 6 contains the following account of the reception of some of these gentry by Buonaparté :—

At the audience which took place yesterday at St. Cloud, Captains Lucas and l'Infernit, who have lately arrived from England, were presented to His Majesty. Captain Lucas commanded the Redoubtable, in the battle of Trafalgar, and conducted himself in the most gallant manner; he attempted to board the Victory, Lord Nelson's ship. Captain l'Infernit also behaved in the bravest manner. After an unfortunate affair, it is gratifying to acknowledge such conduct. His Majesty said to the Captains, Lucas and l'Infernit, "If all my vessels had conducted themselves as well as those which you commanded, the victory would have been ours. I know that there are several who have not imitated your example, but I have ordered their conduct to be investigated. I have appointed you Commanders of the Legion of Honour. The Captains of the vessels who, instead of boarding the enemy, kept out of cannon-shot, shall be prosecuted, and, if convicted, made a dreadful example of.

DEATH OF ADMIRAL VILLENEUVE.

THE following account of the death of this officer, who is said to have terminated his existence by suicide, is given in one of the French papers:—

Admiral Villeneuve, who commanded the French fleet at Trafalgar, and of whose death we have been informed from Rennes, is known to have been landed at Morlaix from an English flag of truce, in the night between the 22d and 23d of April. The motive that induced him to commit an act of suicide in the *Hotel de la Patrie*, at Rennes, is unknown. He was found in his chamber quite undressed, and with five wounds given by a knife in his left side. According to the position of his body at the time, it is supposed that after he had stabbed himself he threw himself upon the bed, pressing upon the handle of the knife that still remained in his body, to hasten his dissolution.

History will remark, that the three Admirals, French, Spanish, and English, engaged in the battle of Trafalgar, have all lost their lives. The English Admiral was killed outright; Admiral Gravina died of the wounds he received; and the French Admiral Villeneuve finished his mortal career by his own hand.

Suicide can in no instance be justified; yet, from the sanguinary scenes which have been perpetrated in modern France by the reigning tyrant, we can scarcely be surprised at any step that may be taken to avoid his bloody fangs. The Admiral, it appears, had been called to Paris for the purpose of being tried by a court martial; and it is well known, that a trial in that blessed country of justice, happiness, and freedom, called France, is tantamount to an execution in most other countries. Villeneuve was a brave man; but the mean tyrant, his master, actuated by the same infamous spirit that induced him to charge the unfortunate Admiral Brueys with cowardice, at the battle of the Nile, had attempted to stigmatize his professional character. Villeneuve, impelled by a sentiment of bravery, though not of prudence, and anxious to clear himself, even from the shadow of suspicion, disobeyed the orders of Buonaparté, and, quitting the harbour of Cadiz, risked an action with the British fleet. Had he been victorious in that action, Buonaparté, it is probable, would have been compelled to acknowledge his merit; but, as it was, he had little hopes from the clemency, or even justice of the Corsican. With the dreadful fate of the lamented Duke d'Enghien, Pichegru, and the gallant hero, Captain Wright, full in his view, we can scarcely wonder that Villeneuve should seek to shun a protracted death of torture, by a premature termination of his existence.

After all, in our humble opinion, the French account of Villeneuve's death indicates *assassination* rather than *suicide.*

GALLANT CONDUCT OF CAPTAIN SALTWELL, OF THE ADMIRAL GARDNER, EAST INDIAMAN.

THE following particulars of a very gallant action, fought by the Admiral Gardner, East Indiaman, with a French ship of war of 32 guns, are contained in a letter from Captain Saltwell, to John Woolmore, Esq., dated Fort St. George, December 7th, 1805:—

I write overland to inform you of our safe arrival here on the 4th inst. We sailed from St. Helena on the 15th of September, with the Lady Castlereagh, with whom we parted on the 27th of November, in lat. 6° 4′ N., long. 93° 25′ E., and on the following morning, from the mast-head, saw a ship bearing east, which we judged to be the Lady Castlereagh, and at 20 minutes before nine, A.M., from the deck saw a ship steering down upon us. I cleared ship for action, and made a private signal, but finding she did not answer it, took in all my small sails, triced up the boarding netting, and hove to. Thirty-five minutes past nine, A.M., being within pistol-shot, she hoisted French colours, and fired a shot, which we returned with a broadside, and continued engaging until 15 minutes past 11 A.M., when she bore up and made sail to the S.S.W. Her aim was to disable our masts and rigging, which she accomplished: our lower masts, bowsprit, and main-top-mast are damaged, (the main-top-mast I have shifted here); several of the lower shrouds and top-mast rigging a good deal cut; in our hull we received several shot, but not materially to damage us. From the report of a Frenchman on board, whom I shipped at St. Helena, and who formerly belonged to her, I learned that she is la Jeune Adele privateer, of 32 guns. What damage she sustained is impossible to say, but he kept his vessel before the wind until dusk, and the next morning she disappeared.

I received all possible support from my officers, cadets, and ship's company, whose conduct was cool, steady, and spirited; every one appearing zealous in the cause. My chief officer was severely wounded, but no life was lost.—I enclose a list of the wounded, viz.

Mr. J. Young, chief officer; Mr. Love, Midshipman; and Emanuel Peter, seaman, severely wounded; William Skeen and John M'Dougall, seamen, dangerously wounded; and Charles Grey, Thomas Kirk, and three Lascars, seamen, slightly wounded

NAVAL CHAPLAINS.

THE important addition of a Chaplain to the establishment of our ships of war seems, from the following letter of George Duke of Buckingham, to have been first adopted in the year 1626:

The Duke of Buckingham to the University of Cambridge.

After my hearty commendations. His Majesty having given order for preachers to goe in every of his ships to sea, choyce hath been made of one Mr. Daniel Ambrose, Master of Arts, and Fellow of your College, to be one. Accordingly upon signification to me to come hither, I thought good to intimate unto you, that His Majesty is so careful of such scholars as are willing to put themselves forward in so good actions as that he will expect, and I doubt not but you will accordingly take order, that the said

Mr. Ambrose shall suffer noe detriment in his place with you, by this his employment, but that you will rather take care that he shall have all immunities and emoluments with advantage, which have been formerly, or may be, granted to any upon the like service. Wherein not doubting of your affectionate care, I rest

Your very loving friend,

York House, July 29, 1626. G. BUCKINGHAM.

It was accordingly ordered that Mr. Ambrose should have the benefit of his fellowship during the whole period of his service at sea.

RUSSIAN VOYAGE OF DISCOVERY.

THE following letter, dated from the port of St. Peter and St. Paul, in Kamtschatka, the 24th of August, 1804, has been received from an officer in the Russian expedition under M. de Kreusenstern:—

On the 6th of May we perceived Hood's Island, and about noon of the same day Riou's Island, which form a part of the group called Marquesas, which the French navigator, M. Marchand, has denominated the islands of the Revolution. That which is considered the largest of them received from him the appellation of Baux, but in the language of the country it is called Nukahiwah. On the 7th, one of our ships, the Nedeshda, made that island: the natives immediately came on board in crowds, and appeared highly delighted at our visit: we observed among them an Englishman and a Frenchman, who have been naturalized in the country. About noon our vessel came to an anchor in the gulf of Anna Maria, and the next day went on shore. After viewing the country we thought fit to pay a visit to the chief of these savages. The women of this island are all excessively ugly; but this proceeds rather from the disproportion of their limbs, than the coarseness of their features: they generally go naked, their whole dress consisting of a few leaves rudely sewed together, with which they cover the parts of generation. Nature, who has been niggardly of her favours to the women, seems, by a singular caprice, to have lavished them all on the men: these savages are of a noble stature, and perfect proportions, and we met with none diminutive or deformed: their dress is very extraordinary; they make use of none excepting for the head, the arms, and the legs, the other parts of the body being entirely naked. Their food is the bread-fruit, cocoa-nuts, fish, pork, and even human flesh: these islanders devour not only their prisoners of war and the enemies whom they have killed, but even their wives and children in times of scarcity. Their arms are slings, lances, and clubs made of the wood of the *casuarina*. The Englishman, whom we had on board, and who appears to have resided a considerable time among these cannibals, warned us not to place too much confidence in their apparent joy. As nature seems to have made ample provision for their ordinary wants, they spend their time in feasting and drinking; they however manifested great solicitude to serve us. They use the skin of a whale for making a kind of drum, which is their national music. Their chief or king, whose name is Topeka Ketenue, exercises no authority over them; but he and his family are considered as inviolable: they pay him a heathen tribute on the fishery, because they look on him as the master of the ocean. They worship a certain god called Atua, who is nothing more than the corpse of their high priest; for as soon as he dies his body undergoes various operations: after he has been cleansed and washed with cocoa-nut oil, it is exposed in the air to dry, and then embalmed: it is then wrapped in skins sewed together, and deposited in the place consecrated to this purpose: they sacrifice to him their prisoners of war, whose flesh they devour with great avidity. The 8th of June the Nedeshda arrived at the island of Owhyhee, the inhabitants of which are much more industrious than those of the Marquesas, but they are less handsome. On the 15th of this month we arrived at the port of St. Peter and St. Paul. The number of the Kamtschadales has diminished exceedingly, in consequence of epidemic diseases, which have made dreadful ravages among them. During our residence in these parts, our crews opened a subscription for the erection of an hospital, which soon amounted to the sum of four thousand rubles.

VARIATION OF THE COMPASS.

A CURIOUS paper was recently laid before the Royal Society, relating to the "Differences in the Magnetic Needle on board His Majesty's ship the Investigator, arising from an alteration in the direction of the ship's head." In this Captain Flinders infers—1. That there was a difference in the direction of the magnetic needle when the ship's head pointed to the east, and when it was directed westward. 2. That this difference was easterly when the ship's head was west, and westerly when it was east. 3. That when the ship's head was north or south, the needle took the same direction, or nearly so, that it would on shore, and showed a variation from the true meridian. 4. That the error in variation was nearly proportionate to the number of points which the ship's head was from north to south. Hence the Captain supposes, 1. An attractive power of the different bodies in a ship, which are capable of affecting the compass, to be collecting into something like a flat point, or centre of gravity, and this point is nearly in the centre of the ship, where the iron shot are deposited. 2. He supposes this point to be endued with the same kind of attraction as the pole of the atmosphere where the ship is: consequently in New Holland the south end of the needle would be attracted by it, and the north end repelled. 3. That the attractive power of this point is sufficiently strong in a ship of war to interfere with the action of the magnetic poles upon the compass, placed upon or in the binnacle.

Captain Flinders in the course of this paper has given several tables, the inference of which is, that the variation is more westerly when taken upon the binnacle of a ship whose head is westward in north lat., than when observed in the centre of the ship. He thinks it will be found, that the variation of the compass is greater when going down the English Channel, than when coming up it; and then it will follow, that from a high south latitude, where the differences are greater on one side, they are most likely to decrease gradually to the equator, and to increase in the same way to a high north latitude, where they are great on the other side.

CORRESPONDENCE.

MR. EDITOR, *Saville Row, Walworth, May 22,* 1806.

I HAVE taken the liberty to send to you a list of several vessels, principally those trading with the people in the Archipelago of India, generally called Malays; which have been attacked or cut off by them.

The NAVAL CHRONICLE being in the possession of most commanders; such a list of ships taken through the perfidy of this people, if inserted in the Chronicle, might probably be useful, as a caution to those who have any dealings with them, to be constantly guarded against their treacherous disposition.

for most of these disasters have been owing to the sufferers having had a better opinion of this race of men than they deserved. Even in some publications, which ought to be guides to nautical men, they are led into error, by trusting too much to the descriptions given of uncivilized people. As an instance of this the following may be adduced :—

A few years ago an American ship bound to Bengal, was on the west side of the great Andaman Islands, in the Bay, and a calm commenced when she was within a few miles of the shore. Having on board Brooks's Gazetteer, one of the gentlemen observed, that under the words *Andaman Islands*, it said, " The inhabitants are an inoffensive people, though in a state of barbarism." From the favourable description of the natives given in the Gazetteer, some gentlemen on board as passengers proposed to go on shore, as a small relaxation from confinement on board; and to endeavour to procure a few fruits or vegetables. Several of them therefore proceeded on shore, and when they were stepping out of the boat, a volley of arrows was poured amongst them from a party of the natives, who had concealed themselves behind the bushes: they now returned into the boat, assailed at the same time by the natives, who had rushed from their lurking place, seized the rope, or penter of the boat, and endeavoured to pull her on shore: it fortunately happened there were some loaded small arms in her, which were discharged on the natives: this intimidated them a little, and allowed time to cut the boat's penter close to the stem, and to shove her clear of the shore. Some of the arrows wounded the Americans; one of them stuck fast between the ribs of one of the gentlemen, which could not be extracted until the boat got on board, when it was accomplished by the Surgeon.

This transaction was related to me in Calcutta, by a gentleman who was in the American ship at the time. I have also sent a list of several vessels known to me, which have been lost in the China sea of late years.

I have been considering, that should you think the list of vessels cut off by the Malays deserving of a place in the Naval Chronicle, there still appeared a sort of objection to its insertion; which is, whether it might not in some degree augment the grief of some of the relations of those who have fallen a sacrifice to the perfidious Malays. This is far from my intention; my whole aim being in this case to prevent, if possible, any lives from being sacrificed so unprofitably, and so prematurely, as those in question. So I must leave you to decide how far the insertion may be proper, if you think any part of these deserving of a place in your valuable Chronicle.

I am, Sir,

Your most obedient and humble Servant,

JAMES HORSBURGH.

P.S. Most of the commanders mentioned in the list, who suffered from the treachery of the Malays, I personally knew.

SIR,

Since I sealed the letter enclosing a list of vessels cut off by the Malays, a friend of mine just arrived from India informs me that the ship Wollajee, of Bengal, Captain Bowman, was assailed by the Manilla helmsmen whilst at sea, and the commander severely wounded. The ship Perseverance, of Madras, Captain James Johnston, was assaulted by the Manilla helmsmen on board,—the commander and officers cruelly murdered. This happened last year.

Your most obedient servant,

May 23, 1806. JAMES HORSBURGH.

A LIST
OF
SEVERAL VESSELS
LOST IN THE CHINA SEA.

IN 1761, Frederick Adolphus, Swedish ship, about one thousand tons burthen, from Europe bound to Canton, was lost on the Pratas Shoal, on the evening of the 4th September, having been set greatly to the eastward by a current, from leaving Pulo Sapata. The crew were saved in the boats, and arrived at Canton; from whence the long boat was fitted up, and sent to the shoal, accompanied by several Chinese boats, with divers in them. They discovered the bottom of the wreck, from whence the upper works had separated; and by the help of the divers recovered about thirty chests of treasure.

In December 1773, ROYAL CAPTAIN, six or seven hundred tons burthen, Hon. Company's ship, from Canton bound to Balambangan, was lost on a shoal near the west coast of Palawan. The crew saved in the boats, and arrived at Balambangan, at this time a British settlement.

In November 1787, RUSSELBUX, about five hundred tons burthen, belonging to Surat, Captain Ramsay, Commander, with the wind from the eastward, and thick weather, was running in with the coast of China, and finding the island Grand Ladrone close under their lee, let go the anchors, but after parting the cables she drove on shore. Crew all saved.

In August or September 1788, DADALOY, belonging to Bombay, about five hundred tons burthen, Captain Richardson, from Bombay towards Canton, foundered on the coast of China, near the island of St. John's. Crew saved.

In 1789, a small ship belonging to Bombay, commanded by Captain Newton, from that port bound to Canton, was wrecked in the night on one of those shoals in the western part of the China Sea, generally called Paracels, which happened in August. The commander and eight or ten persons arrived at Macao in a small boat; the remainder of the crew, about forty in number, left the wreck on rafts, which were constructed on a sand bank near it, and were supposed to have perished.

In December 1789, ship HASTINGS of Bombay, burthen about eleven hundred tons, Captain Sampson, from Canton in ballast bound to the former port, proceeded by the outer passage; blowing strong with a high sea, she laboured greatly, and started a butt end, which occasioned her sinking between the Macclesfield Bank and Pulo Sapata, with about eighty or ninety of the crew. The commander, officers, and about thirty of the people, were saved in the boats, and taken up by the Milford, which was in company. The ship Neckar, of Bombay, burthen about six hundred tons, was also in company, and sprang a leak; with great exertions this ship was kept above water until she reached Malacca, where she sunk. The Neckar had been a French frigate. The Hastings was built in Pegu.

December, January, 1789-90, ADMIRAL SUFFREIN, Dutch Europe ship, about seven hundred tons burthen, from Canton bound to Batavia and Holland, by the outer passage down the

China Sea; by not keeping sufficiently to the eastward, she ran upon one of the shoals (north-east part of the Paracel group) in the night, and was wrecked. Crew saved, and carried to the island Hainan, in fishing vessels (or free-booters,) which were lying in a bason under lee of the shoal. From Hainan they were sent to Macao.

About 1790, a Portuguese ship, from Manilla bound to Macao, was said to have been lost on the east side of the Pratas Shoal; being calm at the time, and the current setting her towards the shoal, the anchors were let go; but with all the cables veered out, the anchors did not take the ground, on account of the deepness of the water close to the shoal.

In October 1790, a Danish Europe ship, about eleven hundred tons burthen, from Europe bound to Canton, encountered a Ty-foong on the coast of China, which made her a complete wreck; she was sold for firewood, and a new large American ship purchased in her place.

In 1792, ARGYLESHIRE, of Calcutta, burthen about five hundred tons, built at Calcutta, perished in the China Sea, no traces of her known. The crew, about seventy or eighty in number, supposed to have perished.

In October 1792, BOMAIN YAID, built at, and belonging to, Bombay, burthen about eight hundred tons, Captain Douglas, from Canton bound to Calcutta, ballasted with tuthenag or zinc; it began to blow strong when she left the land, which forced up a confused sea, and the tuthenag being low in her bottom, she laboured and strained greatly, lost her masts, and finally sunk in about 40 fathoms water, the night after departing from Canton river. The commander, officers, and part of the crew, reached the coast of China in the long boat, and arrived safe at Macao; the remainder on rafts, supposed to have perished.

In October 1793, NERBUDDAH, built at Surat, burthen eight hundred tons, belonging to Bombay, sailed from Canton for this port, and was not heard of after her departure from China; supposed to have been lost on one of the shoals. The crew, upwards of one hundred persons, consequently perished.

September 1793 or 4, KING GEORGE, built at, and belonging to, Bombay, about one thousand tons burthen, from this port loaded with cotton, sandlewood, gumolibanum, &c., was burnt by lightning near Lintin Island, in proceeding up Canton river. A few of the people were killed by the lightning.

December 1796, SHAH MUNCHAH, of Bombay, built at this

place, burthen about one thousand tons, from Canton bound to Bombay, was lost on Pedro Branco, in the entrance of Sincapour Strait. The crew arrived at Malacca in the boats.

About August 1797, ship SETON, of Bombay, about six hundred tons burthen, from Bombay bound to Canton, was perceived to be on fire when near the coast of China, which could not be extinguished by the crew; but a strong breeze being favourable for running towards the land, they were enabled to run her on shore near Macao, which saved the crew.

About December 1798, ONTARIO, American ship, about six hundred tons burthen, from Canton bound to New York, was wrecked on a rock (before unknown) in the fair Channel near Carimata, on the west coast of Borneo. Crew saved, and taken on board by the American ship Swift, which was in company.

October 1800, EARL TALBOT, Hon. East India Company's ship, burthen about fifteen hundred tons, from Bombay bound to Canton, in a gale of wind supposed to have foundered, or lost on the Pratas Shoal. Crew, upwards of 150 persons, perished.

October 1800, a Chinese TCHUAN (ship) from Java to Borneo, foundered near the Pratas Shoal, in the gale which occasioned the loss of the Talbot. The crew saved in their launch.

July 1801, INTREPID, a ship, and COMET schooner, Bombay vessels belonging to the Hon. East India Company's marine, destined to explore some of the dangers in the China Sea, &c., passed out from Sincapour Strait in July, and their further progress unknown; but supposed to have perished on some of the Paracel shoals, with their crews, amounting to near one hundred persons.

In November 1801, GENEROUS FRIENDS, of Madras, burthen about four hundred tons, was wrecked on her passage from Canton, about ten o'clock at night, on one of the shoals of the Paracel group. One European, and about fourteen Lascars, saved by the free-booters, who visit the shoals for plunder from wrecks, and to fish. The commander, officers, and passengers, with the principal part of the crew, who left the wreck on rafts and in the jolly boat, were supposed to have perished, consisting of about forty persons. There were also a few said to have been killed in an affray with the Chinese free-booters.

About September 15, 1802, NAUTILUS, a ship about from three to four hundred tons burthen, of and from Calcutta, bound to Canton, was wrecked on the Iron Islands, near the Great Lema, on the coast of China, during a gale of wind from the eastward. The second officer, and six or eight Lascars, were thrown up on the rocks by the surge of the sea, and saved, though much bruised; the other part of the crew, in number about forty, with the commander and first officer, perished.

The same night in which the Nautilus suffered, a Spanish frigate from Manilla, bound to Canton, with dollars, was wrecked in Brandon's Bay, near Pedro Branco, on the coast of China. The crew saved, but most of the treasure (said to have amounted to upwards of eight hundred thousand dollars) lost.

August 1803, HOUGHTON, built in London, of and from Bombay, bound to Canton, about seven hundred tons burthen, was supposed to have sunk in a gale, near the coast of China; and the crew, about one hundred and twenty persons, perished.

August, 1803, in the same gale that the Houghton suffered, three Chinese TCHUANS, from Java, Borneo, Siam, or some of these southern countries, bound homewards to China, foundered near that coast. In these vessels there were about five hundred men, out of which twelve or fourteen were seen floating on a tank, and taken up by the Hon. Company's ship Warren Hastings.

October 1803, ship Fanny, of and from Bombay, bound to Canton, about six hundred tons burthen, was wrecked amongst the shoals in the south-east part of the China Sea, lat. 9° 44′ N. The commander, officers, and about half of the crew, were saved, and reached Malacca in a boat they built upon the wreck of the ship. In another boat built at the same time, and of equal size with the former, the other half of the crew embarked; their fate unknown, having separated from each other in the night.

In September or October 1803, ship ANSTRUTHER, about six hundred tons burthen, of Calcutta, from Malacca bound to Balambangan with troops, stores, &c., was wrecked on one of the shoals near the north-west end of the island of Banguey; part of the people are said to have perished; a strong south-west wind drove them past the north end of Balambangan, amongst the shoals. A few days after this happened, the General Baird, a ship of the same squadron, belonging to Calcutta, was burnt in the harbour of Balambangan.

July 22, 1804, ST. ANTONIO, a ship belonging to Macao, returning from Saigon in Cochin China, to the former port, burthen about five hundred tons, was wrecked on one of the shoals of the Paracel group, in lat. 16° 45′ N., consisting of a high sand bank, with a single high Palmyra tree in the centre of the bank, which is surrounded by a coral reef. The commander and most of the crew got to Manchow, on the east side of the island Hainan, on rafts, and were three or four days on the passage from the wreck to Manchow. The cause of the loss of this ship was a hard gale of wind from the westward, which drove her to the eastward amongst the shoals, not being able to carry any sail.

December 1804, ship FRIENDSHIP, of Madras, from Canton river bound to Cochin China, sprung a leak, which obliged them to run her on shore on the island Hainan, where she was lost. The crew were said to have been treated very indifferently, in their journey from Hainan to Canton by land.

Exclusive of the vessels here mentioned, several others have been lost in the China Sea of late years: it is said that several foreign ships have been lost, whose names, and other particulars relative to them, are not known; and also a ship belonging to Madras, missing from the time she entered the China Sea.

A List of several Vessels which have been assaulted or cut off by those People generally called Malays, spread over the Indian Archipelago; evincing the Propriety of Europeans, who trade with those People, to be constantly guarded against the Perfidy of the Natives of many of the Eastern Islands; or having any of them on board as Passengers, or otherwise, to have no Reliance upon them.

IN 1785, the ship FLOYER, about 350 or 400 tons burthen, Captain Bain, an experienced eastern trader, was on the coast of Pedier, north part of Sumatra. Some of the chiefs having arrived in proas (boats) to trade, were invited into the cabin, and with their cresses (or daggers) which had been concealed, they stabbed the commander and officers of the ship, whilst at breakfast; at the same instant, the Malays, with concealed cresses in the proas alongside, boarded the vessel by signal from their chiefs, and murdering the few remaining Europeans, possessed themselves of the ship. This ship belonged to Calcutta in Bengal.

It has been mentioned, that a ship belonging to Bengal was taken possession of by one Malay, previous a little to the time when the Floyer was taken; and the method this man followed to accomplish his purpose, was this:—In a serene night, when all the crew were asleep except the man at the helm, this desperate Malay stabbed him without noise, and also the officer of the watch, who was asleep on deck; then going below, he terminated the existence of the commander and another officer, who were asleep, in the same manner. At this time the third officer, a young man, being asleep in one of the boats, was secretly apprised of his danger by one of the Lascars, and he was prevailed upon to conceal himself in a large empty chest, belonging to the sarang, or principal native of the crew. The Malay, whilst in search of this young officer, was informed by the sarang, that he had jumped overboard through fear, on perceiving the fate of the others, which satisfied the Malay. He continued in command of the vessel for a few days, giving his orders to the sarang, and kept his cress in a menacing position, when any person approached him with victuals or otherwise, securing the door of the cabin where he slept in the night. At last a plan was concerted between the sarang and the young officer, to retake the ship, which was accomplished by rushing upon the Malay, followed by the Lascars, at a time when he was a little unguarded.

In 1782 or 3, the Snow INDUSTRY, of Calcutta, burthen four hundred tons, Captain M'Ewen, sent his boat for wood and water at Pulo Varela, near the north-east coast of Sumatra, with Mr. M'Intosh, the first officer, in charge of the boat. This island is not always inhabited, but some Malay proas were there at this time. The Industry's people were sent by the officer to cut wood, and fill the casks with water, whilst he remained to cultivate the friendship of the Malays belonging to the proas; but they were not susceptible of friendship to strangers, for they cressed him to the heart, and seizing the arms which had been brought from the vessel for the protection of the wooding and watering party, assailed the Lascars, who were at work, killing several of them. Three of the Industry's people escaped from the Malays, by secreting themselves among the bushes during the first part of the night, and afterwards swam to the snow, which was anchored near the shore. These Malays committed this barbarous deed for the possession of a few muskets brought on shore in the Industry's boat, as a protection to the parties on shore whilst wooding and watering. After this misfortune, the Industry had no boat, very few people left, and only one cask of water remaining: in this state, with a leaky vessel, (on account of the Dutch war,) Captain M'Ewen resolved to proceed direct to Madras, and by obtaining a large supply of rain water in the Strait of Malacca, he was enabled to arrive at the destined port.

In 1788, a boat was sent from the ship DADALOY, of Bombay, to Pulo Varela, in Malacca Strait, for water or wood; some proas belonging to Battabarra, a town on Sumatra adjacent, being at Pulo Varela at this time, the Malays belonging to them made prisoners of the officers and boat's crew, carried them to Battabarra, where they were sold. Some of them were re-purchased from slavery afterwards, by an officer sent to Battabarra from Prince of Wales Island.

In 1788, the ship MAY, of Calcutta, burthen about four hundred and fifty tons, commanded by Captain Dixon, a person experienced in the eastern trade, and well acquainted on the Borneo coast, arrived at the entrance of the river of Borneo Proper, to trade. With a view of expediting the trade, he was prevailed on by the chiefs to proceed with the ship up the river, and moored her close to the town of Borneo Proper. He then went on shore to consult with the Rajah and chiefs relative to trade, and was cressed. The natives from the town then crowded into large proas, boarded the ship in all directions, cut the three officers and other Europeans to pieces, and took possession of the ship and cargo.

About 1789, the Grab Snow GENEROUS FRIENDS, Captain Lunn, belonging to Calcutta, burthen about two hundred tons, on her passage from Mocha in the Red Sea, bound to the coast of Coromandel, had on board some Malay passengers. These being Mussulmans, had been on a pilgrimage to the Prophet's tomb at Mecca. During the passage much rain was experienced, and there being but little spare room in the vessel, Captain Lunn humanely entreated these sanctified pilgrims to spread their mats in his cabin, where they might sleep comfortably in the night; his own hanging cot being in the same apartment. In return for this humane and hospitable behaviour, these *holy Malay Hodjees* *, when Captain Lunn was asleep, cressed him to the heart, and served his two officers in the same manner. These Malays then ordered the sarang to navigate the vessel to some part of the island Sumatra, on which he declared his incapacity to navigate them to any place. They threatened him with death, if he did not conduct them to some Malay port; but the sarang and his people steered towards the Malabar coast, in hopes of meeting some ship, and got sight of one of the Maldiva Islands, near to which the vessel was carried by the current in a calm night. Some of the Lascars at this time secretly left the vessel, and being assisted with the current setting towards the island, reached it by swimming, from whence they were sent by the King of the Maldivas (who has

* The venerable name acquired by a pilgrimage to the holy tomb of the Prophet Mahomed.

always treated with great humanity shipwrecked mariners) to the Malabar coast, and ultimately to Bombay, where they gave the narration here described. There is reason to conclude, that the Generous Friends was never heard of after these Lascars left her.

It may be here observed, that humanity appears to be but little regarded by the *Holy* of Mecca, which their recent outrage upon a King of the Maldiva Islands seems to confirm. A few years ago, the King of the Maldivas ardently wishing to become a better Mussulman, resolved on a pilgrimage to Mecca, as the surest means to accomplish that end; and, with his family, proceeded in one of his own vessels, to visit the tomb of Mahomed. He had collected a sum of money, as large as he could conveniently obtain, to present to the *Holy* in possession of the tomb; but their rapacity was not satisfied. They detained him in a vexatious manner for a considerable time, in hopes of being able to extort from him more money: this was impossible, for he had no more. These *holy* men were therefore displeased, they plundered his Queen of her trinkets, deprived him of life, and kept the family in bondage a considerable time.

In March 1789, two Chinese Tchuans (vulgo tunks) bound to Rhio, were surprised by the Malay pirates near Point Romania; the crew of one of them were said to have been all massacred; the crew of the other were carried to Siak, on the north-east coast of Sumatra, nearly opposite to Cape Rachado, in the Strait of Malacca, to be sold; but the Chinese escaped from the place of confinement in the night, seized the launch which belonged to their tchuan, and put to sea. Two days after we met with this launch, in which there were about seventy Chinese; several of them much cut and mangled, in an affray they had with the Malays, who discovered them effecting their escape. Several of the Chinese were killed in the affray, and some of those in the launch had their hands nearly severed from their arms; a few were taken on board and conveyed to Canton, and those which remained in the launch were supplied with water, provision, dressings for the wounded, &c., and directed to proceed to Malacca, where they arrived on the following day.

Nearly about the time the Chinese tchuans were taken, a snow, in the Malay, or eastern trade, commanded by Captain Robb, had on board as helmsmen (vulgo seconies) natives of Luconia, or some other of the eastern islands; these formed a conspiracy, murdered Captain Robb, &c., and carried the vessel into Battabarra, near Pulo Varela, in Malacca Strait, where most of the crew, consisting of Lascars, were sold.

In 1789 or 90, the ship MARIA, Captain Wilcox, was at anchor in Madras Road. The Manila seconies belonging to this vessel, murdered the chief officer in the night, when he was asleep, and threw him overboard.

About 1791, the snow BETSEY, of Bombay, burthen about three hundred tons, Captain Nelson, from Bencoolen bound to Batavia, had on board as passengers some natives of Java; these, in concert with the gunner and seconies, who were Manila-men, assassinated the commander and officers in the night, and took possession of the vessel; but the sarang and Lascars took courage, and retook her from the Malays, some of which were killed in the affray. A few days after this happened, the ship Jane, from China bound to Bombay, fell in with the Betsey, near Java Head, and conducted her to the owner there, where the remaining murderers were tried, executed, and placed on gibbets. Previous to the retaking of the vessel by the Lascars, several of the principal assassins had proceeded in a boat to Java.

About 1791, a snow belonging to Prince of Wales Island was commanded by a Captain Stewart, who was assassinated by Malays.

Captain Gray, an experienced trader to the eastward, was assailed and wounded by the Malays on the Pedier coast.

In March 1793, the long boat of the ship Anna was sent for water to Maloza River, south part of the island Baseelan, near Mindano; the ship at anchor about three leagues from the river. The long boat went three times to the river for water. Prior to her arrival the last time, the natives had concerted a plan to entice the officer on shore, then to attack the boat and murder the crew, on purpose to obtain a few muskets and cutlasses, and a few pieces of linen cloth, brought from the ship to barter with them for poultry and vegetables. Being aware of the perfidy of most of the natives in this part of the eastern Archipelago, their feigned kindness was rejected; and by continuing in the boat with three European helmsmen under arms, we frustrated their plan; for they had not courage to make an open attack, although nearly one hundred men had assembled, armed with cresses and long spears, to execute their bloody scheme, had any favourable opportunity offered for secret assassination.

About two years subsequent, the ship GLOCESTER, of Bombay, sent two boats to Maloza river for water; they were seized by the natives, and most of the crews murdered.

In 1793, an American ship from Batavia, bound to Manila, had a boat with an officer and four men in it, which landed on the west coast of Celebes, near Cape Temoel, which is exactly on the equator; one of the boats' crew was murdered by the natives, the others remained in servitude about two years, during which time one of them died; the remaining two, with the officer, escaped in a canoe to Macasser, where they were humanely treated by the Dutch, and sent to Batavia. This officer, whose name was Woodard, published in London a narrative of their sufferings, &c., comprised in an 8vo volume.

In 1794, a snow belonging to Madras, commanded by Captain Gray, went to trade on the coast of Pedier, north side of Sumatra. When he was on shore examining some beetle nut, which had been purchased by him, was cruelly murdered by the natives with whom he was trading; then they boarded the vessel in their proas, and got possession of her.

About 1794, Captain Piercy, in command of a snow at Tolloo Samwai, on the coast of Pedier, was with his officers murdered, and the vessel taken by the Malays.

Nearly about this period a vessel from Manilla was commanded by an English gentleman, most of the crew were natives of the islands situated south-eastward from Luconia, who are said to be cruel and treacherous, and are known by the appellation of Bassias. When the vessel was near the Natuna Islands in the China Sea, these Bassias wounded the commander, and took possession of the vessel.

In 1796, the ship TRANSFER, of Calcutta, commanded by Captain Sadler, an experienced eastern trader, was at Pontiana, or Monpava, on the west coast of Borneo. He went on shore to transact business with the Rajah, and was returning down the river in the evening in his boat towards the ship, with some gold dust which was due for goods sold, when the boat was assaulted by natives, (supposed to have been sent by the Rajah,) who murdered Captain Sadler, and robbed the boat. The officer on board left the coast, to preclude any attack on the ship.

Nearly about the same period, a vessel belonging to Calcutta, said to have been commanded by Captain Stalker, an experienced eastern trader, was taken by the Malays, and the Europeans on board murdered.

About 1797, Captain Page, commanding a small American ship, was assassinated in the Strait of Banca, by Malay pirates.

In 1799, His Majesty's ships SYBILLE and FOX were at anchor in Pollock Cove, on the north-east side of Bongo Bay, near the town of Mindano. Two unarmed boats belonging to the Sybille, sent on shore for water, were assailed by the natives, who were at war with the King of Mindano; part of the crew murdered, and the rest carried into slavery. About one year afterwards, these were liberated by the humanity of Captain Lynch, who paid a ransom for them, and carried them to Amboina, at that time a British settlement.

About 1799, a ship belonging to Calcutta, commanded by Captain Drysdale, had on board as seconies, Manilla men, or natives of some other of the eastern islands. These concerted a plan to murder the commander and officers, and seize on the ship, then at sea in the Bay of Bengal. They began to execute their plan in the night, by stabbing the officer on deck who had the watch; this occasioned some noise, and alarmed the commander, who was asleep in his cabin. He instantly jumped on deck armed, which intimidated the conspirators, and saved himself and the vessel.

In February 1800, the ship ANNA, of Calcutta, burthen about six hundred tons, commanded by Captain Gilmore, bound from London to Bengal, had on board about thirty or forty natives of Java, part of the crew of some captured vessels or vessel from Batavia; which were sent on board the Anna, as passengers to India. During the passage, these Javans formed the dreadful plan to murder all the Europeans on board, on a Saturday night, when mostly below; although there were several English gentlemen in the ship, exclusive of the commander and officers, and also from eight to twelve English seamen; besides the Lascars. The crisis of slaughter had nearly approached, when the conspiracy was discovered, and means of security adopted. These wretches, when interrogated, did not deny the cruel plan they had formed, nor offered any reason for such an undertaking, or what they would have done with the ship. At this time the Anna was in a high southern latitude, off the Cape of Good Hope, but far distant from the land.

In 1800 or 1801, Captain R. Pavin, in the ship Ruby, of Calcutta, arrived at Sooloo, and went on shore to transact business with the Sultan, relative to trade. He was cressed whilst sitting in conversation with the Sultan, by some of those in waiting. An immediate attack was made on the vessel by a number of proas, assisted by a battery firing on her from the shore: fortunately there was a fresh breeze of wind; the cable was cut, and the vessel being well armed, destroyed some of the proas in a running fight, by which she escaped.

About this time, a ship belonging to Madras, commanded by Captain Henderson, part of whose crew were natives of some of the eastern islands, murdered the first officer at sea.

In 1800, a small ship belonging to Calcutta, which Captain Langlands commanded, was proceeding from Amboina, the crew mostly natives of Java. A few days after their departure from that island, about two o'clock in the afternoon the Javans rushed on the quarter-deck, armed with cresses, knives, bludgeons, &c., stabbed the Purser, who was walking the deck with Captain Langlands, in a vital part. The latter being unarmed, ran below, and grasping a musket with fixed bayonet, forced his passage on deck; he being a powerful man, and perfectly acquainted with the practice of the musket and fixed bayonet, after fighting singly with from fifteen to twenty of these Malays for some time, the victory was gained by him. Although much cut and bruised, by bayoneting several, and pushing others overboard with the but end of the musket, or with the bayonet, a panic began to pervade them, several of them jumping into the sea, which enabled him to secure the others, with the assistance from a few Lascars he had on board, and returned to Amboina for a supply of men to his vessel.

In November 1800, a small ship from Prince of Wales Island, bound to Calcutta, commanded by Captain George, whose gunner and seconies were Manilla men, or of the Malay tribe, near the coast of Aracan, assassinated the commander and officers in the night, and an English female passenger. Having perpetrated this deed, they prepared to leave the vessel, and to proceed in the boat to Chittagong, at this time not far distant; and to preclude every means of detection, a train of gunpowder was laid, communicating with the magazine and that part of the vessel where they were to step from into the boat. The plan was, to have set fire to the train when they went into the boat, that by the time they got at a safe distance from the ship, she might explode with the remainder of the crew, who were Lascars, so that none might survive the catastrophe but themselves. The Lascars perceiving the danger near, of being all blown in the air by one explosion, were roused from their natural apathy, by the innate principle of self-preservation; and when the last man was going into the boat, several Lascars rushed on the gunner and seconies, and dispatched all of them except one, who took refuge at the mast-head of the ship. The Lascar who headed the others in this affray, was drowned in struggling with one of the seconies in the boat. In the struggle they both tumbled out of the boat, and were drowned. Although near Chittagong, and not far distant from the entrance of Hooghly river, the Lascars knew not how to proceed to either of these places, but they found means to navigate the vessel back to Prince of Wales Island, from whence they came, and there delivered up the surviving assassin, who was sent to Calcutta for trial.

In 1803, a small snow belonging to Prince of Wales Island, bound to Malacca, was assaulted by Malay pirates in Calam Strait, and after expending all their ammunition in a running fight, was obliged to return to Prince of Wales Island.

In 1803, Malay pirate proas assaulted a small brig in Sincapour Strait; but His Majesty's sloop Rattlesnake coming up, and dispersing the proas, prevented this vessel from being taken.

In July 1803, the ship SUSANNAH, of Calcutta, Captain Drysdale, at Pontiana, on the west coast of Borneo, with a valuable cargo on board, was surprised by the natives, all the Europeans massacred, and the vessel taken by the chiefs of the place.

About this time, an American vessel was surprised, and taken by the Malays of Sumatra.

In 1804, or 1805, another race of men than Malays have been guilty of a like barbarous action with the foregoing. The ship Alert, from Bengal bound to Bombay, had a part of her crew, consisting of Muscat (or Arab) seedies: these are woolly headed men, originally slaves procured from the east coast of Africa by the Arabs, and by these metamorphosed into mussulmans. Those of this class which were in the Alert, put the commander and officers to death, and carried the ship into Maculla, on the south coast of Arabia; the Shick of which place delivered her to the Bombay Government, when applied to for this purpose.

PLATE CCVI.

THE HYDROGRAPHER, (No. 4.)

ST. LUCIA.

THIS third and last Island in the West Indies belonging to the French, is one of the Caribbees, about 27 miles long, and 12 broad, and was so named because it was discovered on St. Lucia's day. It lies in north lat. 14°, west long. 60° 58'. It is nearly as large as Barbadoes. The interior is very mountainous. Two of the mountains, terminating in sharp points, are called the pin-heads of St. Lucia. The sea coast is very fertile, well watered with rivers, and abounds in good harbours and bays. The little careenage has many advantages: a sufficient depth of water, and

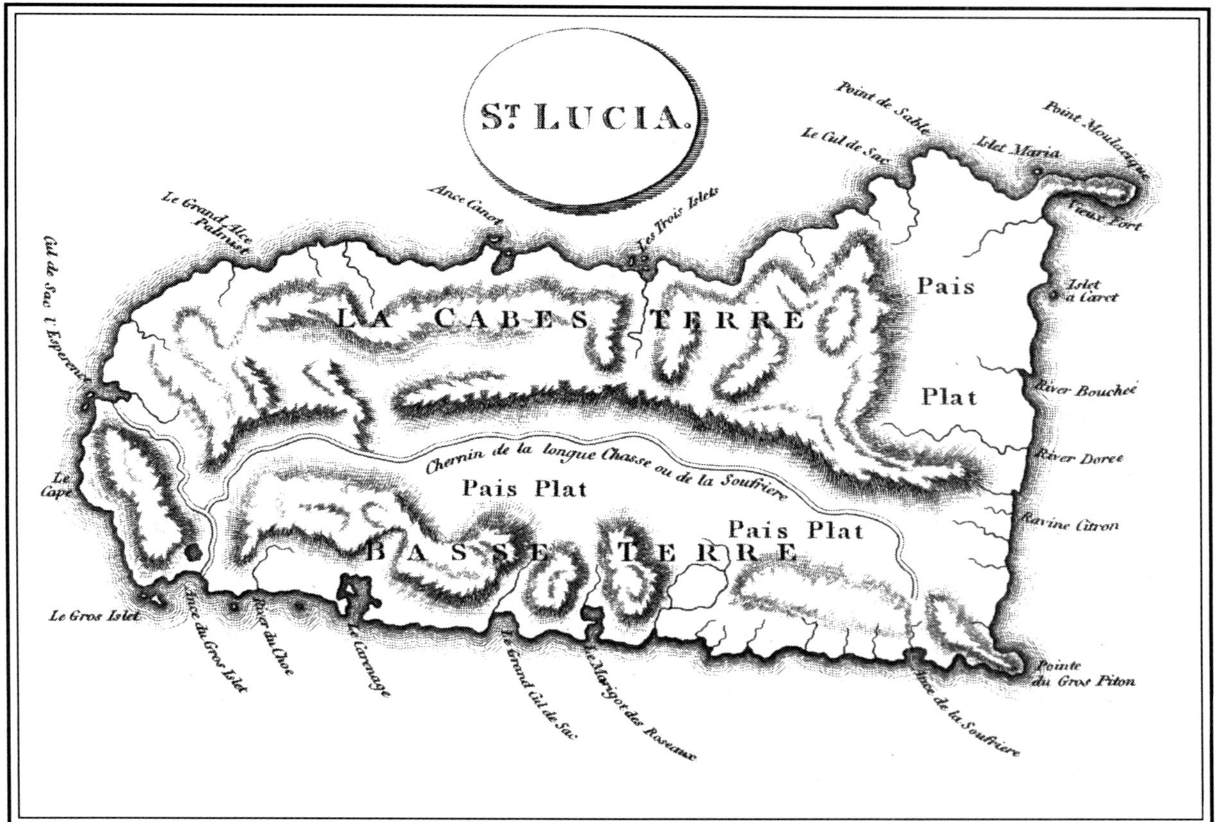

London, Published June 30th 1806, by J. Gold, 103, Shoe Lane, Fleet Street.

an excellent bottom; three carening places, which have no need of a quay, and require nothing but a capstern to turn the keel of a ship above ground: thirty ships of the line may lie in it sheltered from hurricanes, without being moored; and the boats of the country, which have been kept a long time in this harbour, have never been attacked by worms. The winds are always good to go out with, and the largest squadron might be in the offing in less than an hour.

The English took possession of this island in 1637. After the dreadful massacre of the settlers in August 1640, the French in 1650 sent over forty inhabitants, under the conduct of Rousseban: three of his successors were murdered by the Caribs; and in 1664 the colony was taken by the English, who gave it up in 1666. By the peace of Aix la Chappelle, St. Lucia was declared to be a neutral island; but the French, with their usual perfidy, afterwards settled the island, built a fort, and appointed a Governor. In 1762 St. Lucia capitulated to the following squadron:—

Ships.	*Guns.*	*Commanders.*
Dragon	74	Capt. Hon. A. J. Hervey.
Norwich	50	—— William M'Cleverty.
Penzance	40	—— J. Boyd.
Dover	40	—— Chaloner Ogle.
Baselisk	8	—— Robert Price.

In 1763 this island by treaty was ceded to France. Raynall informs us, that it contained in 1777, fifty-three sugar plantations, which occupied 1541 pieces of land; five million, forty thousand, nine hundred and sixty-two coffee trees; one million, nine hundred and forty-five thousand seven hundred and twelve cocoa plants; and five hundred and ninety-seven plots of cotton. These united productions were sold in the island for little less than £. 125,000.

TRIAL

OF

HENRY LORD VISCOUNT MELVILLE,

BEFORE THE HIGH COURT OF PARLIAMENT.

ON Tuesday the 29th of April, the trial commenced, when ten charges were exhibited against Henry Lord Viscount Melville, by the Commons of England, viz.

FIRST.—That Henry Viscount Lord Melville, whilst he enjoyed the office of Treasurer of the Navy, and previous to the 10th of January, 1786, did fraudulently and illegally convert to his own use 10,000l. of the public money; and did continue such fraudulent and illegal conversion after the passing of an Act for the better regulating the office of Treasurer; which sum of 10,000l. Lord Melville did declare in the House of Commons, on the 11th of June, 1805, that he would not reveal the application of, as he felt himself bound by motives of public duty and private honour to conceal the same; all which was contrary to the duties of his high office, a breach of the high trust reposed in him, and a violation of the law.

SECONDLY.—That the said Henry Viscount Lord Melville did connive at and permit Alexander Trotter, his Paymaster, to draw divers sums of money from the Bank for other purposes than for naval services; and did connive at and suffer him, the said Alexander, to place such sums in his own name, at a private banker's, Messrs. Coutts and Co., subject to his sole controul and disposition, against the statute, &c.

THIRDLY.—That the said Henry did fraudulently and illegally permit the said Alexander, after placing such sums of money at his private banker's, to apply such sums for purposes of private advantage, profit, and emolument; by which the public money was exposed to great risk and loss, against the statute, &c.

FOURTHLY.—That the said Henry did connive at the said Alexander's placing in the hands of Mark Sprott, and others, divers sums of public money, for purposes other than for naval purposes, and for the purpose of private emolument and advantage, against the statute, &c.

FIFTHLY.—That the said Henry did take from the public money a sum of 10,000l., and did fraudulently, corruptly, and illegally, apply the same to his own use, &c., against the statute, &c.

SIXTHLY.—That the said Henry did, for the purpose of private emolument, receive divers large sums of the public money from the said Alexander, fraudulently concealing the illegal use and application of the same; such sums being mixed and undistinguished from the proper monies of the said Alexander; that the sums so advanced were entered in a book by the said Alexander, entitled, "Lord Melville's Account Current;" which book, by agreement, dated the 18th and 23d of February, 1805, together with all vouchers, memorandums, and writings, were cancelled, burnt, and destroyed, with a view to conceal and prevent the discovery of such advances of money by the said Alexander to the said Henry, against the statute, &c.

SEVENTHLY.—That amongst other advances so made, was one of 22,000l., without interest, part advanced from the public money so illegally drawn from the Bank, and part advanced from the mixed fund at Coutts's, composed as well of the public monies as the proper monies of the said Alexander, wholly mixed and undistinguished.

EIGHTHLY.—That amongst other advances, was another sum of 22,000l., for which the said Henry agreed to pay interest.

NINTHLY.—That during the greater part of the time the said Alexander filled the office of Paymaster, he did gratuitously transact the private business of the said Henry, as his agent, and was from time to time in advance to the said Henry from 10 to 20,000l., all which advances were taken from the mixed fund at Coutts's; whereby the said Henry derived an illegal benefit from the public money; and further, that such advances were made in consideration of the said Henry's conniving, permitting, and suffering the said Alexander to use, appropriate, and apply the public money to his own interest, profit, and emolument. All which proceedings of the said Henry were contrary to the duties of his office, and in gross violation of the law; and by all and every such acts done and committed, the said Henry was guilty of high crimes and misdemeanors.

To the above *Nine* charges his Lordship pleaded generally "*Not Guilty,*" matters of error and want of form excepted, and relied upon the goodness of his cause, and their Lordships' justice, for an acquittal.

The TENTH, in other words the *additional Article* of charge, was to the following effect:—"That between the 1st of January, 1784, and the 5th of January, 1786, the said Henry Viscount Melville, did illegally apply a sum of 20,000l. for purposes other than naval, with a view to promote his own private emolument and advantage," and did continue such illegal application of the public money, after the passing an Act for the better regulating the office of Treasurer of His Majesty's Navy."

To this his Lordship pleaded, that he was no ways bound to answer, either by the law of the land or by the constitution; nevertheless he would plead *Not Guilty*, relying upon the goodness of his cause, and the justice of their Lordships, for an acquittal.

After the charges were read, Mr. Whitbread rose, and addressed the Court for three hours and forty minutes.

Mr. Whitbread said it was his intention, as it was the wish of the Managers of the Impeachment, on the part of the House of Commons, to open all the charges at once. This course of proceeding had been adopted, because it would have been extremely difficult to separate, in detail, the matters contained in the different charges, intimately connected and interwoven as they were; and also because the Managers were extremely anxious to avoid every proceeding that might tend to create unnecessary delay. It would probably be necessary for him, in performing the task he had undertaken, to enter into a long detail of dry facts, many of which had already become matter of public notoriety. He should not, however, offend their Lordships, by asking for their patience, since their Lordships were fully aware that patience was indispensably necessary to the due administration of justice. It should be his endeavour to make the detail he had to submit as perspicuous as the powers of his mind would enable him, with, at the same time, as much conciseness as the nature of the subject would admit. He was well aware that the task he had undertaken was one of the greatest magnitude and importance; he was well aware that the post he now occupied had formerly been filled by persons possessed of the most splendid talents. He knew the strength against which the Managers of the Impeachment had to contend; he knew the ability of the learned Counsel for the Defendant; he knew that to that ability they added all the experience which could be acquired in this mode of trial, they having been, on a former occasion, one for, and one against, a prosecution of this nature. Far, however, from being appalled, if there was any energy in his mind, these circumstances quickened it, and called for all its exertions. When he looked back to the memorable day when the seeds of this trial were sown, and reviewed the proceedings until the charges were brought to issue, he felt a satisfaction that this mode of trial had been adopted, since it was that which had been chosen by the dearest friends and connections of the Defendant. He felt also a satisfaction at the means employed for the defence, inasmuch as every mistake made in propounding or supporting the charges, would be immediately rectified by the learning and experience of the learned Counsel for the Defendant. [A short pause ensued, for which Mr. Whitbread apologized, and proceeded.] I trust that whatever exertions I may make, I shall not be betrayed into intemperate expressions—truth delights in the language of temperance. Whilst, however, I endeavour to avoid the language of intemperance, I will speak for justice; if the party accused be guilty, the fault is double, because he came into office on the pretext of reforming the abuses of others. Errors may creep into the best regulated offices, in spite of every care and attention; but, if abuses are wilful, spare them not. The preamble to the Articles of Impeachment stated, he said, a self-evident proposition, that the office of the Treasurer of the Navy was one of great trust and importance. He need not dwell upon another proposition, that all great officers ought to act with honour and integrity. If these qualifications were required more in one office than in others, it was in that of the Treasurer of the Navy.—As to the origin, or constitution of the office of Treasurer of the Navy, it was not necessary to say much. Large sums of money necessarily passed through the hands of the Treasurers of the Navy, who had been accustomed to make use of the public money, whilst remaining in their hands, for the purposes of private emolument. This practice, though not legally recognised, was allowed. At the close, however, of the American war, when the situation of the country loudly demanded inquiry, Commissioners were appointed for the purpose of inquiring into the past expenditure of public money, and also as to what enactments might be necessary for the future. These Commissioners, in the execution of the trust reposed in them, made a special report respecting the office of Treasurer of the

Navy, in which they advised measures to be taken for the purpose of preventing accumulations of public money in the hands of the Treasurer of the Navy: and that future Treasurers should be precluded from making use of the public money for the purposes of private emolument, as had been done by former Treasurers. In consequence of this report, several resolutions were passed by the House of Commons, on the 19th June, 1782, [Mr. Whitbread read the resolutions,] stating the expediency of granting to the Treasurer of the Navy a fixed salary, in lieu of all fees and perquisites. From that moment a new æra commenced in the office of Treasurer of the Navy; from that moment it became illegal to make use of the public money for the purposes of private emolument, and the person doing so was, he contended, guilty of an impeachable offence. Mr. Barré, at the time the resolution passed, held the situation of Treasurer of the Navy; but, after that period, never made use of the public money in the manner before stated. The salary was then increased to 4000l. a year, in lieu of all fees and perquisites. It was worthy of observation, however, that, during the treasurership of Mr. Barré, the public money was invariably deposited in the Bank of England; for although it was the custom of the office for the Treasurers to make use of the public money as before stated, still the usual place of deposit was the Bank of England. None of them had lent any sums to private individuals, except the Noble Defendant. Mr. Barré soon afterwards quitted the office, and was succeeded by the Noble Defendant, who had some years before began his political career, having first been attached to Lord Guildford, and who subsequently connected himself with that prodigy of talent, whose sun had prematurely set, but who carried with him the regret of all men who admired or esteemed personal political purity. The Defendant, on coming into office, appointed Mr. Douglas his Paymaster, who had held that situation, under several Paymasters, for 18 years, and who was recommended to the Defendant by Mr. Barré. He charged the Noble Defendant with, at the time Mr. Douglas was Paymaster, and previous to the Act of Parliament, a breach of his duty, in possessing himself of certain sums of the public money. With respect to the circumstances of that period, he begged their Lordships to consider in what situation the Commons stood. At the time the first articles were framed, they were not in possession of the greater part of the evidence relating to this charge. In the lapse of 24 years, many of the persons who could have given evidence were dead—many of the documents had been destroyed, and many had been accidentally lost. By means, however, of the evidence which the Managers had been able to resort to, he trusted their difficulties had been surmounted, and that they should be able to lead their Lordships, first by circuitous paths, and small steps, and afterwards by a plain and open road, until they reached an eminence from whence they might survey, with a clear and comprehensive view, all the transactions of the Defendant. The exertions of the Managers had been unremitting; but, though they had been able to conquer all the difficulties which stood in the way of their procuring evidence, they had not been able to conquer their feelings. Their Lordships might know, the Managers did know, that, in the course of last spring, the Defendant wrote a letter to the Commissioners of Naval Inquiry, denying that he had derived any interest or advantage from the use of the public money in his hands, during the paymastership of Mr. Douglas. The Noble Lord had been elevated by His Majesty's favour, on account of his services, to a rank in which he was only bound to answer upon his honour.—"The Noble Lord said he never did that which we undertake to prove that he did. The Noble Lord said he was ready to verify his statement upon oath. Under such circumstances, it is a painful duty for us to proceed; but I charge the Noble Lord not only with having taken this money, but with having made use of it for his own advantage and emolument." He would now advert to the first charge, stating that the Noble Defendant had possessed himself of a certain sum of 10,000l. of the public money. This was connected with the 10th article, by a reference to which it would appear that this sum was increased to 27,000l. How were the Commons prepared to prove this? By the confession of the Defendant himself. The Defendant had avowed that he had taken 10,000l. of the public money, and he told the House of Commons this remarkable fact—"That he never would reveal in what manner that sum had been applied." That expression the Defendant used in the face of the House of Commons; and that, I say, is an impeachable offence. Neither the Defendant, nor any man breathing, has a right to set himself above the law, to say that he has taken 10,000l. of the public money, and refuse to tell to whom it was paid, and for what purpose. I was apprehensive that it would be, and it may be still necessary to go into an elaborate and detailed proof, with respect to this 10,000l., of which the Defendant possessed himself. I hope, however, that our labours, in this respect, are cut short. Whilst the Managers were employed in the exercise of their duty, and within a few hours of our appearance here, I have learnt that the Counsel have got a short cut to the secret of the employment of this 10,000l., and I propose to carry your Lordships along with them. We may now be enabled to settle the point at once, as I know that the receipt of the person to whom this 10,000l. was paid, was, within these few days, in possession of the Defendant's Counsel. I shall call, therefore, for this receipt; and I hope that neither private honour, nor personal convenience, will interfere to prevent its production. As to the concealment of the application of this 10,000l., could private honour, could public duty, be pleaded as the motive? The public themselves asked for the information. He strongly suspected that the person to whom the money was paid, was one who was long known as being engaged in mercantile transactions, and who, from a subsequent failure in his concerns, was subjected to a commission of bankruptcy, in consequence of which the whole transactions of the House were exposed to investigation. Private honour, therefore, must, in the case, cease to be a motive for concealment. As to personal convenience, it was most convenient that the Defendant's Counsel should produce the paper to which he had alluded: not only this, but justice required its production. He not only charged the Defendant with possessing himself of this 10,000l. of the public money after the new æra had taken place in the Navy Pay Office, but he knew that the Defendant had not only confessed to the House of Commons, but also to Mr. Trotter, in 1786, that he had possessed himself of other sums of public money to the amount of 10,000l.; and though it might be true that the Defendant did not possess himself of that sum at once, and as a whole, yet he did possess himself of that sum, made up of fractional parts, not one atom of which was applied to the public service, but which was applied to the purposes of his own interest and advantage. On the 19th of August, 1782, Lord Melville (then Mr. Dundas) was appointed Treasurer of the Navy. On the 20th of the same month, Mr. Douglas paid into a banking-house, at which the Noble Defendant then and still kept an account, 1000l. on account of Lord Melville. Who was Mr. Douglas? He was appointed to his situation by Mr. Dundas; every act he did was with the sanction of the Defendant, who was legally responsible for such acts, and who at the same time placed the greatest confidence in Mr. Douglas. It would be shown that this 1000l. was part of the public money. Early in November a payment of a different description was made into the banking house on behalf of the Defendant. The then mode of managing the business of the office of Treasurer of the Navy was, for the Paymaster, after a warrant had been received, to go to the Exchequer with a Bank Clerk to have the greater part of the sum written into the bank book, whilst the rest was delivered to him in any way he chose. On the 6th of November, 1782, Mr. Douglas went to the Exchequer to receive 45,000l.; he chose to write into the bank book 40,000l., and to take the remaining 5000l. with him, in five bank notes of 1000l. each. A similar transaction had frequently taken place before; but as far as could be traced, the sum so received in cash or notes, had uniformly been set apart to pay exchequer fees. This 5000l. was never carried to the public account. It had been the custom to deposit sums of money in the iron chest in the Navy Pay Office, as a place of safe custody. Cash was thus frequently deposited there previous to being sent to the out ports. In process of time, however, when payments in cash were much narrowed, the iron chest became the place of deposit for the papers, books, and floating securities of the office. The iron chest was, however, at the time of which he was speaking, the regular place of deposit; but this 5000l. never was deposited there. One of the bank notes for 1000l. which had been traced, was paid out of the hands of the Treasurer of the Navy to his private account at Messrs. Drummonds. Of the remaining 4000l. the Defendant also possessed himself. In December, 1782, another sum was subtracted from the public money; one of the bank notes forming a part of which, had been traced, and it was found was applied to liquidate a private debt of the Defendant, and was paid into the hands of Messrs. Moffatt. If he could show this, it would be as clear as that the sun shone that the Defendant made use of this money for his own private advantage. Unquestionably he did. Between the 20th of August, 1782, and the 10th of April, 1783, subtractions were made by Mr. Douglas, on receiving money at the Exchequer, to the amount of 16,000l.—only 3000l. of which was paid on official account. Including the two bank notes of 1000l. each, which he had mentioned, (he would not trouble their Lordships with the different items,) 13,000l. was paid to the Noble Lord. The Managers had been fortunate in making this discovery, and he trusted that all the papers respecting the paymastership of Mr. Douglrs, which must be in possession of the Defendant, would be produced. When the Defendant went out of office on the 10th of April, 1783, there was a debt due from him of 13,000l. On that day Lord Bayning succeeded to the office of Treasurer of the Navy. Notwithstanding this, however, on the 14th of April, Mr. Douglas drew an order upon Mr. Jellicoe for 10,000l., of which the Defendant possessed himself. He had heard the Defendant tell the House of Commons, that at the time he was Treasurer of the Navy he held various confidential situations, with respect to which great caution and circumspection were necessary; and it appeared that the Defendant would not even communicate to his colleagues the circumstances respecting this sum of money, although he himself, at that time, formed no part of the Ministry; but he takes 10,000l., and then says that it was for the service of the public, but will not tell to whom it was paid, or for what specific service. The Managers had, however, obtained sufficient information as to the real application of this money. There existed at the time of which he was speaking, a house well known in the commercial world, the house of Muir and Atkinson, who were at one period largely concerned in government contracts. Long, however, before the payment to them of this 10,000l. with which they were accommodated, they had ceased to have any concern in government contracts. Was this a fit place to deposit the public money? Were the circumstances of these individuals such at that time as to render a loan to that amount highly desirable?—He could show that the circumstances of the house were such, that the loan of 10,000l. was to them of essential importance. If that was proved, would the Defendant say that he received no advantage from advancing this loan? Could it be said that there any consideration of safety operated, when the Defendant must have known the situation of their affairs? The Managers had the account of Mr. Atkinson, in which the 10,000l. formed only one item, and the entry was signed Henry Dundas, in the hand-writing of the Defendant. He had already stated that the Defendant's Counsel were in possession of the receipt given for this 10,000l. During the time the Defendant was out of office, there was a sum received by a person of the name of Gray, now dead, which was applied to the payment of the Defendant's private debts. Having touched on this, he could not help observing, that nothing had been so painful to the Managers as the knowledge they were obliged to obtain of the private affairs of the Defendant: it was still more painful to be compelled to state them to the public. Gray was the private agent, at that time, of the Defendant, and the Managers were in possession of a letter written by the Defendant to Mr. Douglas, (Gray was a Clerk in the Navy Pay Office, and not a public accountant,) in which the Defendant stated, that if Mr. Douglas wanted any money in a particular way, (in what way was not stated in the letter,) upon application to Gray, the latter would supply him with 4 or 5000l. In June, 1783, Gray paid into the bank on account of the ex-treasurership 1000l. This could not come from any public source. The debt due from the Defendant to the public was thus reduced to 22,000l. In July, 1783, the Navy Pay Office was in a situation of great difficulty, having to pay a demand of 10,000l., and there being only 3000l. in the office to discharge it. Under these circumstances the Defendant was applied to, and recourse was had to Mr. Atkinson, who finding that there was 4000l. in the office, advanced 6000l. to make up the sum wanted. Sundry payments besides these, with the enumeration of which he would not trouble their Lordships, were made by the Defendant, by which the debt was reduced to 7600l. At this sum it stood, when another memorable revolution took place in the political affairs of this country, and the Defendant, on the change of ministry, became again Treasurer of the Navy in January, 1784. In this situation, the old Henry Dundas need only apply to the new Henry Dundas to accommodate him in any way that he wished, with respect to the debt due from him to the public. This accommodation was given; an unauthorized transfer of 2000l. was made from the account of the second treasurership to the first; and afterwards other transfers, equally unauthorized, to the amount of 4000l., leaving only 1600l. due on the account of the first treasurership, and creating a fresh debt of 6000l. to the account of the second. Besides this, there were two drafts of the Defendant for 2000l. each, which were sent by the Defendant to the bank, (and for which he received the money,) one of them on the 25th of May, 1785, a day most memorable, as it was on that very day that the Defendant carried a bill to the House of Lords for the better regulation of the office of Treasurer of the Navy. That very day the Defendant took 2000l. of the public money, and paid it to his account at Messrs. Drummonds, which had been overdrawn. These sums increased the debt to 11,600l. A payment of 1000l. was subsequently made out of the Defendant's own salary, which reduced that sum to 10,600l. In this situation the account stood up to the death of Mr. Douglas—the public account at the bank being deficient at that time in the sum of 10,600l. This statement was confirmed by all the public accounts, which gave the same result. All of them proved invariably that this was the deficiency. He thought, however, it would be discovered that this was not any specific sum, but was composed of different fractional parts, which had been appropriated by the Defendant for his own private purposes. Did the Defendant call upon the executors of Mr. Douglas to make good any deficiency? On the contrary, the only balance which the Defendant thought of calling for from the estate of Mr. Douglas, was a trifling sum on account of exchequer fees, on the payment of which he gave Mr. Douglas's son and executor a receipt in full. Was this out of tenderness to the memory of Mr. Douglas? No. The character of Mr. Douglas was unimpeached; and he could call many most respectable persons, some even amongst their Lordships, to speak to the high character of Mr. Douglas. This circumstance, therefore, proved that the Defendant was conscious the deficiency rested with himself, and resulted from his own acts. He had thus gone through the detail of the statements relative to the 1st and 10th articles, and which, he had no doubt, would be completely proved. He had brought down the transactions of the Defendant to January, 1786, and he believed it would be found, with reference to those transactions, that the Defendant had forged a chain for himself, with a shackle at the end of it, from which he would not easily free himself. He now proceeded to the second grand division of the charges.

The Honourable Gentleman professed his readiness to do complete justice to the meritorious conduct of Lord Melville in the Navy Pay Office, particularly with regard to the arrangement upon the subject of payments to seamen, their families, and their heirs.—In those arrangements it appeared the Noble Lord was assisted by Trotter. Indeed the Noble Lord himself acknowledged this assistance, and very manfully bore testimony to the character of Trotter.—To the testimony of that character then he (Mr. W.) called upon their Lordships to give ample credit, and it would go to the conviction of the Defendant. Upon that testimony alone, however, he would not desire their Lordships to rely, for he had ample corroboration for every part of it. After the evidence he had to adduce should be heard, he was at a loss to imagine what ground of defence could be taken by the Counsel for the Defendant. He had heard it rumoured that they meant to contend that the act of 1785 had not been violated, But if the terms of that act were not plain and unambiguous, he knew no act in the statute book which could not be explained away: nay, the meaning of that precept in the decalogue, "Thou shalt not Steal," might be questioned. But unfortunately for the purpose of the learned Counsel, Parliament had put its own interpretation on this statute by the act of indemnity to Mr. Pitt for the loan to Boyd. By this act the violation of the statute of 1785, by conduct exactly similar to that in this instance charged upon the Noble Defendant, was expressly recognised. But it would be an insult to the understanding to suppose, that any doubts could exist upon the meaning of a law prepared and carried through by the Defendant himself, in the character of a Reformer, and avowedly for the purpose of guarding against such abuses as he himself now stood charged with committing. The distinction which he understood was meant to be taken between assigned and unassigned balances in the hands of the Treasurer of the Navy, he ridiculed as absurd. Both these balances were equally in the contemplation of the statute, which was palpably violated by drawing either from the Bank of England for any other purpose than immediate naval services. The assigned balances were estimated to amount, on an average, to 140,000l. a year, and surely it could not be seriously argued that the Paymaster of the Navy should have such sums placed at his disposal. But, in point of fact, Trotter was not confined to those sums, for his power to draw on the Bank was unlimited, and he had made ample use of it; insomuch, indeed, that although it was pretended the first cause of removing the public money from the Bank to Coutts's, was to give facility to the smaller payments at the Navy Pay Office, by a nearer connection between that Office and the place of lodging the public money; it now turned out that the money was seldom at Coutts's, and no small payments whatever were made by the Paymaster of the Navy. According to a comparison of the accounts at Coutts's and the Bank of England, it appeared that at the time there was a balance of no less than 490,000l. at the Bank, there was not a shilling at Coutts's; but on the contrary, that Trotter was actually overdrawn. Persons would be disposed to ask what was become of this immense balance? Why, it was employed in various speculations by Trotter. Thus, the sum of nearly half a million of the public money was placed beyond the controul of Lord Melville, in consequence of his own connivance; it was put to risk by Trotter, and liable to be lost: but not only that, a considerable loss must have actually accrued in consequence of a fall in the price of Navy Bills, which Trotter had purchased, had not the wealth acquired from other speculations, and the accommodation of Mark Sprott, enabled Trotter to meet the loss. In order to show that no small payments, such as a single shilling, and even pence, which were mentioned, had ever taken place by the Paymaster, the Honourable Gentleman mentioned, that out of 332 drafts drawn by Trotter on Coutts, only three were under 1000*l.*; and to prove that no inconvenience could arise from suffering the money to remain in the Bank, until actually wanted for naval service, he referred to the practice which prevailed under the Treasurerships of Mr. Bathurst and Mr. Tierney, and particularly the change which took place under the latter, in consequence of the recommendation of Trotter himself. The result of this investigation would be such, the Honourable Gentleman trusted, as to deter any public officers from ever presuming to meddle with the public money but for the fair objects prescribed by the law; and that as a child was cautioned to dread the fire, every public accomptant should approach the public money with awe— that recollecting the fate of Trotter, and reflecting on the situation to which Lord Melville was reduced by such misconduct, every agent of the public should feel it necessary to beware how he acted.

It must have been obvious to any man at all acquainted with the world, much less to a man possessing the accumen of Lord Melville, that Trotter's advances without interest, could not have proceeded from his own money honestly obtained, for he had no ostensible means of obtaining any such sums, no honest way of qualifying himself to afford such accommodation. Indeed, no pretence for ignorance on this subject could now be alledged; for, spite of the studied confusion of accounts, spite of all the artifices that were used to perplex the understanding of those disposed to inquire, the clue was found out, the labyrinth was unravelled. Although the Noble Defendant kept accounts with several bankers, besides two or three private merchants, and although Trotter kept an uncommon variety of accounts at one banker's, still the complication was not deemed sufficient for concealment; for as soon as it was understood that the business was to be inquired into, all vouchers and documents that could lead to discovery were destroyed, and that in consequence of a release signed by the Defendant and Trotter. In this release a clause was introduced referring to the mutual destruction of vouchers, which he was prepared to prove was entirely without example. Now there were some terms generally used in legal instruments, which were mere formalities and of no avail, such for instance, as "by force of arms," and so forth. But the clause he alluded to was not only unusual, but the object was evident. In order that their Lordships should be able to judge fairly of this release, he requested them to consider the circumstances under which it was executed, and particularly the time, which was a most critical juncture indeed. A commission had been appointed to investigate the affairs of the Navy, a precept had been served on the Navy Office by the said Commissioners, for the return of certain accounts, and at such a moment did Trotter send this celebrated releas. down to Scotland to be signed by Lord Melville, who was then about to come to town, and did actually arrive very soon afterwards. For what purpose, he would ask any man of common sense and candour, could such an instrument have been executed under such circumstances, but for some purpose of concealment? In this release Trotter, it appeared, acknowledged himself in debt to the Noble Defendant in the sum of 1480*l.*, but for this there was no voucher, or account, remaining in the hands of Lord Melville. He seemed to have altogether taken the word of Trotter upon the subject, upon whose honour he had so much reliance, that he thought it quite unnecessary to preserve any evidence by which to ascertain whether Trotter's acknowledgment formed the whole of the sum which he could justly claim. Upon the face of the transaction there did not appear to have been any thing like an investigation of accounts between two fair men bringing their honest dealings to a conclusion; nor did there appear to be any just object for the destruction of the accounts.

Here the Honourable Manager took a view of the several advances made by Trotter to the Defendant, which were of three descriptions: First, money lent for which no interest was paid; secondly, by loans upon which interest was charged; and thirdly, those upon which no interest was charged. Of those classes he took the second first; and called the attention of their Lordships to the sum alluded to in the 8th article of the Impeachment. This sum consisted of twenty-two thousand pounds advanced to the Defendant, and for which it was alledged by the said Defendant that he was to pay interest. It was stated by Trotter in evidence, that he had occasionally, "not frequently," made advances to the Defendant, which were not applied to naval purposes. To enable their Lordships to judge of the nature of these advances, and of their application, the Managers had collected a vast deal of evidence; and, as an apology for the trouble to which their Lordships would be subject, in consequence of the examination of so much evidence, he had to assure them, that no one would be called forth whose testimony did not appear to the Commons to form some link in the chain of circumstances by which they proposed to establish the charges they had felt it their duty to bring forward against the Noble Defendant. He had little doubts that, scattered as the evidence was, small as the links were, in some instances, that the whole were so connected and arranged, as fully to make out the accusations preferred by the Commons.

It would be shown, that, in one of the interviews which Trotter had with the Defendant, in the year 1789, a conversation took place about India Stock. Lord Melville, who was then one of the highest officers in the State, mentioned to Trotter that he thought the value of India Stock was very likely to rise, and that he would, therefore, be extremely happy to possess himself of some. "Why, my Lord, (said Trotter,) should you not do so? the money can be immediately had; there is a large balance of the public money always lying quite useless, which may as well be employed by your Lordship." But this proposition, which marked so much familiarity and friendship, was, according to the deposition of Trotter, indignantly rejected by the Defendant; who desired to hear no more of any such thing as the application of the public money to his private purposes. The suggestion, however, (said Mr. Whitbread,) although it palpably betrayed the disposition of Trotter, did not alarm, in any degree, the solicitude which the Defendant ought to have felt for the safety of the public money. He made no inquiry whatever; and Trotter, whose gratitude for the indulgence and liberality of his patron was very natural, could not endure the idea that his eager wish for the purchase of India Stock should be disappointed. Accordingly, Trotter took occasion to mention to the Defendant, (not, to be sure, until his indignation had subsided, although in the same conversation,) that he had a relative, from whom he knew he could borrow the sum his Lordship required. "Then (said his Lordship, without any further observation) let it be done." That the money was obtained, and laid out in the purchase of 13,500*l.* India Stock, we have ample evidence to present to your Lordships, in the person of Mr. Antrobus, by whom the stock was purchased, and in whose name it stood for some time; and also in Mr. F. Linde, in whose name it also stood for some time. But as to the manner in which the money was procured: Trotter applied to Mr. Montague Linde to lend such a sum to Lord Melville; Linde, however, replied, that he could not—having no money. But Trotter, it seems, told him, that his Lordship must be accommodated; and what did he do? why, he gave Linde so much as was required of the public money, to be lent to the Defendant. The loan was made without the Defendant having given any bill, bond, or security whatever, excepting the mortgage of the stock, as Trotter pretended, to the lender. The dividends upon this stock, which were received by Trotter, Linde, and Coutts, were carried to the credit of the Defendant, in a private account which Trotter had with him. Some time after the purchase, India Stock rose 10 per cent; and when the stock alluded to was finally sold, the produce of the sale far exceeded the amount of the purchase money. Indeed, upon the whole transaction, the Noble Defendant profited very considerably. The original purchase money was 23,000*l.*, upon which interest was charged; but this sum was soon reduced to 20,000*l.* in consequence of a payment of 3000*l.* made by Lord Melville to Trotter. Now, this payment being made to Trotter, who credited the Noble Lord for it in his private account, leaves no room to doubt, combined with other circumstances, that the Defendant knew Trotter was the real lender of this money; and also, that it must have been advanced from the public money, Trotter having no other means of procuring it. Here I shall leave this subject of India Stock, to return to it again at the conclusion of Lord Melville's account with the public, when the Noble Lord's knowledge of the source from which the purchase money came, is rendered still more glaring.

I now proceed to the consideration of about 20,000l. and other sums of the public money, of which the Defendant had the use, without any interest whatever. Trotter states the advance of 20,000l. to Tweedy and others; and we find that Lord Melville himself acknowledged to Trotter, on his first introduction to office, a debt of 10,000l. This debt formed the first item in the chest account, which was an account raised by Trotter, between Lord Melville and the public. There was a still further sum of 10,600l., which was not paid off by the Defendant so late as May, 1800. With regard to the 10,000l., the application of which Lord Melville refused to reveal, we have found out the secret. Notwithstanding the destruction of the vouchers, we have unravelled the mystery. This sum was, it appears, applied in a way somewhat similar to the 40,000l. lent to Boyd, and I have got a complete receipt for the money. It was not lent for any public purpose. Such an assertion cannot now be hazarded. So much for the "public duty," as well as "private honour and personal convenience" of Lord Melville, who would not only have violated his duty, by appropriating the money voted for naval services to any other public purpose whatever, but who now appears, from incontestable evidence, to have applied that money to his own private use, or to the accommodation of personal or political friends, and, therefore, to have lost the excuse which his first letter to the Naval Commissioners intimated, and which his friends have been, heretofore, so forward to press.

There is a sum which will be fully explained to you in evidence, and to which I beg your Lordships' particular attention, because it serves, even taken alone, completely to establish the main charge which the Commons have preferred against the Noble Defendant. Your Lordships will immediately perceive, it would be preposterous to pretend that Lord Melville did not know this sum to have been public money. Indeed, from the nature of the case, it would be quite impossible that he should not know it. The case is this: in 1797, when what was called the Loyalty Loan was collecting, it was deemed right that men holding high offices in the State should subscribe to it, and the Defendant signed for 10,000l., which was paid out of the public money; for Trotter was the guarantee to Coutts, by whom the instalments on this Loan were advanced. Trotter debited Lord Melville for the whole amount, in his private account current. But, after some time, a circumstance took place, which renders, as clear as the noon day, Lord Melville's knowledge of the nature of this money. Trotter being unwilling to continue his responsibility for the 10,000l. thought proper to transfer it from his account current to the chest account, thus at once making Lord Melville debtor to the public for that sum. Of this transfer Lord Melville was apprised in the account presented by Trotter, and he showed no sign of disapprobation whatever. Surely, then, from that moment at least, no man can venture to maintain that the Noble Defendant did not make use of the public money for his own private purpose; that he did not derive profit from it; in a word, that he did not appropriate it in a manner decidedly contrary to the Act of Parliament. This Loyalty Loan continued in Lord Melville's possession for some years, and, when the stock was sold, the proceeds were applied to his benefit.

When your Lordships take these several advances into your consideration, you cannot, I am persuaded, fail to be of opinion, that the Noble Defendant was well aware of the source whence the sums were derived with which he was "occasionally" accommodated by Trotter. But no doubt can exist upon the subject, when the circumstances in which Trotter was placed are taken into view. When Trotter was first in the Navy Pay Office, his salary was but 50l. a year; upon that salary he remained in the office for some time, and left it to become a Navy Agent. This specnlation, however, not succeeding, he returned to the Navy Pay Office, upon a salary of somewhat less than 100l. a year, and that was the amount of his property, exceptiug a legacy of from 1000l. to 2000l. when Lord Melville appointed him his Paymaster, in 1806. Yet soon after this appointment, not more than four months, the Noble Defendant borrowed from this man no less a sum than 4000l. upon his bond, which was not to bear any interest. Now I would ask, whether any man can be so ignorant of the common affairs of life, as to suppose that Lord Melville did not know whence this money came? What, that an agent having only 50l. a year, and but four months in office, could have been competent to lend his principal 4000l. without interest? Trotter would no doubt have done any thing in his power for Lord Melville. He professed to feel for his patron all the gratitude which was due to the Noble Lord. He would, no doubt, have returned favour for favour, and still more, as he was most probably influenced by expectation as well as gratitude; but, at the time I am speaking of, it was not in the power of Trotter to furnish the sum alluded to from any other than the public funds, and the Noble Defendent must have been well satisfied of that. Indeed it appears pretty evident in most cases, that there was a very clear understanding between the Noble Lord and his Agent; they seemed to co-operate very well. In 1792, it appeared, that at a time when Trotter had not much above 200l. at his banker's, 8000l. India Stock were purchased for the joint benefit of Lord Melville and his agent—one half for each. Now, what does this imply? Is it necessary for me to comment upon it? Is it possible that the Noble Lord could have been unaware of the situation and proceedings of Trotter? We have not seen the bond of 1786. It has been cancelled; whether in consequence of a *bona fide* payment we cannot say. The destruction of the books and vouchers has wrapped up these things in the veil of darkness. But the veil has been a little removed by the evidence of Trotter, who admits that no interest was paid for the bond; and when asked the reason, his answer was, that he thought it a proper compliment to the Treasurer of the Navy. Can any man mistake the motive of such a compliment; or can any man believe that Lord Melville could suppose, in the circumstances of Trotter, he was capable of paying it, unless he were practising fraud somewhere? If any agent were to come to any of your Lordships, and tender you the use of 4000l., for instance, which was the first sum lent by Trotter to the Noble Defendant, and that you knew from that agent's salary he was not likely to obtain such a sum by honest means, or that he had not any ostensible way of getting possession of it—you would naturally make some inquiries of him, particularly when he offered the money without interest. As to the latter condition, indeed, I rather think your sense of honour would reject it, whatever Trotter's circumstances might be. But certainly that man could not be alive to a just solicitude for character, who would in such a case accept the loan of money without any inquiry. But what are we to think of the man who accepted, in a similar way, the loan of 10,000l., 20,000l., 23,000l., &c., and what further sums we cannot ascertain, for the records are destroyed? With respect to what we have been told of "large sums" paid by the Noble Defendant to Trotter from private funds, and independently of his salary, as Treasurer of the Navy, upon searching, we do not find whence those large sums could have come. Lord Melville was at the same time Treasurer of the Navy, President of the Board of Controul, Secretary of State, Keeper of the Signet, and Keeper of the Privy Seal in Scotland. But Trotter was his agent only in the Naval Department. The Noble Defendant had other agents: he had a Mr. Le Blanc, a Mr. Wardner, and a Robert Dundas, who was his Receiver in Scotland for the Keepership of the Signet, and also for his private property. We do not find that Trotter received large sums from any of these sources. But great light is thrown upon the conduct of the Noble Defendant by the transactions which took place at the close of his connection with the Naval Department. In consequence of some political arrangements in 1800, the Noble Lord gave up the Navy Office, and Lord Harrowby was appointed in his room. It became a matter of moment, however, that Trotter should retain his situation, for at that time there was a considerable deficiency to be made up, which it was not convenient at once to provide, and therefore to manage and conceal were both material The deficiency was not less than about 220,000l., and how it arose may be easily conceived, when we reflect upon the speculation of Trotter, upon the sums transmitted to the Scotch bankers, Messrs. Forbes and Co. Messrs. Mansfield and Co. and the other more considerable advances, for the use of Lord Melville. It has been stated, that the public accounts were regularly kept, and the balances tolerably even, notwithstanding the proceedings of which the Commons now complain to your Lordships; but those who are inclined to think so, I would only refer to the comparisons between the Bank books and those of the Navy Pay Office. They will then see that a considerable difference always existed between the Bank and the official balances. The deficiency at the time of Lord Melville's retirement from the Navy Office I have stated to be 220,000l., and of this the Noble Defendant was indebted in the sum of 71,000l., the remainder being the debt of Trotter. How the Noble Defendant made up his part will be shown to your Lordships. It will be seen, that the principal means arose from the different descriptions of stock which were before purchased with the public money, and all of which were sold, with the exception of his favourite India Stock, which was only pledged. Now, the manner in which the India Stock was disposed of upon this occasion, clearly manifests that Lord Melville must have known the money was lent originally by Trotter, and no other person; for, if this India Stock had been mortgaged to the friend originally held forth as the lender, how could it have been again mortgaged to the person who accommodated the Noble Defendant in the instance of which I am now speaking? However, with the aid of this mortgage of the Loyalty Loan, of 7000l. 3 per cent stock, and other securities, seconded by a collateral security from one whom it is impossible to mention but with respect, and of whom it is equally impossible to think without a lively feeling for the situation in which he is at present placed—I mean Mr. R. S. Dundas: through these combined securities, the wary Mark Sprott was induce to advance 51,000l. for the use of the Noble Defendant. But this supply was insufficient, and therefore another loan was obtained from Coutts and Co. upon the credit of Lord Melville, and was set down to his private account. Here then let me observe, that if Lord Melville were not a debtor to the public in consequence of the use which he made of the public money, how came he to make up a deficiency from his private funds? But, after all the supplies I have described, still something remained to be done to enable the Noble Defendant to liquidate the claim upon him, and the balance of the 71,000l. was got at by an expedient that will rather surprise your Lordships. The Noble Lord having exhausted all other resources, resorted for the loan of between 5 and 6000l. to a good-natured friend of his, who was Treasurer of the Navy in 1783, and from him borrowed the sum; that is, he added to the balance of his first Treasurership to make up the deficiency upon his second. Can it be necessary for me to animadvert upon such conduct? Can such a farce and mockery be reconciled to any notion existing, of equity or law? It is in the very teeth of both. How contrary is it to the course prescribed by common sense, enforced by public caution, and sanctioned by the example of the great Chatham?—that no public officer should take balances due to the public from the Bank of England, and apply them to his own private purpose. No man, disposed to act fairly and justly towards the country, would do otherwise.

I now come to that point where I feel myself justified in stating, that if the facts I have recited be made out in the evidence I have to adduce, there cannot be a shadow of doubt of the guilt of the Noble Defendant. That Treasurer must be criminal, who permitted his agent to apply the public money for any other purpose than that to which it was assigned by Parliament, and that the Noble Defendant knew of such application, is proved by the loans which he himself had from Trotter; for surely any man must be infatuated, who could suppose that Trotter could make these loans from any other source—unless he were to be a conjurer, or that he had found the philosopher's stone. Where else than in the public treasury could Trotter be conceived by Lord Melville to have made out the 4500l. but a few months after he became Paymaster, and also the advance made for the purchase of India Stock? But Lord Melville did well know these things, and the transactions of Trotter were also known to Coutts, and to Wilson, and to many others; but no one of these could well venture to stand forward as an accuser. Indeed it would have been hazardous in any private individual or individuals to have incurred the ire of persons so powerful as the Noble Defendant, or any one under his patronage, then was. But, strange to tell, that notwithstanding the notoriety of these criminal proceedings, and the ample evidence that has already appeared to prove them, the endeavour of the Commons to obtain justice for the public is charged with cruelty. Compassion, or some much less laudable motive, interesting itself in favour of the Noble Defendant, is forward to set down the pursuit of this business to the score of persecution. But I would ask, how can such a charge apply? What is persecution? An odious compound of malevolence and power. Now, as to the first ingredient of this compound, I feel confident that I can acquit my colleagues of any motive so foul—as to myself, I spurn the base imputation; and as to power, can it be pretended that we have attacked the weak and the powerless? Was there any thing in the situation of the Defendant, that could have enabled us to practise cruelty towards him, or that could have encouraged the hope of success in persecution, were we even so disposed? No; on the contrary, at a time when the sense of public duty, not any feeling of private pique—when an aversion to guilt, not any undue prejudice against the guilty, prompted us to commence our proceedings against the Defendant, he was surrounded by power; he held one of the highest offices in the state; he was, without meaning any imputation upon the dead, supported warmly by the Minister of the day. He had a friend in one of the ablest men this country has ever seen—in the most powerful Minister we have had since the Revolution. He had friends in every department of the state; and against such a man it would be preposterous to suppose that the machinations of prejudice or party could prevail. No; it was the call of justice, seconded by the voice of the country, that succeeded against him. What, indeed, less than that, could bear down the man who had such domineering influence?. who had the disposal of almost every office of power and trust in the state vessel, from the deck to the top-gallant-mast head; without whose approbation not an exciseman or a viceroy was appointed? Against such a man, what had the spirit of inquiry and public justice to encounter, and what a degree of courage and perseverance was requisite in the man who should commence the arduous struggle. Happily for the country, that man was found—the patron of Nelson, he who is now conducting our fleets in triumph, undertook the salutary work—Lord St. Vincent, as soon as he was appointed to a high office, determined to become a reformer in power, and he presented the singular instance of a man in office carrying into effect those plans of retrenchment and reform, the necessity for which he saw in other circumstances. That Noble Lord scorned the spurious addition which power might derive from influence obtained by means of abuse and corruption, and to his immortal honour he suggested the project for cutting off such excrescences. With that Noble Lord, then, rests the merit of the investigation, which has produced such important discoveries. We have only followed the course into which he led us.

We have been asked, whether the Noble Defendant had applied the public money to his own use, and derived profits from it, how comes it that he is not rich? But let it be remembered, that the acquisition of money does not always lead to riches; men desire money from various motives, and perhaps, but comparatively few, to keep it. The love of money, for the sake of money, is by no means the least excusable species of avarice. If a man desire money for the purpose of doing good, his desire is laudable; if it be looked after for the purpose of being disposed of in the festive board, one would not be so forward to condemn him; but, if it be sought for merely with a view to employ it as an instrument of power, as the means of advancing that power by corruption—for the purpose, as it has been suggested, of extending political influence in Scotland, and overwhelming the independent part of that country, then is the avarice of the party actuated by such views, not only highly criminal, but infinitely more mischievous to society, than if he had the miser's sordid feeling, or the spendthrift's prodigal practice.

There are many things, my Lords, of which some people can scarcely be persuaded to suppose a man of high rank, and generally distinguished qualities, guilty, even though the evidence of his guilt were to stare them in the face. I know there are persons who, notwithstanding the force of the evidence which has been heretofore adduced upon this subject, are still disposed to think, that a man like Lord Melville could not have been capable of such offences as are charged against him in the articles which we have submitted to your Lordships. But let such persons look at history, and there they will find, that men equally distinguished for social qualities, and still more distinguished for public talents, have been convicted of similar offences. Let them examine your Lordships' journals, and there it will be seen, that a man who was eminent among men, was not only charged, but confessed himself at this bar, that he was guilty of peculation. The great Lord Bacon, who, in point of ability, was an honour to this country and to human nature—he whose powers of mind were of so high an order as to be acknowledged almost supernatural, was yet stained with this odious vice. Why then should it be deemed so improbable that Lord Melville is guilty of such offences? That he is guilty, we on the part of the Commons allege, and are ready to prove.

SECOND DAY—April 30.

Mr. Giles proposed the reading, as evidence, the 20th of his present Majesty, appointing Commissioners to examine the Public Accounts, and also the Third and Eighth Reports of the said Commissioners, which had been presented to the House of Commons, together with Resolutions of the House thereupon. Here some discussion arose. The Counsel for the Defendant objected to the reading of the printed Journals of the House of Commons, as but secondary evidence; and contended that the original Journals ought to be produced. The Managers argued, that the printed Journals of Parliament had been received as competent evidence in the case of Lord George Gordon, and that this was the first time an objection of this nature had ever been taken in any Court. After some remarks by Lords Ellenborough and Eldon, the Lord Chancellor directed that the Journals should be entered as read, and that persons should be afterwards examined as to their comparison with the original Journals.

Mr. Whitham, Clerk of the House of Commons, was examined, as to the original Reports of the Commissioners for examining the Public Accounts; which Reports he produced.

The entering of the warrant, granting an additional salary of 2150l. to Mr. Barré, as Treasurer of the Navy, was proved by Mr. Mitford, a Clerk belonging to the Treasury. A great deal of discussion arose upon this subject, in consequence of the original warrant being lost. This warrant the Managers deemed it material to have entered in evidence, because it contained the conditions upon which the increase of salary was granted, namely, "in lieu of all fees and profits whatsoever, derived by former Treasurers of the Navy;" which condition was entered into previous to Lord Melville's Act. The Counsel for Lord Melville argued, that no condition entered into with Mr. Barré could possibly affect Lord Melville; still they opposed the admission of the warrant in evidence. However, upon a Mr. Standert, Chief Clerk in the office of the Comptroller of the Navy, proving the entry of the warrant, and his attesting the comparison of the copy with the original, the copy was entered as read.

The warrants of Lord Melville's first and second appointments to the Treasurership of the Navy, and also Lord Bayning's, were proved.

THIRD DAY—May 1.

Mr. Dyson, Solicitor of the Admiralty in 1782, swore to his attestation of the power of attorney, by which Mr. Douglas was appointed Paymaster; and evidence was given of certain acts done by Mr. Douglas, as Paymaster.

Mr. G. Fennel and Mr. Standert were examined as to the nature and business of the Navy Pay Office, in which they stated that no small payments were made by the Paymaster, nor any other payments, excepting those which he made to the several sub-accountants. A book, containing some certificates upon this subject, signed by A. Douglas, as Paymaster, was tendered as evidence, but objected to by the Defendant's Counsel. The objection, however, was overruled, and the certificates entered as read.

The bank book of Mr. Douglas, which was found among his papers, was produced, and Mr. Gimingham, one of the Clerks appointed to attend the Exchequer, on account of the Bank of England, proved several entries. He proved the payment, to Mr. Douglas, of a note of 1000l., No. 12, dated the 24th of October, on the 6th of November, 1782; and also of a note of 1000l., No. 212, dated the 7th of November, on the 22d of the same month; the former note being part of 5000l., and the latter of 3000l., advanced for Navy Services. These two notes were produced, and identified by the witness, who stated, also, that the two notices referring to them in the bank book were in his own handwriting. He was cross-examined as to one of the entries being in the name of Mr. Dundas, although witness stated, that Mr. Dundas never came to the Exchequer. But witness added, that whenever the advance at the Exchequer was not set down to the credit of the Treasurer, Mr. Dundas's name was entered; but when payment was made in bank notes, the name of the person receiving such notes was entered; it was, however, sometimes in one way, and sometimes in the other.

Mr. Heald, a Clerk from the bank of Messrs. Drummond, deposed, that on the 29th of November, 1782, he received, for the private credit of Mr. Dundas, the note No. 212, dated November 7. The entry of this note, which was shown to witness, appeared in the bank waste book, and in his own hand-writing. From this entry it appeared, but he could not swear positively, that he received the note from Mr. Dundas himself. This belief he was induced to form, because, when he received a note from one person to set down to the credit of another, his custom was to mark the entry with the letter "P," which letter did not appear to this entry.

From a comparison of the book at the Navy Office, produced by Mr. Fennel, with the Treasurer's account at the Bank, it appeared that the 5000l. above alluded to was part of 45,000l., and the 3000l. part of 50,000l., advanced at the Exchequer, by Mr. Gimingham to Mr. Douglas, for naval services.

Mr. Buckley, from Drummond's bank, deposed to the entry of this note in the ledger, and it appeared in their book as if paid to Mr. D. himself.

Mr. Rippen, one of the Cashiers from the Bank of England, deposed, that it never happened that more than one note, bearing this same letter, date, and number, was issued the same day.

FOURTH DAY—May 2.

Mr. Oliver (from Drummond's) was examined, and from his evidence it appeared, that Lord Melville, as well as the other customers of that house, kept a banking-book, a transcript of which was inserted in the ledger of 1782. In this transcript, the receipt of the note of 1000l., &c. on the 29th November, was entered. Several other entries are also mentioned, namely, the receipt of A. Douglas for 1000l., August 10, 1782; of 1000l., December 19; and 1000l., March 21, 1783, &c., for account of Mr. Dundas.

Mr. Whitbread proved the declaration made by the Defendant in the House of Commons, respecting the 10,000l. of the public money, which he alleged to have applied to public purposes, but which purposes he refused to reveal.

Mr. Serjeant Praed, one of the Commissioners of Naval Inquiry, produced the depositions of the Defendant before that Commission. They were signed by the Defendant. Upon cross-examination, the witness stated, that the Noble Defendant answered instantly any questions proposed to him. He had, however, sometimes altered the shape of expression, but nothing, in the opinion of the witness, material. After the first day, no wish for alteration was expressed. The questions put to Lord Melville were previously framed and prepared by the Commissioners—not every one, however. Lord Melville required no time to consider about the questions put to him. If he had, it would have been granted. A similar indulgence had been allowed to Mr. Antrobus and Mr. Trotter. There was an interval of three or four days between the first and second attendance of the Defendant, and during that interval he had made no application to see his first depositions. If the Noble Lord had, he had no doubt that the Commissioners would have complied with his request. From the Commissioners the Noble Lord had not, before examination, any intimation either of the specific questions to be put, or the general scope and purpose of the examination.

The depositions of Lord Melville were read, including his letters to the Commissioners, dated in June, 1804, and March, 1805.

Mr. Callander, formerly Clerk to Mure and Atkinson, and Mr. Edgar, from the house of Smith, Payne and Smith, were adduced to prove the payment of several drafts drawn by Mure and Atkinson, or their duly authorized Clerk, Mr. Dixon, on the house of Smith and Co., in favour of the Defendant. These drafts were dated on the 24th of June, 1783, the 2d, 11th, and 31st of July following; and sums of equal amount were proved to have been paid into the Bank of England on the same days to the account of the Treasurer of the Navy. From the books in which these several sums were entered, in the official book at the Navy Pay Office, it was shown by the evidence of G. Fennel, that the money could not have come from a public source.

These Clerks were severally asked by the Defendant's Counsel, whether they had any other recollection of the transactions to which their evidence applied than that which they derived from the books before them?—To which, in general, they answered in the negative.

FIFTH DAY—May 3.

The examination upon the subject of the Defendant's dealings with Mure and Atkinson was renewed this morning, and Mr. Edgar underwent a long examination.

Mr. Fennel's production of the certificate books of the Navy Office, was opposed by Counsel, as they stated, against the wish of Lord Melville, they conceiving such evidence legally inadmissible, as the hand-writing was not proved.

Mr. Serjeant Best, Mr. Giles, and the Solicitor General, contended on the contrary, that the book was similarly situated to the books of account in a Merchant's counting-house, which, though the hand-writing was not proved, might be, notwithstanding, good evidence. The nature of the book was then explained by the Witness as being that from which the Paymaster stated the balances officially. Mr. Plumer declined to support his objection, and the Witness proceeded to read several entries of balances during Lord Melville's first treasurership. In this book, from the month of July, 1783, there were two entries of 10,000l. each, "to carry on payments and recalls."

Mr. G. Swaffield, who had been sixty years in the Navy Pay Office, never met any inconvenience in his business, or committed any mistake in his accounts, until the public money was removed to Coutts's bank, where he was, at the request of Trotter, urged to keep his balances.

Mr. Oliver, from Drummond's bank, deposed, that on the 25th of May, 1805, two notes for 1000l. each were paid into that bank by Mr. Douglas, for account of Mr. Dundas.

Mr. J. Davies, who was Assistant to the Cashier of the Navy in 1785, deposed, that in the month of October, in that year, he made a draft for 1000l. payable to the Defendant, which draft was for his salary as Treasurer of the Navy, for the preceding quarter; this draft was given to Mr. Douglas.

Mr. A. Douglas deposed to his father's death, in December 1785,

Mr. Standart was again examined, and proved the transfer of several sums in 1784 and 1785, from the new to the old treasurership of the Defendant. Of any transfers irregularly made, Witness knew nothing. To a question, "Whether he was understood to be speaking of transfers of the Bank account of the Treasurer at the Bank to the Bank account of the Ex-Treasurer; or the total account of one Treasurer to the total account of the other?"—his answer was, that he knew of no transaction at the Bank.

SIXTH DAY—May 5.

Mr. G. Fennel underwent another examination, as to official balances.

Mr. Oliver proved the receipt of several sums at Drummond's bank, on account of Lord Melville, in the years 1803, 1804, and 1805. Those sums were principally received from Douglas, Newbigging, and Davidson.

Mr A. Douglas proved the payment of 4475l. 4s. 9d. to Lord Melville, being the balance of exchequer fees due by his deceased father.

Mr. Whitbread again gave evidence as to the speech of Lord Melville.

The letters of attorney from the Defendant appointing Alexander Trotter his Paymaster, and authorizing him to draw on the Bank, &c., were read in evidence. These letters were dated in June and July, 1784. The release signed by the Defendant and Trotter in Feb. 1803, was also put in as evidence.

The Counsel for the Defendant, upon the application of the Managers, admitted the serving the notice upon the Defendant for the production of all papers relative to his connection with Trotter, either as private agent or public officer.

Alexander Trotter was then called and sworn.

Witness began by deposing to his first introduction to the Navy Pay Office in 1774, upon a salary of 50l. a year, and he stated these particulars, alluded to by Mr. Whitbread in his opening, as to the advance of his, (Witness's,) salary, (he did not think it was doubled,) and appointment to the office of Paymaster. He was absent from the Navy Pay Office about a twelvemonth, and on his return to it was appointed Paymaster under the Defendant, upon the recommendation, as he believed, of Mr. Coutts, who had applied to Mr. Pitt, and Mr. Pitt, he believed, had made interest with Lord Melville. His first salary, as Paymaster, was 500l. a year, with some deductions of taxes. Upon his introduction to office, the Bank book was delivered to him, and he was told, that the public balance was in the Bank, excepting the sums that were in the hands of the sub-accountants, and a sum which the Defendant mentioned to him. That sum Witness mentioned on a former occasion to be, according to his recollection, 10,000l.; but he was induced, from many things he had since seen, to believe it was 10,600l.; 1,600l. a balance due from the Defendant's first treasurership, and 9000l. a balance due upon the second treasurership. The Defendant told Witness, that he would account for this sum of 10,600l., but did not tell him in whose hands it was. Exchequer fees are entirely at the disposition of the Paymaster, having the sole management of this business. He applies to the Treasury for 3000l. at a time, as he finds his funds are nearly exhausted, or reduced, under the sum of 3000l. Did not recollect any instance of the Treasurer having drawn a draft during the time that he acted as Paymaster. When he entered into office, the balance of Exchequer fees was in the hands of the executor of Mr. Douglas; and the public balance, exclusive of the 10,600l., and the money in the hands of the sub-accountants, were at the Bank. From thence he soon obtained liberty from the Defendant "to draw part of those public balances, and to place them in the hands of Coutts and Co., for official convenience." Whether he meant to pay the public money to the sub-accountants or not, he always drew on the Bank, according to the terms of the Act: He had the public money in other hands besides those of Coutts, viz. Mr. Sprott, Mr. Jellicoe, Mr. Montague Lind, and some bankers at Edinburgh. To Mr. Lind "he did not recolllect having lent any money, but he used him in negociating business." Witness was in the habit of laying out the public money in purchasing Government securities, such as Navy, Victualling, Transport, and Exchequer Bills. He also applied it to discount the bills of private individuals, not by himself, but through "Mr. Lind and others whom he had employed." When absent from the Navy Pay Office, he confided the management of the business to Mr. T. Wilson. "As he did not wish to propose to Lord Melville to authorize any other person than himself to draw from the Bank, he found it necessary, in case of illness or occasional absence from the office, when sudden demands were made upon the Accountants for payment of money, to leave in Mr. Wilson's hands drafts, signed by himself." These drafts were blanks with regard to the sum. They were only on the Bank. But Wilson had also authority, "unlimited," to draw on Coutts, and had "verbal instructions" to employ the public money, during such occasional absence, for his (Witness's) advantage. To a question, "Whether Witness actually made profit of the public money, &c?" the answer was, "I did. I never meant to conceal it." He was introduced, for the first time, to Lord Melville in 1782. After he became Paymaster, he received Lord Melville's salary as Treasurer of the Navy; but did not receive any other regular salary of the Noble Lord, as President of the Board of Controul, as Keeper of the Privy Seal, or Keeper of the Signet of Scotland: nor did he receive any income from his Lordship's private estates in Scotland or in England. He received dividends from public stock belonging to Lord Melville, and kept an account of debtor and creditor. This account he cannot now produce. He had no account in his possession which he can command, excepting one which was in the possession of the Managers of the Impeachment. A copy of the account between him and the Defendant was frequently furnished to the Defendant. There were duplicates made, which were signed by both. He carried all sums received on account of the Defendant to the credit of this account; no interest was charged on either side of the said account. The advances he made to Lord Melville were placed to the debit of this account.

Upon particular advances the following answers were given by Mr. Trotter:—

In 1786, or thereabouts, as nearly as I recollect, I did advance specific sums to Lord Melville, and placed them to the debit of that account.—His Lordship granted me a bond and security for 4000l., which I advanced him in or about that year.—I was enabled to advance that sum of money to his Lordship from the fund which I have already explained, having had the controul of that which was put into my hands for the purpose of paying exchequer fees; and as I had money upon two different treasurerships, which would not probably be called for, but had always been allowed to remain in the Paymaster's hands for the trouble of making up the Ex-Treasurer's accounts, I knew that money would not be called for till I should leave the office, or the accounts should be audited; and from that account I advanced his Lordship 4000l.—I charged no interest to his Lordship for that sum.—The bond did not bear upon the face of it that no interest was to be paid, but no interest was expressed to be paid.—Interest was not expressed to be paid upon the face of the bond.—I did not feel myself entitled to charge his Lordship interest for money which had been put into my hands under the situation which I have described.—I did not describe to Lord Melville the reason why I did not charge interest, nor did I press it upon his Lordship's attention so much as to know whether he ever knew that it did bear interest or not.—I believe this 4000l. to have been the first article in that account; but I can only speak from recollection; and it being at a very distant period, I beg to say, it is only from recollection that I do state it. To the best of my recollection and belief it was the first item in the account.—It was entitled an account current.—As I was in the habit of receiving all his dividends, and his salary as Treasurer of the Navy, of course I debited his Lordship with payments that I made of those sums—I also credited Lord Melville for all these dividends as received upon those sums.

Did you direct a purchase to be made on account of Lord Melville of 2000l. India Stock, in or about the year 1792?—My attention has been called to that circumstance from seeing the entry in the Tenth Report, and I have no reason to doubt that I did. I really have no doubt that I did give such directions, although I have no actual remembrance of it. I can venture to say, that I did give such directions.—I have already said, that I had drawn money from the Bank and put it into the hands of Coutts and Co.; these sums having created credit to me at Coutts's house, I then drew upon Coutts for money to pay for that stock.—I believe that 2000l. stock was bought on the account of, and for the benefit of Lord Melville.—I have no doubt that the dividends of that stock were carried to the credit of his account current.—I am obliged to speak under that reserve, from having no documents of my own to refer to; but, from looking at the account at Coutts's house, I am satisfied, that the dividends of that stock were carried to the credit of Lord Melville's account.—I did not direct to be purchased a certain quantity of stock, commonly called the Loyalty Loan, in or about the year 1797, to the best of my recollection.—There was no such stock subscribed for by me, or purchased by me; I believe the payments were made by Mr. Coutts's house, as far as I can understand and recollect; and they were afterwards repaid by me to Coutts's house.—It was repaid by me to Mr. Coutts for Lord Melville.—The dividends upon that Loyalty Loan were carried to the credit of Lord Melville in the account current.

What was the quantity of that stock so purchased for Lord Melville?—I understood that it was 10,000l.

Did you purchase, or direct to be purchased, a certain sum of 7000l. three per cent. reduced annuities, for or on account of Lord Melville?—I directed stock to that amount to be purchased, I believe.—The dividends of that stock were carried to the credit of Lord Melville in the account current.

Did you direct payments to be made to private individuals on account of Lord Melville?—I have frequently.

Did you direct a certain sum of money to be paid on account of Lord Melville, to the account of Sir William Forbes and Co., in Edinburgh?—I believe I did.

Have you any doubt of that fact?—I have none, but have no recollection of it.

To what amount?—2000l.—That sum was carried to the debit of Lord Melville's account with me.—No interest was charged upon that 2000l.

Do you recollect, from having looked at that document in your own handwriting, and made at the time, any advance directed by you to be made to the account of Lord Melville to the house of Mansfield, Ramsay, and Co., in Edinburgh?—The same letter specifies the sum of 3374l. to have been paid by my direction to Messrs. Mansfield, Ramsay, and Co., on Lord Melville's account.

Was any security given to you for either of these sums from Lord Melville?—None that I recollect.

What was the amount of that sum so paid by you to Mansfield, Ramsay, and Co.?—3374l.

Was any interest charged upon that sum between Lord Melville and you?—I believe none to have been charged.—On the balance of the account current Lord Melville was generally indebted to me.

When was the account current brought to a settlement?—I think upon the 31st of May, 1800.

Was a transcript of that account, or the account itself, presented to Lord Melville at that time?—I made out a general statement of his Lordship's business, as far as I was connected with him, and that account was particularly specified, as well as others.

At that time in whose favour was the balance?—The balance was in my favour.

Have you any recollection of the sum of 3000l. advanced about the 17th of the same month, to Mansfield, Ramsay, and Co., on account of Lord Melville?—I have no recollection of that circumstance.

Then a paper was shown to the Witness, and he was asked:

Is that your hand-writing at the bottom of that paper?—It is.

Read that, and see whether you refresh your memory by it; it is a memorandum dated the 5th of January, 1790, the transaction took place in 1789; can you now state whether you did advance, on account of Lord Melville, to Sir William Forbes and Co. 1000l. in the month of July, 1789?—I have no recollection of that particular transaction.

Whether there was any account besides the account current kept between you and Lord Melville?—There was.

What was the title of that account?—It was entitled "Chest Account."

Do you recollect whether the sum of 10,600l., which it was stated by Lord

Melville that he would account for when you first became Paymaster of the Navy, was carried into that account?—I do recollect that it was stated in that account.

Was the Loyalty Loan, to the amount of 10,000l., which you stated to be advanced to Lord Melville for the purchase of that stock, and carried to the account current, ever transferred to this chest account?—It was.—I considered Lord Melville to be indebted to Government for the sums I advanced upon the chest account.

What was your reason for transferring the Loyalty Loan money from the account current to the chest account?—It was from an anxiety, an attention to my own interest. Lord Melville was indebted to me as a private individual only upon the account current, and I considered him indebted, as I said before, to Government, for the balance upon the chest account.

Did you charge any interest to Lord Melville upon the chest account, when the balance appeared to be against Lord Melville?—I did not.

On which side did the balance on the chest account usually stand?—Lord Melville generally stood debtor upon that account.

When did this chest account terminate?—At the general settlement which took place when his Lordship left the office.

Did you present to Lord Melville a general statement of this chest account, as well as the account current?—I did.

Did Lord Melville sign that account, or acknowledge it?—I believe he did.

Did Lord Melville at that time discharge these two accounts?—He did, to the best of my recollection.

Do you recollect what the amount due to you upon those two accounts was?—I should think nearly about 50,000l.

Did you state, that, in consequence of Lord Melville's intended quitting the Navy Pay Office, there would be a necessity for his providing a sum of money?—I did.

For what purpose was it necessary to provide that sum of money?—To make a repayment of the money which his Lordship had from the public balances.

Where did you pay those balances as soon as you received them?—They must have centred ultimately in the Bank; because I had a larger sum at that time from the Bank upon my own account.

Were your differences as Paymaster at the Bank made good in part by these payments so received of Lord Melville?—As money cannot be identified, I cannot answer that literally; because it may first have gone into Coutts's house, and I may have drawn a larger sum from Coutts's house, which may have made up my balances.

Was your difference, your debt to the public, swelled by the debt owed to you on the account current of Lord Melville?—If I understand the question, certainly not necessarily.

Was it, in fact, so increased on account of the debt Lord Melville owed to you?—I do not know whether it was.

If you had not had any balance due to you from Lord Melville on the account current, on the 31st May, 1800, would you have had so great a difference at the Bank as then existed?—I may have chosen to take the balance which Lord Melville owed to me into another channel, in which case it would have made no difference in the cash in the Bank; and as the fact did not exist, I cannot say what I would have done in such cases.

If Lord Melville had not paid to you the sum due upon the private account, to enable you to pay that sum into the Bank, must you not have been under the necessity of providing that sum of money elsewhere?—Certainly.

Did Lord Melville understand then, that the discharge of these two accounts were to enable you to make good your differences at the Bank?—Certainly not; Lord Melville understood that so much of it was due upon the chest account; I believe he understood that was to make good his Lordship's difference at the Bank, and the other was to be in repayment of a sum of money which he owed me upon my account current.

Whether you gave directions in or about the year 1789, or 1790, for the purchase of another sum of East India Stock for the benefit of Lord Melville?—I gave directions in the year 1789, to purchase a sum of East India Stock for the benefit of Lord Melville.

Are you enabled from your memory to state what passed between Lord Melville and yourself upon that subject?—I will state the transaction as far as my memory will carry me; which was in consequence of a conversation I had with his Lordship, in which he stated his opinion, that the value of East India Stock, from the probable rise that would take place ultimately in that Stock; and I observed to his Lordship, that if he was impressed with so good an opinion of that Stock, that I thought, in consideration of his own interest, he ought to invest a sum of money in that Stock: his Lordship's observation seemed to throw it aside, by saying that he had no money to invest in stock. I had mentioned to his Lordship that there were considerable balances lying at all times in my hands that were not called for, and, in all probability, would not be called for, from circumstances that I need not perhaps relate at this time; but it was money lying unclaimed in my hands, which it would not be necessary to advance to the public until they were claimed, and there was no prospect of that claim taking place soon; and I advised his Lordship to give me leave to lay out so much of that money as would buy about 13,000l. or 14,000l. East India Stock, but which his Lordship refused in the most pointed and decided manner, insomuch, that I was afraid I had incurred his Lordship's displeasure by proposing it. But it occurred to me at the same moment that it would be possible to borrow a sum of money upon the security of that stock, and I proposed to his Lordship that I should endeavour to do so, and that I should lay out that money in the purchase of East India Stock; to which his Lordship readily assented. I mentioned, that I then lived with a relation of my own, who was a man of considerable importance in the City, and that he would be enabled to raise this sum of money for me. In short, I made it an easy matter to his Lordship. But when I applied to Mr. Lind, the gentleman to whom I alluded, I found that I was deceived, and that it was not an easy matter to raise money upon that security; but I was unwilling to disappoint his Lordship in what I had so sanguinely told him I could effect, and I never acquainted his Lordship with the difficulty that had arisen, but I assisted Mr. Lind by advancing money from the public money which I had the management of. I never had occasion afterwards to mention the circumstance to Lord Melville until April in the last year, and he was perfectly unacquainted with my having made use of the public money in that transaction, and I charged his Lordship a regular interest for the whole of the money which I advanced in that transaction, from the first day that it was advanced until the final settlement of our accounts.

Did Lord Melville never inquire the name of the lender of that money?—I do not recollect that his Lordship ever did · I had stated in such positive terms that Mr. Lind could do it, that I never found it necessary to mention the circumstance again to Lord Melville, but took it for granted that he had thought I had concluded the transaction in the manner that I supposed it could be effected.

Did you mention Mr. Lind's name to Lord Melville at the time?—I did.

Were the dividends upon that stock carried to the credit of Lord Melville's account?—They were.

What was the amount of the sum originally expended in the purchase of this stock?—It was about 23,000l.

Did the debt for the purchase of that stock continue to that amount until the stock was replaced or repaid for?—It did not. It was diminished, by payments from his Lordship to me, to the sum of 20,000l.; upon which his Lordship continued to pay interest to me until the final settlement of our accounts.

In what manner was the 3000l. repaid to you?—I have no distinct recollection of it, but I believe I have been paid at two different times.

Was the 3000l. so paid, carried to the credit either of Lord Melville's chest account, or his account current with you?—It was not.

To what credit was it carried?—It was carried to the credit of the debt which was upon the stock.

To whom was that 3000l. paid?—As I had advanced the money for the stock myself, of course it was repaid to myself.

Was that East India Stock in possession, or was it still placed for the benefit of

Lord Melville in May 1800, when he quitted the Navy Pay Office?—It was held in trust by the house of Messrs. Thomas Coutts and Co., and subject to my controul.

Were the dividends always carried to Lord Melville's credit?—I believe they were.

At the time that you proposed to Lord Melville to purchase East India Stock for him out of the public balances lying in your hands unclaimed, did Lord Melville ask you the amount of such balances?—I do not recollect that he did.

Were you ever restricted by Lord Melville in any way, as to the quantity of money you were to keep out of the Bank at the house of Messrs. Coutts?—Lord Melville left the management of the balances in the Bank entirely to me.

Was there any restriction upon you as to the sums to be taken out of the Bank for that purpose?—There were none.

Was this East India Stock in May 1800, when Lord Melville went out of office, either sold or pledged for the purpose of making up your deficiencies at the Bank?—It was deposited at that time.

Was there any increase upon the value of that stock, from the time at which it was bought to the time at which it was either so sold or pledged?—The stock had risen.

To what account was the money obtained upon the stock either sold or pledged carried?—20,000l. to pay off the debt upon that stock, and 8000l. of it went to pay me in part liquidation of the balance upon my account current.

Had Lord Melville in fact the benefit of the rise of that stock?—Certainly he had; and the loss would also have accrued to his Lordship in case the stock had fallen.

Had he the benefit of the excess of dividends above the interest at 5 per cent. paid for the money, during the whole time there was such an excess?—I do not know that the dividend did exceed the interest which he paid upon it; especially at first, I believe it did not.

Was there at any time a rise upon that, between the time the stock was purchased and the time it was sold?—There was a rise upon the dividends on the stock, several after it was purchased upon his Lordship's account.

Was any security, of any kind, given to Mr. Lind for this purchase of East India Stock?—The stock was invested in his name some time after, not immediately, as I have understood from a document which has been lately put into my hands.

Did the accounts which you from time to time delivered to Lord Melville, though not delivered at regular periods, include all the receipts and payments made and received by you on account of Lord Melville?—They did, to the best of my recollection.

Did you, at the close of the year 1790, make up all the balances of the Navy Pay Office at the Bank of England?—The account at the Bank of England would appear by my books to be balanced at that time; but whether the balance was exactly paid in or not I cannot ascertain, because some of my drafts may not have been presented, in which case that would form part of the balance appearing so to be paid in.

Was the balance at the end of the year 1790 exactly struck, and did it appear that there was no deficiency at that time?—It appeared to be exactly struck; I could speak with more precision if the accounts were laid before me.

Did you make up the difference between the balance of the one account and the other, at the end of the year 1791?—I cannot speak from recollection; my documents are in the hands of the Honourable Managers, and I probably should be able to speak with more precision if they were laid before me.

If there was any difference between the office cash and the bank cash, in the end of the year 1791, of what money did that difference consist?—It would consist of drafts of mine which had been presented at the Bank in part, and in part of the sum of money which Lord Melville was indebted to the chest account, and to me upon my account current.

Did that balance you are now speaking of, comprehend both the chest account and the account current?—It did, to the best of my recollection of the accounts.

Did the balances so outstanding, from 1791 to 1799, comprehend those balances so due from Lord Melville?—They did; of the settled accounts always; but a small account may have existed upon the account current, not included in that.

Did the difference between the office and the Bank balance, at the end of those years which you have specified, denote, with a trifling exception, the sum of money which was to be made good by payments from Lord Melville to the public and to you?—They did, to the best of my recollection.

The Witness further stated, that he was upwards of two years in the Navy Pay Office, after the termination of the Defendant's treasurership; and he described the new arrangements which were made under the treasurerships of Messrs. Bathurst, Tierney, and Canning. The balance on the chest account was always against Lord Melville. No security of any sort was signed by himself or Lord Melville on account of the 13,500l. India Stock. Witness never made any cash payments as Paymaster of the Navy, except on account of Exchequer fees. It had happened, as he was told, more than once; but he had no recollection of it, that notes were brought from the Bank without passing through the hands of Coutts. Upon a farther interrogation, he recollected a million of money having been drawn one day from the Bank. The draft for this sum was given to the principal money conductor of the Navy Pay Office, who brought the amount in a great number of small notes, which he put directly into the house of Coutts, as he (Witness) understands. With respect to the destruction of the account books, &c., Witness, after attesting the fact already before the public, identified an account book which was shown to him by Mr. Whitbread. This book Witness said he had been robbed of at one time, and that it was returned to him by one of the Magistrates belonging to the Public Office in Hatton Garden. It contained an account current between Witness and Defendant, and was signed by both parties; Witness gave no directions for the purchase of the 10,000l. Loyalty Loan, to best of his recollection; but did, as to the purchase of the 7000l. 3 per cents, to the house of Coutts and Co., for which he heard that Mr. Antrobus acted as broker.

Cross-examined.—You speak of your being appointed Paymaster in consequence of the recommendatton you stated; had you an opportunity of being useful to Lord Melville in some regulations respecting the office, previous to your being appointed by him to the office of Paymaster?—I very early after Lord Melville's first appointment as Treasurer of the Navy, presented his Lordship with a plan for new regulating the business of the office, which, I have understood, was much approved of by his Lordship.

The first circumstance you were interrogated to, after that of your being appointed Paymaster, was his Lordship's acknowledgment of a balance in his hands of 10,000l.; at the time Lord Melville said that this was in his hands, did he not at the same time say, it was not applied to any private use or emolument of his own, but to public purposes, from whence it was likely there would be a loss?—His Lordship expressed to me, he was afraid there might be a loss.

Whether the sums for the purpose of paying the Exchequer fees, which you have stated, had not for some time been a fund in the hands of the Paymaster, which he used for his own emolument, when not wanted by the public?—I had understood that they had always been in the hands of my predecessors, Paymasters of the Navy; and that the parts which were not immediately required for the payment of the public fees, were made use of.

Whether all the detail and management of the Paymaster's Office has always been left to the Paymaster?—I believe it generally is; it certainly was altogether so in Lord Melville's time; some subsequent Treasurers have thought it necessary to attend the business of the office more minutely.

You stated that permission was given by Lord Melville to draw money from the Bank of England to Coutts's Bank; whether the only reason represented by you to Lord Melville for that measure was not to facilitate the official convenience?—Entirely so. I represented the inconvenience that would attend the payments from the distance of the Bank, and proposed to his Lordship, that a banker nearer should be allowed to keep the money in his hands, till I found it necessary to issue it to the sub-accountants. I represented to Lord Melville the danger of sending in drafts to the Bank every day by messengers, who were obliged to bring out the produce of these in cash to supply the daily payments.

Was there the least mention to Lord Melville, at the time application was made for his permission to make the change you have stated, of any private emolument to be derived to any body from it?—None whatever; it was never in Lord Melville's contemplation, and I do not remember that it was in my own at that time.

Was the permission which was given to draw money from the Bank, to be deposited till it was wanted in Coutts's Bank, entirely confined to the money that would be wanted for official convenience?—I do not know that the conversation extended to so great a length as to go into that minute part of the subject.

But was there then, or at any subsequent time, any permission given by Lord Melville to draw monies from the Bank for any other purpose?—Never.

Besides the salary of the Treasurer which you received, did you also receive, on Lord Melville's account, during the whole period of acting as his Agent, various remittances from Scotland, and other places, on his Lordship's account, to a considerable amount?—I did, to a large amount.

You speak of your attending Lord Melville with the statement of his accounts, which was signed by his Lordship, as you are understood to state, and duplicates of the accounts left by him?—So I stated the fact.

Whether, when you attended his Lordship upon the subject of private business, and business of the nature you have stated, you observed whether his Lordship gave any particular attention to the business?—I was very much concerned that I never could draw Lord Melville's attention particularly to the subject of his private accounts.

Were not, in most instances, the accounts that were produced, brought by you, signed immediately upon the confidence Lord Melville reposed in you, without any examination?—I always debited the accounts to his Lordship, for his examination; and he may have looked at them: but I am conscious that he never attended to them particularly.

Whenever you had occasion to attend his Lordship upon any business of a public nature, or any business that related to the detail and management of the office in which his own private interest was not concerned, did you find Lord Melville equally inattentive, or directly the reverse?—I must state directly the reverse; Lord Melville never interrupted me in any representations that I made to him respecting the public business of the office, unless it was merely telling me he had not time to attend to me at that time, and appointing another time, when I laid the subject before him.

Whether Lord Melville did at any time require or receive from you any receipt, or voucher, or document of any kind upon these accounts?—I do not recollect that I ever gave him a receipt for any money in my life.

Have you any distinct recollection that can enable you to state what was the form or the contracts of the bond of this 4000l., or whether it was not a bond in the usual form?—I have no recollection of it whatever; only I believe it did not bear interest.

The first purchase you speak to was 2000l. East India Stock; whether you have now any memory or recollection upon the subject?—I recollect, generally, that Lord Melville wanted to be possessed of a further qualification of East India Stock; and he begged me to procure it for him; but whether he told me that he would immediately repay me the money or not, I do not recollect.

Whether upon that occasion, or upon any other, Lord Melville ever directed you to lay out any part of the public money in your hands for the use and benefit of Lord Melville?—*He never did under the specific name of public money*, or any money bearing that description.

Is there any instance in which, prior to the purchase of any Stock, it was mentioned to Lord Melville by you, that it was intended to be purchased out of the public money, except in the instance of the purchase of East India Stock?—Never, to the best of my recollection.

Are you to be understood to state, that in the only instance where that was proposed, it was indignantly rejected?—I mean so to be understood.

You are understood to state that you did not originally give directions, nor are cognisant by whom the directions were given for the purchase of the subscription of the 10,000l. Loyalty Loan?—I am unacquainted who gave direc-

Did you ever purchase Navy or Victualling Bills, or other government securities, for Alexander Trotter, and for his benefit and advantage?—I once purchased Navy Bills to the amount, I said, of ten or twelve thousand pounds.

Whether the Navy Bills you so purchased for Alexander Trotter, at any time, were ever at a discount?—I have no memory of that.

Cross-Examined.—Had you any pecuniary transactions with Lord Melville in your life?—Never.

Were not you applied to by Mr. Trotter, in 1800, to advance money to him on certain stock?—I was. Mr. Trotter told me that he wished I would do him the favour of lending him upon India Stock and reduced Loyalty Stock; I agreed to lend it him. He proposed for me to lend it to the Honourable Robert Dundas; I then had a meeting with the Honourable Robert Dundas, and I said I would not lend it upon heavy stock *(a laugh)*, such as India and Loyalty too, which was a heavy stock; but that I wished to lend it upon three per cent. consols and India. The sum wanted was fifty thousand odd pounds, upon which I had a meeting with him next day, and that 1400l. mentioned was to reduce the stock, that the dividend of India and the dividend of Loyalty should be five per cent. equal to the sum lent five per cent.

Then was it upon that account that you received from Mr. Trotter 1427l. 11s. 11d.?—It was.

Had you any intercourse with Lord Melville during the course of that transaction?—None.

Was the stock disposed of or not?—It was rather long winded *(a laugh)*; I was anxious to get my money; I had stayed two or three years, and I wrote either to the Honourable Robert Saunders Dundas or to Mr. Trotter, begging permission to sell the stock; for I did not think things were clear *(a laugh)*.

You say you have had various money transactions with Mr. Trotter, lending money and borrowing money; whether these money transactions with Mr. Alexander Trotter were not all entirely upon Mr. Alexander Trotter's own account?—His own account.

Question by the Counsel.—Whether you had any knowledge, at the time of these transactions, that the money advanced to you at different times by Mr. Alexander Trotter, was public money?—None.

What was the nature of the security you received beside the stock itself?—A missive letter Mr. Robert Dundas gave me, saying he had borrowed so much money upon that stock; and I engaged to account to him for the dividends; and he was to allow me interest for the money.

NINTH DAY—May 9.

Mr. Miheux, an officer at the Board of Controul, stated, that he had received the salary of the Defendant.

Cross-examined. He knew Lord Melville to have performed the whole business of that Board, as President, without any salary for the first nine years of his appointment, namely, from 83 to 93.

Mr. G. Fennel, Principal Accountant, deposed to the dissolution of the Accountant's branch in the Navy Office, during the Treasurership of the Defendant, and its restoration since.

Mr. Wilson deposed to his conduct, as Agent for Mr. Trotter, in Mr. T.'s absence from the Navy Office.

Mr. Tierney deposed to the change which was made while he was Treasurer of the Navy. This change was to write off the sum required to the account of each Sub-accountant at the Bank, instead of drawing each day for such sum. This change was suggested by Trotter.

Mr. Latham, Paymaster to Mr. Tierney, was ten months in the Office, never absent but once, in consequence of illness. Mr. Tierney, during that time, officiated for him in any thing that was necessary to attend to. Witness signed drafts himself. He never delegated that power to any other person. He never made any personal payments whatever; but issued money for every necessary purpose to the Sub-accountants. The balances were, during his Paymastership, uniformly kept at the Bank.

TENTH DAY—May 10.

A letter from Lord Melville to Mr. Huskisson, Secretary of the Treasury, was read, requesting to be freed from the charge of interest, on the grounds that from 1783 till 1800, the money was either in the Bank of England, or in the hands of his Sub-accountants; and since that period in his own hands, liable at any hour to be claimed by the holders of assignments which had been or might be made for payment by the different Boards, to the full amount of the balance due.

Mr. Huskisson deposed that he was the writer of a letter produced to him; which letter was addressed by direction, from the Treasury Board to the Commissioners for Auditing Public Accounts, upon the subject of remitting the interest before alluded to.

The Managers referred to their Lordships' Journals to show that Lord Melville, who signed a certain release in Scotland on the 18th of February, was in his place in the House of Lords on the 20th of April following.

This reference being made, the Managers stated, that they here closed their evidence.

The Solicitor General rose, and with considerable ability, and at great length, summed up and animadverted upon the evidence.

DEFENCE.

ELEVENTH DAY—Tuesday, May 13.

Mr. Plumer opened the defence.—After alluding generally to the charges against Lord Melville, he proceeded to enter upon a defence to the first article of impeachment. With respect to this charge no evidence had, he said, been adduced which could in any degree affect the Noble Defendant on any charge of criminality. He meant to contend broadly and distinctly, that previous to the Act of Parliament, passed in the year 1785, there was no common law, neither was there any statute, which prohibited any public Officer having public money in his hands from using that money whilst it remained with him, provided it was forthcoming when wanted for the public service. This doctrine applied equally to the offices of Treasurer of the Navy, Paymaster of the Forces, Receivers General of the Land Tax, and other offices; and so distinctly had this principle been admitted, with respect to the latter office, that of the Receiver of the Land Tax, that when a Bill was brought into Parliament to compel those Officers to pay the public money into a certain place of deposit, and to prohibit them from making use of it for their own private emolument, a distinguished Member of the House of Commons, now a distinguished Member of their Lordships' House, strongly opposed it, and stated, as a reason, that if the Bill passed, the place of Receiver of the Land Tax would not be worth fifteen pounds per annum. The Honourable Manager (Mr. Whitbread) had quoted the resolutions passed in the House of Commons in 1782, as having established a new æra in the Navy Pay Office; but what did those resolutions prove? They proved distinctly what he had been stating, that there was no law to prevent the Treasurer of the Navy from placing the public money in the hands of whomsoever he pleased. He might then place it in the hands of any banker, in the hands of Messrs. Muir and Atkinson, or with any other house, whether of credit or no credit. The Treasurer of the Navy was alone responsible to the public for the amount. These resolutions of the House of Commons were, it seems, passed with a view of founding a Bill upon them. In point of fact, however, no Bill was brought in until the year 1785, when the Bill for regulating the Office of Treasurer of the Navy was passed. Upon this Bill he should say something afterwards; he should merely now state that the construction of it, in his opinion, was very different to that put upon it by the Honourable Manager. There was no proof, however, that Lord Melville did make any advantage of the public money. He had already stated that Lord Melville had, at that period, a right to place the public money in his possession in the hands of any house whatever. But it was said, that Lord Melville, in the speech he had made in the House of Commons, refused to give an account of the application of the sum of 10,000l. which had passed through his hands, and this was one of the crimes for which he was impeached. Was, then, silence a crime? Was it to be imputed as a crime to Lord Melville, that he had refused to say any thing that might affect himself? If a person charged with any crime were brought before a Magistrate, the latter, in the humane spirit of the law of England, would tell him, "you are not bound to say any thing that may criminate yourself, but if you wish to speak I will hear you." But here, because Lord Melville would not state any thing that might be twisted into a positive charge against himself, he was impeached, for what? for being silent; and thus, for the first time in the law of England, silence was constituted a crime where a person refused to accuse himself. With respect to the speech made by the Noble Defendant in the House of Commons, the Honourable Manager had himself chosen to stand forward as a witness to prove particular parts of it, and that Honourable Manager would probably have, in reply, to comment upon his own evidence. With all respect, however, to the Honourable Manager, and the Honourable Witness, he would venture to state that the evidence of that Honourable Gentleman remained unconfirmed by any of the four hundred persons by whom that speech was heard. The Honourable Gentleman also admitted, in his cross-examination, that he paid attention to the speech for the purpose of answering it; he listened to it, therefore, with a bias in his mind; he listened to it, therefore, in order to catch particular parts of it that would serve the purpose of his answer to it. Added to this, the Honourable Gentleman could not produce the notes which he had taken of the speech, having either lost or mislaid them. He was warranted, therefore, in saying, that the evidence, as to the expression made use of by Lord Melville in the House of Commons, was imperfect. The evidence which had been adduced on this charge was not applicable to any purpose of proving, that Lord Melville had derived any improper advantage from the public money in his hands. He now proceeded to the Tenth Article of Impeachment, which had been preferred some time subsequent to the other Nine, and in a manner very unusual, but which proceeding had, however, been sanctioned by their Lordships' House. It charged, that the Noble Defendant did, at divers times, between July 1782 and January 1786, possess himself of divers sums to the amount of 22,000l. &c. at divers times, and divers sums during four years. Was there ever so loosely worded an article? It happened that during a part of this period, from October 1783, to January 1784, a period of five months, Lord Melville was out of office, and yet he was charged in this loosely worded article, with possessing himself of public money during that period. And yet it was stated that this article was preferred out of candour and fairness towards the Noble Defendant, and for the purpose of more specifically stating the charge against him. But in what manner was the article supported; what was the proof by which it was sustained, general and sweeping as it was?—The Honourable Manager ascends to the attics of a widow, to hunt for old papers, and at length finding a box of papers which he thinks will suit his purpose, carries it away with him; thus the Honourable Manager had appeared in three characters in the course of this business, namely, as a Manager, a Witness, and a Carrier of a Box. After all this, to what did this box of papers, or the other evidence in support of this most specific and particular charge, amount to? Nothing; the divers sums and divers times dwindled to nothing that could in any degree affect the Noble Defendant. The 10,000l. respecting which the silence of the Noble Defendant alone was imputed to him as a crime, was now accounted for, and accounted for in a way that clearly justified the Noble Defendant in the assertion which he made, that private honour and personal convenience precluded him from making the discovery. The charge made against the Noble Defendant before their Lordships' high tribunal, had forced a disclosure respecting the application of that 10,000l., and what did it amount to? Nothing that could criminate the Noble Lord; to nothing that could sustain the inference of criminality that was drawn against him.—The Noble Defendant had filled some of the highest offices of State with the greatest ability and the most splendid talents, and in which he had shown an unremitting anxiety for the public welfare. Was it not natural to conclude, that in the course of the exercise of the duties of those high offices, and more particularly at those periods when the Noble Lord held those official situations, periods of great public danger, in times of great peril and alarm, sums of money must necessarily have been expended, of the application of which it would have been pregnant with public evil to have compelled an account of the expenditure—of which to have rendered an account might have been productive of the greatest danger to the interests of the country? Suppose for instance, with respect to the sum of 40,000l. which had not long since become the subject of Parliamentary inquiry, and in the advancing of which the Noble Defendant, then one of His Majesty's Ministers, was concerned —suppose, that the great and illustrious Statesman, now no more, had been lost to his country at an earlier period, and previous to any inquiry taking place, or the discovery of the sum advanced having been made, the Noble Defendant might have been called upon to account for it,—to give some clue as to its application,—to state the motives and the reasons which induced its application,—what could he have said, but as he did with respect to the 10,000l.,—that he could not disclose the application of the money?—Then it would have been said, "Oh! it was employed to purchase some rotten borough—it was used for the purposes of undue influence and corruption—it was applied with sinister and corrupt views—it was expended for the purpose of attaining objects incompatible with public liberty." Such would have been the outcry upon such an occasion, against the Noble Defendant—such would have been the prejudice excited against him. Yet the application of this 40,000l., after being inquired into, and sifted to the bottom, had been found to be an application of it consistent with every enlightened view of public policy, conducive to the support of public credit, and in conformity with the most patriotic intentions, to maintain the public security, and contribute to the public welfare. Viewing it in this light, Parliament had, as their Lordships well knew, passed a Bill of Indemnity, to indemnify the persons concerned in the advance of that sum of 40,000l.; and in so doing, had justified the motives of those who had advised its application in the particular mode specified. These circumstances, therefore, were amply sufficient to prove that some caution ought to be used before a Nobleman, who had filled high and distinguished situations, was charged with a misapplication of public money In point of fact, however, all the sums of public money, with possessing himself of which the Noble Defendant had been charged, had been accounted for, except two items of 1000l. each, of which there was no account. But was it to be supposed that at the distance of twenty-four years, every minute item in a Banker's book could be accounted for? This, however, clearly appeared from the entries in the Banker's book, from which the two entries to which he had alluded were proved, that very shortly afterwards there was a sum of upwards of 5000l. remitted to Scotland, which was placed to the account of the Noble Defendant at the same Banker's. He concluded, therefore, this part of the charges, by stating, that there was no proof of any criminality on the part of the Noble Lord, either in act or intention; that there was no proof whatever of any corrupt application of the public money, or of any improper advantage made by him of any of the sums included in these charges.——With respect to the Second Article of Impeachment, relative to the breach of the Act of Parliament, a great public clamour had been raised against the Noble Defendant, because being the person who brought in the Act alluded to, for the better regulation of the Office of Treasurer of the Navy, he was supposed to be the first to break it. He conceived, however, that the construction of the Act was far different from what had generally been stated and alleged. The grand object of the Act appeared to him to be to render the Bank of England a primary place of deposit for the money issued to the Treasurer of the Navy from the Exchequer, and by opening there an account in the name of the Treasurer of the Navy for such monies, the balance of which, at the time of his going out of office, was to be transferred to his successor, to put an end to that practice which had prevailed for a number of years, of suffering the public money issued to the Treasurer of the Navy to remain in his hands, to be placed to a private account, such Treasurer retaining in his hands, on quitting office, the balance of such money, and continuing, notwithstanding his being out of office, to answer demands upon his Ex-Treasurership, and only paying over the balance on his accounts being passed. This practice, which had been productive of great inconvenience, it was evidently the intention of the Act to put an end to; the money issued from the Exchequer to the Treasurer of the Navy was to be no longer placed at any private Bank on his private account, but to be deposited at once in the Bank of England, and the balances transferred successively from Treasurer to Treasurer, without the intervention of any private account, or any demands continuing to be made on an Ex-Treasurer, of sums for the public service arising during his Treasurership.—But this only related to the place of primary deposit.—The Act could not, in his opinion, be construed to extend to any place of subsequent deposit for sums taken from the Bank of England, in order to be applied to the public service. What were the directions of the Act? that the money should be drawn from the Bank by the drafts of the Treasurer of the Navy; which drafts should specify the heads of service to which such money was to be applied. The Act stated, explicitly, the heads of service; not that every specific sum paid to an individual was to be paid by a draft on the Bank. It was clear also, from an Act recently passed for the Regulation of the Office of Treasurer of the Ordnance, in which there were clauses introduced, stating the form of the draft to be given by the Treasurer of the Ordnance to the different individuals having demands on that officer in his public capacity. No such provisions were made in the Act for the regulation of the Office of Treasurer of the Navy; and therefore it was clear that the intention of the Legislature in the two Acts was totally different. There was nothing in the latter Act that could at all justify the construction, that every individual having money to receive at the Office of the Treasurer of the Navy, was to be sent to the Bank of England to be paid. If such had been the object of the Act, there could not have been a more mischievous law passed, and the Noble Defendant would have deserved reprobation for bringing in an Act of so injurious and dangerous a tendency. Such an Act must have put an end to the service upon which this country depended for its glory and pre-eminence, as it would have placed an insurmountable bar to the payment of our gallant and meritorious seamen. Could it be supposed that that deserving class of persons would be content, on going to the Navy Pay Office, to receive sums, a large proportion of which were under one pound, to be told, "we have no money here, you must go to the Bank of England to receive it?" Not only this, but under such an Act a large proportion of our gallant seamen could not have been paid at all. By an Act of the 15th of the present King, all drafts for sums under one pound, were declared illegal and void. Thus, therefore, no drafts could have been given under such an Act to the numbers whose demands individually amounted to less than that sum. The Bank of England, as he had already stated, was merely declared by the Act to be the place of primary deposit; but nothing was said in the Act as to any place of deposit, from whence the ultimate payments were to be made. He contended, therefore, that there was no evidence to prove, that there had been any violation of the Act of Parliament on the part of the Noble Defendant, in sanctioning the deposit of sums of money in the House of Messrs. Coutts, or any other Banking-house, such sums having been previously drawn from the Bank of England, according to the form prescribed by the Act of Parliament, under specific heads of service. He admitted, that if the draft was fictitiously drawn, in order merely to comply with the letter of the Act of Parliament, that the spirit of the Act might be violated; but with this the Noble Defendant had no concern.

The Lord Chancellor intimated, that if the Learned Counsel had much more to offer, it might probably be more convenient to postpone the remainder of his speech to the succeeding day.

Mr. Plumer availed himself of this intimation, and the Court adjourned about three o'clock to the next day.

TWELFTH DAY—Wednesday, May 14.

Mr. Plumer resumed the Defence. Having stated the substance of the remaining Seven Articles of Impeachment, he proceeded to comment upon the evidence examined in support of them. Nothing whatever, he contended, had been proved that in any degree implicated the Noble Defendant in any charge of having improperly used the public money. Nothing whatever had been proved that could impeach the public character, or sully the reputation of the Noble Defendant. Their Lordships had been told by the Honourable Manager who opened the charges, that strong and conclusive evidence would be brought forward to prove them. One witness in particular was to be examined, the accomplice of Lord Melville, as it was stated, in making use of the public money, who would make the guilt of the Defendant perfectly clear and apparent, and prove, beyond a doubt, the transactions with which he was charged. That witness was Mr. Trotter. Mr. Trotter was called, and what did he prove? Instead of establishing a single iota of what the Honourable Manager had stated, he proved directly the reverse. The Witness, upon whose testimony so much reliance had been placed, had sworn that the Noble Defendant had not participated—that no human being had participated in the profits which he acknowledged to have made of the public money—that the Noble Defendant had not participated in the profits derived from the use of the public money—that he had not connived at its use—that he did not know of it till long afterwards.——Thus had the very principal Witness called to establish the guilt of the Noble Defendant, completely proved his innocence. The Honourable Managers had failed in their proof, or rather they had proved the direct contrary of that which they set out to establish. At the first establishment of the Board of Controul, in the year 1784, Lord Melville was appointed President, which office he held till the year 1801. In 1791 the Noble Defendant was appointed Secretary of State for the Home Department. In 1794 he resigned this office, and was appointed Secretary of State for the Foreign Department. He held this office during a crisis of peculiar difficulty, and at a period when the country was engaged in an arduous contest, and was threatened with the greatest dangers. The Noble Defendant held this office until the year 1801, devoting his time and his talents to the service of his country during this period of peril and difficulty. Yet it was well known that the Noble Defendant relinquished his salary in the first instance as Secretary of State for the Home Department, and afterwards as Secretary of State for the War Department. The whole amount of the sum thus relinquished and given up to the public was upwards of 34,000l. Could it be supposed for a moment that a person who acted thus, could be actuated by any views of avarice? The whole sum of public money with which the Noble Defendant was charged with having possessed himself of, amounted to only 22,000l. The contradiction, therefore, was too glaring to be entertained, that the Noble Defendant should voluntarily relinquish and give up to the public a sum of 34,000l., to which he was fairly and honourably entitled, and should, at the same time, possess himself of 22,000l. belonging to the public in another department, was an inconsistency not to be accounted for on any rational principle. But it was said, that the Noble Defendant had connived at the improper use of the public money made by Trotter, and that for such purpose he had given his consent to transfer the money from the Bank of England to the House of Messrs. Coutts. To make good such a charge, it must be shown that the Noble Defendant was aware, at the time he gave his consent to this measure, of all the consequences which were to follow. But surely it was too much to charge the Noble Defendant with all the consequences of that measure, when he could not foresee them at the time he gave his consent to it. What had Mr. Trotter sworn?—He had declared upon his oath, that the reason he suggested to Lord Melville for removing the public money from the Bank of England to Messrs. Coutts, was official convenience, and official convenience only. Nay, he had sworn further, that that was the real and *bona fide* reason which induced him, at that time, to make the proposal to Lord Melville; and that, at that time, he had no other view in doing so than official convenience. What then became of the charge against the Noble Defendant, of conniving at the conduct of Trotter, when it was clearly proved in evidence that, so far from conniving, he knew nothing of it; and that so far from giving permission to Trotter to lodge the public money at the House of Messrs. Coutts, with a view to private advantage, it was clearly proved that he gave his consent expressly on the ground of official convenience, and that Trotter himself proposed with that view, and that view alone, at that period. A curious argument had, however, been set up with respect to this evidence of Mr. Trotter. The Honourable Manager who opened the charges had told their Lordships that Trotter was a most material evidence, that he was the accomplice of the Noble Defendant, that he knew every transaction in which the latter had been engaged with respect to the public money, and that every word he said was to be believed. After, however, he had given his evidence, comes the

Honourable and Learned Manager, who sums up the evidence, and tells their Lordships that not one word of what Mr. Trotter had said was to be believed. This palpable contradiction he should leave the two Honourable Managers to reconcile between themselves in the best manner they could, but it clearly showed how completely they had been foiled by their own evidence, and how entirely the evidence called for the prosecution had proved the innocence instead of the guilt of the Noble Defendant. The next transaction to which he would refer, was the laying out the 23,000l. in East India stock for the use of the Noble Defendant. It had been stated that the Noble Defendant, after having negatived the proposition of Trotter to lay out the public money in India stock for his own advantage, had borrowed, through the medium of Trotter, 23,000l. for the purpose, without interest. What in the course of the trial appeared to be the real circumstances of the case? In the year 1789, that is to say three years after it was charged this partnership in iniquity between the Noble Defendant and Trotter had commenced, there was a great probability of a considerable rise taking place in India stock. The Noble Defendant made, in the House of Commons, a very favourable statement with respect to the affairs of India, stating his belief that India would shortly be in a situation to render material assistance to this country, instead of any call being made upon the country to assist the East India Company. These statements were made with every prospect of their being realized. The natural effect was a rise in the price of East India stock. Trotter, it appears, went to the Noble Defendant, and advises him to buy East India stock: the answer of the latter was, "I have no money." This too, after three years, during which it was charged there was a partnership between them in making a profit, for their own private advantage, of the public money. Trotter replies to the Noble Defendant, "There is 100,000l. of the public money now lying at Coutts's, which is not wanted for any immediate purpose, why not make use of that?" Did not Lord Melville know this? if he had been making use of the public money, must he not have known this? Would he have hesitated a moment to make use of this sum for the purchase of East India stock? Was it necessary for Trotter to have hinted to him the expediency of making such an use of the public money, after they had been three years in partnership in turning it to their mutual profit? But Trotter had sworn that this was the first time he had ever talked to Lord Melville on the subject of making use of the public money. In a private conversation between these two supposed partners in guilt, when no third person is present, the Noble Defendant not only refuses to make use of the public money for his own private advantage, but expresses the greatest indignation at such a proposal being made to him. Could there be a more striking proof of the innocence of the Noble Defendant, with respect to all these transactions, in which he was so heavily charged with participating? Trotter then proposes to borrow 23,000l. for the use of Lord Melville; the money was provided, and laid out in the purchase of stock. But what were the circumstances with respect to this loan? It was proved that interest at five per cent. was regularly paid for it, by Lord Melville, to the amount of 1150l. per annum; and this for ten years, until the principal was repaid, in the year 1800, making a total of principal and interest of upwards of 34,000l. Could there be a more *bona fide* transaction on the part of Lord Melville?

The next transaction to which he had to advert, was the share of the Noble Defendant in the Loyalty Loan, amounting to 10,000l. Upon this, however, there was no proof whatever of any improper motive on the part of the Noble Defendant. He had come forward, like many others, patriotically to assist the country, at a period of peril and difficulty, and there was not the slightest evidence to show that he was actuated by any other consideration. With respect also to the 7000l. reduced annuities, there was nothing that could, in any degree, implicate the Noble Defendant in any charge before their Lordships. He had nearly omitted to take notice of the charge against the Noble Defendant, of burning a variety of vouchers, papers and accounts.—With respect to this, however, it was perfectly clear that the burning of vouchers and accounts was no crime in itself, although he admitted that it might, in some cases, afford ground for suspicion. In this case, however, it was proved that there were no public accounts destroyed; and surely there could be no doubt as to the right of individuals to destroy what, ever private accounts they might no longer conceive of any use. Lord Melville, it appeared, had been constantly in the habit of destroying such papers as he deemed to be useless, and had merely in this case pursued the same line of conduct. With respect to the release, it appeared clearly that Lord Melville executed it without being aware precisely of the nature of the deed, or of the circumstances attending it. At the same time there was nothing in that transaction in itself that was unusual and improper; and releases being given, nothing was more usual than the destruction of vouchers and accounts which were thereby rendered useless. Upon the whole of the case, therefore, he was entitled to assert, that there was no proof whatever of any corruption on the part of Lord Melville, of any connivance at the improper use of the public money, or of any guilty knowledge of the transactions in which Trotter was concerned with respect to such public money. The charges against the Noble Defendant were not only unsupported by evidence, but the evidence for the prosecution had proved the case for the defence. The law was not violated by any act of the Noble Defendant. Thus, then, with the law and the facts of the case in his favour, he left it to the decision of their Lordships' high tribunal, trusting that, even if they should think the Noble Defendant guilty of any small part of the charges, that they would consider the degradation he had experienced, the wound his reputation had received, and the destruction of his peace of mind by the anxiety consequent upon such a prosecution, as an amply sufficient punishment; but confiding at the same time in their Lordships' decision, entirely to establish his innocence and declare his acquittal.

The court immediately adjourned till the next day, (Thursday.)

THIRTEENTH DAY—Thursday, May 15.

A short examination of Witnesses took place to prove the relinquishment of his salary by the Noble Defendant, whilst Secretary of State for the Home Department, and afterwards while Secretary of State for the War and Colonial Departments, as stated by the Learned Counsel.

Mr. Adam then addressed the Court at considerable length in behalf of Lord Melville. The Learned Counsel went over the same grounds as those taken by Mr. Plumer, contending for a similar construction on the Act of Parliament, and maintaining that the charges were completely disproved by the evidence brought to support them.

After Mr. Adam had concluded, the Court adjourned to the next day, Friday.

FOURTEENTH DAY—May 17.

The Attorney General begged their Lordships attention to two points, to which the observations of the Learned Counsel on the other side had been principally directed. Those points were with regard to the construction of the statute and common law, as applying to the charges against the Noble Defendant. Without referring to the reports of the Commissioners for examining Public Accounts, or the Resolutions of the Houfe of Commons, grounded upon those Reports; or to the professed object of the Statute of 26 Geo. III, he might appeal to all those who had been Treasurers of the Navy since its enactment, with the exception of the Noble Defendant, and indeed to common sense itself, against the construction of the Learned Counsel on the other side. What, could it be contended that the object of the Act was accomplished the moment the money was put into the Bank, and that it might be drawn from thence the moment afterwards, and applied to private purposes? "Oh, unwise, improvident Legislature, was this the only security devised for the public money?"—But that such was not the object of the law, was evident from the interpretation which it received from the Treasurers, who did not conceive it sufficient to draw money from the Exchequer, place it in the Bank, and draw it out again immediately. The purpose of the Statute was, that public money should not remain in the hands of Sub-Accountants. And if such delinquency as that with which the Defendant stood charged, had occurred prior to the Statute, there was no doubt that the Attorney General might have filed an information against the delinquent. Lord Kenyon, when Attorney General, did file an information against a Paymaster of the Navy, end the conduct of that Paymaster in using the public balances was tolerated only on the ground that his salary was inadequate to the duties. Various Public Accountants saw the mischiefs resulting from such a practice, and forwarded those measures which led to bringing in the Bill in 1786. The Learned Counsel on the other side had stated that the Resolutions of the House of Commons were to be considered as nothing; but His Majesty gave effect to these resolutions by new modelling the Navy Office, and it could not be doubted that His Majesty had power to prescribe the duty of his office, and that it was criminal for them to violate the prescribed line. The Noble Defendant, by accepting the office of Treasurer of the Navy, with an increased salary in lieu of all fees and perquisites, bound himself to follow the rules prescribed, and it was preposterous to say, that he was not guilty of a misdemeanor if he violated them. It had been hinted that no criminal information could, at common law, be filed against a Public Accountant; but it had been only hinted, for it was too absurd seriously to argue. It was not true that a public defaulter stood in the same situation as a private defaulter. A public defaulter was liable to criminal prosecution for breach of duty, as well as to process from the Exchequer for his default. And it was clear law, that when no express punishment was provided by statute for violation of public duty, it was punishable at common law as a misdemeanor, particularly when the offence related to the public revenue. If the doctrine of the Learned Counsel on the other side could hold, a Public Accountant would scarce be under any restraint. But, in truth there did exist an Act of Parliament, which, whatever construction might be put upon it, certainly meant to protect the public interest, and guard the public money. If so, can any rational man, for a moment believe that the Act was satisfied by carrying the money from the Exchequer to the Bank, and letting it remain there but for a moment? In deciding these points, he was sure their Lordships would consult the dignity of their own character, and decide as was befitting them.

Mr. Whitbread expressed his concurrence in the definition of the law, which their Lordships had heard so ably stated by his Learned Colleague, and which served, in his judgment, completely to refute the doctrine so confidently asserted by the Learned Counsel for the Noble Defendant. With respect to other parts of the Defence, it had been stated, that the Noble Defendant declined to receive the salary of the office of Secretary of State. But independently of the consideration that the Noble Defendant held the Secretaryship improperly, and against a Resolution of the House of Commons; his display of generosity in that instance bore a very questionable character. A Noble Lord (Grenville) had recently given up a salary, that of the Auditorship of the Exchequer, and in a manner that, far from being liable to suspicion, was entitled to praise. But how different the character of that sacrifice, which the Noble Defendant appeared to make! He gave up 4000l. a year to be sure, but why retain the Treasurership of the Navy? Because the receipts from the latter were very different from those which could be expected from the Secretaryship of State, as fully appeared from even the case of the 10,000l. which the Noble Defendant affected to have laid out for public purposes, which purposes were never hinted at even by the Defendant's Counsel, and which could never be ascertained. With regard to the assertion of the Learned Counsel, that the Noble Defendant was inaccurate in accounts, he should only refer to that which certainly was inconsistent with the idea; namely, the arrangements made in the Navy Office in 1784; and also the adjustment of his own salary in that office, in order to make it up to 4000l. a year. This idea of inaccuracy was also contradicted by the Noble Lord's management of the finances of India. In his statement of those finances in the House of Commons on the opening of the Indian Budget and other occasions, there certainly never was the least appearance of inaccuracy, or embarrassment in accounts. The Learned Counsel had maintained the impossibility of disproving all the objections that might apply to the conduct of a man in office for twenty-four years. When told that evidence appeared to prove that money was applied to the private use of the Noble Defendant by Douglas; then the Learned Counsel stated; that as Douglas was dead, the business could not be explained. But when the case of 1805, at which period the balance incurred during the Paymastership of Douglas was discharged, the same apology of Douglas's death, aided by the destruction of the papers, was relied on. How fortunate for the Defendant was the act of death and the destruction of his papers! If the Managers could only avail themselves of the evidence of Douglas—if they could but read the accounts between the Noble Defendant and his deputies, and ascertain the manner in which he applied the sum to which his confessions in the House of Commons referred—could they but penetrate that triple shield of brass in which the Defendant was enclosed—how much, from what they had already discovered, were they justified in expecting!

The Honourable Manager proceeded to detail the Evidence relative to the First and Tenth Articles, commenting upon it as he went on, and contending upon similar grounds to those urged by the Solicitor General, that it was conclusive against the Noble Defendant.

The Honourable Manager concluded with observing, that having gone through the 1st and 10th Articles, he should now, not from any desire of time for preparation, nor from any want of personal strength, but merely to consult their Lordships' convenience, beg leave to pospone the remainder of his reply till to-morrow.

FIFTEENTH DAY—May 17.

Mr. Whitbread resumed his speech. He commented at length on the confession of the Noble Lord respecting the application of 10,000l. to purposes which he avowed he would not disclose. He then adverted to the demeanour of Mr. Trotter in giving his evidence, and insisted that from his manner as much was to be inferred as from the plainest testimony. He argued from the fourth and fifth clauses of the Act of 1786, and contended that they were notoriously violated by the Noble Defendant: with respect to the want of care in the Noble Defendant in examining his accounts, it did not appear that such was his character by his subsequent conduct. He had had the caution to insert an unusual clause in a release for the destruction of all vouchers, and he had not neglected to perform that agreement. With regard to the removal of the money from the Bank to Coutts's, it was argued that the Noble Defendant had done it for reasons of official convenience, when the Pay Office was removed from Broad-street to Somerset-House. But, in fact, it was in 1786 that the money was removed to Coutts's, and the office was not removed until the year 1787:—the falsity of that pretence was then most evident. The Honourable Manager next adverted to the refuge taken by the Noble Lord under the 5th Clause, and refusing to answer the Commissioners of Inquiry. He considered this a strong indicative of what were the Noble Lord's feelings—He fled to the 5th Clause, and exclaimed in the words of the Scotch song, "Throw your auld cloak about me." He then entered into a detail of the transactions of 1800, and observed, had not that been negotiated, the Noble Lord would not probably have been enabled to pay his balances, and the public must have suffered a loss. In adverting to the conversation stated to have passed between Lord Melville and Trotter, he observed, that though the latter would not recollect any of the conversations with precision, it was not to be doubted but that they understood each other: there were many modes of communicating ideas besides by words. When our immortal bard represents King John as wishing the death of his nephew Arthur, without daring to speak his wishes direct to Hubert, he thus addressed him:—

" If that thou could'st see without eyes,
" Hear without thine ears, and make reply
" Without a tongue, using conceit alone,
" Without eyes, ears, and painful sound of words,
" Then, in despight of blooded, watchful day,
" I would into thy bosom pour my thoughts."

Similar, most likely, was Lord Melville's directions to Trotter, respecting India Stock; but if any doubt remained as to this point, there could be none to those services to which the Noble Lord admitted he had applied, contrary to the purposes of the Act. In conclusion, the Hon. Manager adverted to the manner in which the Counsel had attempted to defend their client. Instead of attempting to rescue his impeached honour, and restore his character, they had only attempted to save him from punishment: "Oh, miserable man, to be so defended!" said the Honourable Manager. Every one of the charges, which the Managers have presented against you, have been completely substantiated. By your own confession, you have shown that you have illegally applied a large sum of the public money; and for that alone we are justified in seeking a verdict of condemnation against you. You expressed your readiness to swear that you did not derive any profits from the public money during the Paymastership of Douglas, and we have proved that you did. You have also declared, that you derived no profits during the Paymastership of Trotter, and we have proved that you did. And what has been deposed by our evidence, not a single witness has been called on your part to controvert.—No, your Counsel have not ventured to repel it. Their strength has been to secure a retreat. We attacked them in their fortress—we pursued them in their flight for refuge, first to the bastion, and next to the citadel.—When being unable to make a stand, they endeavoured to carry off the body of their client; but in this, too, it will be seen that they have failed. They have not fought, but bled. We, however, have overtaken and conquered, and we claim from your Lordships the just reward of our success—a Verdict against the Noble Defendant.

The Lord Chancellor asked the Learned Counsel for the Defendant, if they wished to say any thing upon the cases quoted by the Attorney General.

Mr. Plumer merely observed, that he thought the case of Bembridge and Powell did not apply.

The Attorney General stated, that he quoted the case for the principle it established, which he insisted was analagous to the present case.

The Court then adjourned to the Chamber of Parliament.

SIXTEENTH DAY—June 12.

The Court having assembled in the usual form, about twelve o'clock, the Lord Chancellor stated that the first question he was to put to their Lordships was, Whether Lord Viscount Melville was guilty of the high crimes and misdemeanors charged upon him in the first article of charge, or not guilty?—His Lordship then proceeded to ask the opinion of each Lord, beginning with the junior in rank present, in the following form:—"John Lord Crewe (the junior Baron), what says your Lordship to this first article of charge?" Lord Crewe answered, "Not Guilty, upon my honour," laying his right hand upon his breast. "James Lord Lauderdale, what says your Lordship to the first article of charge?"—"Guilty, upon my honour." The same question was repeated to each Lord, who answered in like manner, either "Guilty," or "Not Guilty, upon my honour." The Lord Chancellor voted last, and laying his hand upon his breast, said, "I, Thomas Lord Erskine, Lord High Chancellor of Great Britain, give it as my opinion to your Lordships, that Lord Viscount Melville is not guilty of the High Crimes and Misdemeanours contained in the first Charge."

A similar question was put on the second and other charges, and the following are the numbers on each:—

CHARGES.	NOT GUILTY.	GUILTY.
1	120	15
2	79	56
3	83	52
4	Unanimous.	
5	131	4
6	89	46
7	85	50
8	121	14
9	119	16
10	123	12

There being 135 Peers present.

Soon after three o'clock, the Lords had given their votes upon all the articles of charge. About half an hour was occupied by the Clerk, in casting up the numbers on each side, on the different charges. About a quarter before four, silence was again proclaimed, and

The Lord Chancellor declared, that, by the vote of their Lordships, Lord Viscount Melville was acquitted of all the High Crimes and Misdemeanors charged upon him in the different Articles of Charge; and then, addressing himself to Lord Melville, said, "Henry Lord Viscount Melville, I am to declare to you that you are acquitted of all the Charges exhibited against you, and of every mattter and thing therein contained."

Lord Melville, who stood while the Chancellor addressed him, bowed and retired.

The Lord Chancellor put the question to adjourn to the Chamber of Parliament, which was immediately ordered.

INDEX

TO THE

MEMOIRS, HINTS, PHILOSOPHICAL PAPERS, MEDICAL FACTS, NAVAL LITERATURE, POETRY, REMARKABLE INCIDENTS, &c. IN VOL. XV.

E.

O.

P.

Q.

R.

INDEX *to the* GAZETTE LETTERS *in* VOL. XV; *containing Accounts of the Captures, Proceedings, &c. by and of the under-mentioned Officers.*

INDEX *to the* PROMOTIONS *and* APPOINTMENTS.

INDEX *to the* MARRIAGES.

INDEX *to the* OBITUARY.

END OF THE FIFTEENTH VOLUME.

JOYCE GOLD, PRINTER, SHOE-LANE, LONDON.

Lightning Source UK Ltd.
Milton Keynes UK
05 September 2010

159422UK00001BA/9/P

La Belle et le Clochard

HACHETTE ÉDITION

« Oh ! Jim chéri, que ce chien est joli ! C'est le plus beau cadeau de Noël que tu pouvais me faire !

– Ce n'est pas un chien, c'est une chienne, Darling ! Je suis heureux qu'elle te plaise… »

Nous sommes à Londres, dans une maison des beaux quartiers. C'est le soir de Noël. Darling vient de trouver au pied du sapin un petit paquet gigotant, couinant, car on ne peut pas appeler cela des aboiements…

« Comment allons-nous l'appeler ?

– Baptisons-la Lady, car, élevée par toi, je suis sûr qu'elle deviendra une vraie demoiselle ! » répond son mari.

Le temps passe et Lady grandit. Ses maîtres l'adorent.
« Darling, ma chérie, il n'est pas question que cette chienne dorme sur notre lit.
– Mais non, Jim chéri. C'est juste pour cette nuit. Pas vrai, mon trésor ? »
Et le trésor, qui sait bien qu'elle règne en maîtresse sur le cœur de ses maîtres, s'installe douillettement au creux de la couette… Elle ne veut surtout pas perdre Jim chéri et Darling de vue ! Que deviendraient-ils sans elle ?

Lady a deux voisins, deux chiens d'un certain âge, qu'elle apprécie beaucoup : voilà Jock, le petit noiraud, et César, le grand brun. Ces deux-là sont amis depuis longtemps. La petite Lady, si jeune et si charmante, leur plaît. Et puis, elle a de si bonnes manières…

« Bonjour, messieurs ! Avez-vous remarqué le joli collier que mes maîtres m'ont offert ?

– Mon Dieu, Lady, il vous va vraiment à ravir. Vous avez l'air d'une demoiselle, à présent.

– Eh bien, ma poulette, tu viens te promener ? »
Qui ose lui parler avec autant de familiarité ? Lady ne l'a jamais vu, ce grand chien gris, qui n'a pas l'air très soigné, mais qui a tout de même si fière allure… La jeune chienne est bien trop timide pour lui répondre.

À la maison, grand chambardement ! Darling vient d'avoir un bébé ! Il est beau comme un ange et Lady l'aime tendrement. « Lady, nous sommes obligés de partir quelques jours, déclarent un beau matin Darling et Jim chéri. Tante Sarah s'occupera du bébé en notre absence. Sois bien sage et ne fais pas de bêtises. Nous comptons sur toi. » La tante Sarah n'est pas bien belle, elle a une voix de crécelle. Quand elle se déplace, on dirait un troupeau d'éléphants. Ses siamois, Si et Am, au contraire, ne font aucun bruit. Mais c'est à qui sera le plus méchant, le plus sournois. Pauvre Lady ! Le cauchemar ne fait que commencer…

« Mais… mais, qu’est-ce que vous faites ?
Voulez-vous lâcher cette cage !
Vous n’êtes pas chez vous, ici ! »
Lady est indignée : elle a beau crier, sauter, aboyer, les deux chats n’en font qu’à leur tête. Un petit coup de patte, et bonsoir ! le poisson rouge ! Un grand coup de queue, balayé, le canari…
« Il est formidable, ce salon ! Ya vraiment plein de choses à casser ici !
– T’as raison, frérot ! Eh ! pousse-toi, la chienne, tu nous gênes… »

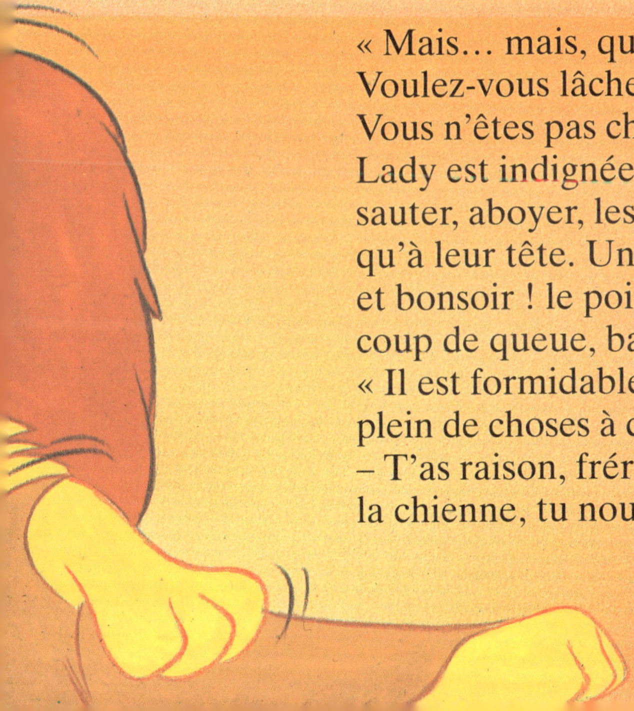

« Mais qu'est-ce que c'est que ce carnage ? Tu ferais mieux de garder la maison, espèce de sale chienne, plutôt que d'embêter mes gentils chatons ! » crie tante Sarah, folle de rage.
« Sale chienne ! » Lady n'en revient pas. Jamais personne ne l'a appelée ainsi. Jamais personne ne l'a grondée aussi injustement. Elle essaye faiblement de se défendre, d'expliquer.
« Ah ! Et puis n'aboie pas en plus ! Venez, mes amours, laissez cette sale bête réfléchir à toutes ses bêtises... »

Lady n'a pas eu beaucoup de temps pour pleurer sur son sort. Tante Sarah est vite revenue avec un monsieur inconnu.
« Viens, ma toute belle ! Viens donc, que je te mette cette jolie muselière. Comme ça, tu ne feras plus peur à personne... »
« Muselière, faire peur... Mais de quoi parle-t-il ? » se demande Lady en se débattant de toutes ses forces.

Décidément, c'en est trop ! Trop de malheur et trop de tristesse ! Sans plus réfléchir, Lady s'enfuit à toutes pattes, loin de la tante Sarah et de ses horribles chats ! Elle court droit devant elle, elle, la petite chienne des beaux quartiers qui se promène toujours en laisse… Attention, Lady, il y a des voitures…

Depuis longtemps, Lady ne reconnaît plus rien des rues autour d'elle. Elle est complètement perdue.
« Ouah ! Ouah ! Ouah ! »
Plus elle fuit, plus une meute d'affreux molosses grossit derrière elle.
« Tiens, il y a de la bagarre dans l'air, se dit un grand chien gris. On dirait que cette poulette a besoin d'un peu d'aide. En route, mon vieux Clochard ! Vole au secours de la demoiselle en danger ! »

« Bonjour, ma petite ! Mais… on se connaît ! Qu'est-ce qui t'amène aussi loin de chez toi ? Que je suis bête ! Tu ne peux pas répondre. On va s'occuper de ça ! Suis-moi, je connais un endroit parfait pour arracher cet engin de torture… »

Pauvre Lady ! Elle aimerait bien remercier ce grand escogriffe qui a mis tous les affreux molosses en fuite, mais… la muselière… ! Elle hoche la tête de toutes ses forces et lui jette un long regard mélancolique. Comme c'est bon de ne plus être toute seule et de sentir que quelqu'un est prêt à vous protéger… Elle pousse un grand soupir de soulagement.

L'une suivant l'autre, les voilà au zoo. D'abord, une petite visite au Crocodile. En voyant le joli petit nez de Lady, il se pourlèche déjà les mâchoires…
« Viens, Poulette ! Cet animal a vraiment de trop grandes dents ! Il te croquerait toute crue… »

Le castor est bavard, mais il est très efficace : et ronge, et ronge, et ronge… adieu muselière, bonjour la liberté !
« Oh ! merci, s'écrie Lady. Maintenant, je peux tout vous expliquer… »
Et elle raconte son histoire, tandis que Clochard l'écoute, tout ému de ses malheurs.

« Et maintenant, Poulette, à table ! On va dîner chez Tony, le champion de la pizza ! Tu m'en diras des nouvelles... »
« Ce Clochard ! Il a vraiment des amis partout », pense Lady, de plus en plus contente de son escapade.

En voyant Clochard en aussi galante compagnie, Tony, aussitôt, met les petits plats dans les grands : spaghetti, chandelles et surtout… musique !
« Bon appétit, les amoureux ! »
Clochard et Lady échangent un long regard, puis, sans plus attendre, se jettent sur les pâtes. Lady en est bien sûre : jamais son repas à la maison n'a eu aussi bon goût… Et si c'était l'amour ?

Après un bon dîner, rien ne vaut une promenade romantique au clair de lune… Les yeux dans les yeux, patte contre patte, Clochard et Lady se promettent mille merveilles.
Brusquement, la fatigue s'abat sur eux sans prévenir : la journée a été rude et ils s'endorment serrés l'un contre l'autre, au pied d'un arbre, sur la pelouse d'un jardin public.

Le lendemain matin, Lady et Clochard se réveillent en même temps.
« Allez, Poulette, il est temps de se mettre en quête d'un petit déjeuner...
– D'accord, mais après, il faudra quand même que j'aille prendre des nouvelles de mon bébé.
– Pourquoi ? Reste avec moi, j'ai encore tant de choses à te montrer...
– Mais que diraient Jim chéri et Darling si je les abandonnais ? C'est toi qui viendras me voir à la maison.
– Si tu le dis... Je vais t'apprendre quelque chose d'amusant avant que tu ne rentres.

Ces poules sont idiotes, elles ont peur de nous. Vole-leur dans les plumes et tu entendras un beau concert… », crie Clochard tout excité. Il se met à courir en aboyant comme un fou.

Le poulailler en entier s'enfuit en piaillant. Lady est abasourdie par tout ce bruit. Elle a un peu peur aussi. Décidément, ce Clochard ne ressemble guère à Jock et à César. Pris par son jeu, Clochard oublie Lady derrière lui…

Et voilà ! Quand le fermier est venu voir pourquoi ses poules étaient si agitées, il n'a vu que Lady. Clochard, lui, s'était enfui pensant que Lady le suivrait. C'est comme ça que cette pauvre Lady s'est retrouvée à la fourrière. On l'a balancée dans une cage malodorante, avec un tas d'autres chiens, des gros et des petits, des à poil long, des à poil ras. Ce qui est sûr, c'est qu'elle était la seule à avoir un collier.

« Pleure pas, ma jolie, sapée comme tu l'es, tu feras pas de vieux os ici ! »

Effectivement, au bout de quelques heures, on vient chercher Lady.
Sans douceur, un employé de la fourrière passe une laisse autour de son beau collier.
« Avance, tes maîtres te réclament. Tu as bien de la chance de ne pas rester ici », déclare-t-il.

Lady se retourne une dernière fois avant de quitter le chenil.

« Au revoir, les amis ! Bon courage !

– Au revoir, ma jolie ! Pense à nous, quand tu seras revenue chez toi... » aboient ses copains de cage.

Le retour à la maison n'est pas très gai. Jim chéri et Darling ne sont pas encore rentrés. Tante Sarah l'enchaîne immédiatement dehors, dans le jardin. « Allons, Lady, ne vous découragez pas ! Quand vos maîtres rentreront, tout s'arrangera. » Jock et César ne l'abandonnent pas, mais Lady est triste, triste et malheureuse.

« Salut, Poulette ! Alors, finalement, tu t'en es bien sortie de toute cette histoire ? On a passé un moment formidable, tous les deux, non ? On recommence ce soir, d'accord ?
– Ah ! je vous en prie ! Vous vous rendez compte de ce que vous avez fait ? Vous m'avez abandonnée ! À cause de vous, j'ai été en prison. Et maintenant, vous osez me proposer de sortir !
– Ne t'énerve pas, ma jolie. Je ne t'ai pas abandonnée. J'étais sûr que tu me suivais. Et puis, je suis venu prendre de tes nouvelles…
– Pas un mot de plus !
Vous avez l'audace de me proposer une promenade alors que je suis attachée : vous vous moquez de moi… Maintenant, partez, je ne veux plus jamais vous revoir ! »

« Ma petite Lady est très fâchée contre moi. C'est sûr, je ne suis pas toujours parfait. Mais tout de même, je l'aime, et je saurai bien le lui prouver. »
Clochard s'en va, le cœur gros, en espérant que Lady va le rappeler. Mais elle a beau être la plus malheureuse des chiennes, elle tient à sa dignité.
« Non, mais ! pour qui se prend-il, ce Clochard ?
Ce n'est pas comme ça qu'on me traite, moi, Lady… »

Lady s’est couchée au fond de sa niche, pour pleurer tout à son aise.
« Moi qui avais une si bonne vie : mes maîtres, le bébé, mes deux copains les voisins. Tout d’un coup, tout s’est compliqué. Clochard, où es-tu ? »

« Ouh, là là ! pense ce gros vilain rat. Cette chienne ne veut donc pas s'endormir ? Moi, il faut que j'aille faire un tour dans la maison : ça sent trop le bébé frais… Tant pis, je n'y tiens plus. J'y vais ! De toute façon, elle ne surveille rien… »

Lady est brusquement arrachée à ses pensées moroses par une odeur qui lui déplaît énormément. Un rat ! Elle se lève d'un bond, elle s'élance en aboyant… Attachée ! Elle retombe, à moitié étranglée. Le bébé ! Le rat ! Il faut prévenir quelqu'un. Elle continue à donner de la voix. « Ne t'affole pas, ma Poulette. J'ai compris et j'y vais ! Je m'occupe de ce rat. » Clochard n'était pas bien loin et dès qu'il a reconnu la voix de sa Lady bien-aimée, il s'est précipité…

« Je ne connais pas la maison, mais il n'y a qu'à suivre la piste de ce rat, l'odeur est toute fraîche. Elle va me mener directement à la chambre du bébé. C'est là ! Maintenant, à nous deux, mon petit gars ! »
En arrivant sur le palier, Clochard n'hésite pas : d'un bond, il saute sur la poignée et la porte s'ouvre à la volée.

Le rat est bien là, tout à côté du berceau. Babines retroussées, yeux fixes, Clochard bondit sur l'ignoble bête. Mais l'autre est malin : il se retourne et fait face à l'attaquant. Une terrible mêlée s'ensuit. Clochard est plus grand, mais le rat est rusé et ses dents sont sacrément pointues ! Clochard ne pense qu'à une chose : l'éloigner du berceau d'abord, le tuer ensuite…

À force de tirer, Lady a réussi à casser sa chaîne. D'un bond, elle se précipite en haut de l'escalier. Mais la bagarre est déjà finie ! Clochard vient de tuer le rat.

« Clochard ! Tu es formidable ! Si tu n'avais pas été là…

– Pour toi, je serai toujours là quand il faut. Ne t'inquiète pas, ma Poulette ! » répond Clochard un peu essoufflé.

Tout ce bruit a réveillé le bébé et surtout tante Sarah.
« C'est donc encore toi, sale bête, qui nous empêches de dormir ! Quelle idiotie as-tu encore inventée ? Et en plus, tu nous amènes tes copains ! Ah ! ils sont jolis, tes copains… Ils ont vraiment l'air aussi mal élevés que toi ! Lady, je t'enferme pour de bon ! Quant à ton copain, direction la fourrière ! » vocifère la tante, hors d'elle.

À grands coups de balai, elle chasse la pauvre Lady dans la cave toute noire.
« Allez, disparais, sale bête !
– Tante Sarah ! Où êtes-vous ? Nous sommes rentrés ! »
C'est la voix de Jim chéri. Lady en pleurerait de soulagement.
Puisque ses maîtres sont là, tout va s'arranger.

« Jock, vois-tu ce que je vois ?
– Oui, César, et je ne suis pas d'accord.
Même si ce Clochard est parfois un peu mal élevé, c'est un chien de cœur et puis je crois… que Lady l'aime.
– Clochard, crient les deux chiens, ne t'inquiète pas. On ne te laissera pas tomber… »

Jim chéri a libéré Lady de la cave, mais il est très en colère.
« Si j'ai bien compris, tu as fait beaucoup de bêtises et tu as été très désagréable avec tante Sarah. Je ne comprends pas, ce n'est pas dans tes habitudes.
– Mais suis-moi, et tu comprendras » , aboie Lady en essayant d'entraîner son maître dans la chambre du bébé.

En haut, Lady pousse le rideau du bout de son museau. Le cadavre du rat apparaît.
« Tu as sauvé le bébé ! crie Darling. Merci, Lady !
– Mais ce n'est pas moi, c'est Clochard ! aboie Lady.
– Vite, il faut le rattraper ! » crie Jim, qui a tout deviné.
Sa femme le regarde, sans rien comprendre.
« Le chien gris que tante Sarah a trouvé avec Lady, c'est lui qui a tué le rat. Et nous, pour le remercier, on l'a envoyé à la fourrière, explique Jim d'une traite. Il faut le reprendre… »

Jock et César, eux, n'ont pas attendu que Jim parte sur les traces de Clochard. Après tout, jadis, César était chien policier. Il lui reste du flair…
« La voiture est passée par là, j'en suis sûr !
– On n'y arrivera jamais ! Il y a trop d'odeurs différentes…
– Tais-toi, Jock, et avance ! » rétorque César.

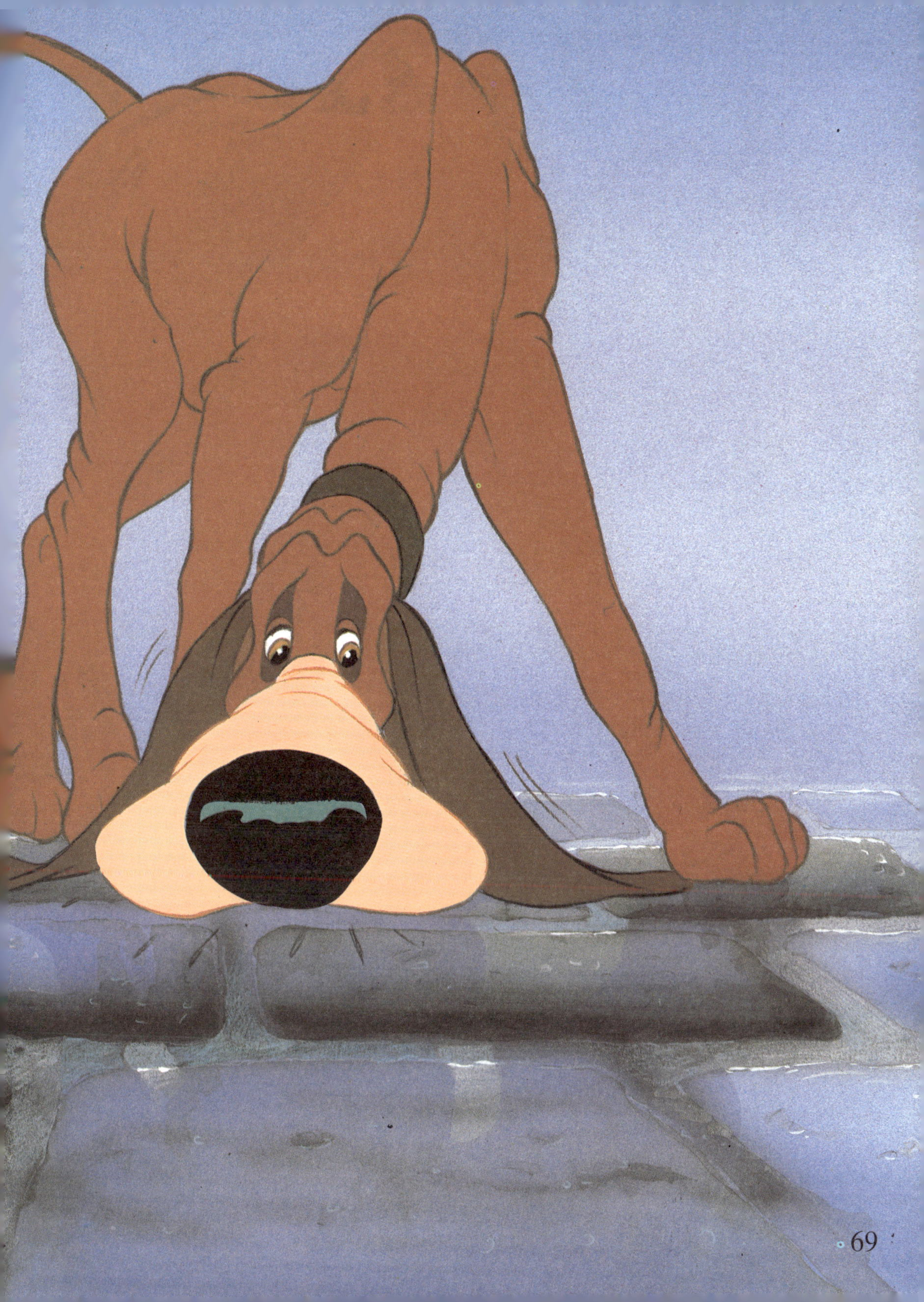

« Plus vite, chauffeur, crie Jim.
C'est une urgence ! »
« Comme il a raison, pense Lady affolée. Il n'y a rien de plus urgent au monde que de rattraper cette maudite voiture. Dès que je verrai Clochard, je lui dirai… Oh oui ! je lui dirai que je l'aime ! Même s'il est mal élevé, même s'il n'est pas très galant, tout ça n'a aucune importance…
Parce que je n'en veux pas d'autre ! »

César est formidable ! Il a réussi à rattraper le fourgon de la fourrière. N'écoutant que son courage, il se jette devant, pour obliger le conducteur à arrêter ses chevaux. Mais le mouvement est trop brusque et le fourgon bascule.
« Clochard ! C'est nous ! On va te libérer ! »
crie César en faisant un bond de côté pour ne pas se faire écraser.

La voiture de Jim n'est pas loin derrière. Lady saute en marche et se précipite à la porte du fourgon.
« Clochard ! Clochard ! Tu es là ? C'est moi, Lady ! Je voulais te dire…
– Ah ! tiens ! Te voilà ! C'est gentil d'être venue me voir… »

Dans l'accident du fourgon, ce pauvre César a eu la patte écrasée. Mais il ne regrette rien, car, grâce à lui, la petite Lady a retrouvé son bien-aimé.
« Alors, les petits, vous allez bien ce matin ?
Dis-moi, ma chère Lady, voilà bientôt un an que nous nous connaissons, puisque c'est Noël dans quelques jours.

– Eh oui ! Le temps passe vite quand on ne s'ennuie pas, répond Lady en soupirant doucement.
– Chers Jock et César, annonce Clochard, nous avons une grande nouvelle à vous annoncer. Lady et moi, nous avons décidé de nous marier.
– Toutes nos félicitations, répondent en chœur Jock et César. Nous espérons bien être les parrains de vos premiers enfants. »

Beaucoup plus tard, chez Jim chéri et Darling.
« Ne bougez plus ! Le petit oiseau va sortir... Jim a bien du mal à cadrer tous ces chiens, grands et petits. Il faut dire que si les trois demoiselles sont aussi sages que leur mère, le dernier est un sacré gaillard. Aussi terrible que son père. D'ailleurs, c'est son portrait tout craché ! Heureusement, tonton César veille :
« Mon garçon, si tu n'es pas sage, je vais m'occuper de toi ! N'oublie pas que j'étais chien policier ! »
Mais l'oncle César ne fait peur à personne. Rien ne sauvera le manteau de Jock et c'est très bien comme ça !

– Eh oui ! Le temps passe vite quand on ne s'ennuie pas, répond Lady en soupirant doucement.
– Chers Jock et César, annonce Clochard, nous avons une grande nouvelle à vous annoncer. Lady et moi, nous avons décidé de nous marier.
– Toutes nos félicitations, répondent en chœur Jock et César. Nous espérons bien être les parrains de vos premiers enfants. »

Beaucoup plus tard, chez Jim chéri et Darling. « Ne bougez plus ! Le petit oiseau va sortir... Jim a bien du mal à cadrer tous ces chiens, grands et petits. Il faut dire que si les trois demoiselles sont aussi sages que leur mère, le dernier est un sacré gaillard. Aussi terrible que son père. D'ailleurs, c'est son portrait tout craché ! Heureusement, tonton César veille :
« Mon garçon, si tu n'es pas sage, je vais m'occuper de toi ! N'oublie pas que j'étais chien policier ! »
Mais l'oncle César ne fait peur à personne. Rien ne sauvera le manteau de Jock et c'est très bien comme ça !

Imprimé en France par Jean Lamour
54320 Maxéville
Dépôt légal n° 5660 - Septembre 1993
46.29.0848.02/5
ISBN 2.23.000201.5
Loi n° 49-956 du 16 juillet 1949
sur les publications destinées à la jeunesse